SURVIVING ROME

Surviving Rome

THE ECONOMIC LIVES OF THE NINETY PERCENT

KIM BOWES

PRINCETON UNIVERSITY PRESS
PRINCETON & OXFORD

Published by Princeton University Press
41 William Street, Princeton, New Jersey 08540
99 Banbury Road, Oxford OX2 6JX

press.princeton.edu

ISBN 9780691273334
ISBN (e-book) 9780691273358
Library of Congress Control Number: 2024057621

British Library Cataloging-in-Publication Data is available

Editorial: Rob Tempio and Chloe Coy
Production Editorial: Natalie Baan
Jacket Design: Karl Spurzem
Production: Erin Suydam
Publicity: Carmen Jimenez and Alyssa Sanford

This book has been composed in Arno

Printed in the United States of America

10 9 8 7 6 5 4 3 2 1

CONTENTS

ILLUSTRATIONS

Maps

Figures

Tables

ACKNOWLEDGMENTS

ALL BOOKS are produced through the kindness of others. This book owes its completion to many people who gave the greatest gift one scholar can give to another—their time.

Many helped me understand aspects of the ancient economy that had left me puzzled: Dominic Rathbone and Kevin Butcher on details of the coinage of Egypt and Ephesus, respectively; David Parsons on crop modeling; Janet Monge on the heuristics of physical anthropology; Lin Foxhall on spinning technology; Jeremy McInerny and Julia Wilker on the Greek vocabulary of pawning and pawnshops. Others very generously shared their data prior to its publication: Ben Kelly shared his unpublished data on petitions; Chris Evans shared some new work on Cambridge-area archaeology; Ted Peña gave permission to use some unpublished data from the Pompeii Artifact Life History Project, and Rob Witcher excavated some amphorae data from the Tiber Valley database. Jessica Pearson, collaborator without peer, collected isotope data from the whole of the Roman empire with me, a tiny sliver of which is reproduced here thanks to her generosity.

A great many people read chapters in progress, offering their criticisms, bibliography and often their own work in exchange. Gilles Bransbourg, Seth Bernard, Rob Bloomfield, Jane Buikstra, William Harris, Duncan MacRae, Janet Monge, and Ellen Muehlberger all gave of their time and intellectual energies. Tim Guinnane lent an economist's eye to the first and last chapters. My staunch friends and colleagues Cam Grey and Tina Sessa gave their frank critique on the prose. These are the members of the academic 90 percent—the majority whose care for their peers and passion for the ancient world leads them to set aside their own work to help their colleagues. Errors remain my own: without their help, there would have been many more.

Some truly kind friends read the whole manuscript—carefully, incisively, lending their keen eyes for missing fact, missing bibliography, or missing ideas to its final form. The two anonymous reviewers made especially helpful suggestions. I also owe a special debt of gratitude to several others: to Brent Shaw for his attentive reading and insistence that the deeper past of the subject still matters; to Ed Cohen for thinking with me so carefully about the concept of the 90 percent; to Peter Brown, my mentor past and present, for his encouragement and model of historical empathy; and to Betsy Brown for spotting arcane language and not-so-obvious facts. Finally, my husband, Richard Hodges, suffered through several chapters in their worst state and is doubtless looking forward to hearing less about Roman agriculture around the dinner table.

Books also require time. I'm grateful to the University of Pennsylvania, the Guggenheim Foundation and the National Endowment for the Humanities for their financial support of a sabbatical during which this book was written.

Books are also the product of book professionals. Matilde Grimaldi produced the graphs, maps and many plans with an attentive eye for making the "poetics of muchness" legible and interesting. Rebecca Stuhr, librarian extraordinaire, helped find many a book and resolved many a technical issue. And Rob Tempio, editor for Princeton University Press, helped squeeze the dregs of jargon from the manuscript, lending his long experience in transforming academic books into something other people might want to read.

Finally, books are the product of tolerance. While I was writing this book, we asked our son what he and his sixth-grade friends talked about during lunch hour at school. "Communism and capitalism," he replied. For putting up with too many conversations about economic history, and for their ideas and their patience, I'm grateful to my family.

MAPS

MAP 1. Roman empire

MAP 2. Roman Italy, with sites mentioned in the text

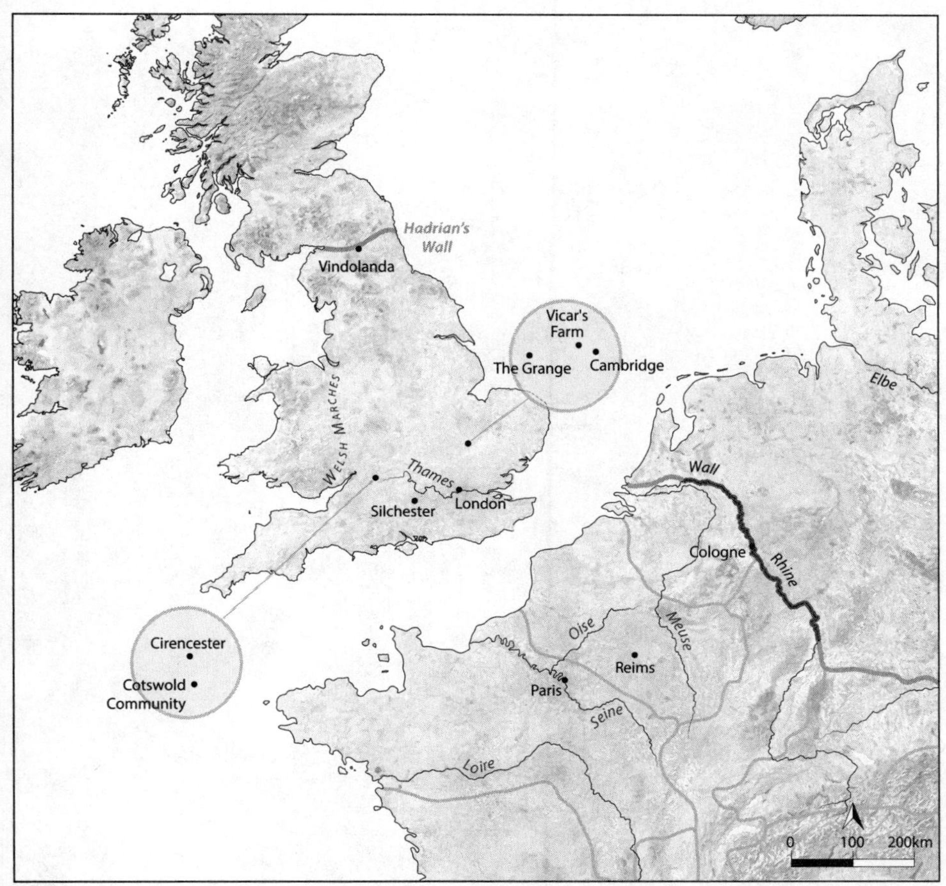

MAP 3. Provinces of Northern Gaul and Britain, with sites mentioned in the text

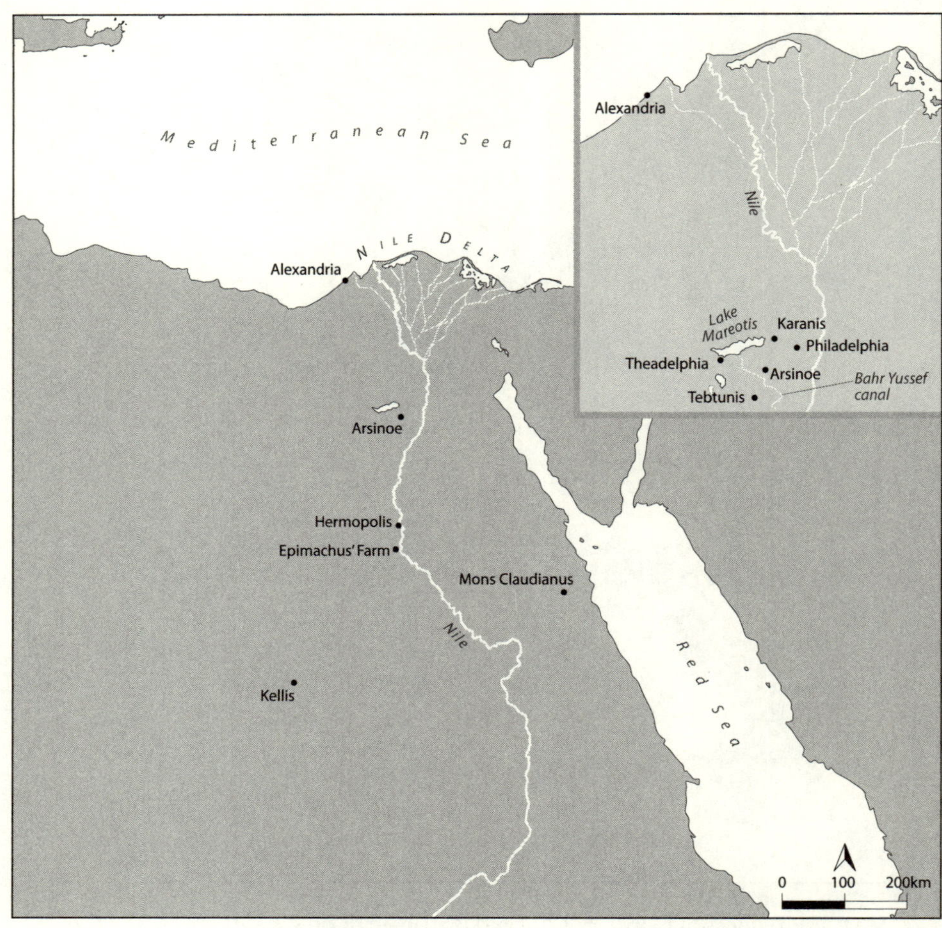

MAP 4. Roman Egypt, with sites mentioned in the text

SURVIVING ROME

Introduction

GETTING DOWN TO WORK

THE YEAR was 78 CE. The emperor Vespasian had been on the imperial throne for nine years, ruling over an empire that stretched from Syria to Wales. In Italy, Mount Vesuvius was beginning to rumble over Pompeii. And at dawn on October 11, an Egyptian farmer named Epimachus went to work.[1] With him trudged another farmer and three slaves. For two weeks during that October, the five of them worked side by side, running the backbreaking hoist pumps that lifted the Nile floodwaters onto their parched lands. Epimachus and his landlord split the costs of the work: Epimachus worked himself and paid one of the slaves, while the landlord supplied the other slaves and some day-wages. Those wages, the workers' names, and each day's work were all carefully entered into the landlord's account books, until October 25, when the accounts break off and Epimachus, the farmer and the slaves all vanish from history.

The history of Rome is peopled with the rich. It was a history written by and for men who made their living from the labor of others. How people like Epimachus and his comrades made their way in this world has yet to be told. How did ordinary people survive? How did they work and earn, sell and save, borrow and lend? This book tells their story. This is a history of the 90 percent of Romans who worked with their hands, a history of shopkeepers and farmers, spinners and potters, and the even more numerous who had no single profession, but many. It's a book about both enslaved and free workers, women, men and child workers. It's a group of people who have stood on the sidelines of history, even as they are sidelined today. This is the story of how they got by.

As the following pages will describe, they got by in a world in which the expansion of coined money, consumer goods, markets—in short, the world's first "global economy"—created bitter challenges and opportunistic hustles.

Theirs was a world awash with things: even miners and farmers might eat off well-made plates and drink imported wine. But their many things concealed and produced a constant precarity. Theirs was a world in which most farmers produced and sold small surpluses—to cities, to the state, and to each other. Yet their astonishing productivity was driven as much by the whip of high rents as it was by the lure of high profits. It was a world where working for wages was probably more common than at any time before early modernity. But working for wages meant working multiple jobs, hustling a living from many kinds of income. Theirs was a world where most everyone used credit—to invest, to supplement periods of low income—but saving was wrenchingly difficult.

The categories to which history has assigned these people—slave and free; urban and rural; butcher, baker and trinket-maker—have obscured all these strategies for survival. Preoccupied with their identities, we've missed what they did. While they may have differed in their jobs, their income bracket or their status before the law, the 90 percent shared a set of economic practices and strategies, managing risk, living with precarity, while doubling down on opportunity.

Their story often bears an uncanny resemblance to that of modern working people. Like the modern poor, Romans were cagey managers of small resources. Like modern Americans and Kenyans and Indians, they held multiple jobs to make ends meet. As one of the world's first "global" economies, they, like us, lived in the near and interacted with the far, using money and markets and credit to do so. And like us, they suffered from these things as well. But as we shall also see, the past is a foreign country: the Roman world was not ours. Most Romans were farmers. Most Romans didn't live by wages alone. While they used credit, they rarely used banks. With few machines to do their work, physical labor took an unprecedentedly high toll on their bodies. And a great many Romans, even working Romans, routinely enslaved other human beings to do some of their work. The world of the Roman 90 percent is both eerily familiar and ineluctably distant from our own.

This is a history set in the crucible of the Roman empire, from its advent in the late first century BCE through the first half of the third century CE. Our subjects were already subjects of a massive empire, one that, by sword and by tax, had unified unprecedentedly diverse peoples and ecosystems under a single political umbrella. They lived in one of the world's first "global" economies—where "global" embraced the lands between Britain and Syria—connected by fast ships but divided by slow roads. Theirs was a dense and populous world of some 50–60 million inhabitants, probably even more. Most of them lived in the countryside, small farmers like Epimachus owning or leasing small or smallish plots. But many more than we used to think lived in cities. Cities were bigger and thicker on the ground in most parts of the empire than at any point before the nineteenth century. This meant more craftsmen, traders, seasonal laborers and commuting farmers than ever before. They lived in a world where cities and countryside were linked by trade and religion and labor, and where people were constantly on the move in short and long trips. This world included the megacity of Rome with its million inhabitants, its thousands of specialized craftsmen, its huge number of slaves. It included the cities of Herculaneum and Pompeii, buried in 79 CE by the eruption of Mount Vesuvius and thus preserving two of the best-documented cases of working people's lives—their houses, shops, and savings. It included the lands of Egypt, where farmers like Epimachus had managed the Nile flood for millennia, and from whom Egyptian, Greek and now Roman overlords extracted rents and taxes. It included the northern provinces of Britain and Gaul, where farming meant cows and beer, while backbreaking work was to be had in new cities. And, although less prominent in this story, on the other side of the Mediterranean it included the ancient cities and villages of Greece and Asia Minor.

This is a history that can only begin to be told now. Even thirty years ago, had anyone wanted to write an economic history of working Romans (which, with some exceptions, they mostly didn't) they would have run aground from lack of data. New archaeology, new texts, and old texts newly reconsidered have radically altered the picture. The archaeological data alone is staggering: hundreds of farms and shops and workshops, and reams of new scientific data—studies of ancient plants and animals, ancient coins, and ancient skeletons. Those same excavations—as well as excavations in libraries and archives—have uncovered the writings of working people: graffiti and papyri record their contracts, loans, wage payments, even their bar bills and receipts for trips to the baths. All this new evidence reveals working people to a degree unimaginable three decades ago. Much of this new material has been published in big datasets, releasing a refreshing shower of quantified data onto the parched landscape of ancient history. This data makes it possible to do the work of this book, to give voice to the lives of the 90 percent in their complexity and diversity.

Only now, too, do we have tools and perspectives to do justice to that data. For some time now, we've realized that the lives of working people—in the present and in the past—aren't always well represented by macro-models and aggregate measurements. High gross domestic product and high average wages often conceal grinding poverty and hunger, while real financial hardship lurks in erratic incomes, high interest payments or low credit scores. Top-down theories are particularly bad at making sense of the life-critical messiness of lives lived on the edge. Economists have come to realize that the 90 percent themselves are often the best source of information on their economics: how they use money, how they juggle multiple jobs, how they save—or don't—for the future. This is as true of the past as it is of the present. Understanding how the ancient Roman 90 percent or the contemporary American 90 percent survive means taking their own lives and choices seriously. New data, combined with new ways of thinking, make that newly possible.

Who Cares About Working People?

An account of why no one cared about working people in ancient history barely needs to be written. The field has been famously focused on rich men ever since the rich men who are its subjects—Cicero, Livy, Tacitus—wrote it themselves. Classics, as the study of those rich men's literary production, only slowly shed this bias, and ancient history, its bedfellow, more slowly still.[2] But there are still some understandable reasons why this should have been so. For one, our ancient sources were biased themselves. Cicero, to whom we listen more often than we ought, famously said that "the wages of the laborer are the badge of slavery," "no workshop can have anything noble about it," and other disparaging *bon mots*.[3] Work, it would seem, was bad, and workers to be despised. Cicero wasn't alone—he was parroting a long Greek tradition that included Plato and Aristotle—but we can find the same general ideas repeated by many Roman writers. Following their lead, historians long assumed that ancient people (elites at any rate) looked down on work as well as working people, and that this was true in some kind of operative way.[4]

That we long believed that these ancient prejudices reflected something real about ancient economic behavior is down, in part, to Sir Moses Finley. Finley—a child prodigy of immigrants, pushed out of America for his communist sympathies and welcomed at Cambridge University—was one of the subtlest, if stubbornest, thinkers about the ancient world the twentieth century ever produced.[5] His 1973 publication of *The Ancient Economy* deployed an enormous range of elite sources and, in readable, citation-light prose, internalized their prejudices.[6] As Finley saw it, Cicero & Co. didn't hold labor as a value, or profit as a motivation. As a result, he believed, ancient people had no properly economic thinking. Elites didn't think about profit maximization—they thought about status. Happy to get rich off their estates, they showed scant interest in innovation, trade, banking or anything resembling "modern" economic activity.[7] Nonelite people, according to Finley, were mostly subsistence farmers, producing just enough for survival, tools and taxes. Their "just-enough-ism" also lay outside anything we might describe as distinctly "economic."[8] In short, by failing to value either labor or profit, and being disinterested in "getting ahead," neither Roman elites nor Roman working people had anything we would recognize as an economic mentality.

Much of this, we now know, is wrong. For someone as well-versed in economic theory as Finley was, his definitions of "profit-seeking" or "maximizing" seem lumpen. But his certainty that there was some essential truth in Cicero was real. In part, the problem Finley faced was his almost total reliance on elite sources. If you follow Cicero & Co. around, you're going to be left with the impression that work was undervalued and working people's activities lay outside of anything discernibly economic. While Finley knew that no politician or philosopher is ever to be trusted when talking about working people, neither did he appreciate the subtleties contained in those politicians' arguments. Cicero & Co. were much less interested in the value of labor or the laborer than they were in the nature of civic responsibility. And beneath civic responsibility lay even deeper waters—the philosophical relationship between objects and their makers, metaphysical cul-de-sacs where a shoe could be good, but a shoemaker was without honor.[9] In short, behind these seemingly damning statements against workers and work was a kind of cultural double-think, rolled out in political-philosophical texts, but set aside when living one's life.

Ancient and modern thinkers made one exception to all the anti-worker speak: the farmer or peasant.[10] For ancient writers, small farmers were the protagonists of a national, tragic myth. Farmers like Cincinnatus farmed a Republican golden age, when smallholders worked the land and served the state, setting Rome on its course to political and military greatness. Then followed these farmers' ruin: pushed off their land through years of military service, ensuing debt, and slave-run agriculture, the death knell of the small farmer was the death knell of the Roman Republic. For Finley and his predecessors, it wasn't so much the equation of farmers with a doomed Republic but their presumed subsistence economic behavior that made them so interesting. For Finley particularly, the ancient economy was dominated by just-getting-by farmers, intent on self-sufficiency with only negligible surpluses and only a glancing interest in markets or specialization.[11] That is, unlike his ancient sources who imagined an occupation—farming—Finley imagined a category of person complete with their own particular kind of economy: the peasant. Together with status-oriented elites, self-sufficient peasants anchored Finley's noneconomic ancient economy. In different ways, then, for both ancient and modern historians, farmers were a kind of mascot, good to do history with, no further thought on their hows and whys required.

Many of Finley's ideas about ancient economics have long been swept away, undone by new evidence and new models. The sophistication and extent of nonagricultural activities—trade, craft production and infrastructure as revealed by archaeology—all describe something much bigger and more complex than Finley's underdeveloped world.[12] Some of this world was funded by what appear to be entrepreneurs, investing in risky businesses with the expectation of robust returns. So, too, new work on Roman money has discovered a world awash in coins and credit, where Cicero & Co., rather than disdaining finance, actually used reasonably sophisticated accounting and financial instruments.[13] A mountain of new data has revealed a world Finley never imagined or took seriously.

And yet, this new data has been grafted onto what is now a rather old model of economic behavior. This model casts institutions, particularly the state, as the star in history's drama.[14] According to this more recent view, the Roman state guaranteed the value of money through its mints, enforced contracts with its laws, and through a set of carrots (infrastructure) and sticks (taxation), it encouraged trade and exchange and investment at a historically unprecedented volume. The Roman state, some argue, produced a Roman economic revolution. Rejected, too, is Finley's contention that modern economic models and metrics were useless in a world without proper economic thinking. Historians have now enthusiastically charted the details of Roman economic performance, estimating a Roman price index, taking up the question of economic growth, even providing a number for Roman gross domestic product (GDP).

Yet even in our own world, economists and workers alike no longer trust that either institutions or macro-performance measurements represent the economy as experienced by ordinary people. Working people's challenges are routinely masked by national production calculations or estimates of average income. In the same way, the recent emphasis on ancient economic performance and the state has pushed poor and working Romans to the sidelines of history. The rejection of Finley's peasants has meant tossing out the small-farmer majority—small-scale agriculture not being an obvious agent of economic performance. Questions about money have become questions about gross state outputs, leaving aside the supply of small change and its use by ordinary people.

Even labor, posed as a problem of market efficiencies, wage formation or market integration, takes large-scale employers' and owners' perspectives rather than that of workers. Cicero & Co. get as much attention as they ever did, while the 90 percent are submerged within institutions, like the slave villa, or swapped for abstract categories, like wage-labor. In short, these models of Roman economic performance swerve away from both the working majority and the complex realities of their lived experience.

But if the recent macroeconomic studies have sidelined the 90 percent, other disciplines and other kinds of data have revealed their lives in astonishing detail. Driven by the desire to plumb all corners of Roman life—not just the elite—this new data has exploded in quantity and quality in the past twenty years. Three profound revolutions in our knowledge of the Roman world have transformed what we know about working people, revolutions that, although they speak at tangents to economic performance, are eloquent on matters of economic life.

The first knowledge revolution pertains to making. Each step in large-scale bread baking, how shopkeepers set up their shops, the complicated processes of potting, cloth-making and glassmaking—have all been revealed in granular detail, thanks to two decades of new archaeology.[15] Unearthing craft has also revealed the extraordinarily specialized knowledge produced by Roman working people. These examinations have tended to linger on products and processes—retail and baking and weaving—and somewhat less on the economics of shopkeepers and bakers and weavers.[16] This is understandable: it's not easy to get from the product to the people, and archaeologists are justly cautious in assuming a loaf of bread tells us anything about a baker. Furthermore, much of this new data is qualitative, not quantitative: we are still woefully uninformed about the scale of artisanal outputs, wages or profits—the basic building blocks from which to reconstruct artisanal economic life.[17] Nonetheless, this book amasses what we do know about makers and their economic strategies to ask how they made a living—their various sources of income, how they managed credit and debt and labor.

In no sphere of ancient activity has there been a greater knowledge revolution than farming. We can never pay enough attention to farming and farmers. Sadly, that's not how decades of archaeology saw it. Cities were held up as the yardstick of a civilization, and Roman archaeologists long lingered on urban monuments and urban design. When they spared time for the countryside, they tended to focus on the villas of elites.[18] These villas were big and attractive, produced mosaics and sculpture, and recalled the world of the city. As a consequence, their agricultural apparatus was mostly ignored. Less sensational, but ultimately more important, were the meticulous surveys of the countryside itself, mapping where people lived and the changes in those places over time.[19] But it is only with excavations, particularly big excavations done in advance of big construction projects, that we can now see Roman farming in its true light. Over the last thirty years, the construction of modern train lines, highways and airports, carried out in what had once been the Roman countryside, has done more for Roman farmers than a century of academic projects.[20] The result has been a shower of information about Roman farms and fields, crops and herds, and the geology and soil science to make sense of it all.

Finally, the last twenty years has also seen a revolution in ancient texts. Roman texts used to mean Cicero and Livy. Now they also mean dirty jokes penned by bored Pompeiians, land leases signed by illiterate farmers, and beer deliveries tracked by London publicans. Graffiti scratched on walls, wooden tablets, the thousands of papyri and ostraca (writing on broken pottery) from Egyptian towns and villages—all these constitute what has been termed "everyday writing."[21] Only recently have scholars realized its importance for revealing the extent of ancient literacy. Yet much of this writing also constitutes the economic archives of working people—their expense lists and receipts, contracts and loans. Everyday writing contains the residues of everyday economics, overwhelmingly produced by and for working people.

These three knowledge revolutions—on making, on agriculture and on writing—have made the lives of working Romans visible as never before. This new data sets the stage for a new kind of history, centered on what working people actually did to survive, not simply the distilled metrics of their economy. They make possible a bottom-up economics, one rooted not in economic performance, but in economic practice.[22]

Who Are the 90 Percent?

When the British historian E. P. Thompson set out to write *The Making of the English Working Class*—one of the all-time great books on working people's lives—he could rely on some basic things.[23] He had as his subject late-nineteenth-century people who earned their living mostly from wages. They worked principally at a single trade, and increasingly in factories. These people came to regard themselves as a group—as a working class—and demanded improved labor conditions in part on the basis of this identity.

We cannot rely on any of these things in defining our group of working Romans. The group we're interested in didn't, despite some claims to the contrary, work principally for wages. Some worked at a specific trade, but many didn't. They occasionally grouped themselves by profession, but on the whole, they tended to describe themselves in other terms. And there is no Latin or Greek equivalent for "working class" or "blue-collar." So who are the people that are the subject of this book, and, in the absence of an ancient term for them, what's the logic to considering them together? Put another way, who are the proper subjects of a history of economic practice?

In a modern context, we would probably speak of a "class" of working people. But ancient history has often had an allergy to the concept of "class," one that is both wholly appropriate and not always helpful.[24] It's amusing, in a way, that the class allergy began with Finley—the alleged communist. Finley strenuously objected to the use of the term "class" to define ancient working people. "Class" defined around a Marxist means of production placed slave and free, not to mention nonworking members of different political orders, on the same analytical footing.[25] Class seemed to open the door to the notion of a "middle class," a capitalist bourgeoisie invented, he felt, by modern scholars. "Working class" was to be avoided for the same reason. "Status" was Finley's favored heuristic for dividing up ancient society, defined around Max Weber's "admirably vague" blend of legal status, political order, economic resources, family background and a self-defined sense of belonging.[26] Notwithstanding some recent attempts to reinsert a "working class" back into the conversation, Finley's aversion to class and preference for status continues to frame most work on the group under discussion here.[27]

Finley was, again, following his elite sources, for the Roman elite and juridical sources don't use anything like a class vocabulary. They employ legal terms for people according to their political status (*plebs, humiliores*), or their property status, like tenants (*coloni*) or landowners (*possessores, domini*). They have terms that are place-specific: country people are *rustici* or *pagani*, for instance. They have terms for specific kinds of activities or professions—shippers (*naviculari*), deposit bankers (*argentarii*), sex workers (*meretrices*)—some of which they use pejoratively and some they don't.[28] What Roman elites didn't have is a term for people who work with their hands generally. Even the people who did work with their hands didn't have a blanket term for it.

In fact, it's not so easy to find working people talking about themselves with anything like a consistent vocabulary. In the late Republic, the *plebs* of the city of Rome identified themselves through their neighborhoods, but above all through their shared access to the grain dole—a legal status that led to a form of messy group identity.[29] During the imperial period, much of our evidence for workers' perspectives comes from tombstones. Most Romans did not put their economic occupation on their tombstone, which shouldn't surprise us because neither do we: they, like us, emphasized their family relationships. This isn't to say there aren't exceptions. Much of the evidence for that work-identity on tombstones comes from the city of Rome and much of it from enslaved and freed people.[30] Enslaved and freed people were more likely to describe themselves by their work identity, having no legal families to relate themselves to. And a great many of those enslaved and freed worked in great elite households where work identities were particular and hyper-specialized, not unlike an English manor: hairstylists, pearl-setters, seamstresses. In other places, like Gaul, work identity in funerary contexts isn't so tied to enslaved/freed status, but it's still not the norm. Work identity clearly mattered, but, at least on tombstones, we can only see it mattering in quite particular circumstances.

What about a collective identity, like "working class"? Roman working people sometimes did join collective organizations, called *collegia*. These clubs were often (but not always) formed of people from the same profession, who organized themselves for a variety of reasons—to make business connections, to lobby the state on particular issues, to show their fealty to that same state, to have parties, or to provide for members' burials.[31] Professions-based *collegia* proudly declared that profession in public inscriptions: the cloth traders from a town in southern Spain made dedications in honor of the emperor; the builders of Ostia built a temple ditto.[32] Surely here is "class consciousness" on display? Not quite. It's not at all clear that the builders of Ostia or those cloth traders from Spain were bound by any abstract idea of their profession: local ties and interests were what drew them together. Although they may have banded together for mutual benefit, *collegia* didn't have the abstract labor identity and explicit aims we associate with the nineteenth-century development of a "working class."

There's another category that both ancients and moderns have used around our subject, and it's one that also forms part of this book—the poor. When Roman social historians have addressed this subject—which, again, has only happened recently—they sometimes conclude that "the poor" were actually most people, or they tend to treat the very bottom end of the spectrum—the homeless and destitute.[33] More nuanced studies use "poverty" as an opportunity to ask what Romans meant by the term, for ancient writers made abundant use of the idea of the "the poor," particularly as part of a dichotomy of rich and poor.[34] Cicero (again) uses the rich/poor contrast to probe the boundaries of civic virtue—is the rich-but-immoral citizen to be preferred over the poor-but-virtuous citizen? For lawyers-in-training, the rich-man/poor-man duo were stock characters in textbooks, stereotypes to be deployed in speeches. Even social satire relied on it: in the satirist Juvenal's Rome, the rich ride in their sedan chairs like ocean liners, parting waves of the begging poor. This ancient literary dichotomy of rich and poor, along with the contemporary interest in poverty, has again left us with a category of people, rather than questions about what those people actually did—their practices.

In fact, many of our challenges in defining working people come down to what we might term categories of analysis, versus categories of practice.[35] Categories of analysis are types, like "the poor," categories we use to divvy up people into abstract entities. These are categories helpful for making sense of the world at a distance. Categories of practice, on the other hand, are based in experience—the categories ordinary people use in their day-to-day lives. These categories overlap. For example, in contemporary society, race is used to make particular political, social and historical arguments: this is race as a category of analysis. But race shapes daily life in inescapable ways for many people—racial slurs, racial profiling. Here is race as a category of practice. In the ancient world, *colonus*, or tenant, was a category of analysis: a person defined by their legal obligations to another. That analytical category really mattered when you paid your rent. But the practices and daily experiences of being a tenant overlapped with the analytical category only in part.[36] Think of the tenant Epimachus' weeks of raising and pouring the hoist pump alongside four slaves and a wage-laborer: "tenant" doesn't make sense of that. The point is that we shouldn't mistake analytical and practice categories as being the same thing. When we do, we mistakenly assume that one kind of identity—typically the categories we make as scholars, or categories made by the law—tells us something about people's lived experience, their practices. It's our job as historians or social scientists to unpack the overlap, as well as the differences.

One of the reasons we've struggled with a working people's economics is that we've often confused analysis for practice. The absence of an ancient concept of a "working class," and the more general noncorrespondence between ancient and modern socioeconomic categories, have closed off the space to think about practice. We have thus, quite understandably, prioritized discussions of legal status, or professions, or the poor. These categories seem safer or more relevant, for they echo what Romans said about their own world, they hint at a modern notion of "professional identity," or they speak to modern preoccupations with poverty. All of this sidesteps the lived experiences and economic practices of actual working people, as experienced by them.

These problems of category make us particularly blind to the messiness of work as a practice, as opposed to work identity as an analytical category. There were over 200 specific job titles used in the Roman world, and we've already noted the specialized training and knowledge required in many of them.[37] But one's profession was not necessarily identical with the work one did to get by, nor did it define a discrete set of economic practices or thinking. Most households did many things, relying on a variety of activities to get by: hauling and potting, farming and building and carting—to name just a few. That kind of multitasking elides analytical professional categories, categories we like because they remind us of our own modern professional identities. Analytical categories like profession also privilege the individual (usually male) head of household: they ignore the often-critical labor inputs from women and children.[38] Those inputs may be supportive of the male "profession"—the woman from Rome who managed the books for her family butcher shop—or they may be different—Egyptian children who earned cash wages sweeping leaves while their parents farmed a small plot.[39]

The analysis/practice problem is particularly important when it comes to integrating enslaved and freed people into a history of labor. Slave (*servus*) and freed (*libertus*) were fundamental legal categories. Following this preoccupation with legal categories and using the slave systems of the Americas as a comparative guide, ancient historians have often placed the enslaved apart, in separate books, in separate interpretive frameworks—the slave villa, slave labor, the slave experience.[40] And yet, the recent shift to the term "enslaved" rather than "slave" labor opens to the door to the practical fact that this legal category, imposed by others, did not constitute an entire identity.[41] The labor of enslaved people was also a category of experience, of daily practices and work, some of which they shared with others who were not enslaved. We have already witnessed this with Epimachus, where a tenant and three enslaved men—all categories of analysis—all did the same work side by side for weeks. Similarly, even though slaves, as legal nonentities, were prohibited from owning anything, this didn't prevent them from owning money, real estate, even other slaves, via a legal fiction that prioritized practice—particularly the economic needs of their owners—over the analytical category of enslavement.[42]

Any history of Roman working people would be incomplete if it did not include the enslaved people who did so much of the labor. And much of that labor was of the same kind as, and often done side by side with, free people. But this does not mean that their labor was the same, and this is where the legal-analytical category of slavery diverges from the shared practice of work. The slaves Epimachus worked beside were not paid, and even the wages for one slave, Ambyron, were paid directly to his owner. Enslaved labor was patently not the same labor because it was owned by someone else, and enslaved bodies were legally an instrument—a tool. The role of the enslaved in an economic history of working people will necessarily be messy, far messier than an easy comparison with the slave-driven American South sometimes intimates. Roman slaves formed a major part of the workforce in some areas and were largely absent in others. They sometimes earned, saved and spent money like free people; they were sometimes the property of other working people and thus part of their capital.[43] Some freedmen used their earnings and their master's capital to become so wealthy they left working people's history and became part of the nonworking elite—like the fictional character Trimalchio.[44] Including the enslaved in working people's economics means being attentive to legal distinction—as we shall see on the issue of savings and capital—while at times trampling all over it—when, for example, discussing the working body.

Where does this leave us as far as defining working people? This book uses "the 90 percent"—a demographic guesstimate and majoritarian slogan—or "working Romans"—an activity descriptor. These terms gesture to the majority of Romans—maybe something like 90 percent of the population—who depended on their own labor, overwhelmingly manual labor, for their survival. They are distinguished from the minority of Romans—maybe something like 10 percent or even less—who didn't need to labor, earning their income from investments, from rents, from the labor of others.[45] The 90 percent might also be termed the nonrentier class, although they might have had some income from rents. They are often called nonelites, although this term simply begs the definition of an elite. The "90 percent" or "working Romans," are terms that, if nothing else, gesture through positives, not negatives, to the laboring majority.

The gesturing, not strict defining, is deliberate. Like E. P. Thompson, instead of defining a group in advance and then studying it, here we want instead to observe and dissect a series of activities. Words will not be helpful. We will have no choice but to use identity categories and terms like craftsmen, builders, farmers, traders, spinners. Enslaved and free, men, women and children. But what this book is really about is what they did as economic actors—growing, making, earning, saving, spending, borrowing, lending. People we might term "knowledge workers" today—teaching, scribing, managing—also sometimes form part of this story. Others, like a harvester from North Africa who worked for many years, eventually accumulating enough capital to enjoy leisure later on, drop in and out.[46]

Indeed, it is the very messiness of this big-tent category, its noncorrespondence with narrower ancient categories, that allow it to be so useful—and so revealing. It includes people who may have worn different identity-hats but shared complex strategies for getting by.[47] It includes an urban fisherman whose status as a manual laborer didn't stop him from applying for membership in an elite club. It includes a family of shepherds, unable, seemingly, to own their own animals but nonetheless capable of leasing big flocks, handling big cash flows, and taking out big loans. It includes a priest who, despite his impressive office, routinely rented out his children to pay off his debts. It even includes (possibly enslaved) salt workers whose bodies show the signs of the most punishing physical labor, but who lived unusually long lives and made dedications, ironically, to the god of the sea. These are just some of the Roman 90 percent whose very different job titles, gender or legal statuses conceal shared practices of survival in a harsh world. It's those practices we'll be interested in here.

As a consequence, and in sharp contrast to the categories extracted from performance metrics, our 90 percent will also include people of very different economic status. As a demographic guesstimate, the 90 percent refers not to a singular income bracket but to a diverse group who were reliant on their own labor. The impoverished hauler of salt, the struggling shopkeeper, and the owner of a medium-sized farm had very different incomes but shared strategies for consuming, accounting, borrowing and lending—strategies shaped by the particular challenges of living in the Roman world. As we will also see, whatever their economic status, the 90 percent shared the specter of precarity, a precarity hinted at by income but really lurking in spending, borrowing and hustling—that is, in practices. Income, this book argues, is just the beginning of the story. At the same time, the sources of that precarity will vary enormously—from tenant farmers versus owner-operators, from those who lived on wages to those who lived with them. The purpose of the category of "the 90 percent" is thus to cast a big net; the work of the rest of this book is to demolish it.

The Right End of the Telescope

In the 1950s, when economists began to wake up to the problems of global poverty, they initially used the tools developed for national economies.[48] Aggregate indicators of economic performance—like GDP or capital accumulation—were imagined to follow evolutionary developments, with "developed" nations simply further along the same curve as "underdeveloped" nations. Institutions like the United Nations or the World Bank tried to foster economic growth as measured by these gross indicators through a whole range of means, from sponsoring industrialization to incentivizing free markets.

Big problems attended both the theory and the practice of this approach. Aggregate indicators are useful for some things: they provide a general basis for comparison among different kinds of economies. But as measurements of the things that matter to working people or that impact their lives, they turn out to be pretty bad. GDP in particular suffered from the "power of a single number" phenomenon.[49] As an information-dense aggregate of millions of transactions, GDP was both incredibly seductive and potentially incredibly misleading. In 2009, the Organisation for Economic Cooperation and Development commissioned a study on economic metrics like GDP. It concluded that "there appears to be an increasing gap between the information contained in aggregate GDP data and what counts for common people's well-being."[50] Production, big business, financial markets—all turn out to be overrepresented in GDP metrics, while the economic well-being of the "common people" was experienced more in consumption, in household-level transactions, and in many nonmarket interactions. Put another way, average people's economic lives are composed of somewhat different variables—different in nature and in scale—than those that go into gross performance measurements.

A new approach to working lives—not just of the poor in developing countries but of working people everywhere—was needed. The winners of the 2015 and 2019 Nobel Prize in Economics represented that new approach, which can be summarized as: don't start with models, start with people.[51] By gathering detailed information from working households on how they earned, spent, saved and borrowed, a new generation of economists were able to get at those activities concealed by GDP measurements. They also learned surprising things: that most of the world's most impoverished people rarely ended the month in the red; that most used sophisticated, if tiny-scale, financial instruments to boost their earned income; that illiterate street traders in India kept precise mental financial diaries while working Americans had only a general sense of their household finances. Above all, they learned that the aggregate measurements miss the all-important flows of money within households, complex balance sheets of incomings and outgoings, of wealth alternatively frozen and thawed by loans and borrowing.

Many of the problems addressed by this newer "poor economics" don't apply to the ancient world: Romans, after all, lacked microfinance, NGOs and health insurance. But its realignment in scale—from the macro to the micro—was important. The relationship between macro and micro—in economics and in history—has been a matter of debate for some time. In economics, there's a long-running argument that macroeconomic aggregates behave in ways different from individual actors.[52] Historians have been puzzling over the problem for a while too: Is the macro-micro distinction just scalar—big histories address institutions and the state, while microhistories tell stories of individuals and households? Or is the distinction temporal—long- versus short-term histories?[53] This debate produced nagging doubts that aggregates of any kind—be they GDP or "big" histories or institutions—are simply the sum total of lots of small kinds of actions or people.[54] They are different, and the shift in scale constitutes a shift in kind. In choosing the scale of measurement, we don't just choose which end of the telescope to peer through, but in doing so, we shift the nature, the subject, and the results of our observation.

Here we opt to look through the right end of the telescope, examining little people who lived at a great distance from our own time in such a way that they leap up large in our field of view, full of their original complexity and contradiction. This book is built from "micro" data—the actual remains and records from households and individuals. It takes most seriously what they took seriously—how much they spent and consumed. Consumption and expenditure help shed light on labor and income, and, to a lesser extent, on production. The flows of money within households were the daily micros of economic experience and the real basis of precarity or prosperity. It's those flows, concealed by the aggregates, that interest us here.

As a consequence, we view income and savings as working people experienced them, at the level of the household. The household here is not the "primitive" economic unit of Finley and his predecessors, nor the institution-in-miniature of some economists, but a messy, often conflicted group of people.[55] Roman families lay somewhere on a spectrum between the nuclear model that populates modern economics to various kinds of extended kin: Roman families in Italy probably lay more toward the nuclear end, those in Egypt often included sibling couples and grandparents, while British farming families may have preserved traditions of older extended-family tribes.[56] Better-off families included their slaves and freedmen. These complex groups, as we'll see, acted as units when they made decisions about expenditure and labor allocation but had more tangled relationships when it came to debt and savings. Individualist or collective behavior depended on what they were doing. However, by looking at things like wage earning and labor strategies from household rather than institutional perspectives, "wage labor" and "professions" look very different, sometimes fading altogether.

It's probably worth noting, too, that we're also doing something quite different than Karl Marx.[57] Marx reoriented the subject of history to include working people, and all historians who think the 90 percent matter owe him a debt.[58] But Marx was a quintessential categories-of-analysis man. Proletariat, modes of production, slave society: Marx wrung these categories from the detritus of history, not chats with his working neighbors. Marx's aim may have been the improvement of the lives of workers, but their actual, messy lives were often sacrificed on the altar of historical materialism. This is particularly true of the lives of the ancient people who populated his historical arc. Our aims here are not Marx's aims, and indeed, by letting the practices come before the theory, we'll find many of Marx's categories to be less than helpful.

Little People, Big People

There's another contemporary question that seems to sit somewhere between the macro-measures and economic life, and that's inequality—the disparity in wealth or income among groups. Inequality, as a category of analysis, will be treated only glancingly by this book, a move that will strike many as bizarre. After all, one might argue, surely the new (or rather, more avowedly passionate) interest in wealth inequality—beginning with the financial crisis of 2008 and picked up by historians—heralds a genuine swerve toward the working majority? The answer to this would be to ask any working person today to read Thomas Piketty's *Capital*—a book on long-term wealth inequality that, if it didn't start historians thinking about inequality, certainly opened the floodgates.[59] It's a marvelous book, rich in data and metaphor alike, trying to put some real depth and calculus on Marx's claim that capital just yields more capital. I have not asked my Philadelphia neighbors—who work three jobs during the day and look after other people's children at night—to read *Capital*, but if I did, I suspect their response would be, "Right, another book by so-called liberals about rich people." Which would be correct, and not just about Piketty and his project.

Piketty's book on inequality describes how rich people hang on to their money and grow it. The money of working people—even what we could legitimately call the working class of the eighteenth through twenty-first centuries—doesn't even factor in his book, so statistically irrelevant is their wealth. In short, the inequality question, as it has driven Piketty and the Occupy Wall Street Movement and most of the new work on inequality in the ancient world, is yet another conversation—an angry one, to be sure—about the rich. This is an important conversation in the present, as it touches on the rich's hoarding of limited resources, their control over political decision-making and the resultant sullying of our democracies. This is not a rationale any ancient person would have recognized: insofar as Romans cared about inequality, theirs was an elite concern about moral corruption. Eating fish purchased at 1,000 sestertii a pound hollowed out your soul, but that didn't lead to any efforts to eradicate poverty.[60] As for the Roman scholarly conversation about inequality, following Piketty, it tends to be rich people's economics by other means: political instability, monetary inflation, or Roman senatorial wealth portfolios, all a putative product of inequality as experienced by the rich. How the unequal distribution of wealth in the Roman world mattered for the 90 percent is not so much on the menu.[61] We shall have many things to say about inequality in this book, but inequality of a different kind. The inequalities separating farmers who owned land from those who rented; between weavers who earned wages versus those who were paid by the piece; between the enslaved with access to their master's capital and those without—these are the inequalities of everyday practice that will occupy us here.

The inequality question also highlights one of the hazards of a project like this: how to do justice to regimes of power without simply writing about regimes of power. To date, Roman economic history has mostly been a history of the state and how, in part by accident and in part by design, it produced an extraordinarily productive moment. Increasingly, too, we're aware that the Roman state wasn't some socialist democracy, building roads, enforcing contracts and reducing transaction costs. It also behaved in brutal ways, killing and enslaving millions of people, forcibly resettling other millions, and subjecting newly conquered peoples to tribute and tax.[62] The 90 percent, by definition, lived at the thin edge of that wedge of power, exposed to landlords, employers, tax collectors, soldiers and slave owners, all as part of their daily bread.

We do yet a further injustice to our working subjects if we render them as simple victims in yet another history of the powerful. As we shall see throughout this book, the Roman 90 percent were canny and shrewd. They were adept exploiters—of the systems that exploited them, as well as of each other. The following pages will find them robbing each other of pennies, reserving the right to pursue their mothers for debt, and selling their children into something close to slavery in order to live another day. They were litigious when they could be and rarely trusting. Many of them were doubtless ruined by the big powers that surrounded them, but few of them went quietly. "Agency" is often used to describe people's ability to act within the structures that confine them.[63] It seems too sanitized, too optimistic for this hard world. "Grit" may be more accurate.

The Past Is Many Foreign Countries

One could argue that economics—or, at any rate, the theory of supply, demand and price that has dominated economic thinking since the early twentieth century—has no real need of history. If, as neoclassical economic theory argues, human actors are rational and human behavior therefore universal, then change over time is uninteresting.[64] We could also say that these same certainties make all history the same: if rational actors making informed decisions around price and profit are ever-present, then all economies share some fundamental metrics, like price-earnings ratios or wealth distribution. Wearing the sheriff's badge afforded by this theory, a historian could confidently move between, say, the Roman empire and eighteenth-century France, armed with some economic performance statistics, and say something meaningful about the comparison. By this same logic, things we do know about, say, the cost of living in eighteenth-century France, could be used to fill in what we don't know about the Roman economy.

There are many things that we don't know about the Roman economy: the overall population, per capita consumption, wheat yields, the tax rate, land rents outside of Egypt—the list is depressingly long and contains some pretty important variables. So it's doubly tempting to rob statistics from better documented societies. The neoclassical sheriff's badge would appear to give us the right to do so. But even if we think that badge is bunk, some genuine similarities appear to make comparison not unreasonable. As a highly monetized, nonindustrialized, agricultural world that had simple but sophisticated accounting and did lots of trading, the Roman world had some things in common with, say, the Abbasid empire or Tudor England. However, these economies' shared "premodern" label has done some thinking for us, thinking that needs to be rethought.

The growing fascination with so-called deep or big history has not only made use of the increasing amounts of "big data," but when such data isn't forthcoming, it has proven very tempting to simply retroject what we do know onto the deeper, uncertain past.[65] With economics, this has been an exercise in making less do more—that is, using a few data points to recreate a whole economy. A few mega-data projects have applied this method to create performance metrics for economies from 1 CE to the present.[66] These re-created performance metrics have been used by lots of people, from those interested in wage series or long-term inequality to those estimating GDP.[67] They all postulate a static "premodernity"—little growth, little significant change in output measurements. Population ups and downs, not economic behavior, produce the only real blips in the growth curve. The action only really starts in the seventeenth or eighteenth century, when mercantile capital, trade and eventually industrialization start the pot really boiling.

This blasé premodernity is, in large part, a product of self-determining math. The performance measurements from the early economies—the Roman empire, the Byzantine empire or twelfth-century France—look the same because they have been constructed with the same bad data—subsistence calories times the cost of wheat, tweaked by population guesstimates.[68] Pre-modern economies tend to look alike in part because the numbers used to calculate activity are mostly the same.

Static premodernity is also a product of the scale—the graph—thinking for us. It's true that compared to the massive economic growth of the past 150 years, the premodern space does look pretty static and dull.[69] If we're interested in the present, that's an important observation. If we want to understand the Roman (or Byzantine or medieval) world on its own terms, it's less so. But it's also a case of a model driving interpretation to a place that is inductively absurd: the idea that the Byzantine empire, with its tiny population, small production of surpluses and consumer goods, smaller levels of trade, and limited use of money for everyday exchange is somehow economically "the same" as the Roman empire, seems strange.

But even this example highlights that what we choose to measure and compare has a big impact on what the comparison looks like. Comparing the cost of minimum requisite calories in different societies (which are erroneously assumed not to change) produces lots of sameness. Comparing the breadth (not the rates) of monetization and the use of credit and patterns and quantities of consumption will emphasize difference. Comparing *how* things happened—how small farmers grew crops, to whom they sold their surplus, the uses to which they put credit—this all introduces the fine-grained stories of practice, which are more different still.

Baked into this notion of an unchanging premodern world is another equally unhelpful idea: "subsistence." Subsistence, despite some important cautionaries to the contrary, usually means producing enough to survive, plus reserve for bad times.[70] Even for those who accept that such a concept is absurd—for virtually nobody deliberately produces just enough to survive—subsistence continues to define an attitude, a just-enough approach to getting by tinged with pessimism and risk-aversion. More than that, subsistence is mostly presumed to be unchanging. Subsistence-oriented people are not, by definition, hugely variegated because the subsistence ideal is all-encompassing and consistent. "Subsistence" is dredged up to characterize everyone from hunter-gatherers to medieval serfs. In this way, subsistence worms its way in to become a historical constant, only finally undone for the masses by industrialization. Wearing the neoclassical sheriff's badge again, this means that subsistence can also be used to fill in missing data in economic performance models, while it also has a contagion effect on lots of other economic variables—like diet, well-being, trade and consumption. In any premodern society, the former two must be depressingly low, and as for the latter two, working people need not apply—they are all just living at subsistence, and their consumption or trade is negligible. Subsistence is another one of those ideas that seems to address the 90 percent but, by flattening them into an ahistorical, timeless abstract, ultimately erases them.

How do we get around these temptations to fill in what we don't know with people and places we know better? How do we preserve the emphatic then-ness of then—the particular, often weird and distressing Romanness of Roman working people? In this book, we do so by sticking to ancient data from the hands and households of the 90 percent themselves. This book is constructed on such data. It steers clear of ethnographic interviews, data from modern agriculturalists or artisans, early modern household budgets, and all the other siren songs from better-known worlds. Perhaps as controversially, it draws only sparingly on the writings of Cicero & Co.: filling in the lives of the 90 percent with the opinions and prejudices of the 10 percent has been done for long enough. The payoff, though, is worth it. It is amazing how much we can know about the ancient 90 percent just by listening to them. The triple revolution in making, farming and everyday writing has produced mountains of information that allows them to write their own history.

While it may be more their own history, this doesn't mean it's necessarily a smooth or complete one. Archaeological data is often not quantified, and when it is, it can't be easily compared with texts. The texts—receipts, expense accounts, contracts—come overwhelmingly from a couple parts of the empire and are missing critical variables. We'll overemphasize some places—Pompeii, Britain, Egypt—and have less to say about others—the city of Rome, Asia Minor and North Africa—places that were more central economically but for which we have less robust data of the kind used here. Much of our data probably privileges the working middle and bottom-middle. The very bottom—the indigent, the homeless—are hard to see by any means. Comparative macroeconomic aggregates paper over these cracks; we shall have no choice but to confront them.

This book's comparative debt is not data but scale. It aspires to the granular, household budget-driven stories that the new poverty economics now tells—dense stories about how working households manage their resources.[71] Aspiration is the key term here: we don't yet have the data to write these kinds of dense household histories, so this book offers more fragmented versions. Throughout, too, we'll be reminded that the Roman world was not, in fact, sixteenth-century England or twentieth-century India. We owe working Romans, so long relegated to the sidelines, a history that is properly theirs, rather than rendering them in the clothing of an English manor farm servant or a Mumbai textile worker.

The Math of Small Things

It's one thing to know something about economic practices in the past. It's another to quantify them. The passion for numbers in economics is a product of the discipline's quantitative turn, and economic history's turn with it.[72] Beginning in the 1970s, economic historians began the search for big data in the past—what they called cliometrics. Wages paid to English builders, the height of American slaves, ages reported in the census or on tombstones—all these numbers could be gathered and analyzed to understand something about economies over the long term. What historians assumed those numbers meant sometimes turned out to be wrong: wages were often not equivalent to take-home income; slave heights didn't reflect only diet; age-accuracy doesn't always reflect numeracy. Those mistakes have sometimes led to better numbers, sometimes to new questions that can't be answered with numbers.

Finley was suspicious of numbers. He didn't think there was enough coherent evidence from the ancient world to scrape together even a single coherent data set, and since ancient people didn't think quantitatively about their economic lives, what would be the point? For a long time, historians and archaeologists mostly followed his lead. Now, with skepticism thrown to the wind and huge amounts of data piling up, we have quantitative analyses of everything: Roman loans, city sizes, coin-outputs and a myriad of other subjects.

Numbers save us from raiding the already bare cupboard of ancient evidence for a handful of compelling examples. Used correctly, numbers reveal differences even as they reveal patterns. For instance, only now that we have thousands of excavated farms can we see that most of them were pretty big, and the few very small ones had to cope with particular challenges. The thousands of moderate-sized loans throw the tiny ones into sharper, more desperate relief. The poetics of muchness, as one economist termed it, doesn't need to be obfuscating: it can reveal the majority's struggles in emphatic, even sympathetic ways that stories alone cannot.[73]

This book is based on lots of numbers as well as lots of stories. It draws on a wide range of datasets, many of which are wholly new. While the curious reader can find the raw analysis in the appendixes, the text and many figures provide an easy guide for even the number-allergic. For while quantitative data underlies this book, it has not been wrung particularly hard to yield up its stories. While statistical work has produced some important breakthroughs in working people's economics and the numbers that underlie this story are more robust than they once were, they are still fragile enough to collapse under too much pressing.[74] The kind of questions we're interested in here also don't necessarily require complex math. Ours is the math of household expense lists and interest rates and fractions of fractions—the math of small things.

The Road Ahead

The Roman 90 percent, as they emerge from these numbers and stories, were both/and-ers. They were avid trackers of their economic lives, but they only rarely used their accounting skills for future-oriented planning. They produced more than we thought, and they consumed more than we imagined. Neither of these was necessarily a sign of affluence. Their acquisitive society, awash with new goods and foods, produced its own consuming imperative. To belong, particularly but not only in cities, meant high costs of social inclusion. Their sophisticated, specialized agriculture was, in many places, the product of both opportunity and compulsion—new markets, shrinking amounts of land. Robust incomings were often quickly eroded by high outgoings, while erratic incomes required a robust portfolio of loans to bridge the gaps.

"Poverty" and "affluence" as simple descriptions of income poorly capture their constantly changing circumstances. Precarity—the high-wire act of balancing income with outflows—was the 90 percent's constant companion.

As the 90 percent carved a living from an unforgiving world, the sources of that precarity were somewhat different than we had imagined. Getting enough to eat was less of a problem for many than controlling expenses in a world of things. Producing higher wheat yields may have been easier than we thought, while finding enough land to feed one's cows was harder. Taxes appear to be less extortionate than bogglingly high rents. An obsessive tracking of expenses made sense in a world in which constant outflows—and thus the real challenges to savings—constituted the biggest threat to survival for many.

Our subjects will defy our efforts to categorize them. We will linger over small farmers, because farmers constituted the majority of the 90 percent, and because they have been ignored for too long. But these farmers were never just agriculturalists: they worked for wages, acted as small-scale traders of their own and others' produce, and were key players in the great craft industries. We will spend equal time in cities and very large villages, where professional titles—butcher, baker, jug-maker—will matter less than a shared gusto for things, and the frantic efforts to manage money flows in a world saturated with both cash and credit. Indeed, the divide between urban and rural people was constantly eroded in this world, as farmers moved to cities for trade and work, while city shopkeepers and artisans often kept small plots. Animals—key agents of both transportation and disease—followed them all from place to place.

The people we will meet in this book, like a great many modern people, lived in moments of plenty and dearth. One of the arguments of this book is that, like modern Americans, working Romans found it very hard to save. Much of an Egyptian farmer's plentiful harvest vanished into the pockets of his landlord; urban craftsmen's astonishing outputs were eroded by the social obligation to decorate their houses and keep a good-looking table. Socking away small sums without spending them the next month was particularly challenging. As a consequence, the Roman 90 percent lived in a world of risk, with limited buffers to cushion the bad times.

Working Romans' response to their risky, precarious world was an intense and relentless doing. The villager who used his wage account to buy wine on credit to sell for a profit: living in a monetized world meant squeezing the spaces between different kinds of money for maximum advantage. The Gallic small farmers who sold mustard and pigs to the city, or the Tuscan farmers who sold their excess wine to their neighbors: producing meant a high-wire act between selling your crops and eating them. The mine workers running futures markets on their meager rations; the sutlers who sold fish and prostituted their sisters to the army; Epimachus and his renting, wage-hustling and water-sharing: the Roman 90 percent confronted their complex, exploitative world by wringing its neck. Hustlers and operators, the subjects of the following pages bear witness to an economy of tenacity, maneuvering, and white-knuckled grit.

1

Let's Settle Up

FIGURE 1.1. Relief of an innkeeper and his client (Museo della Civiltà Romana/*CIL* 9.2689. Photo: © DeA Picture Library/Art Resource, NY)

Lucius Hot-Lover made (this monument) for himself and Fannia Delight while he was alive.
"Innkeeper, let's settle up."
"You have one sextarium of wine, and bread: one *as*; relish: one *as*."
"Agreed."
"The girl, eight *asses*."
"Agreed again."
"Hay for the mule, two *asses*."
"That mule will be the death of me!"[1]

THIS INN sign, posted over a tavern in the central Italian town of Isernia, made funny with the serious business of money. The innkeepers advertised their place with raunchy nicknames (Lucius Hot-Lover was almost certainly not his real name), a mock-monument ("while he was alive" is classic tombstone-speak), but above all through accounting. The fact that the hay costs less than the prostitute, but elicits the most buyer's remorse, is the funny bit. But the cheap prices for wine and bread, even the cost of a high-price prostitute, are all clearly accounted for—"we won't cheat you here" is the message. To make that doubly clear, the image shows innkeeper and the client, the latter clad in a hooded traveling cloak, using the particular Roman hand-signs for numbers—perhaps a two or a three, and a 13 (the total bill), respectively.[2] The image confirms the text, which is itself a confirmation of the bill. This may be a dive bar, the sign proclaims, but it's an honest one.

Working Romans were canny, deliberate and anxious accounters. While most of them were mostly illiterate, this did not prevent innkeepers and food-sellers, potters and miners, even some farmers, from tracking their economic lives in coherent ways. Today the very poorest on earth, those who live on less than two dollars per day and are often illiterate, keep track of their economic transactions in hyper-detail. They have to, for money is a matter of life and death. We'll see something similar in the Roman world. We'll find working Romans using basic accounting to track expenses and income, calculating interest on loans and speculating on future prices. We'll find them thinking insistently in money and worrying about it. Like the very poor today, working Romans did not need to be literate to be highly numerate. In fact, the degree to which a working person was literate was heavily determined by the degree to which their livelihood required them to make detailed accounts. For working Romans, on-the-job accounting drove reading and writing.

Deliberate the 90 percent may have been, but kin to the *homo economicus* of modern economics they were not. Their accounting thinking had particular qualities. They were capable of fairly high levels of abstraction—in terms of units and money. They were frantic keepers of expenses and, like the traveler, kept those lists to verify what they paid. But they more rarely used them to calculate or analyze. While working people had all the data and the tools to make calculations and decisions around profit, it's less clear that they did so, at least in any systematic, long-term way. Theirs was the planning born of precarity, of anticipating the arrival of the tax man or the repayment of loans, not of the strategic plan. As we shall see, this kind of shorter-term, less analytical accounting has much in common with the way working families think and plan today.

Although much of our evidence will come from cities—from shopkeepers, artisans and traders—we'll also try to pay attention to farmers. Not only were farmers the most numerous of the Roman 90 percent, but they have been imagined to lie outside any specifically accounting thinking.[3] Theirs, it was long assumed, was the business of family survival, of household production that did not require money or accounting or planning beyond the next harvest. Many scholars have long been convinced that farmers had an aversion to money, to monetary exchange and to accounting based on numbers and weights. We'll see that this mostly mispresents the Roman farming majority. Understanding how and why Roman farmers did, in fact, account and plan and engage with economic worlds outside family subsistence is thus doubly critical. Hard though it may be to see, farmers' accounting thinking, was, to a certain extent, the majority of Roman accounting thinking.

Indeed, the problem of farmers allows us the first of many opportunities to explode the Roman 90 percent as a group and see instead its enormous diversity. Working Romans displayed a spectrum of accounting thinking that varied not so much by their relative wealth or even by their profession, but by how much their lives brought them into contact with certain institutions and activities. The army, the state, surplus production and trade—these were the contexts that inculcated dense and persistent accounting practices into people who came in contact with them. This chapter argues that, to a degree that is historically remarkable, many more people intersected with these institutions or activities than we had appreciated—from small-scale artisans and family traders to many farmers.

Economic Thinking, Accounting Thinking

The development of capitalist economies since the nineteenth century has prompted scholars to ask hard questions about what economics actually is, and what distinguishes our contemporary attitudes to profit, risk and money from those of people who lived in the past. Sharp debates once divided those who thought that rational decision-making around concepts of value determined by a market could be traced back to the very ancient Near East, and those who thought such concepts were purely a product of modern capitalism.[4] This latter camp regarded the *oikonomia* (they used the ancient Greek term deliberately) of premodern societies as being entirely embedded in social entities—the family and household first (the *oikos*), and then the broader community. Social values and social hierarchies determined how people thought and made decisions about what they grew or produced. Abstract concepts of value, and thus the accounting of those units and making decisions around them, were not, so the argument went, how ancient people thought.

In retrospect of the past fifty years—of behavioral economics, of economic sociology, of many market failures—the distinction between rational versus socially embedded thinking seems a pointless one. It's clear that our contemporary economic decisions are embedded in social or political values. It's clear that economic actors are often irrational. Conversely, it's also clear that premodern people were debt-quantifiers and gain-seekers.[5] The modern *homo economicus* has turned out to be as much of a mirage as the so-called primitive market. But while the debate may seem overly polarized today, it left a lasting imprint on Roman history. Moses Finley, very much in the second camp of thinkers and taking seriously what Cicero & Co. said about their own affairs, firmly believed that Romans of all stripes didn't think "economically" in any way a modern person would recognize as economic. Their decisions about production and exchange were embedded in their concern for status, and their financial thinking and bookkeeping were therefore rudimentary.[6] A Roman senator farmed not to make a profit, but because land was the basis of his status, and he managed his land with an eye to preservation and risk avoidance. For many scholars who accepted (and still accept) this view, ancient workers—including the farmers and potters and spinners who are our subject here—lived subsistence lives. This meant not only that they produced just enough to survive through the next harvest, but also that they thought in "just-enough" ways. They practiced risk avoidance and rules of thumb, and avoided trade, money and the abstract thinking that went with them.[7]

As we noted in the introduction, the pendulum has recently swung the other way. Economic thinking has been imputed mostly to institutions and to the structures—law, monetary policy, taxation—that impacted performance. Recent work has argued that these institutions, from the imperial mint to large estates to clubs of traders, often made rationalizing decisions intended to expand market access and improve efficiencies.[8] Romans, or Roman institutions at any rate, now appear to have at least some characteristics of the rational-actor *homo economicus.*[9]

How we evaluate ancient people's economic thinking—or lack of it—depends in part on how we evaluate markets. So-called primitive markets, where exchange is centered on barter or small-scale exchange of nonessentials, appear to require a different kind of thinking and a different set of tools than capitalist markets where exchange is more frequent and based on fluctuating prices set in money.[10] So if, as Finley thought, Roman markets were relatively small in scale, erratic and unintegrated, they might be readily managed by a small group of accountants doing basic tallies. Were Roman markets much larger in scale, relatively stable at the regional level, and pretty well integrated—as we now believe—this would have required a different set of practices, both on the part of institutions and individuals.[11] In short, while the different "types" of markets are categories of analysis, used by anthropologists or historians to chop up societies, they do have some implications for everyday practice.

Rather than using economic structures like markets or analytical categories like subsistence to deduce economic thinking, we'll take a leaf out of studies on the contemporary poor, studies that make sense of working people's thinking based on what they actually do.[12] We'll refrain, for the moment, from categorizing our subjects: we'll meet them where they lived and worked to unearth how they thought about, planned and tracked their material lives. Put another way, we shall be more concerned with accounting—as practice—than economics—as structure. Accounting thinking—not economic thinking—is where the pressures of daily life meet the tools, contexts and practices used to order and act on them.

How can we possibly know how a Roman carpenter or farmer thought about the business of getting by? A whole range of evidence is now available that didn't exist in Finley's time, and that is only now starting to make its voice felt in the study of ancient history. Most important are the accounting tools written or signed by working people's own hands: expense lists they kept to track their outgoings; contracts for labor or leases or loans; receipts for sales or wages paid; even letters, which very often mix economic matters—a plea from a widow for spinning work, or a suggestion to speculate on peaches—with the personal.[13] Also part of working people's lives were the records kept by "the man": the account books of medium to large rural estates; the pay-books and ration receipts of the army; the tax records of the state. All these records are best preserved in Egypt, where the dry climate preserved the papyri and pottery sherds (ostraca) on which these accounts and loans and letters were written. The waterlogged soils of rainy Britain have done similar work, preserving wooden tablets used by innkeepers in London and army sutlers near Hadrian's Wall. Finally, a plastered wall was all that was needed for many working people to jot down their expense lists, loan documents, or pay acknowledgments in the form of graffiti.

All of these records are, of course, written, and thus privilege those who could write or who could find people to write for them. But a majority of people in the Roman world could not write: How do we excavate their accounting thinking? In part we shall find their thinking in images and in archaeology—from the sophisticated finger-counting systems used in the humorous inn-sign to the discovery of weights, coins and writing instruments in Roman farmhouses. Here we'll also need to pay particular attention to pragmatic contexts: In what contexts would working Romans have needed to track expenses, estimate yields or calculate interest, even if we don't have explicit records of them doing so? In what contexts didn't it matter?[14] Above all, we shall have to be attentive to variety, for not all working Romans needed or used the same economic toolkit. From a vast, highly numerate accounting underclass staffed by enslaved people to the illiterate small farmer, those who worked with their hands did not all account—or need to account—the same.

As we'll see, working Romans were steeped in a world of money, and we'll look in detail at their financial instruments in chapter 5. But their money was quite different from our money. The modern reader may find a word of two of explanation useful before diving into their accounts.[15] Residents in different parts of the Roman empire used different money systems, anchored, at least in theory, around the principal coin of the realm—the silver denarius. The coins of daily use, those that dominate everyday accounting, were bronze—the *as* and sestertius in the Roman West, the obol and the drachma in Egypt, and the drachma, the assarius and the obol in the Roman East. As a rule of thumb, the Roman sestertius and Egyptian bronze drachma were broadly equivalent (each four to the silver denarius). Four asses made a sestertius, and six or seven Egyptian obols made a drachma.[16] As much as the modern reader might wish it, it's impossible to provide modern dollar or euro equivalents to these coins. It's more accurate to give a sense of what they could buy. A loaf of bread cost around three *as* in Pompeii, an obol in Egypt, or two obols in cities of the Greek East.[17] Thus, the *as* and the obol were somewhat more valuable than small change today, while the sestertius and the drachma were used for more significant but still daily purchases. Prices for nonwheat items increased slowly through the first two centuries of empire, punctuated by moments of more pronounced inflation in the 160s and again in the 270s CE.[18] So expenses from later first-century CE Pompeii, for instance, are not readily comparable with those from the mid-late third-century city of Ephesus. For this reason, we restrict our discussion, here and throughout this book, to working people of the first two and a half centuries of empire, when we can more readily compare their economic lives.

Accounting Tools: Beyond (Il)literacy and (In)numeracy

Working Romans' ability to keep track of their economic lives is clearly tied to their ability to do basic arithmetic, and secondarily to their ability to record their arithmetic in writing. Numeracy and literacy are distinct skills.[19] Highly numerate people may be capable of doing and storing complex arithmetic procedures in their head (ancient people had to remember a lot more than we do), while literate people (even today) might be incapable of basic mental addition.

In the modern world of mass literacy and numeracy, we tend to ask, "Can you read and write?" or "Can you do long division?"—posed as a yes-no question. But in earlier worlds, where the ability to read, write and do math were much less widespread, there was a wide spectrum of literacy and numeracy, from being able to read some words or count to a hundred, to writing one's name or adding and subtracting, to keeping written accounts or calculating compound interest. Rather than an on-off switch—literate or illiterate, numerate or innumerate—accounting thinking involved a range of processes, many of which did not require writing, although they could be facilitated by it. Accounting thinking involves number operations from counting, measuring and labeling, to adding, subtracting, fractions and percentages. It also involves intentions—to verify a total, to keep track of expenses.

In the first instance, accounting thinking requires accounting tools. Those tools might be mathematical operations, from adding to percentages, or physical objects to facilitate those operations, from counters to account books. Objects and operations are necessarily entangled, the physical tools revealing the kinds of thinking required to use them. As we'll see, working Romans had a simple but efficient and very particular accounting toolkit: a range of both basic and more complex tools to do a range of operations, from expense tracking to calculating long-term interest.

Unwritten Tools

While today counting and writing are taught together—math and reading—this is a recent invention. Many cultures had complex systems of nonwritten counting and accounting. It's no accident that one of the most complex of these nonwritten systems was developed by the Romans, seemingly first in Italy, from which it spread to the northern and eastern provinces. This was a system of finger counting, in which the left-hand fingers were used for numbers up to nine and the tens while the right hand counted hundreds and thousands.[20] The system is preserved for us in a medieval text and confirmed from ancient game tokens, which had the hand sign on one side and the Latin numeral on the other (figure 1.2), and from images like the humorous inn-sign with which we began this chapter. While it's called a "finger-counting" system, it was not only used to count, but also to do basic arithmetic operations—addition, subtraction, multiplication. Cicero even suggests it was possible to calculate interest—that is, division—through this system.[21]

Historically, finger-counting systems develop in contexts where accounting is constant and public, a matter between two or more parties. Trading and mercantile communities are big users of finger-counting systems.[22] These are also the contexts where the Roman finger-counting system thrived. We find it in contexts of buying and selling, as in an image of a woman selling vegetables from the port city of Ostia (figure 1.3), in manufacturing or tax collecting. As with our inn-sign, in all these contexts finger counting had a secondary function—transparency. Both parties can literally see the math.[23]

Another historically common, nonwritten tool for accounting is the counter: a physical board or grid with objects used to represent quantities. Most readers will be familiar with the so-called eastern or Chinese abacus—a mobile arrangement of wires and sliding tokens. In the Greek and Roman worlds, more common and easier to use was the board or western abacus, composed of a grid of lines drawn on a flat surface with any small object used as counters, or a metal version with attached counters.[24] Like the finger

FIGURE 1.2. Bone tessera showing the finger-counting gesture for the number seven on the obverse and the Roman numeral seven on the reverse (MMA Froehner 322a and b. Photo: Bibliothèque Nationale de France, Médailles et Antiques)

FIGURE 1.3. Relief of vegetable saleswoman using finger counting to show the number eight (Museo Ostiense, inv. 198. Photo: Erich Lessing/Art Resource, NY)

counting systems, one column (usually on the right) was used for numbers up to nine, and other columns to the left for tens, hundreds, and so on. Alternatively, the different columns could stand for monetary divisions—asses, sestertii and denarii, or obols, drachms and tetradrachms—or for weights. The board version could be drawn up on any surface—many were scratched ad hoc on floors—and any small object—pebbles, pottery sherds—used as counters. Like the finger-counting systems, the table abacus could be used for addition, subtraction, multiplication and division. And like that system, it made for good public math: a second party could watch the tallies being made. Many of the preserved abaci come from the floors of urban marketplaces, while images of these items appear in scenes of commerce.[25]

The Roman finger-counting system and the abacus provided quick and easy-to-use tools for not necessarily literate users to do the math required in exchange contexts. It is not a coincidence that we find them in places thick with the need to account—marketplaces, traders' warehouses, inns, tax-collection points—and to verify those accounts to another party. Their limitations were obvious: both systems were ephemeral. They could not preserve calculations or verification for future reference. This, of course, is where writing comes in. But even here, one need not know how to write to preserve some accounts. Tallies—lines representing numbers—are found etched into walls and on pots all over the empire, the result of people counting—counting objects produced or delivered, sums received or spent. Tallies are the most common form of economic graffiti found on the walls of Pompeii.[26] Rarely do we know what was being tallied, only that the need to count and record that count was common.

These nonwritten accounting tools reveal both the need, and the partial openness, of basic accounting to the nonliterate. As we turn to writing and written accounting, we must imagine a similarly open field. Ancient writers occupied a much wider spectrum of "literacy" than our mass-literacy world tends to admit. And much of that spectrum was occupied by people who needed to do accounting things with writing—from using written numbers to do math or keeping a basic list of expenses, to adding an affidavit to a contract.

The Many Forms of Written Accounting

Written accounts have the obvious advantage of durability and confirmability: they preserve transactions in the now for use in the future—for checking, for more complex calculation, and, like finger counting, for confirmation to third parties. Roman people who could write, or have someone write for them, kept a range of accounting documents. Some of these we would consider accounting tools, like shop account books or expense lists. Some of these we would probably classify as legal documents. But most had an accounting function, even if they appear not to. Between their badly spelled words and unfamiliar technical language, these documents also reveal the particular kinds of accounting thinking used by everyone from travelers to farmers, whether they could read or not.

FIGURE 1.4. Expenses tracked on an ostracon from the Red Sea port of Berenike (*O. Berenike* 2.210. Photo: S. E. Sidebotham. Creative Commons Attribution 4.0 License)

The most basic and common form of written accounting preserved from the Roman world is the expense list.[27] Here's a short example, scribbled on a potsherd from a port on the Red Sea, transcribed with its original formatting (see figure 1.4 for the original):

Account 22nd bunch of cabbage, [ ]
bunch of parsley, 1 obol
23rd salt fish [or meat], [ ]
salt fish [or meat], 2 obols

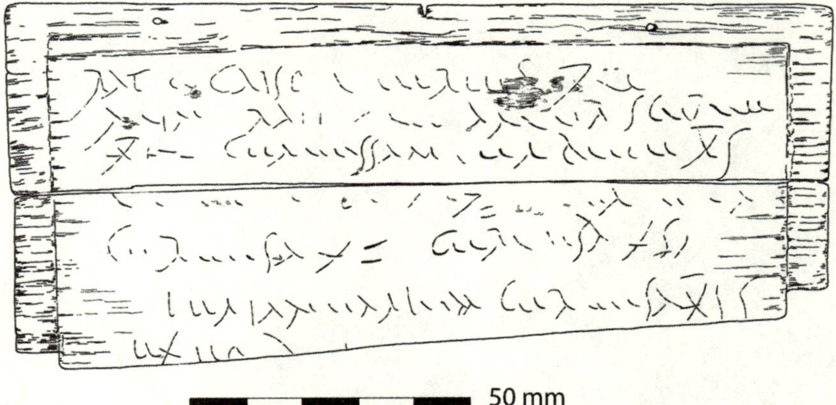

FIGURE 1.5. Accounts of a Roman beer buyer from London (*T. Lond. Bloomberg* 72. Photo: © MOLA [Museum of London Archaeology]/Roger S. O. Tomlin)

revenue [?], 3 obols
cabbage, 4 obols
bread, 2 obols
salt fish [or meat], 2 obols

26th bread, 2 obols

27th bread, 2 obols

artabai (of wheat), 2 obols[28]

In their small sums spent on small amounts of things—principally food—these lists describe the expense-keeping of those who had to count their pennies. Whether written on the back of a potsherd, scratched on a wall or written on papyrus, such lists usually include a list of items and their costs, with the longer examples, like this one, organized by date.[29]

Small business tracked their transactions in similarly basic ways. An innkeeper or beer-dealer in Roman London tracked his beer deliveries on a wood-and-wax tablet, made from reused barrels (figure 1.5):

Account of Crispus. Beer: 5 denarii
. . . 105 [units]: 7 denarii
(and) 3 asses. Beer, through Brutus: half a denarius
. . . 2 asses . . .
Beer: 2 asses. Beer: half a denarius (and) one-quarter. Through Januarius, beer: one (and) a half denarii[30]

While the account is fragmentary, the account lists what appear to be deliveries by the suppliers' name (an example of third-party accounting) and amounts paid.

The dozens of expense lists that come down from the Roman world reveal some basic accounting tools. We find a mania for recording the cost of things in money, and a tendency to order those costs in chronologically organized lists. We also find a disinclination to record the quantities of the items listed—the quantities of beer or bread and fish—and a reluctance to tally the totals, two seeming oddities we'll discuss further below.

Working Romans also kept track of their loans, even for tiny sums. These were recorded on the same cheap media as expense lists, scribbled on papyri, potsherds or tablets. They reveal somewhat more complex accounting thinking—the ability to calculate interest and, often, to track future repayment dates. A graffito from a bar in Pompeii lists the date, name of the lenders—in this case two woman, Vettia and Faustilla—the amount loaned and the interest, presumably deducted from the amount loaned:

> 4 days before the Ides of February. Vettia, 20 denarii, interest 12 asses.
> The Nones of February from Faustilla, 15 denarii, interest 8 asses.[31]

A loan between a mine worker and a soldier in the Egyptian desert, written on a pottery sherd, is much more complex:

> Ammonios, son of Vergilius, worker in the Porphyrites quarry, to Hareotes, soldier of the Alexandrian fleet, greetings. I acknowledge the loan of four drachmas which I will pay back promptly in two monthly installments of two drachmas each, one in Phaophi [October] and the other in Hathyr [November]. The 5th year of our emperor Antoninus [141 CE], Toth 21 [18 September].
>
> [different hand] I have received as indicated above. Ammonius.[32]

Even though the amount loaned is very small, the ostracon is laid out in proper chirographic form—the letter-like format that had legal validity in the Roman East—complete with a greeting, the name of the borrower, the lender, the amount loaned and the due dates for repayment.[33] The borrower, Ammonius, even adds his affidavit at the bottom.

Papyri, protected by the dry climates of Roman Egypt and Judea, preserve some of the most complex accounting documents used by working people. These include both expense lists and loan documents, as well as other accounting tools found only on papyri—shop accounts, wage accounts, plus a whole array of receipts, from wheat purchases to loan quittances. We'll encounter these documents throughout this book, but will pause here to describe two forms, documents which, while not strictly accounting tools, have much to reveal about accounting thinking throughout the empire. These are the land lease and the tax declaration.

Hundreds of agreements to rent land survive from Egypt.[34] Leases were most often written by professional notaries, although some were written by the parties themselves. An example for some land leased near the city of Oxyrhynchus allows us a glimpse of their parameters:

> Tryphon son of Aristandros and Sarapion son of Herodes, inhabitants of Oxyrhynchus, have leased to Apollonius son of Horus, of the village of Senepta . . . for the present 6th year of the emperor Hadrian [121 CE], from their property at the said village in the holding of Dion, the 10 1/2 arourae [2.8 hectares] upon which grain has been grown, of which the adjacent areas are on the east the land of Didymus, on the south that of the aforesaid lessors, on the north the same, on the west the land of Seuthes son of Potamon. [This] land is to be cultivated with grass for cutting and grazing at a rent for each aroura, without a survey being made, of 36 drachmae of silver, guaranteed against all risks, the taxes upon the land being paid by the lessor, who shall be the owner of the crop until he recovers the rent. If this lease is guaranteed [made official], the lessee shall pay the rent in the month of June of the said year and shall forfeit any arrears increased by one half, and the lessor shall have the right of execution upon the said Apollonius and upon all his property as if in accordance with a legal decision.[35]

Here Apollonius has leased a small plot of land, currently in grain but to be planted in grasses for hay. The lease, while not an accounting tool itself, reveals a whole raft of tools with which Egyptian farmers must have been familiar: the measure of land in units of area (in Egypt, the unit was the aroura, around 0.27 hectares), rent in cash or in kind per land unit, and in this case, fractions of that rent for the calculation of penalty payments. Calendrical deadlines, expressed in months, were also part and parcel of these farmers' lives.

The other, all-too-familiar accounting document was the tax declaration. We'll return in a moment to taxation and the enormous impact it made on accounting thinking. In the meantime, it will be useful to get a sense of what one such document might look like. One of our most complete examples was found in a cave near the Dead Sea and was made by a Jewish woman named

Babatha.[36] Among Babatha's letters, marriage contract, loan documents and many legal complaints was a declaration of her ownership of four date orchards, made to the local tax authorities in Maoza (near Petra in Jordan) (figure 1.6). A portion of the declaration provides a sense of the complex accounting required by all owners of land:

> . . . As a census of Arabia is being conducted by Titus Aninius Sextius Florentinus governor, I, Babatha, daughter of Simon of Maoza in the Zoarene [district] of the Petra administrative region, domiciled in my own private property in said Maoza, register what I possess . . . as follows: within the boundaries of Maoza a date orchard called Algiphiamma, the area of sowing being one *saton* three *kaboi* of barley, paying as tax, in dates, Syrian [dates] and mixed [dates] fifteen *sata*, "splits" 10 sata and for crown tax one "black" and thirty sixteenths. [The property] abuts a road and the sea. [Also] within the boundaries of Maoza, a date orchard called Algiphiamma, the area of sowing being one *kabos* of barley, paying as tax a half share of the crops produced each year. [The property] abuts the *moscantic* estate of our lord Caesar and the sea. . . . [37]

In among the all-too-familiar legalese of the tax document, and the very unfamiliar weights and currencies, we catch a glimpse of some more accounting tools, tools with which any owner of land must have been acquainted. Unlike the land lease, here no land units are used, only the volume of seed required for sowing—a less abstract, less precise method of representing area. On the other hand, the statement of taxes previously paid is complex, for these taxes were paid both in kind (in various kinds of dates) and in cash (probably a combination of imperial and local currencies). A comparison of the different land sizes with the amount of tax paid makes it clear that the tax was based not only on the area of the land, but also on its different yields.[38] The Babatha declaration thus throws into stark relief the kind of accounting tools required by the Roman tax apparatus, at least in some regions: calculation of land area either in sowing volume or unit area, a general knowledge of agricultural yields translated into both volume and monetary value, and an ability, at first or second hand, to communicate those facts in what may not have been one's first or second language, but even a third.[39]

For Babatha's declaration raises yet again the question of literacy and its intersection with accounting tools. Babatha, a modest property owner and a native Aramaic and/or Nabataean speaker, was not only unable to write in the Greek in which she transacted most of her financial life, but her land/tax declaration

FIGURE 1.6. Babatha's land declaration (*P. Yadin* 1.16. Photo: Najib Anton Albina. Courtesy of The Leon Levy Dead Sea Scrolls Digital Library, IAA)

was penned and even signed by others on her behalf. Her document, like so many of the accounts and loans and leases we'll examine in this book, describes the widespread use of written accounting by a spectrum of illiterates.

Many of the accounting tools we examined above—the expense lists, loan documents, land leases—were used by people who could not read or write them. Some, like Babatha, could not write or read in any language. Others included a large group of self-described "slow-writers," people who could write slowly and with difficulty in either their first or their second language, and indicated this when they asked others to write for them on legal documents.[40] In the provinces, their ranks were swelled by those whose native languages, like Celtic, were mostly not written, or, like Demotic, were not allowed in legal documents. These slow-writers even included those who had accounting jobs. A priest from the village of Soknopaiou Nesos in Egypt was a slow-writer, but it didn't prevent him from taking up an extra job as an estate bookkeeper. Even some village clerks—people who were involved in the village tax collection, among other things—were only able to sign their name and copy some basic phrases. These people filled the vast ranks of the not-quite-illiterate who nonetheless used writing, particularly accounting writing and its legal accessories.[41]

Accounting Contexts

How representative were people like Babatha? Was a knowledge of area, of yields and of volumetric measures, but an inability to write, typical? How many Roman working people could do basic accounting math? How many people could read?

Ancient history's answers to this last question have ranged from "almost everyone," to "virtually no one," to, most recently, "probably more than we thought."[42] We've suggested that these aren't quite the right questions to ask. Our quick survey of accounting tools and a spectrum of numeracy and literacy points beyond an easy answer, beyond a number of the kind the World Bank might produce. That spectrum, above all, points to contexts. That is, rather than asking how many people could perform basic accounting arithmetic or read or write at any of a range of levels, it's more useful to ask—who would have needed to do these things? What were the activities in which accounting thinking was particularly critical? These are what scholars of literacy term "cognitive contexts," the real-world situations where our innate cognitive skills are kindled to life by particular needs.[43] In the modern world, this context is mostly school—the context in which we are taught to read and write. But in premodern societies, where formal schooling was mostly restricted to cities and wealthier families, other contexts were more important—the context of work and the business of survival.

In the Roman world, the cognitive contexts for accounting thinking were particularly thick on the ground, due to a combination of the violent, extractive nature of its empire and the historically unprecedented scale of its trade.[44] This doesn't mean that everyone could or needed to engage in accounting practices. It means that the situations in which people encountered accounting practices were unprecedentedly common, and the kinds of people who encountered them unprecedentedly diverse. Thus, the full spectrum of accounting tools—from mental arithmetic of the farmer calculating sowing ratios, to finger-counting by a vegetable merchant, to a poll-tax declaration from a camel driver—were used by more people. This still means that lots of people didn't account—that is, they didn't keep mental or written accounts—but more probably did.

Taxing, Fighting, Trading

The Roman contexts around which accounting practices particularly concentrated were the state, the army, and trade. These are, not coincidentally, the same contexts that, throughout history, have tended to stimulate literacy, the particular literacy that is rooted in the need to account.

The Roman state, like most states, needed large amounts of accounting and maintained a small army of scribes to do this work.[45] The state also impacted its subjects' accounting thinking in particular ways. In classical Athens, mandatory participation in democratic governance regularly immersed citizens in counting systems—ballots, randomized jury selection, budgets.[46] The Roman state inculcated accounting thinking through a more ruthless process—taxation.[47] Most working Romans living outside Italy—that is, in the provinces—were required to pay property taxes. Most, too, would probably have paid a head or poll tax. Everyone, Italians included, paid toll taxes levied on goods in transit. Sales tax was applied to goods sold at auctions. In Egypt, where we have the best evidence, we know of dozens of other kinds of taxes, from taxes on livestock to taxes for use of the baths to taxes paid in lieu of work on the irrigation dikes.

Paying different kinds of taxes inculcated different kinds of accounting thinking. For instance, anyone moving goods between two urban territories had to know the value of those goods in order to declare the toll tax, which was calculated as a percentage of value. Larger-scale traders would have required more sophisticated accounts than smaller ones, but the difference was a matter of scale, not of kind.[48] Some of the most complex accounting thinking, however, was required by potentially the most numerous group of people: this was the calculative thinking required for property taxes.

The Roman property tax system was a hodgepodge of newly imposed rules and inherited traditions. Some provincials—in Sicily, for instance—may have paid a simple percentage of their crops in cash or kind.[49] In Egypt, the Romans imposed a new flat rate per unit of area for arable land. Increasingly, however, the Roman state relied on granular data to assess the tax potential of all of its possessions. Every ten years (14 years in Egypt), the Roman state required provincial residents to make a statement not only of their persons, but, in most places (except Egypt), also of their property. This was the dreaded census.

The goal of the census was to establish not only the basis of the head or poll tax, but also (again, except for Egypt) the general basis of the property tax. Property owners, even the smallest holders, were required to know the area of their land. They also had to declare the quality of its soils. In the case of vineyards and olive groves, they had to count up the number of plants. In many regions, as in Babatha's case, property owners also needed to provide, or at least understand, an average yield on the land's agricultural output. In Egypt, land taxation was less invasive: village clerks maintained property records, and the census didn't include a redeclaration of land.[50] Apart from Egypt, however, as the Roman state relied less and less on the hated tax-farmers for the mechanics of tax collection, the more granular and more important became the declarations from individuals themselves. It's no wonder that peoples new to such systems of accounting—like the British and the Gauls—rebelled when it was instated. Taxation would not only have made demands on their wealth; it also forced upon them an unaccustomedly invasive accounting.

It's important to keep Roman taxation thinking in perspective. Its requirements were considerably less than those of income-based tax systems. In fifteenth-century Tuscany, for instance, farmers appeared at the tax office with accounts tracking their yearly earnings from multiple income streams.[51] Nor were the Roman taxation strategies invasive on a daily basis. In comparison, the early-twentieth-century *mezzadria* or Italian sharecropping accounts required landlord and farmer to physically share a daily account book.[52] On the other hand, the Roman assessment by individual plot size and productivity introduced a level of individual responsibility: this was absent in tax systems like those of mercantile Venice, where tax was assessed by outsiders on villages with little farmer input.[53] Roman land tax systems required that families had numerical knowledge of land area, trees or other productive units, and possibly even their yields over time. The latter requirement in particular, if widespread, would have required recordkeeping—mental or written—and the ability to calculate a rough average.

The number of people caught in the net of land-tax accounting thinking was enormous. As we'll see, even urban artisans often owned tiny plots of rural land, let alone the millions of rural smallholders. The net would have tightened every ten years, when the census came around, and may have lain loosely at other times. It impacted only those who owned land, not tenants, although their landlords may have demanded a yearly accounting of yields for their own tax declarations. Even with these caveats, the impact of the Roman land tax on accounting thinking can scarcely be overestimated.

More limited in its overall impact on accounting thinking was the army.[54] The Roman army, like all armies, ran on accounts: manpower estimates, supply registers, payrolls. Once in the army's grip, legionaries and auxiliaries, officers and common soldiers, army wives and sutlers were all caught in the army's accounting web. Officers were responsible for the accounts of their units, and were thus the most insistent account keepers, while simple soldiers signed for their pay and its myriad deductions, signed for rations while on patrol, and so on. For soldiers lived in a world of account money: their pay was often paid on account rather than in cash. We have such accounts from the forts of northern Britain and Switzerland, from the fortress at Masada in Israel, and from the eastern desert of Egypt: soldiers' pay accounts with perquisite deductions; sutlers' accounts, ration receipts for pack animals.[55] The army functioned like an overgrown, violent company store, and those in its grasp, literate or not, would have absorbed its habit of account money and, perhaps, account keeping.

The second-century army counted only some 400,000 men—less than one percent of the overall population but still substantial by premodern standards. It was concentrated heavily in the northwest and easternmost provinces, where its tentacles of accounting practices would have wound themselves into many aspects of daily life. The Vindolanda tablets from near Hadrian's Wall, for instance, find soldiers of all ranks putting bacon and socks on account, making up loan documents and tracking their constant debts.[56] But the impact of those practices would also have been spread by its veterans, particularly auxiliary veterans who, recruited overwhelmingly from among rural provincial farmers, very often returned to their home villages.[57] Once discharged, we often find them putting their accounting thinking to work as sutlers, traders and large-scale farmers. The auxiliary veterans were potentially as important a vector of accounting thinking as the army itself.

The third major context that required accounting thinking was trade.[58] The trade networks that moved wine from Italy to Asia Minor, wheat from Egypt to Rome, or textiles from Gaul to the frontier armies required whole chains of accounting thinking. Waybills, tax receipts, seals tallying the contents of sacks—all are the detritus of such accounting. From Sotas, a small-scale farmer and trader who paid the toll tax on his surplus vetch and grain, to the clothing merchants using lead sack-tags so the contents could be readily valued, to potters who made transport amphorae to standard volumes and etched the names of shipper or receiver on the stoppers—all these people found themselves in contexts of certain kinds of accounting thinking.[59] It has often been assumed that only large-scale, long-distance traded goods required such accounting. But the ubiquity of poll taxes made all traders, large-scale or small, long-distance or short, keep some kind of accounts.

If trade was an accounting-dense activity, cities were accounting-dense spaces. Roman cities were hot spots of trade and exchange, and the folks we met earlier, from the vegetable seller in the great port of Ostia to the innkeeper from small-town Isernia, lived in a world of goods received, credit accounts for customers, and, as we'll see, a monetary value for pretty much everything. Retail and artisanal work, which tended to be centered in cities, were accounting-dense occupations. Cities housed the state's bureaucratic apparatus, including its tax collection offices and its dozens of officials and their staff. Cities also hosted army garrisons: the same wooden tablets from London that preserved those beer deliveries contained dozens of loan documents witnessed by soldiers.

Consuming, Producing, Wage Earning

The state, the army and exchange were the most obvious contexts of accounting thinking. But other contexts required more daily kinds of accounting practices, activities that were essential parts of Roman working people's experience. The first, most basic context was buying things from other people, with money. An autarkic world in which families produce most of what they need has little need for money, and thus little need for monetary exchange and keeping track of money. As we shall see in chapter 2, this autarkic world was not the Roman world. Romans of all stripes, including farmers, bought consumer goods with great gusto. In the wake of their consumption would have followed the basic practice of valuing things by their price. For some, consumption also meant tracking those purchases through expense accounting.

Selling crops off the farm also carries with it the need to account.[60] Rather than eyeballing the amount needed for next year's seed and family needs, surplus-producing farmers were pulled into market exchange. They sold their excess crop to consumers or to middlemen or doled it out for the tax man. They were enmeshed in fluctuating prices, transport costs, toll taxes and future-oriented thinking. As we'll see in chapter 3, most Roman farmers were engaged in surplus production to a greater or lesser degree. Some, even some small farmers, elected to specialize in certain crops destined for nearby cities. In this way, a sizable chunk of the farmer-majority Roman world was pulled into accounting thinking.

Wage-labor also enforces a certain kind of accounting thinking in those it touches. One must be familiar with going rates, equate time with money, and, in some contexts, contend with payment by account, not only in cash. As we'll find in chapter 4, working for wages was ubiquitous in the Roman world—in cities, the countryside, in all kinds of activities from grape harvesting to clay hauling. Labor was a commodity, and the many kinds of people who both bought and sold it, as workers or employers, were involved in accounting its value.

Accounting for Slavery

If labor was an accounted commodity, what about the labor of those who were themselves a commodity, namely slaves? In the American South, the rise of large-scale slave agriculture was bound up with developments in large-scale bookkeeping—in particular, the detailed accounting of labor and time that was also crucial to industrialization. Slavery's brutal accounting and American capitalism thus share a rationalizing mentality.[61] It's unlikely the same was true in ancient Rome, at least in any direct way. The most explicit statement we have about the accounting on a slave-run farm comes from Cato the Elder, who records slave manpower requirements and rations for a wine estate—a brutally stark reckoning that somewhat recalls those of an American plantation account book.[62] But much of Cato's account also recalls the manpower assessments and rations of the Roman army, an accounting system with which he, like so many of his contemporaries, was intimately familiar as a long-time army officer.[63] Army accounting and slave-estate accounting have so much in common—the dehumanization and enumeration of people for tasks, tracking of materiel, ration requirements—that it would be hard to disentangle the accounting footprint of one from the other. So, too, our most detailed accounts of rationalized labor and its deployment come from Egyptian estates, where slaves were less commonly used.[64]

Slavery and accounting did go hand-in-hand in other ways, for enslaved people filled the ranks of a vast accounting underclass.[65] Scribes, accountants, bookkeepers—the key figures in most professionalized accounting—were often (although not always) slaves. In many of the contexts we explored above—larger farms and trading enterprises—slaves maintained and expanded the accounting praxis. Enslaved and freed people were key figures in banking and moneylending: the accounts of Caecilius Iucundus, a former slave from Pompeii, form one of our most detailed records of business accounting as it related to moneylending and sales-at-auction. It's not too much to say that it was the enslaved who both perfected and expanded Roman accounting through many areas of commercial activity.

Slaves also had their own particular relationships with money. Roman slaves might receive a *peculium*—money or valuables gifted to them by their masters.[66] This could range from a few sestertii to huge fortunes. But even smaller *peculia,* and slaves' income and expenditure generally, demanded unusual accounting. Because they were so often spending their master's money—either as their master's representative, for their own upkeep, or using their *peculia*—slaves were particularly needful of keeping accounts. As we shall see in chapter 2, some of the expense lists that have come down to us—graffiti scratched on the walls of a fine dining room or accounts kept by gladiators or their trainers—may have been generated by enslaved people, their use of verificatory accounting a product of their dependency, their enslavement. The relationship between slavery and accounting, then, was a powerful one, albeit quite different from the slave-capitalism of early America.

Accounting Histories

The final important accounting context was not an institution or an activity or a group of people, but history. The Roman empire included regions with wildly different histories of the written word, of measurement and taxation. In other words, the empire was a collection of different accounting histories. These different, pre-Roman accounting histories had an enormous impact on literacy, numeracy and their entanglement with accounting thinking. The experiences of the residents of Roman Egypt compared with those of Roman Britain provide a stark comparison.

For more than a thousand years before the advent of Roman rule, since the time of the New Kingdom pharaohs, the farmers and artisans of Egypt paid rent and taxes, knew the value of even the humblest objects in their tombs, and maintained written records of all these things.[67] The history of verificatory accounting—accounting for the purposes of proving something's value, or demonstrating that a transaction had been accomplished—was powerful in Egypt. It continued under the region's Greek Ptolemaic kings, whose tax and accounting bureaucracies reached right down into smaller rural villages. Changes to the region's land tax assessment under the Romans—from a percentage of the harvest to a unit per area tax—would have required yet more granular accounting. Accounting thinking was already a millennium-long and reasonably deep cultural habit, one that was maintained and deepened under Roman rule.

The impact of this long accounting history—and its limits—peers through some proxies for accounting thinking. One of these was knowing your real age. Today, governments, schools and banks all require us to know our age and birthdate. In the historical past, the ability to recall one's specific age varied enormously, depending how much age mattered in a particular society, and to what extent institutions inculcated age-recall as part of daily life. In historical terms, Roman Egyptians' ability to accurately declare their age for the census was reasonably high.[68] In large part this was a product, again, of the census: every 14 years, Egyptians needed to declare their age, and census receipts helped them recall what age they had declared before. Bureaucracy here inculcated its subjects with high levels of a very particular kind of numeracy—age counting.

Another widespread Egyptian skill was the ability to engage with financial and legal documents. The great majority of Egyptian men and women who signed legal documents were identified not only by their names, but also by the physical scars on their body. These scars, as it turns out, are those particularly associated with farm work.[69] That is, to a degree that is historically quite unusual, our corpus of Egyptian financial documents is a corpus overwhelmingly produced by and for people who worked with their hands. But there's a big difference between financial documents produced "by" versus "for." In one Egyptian territory, some 75 percent of documents—leases, loans and other, mostly financial, agreements—were produced by a notary. Clearly very few working people felt competent to draw up such legally binding documents by themselves.[70] But comparing the number of parties who added their confirming affidavit—usually two or three lines summarizing the document's main points—in their own hand, versus illiterate signers who required the assistance of another, reveals more widespread, basic skills.[71] Some 43 percent of people in cities and larger villages could summarize and sign a financial document in their own hand, an astonishingly high number. But only three percent of people from a small village could do so. Lessors were more likely to be able to write their own affidavit than lessees. Men were five times more likely than women.

In short, even Egypt's long history of written accounting left distinct pools in its wake, with women and the residents of the deep countryside less able—or less required—to engage in written legal accounting practices than men and those from bigger villages. Even much of this apparent "illiteracy" was in part driven by illiteracy in Greek, versus the native Demotic of many country-folk. In comparison, it might be useful to recall that in Britain, on the eve of the Industrial Revolution, only 24 percent of rural villagers were able to sign their full name on a legal document. This signature was a far cry from a two- to three-sentence affidavit, in what was mostly their second language, that Roman Egyptians had to manage.[72] That so very many Egyptians could do so is not general to the Roman experience, but a particular product of Egypt's long and deep experience with bureaucracy and accounting.

Turning to the Britain of Roman times, we find a very different world.[73] Prior to Roman rule, Britain, unlike Egypt, had no tax system or any consistent use of writing. Periodic tribute to local tribal rulers would have been spectacular and occasional—cattle for feasting, corvée labor at moments of war—rather than systematic and quantified, while Celtic writing systems were largely unused. The Roman experience with accounting thinking—both its numeric and written components—thus took place against a historical backdrop very different from Egypt. On the other hand, after the Roman conquest, Britain was saddled with among the densest military presence in the empire: some 55,000 soldiers were stationed in the province in the second century, versus a population of perhaps around three million.[74] While many garrisons were concentrated in the north and on the Welsh Marches, soldiers were also present in most British cities. As we've seen, the military brought accounting in its wake, and it's no accident that the wooden tablets from Roman London, whose beer receipts we've already examined, date to the years of the conquest itself.[75] Soldiers, many recruited from nearby Gaul and themselves relatively new to accounting-thinking, feature prominently as authors or witnesses in these documents, their accounting part of the immediate apparatus of conquest.

Outside the cities and garrisons, the British countryside must have seen much less need for accounting. The mechanisms of land tax in Britain remain something of a mystery.[76] At one point, early in the Roman conquest, taxes were collected by a forced sale of grain at a set rate. But whether this was the regular method is less clear. Britain, like the rest of the empire, eventually underwent a census, and thus some kind of land declarations, with their statements of size and yield, would have been part of many British farmers' toolkits.

While the British countryside lacks the preserved writing of Egypt, it does have one of the best-studied archaeological records anywhere in the Roman rural world. Those records can be combed for proxies that speak to, although don't directly describe, accounting practices. Writing implements like tablet styluses, weighing tools that speak to quantification, and coins that document the use of money are all found on Roman British farms and villages, and reveal some interesting patterns.[77] Only around 10 percent of small farms from south central Britain produced any material vestige of writing or weighing, and only 25 percent yielded any evidence for money use. But these tools are much more common in larger farms, roadside sites and villages. As we'll see, it's those larger farms and villages that were centers of both surplus production and exchange, and thus were more likely to produce the vestiges of accounting thinking. It's also interesting that the same patterns mostly accrue to elite villas as to rural roadside villages: contexts mattered as much as class when it came to accounting thinking. But whether small farm or villa, less than half of British rural places overall have these vestiges, the product of a world where accounting thinking was newer and probably remained thinner on the ground.

The Egyptian document affidavits and the British styluses, weights and coins are proxies, mere shadows of accounting thinking or its absence that don't translate into literacy or numeracy statistics. They do, however, dispel any notion we have of "Roman" accounting thinking and reveal the all-important differences in contexts—contexts produced by history, by the army and the state, and by different concentrations of exchange and surplus. These contexts don't determine whether a farmer would keep track of his wheat yields or a vegetable seller her daily sales. Rather, they provide a density-plot of places and moments where such thinking was necessary. Because of its particular political economy, the Roman world was relatively thick with such places, even if the form, written or not, and the skills required, from addition to geometry, would have varied considerably.

Accounting Practices

When we think of accounting practices, we might think of a shopkeeper's ledger, a tax declaration, or a corporate profit-and-loss statement. In other words, we think of bookkeeping of a particular modern kind. Prior work on Roman accounting practices went off in enthusiastic search for such modern practices—and mostly didn't find them.[78] For instance, there's no evidence that Romans ever developed double-entry bookkeeping, a practice of late medieval mercantile origins in which each transaction has a double existence as a credit and a debit, and in which these terms take on abstract, not just transactional, meaning. It's also now clear that double-entry bookkeeping was not some gold standard of accounting, a Rubicon that, once crossed, plunged the world into capitalist thinking. A whole range of historical accounting practices achieved the same ends, managing expenses and income and making possible future planning.[79]

So, too, Roman accounting had its own sophisticated procedures and logic.[80] Roman businesses large and small kept running logbooks where all transactions were recorded as they happened, day by day. Larger entities, like large estates, aristocratic households or the army, then redacted these daybooks into consolidated accounts of debts and expenses, credits and earnings. Only in Egypt, however, can we see large entities with multiple administrative units, each separating income and expenditures by various subtypes, consolidating daily logs into compressed monthly totals, and consolidating these individual accounts to arrive at calculations of total income and expenditure.[81] A newly discovered school textbook from Egypt even illuminates the training professional bookkeepers may have had—calculating area, converting units—a training centered on memorization rather than process-based solutions.[82]

What appears to differentiate the practices of these large Roman entities from the double-entry systems of the Florentine bankers and Genoese merchants is their concreteness and backward gaze.[83] Even very large-scale Roman accounts retain, in their tallies of incomings and outgoings, the detritus of actual transactions. As a result, they tend to be less standardized, less immediately legible for cash-flow calculations. Most tend to be past- rather than future-oriented, composed at the end of the calendar year looking backward at transactions that have already taken place. These qualities didn't necessarily hinder financial management, for these systems lingered above all on expenses, and it was on expense management where, at least in agricultural estates, the efforts toward profitability appear to have concentrated.

These practices mostly pertain to the practices of Cicero & Co.—the state, aristocrats, large estate owners and "men of affairs"—whose transactional life was large in scale and distributed in space. What about the Roman 90 percent? What practices did small shopkeepers and farmers, artisans and innkeepers use to keep track of their economic lives? We've already seen the different contexts in which they were—and weren't—incentivized to do so, and we've seen the various physical tools, from finger counting to papyrus records, they had at their disposal. When we ask more specifically about their accounting practices, we're reliant on the written accounts alone, the graffiti and broken potsherds, papyri and wooden tablets, which constitute the very fragmentary record of those who wrote their accounts. As we discussed above, this would not have been everyone, but these accounts and records nonetheless provide a precious window into how a portion of the 90 percent managed their economic lives.

The Account Books of the 90 Percent

The 90 percent's most obvious accounting practice was a habit of thinking in monetary value. This is wholly at odds with earlier assumptions that ancient people, particularly farmers, avoided money and thus didn't think in it. From the innkeeper's sign we began with to farmers like Babatha who knew the cash value of their taxes, working people's accounting practices begin with money. Throughout this book, we'll refer to this as one definition of a "monetized" society—a world in which most things had a widely known monetary value, even if the use of actual coined money varied.[84]

That monetary thinking had particular qualities. Most working Romans' accounts consisted of whole money units, the unit defined by the various circulating coins of particular regions.[85] Thus, most Pompeiian accounts are in whole *as* units, while accounts in Egypt or the East are in whole drachma or obol units. There are exceptions—we occasionally see a half an obol or half a semis, fractions of the lowest common coin denominations—but whole numbers tied to actual physical coins are the rule. Thus, the Roman 90 percent's tendency to think in money included, even in written accounts, a preference for sums readily added in the head, and an attachment to actual coin denominations, even in instances where coins may never have changed hands. Both of these tendencies recall the physical acts of exchange between people, even when rendering those transactions into writing.

As we noted, one of the most common accounting tools used by the 90 percent was the expense list. Here's an example from Pompeii, which we'll encounter again in chapter 2. Scratched on a wall in a gladiator's training barracks, it appears to cover the transactions of a day or at most two (figure 1.7):

bread 2 asses
relish [?] 3 asses
oil 1 as
XC [?] 4 asses
wine 1 as 1 semis
cheese 1 as 1 semis
O[?]M[?] 4 asses
wine 1 as 1 semis
on the 11th day (before the) Kalends accepted 1 denarius
wine 1 as
pork 1 as
wine 1 as 1 semis
cheese 1 as 1 semis
Accepted 1 denarius 4 semis from Lucius Gavius
wine 1 as 1 semis
meat 1 as
wine 1 as[86]

FIGURE 1.7. Graffito expense list from the Campus ad Amphitheatrum, gladiator barracks (II 7.1), Pompeii (*CIL* 4.8566/EDR128734. Photo: Epigraphic Database Roma. Creative Commons License 4.0)

Aside from a penchant for large quantities of wine, the list has many of the characteristics common to working people's expense accounting, much of which it shares with Roman organizational thinking more broadly.[87] It's organized as a roughly spaced list, not quite in columns, with the item on the left and cost on the right. It contains no volumes or quantities—thus no real "prices" (that is, value per unit), only costs.[88] As noted above, moneys are recorded in the coins received—so four semis are not reduced to the two asses that they equaled, somewhat as if an American recorded "two nickels" instead of ten cents.[89] Expenses and income are mixed together, distinguished only by the verb "accepted" (*accepit*). And no totals or other mathematical operations are performed on the list.

A smaller number of lists do have totals—particularly those that were composed for verification by a third party. An example of such a list comes from the trash heaps outside the Egyptian city of Oxyrhynchus. Below is a sample—three days of an eight-day account, made for an unknown month:

Isas has received from Apollonius, an inhabitant of Cynus, 4[.] drachmae. Deduct on account of expenses:

price of . . . paid to Nechtheus 28 drachmas
for making bread 1 dr. 4 obols
~~for oil 4 drachmas 2 obols~~
on the 4th: for grinding 5 obols
powder [?] for a fish 1 obols
on the 5th: 3 baskets 4 1/2 obols
on the 6th: plates 2 obols
a fish [?] for the builder 1 obols
a chous of oil 4 drachmas 2 obols
Total 40 drachmas 3.5 obols[90]

Isas tracked his expenses for eight days and, as is clear from the first three days, periodically ran the totals. Each day was labeled and its expenses tracked. Mistakes were deleted. In addition to food and consumer goods, we find small expenses for third-party dependents—food for workmen, seemingly paid as part of their wages, and payments for services, like baking bread or grinding wheat. Isas also tracked fractions of obols, not just whole numbers. Finally, we're given a motivation for the list—tracking of expenses to be deducted from an unknown sum given to Isas from one Apollonius.

We have fewer small-business accounts, and while they retain some of the features of the expense lists—often not-quite-columnar arrangement, a preference for whole numbers based on coin denominations—in general they are more complex. They even include elements proper to small-business accounting used in the smallest "micro" businesses today. Portions of a storekeeper's account, again from Oxyrhynchus, recount sales made in the month of June or July in 143 CE:

July 24th, Chares' shop. Report of the shop . . . of Chares, to Ammonion, Hephaestas and Lycarion, overseers, in the 6th year of Antoninus Caesar [143 CE].

Nicus 2 double jars of pickled fish 2 drachmas
Didymus 6 ropes . . .
Ptolemaeus 1 double jar of pickled fish 1 drachma [marginal note reads "2 obols too little"]
[. . . .]
Iulas 3 mattresses . . .
Seras 2 double jars of pickled fish 2 drachmas

> Sarapion 2 artabai of meal . . .
>
> another Sarapion 3 loads of . . . and 2 minae of wrought iron . . . drachmas
>
> Parodus 2 minae of wrought iron . . . drachmas
>
> Arius 24 mats . . .
>
> Isidorus 6 couch-legs . . . , and 4 staters of purple . . .
>
> [. . .]
>
> Total 34 drachmae 1 obol [marginal note reads "making 34 drachmae 3 obols"], which sum was paid over to Ammonion, Hephaestas and Lycarion, overseers.[91]

The accounts appear to be for a small general store, which for some reason was being supervised by three overseers. Like Isas' account, this one was, at least in part, generated for verification by others. As far as accounting practices are concerned, there are additional things to note. The first is the use of a basic third-party accounting structure: each customer has an account within the account, to which is charged the total of his purchases. We find third-party accounting in other small business accounts—from other shops in Oxyrhynchus, to a village pawnbroker, to the beer account we examined from London—so this appears to be common practice.[92] It's possible that the costumers in Chares' shop were charging their purchases on credit, and Chares is tracking their individual purchases and debits. The fact that the total for all transactions is paid over at month's end to the overseers indicates that the customers paid up in cash (except Ptolemaeus, who was two obols short).

What's notable, too, about this account and many like it is that expenses—that is, the cost the shopkeeper paid for the goods—are not accounted alongside and against receipts. Indeed, in only a handful of examples do we find small businesses calculating expenses against receipts. An account of the baker Onnophris, also from Oxyrhynchus, is a rare exception: Onnophris tallies the costs of flour and fuel against his receipts for bread and cakes sold.[93] Seemingly only when organizations or family businesses reached a certain size did the balancing of income and outflows become more typical.

It's important to note that this isn't some Roman accounting failing: a disinterest in balancing receipts and expenses continues to be characteristic of the very smallest microbusinesses today.[94] The Roman 90 percent's individual and small-business accounting practices aren't primitive: rather, they reflect the priorities of small-scale entities who, while they manically track expenses, somewhat less manically aggregate them. It's only when those entities—ancient and modern—get somewhat bigger that other impulses take hold.

Show Me the Money

One such medium-to-large business was owned by one Epimachus, on whose farm we began this book. His accounts displayed another of Roman accounting's particular impulses: the need to verify.[95] Epimachus (the landowner, not his tenant of the same name) owned around 14 hectares of dispersed, small plots near the city of Hermopolis in the Nile Valley. He was a hands-on owner-operator, and appeared to have spent much of his time on his farm. He used four or five slaves and lots of daily wage labor to work his plots. The multiple, dispersed nature of his holdings—which, as we shall see, was normal for all Mediterranean farmers—as well as his use of daily wage laborers probably drove his use of more complex accounting. He employed a slave, one Didymus, to keep his books, which were taken over by Epimachus himself when Didymus became ill. Those books, as was typical for larger Egyptian agricultural enterprises, began each month with receipts, chronologically organized, and followed with a daily record of expenses. At the end of the month receipts and expenses were balanced, and any deficit or profit carried over to the next month.

The accounts that Didymus kept for Epimachus, like many accounts preserved for us, appear to be at least partially driven by the need to verify transactions to a third party.[96] Kept by slaves reporting to a master or a shopkeeper to a group of overseers, such accounts are born from a need to justify, to prove. This is not dissimilar to what is termed "financial accounting" today—records kept for verification by shareholders or by government agencies.[97] Verificatory accounting has peculiar qualities. Like financial accounting, these Roman verificatory accounts tend to be backward-looking—that is, enumerations of transactions that have already taken place—and focused on specific items of interest to third parties. This particular function may explain why so many of our accounts extend only for short periods, are made by travelers while on a journey, or omit major expenses like housing.[98] Indeed, we have no examples from the Roman 90 percent of a real household budget—a long-term effort to track all expenses and income. Just like working families and very small businesses today, the ambitions of most of our accounts are short-term and never totalizing.

The need to verify may also explain another peculiarity of working people's accounting practice. Lurking in Epimachus' accounts, those of Onnophris the baker and even those of the London beer dealer are all the ingredients for decision-making around profit and loss. But we cannot see any working Romans taking this step. Indeed, while accounts from large estates are more complex, we can't be certain that even their abundant data was used for future planning.[99] It may be that Romans didn't account in this way. Or it may be due to the verificatory character of the accounts we have. Not unlike income tax statements today, verification-driven accounting isn't intended for planning purposes, although it can be used for it. Rather, its purpose is historical, to track and affirm transactions that took place in the past.

But even in accounts that don't appear to be verificatory, the same logic persists. The many lists with no totals, the mixture of expenses and receipts in the same lists: while these may be relics of preliminary stages of accounting—like the distinction between the journal versus the general ledger in modern accounting—it appears that they, too, stopped short of using their abundant data for further analysis. Even the format of the lists, which never completely commit to tabular columns, suggest that tracking—not adding and analyzing—was their goal.[100] The accounting of the 90 percent, when we can see it, appears feverishly enumerative: it's much less clear that it was analytical.

A Document-Clutching World

The need to verify, to justify, also appears to have motivated illiterate people to keep collections of financial documents. Scholars refer to these as "archives"—sets of documents deliberately retained by families, even over multiple generations, before being abandoned or thrown out.[101] "Archives" is a term we associate with institutions or with the rich. But working people, even illiterate working people, keep archives, too—the kitchen drawer filled with receipts, the dog-eared folder containing mortgages and birth certificates. We've already seen a Roman example of such an archive—that of Babatha, retained by her when she fled war and revolt in Judea and later buried in a desert cave. But others with more meager means than Babatha kept archives, too. A weaver's family from Oxyrhynchus retained their loan, house purchase and apprenticeship contracts; a tenant farmer's family in the Fayum retained their tax receipts and contracts leasing out their children in exchange for loans. Working people's financial archives are no uncommon phenomenon among the papyrus archives of Egypt.[102]

On the one hand, these archives permit a glimpse of the complex financial worlds that working families crafted for their survival. A farmer with multiple lease holdings, labor contracts, and tiny plots of his own land, or a weaver who owned and/or rented at least two homes together with a complex portfolio of loans: working-family archives allow us to see the many strands of income and expenses that even illiterate workers tracked and managed.

But even though the archives allow us to reconstruct financial lives, they could scarcely have been used for financial planning by their keepers. Family archives almost never track daily expenses, and they usually omit huge chunks of income (like artisanal goods made, store sales or farm produce sold). Family archives were not tools of financial analysis or management. Instead, they preserved legal-financial documents of a particular character. The archive of Soterichos, an Egyptian tenant farmer whom we shall get to know better in a later chapter, is a useful example.[103] For two generations, he and his family kept their leases, receipts for rent paid, receipts for the poll tax, debt quittances, a sales receipt for the purchase of a donkey, even a receipt for compensation paid to a neighbor whose grass Soterichos' cattle had eaten. Soterichos was illiterate in Greek, as were the rest of his family; nonetheless, they appear to not only have negotiated a portfolio of leases and loans and demanded receipts for payments, but they retained these documents for many years after their expiration. Why?

Verification must be part of the reason: should anyone question a poll tax paid or a rent in arrears (and Soterichos' rent was almost always in arrears), they could refer to the appropriate document. The many vertical financial relationships engendered by money, tax, land markets and exchange—in other words, all the things that we have seen drove accounting thinking—also drove archiving. In a world where accounting thinking was inculcated in so many people, through so many means, the need to verify those accounts was paramount. The Roman 90 percent lived in and helped perpetuate a document-clutching world.

Backward Thinking and Forward Thinking

The granular glimpse of economic lives provided by archives give us a particular, and potentially misleading, sense of Roman accounting thinking. It's like looking at our own financial world through the contents of safety deposit boxes, with their marriage licenses, house deeds and automobile titles. These are the backward-looking pieces of accounting thinking, pieces that verify transactions and legal arrangements of the past. The overwhelming evidence for verificatory accounting is likewise backward-looking, and thus like looking at modern accounting practices solely through modern tax filings. As we have noted above, it's much harder to find working Romans doing things with their accounts—tallying, organizing and using assembled data for future planning. But plan around futures they did, although in ways quite different from P&L-statement kind of thinking.

A whole chapter of the present book (chapter 5) is dedicated to lending and borrowing. Debt and credit were an integral part of working lives—loans to bridge income shortfalls, loans to put more land under cultivation, loans made to family members or friends-of-friends with the expectation of interest or a future favor. Credit was everywhere, and everyone from soldiers to farmers, artisans' wives to enslaved quarrymen lent and borrowed.

Futurity lies at the heart of all credit transactions—the creditor forgoing the present use of something in anticipation of future interest (or obligation), the debtor getting immediate use at the price of future payment. The ubiquity of Roman debt relationships embedded futurity into Roman accounting practice. It was necessary to think in terms of future due dates, to calculate interest and penalties around those dates, and to plan one's incomings and outgoings with future repayment or quittances in mind.

Roman elites liked to imagine the countryside as a debt-free space, its serene agricultural rhythms a world apart from the jangling alarms of monthly due dates.[104] In reality it was the seasonal variability of the agricultural world that drove many Roman credit relationships—borrowing to put seed in the ground, to convert crop to cash, and vice versa. Seasonal change also drove variations in commodity prices, variation that seems to have produced another kind of future thinking: agricultural speculation. A third-century letter from one Ammonius to his brother, Apion, describes an effort to buy peaches in advance of some regulation on their sale:

> Ammonius to his brother Apion, greeting . . . . . . If you can, gather all the peaches on the market. Don't neglect it as you know that, if the gods will it, these things will soon be brought under regulation and I am to be with you. Therefore, don't neglect the purchase and buy some at once.[105]

We have no idea who Ammonius is, aside from that fact that he may have lived in the city of Oxyrhynchus, could write, and had a solid amount of spare cash—some 100 drachmas—to devote to this speculation. Another letter, from a wealthy woman to her steward, instructs him to take advantage of low wheat prices to buy up some 1,000 artabai (some 29,500 kilograms)—a large-scale speculation.[106] Speculation around agricultural products was probably rife. The bustling auctions whose records we have from Pompeii and environs saw wealthy businessmen and estate owners buying wine, oil, wool and other commodities with plans for future resales and profit. To what extent people of more modest means like Ammonius engaged in such speculation is less clear: those who had no reserves were at speculators' mercy, while, as we'll see in chapter 5, even wage workers might borrow tiny sums to engage in small-scale speculation.

Other kinds of agricultural speculation involved selling agricultural produce before it existed, a very basic form of futures. Futures sales were particularly common in the wine business.[107] Grapes were—and still are—a notoriously finicky crop, and thus subject to lots of price variation and future-thinking. Buyers might purchase grapes still on the vine, or they might purchase the newly pressed juice (called must) for future delivery after vinification. Much, although not all, of this purchase of wine futures was large in scale, part of aristocrats' and *affairistes*' portfolios of agricultural speculation.[108] But farmers and other working people may have also dabbled in wine's many futures. In Egypt, farmer-specialists in grape harvesting (called *karponai*, "fruit-sellers") organized the grape picking in exchange for a portion of the harvest, which they would then resell. The *karponai* would provide the labor and supervise the work and reap the potential risks and benefits of varying quality and fluctuating prices.

Dabbling in futures also doesn't appear to be limited to wine. In the Egyptian Fayum, we have a contract made by one Pasis, a herder, selling his sheep's future wool to a villager some nine months before it was sheared.[109] In doing so, he assumed the risk that his sheep would not die or be stolen before shearing season. Pasis leased, rather than owned, his sheep, and may have needed the ready cash to pay the lease. In other words, what looks like futures could really be a loan. Alternatively, Pasis was betting that wool prices would be lower in nine months—when everyone was shearing—and was assuming the risk in hopes of closing on a higher price. Futures, and the uncertainties they involved, appeared to be part of at least some Roman farmers' accounting practice and thinking.

Related to Pasis' futures sale are a group of documents, all of which come from Egypt and almost all of which date to just after our period of interest. They are sometimes called "sales on delivery."[110] Here a seller, most often probably a farmer, sells a commodity in advance in exchange for cash in hand, with interest deducted from the cash payment. "Sales on delivery" are thus a kind of loan, with part or all of the loan repaid with a commodity.[111] The late date of most documents has suggested that the practice arose in response to the inflation of the later third and fourth centuries: while the future value of money might decrease, the creditor was protected with a repayment in foodstuffs. An economist's eye on these documents has suggested that they were also speculations, the seller/borrower offloading the risk of decreasing prices onto the purchaser/creditor, while reserving the possibility of defaulting on the loan, selling the promised commodity at a higher price if the market rose, and paying the contractual penalty. This is an intriguing possibility: Roman farmers, particularly in Egypt, would have been alert to, if not wholly fixated on, changing agricultural prices. Offloading risk while reserving a potential price-point for profit is just about within the range of what we've seen of their accounting-thinking. If so, the "sales on delivery" practice becomes not just a later tool to combat inflation, but evidence for a more deep-seated practice of hedging—offloading risk associated with declining prices while reserving possible gains if prices decline less than anticipated. If used in this way, "sales on delivery" transactions would reveal a particularly complex form of future thinking.

Using the Man

Working Romans' use of writing, their document-clutching habits and willingness to use legal language—even when they themselves could neither read nor write—point up a final feature of their accounting practice: a readiness to use the law. Those Egyptian slow-writers who struggled to sign a long affidavit, or who registered their loans, leases and work contracts in notary offices, did so with the expectation that they were enforceable in law. This might seem strange. On the one hand, the Roman court system was not kind to working people: there existed no public defenders, lawyers were expensive, and cases dragged on for months or years.[112] Even elites tried to avoid going to court over contract disputes and enlisted arbitrators—often slaves or freedmen, known to all parties—to help negotiate solutions. Noncitizens, who were the majority of provincial inhabitants for much of our story, had, in theory, no recourse to Roman courts. In practice, though, the line between local and Roman legal jurisdiction appears to have been blurry: provincial governors and local magistrates often heard cases of locals in their courts, while provincials used elements of Roman legal language and practices in their dealings with each other. We find lawyers' expenses included in some expense accounts kept by working provincials—a freedman trying to get out of his mandatory work obligations in Egypt, or a possible slave tracking his expenses, including a lawyer's fees, on the wall of a fine house in Ephesus.[113] In Roman London, two non-Roman locals appear to have involved the Roman judiciary to resolve a legal dispute between them.[114] Employing lawyers and involving the judiciary was not the sole preserve of the elite or even citizens, and while this was probably a "nuclear option," out of the reach of most, legal or citizenship status were clearly not hard barriers.

A far cheaper option was to write to the provincial governor or his representative and complain.[115] Petitions registered in notary offices appear to have cost only pennies and were often done for free. Hundreds of these petitions are preserved from Roman Egypt—petitions complaining of usury, of theft, of nonpayment of loans or rent. While in theory this meant a wide range of people could avail themselves of official intervention in case of financial malpractice, in practice the literate were more likely to petition than the illiterate, urbanites more likely than rural dwellers, men more than women. A willingness to use the law to one's enforce financial transactions thus seems to have followed the same patterns as written accounting-thinking—used by many, out of reach of many others.

A final court of appeal was the gods. The Roman world was one of present, interventionist deities, deities who were believed to own their own land and lend money at interest. Thus, asking the gods for financial mediation was considered a normal extension of legal practice.[116] Asking for divine aid appears to have been the ultimate "nuclear option," and asking the gods to curse the malefactor was the appropriate accounting practice. The hundreds of curse tablets flung into the sacred pool of Minerva at Bath in England almost all relate to theft: a farmer whose plow was stolen, a man whose gloves were filched, the theft of five denarii.[117] Some plaintiffs asked the goddess to return their money; others begged only for revenge—that the thief's intestines be expelled, their eyes go blind, their mind lost. Most of these tablets are written by slow-writers. Most would have come from the surrounding deeply rural district. In their ALL-CAPS, local vernacular Latin, sometimes even using the legal language of petitions, these curses find working people availing themselves of another kind of financial law with its own expectations of recompense.

Adding Up

The specter of modernity and its own capitalist economies will be our constant companion in this book. Despite the existence of Latin and Greek terms for it, "accounting" feels inescapably like a modern category of analysis transplanted onto ancient people who would have never described their activities this way. Hopefully, we've shown this to be both true and false. Working Romans had many ways of thinking about and managing their financial lives. Some of them are recognizable to us, like keeping a list of expenses, even if others are not, like failing to tally them up. Many of the tools they used, like finger-counting, we might not recognize as such, while others, like farm account books, at first glance look like their modern versions but were governed by a subtly different logic.

Comparisons between working Roman and "modern" or "capitalist" thinking are also at risk of comparing big institutional apples with smaller, family-sized oranges. When we conceive of "modern" accounting, we conjure up corporate profit-and-loss sheets, or ledger accounting proper to banks and larger retail outlets. We never include in this modernity the quite different kind of accounting thinking practiced by families and tiny "micro" businesses.[118] We ignore the fact that even at the dawn and birthplace of capitalism—nineteenth-century England—most owner-operator farms did not keep double-entry books or, indeed, any books at all. We discount that the truly poor in developing countries today manipulate their household finances more like hedge fund managers, while only 30 percent of American households bother to keep a budget. We forget that modern family accounting practices, just like Roman ones, are often geared toward document-clutching and only rarely use those receipts and contracts to construct budgets, or that most working and poorer American families today have future-oriented accounting that amounts to a few months, rarely a whole year or more. A top-down lens distorts the accounting thinking of modern families and family businesses as much as a primitivizing lens has distorted that of Roman farmers and shopkeepers.

Many of those habits—both Roman and modern—are driven by a shared precarity. As we shall see in the next chapter, the overwhelming numbers of expense lists, versus other kinds of accounting, point to a real need to track and control expenses. It was expenses that, as we shall see, constituted one of the biggest threats to Roman working people's economic security, just as it does today. So, too, document-clutching, like keeping old pay slips, census declarations or expired leases, was motivated not by methodical recordkeeping, but a sense that transactions could be like revenants, coming back from the past to challenge those whose sole ability to contest them depended on having kept a record. Document-clutching and expense tracking—these were and are the accounting practices of the anxious.

Working Romans' accounting thinking may appear to be characterized by contrasts: thoroughly numerate but often disinterested in calculation; engaged in commodities futures while perpetually worried by past transactions; immersed in credit while continuing to account coins in denominations. But those contrasts are of our making. The accounting thinking of the 90 percent was born of daily practices evolved to survive in a complex world.

2

A World Full of Things

FIGURE 2.1. View of kitchen, Fullery of Stephanus, Pompeii (Photo: Miguel Hermoso Cuesta. Creative Commons License 4.0)

ANOTHER INN, another city, another traveling family. Sometime in December of 74 CE, a couple and their slave traveled to Pompeii.[1] Perhaps a family of small-time herders, they stayed for a little over a week in a small backstreet hostel. During that week, they kept track of their expenses by scratching them on the wall of their room: frugal meals of bread, oil, cheese and wine; a more festive meal with sausages and steaks and dates; bread for their slave; hay for their animals; and some basic supplies—a pot, a lamp, incense, a bronze bucket. Some days they consumed a lot, other days they penny-pinched. By the time they left, they had made some 46 purchases of some 20 different items and spent some 56 sestertii on consumables alone.

Consumption matters. It mattered enough to this small trading family to track and monitor their expenses. Consumption matters to poor and working people today, dominating their economic activity and thinking.[2] And it matters to economists and economic historians. Consumption, more than production and hard-to-track income, provides the best indication of families' economic well-being. Consumption data—from the Pompeiian family's expense list to modern American household surveys—are the "first-best" bellwether for the welfare of any population. One of the most profound shifts in development economics of the past three decades has been the use of household-level surveys, information that documents families' consumption as a window onto their economic health. For all these reasons, we begin our exploration of how working Romans got by through examining how—and how much—they consumed.

The Roman world is said to have witnessed a "consumer revolution."[3] Pots and glass, imported and local foods, silver plate and pearl earrings, houses with painted walls and paved floors—the Roman world was awash with more and different food and things. Cities were reshaped by this revolution, as long lines of shops, selling everything from songbirds to sieves, came to define the urban landscape. And for elite Romans, this world of things provided the fodder for social satire, cultural critique and the stuff from which identities were made and contested.

Working people, this chapter argues, not only participated in this consumer revolution but were also central to it. New data from archaeology, and newly reconsidered texts like the Pompeii graffito, find working people, even some of the poorest, consuming far in excess of our previous expectations. From small-time traders to enslaved servants, farmers to craftsmen, Romans ate more and different foods, purchased rather than made many of the items they used, and used those purchases to distinguish between different kinds and qualities of goods. Their levels of household consumption were thus historically quite high, and, not surprisingly, highly unequal—the Pompeiian couple consuming, at least in theory, some nine times more than their enslaved servant.

John Kenneth Galbraith, chronicler of the American consumer economy, once complained that "wants are increasingly created by the process by which they are satisfied."[4] Galbraith might have found food for thought in imperial

Rome. For working Romans cocreated a world where greater levels of consumption became increasingly necessary. Different kinds of sausages, more than one tunic, a selection of dinner plates—not only did more people have access to and consume such things, but these things were necessary to social belonging. The consumer revolution, in short, brought about a consuming imperative. This consuming imperative not only rendered consumption historically high, it also raised the threshold required to participate in society. Those historically high levels of consumption were thus a sign not of an affluent society, but of an expensive and often precarious one.

Galbraith, like many economists before and since, found it easy to slide from "consumer" to "consumption" to "consumerist," blaming the first for the economic (and now environmental) disequilibrium inherent in the latter.[5] Consumption as a category of economic analysis has lent itself to a certain preachiness. This chapter, like much new poverty economics, approaches consumption not from the pulpit but from the shopping cart, taking seriously the decisions of working families as it finds them. It thus takes particular care with some first-order questions: How much, and what things, did working Romans consume? Did they make them or buy them? How did rural farmers consume differently from urban laborers? And what impact did these decisions have on their household budgets? By plunging into the details of what the 90 percent consumed, we also get an intimate entrée into their houses and lives. Those minutiae—of sausages and children's toys, sandals and window glass—serve not only as the basis for quantitative reconstruction, but also as an insistent reminder of real people and messy lives, lives laden with, and made more precarious by, a world full of things.

Marx's Two Coats

Insofar as Roman economic history has been concerned with consumption, it has been embroiled in a centuries-long fascination with elite consumption. It's a fascination begun by elite Romans themselves and their combined commodity fetishism and commodity self-critique.[6] The imperial biographies written by Suetonius or the Stoic meditations of Seneca are texts that ooze with things: 5,000-sestertii fish, women weighed down by pearl earrings, even fish with earrings.[7] These things were believed to be the cause and the symptom of a widely felt social illness, one brought about by too much foreign wealth—a result of the spoils of and contact with the Greek East. A person's things were a symptom of this malaise, a sign of how far they had fallen from the ideals of a frugal Republican Golden Age. The *Gray's Anatomy* for this malaise was Petronius' *Satyrica*, a novel whose humor relied on gauche consumption and whose dissection of the freedman Trimalchio's gauche banquet not only oozed with things, but reeked of outré choices—silver urinals, boar stuffed with thrushes, and too, too, too much of everything, a world gone hilariously and ominously wrong.

It's this world that Finley and his predecessors took for granted as defining Roman consumption. Consumption, insofar as it constituted an economic activity of interest, was centered on rich people living in cities.[8] Finley, as noted in the introduction to this book, assumed that elite literary sources constituted a reasonable proxy for what elites ate and bought, and, lacking any nonelite, nonurban evidence, he concluded that the world of things was a world of rich, urban things. The model of the "consumer city"—Roman cities whose elite-driven consumption sucked dry the production of the surrounding countryside—thus dominated economic theories of Roman consumption until the 1990s. It's a model that has largely seen its day.[9] But if we no longer accept the consumer city model, it's because of new evidence for urban-based *production*, or expanding what is meant by "city" to the dense suburbs that surrounded them. We still tend to assume that *working* urban folks were not big consumers, and as for farmers—the consumer revolution took place without them.[10]

If Finley shoved consumption to the side of economic history, more recent work has placed its doppelganger front and center. Per capita consumption estimates form the core of estimates for Roman economic performance.[11] These are not the consumption figures used in modern performance estimates, the thousands of food and car and sneaker and cellphone purchases representing what modern people actually consume. In the absence of these millions of data points, two basic proxies are used: minimum calories and/or a selection of ancient prices for goods. The first proxy uses the minimum calories required for human survival, rendered into the price of wheat that might supply those calories.[12] Alternatively, a so-called commodity basket of things Romans might have consumed is populated with prices for those things.[13] Consumption in these estimates is thus notional, not actual, and uses the bottom, barely surviving at minimum calories, to stand for the majority. These estimates, not surprisingly, are quite grim, on par with some of the poorest countries today.[14] These low estimates for per capita consumption anchor a "typical" premodern world, analogous to very poor countries today, whose denizens mostly consumed enough to keep body together, and in some calculations, barely that.

Using different, albeit still notional proxies, economic historians who use archaeological evidence arrive at quite different results. Impressed by the sheer quantity of stuff that has emerged from Roman-period archaeological excavations, they point to the pots and glass and animals consumed by a wide range of people (mostly in cities) and view this as a proxy for high income and economic well-being.[15] Since there seems to be so much of this stuff—so many pots and glasses and steaks—Roman populations, it is argued, should have been living well over subsistence.

There's a third perspective on consumption, one that considers the things we buy as not just economic transactions, but also as social ones. Archaeologists have discovered that not only were there more things in the Roman world, and that most of those things were consumed by a huge range of people, but also that those things were made to commonly shared standards. These standards were shaped by consumer tastes.[16] These tastes—for cups and shoes and new foods—could not have been simply the product of working people aping the tastes of their betters, as Finley might have assumed, or of gormless provincials buying an imported package of "Roman" goods.[17] Instead, it's now clear that working people were discerning consumers, choosing objects that both reflected and shaped their social bonds. Working people in Pompeii commissioned paintings and sculpture that celebrated their labor and commercial success.[18] Farmers in the British fens produced and consumed their own distinct brand of fine ceramics. Local auxiliary soldiers in Gaul were buried with the pots and pins that recalled their military service.[19] In short, whether through shop paintings or drinking cups, even working people used stuff to signal their belonging to a group, and to make statements about taste and distinction. Roman social belonging, it's now clear, was shaped by the things one consumed.

Economists have a long history of not taking social belonging as seriously as food and shelter.[20] Economic theory long divided needs from pleasures, commodities from luxuries, even going so far to assume that the poorer one becomes, the less one needs things other than food. The US poverty line is an antiquated byproduct of this thinking, still based on the costs of food, clothing and shelter alone.[21] But this blind spot around social necessities isn't limited to capitalist welfare models. Even Karl Marx made this mistake. At the very moment in the 1860s when he was writing about the coat as the quintessential commodity, a cash-starved Marx was repeatedly forced to pawn his and his family's coats to pay for food and rent.[22] In nineteenth-century England, he was not admitted to the library without a coat; without coats and shoes his children were not permitted to attend school. Marx, fixated on the coat as commodity, failed to see his own coat as an agent of social inclusion.

Here we try to take both of Marx's coats seriously. Food and pots and cloaks (instead of coats) are part of the package of goods necessary for survival. They are also agents that help produce and maintain human identities and relationships. Economists call these social inclusion costs: the value of things, and in some instances services, without which a person finds themself outside the bounds of society.[23] Social inclusion costs include things that bind us to society—customary food, shared clothing norms. They also include special things that distinguish us from others—better food, distinctive clothes.[24] Inclusion—showing we belong—and discernment—showing up—are the flip sides of the same social coin, both equally necessary to social functioning.

Far from being nonessential, social inclusion costs are part of the cost of living. In fact, they are particularly critical for working people. Working people often live on the knife's edge of economic exigency *and* social inclusion. The poorer you are, the more critical is social inclusion—connections for work opportunities, neighborly aid to paper over the cracks of erratic income, signals to distinguish yourself from the even-poorer. Consumption for both biological survival and social inclusion thus together constitute "necessities."

Economists categorize these different order of goods as two different kinds of "capabilities"—the capability for survival and that of inclusion.[25] We might also term them first- and second-order needs.[26] Both concepts recognize that all people's consumption needs are not limited to food and shelter, and many economists now include these goods in the calculation of relative poverty lines.[27] In many countries today, for instance, a cellphone is included among social inclusion capabilities. What those first- and second-order goods and costs were for the Roman world is our job to discover.

Here we toggle between consumption as a set of economic practices and consumption as a process of social formation. As the historian Daniel Roche put it, we try to observe working consumers in a place between the cellar and the attic.[28] We'll follow Roman families like our Pompeii travelers to see what they actually consumed, using quantitative data from expense lists, and more qualitative evidence from archaeology. This kind of data is messy: expense lists, as we saw in chapter 1, miss some critical quantities, while archaeologically derived consumption is hard to quantify and preserves only certain kinds of durable goods. The payoff is worth it: a shift from proxy to practice. In the process, we'll also build a picture of what constituted Roman first- and second-order needs—the amounts and varieties of food regarded as essential to survival, as well as the Roman equivalent to the cellphone or coat: those objects on which social inclusion rested. All of these necessities had costs, costs that—just like in our own world—were borne by working people's budgets. As we'll see, neither "subsistence" nor "affluence" captures the conundrum of living in a world of things.[29]

Food

Food is the most important first-order consumable. Poor people generally spend more on food than rich people. In some times and places, food constituted some 70 percent or more of working people's expenses. The qualifier here is important: while one often sees numbers like 60 or 70 percent as a fixed budgetary percentage, the amount that the working poor spend on food is not a constant, but historically contingent. In eighteenth-century England, food occupied some 70–75 percent of farmers' expenditures. But it also occupied a greater percentage of some aristocrats' expenditures than those of poorer merchants.'[30] In Nigeria today it's some 60 percent of expenses, while in neighboring Cameroon it's only 45 percent. Engel's "law," which stipulates that as income rises the percentage spent on food decreases, should really be Engel's "guidelines": urbanization, local food costs and above all social practices and the particular caloric requirements of certain kind of labor—all these things matter, too.[31]

In a preindustrial world, food was the principal energy source. Labor was almost entirely manual labor, and food the chief fuel-source. How energetic a society is must not only be a product of its culture: it's also simple access to calories. Economic history has largely tended to treat the premodern world as being equally energetic—or rather, equally unenergetic: the whole of the premodern majority is often assumed to have subsisted at a caloric minimum. This was not, as we'll see, the case in the Roman world.

Survival Rations

When, in the 1990s, the United Nations began to focus on the eradication of world hunger, it set out a series of caloric minima for different genders, ages and jobs. Intended for contemporary economists and policymakers, these minima have become "data" for economic historians, who, confronted by an uncertain past, have used them in place of actual diets and consumption. These caloric minima aren't a bad proxy: something around 1,900–2,000 calories is often used.[32] But what humans "need" as a minimum diet is not only a biological question, impacted by height, age, sex and body mass, but also a historical one, humans' changing physiology and cultural norms reciprocally impacting one another. As such, "need" is not a biological constant but a historical variable. We will begin our analysis of what working Romans ate by understanding what Romans regarded—rightly or wrongly—as the minimum food required for working people's survival. We'll begin, in short, with the rations for slaves.

> Food for the enslaved workers [*familia*]: for those who do farm work, four *modii* [34.4 liters] of wheat in winter, and in summer four and a half. The farm manager, the farm manageress, the foreman, and the shepherd should receive three. The slave gangs [*compediti*] should have a ration of four pounds of bread through the winter, increasing to five when they begin to work the vines, and dropping back to four when the figs ripen.[33]

Sandwiched between recommendations for wood storage and the feed requirements for cattle, Cato the Elder's treatise *On Agriculture* contains recommended monthly rations for agricultural slaves.[34] He prescribes wheat or bread, and, in a later section, wine and olives (with a mention of figs) for different moments of the agricultural year, and for different members of the enslaved community, including slave gangs. In his clinical allocation of food according to the strenuousness of labor, Cato's rations have been mined for their wheat allowances even as they have been decried for the exploitative regimes they prescribe.

Cato's *On Agriculture* is an odd sort of text: ostensibly a manual on farming, its hyper-specificity on subjects as diverse as cattle diseases and the best kind of manure presents a seductive sense of comprehensiveness. But this was no how-to guide: it provides numerous details on some things (the materials and costs to build an olive press) and none on others (how to actually use it). It is a performance of knowledge, not a manual.[35] The slave rations, just like the olive press instructions, are very specific and very selective. They appear in a section dedicated almost entirely to storage—stored wood, stored hay, stored animal feed—and the particular contents of the slave rations, all of which are preserved items, should be read in this regard. Fresh things—like fruit and vegetables—are nowhere mentioned because they don't fit the theme, and elsewhere Cato assumes that enslaved workers kept gardens and animals.[36] This, then, is not a report of a diet, but a stylized, selective portion of one.

If, for a moment, we take Cato at his word and add up all the foodstuffs he recommends, we arrive at some 3,700 calories per day.[37] This is low compared with the diets of seventeenth-century English farmers (4,000–6,000 calories), but similar to that supplied to inmates of eighteenth-century workhouses (2,900–3,600 calories).[38] It's almost twice the minima used in most Roman per capita consumption reconstructions (1,940 calories). And this without the missing fresh fruit, vegetables and occasional meat. As a rhetorical statement on the nourishment and control of slave bodies, this 3,700-calorie portion of a diet is one elite Roman's idea of what constituted subsistence.[39]

Some actual rations paid to actual enslaved and free workers were surprisingly similar and constituted in similar ways. The mixed enslaved and free work force (termed the *familiares*) at the quarries at Mons Claudianus in Egypt's Eastern Desert, whom we shall get to know much better in chapters 4 and 5, were given clothing and food rations together with a tiny "wage" in money, presumably to complement their rations.[40] Because these workers often had need for an advance on those rations, hundreds of advance receipts have been preserved, and thus we can reconstruct their rations with some accuracy. Wheat, lentils and oil constituted a daily diet of some 3,800 calories, plus whatever the workers could grow in the quarry's small gardens or purchase with their wages. What they might have purchased is suggested by the archaeology.[41] Well supplied with basic staples—fruit, vegetables and basic spices—it was still a relatively monotonous diet. Meat was available, mostly in the form of donkeys too old to haul stone, which these mostly enslaved workers ate less frequently than their free comrades.

The role of wheat in both sets of rations deserves special mention. It constitutes the lion's share of the calories—as much as 80 percent—as doled out by the owner or employer. But ration-calories are only part of the total calories the owner imagines the slave or worker obtaining by other means—with garden, flock, or wage. When we can quantify this imagined whole, as at the imperial quarries, wheat constitutes some 77 percent of the value of the doled-out food, but only around 50 percent when complemented by fruit, vegetables and meat of the slave/worker's own choosing.[42]

We have a final precious record of what one group of Romans thought was the rock-bottom minimum for survival. Reports from a Jewish community's soup kitchen, penned in third-century Galilee, describe weekday rations doled out to indigent beggars:

> They do not [give] to a poor person, who travels from place to place, less than a loaf of bread worth a *pondion*, [made from grain valued at] four *seahs* per *sela*.

> [If] he lodges overnight, [then] they give him provisions for lodging, oil, and beans.[43]

Here the truly needy receive a minimum of 500–600 grams of bread, plus beans and oil. The bread together with a cup of beans and the equivalent of Cato's slave oil rations could have amounted to some 2,375 calories. Note that the staple foods for the beggar are the same as the enslaved workers: there are just less of them and fewer calories as a consequence.

Rations aren't reality. They are useful as evidence of what Romans thought constituted "necessary"—necessary for a beggar, necessary for enslaved men doing heavy work. For the latter, 3,700–3,800 calories were hardly generous rations: they were, however, considerably more than the figures used by economic historians to model the majority. These working rations were also a minimum of a minimum. The benefactor/owner/employer provided wheat and a modicum of other staples: the recipient/worker was expected, through gardens or cash, to provide the rest. We shall take these, then, to represent a particularly *Roman* consumption minimum, and return to them throughout this book when we need to represent the bottom ranges of the 90 percent.

Beyond Wheat: Food Consumption in the City

If Roman caloric "subsistence" has relied on the United Nations, the composition of the Roman majority's diet has relied on wheat. Encouraged by the slave rations we just saw, and army rations we'll meet later, scholars have assumed that wheat and other cereals constituted some 70–75 percent of the diet.[44] Meat has been assumed to be beyond the reach of most everyone, while other protein sources—except for legumes—were few and far between. This apparently cereal-dominated diet has been judged to be nutrient-deficient and the Roman majority consequently presumed to have suffered widespread, if intermittent, malnutrition, poor resistance to disease, and low stature. As we noted above, the wheat-majority diet also anchors the very low consumption estimates used to calculate Roman economic performance.

This tyranny of wheat is not new: wheat and cereals more broadly cast a long shadow over economic history. Wheat production and consumption were the yardsticks of economic activity for thinkers from Adam Smith to David Graeber.[45] Wheat lay behind the world's first markets. Wheat allowed the growth of the first states, which taxed and levied rents in it. One of the first per capita consumption estimates to inform economic policymaking—made by Sébastien Vauban in 1707 for the French government—was made in wheat.[46] What is evident from all these uses of wheat is their notional—that is, their analytical—value. Wheat is good to measure with and to calculate from, both for the state and for scholars. There's no doubt that ancient people, like modern ones, ate a lot of wheat and other cereals. But a dietary staple isn't a diet, and wheat's relative contribution to Roman diets ought to be the question, not the presumed answer.[47]

The presumed wheat-majority in Roman diets has derived in part from a partial reading of those slave rations we analyzed above. There, wheat anchors the owner/employer's contribution, hence its prominence: the nonration, nonwheat portion of the diet is left to the worker's choice and is thus largely invisible to us. Enslaved workers doubtless ate a wheat-dominated diet, but the ration's controlling prism obscures what lay outside it.

If we leave the ration-controlled bottom of the 90 percent and move up the spectrum to the more middling workers of Roman cities, we find a world beyond wheat. The accounting habit described in chapter 1 has preserved for us a series of expense lists, many of them newly discovered. Composed by a whole range of working persons—gladiator trainers, travelers, a notary, perhaps even some slaves—they come from cities around the empire.[48] Scribbled on walls, on potsherds or on spare pieces of papyri, these expense lists were accounts kept by those who could write but had to carefully count their pennies. Thus, they probably record the consuming habits of a more middling or upper band of working people. These lists are not food diaries: they include a whole mishmash of expenses, usually for unknown numbers of people over an often-unknown period of time. They are hedged around with problems. But they have one important virtue: they are dominated by food expenses.

The graffito with which we began this chapter, tracking the expenses of a couple and their slave during their stay at an inn, is one such example (figure 2.2).

Lists like this one provide a new window on what working urbanites ate—both the kinds of foods and their frequency. From these lists, we can see them consuming wheat and cereals—mostly bread—regularly (figure 2.3). But we can also see them consuming a much wider range of foodstuffs than wheat, or even the so-called Mediterranean triad of wheat, wine and oil. In Pompeii, the working majority regularly ate a dietary tetrad of bread, wine, oil and cheese. Cheese is consumed even more often than oil. In Egyptian cities and large villages, wine is a rarity, but oil is consumed regularly together with a wide range of vegetables, including onions, cabbage and beans. In the city of Ephesus in Asia Minor, bread, wine and oil anchor the daily diet but are almost always accompanied by other things—fruit and various vegetables.

8th day before the Ides cheese 1
bread 8
oil 3
wine 3
7th day before the Ides
bread 8
oil 5
onion (*cepas/fecias*) 5
cooking pot 1
bread for slave 2
wine 2
6th day before the Ides bread 8

bread for slave 4
spelt 3
5th day before the Ides
wine for *domator* 16
bread 8 wine 2 cheese 2
4th day before the Ides dried fruit 6
shanks (*femininum*) 8
wheat 17
beef 1 dates 1
incense (thus) 1 cheese 2
sausage 1
soft cheese 4
oil 7(8)

servato....
(montana) 17
oil 26
bread 4 cheese 4

leek 1 for a plate 1
bucket (*situlae/Sittiae*) 9 lamp wick 1

3rd day before the Ides bread 2
bread for slave 2

day before the Ides bread for the slave 2
coarse bread 2
leek 1

bread 2

on the Ides bread 2
coarse bread 2
oil 5
spelt 3
fish for the *domator* 2

FIGURE 2.2. Multiday graffito expense list, Pompeii (*CIL* 4.5380. Translation: author)

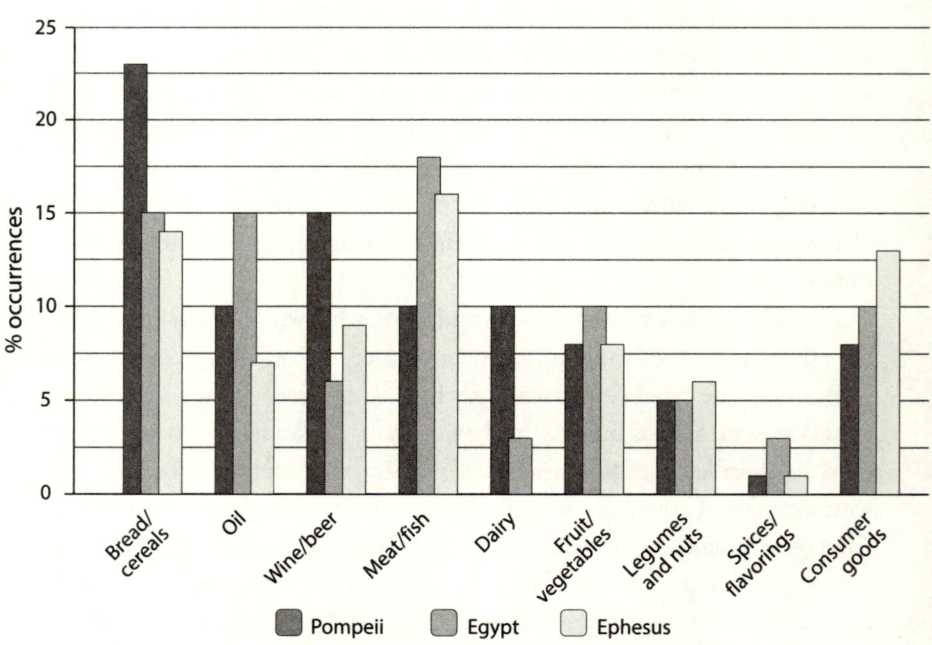

FIGURE 2.3. Frequency of foods consumed on Roman expense lists, first through second centuries CE (Data: appendix 1, table A.1)

Vegetables and fruit appear on these lists less frequently than we might expect, particularly for working people often assumed to be largely vegetarians. In Pompeii, onions and leeks appear on two lists, and fruit is never mentioned. In Egypt turnips, cabbage and asparagus appear in descending order of frequency, along with pomegranates and dates. In Ephesus, aside from an artichoke, the lists name generic fruit or vegetables without specifics. Also surprisingly infrequent in all lists are legumes. Roman literature is fond of ascribing a dish of cooked beans and grains (*puls*) to lower-status people, and soldiers are also known to have eaten it. Nonetheless, beans and pulses appear only four times.

These missing fruits, vegetables and beans should give us some pause. Archaeological evidence from the Vesuvian cities, for instance, shows that working Romans consumed large quantities of things that don't appear on these lists—berries, figs, plums, cherries and lentils. Indeed, the lists that have fruit and legumes in abundance—that of the freedman Gemellus from the Egyptian city of Oxyrhynchus, for instance—are those which appear in other respects to be from wealthier people.[49] It may be that fresh fruit and vegetables were harder to come by in cities, where working people's staples were more often drawn from preserved foods. Or it may be that they just didn't make it onto these lists, the tip of an iceberg of other missing food items.

If vegetables and fruit are relative rarities, the true fourth staple was meat or fish (figure 2.4). In Pompeii, of five lists that include bread, three also include meat and, on the multiday list, meat or fish is consumed one day in eight. In the Ephesus and Egypt lists, meat or fish appears even more frequently. In the Egyptian lists, *opson* and *prosphagion* make regular appearances: although sometimes translated as "relish" (their older meaning), by this period both likely refer to a cooked dish of meat or fish—maybe something like a kebab.[50] In the multiday Egyptian lists, meat or fish appears an average of one day in two, while in the Ephesus lists, meat or fish is consumed nearly five of seven days. Meat and fish appear to have been, if not daily staples, then regular components of the diet.

The data from these lists matches the more qualitative archaeological data we have for meat and, in some places, fish consumption in Roman cities by working people. In Herculaneum, Pompeii's sister-city, the sewer beneath a modest apartment building was stuffed with some 77 types of fish and shellfish, as well as 19 varieties of legumes, fruit and vegetables. As the excavators noted, the remains described a standard package of cereals, fruit, vegetables *and* seafood that most people shared, with occasional injections of "special foods," like imported black pepper or citrus, that would have been more

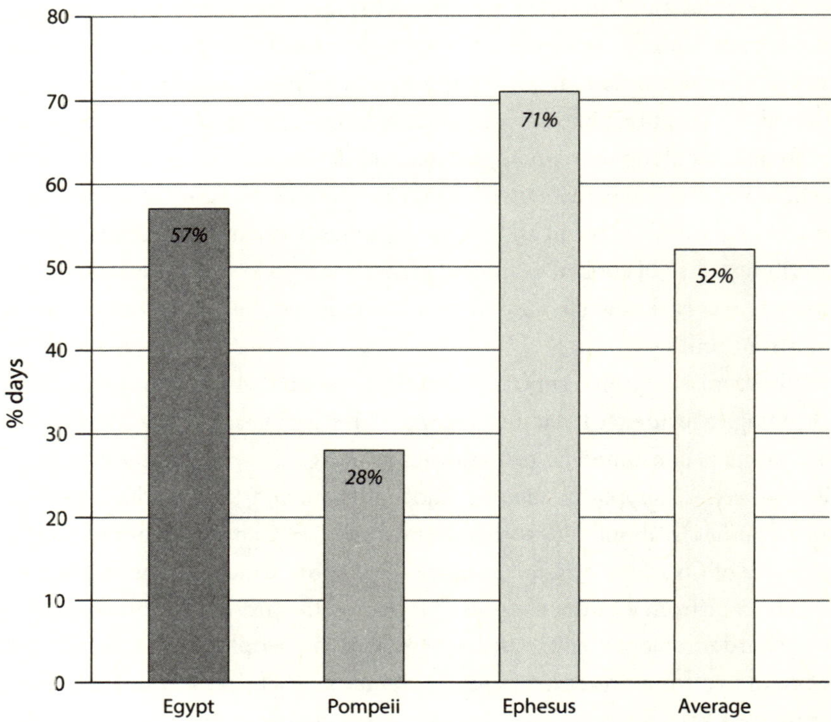

FIGURE 2.4. Meat on the menu: frequency from expense lists (Data: appendix 1, table A.1)

regularly consumed at the tables of the elite.[51] In a provincial city like Meaux, in Gaul, another dump outside another nonelite house complex contained the remains of hundreds of cattle, pigs and chicken—the detritus of a robust appetite for meat among the working majority.[52]

Outside of cities, meat-eating as a regularized habit was perhaps most strongly experienced in the army. Literary anecdotes about a soldier's life frequently mention bacon—which, together with wheat, cheese and sour wine, formed the standard military diet.[53] The military supply records from around the empire—from Egypt, from Vindolanda on Hadrian's Wall and Vindonissa in the Swiss Alps—regularly mention meat of various kinds as part of army rations. Faunal remains from those sites are also particularly rich in cattle, pigs, sheep and deer. The Vindolanda wooden tablets give a sense of how much meat both officers and nonofficer civilians might consume. An account from the later phases of the site finds a centurion buying 60 libra (19.6 kg) of bacon and lard for his own use; one Ircucisso, seemingly an ordinary soldier, bought even more—at least 100 libra (32 kg).[54] The purchases are almost certainly meant to last an extended period—a month perhaps—but that's still a lot of bacon.

The evidence from isotopic carbon and nitrogen preserved in human bones is another indicator of urban working people's meat consumption. As we'll see in more detail in chapter 6, the skeletal remains of Roman working people's bodies have left a robust record—albeit an indirect one—of their food consumption. In both Italy and Britain, where many skeletons have been preserved and studied, working people are clearly consuming fish, meat or both.[55] Gauging how much meat or fish they are consuming is much harder to deduce: isotope values are not straightforward metrics of dietary composition, and far more work remains to be done to reconstruct a whole diet. The only place this has been done with some plausibility, Herculaneum, has suggested a diet composed of some 5–15 percent of calories from seafood, 40–60 percent from cereals and another 30–50 percent from terrestrial protein (meat, dairy and legumes).[56] That amounts to around half of dietary calories coming from meat, seafood, dairy and/or legumes. This is a small sample from one city: our expense lists attest to a variety of practices within a meat-normal diet, a caution against generalizing from this one population. Nonetheless, it's a further sign of a world where meat and seafood were not limited to elites.

It's important to qualify this meat/fish-eating habit, for this is clearly not the world of, say, nineteenth-century England, where beef had become a staple food for pretty much everyone.[57] In the Roman expense lists, meat or fish is not eaten every day: that is, unless you were a soldier, it was not a staple. In the multiday list from Pompeii cited above, it appears as part of a single-day splurge, as both sausage and shanks, together with dates, incense, a lamp and two different kinds of cheese. Here sausage and shanks seem like quasi-luxuries.[58] On average, however, meat appears somewhat more frequently in Pompeii, about once every other day. These lists suggest that meat and/or fish thus constitute something between a luxury and a staple: for many urban working people, they formed regular punctuation marks in the weekly diet.

But what about for the truly poor? That same destitute vagabond living off Jewish communal charity in the Galilee was given fish only once per week, on the Shabbat.[59] The quarry workers in Egypt didn't get any meat or fish with their rations, but probably ate it occasionally as dried fish or old donkey or camel. This may have represented the bottom end of a more frequent habit of meat/fish eating than we have previously assumed.

TABLE 2.1. Food expenses, averages (first–second centuries CE)

	Calories	Value (HS/dr) per day	Value (HS/dr) per month	cereals (% of value)
Italy				
The enslaved: Cato's slave rations (w/o garden)	3,700	0.4–1.4	12–42	28–71%
Urbanites: Pompeii	?	3.3 (1.5–6.8)	99 (45–204)	30%
Egypt				
The (partly) enslaved: quarry worker rations (*w/wages)	3,875	0.44	13.2	77%/50%*
Urbanites/large villages	?	1.2 (0.6–2.2)	36 (18–66)	[47%]
Asia Minor (3rd c. CE)				
Urbanites: Ephesus				40%

Source: Appendix 1, table A.1.
Note: Ephesus for cereal frequency only.

If Roman urbanites were eating more than just wheat, they must have been spending differently, too. How much did city dwellers spend on this much-expanded dietary package? Again, the expense lists provide some answers, recalling, again, that those lists document the middle to upper end of the 90 percent (table 2.1). Working urbanites' food expenses—at least for those who kept lists—averaged around 1–3 sestertii/drachmas per day.

Those averages conceal an enormous range, from those who spent the equivalent of slave rations to those spending more than twelve times that. On average, though, the working urbanites we can see spent between two to fourteen times more on their diverse food packages than wheat-subsistence estimates would have it.

That higher-than-expected consumption was a product of food items that cost relatively little. Bread is strikingly consistently priced and, even in places with no state-supported food dole, quite cheap at around one *as* per libra (329 g) in first-century CE Pompeii, two obols per libra in second-century CE Ephesus. But other staples are similarly cheap—a portion (probably a *sextarius* or half a liter) of wine cost around two to four *as* (depending on the quality), a portion of cheese similarly so.

Indeed, the nonluxury status of meat/fish is further indicated by its low cost, no more expensive than most other items on the list. The beef and sausages consumed on the Pompeiian multiday list cost only an *as*. Other Pompeiian lists give the price of bacon at three *as* per *libra*, while at the military camp at Vindolanda, it cost only around two *as*.[60] While meat and fish aren't the most expensive item on most lists—a kebab in the Egyptian mega-village of Tebtunis costs only around two obols, while salt fish was two obols in the first-century port city of Berenike—they were not uniformly cheap. Kronion, the notary of Tebtunis, spent four drachmae on some fishes, and the "shanks" purchased in the Pompeiian inn were eight *asses*. The range of meat/fish prices suggests not only a range of quantities, but also a range of quality: common versus rarer fish, better or worse cuts of meat, thyme-flavored versus regular sausages.[61] When meat or fish slide into the "luxury" category, it seems to be around these gradations of quality.

The chronic lack of quantities in workers' expense lists almost never allows us to gauge how much of each type of food they were eating. Only one list from Pompeii includes enough quantitative clues to reconstruct diet by calories. Here, in a list from a gladiatorial training barracks, an individual obtained about 30 percent of their calories from bread, the rest from lard, pork, wine and oil. Without the lard (perhaps used in part for cooking), bread would have been 50 percent.[62] One list, alas, does not get us very far, although it's perhaps worth noting that the aforementioned isotope reconstructions from nearby Herculaneum put cereals in this ballpark, at 40–60 percent of calories. Just to put this in perspective, residents of wealthy countries today get about 25–35 percent of their calories from grains—those in poorer countries, around 70 percent.[63]

But if we can't know exactly how much bread or cereals working Romans were eating, we have a better idea how much they were spending on them (see table 2.1). On those lists with bread or cereal expenses, on average only 30 percent of expenditures went to bread/cereals, while 70 percent was spent on other items. Bread was often, as it was in most of the Pompeiian and Ephesian lists, the single largest food line-item, but was dwarfed in the aggregate by expenditures on wine, oil, cheese and meat/fish. This average overrepresents the data from Pompeii and Ephesus, and underrepresents that from cities in Egypt, so it, too, should be taken with some caution. Together with all the other data, however, it again suggests that, for urban dwellers, cereals were less important to overall consumption than we have supposed.

In fact, the greater-than-expected amounts that working Romans spent on food were driven by a desire to consume beyond cereals. A working Roman who spent some eight times more than the bottom-end slave rations put that extra money not into more of the same foods—that is, more bread—but into an expanded variety of foods, particularly meat and fish, which could be obtained at low cost. Like poor and working people around the world today, more money wasn't necessarily used to buy more of the same food—more cereals or lentils. It was used to buy more interesting, better-tasting food.[64] These appear on the lists with special adjectives: soft cheese, white or pure bread, particular kinds of shellfish. Romans' higher food expenditure paid for small moments of pleasure, of distinction.

These expense lists get us some way to reconstructing a new set of first-order foodstuffs—staples and near-staples—consumed by middling working urbanites. In Italy, bread, wine, oil, cheese and meat were consumed regularly, if not daily. In Egypt, it was bread, oil, meat or fish and a wider range of vegetables, while in the cities of the Roman East, bread, wine, oil and meat or fish were the dietary core. Luxuries like pepper and citrus were added periodically, but more often it was higher-quality or distinctive versions of everyday foods—better bread, certain kinds of fish, finer cuts of meat or distinctive cheese. These tended to cost more, and appear less regularly, but nonetheless make it onto these quotidian accounts—little weekly luxuries rather than once-a-year splurges. Although all of these staples and near-staples were low in cost, cumulatively they cost their consumers around one to three sestertii or drachmas per day, some three to eight times the value of slave rations.

Food Consumption in the Countryside

Rural peasants have often been assumed to be largely subsistence vegetarians.[65] The vegetarian peasant is the silent companion to the subsistence peasant—a small farmer who, because they grow only enough to feed their family, subsists principally on wheat, garden vegetables and foraged fruits. The vegetarian subsistence peasant is also assumed to live farm-to-table: the quintessential model of autarky, they produce virtually all their own food and purchase virtually none.

We'll take on the assumptions around smallholder production in the next chapter. Here we'll consider what these smallholders ate, focusing on the smallholder farmers of the western empire, for which we have the most evidence. Untangling the remains of what farmers ate from what they produced is tricky: the remains of consumption and production are conjoined, in some ways hopelessly so. The sciences of archaeobotany—ancient plant remains—and archaeozoology—animal remains—as well as ceramics, provide some help, and give us the "what" of farmers' diet. Unlike the expense accounts from cities, however, they are largely mute on "how much."

Qualitative and fragmentary as it is, all this new data has largely exploded the idea of the vegetarian, autarkic peasant. Rural farmers ate meat and dairy, and they purchased a wide variety of foods from off the farm, even foods they also produced. It is thus possible, even probable, that some portion of the expanded dietary package of staples we observed in cities—cereals, wine, oil and meat/cheese—were also consumed in the countryside. However, while we probably need to bid farewell to the concept of the farm-to-table vegetarian peasant, this new data reveals emphatic differences between their food consumption and that of their urban comrades. Rural dietary variety was more limited, meat consumption was probably less frequent, fish very rare, while seemingly easy sources of wild meat were largely bypassed.

We know that smallholder farmers grew a variety of cereals and ate them.[66] We also know they grew and ate a variety of vegetables and fruit.[67] The more pressing question is: Did farmers eat the same range of fruits and vegetables as their wealthier, villa-owning neighbors or their urban working brethren? Britain is the only place we can answer this definitively. Here, it's clear that the fruits and vegetables eaten in farmer households were more or less the same as those consumed by wealthy villa owners. It was the urban/rural divide that really impacted fruit-vegetable diversity.[68] Only in cities were rarer vegetables like cucumbers or imported fruits like citrus available. We've seen that in cities, even poor residents might get to eat these exotics occasionally; in the countryside, they were almost entirely absent.

Cereals, fruits and vegetables are obvious components of a farmer's diet. More revealing are three aspects of their consumption that suggest a historically unusual dietary range—namely, imported wine, oil and meat.

Italian farmers produced and consumed their own wine and oil, while British farmers produced and consumed their own beer and butter. More interesting is the fact that they also purchased alcohol and fats from off the farm. The traces of these purchases come from the remains of transport amphorae: containers especially designed to transport oil, wine or even fish sauce (*garum*) from their point of production to more distant points of consumption. Amphorae hold anywhere from 5–150 liters of liquid, and thus represent bulk purchases by farmers of things that came from afar. How far afar is indicated by their forms: the forms we know about tend to be those designed for very long-distance transport, in ships, from major places of production—oil from southern Spain, wine from Campania, fish sauce from Portugal. Increasingly, however, archaeologists are unearthing a whole range of smaller amphora types, flat-bottomed so as to be carried in barges or

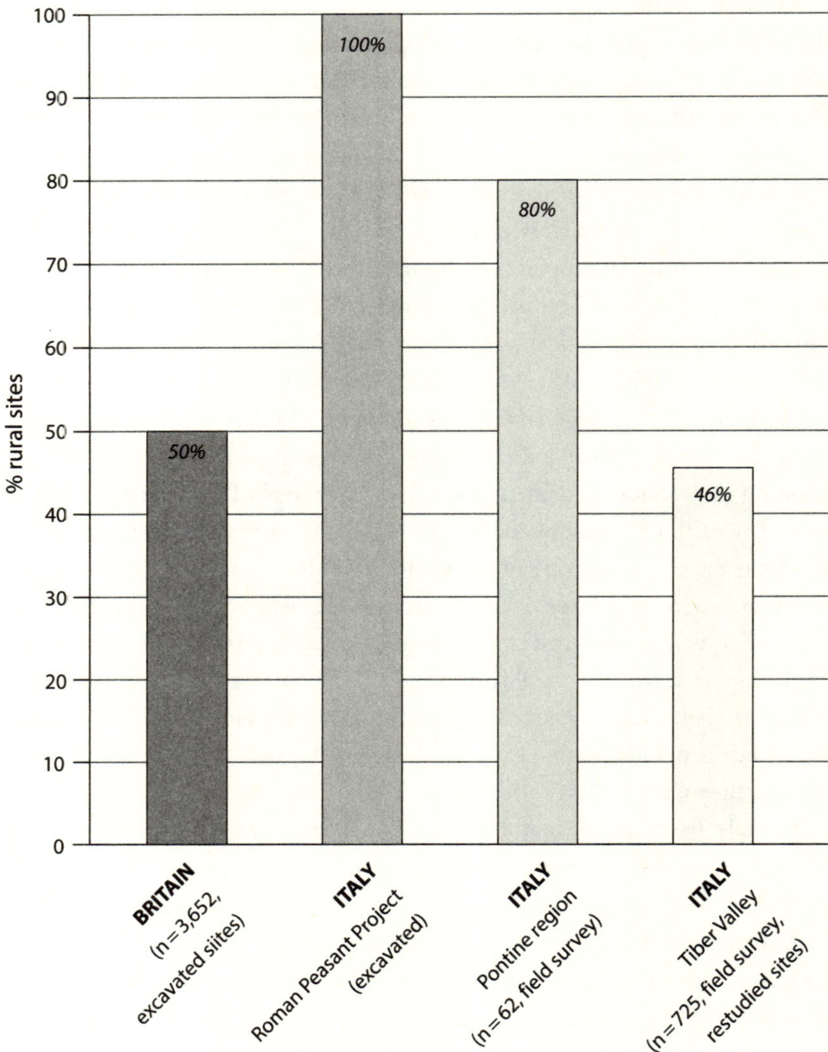

FIGURE 2.5. Buying food from off the farm: amphorae from farms (Data: Britain: Fulford et al. 2017, fig. 7.1; Pontine survey: Haas 2011, tables 3.1, 3.3, 4.1, 4.3, 5.1, 5.3; Tiber Valley: Witcher, pers. comm. (336 farms) and Patterson, Witcher and Di Giuseppe 2020, fig. 2.31b)

carts, which moved wine and oil shorter ranges—within regions or between neighbors.

All this new evidence finds farmers in Italy and Britain purchasing wine, oil and, to a lesser extent, fish sauce, from off the farm (figure 2.5). In central Italy, the home of Roman wine production, some 80 percent of farms south of

Rome were purchasing wine or oil from off the farm. In an inland Tuscan region, farther from the coast and several days travel from the capital, all of the farms and worksites studied were purchasing imported wine or oil. Here on these Tuscan farms, the wine came mostly from nearby—the Tuscan coast or even closer to home, bottled in small local amphorae. Occasionally, these farmers drank wine from farther afield—Campania or Tunisia—and ate even rarer fish sauce from southern Spain.[69] In one region of central Britain, where imported olive oil and wine were still exotic outsiders compared to beer and butter, half of excavated farms and villages were purchasing imported oil and wine. Folks who lived in places that had access to goods on the move—villages and roadside settlements—were most likely to consume these imports, but some 45 percent of larger farms also had them, although in small quantities. Most of the wine consumed by British farmers came from central Italy, while their oil came from southern Spain.[70]

These trends are surprising in both regions, but for different reasons. British farmers are not obvious consumers of imported wine and oil. The fact that a family of presumably "modest" farmers from Wiltshire even occasionally drank Italian and French wine and used oil from Spain, in addition to their likely supplies of home-produced beer and lard, points to not only a greater range of foods, but a willingness and ability to purchase them, albeit in small quantities.[71] In central Italy, the empire's largest wine-producing region in the first centuries BCE/CE, farmers who were seemingly producing their own wine were also purchasing it from off the farm. In both of these regions, amphorae are the tip of an iceberg of preference, of a willingness and capacity to consume something beyond one's own products.

Not all farmers had the means or inclination to do this. British archaeologists have tended to view those 50 percent of British farms without amphorae as a glass half-empty, a majority of rural dwellers alienated from the diets and tastes of their colonizers.[72] It's harder to see the 20–30 percent of Italian farmers who didn't consume imported wine in quite this light. Access and economic capacity shaped rural consumption as surely as did colonial disenfranchisement, a fact we'll return to when we examine farmers' consumption of pottery. Nonetheless, it's clear that not all farmers purchased wine, oil or fish sauce from off the farm, and that it was obviously easier to do in places where the distribution networks along which such goods traveled also ran through your backyard. It is surely equally significant, though, that so many farmers actually did consume these things. We have assumed that only elites and aspiring elites like Trimalchio were discerning wine-drinkers: we should now add at least half of Roman farmers to that list.

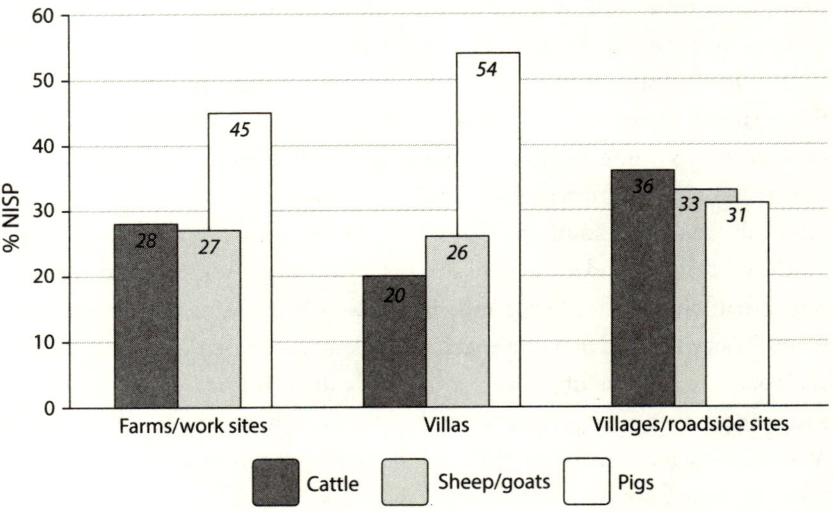

FIGURE 2.6. Eating meat in the countryside, central Italy, first century BCE through third century CE (Data: MacKinnon 2021, table 13.17; sites with less than 10 NISP removed)

Finally, what about meat? Did rural farmers eat meat as frequently as did their urban comrades? The frequency question is, alas, still beyond the ability of archaeology to answer. However, it's unequivocally clear now that smallholder farmers did eat meat. The remains of animals from farms and villages throughout the western empire find farmers eating the same general package of major domestic animals consumed by their elite rural neighbors. In first-century BCE/CE Italy, for instance, inhabitants of farms, villages and roadside settlements were eating more or less the same selection of animals as did elites in their rural villas—a preponderance of pork, followed by beef and sheep/goat (figure 2.6).

The differences in meat-eating between working and rich rural-dwellers in Italy are ones of nuance. Smallholders generally appear to consume somewhat more beef than elite villa-owners, particularly those folks living on roadside sites or rural market centers. Pork-eating peasants appear to slaughter their pigs somewhat later, probably to maximize their weight, while elites appear to eat younger, more tender animals.[73]

In southeast Britain, too, British elite villa owners appear to have the same meat on the menu, in more or less the same relative quantities, as their poorer neighbors: beef, followed by sheep, then pork and horse (figure 2.7). Again, the differences are of quality, not type: piglet and lamb were on villa-owners'

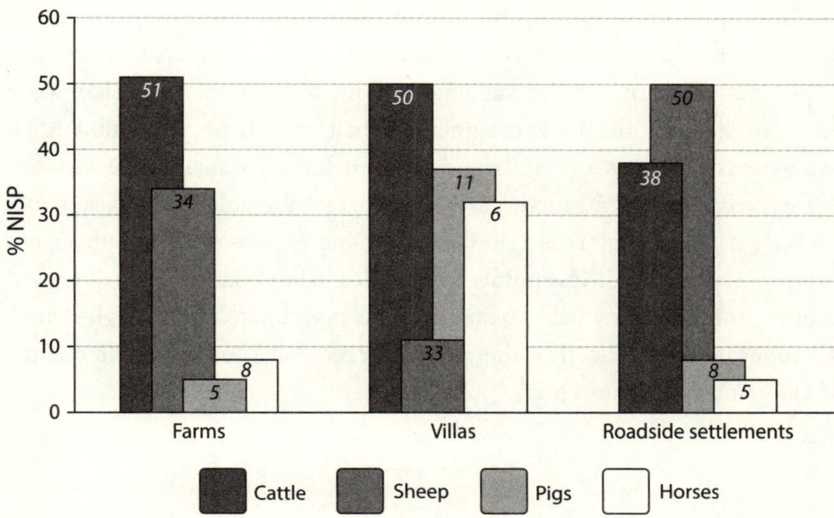

FIGURE 2.7. Eating meat in the countryside, Britain, Cambridgeshire/West Anglian Plain (Data: Allen and Lodwick 2016, fig. 4.6)

tables, pork and mutton on farmers'. It's the denizens of roadside sites who had the really different meat-eating habits, here with much more mutton: these villages were centers of sheep-based dairy and cheese production, and probably ate mutton as part of dairy-oriented farming.

While seemingly very similar in their consumption of meat staples, farmers and urbanites differed in their consumption of less-popular meats. Somewhat surprisingly, chicken was rare in all countryside places.[74] Chickens appear to have been largely creatures of the city and, to a lesser extent, elite villas. The villa-owning elite also ate hunted animals—deer and boar principally—which are almost never found on smaller farms. Finally, farmers almost never ate fish. Fish are vanishingly rare on farm sites in Italy, Gaul and Britain.[75] This is in sharp distinction from what we've seen on those urban expense lists, where fish turned up quite regularly.

The new archaeological data, then, finds the farmers of the western empire consuming an expanded range of food basics. They may have eaten a wider range of fruit than their comrades in towns, but shared with them a dietary tetrad of cereals, wine, oil and meat in Italy, and cereals, dairy, meat and some wine or beer in Britain. They rarely ate fish or imported plant foods. Staples, then, appear to be broadly shared; near-staples and luxury foods less so. In other words, it's at the edges of the core diet where farmers appear to have most differed from their urban brethren or the wealthy.

The nagging question of "how much," however, particularly how much meat, limits what we can say about this evidence. Again, the still-nascent isotope evidence from human bones may provide some clues. As we shall see in detail in chapter 6, the bones of rural and urban working people exhibit different values of isotopes for carbon and nitrogen. In Italy, farmers appear to have lower carbon and nitrogen, this at least in part attributable to that lack of fish. In Britain, carbon values are similar in city and countryside, but nitrogen is lower among farmers. This points, potentially, to less consumption of higher-trophic foods—principally meat. It is thus possible that, although British farming families are clearly eating meat, they may have done so less frequently than their urban counterparts.[76]

From enslaved workers to middling urbanites, all this new evidence finds the Roman 90 percent eating differently than we have imagined. Rations for enslaved people doing hard labor were more robust in calories, but still at the limits of what was necessary for their taxing lives. Most of the rest of the 90 percent regularly ate a whole range of things that we had imagined they ate only rarely, from imported wine to cheese to the surprisingly frequent meat or fish. They didn't eat these things all the time: even the Pompeiian family with whom we began had moments of low ebb. And at high ebb, they didn't just eat more, they ate differently. Food diversity in these moments meant not just an expanded menu, but also variety within the variety—soft cheese, not hard; oil, not butter; Campanian wine, not local rotgut. Food consumption included both subsistence and distinction. A higher price tag was the result of this variety: working Romans spent far more on their variegated diets than simply the cost of wheat, maybe as much as ten times more. Living in a world saturated with imported wine, salted fish and even tough mutton came with a cost, a cost made even higher by the equally seductive world of things.

A Gusto for Things

Working people included more than just food in their accounting of expenses. On those urban expense lists, scattered among the bread, wine and meat, are payments for a pot, a lamp, wool, a basket. These appear to be basic maintenance items for an individual or a household, purchased on a daily or almost daily basis (see figures 2.2 and 2.3). Like the food, they are consumables. In this context, it's remarkable how many things were required for basic maintenance: from pots and wool and soap, to toys and birthday garlands and purple thread. Some appear to be what we might term staples—a pot for cooking, wood for fire. Others appear more like luxuries—the toys and purple thread. Daily necessities or more occasional splurges: these are the detritus of lives lived among an abundance of things.

The so-called Roman consumer revolution refers to the massive expansion of these things, beginning in second-century BCE Italy and expanding to the provinces. It was a kind of conquest by stuff, as a wave of all manner of goods, from household items to jewelry and clothing, swept first over the Italian peninsula and later the provinces. These goods were increasingly standardized and homogenized, so that by the second century CE the plates a senator ate off in Rome looked very similar to the plates used by a farmer in Gaul.[77] It was an IKEA world. With all that similar stuff probably came some homogenization of habits: the dietary package we unearthed above was remarkable as much for its homogeneity as for its regional flavor. Food and cooking, shoe and clothing fashions began to resemble one another from Cotswold farmhouses to Egyptian villages.[78] Lurking behind the standardized forms, however, were a wide range of qualities: cheap and expensive versions of the same objects were produced for consumers of different means. We've already caught a glimpse of this through the expense lists: fine white bread, slave bread; soft cheese, regular cheese; a thousand different kinds of fish.

This was not a world where e-commerce availability produced any object desired by any consumer.[79] Most of this standardized, thing-rich world was produced locally, in local ceramic, glass and cloth workshops, and the majority of objects probably didn't travel more than 50 or 100 kilometers from their place of manufacture—already quite a distance in a premodern world. But as we've already seen with food, "local" and "imported" don't readily map onto cost: humble cooking pots might be traded long distances, seemingly with little increase in price.[80] This simultaneously abundant and contingent, local and global consumer world makes understanding "choice" particularly challenging. Did those 50 percent of British farmers not drink imported wine because they couldn't get it, couldn't afford it, or didn't want it? Was this a product of a deliberate rejection of the Roman cultural package, or of folks living outside the range of the nearest "grocery store"?

Pottery is the consumer good most beloved by archaeologists and scholars of the Roman consuming habit. Durable and abundant, it is perhaps the most studied and least understood of all Roman commodities, in part because—ironically—its study has been so little standardized.[81] In the Roman world, virtually all pottery was wheel-made in specialized workshops: it was among the most frequently purchased goods, virtually never made within the household itself. It is thus a useful barometer for households' purchasing habits. It's also an aspect of the consumer revolution most clearly driven by the 90 percent. Working households' aggregate demand for ceramics was what drove the huge expansion of the Roman ceramics industry, from fine wares to cooking pots.

Glass, iron and bronze objects were similarly ubiquitous, even if less often found on archaeological sites (bronze and iron) or less comprehensively studied (glass). Glass is a false aristocrat. Starting in the Augustan period, huge quantities of glass, produced in bulk in the eastern provinces and Italy but probably blown locally, flooded the markets of the empire.[82] While the delicacy and color of glass vessels have led many archaeologists to label it a luxury good, in most parts of the empire glass is second to pottery in ubiquity, and in towns, at any rate, was as often found on the table as ceramic tablewares.[83] Bronze and iron objects were equally common, if more expensive: from keys to kettles, hinges to sickles, working households ran on metal objects. Because they were costly and because they could be easily melted down, they were usually recycled at the end of their use-life and thus are underrepresented in archaeological sites. Only in catastrophic contexts—like Pompeii—do we catch a glimpse of the superabundance of metals.[84] And like pottery and glass, metal objects were purchased, not homemade.

These are the durable tip of an iceberg of things that Romans consumed along with food. But what difference did all this stuff make to working people and their economic lives? How much did it all cost? How much did they actually buy? What constituted first- and second-order needs? These questions have been obscured by the various disciplines' first-order needs to classify and date these objects, and the third-order desire to use pots and pans as windows into cultural identity. In the current state of Roman consumption studies, it's as though we've labored over the measurements and the cultural significance of the iPhone without ever considering how much it costs.

Urban Things

To stroll down the main streets of Pompeii is to walk among the detritus of the Roman consumer revolution. The long rows of shops, workshops and bars are the standing remains of a retail universe, one of the world's first shopping cultures.[85] We've already caught a glimpse of this urban gusto for things in the urban expense lists—bronze buckets, incense, lamp-wicks and purple thread. These provide a very partial accounting of nonfood goods purchased as part of daily consumption. As we've already seen with food, these consumer goods constitute a broad range of things, much broader than a simple cooking pot and some firewood. These lists also give us a sense of the minimum that working consumers might spend on such goods. Unsurprisingly, these costs constitute only a fraction of the amounts spent on food—a tenth to just over half.[86] Partial as they are, expense lists provide a useful minimum for nonfood expenses.

A better way to understand how much working Romans spent on their world of things is from the contents of their houses. In other periods, probate inventories or wills provide lists of families' objects, and thus a precious glimpse of consumer practices and their price tag.[87] Such sources are mostly absent for the Roman world. Instead, the best way to see house contents is through archaeology, and the best place to do it is Pompeii. Normally, archaeology preserves a selective palimpsest of household consumption over centuries of occupation. Pompeii, the city destroyed over eighteen hours by a volcano, provides something closer to whole-house contents captured in a moment in time.

But even Pompeiian house contents aren't complete: many objects, like textiles, simply didn't survive; many houses were already abandoned by the time of the eruption; while during the eruption, houses were stripped of some movable valuables.[88] The later centuries of excavation unevenly recorded what remained, focusing on prestige objects—pretty things and anything with writing on it—while failing to record mundane objects like cooking pots.[89] Pompeii preserves as good an image of what working people consumed as we are ever likely to have, but it's still only a sketch.

The category of "poverty" that we examined in the introduction to this book has been particularly thorny at Pompeii. If poverty is defined by not owning any things, what does an archaeology of poverty look like? At Pompeii, the ubiquitous presence of paintings and bronze pots and glass led some early excavators to assume that most of the extant houses must, by definition, be the homes of elites or very top-end merchants. The poor majority, by definition, must needs be crammed into apartments and shop backrooms. However, a recent study determined that most inhabitants—something like 70 percent—may have lived in a proper house, however small.[90] That is, the working majority were not only crammed into the backrooms of shops and small second-story apartments, as we had once supposed. They certainly lived in those spaces, but these

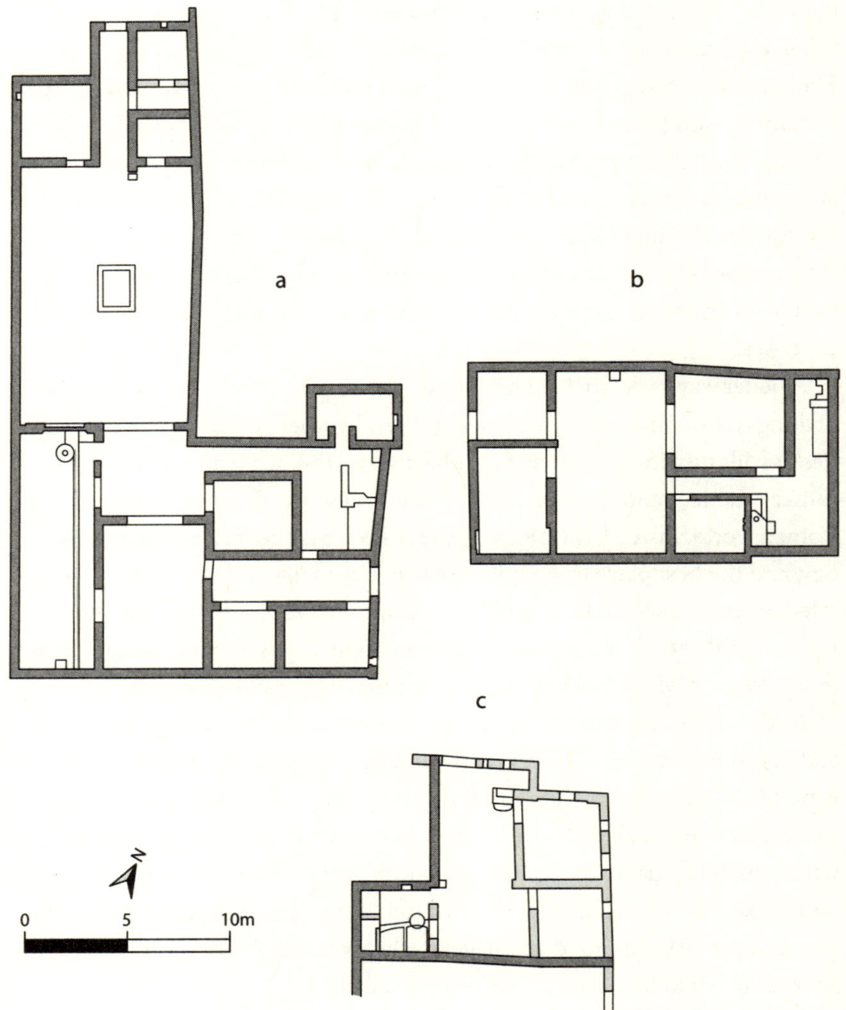

FIGURE 2.8. Three Pompeiian houses: (a) House of Habonius Primus (I 11, 5–8), (b) House of L. Caecelius Ianuarius (I 11, 17), (c) House at I 10, 1 (Illustration: Matilde Grimaldi, after Peña, in press, and Allison 2006)

constituted the bottom end of a range of housing in which the majority owned or rented some kind of multiroomed space.

Three examples provide a sense of what constituted housing for middling to upper-level members of the Pompeiian 90 percent, a range of house sizes and configurations that reflected, albeit dimly, a range of working families' economic circumstances (figure 2.8).

At the top end, some two to five people were thought to be living in the partially abandoned House of Habonius Primus, a medium-sized house with a small atrium and gaggle of ground-floor rooms, only some of which were occupied. A more modest example was perhaps occupied by one L. Caelius Ianuarius; he and his family lived in the four small rooms around a small courtyard. Toward the bottom of the range—although still a house rather than a single room—was a workshop and cluster of tiny rooms at address I 10, 1.[91] Each of these houses had a tiny kitchen and latrine—distinct spaces for cooking and toilet—and some had upper-story rooms. Most of these houses, too, had some kind of decoration—basic paintings in their atrium or largest rooms. Even so, living in these smallish houses with their more cramped, dark rooms and often modest decor constituted a different experience of space and set of tastes than did the spacious houses of the wealthy.[92]

For our purposes, it's also critical to note that these spaces involved costs: the purchase or rent of something more than a room, and its decoration. We have no idea what these costs were: a room in Pompeii may have rented for 1–2 sestertii per night.[93] The rental or purchase price of small houses is anyone's guess.[94] But the fact that many incurred such costs and invested in decoration is something to note.

If we turn to the contents of these same three houses, we find they contained a huge number of objects, objects that, peering through the problematic record-keeping of earlier archaeology, describe a wide range of basic goods owned by a range of middling to upper band of working families (figure 2.9).[95]

They included, as expected, a wide range of cooking and tablewares, not only in ceramic but also in bronze (mostly for cooking) and glass (mostly as tablewares). Through their different forms and materials and size, the different eating and drinking wares made different kinds of distinctions—by food type or by formality: big and small plates; jugs for wine or for oil; plates for a normal meal versus those for a special one. Lamps, mostly ceramic, provided light, and metal tools supported labor. Simple ornaments, such as earrings and rings in bronze or silver, adorned the body, while small objects for hygiene—tweezers, perfume bottles, strigils—kept it clean. Finally, gaming pieces and libation cups speak to modest entertainments and a need to propitiate the gods. This multitude of objects, on average around 80 per household, appear to comprise a range of first-order (food preparation and serving) and second-order (ornament, entertainment and ritual) goods, as well as basic forms of social distinction.

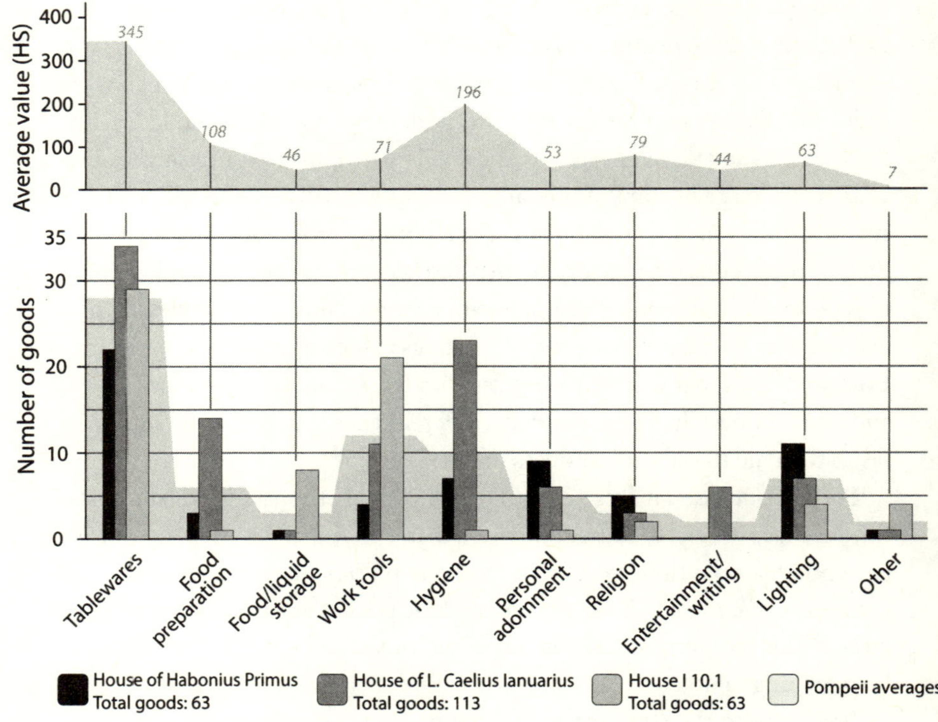

FIGURE 2.9. Three Pompeiian houses and their contents (Data: appendix 1, tables A.2 and A.3)

These very differently affluent working households—from the tiniest to the largest—appear to have owned objects that served most, if not all, of these functions. This was possible because function only lightly correlated with value. In other words, households might own cheap or expensive versions of goods that served roughly similar functions. Difference in value lay in the materials (a lamp made of clay versus a lamp in bronze) or in size (large serving vessels versus smaller ones). Larger houses like that of Habonius Primus had the same functional range of goods as a tiny house like I 10, 1, but more expensive versions of them—silver cups instead of glass, more bronze tablewares than ceramic.

How working people could afford so many things is evident from an estimate of the value of those objects.[96] The value of this basic package of objects averaged between 600 and 1,300 sestertii, a surprisingly low figure considering that these represented the accumulated possessions of, if not a lifetime, then an extended period, and for a whole family. Low cumulative value was a product of the cheapness of most objects: the average value of an individual object ranged from around four sestertii in the smallest, partially occupied house to still only 20 sestertii in the wealthiest. There's an important bias in the archaeological record to remember here: the cheapest goods—ceramics and glass—are well preserved and numerous, while the more expensive furniture and linen are not. Total overall values that included beds and cupboards and mattresses—all of which exist in enough Pompeiian households to appreciate their ubiquity—would have been much higher. Nonetheless, to put the low overall cost for more portable household goods in perspective, documented urban food expenditures for middling individuals in Pompeii, it will be remembered, averaged as much as 100 sestertii per month for an adult. Many household goods were cheap by comparison.[97]

Putting this combined multitude and cheapness of household goods into historical context gives a sense of how particular Roman working people's consumer world was. Early modern Europe also experienced a much-discussed "consumer revolution," in which cheap stuff, from clocks to linen, was increasingly available to and desired by working people.[98] By the later sixteenth century, an English artisan or merchant might have owned as many as 200–300 goods. A great many of these, though, were perishable furniture and linens missing in our archaeological records, so the disparity between the Pompeiian average of 80 goods would have been considerably less. A better sense may come from tablewares alone: a sample of modestly affluent seventeenth- and eighteenth-century English households had on average only about 18 pieces of tableware; our Pompeiian households appear to have had some 28. For at least some kinds of consumer goods, the Roman world may have been a more abundant world of particularly cheap things than even this prequel to modernity.

Rural Things

Roman farmers are not imagined as being consumers of lots of things.[99] Particularly in the Finleyan model, they are producers only, while the fruits of their labor—both agricultural and artisanal—are shipped off to parasitic cities. Recent work in a postcolonial vein seems to have returned to this idea, assuming, again, that the Roman colonizers were mostly urbanites, gobbling up the products of rural indigenous labor.[100] But again, the new archaeological data from the countryside finds farmers with their own gusto for things, albeit somewhat different things in probably different quantities than their urban comrades.

FIGURE 2.10. "Villa Regina" farmhouse, Boscoreale (Photo: Norbert Nagel. Creative Commons License 3.0)

We need look no further than the countryside outside Pompeii, where excavations in a farm uncovered a precious, whole-household comparison with the urban households we just examined.[101] The farm was a largish one: in the typologies we'll lay out in chapter 3, it was on the big side, with twelve rooms organized around a courtyard (figure 2.10). However, at the time of the eruption it was partially abandoned, occupied only by perhaps three day-laborers who were repairing the building and perhaps working in the nearby vineyards. Judging from graffiti on the walls, one or all of these workers may have been enslaved.[102] The house contents at Villa Regina, then, provide a precious counterpoint to urban consumption, while shedding some light on the objects used by enslaved workers.

Figure 2.11 lays out the contents of those workers' temporary quarters.[103] The differences with the urban households are immediately obvious: while the overall number of goods is similar to the average for working houses inside the city, those objects are of a different kind and value. Composed largely of ceramic, rather than bronze or glass, the contents consist of vessels used for food preparation and consumption, water storage, iron tools (including a valuable wagon), and the odd bronze vessel. First-order needs thus constitute the bulk of their things. Second-order needs are not totally absent—some small playing

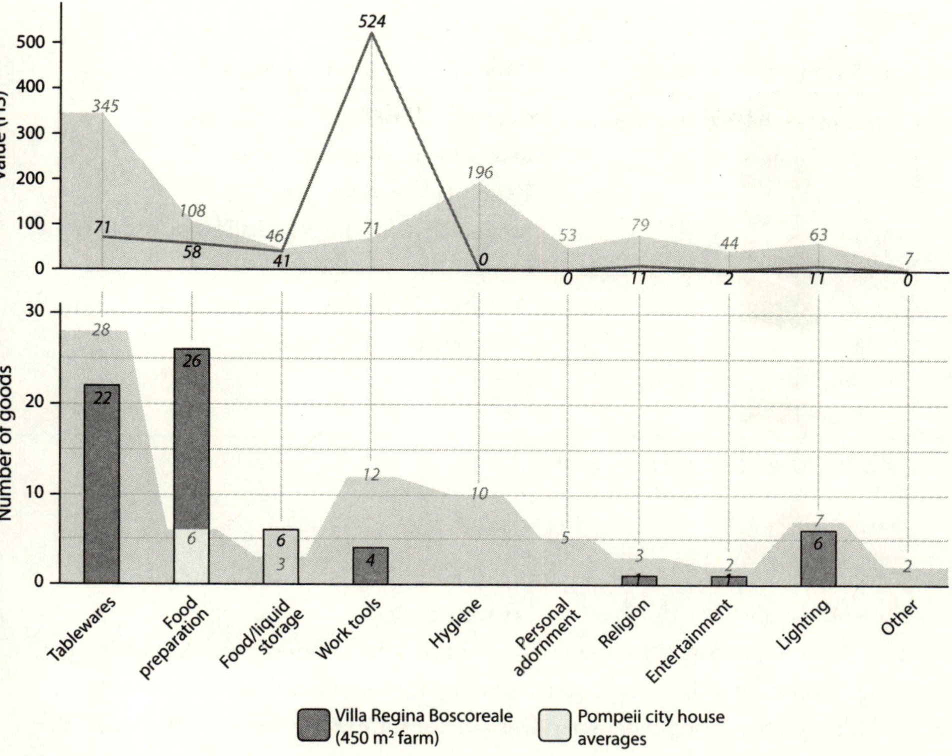

FIGURE 2.11. Some rural workers and their things: the contents of the "Villa Regina," Boscoreale (Data: appendix 1, tables A.2 and A.3)

discs suggest a rudimentary game—but they are few. That being said, the variety of vessels for food serving deserves some note: cups, plates, bowls, and a number of different kinds of jugs, plus a whole range of pots and lids and basins for cooking. The urge to distinguish course and food type is found here, although the limited range of vessels and the absence of glass suggest little distinction by formality. The inhabitants, in short, while having mostly food-related items, had a whole range of them: dining was not simply eating out of the pot.

The overall value of these objects, some 630–800 sestertii, is largely a product of one utilitarian object—the valuable wagon (500 sestertii). The cooking, dining and storage wares are worth only around 130–280 sestertii. In general, the value is lower than the urban assemblages, largely due to the absence of higher-value items in bronze and glass. Assuming these constituted the objects owned or used by the enslaved workers, this modest, ceramic and

TABLE 2.2. Two farms' objects

San Mario (Volterra, Italy)	Cotswold Community (Gloucestershire, UK)
Common ware: local and regional	Common ware: local and regional
Fine ware: regional	Fine ware: regional, imported
Vessel glass	Vessel glass; window glass
Amphorae	Amphorae (Spain [oil], S. Gaul [wine]; Italy [wine])
Bronze statuette (Jupiter Silvanus)	Lamps/candle holders
Gem	Personal adornment (brooches, bracelet, rings)
Fibula	Leather shoes (hobnails)
Glirarium (vessel for raising dormice)	Iron tools

Source: Camin 2005; Smith, Powell and Booth 2010.

first-order needs–centered package resembles Cato's slave rations: a sufficiency of the basic things necessary for survival.

How very basic were the contents of this day-laborer household is highlighted by the relatively richer contents of farmers' households elsewhere. Although the product of generations of consumption, a simple list of the objects found on two farms gives a sense of the complexity of farmers' consumption habits (table 2.2). A tiny two-room farm near Volterra in Italy possessed an astonishing range of goods.[104]

A range of fine and common wares, as well as glass vessels, allowed this farming family to distinguish course and formality. A small bronze statuette of Jupiter Silvanus propitiated the rural gods, while a cut gem and fibulae show the family dressing to impress. First- and second-order needs, even a distinction in materials, are all present on this tiny farm.

Most farms didn't have quite this range of luxury materials. A farm in the British Cotswolds, termed "modest" by its excavators largely on the basis of its household objects, had a remarkably similar list, but in less expensive materials.[105] A range of tablewares distinguished food, course and even occasion. Most of these wares were of regional manufacture, with a small quantity of imported sigillata wares from Gaul. The site also had window glass—a rarity, as we'll see, on British farms—together with a couple of lamps and candlesticks. These farmers were among the 50 percent who also drank imported wine, and they owned a few modest rings, bracelets and brooches, as well as leather shoes. The principal difference with the Italian farm household was the absence of those few objects made of more precious materials. Most goods in both farms were of regional manufacture—the exception may be the glass and the sigillata in the British farm—and these regional goods were purchased from off the farm in an abundant variety.

A more quantitative sense of rural household goods comes from studies of fine ceramic. The Roman period witnessed an explosion of consumption of fine-ware pottery by farmers, as farmers from North Africa to Britain were purchasing in some quantities what had been a rarity. In Italy, the home of the canonical red sigillata pottery, most of our data comes from field survey—which probably underrepresents it. Some 70 percent of farms from a region south of Rome had either sigillata or its earlier black-glazed predecessor.[106] At the other end of the spectrum, much has been made about the fact that many farmers in Britain didn't have an abundance of what for them was an imported ware: red sigillata pottery was made throughout the empire but not in Britain.[107] In fact, some 77 percent of British rural sites had at least one piece of it, but it was especially consumed in larger farms and roadside sites. In North Africa, consumption of fine-ware pottery by Roman farmers was similarly skewed: while perhaps a third of small farms in some Libyan valleys were buying it, for the most part it was large farms, and in some regions only large farms, where such pottery was used. It was only later, in the fourth century CE, when the consumer revolution would really impact the region's smallest smallholders.[108] Farmers' consumption of fine pottery, then, had its limits.

It's one thing to note the farmers' consumption of pottery as a commodity, but pottery was intended to be used for eating and drinking, and the forms of that pottery—plates, jugs, bowls—are equally eloquent about farmers' table habits and preferences (figure 2.12). In Italy and Britain, closed forms like jugs and jars were common. Italian farmers, however, regularly owned a wider range of forms: jars, jugs, cups, beakers and some basins and bottles. The forms on southeastern British tables were much more limited, largely consisting of jars and some bowls.[109] Again, it's clear that some provincial farmers were consuming in more limited ways than others. What's equally interesting, however, is that, despite these regional differences, farmers in both places began to purchase more open-form vessels—plates, basins and bowls—in the later second and third centuries CE, and fewer jugs and jars. This shift toward more open table forms by the later empire appears to be an empire-wide fashion—perhaps part of new collective dining practices like eating out of shared dishes.[110] Rather than lying outside these trends, farmers appear to be changing their tablewares along with everyone else.

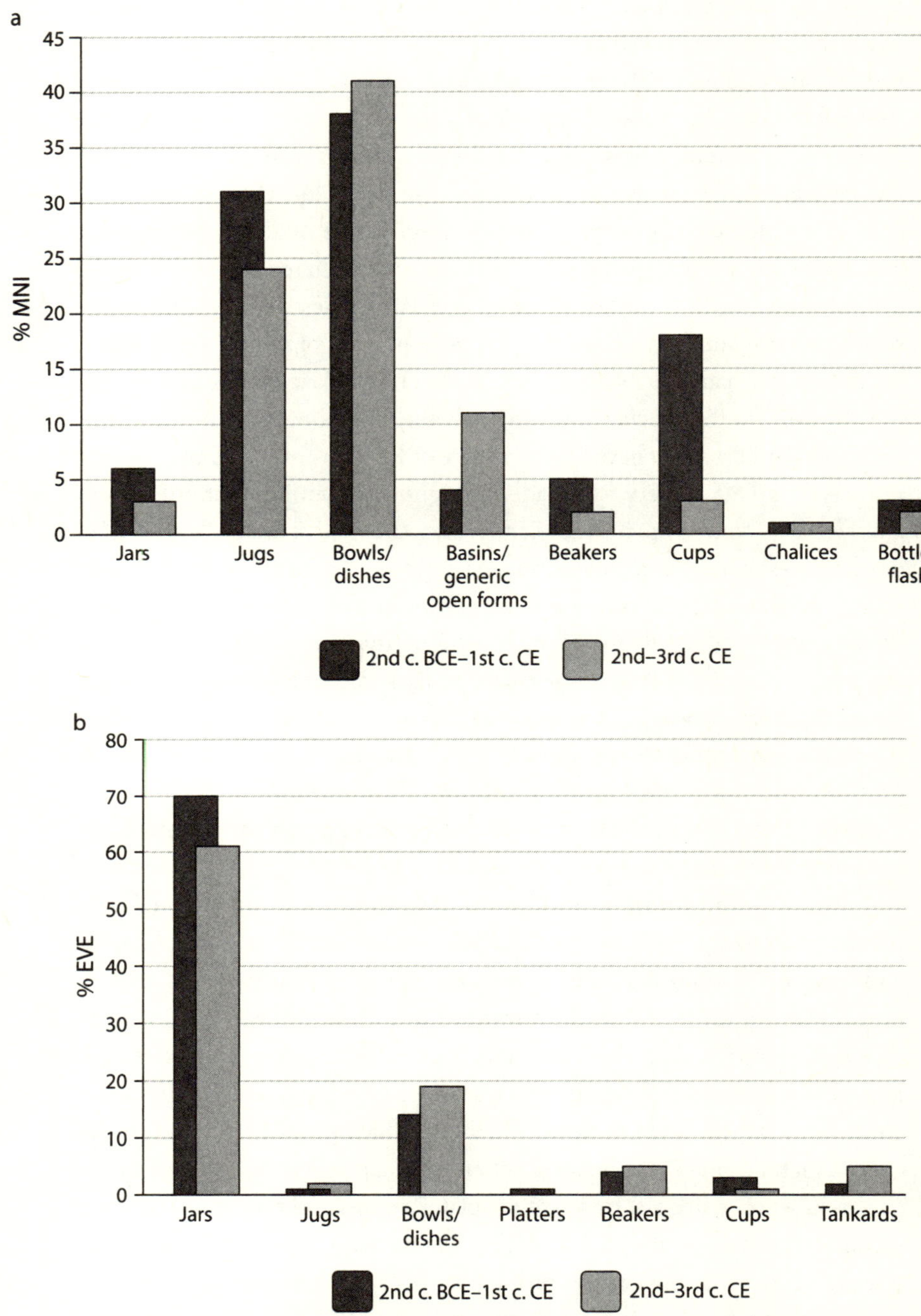

FIGURE 2.12. The changing rural table: ceramic tablewares from (a) Italy and (b) Britain (Data: Italy: Roman Peasant Project; Britain: Fulford et al. 2017, figs. 7.34–35)

By now it ought to be clear that Roman farmers were major consumers and purchased, rather than made, many of the objects they used every day. But there are equal indications that, as with food consumption, their purchase of consumer goods was different than that of urban workers in important ways. Despite hundreds of hectares of excavation throughout the Roman West, virtually no small or even medium-sized Roman farmhouses have been found bearing signs of frescoes or other wall decoration. Very few farmhouses, except the very largest, even had paved floors. In most of the western empire, as we shall see in chapter 3, it is difficult to separate habitation space from production spaces in such farms, let alone distinct spaces for particular domestic activities like dining or sleeping. In the Italian or British farms whose contents we've been impressed by above, it's not easy to locate bedrooms or dining rooms or even be certain which spaces were for animals and which for humans. In other words, if all but the very tiniest back-of-shop houses in Pompeii showed the desire—and costs—of social distinction using the house, all but the very largest farms lacked those indications. Social distinction through houses was a lower priority for farmers.

Apart from their houses, farmers consumed differently—and perhaps less—than their urban comrades. In Pompeii, every house had glossy fine wares, every house had glass, every house had metal vessels. The absence of these things in the farm just outside Pompeii could be explained by the temporary slave or day-laborer inhabitants or by partial abandonment, but other indicators suggest that these things were just not as ubiquitous or as numerous in rural households *tout court*. In Roman Britain, while the majority of farms had some imported fine ceramics and the odd amphorae, at least in the first and second centuries CE, the overall numbers of these and other harder-to-come-by goods is far lower than in an urban apartment in nearby Silchester, a major Roman town.[111] Only 25 percent of British farmers had glass vessels in their homes.[112] Objects used for entertainment—dice, gaming boards and the like—were far less common in farms than even in larger villages, let alone urban houses.[113] Perhaps even greater disparities distinguished North African rural-dwellers from their urban comrades.[114] These studies not only point up the rural-urban distinctions, but also the different levels of consumption between different kinds of farming communities: small farms consumed fewer fine wares, glass, and personal ornaments than large farms, and larger farms fewer than the denizens of roadside settlements or larger villages. These differences may be driven by access—particularly access to transportation networks—as much as by economic capabilities. Nonetheless, while perhaps rather too much has been made of the gap between rural and urbanite consumption in Britain and North Africa—these same gaps appear in Italy, too—it's also clear that farmers everywhere had somewhat fewer movable goods, and these from local, versus imported, origins.

Whether or not the overall *value* of farmers' goods was lower than urbanites' is less obvious. While the contents of the farm outside Pompeii were more modest in quantity and materials than those of, say, the small urban house of L. Caelius Ianuarius, the overall value of those contents was similar. This was due to the comparatively greater value of one object—a wagon, parked in the courtyard of the farm. Although they are almost never found on archaeological sites, there is little doubt that farmers had wagons—either owned outright or shared—and animal harnesses and plows and lots of iron tools. The remains of horse bits, pieces of axes, fragments of sickles and knives are the barest detritus of this working apparatus of farms. The known value of these objects was considerably greater than pottery: basic iron tools were some five to twenty-five times more valuable than a pot, and a machine like a wagon was worth some hundreds of sestertii.[115] Alas, tool finds are vanishingly rare on rural sites, particularly on farms, almost certainly because they were reused and recycled.[116] A rare discovery from a large farm in Tuscany included a hoe, a billhook, two axes, and a knife. The value of these objects alone would have been around 30–60 sestertii—equivalent to some dozen sigillata bowls.[117] Iron tools were also repositories of stored wealth, as they might be melted down for their metal value: as we'll see in chapter 5, they appear in dowry records and among the objects fleeing victims carried when they ran from Vesuvius' eruption. Thus, while the quantities of such tools owned by farmers is impossible to reconstruct, we forget them at our peril. They most likely constituted the majority of farming families' durable consumption in terms of value.[118]

A visceral sense of the differences between rural and urban consumption comes from a seeming noncommodity: light. Light, of course, *is* a commodity when it's artificially made or enhanced, for light extends work. It makes dark houses light enough for crafts like weaving. It prolongs the working day by pushing back sunset. Historically, the countryside was darker than the city: even the massive expansion of public light in Victorian England saw an equally massive disparity between newly illuminated cities and still-dark rural villages.[119] The Roman period was no exception. While the farm outside Pompeii had some six small ceramic lamps, only half of the farm sites excavated in Tuscany had them, and only one percent of British farms had lamps or candlesticks (figure 2.13).

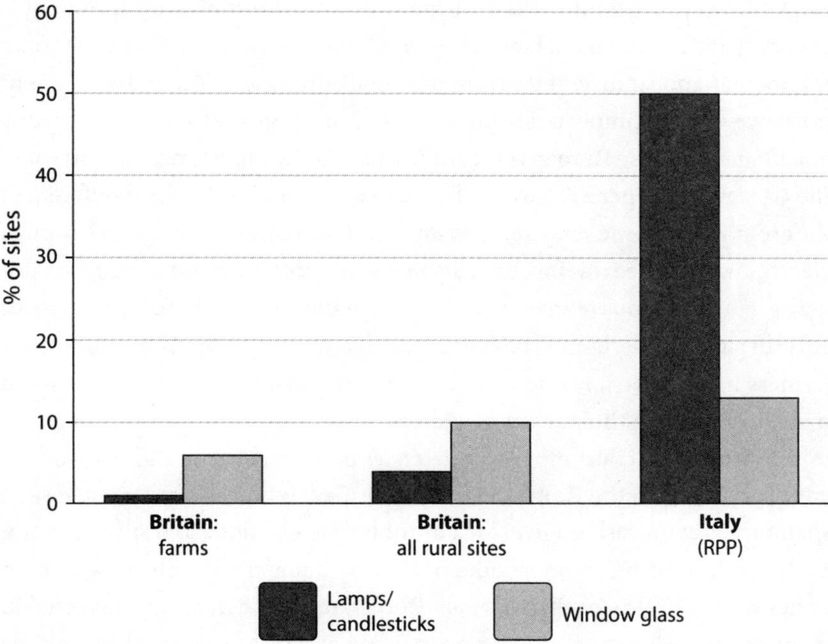

FIGURE 2.13. The dark countryside: percentage of farms with lamps/candlesticks and window glass (Data: Britain: Smith 2018, 52–53; Allen et al. 2018; Italy: Mackinnon, Vaccaro and Bowes 2021, table 14.1; Bowes, Vaccaro and Collins-Elliot 2021, table 15.9)

The same light disparity was present in farmhouse construction. Roman houses were naturally dark, with few windows and most light coming from an internal courtyard or peristyle. The very smallest back-of-shop spaces would have been almost wholly dark, but with their ubiquitous use of lamps, urbanites would have been able to push back at the darkness. As we'll see in chapter 3, most Roman farmhouses were not organized around internal courtyards, and the principal light would have come from doors. Windows there may have been, but window glass is our only clue, and window glass was incredibly rare in the countryside. Rural families, then, often lacked these day-lengthening, space-expanding properties brought by artificial light.

These observations—about lamps and tablewares, tools and glass and light—are necessarily crude, and we are still a long way from being able to view farmers' consumption patterns with the same detail we can for other periods. The lack of detail shouldn't obscure the extraordinary number of things that Roman farmers consumed, most of which were purchased, not made. While availability clearly limited the consumption of some things, discernment is everywhere. The variety of tablewares in different fabrics, forms and materials, the regular appearance of items of personal adornment, the not-infrequent presence of items imported from afar: the Roman gusto for things is readily apparent among the Roman rural population. At the same time, that taste, and the consuming imperative, was different in the countryside—and different in different parts of the empire. Consumption around social distinction was clearly lower: we see this most readily in house decoration and design, but also in the less ubiquitous tendency to use glass at the table, or, in British or North African farmhouses, limited tableware forms more generally. At the same time, farmers had higher "productive" consumption, that is, capital expenses—in metal tools—than their urban neighbors.

These different consumption preferences between farmers and city workers aren't particular to the Roman world. Later medieval peasants often chose to spend their extra cash on livestock or tools over cushions and silver spoons. Early modern British farmers bought mirrors but eschewed the new fashion of hot drinks.[120] The extent to which Roman farmers actually participated in many consumption trends common to urban and rural workers alike, and the sheer quantity of things they purchased rather than made, is still pretty historically remarkable.

Clothing: From Adam Smith's Linen Shirt to Nonna's Linen Tunic

Clothes and shoes were, and continue to be, at the front line of social inclusion. They are our social skin.[121] For Adam Smith, a linen shirt was the social inclusion line-in-the sand, without which "a creditable day-laborer would be ashamed to appear in public."[122] Its cost, for Smith, was part of those second-order essentials required for social survival. Marx's pawned coat served the same purpose. Clothing thus has long history as a marker—the most visceral marker—of those who lie within and outside society. We now know a vast amount about clothing's function as a social agent: the complex social codes conveyed by jeans and sneakers, the attempt to co-opt those codes by multinational firms, and their subversion by youth consumers.[123] Those who work with the contemporary poor think about more urgent distinctions—like the minimum shoes and clothing required to apply for a job.[124] These are the more basic order of needs that we must address: How many and what kinds of clothes did working Romans own? What forms and how many of them were necessary for social inclusion? And how much did those clothes cost?

These questions, rather extraordinarily, have never been asked.[125] We know in some detail what Cicero & Co. wore, but much less about the working majority. Given the discipline's biases, this isn't surprising. What's surprising is that we are, for once, actually reasonably well informed about what working, poor and enslaved people wore, because the rich people who wrote our Roman texts were forever snidely commenting on them.[126] Toward the end of our period, Jewish and Christian sources, more compassionate of impoverished people's dress, also have much to tell us. From them we can gauge the changing character of what constituted minimum clothing requirements, which, together with the visual evidence, describes the subtly different minimal costume for, say, a Pompeiian laundress in the first century, a Gallic carpenter's wife in the second century or an Egyptian weaver in the third. But these are all descriptions of what working people *should* wear: we have much less evidence for working people's own expenditures on clothes, less than we have for food or consumer goods. Here, more than the other components of baseline expenses, we shall be forced to reconstruct a set of theoretical minima, bolstered by some occasional pieces of firsthand evidence.

Clothes were not cheap: like metal tools, clothes were among the more valuable consumer goods that working Romans owned. Despite the massive expansion of wool and linen working in the Roman period, cloth was still laboriously made by hand—wool or linen washed, carded, spun, and woven into garment-ready shapes on increasingly large looms.[127] The prices for various kinds of basic clothes preserved in the papyrological corpus are several orders of magnitude greater than those of ceramics, and could be far more. The average cost for a basic tunic in later first- through second-century CE Egypt, for instance, was some 23 drachmas—almost a month's worth of food as documented by the local expense lists. Hence why, together with metal objects, clothing makes up the majority of moveable objects provided in dowry payments as well as loan agreements. Clothing was a container of wealth as well as a marker of social inclusion.

New work on Roman textiles has suggested that working people were probably more likely to purchase their clothes than make them.[128] The output and trade in woolen and linen garments in Gaul, Egypt, and parts of Asia Minor point to a large and professionalized but diffuse apparatus. Home-based spinning fed into home-workshop-based weaving; dyeing took place at yet larger scales in cities.[129] Even in the countryside, where the initial stages of cloth-making—cleaning, carding, spinning—were probably carried out at home,

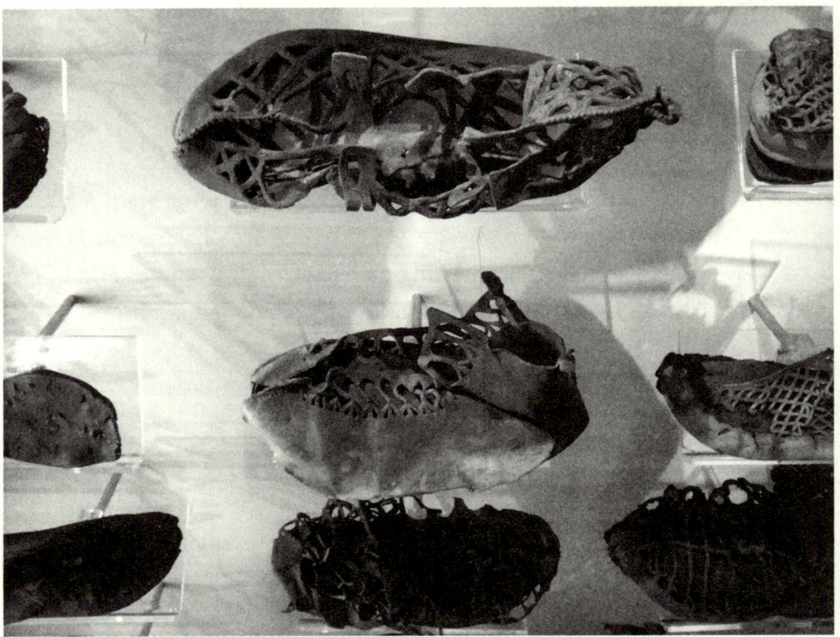

FIGURE 2.14. Working people and their shoes: shoes for soldiers, women and children from Vindolanda (Photo: Victuallers. Creative Commons Attribution License 4.0)

weaving was often done by local professionals in neighboring villages.[130] In Britain, the concentration of weaving apparatus in roadside and larger settlements has suggested the concentration of these activities in larger workshops, not simply home-based production. At remote Kellis, a village in Egypt's Western Oasis, a woman weaver, Tehat, ran a weaving business that not only produced for the village but exported goods to the distant Nile Valley.[131] Even the marketing of clothes and cloth fell to professionals—the *centonarii*—who supplied the army, urban markets and rural consumers, while used-clothing dealers—a larger and more organized profession than simply rag merchants—managed the huge market for secondhand textiles.[132] Just like other consumer goods, a bigger, specialized textile apparatus meant that clothes were more often purchased than made, and in an ever-wider range of fabrics and colors.

Shoes, which are better preserved, display even greater signs of not only standardization, but an empire-wide, consumer-driven market.[133] Well-preserved leather shoes from the northwest provinces have surprisingly standardized sizes, as well as nail placement and decorative patterning (figure 2.14).

Styles appear to change together in relatively short windows. Diamond decoration was au courant after 150 CE, tendril decoration was the thing after 170 CE. All these indicators point to a deep and wide habit of consuming shoes, a habit that appears to have stretched into considerable portions of the working population—soldiers, craftsmen and women, sailors, even farmers.[134]

It's helpful to begin minimum clothing estimates at the boundaries of social inclusion, with those who were, by law or by age, outside of society. Cato, in his *De Agricultura*, the text that provided those slave rations, imagines a short tunic, a cloak and wooden shoes as sufficient for an agricultural slave (men and women?) and suggests replacing these every other year.[135] In keeping with our other observations about this text, this ought to represent a stylized minimum for someone by definition outside a society composed—and controlled—by the free. Another source provides a similar minimum for others at society's edge—underage children being given out for apprenticeship. The apprentice contracts for minors from Egypt typically stipulate one tunic per year or its monetary equivalent be given to the boy or girl in question.[136] Literary sources likewise assume their readers can recognize the enslaved or the destitute by their single tunic, shortened or hiked up above the knees.[137] The enslaved's tunic would have been even more worn and tattered than the apprentice's. Owning just a single, possibly short tunic and a cloak was thus just outside the boundaries of social inclusion.[138]

The inner boundary was defined by more than one tunic, worn in layers. For men, at least two tunics that could be alternated for cleaning, and one or even two kinds of cloak—a mantle (*pallium*), plus a more practical shorter version (*paenula, abolla*) for inclement weather—appear to be minimal dress. A hat and socks also appear to have been, if not socially necessary, practically so, as well as a scarf worn round the neck. This sense of multiple essential items is reinforced by a text from the later Jewish world, specifying what a person was permitted to rescue from a burning building if they were so unfortunate as to have their house burn down on the Shabbat.[139] Eighteen articles of clothing were deemed absolutely essential: three tunics, two cloaks, plus a hat, shoes, scarf and undergarments.

The physical remnants of these multiple-item working men's wardrobes have been found in Egypt's Eastern Desert, in mines and army camps and ports, and in the caves of the Judean desert. Usually professionally made, often imported from afar, and very often ornamented with purple stripes and chevrons, these cloaks and tunics and socks and hats are better made and more colorful than we have imagined.[140] They were, however, constantly patched and reused: a working man's clothes bore the signs of his labor, just as lack of wear identified the rentier elite.

We are better informed about what constituted respectability for women, both because their clothing was more constantly surveilled by male writers' gaze, and because those clothes formed part of dowry agreements. One such dowry may present the very outer edge of respectability. A third-century agreement from the village of Euhemeria in the Fayum finds one Aurelius Hatres promising to provide to one Nonna (it's not clear if she's his daughter) a linen dalmatic—a long, wide-armed tunic—with purple borders, a headband, a face cloth, a bath towel and a pair of sandals.[141] The dalmatic is a more expensive tunic than the basic short-sleeved type, and the purple borders added value.[142] The other cloths to cover face and hair were requisite indicators of female modesty. Sandals, rather than shoes, probably marked the bare minimum for foot covering in Egypt.

More properly, though, women, like men, should have had at least two tunics, to be layered one atop the other. Only the enslaved, prostitutes (also often enslaved), or the destitute would leave the house wearing just one.[143] A mantle, too, provided not only warmth but also the most basic nod to further protective modesty, plus a head covering of some kind. The property one Paulus left to his wife Aurelia Sapias after his death, again from a Fayum village, marks this step into a less fragile respectability: two tunics (one new, one used), a shirt, a decorated head covering, a kerchief and 12 towels. Two tunics appear to be the minimum in Gaul as well: while different in styling—close-fit rather than loose—they appear to be layered, together with a rectangular cloak and a bonnet.[144] In Judea, the requirements were not dissimilar: the Mishnah required a poor man to provide his wife three pairs of shoes, a belt and head covering, plus sufficient money for two tunics and a cloak, per year.[145]

Footwear requirements are less a point of discussion and, because they were cheaper, less often mentioned in dowry or loan agreements. There are strong reasons for believing that a pair of shoes or sandals was the minimum for respectability. Again, the Jewish sources are explicit on the matter: only the wretched or enslaved were regularly barefoot.[146] Most people probably had two pairs of shoes: Egyptian miners and sailors, even a bargeman from the Rhine, seem to have had closed-toe work shoes (which could in a pinch be made of wood or fiber) as well as open-toe sandals.[147]

The costs for various clothing packages (without the shoes), from a slave minimum to Paulus' estate, can be gathered from loan, dowry and other records.[148] The apprentice and slaves' clothes at the outer boundaries of respectability would have cost only between 14 and 23 sestertii/drachmas per year, while the socially acceptable collection of clothes for men and women ranged between 30 and 150 sestertii/Egyptian drachmas. Yearly clothing allowances from Roman legal and Jewish sources land in roughly the same ballpark—around 100 sestertii per year.[149] It's important to note that much of our actual consumption data comes from large rural Egyptian villages: as we've noted throughout this chapter, the costs of social inclusion were consistently higher in cities.[150] None of our estimates include brooches, belts and ornaments—critical accessories for social inclusion. These estimates thus represent a minimum.

Readers may be wondering at the absence from these lists of those canonical Roman garments—the toga for men, and the stola, or heavy woolen overtunic, for women.[151] In theory, any Roman male citizen appearing at any religious or civic event—even as a bystander—was required to wear a toga, at least in the earlier part of our period. The stola had no such legal force and appears to be more consistently an upper-class garment. Both garments were voluminous and thus expensive: the amount of fabric required would have made them at least double the price of a tunic.[152] For most of the citizen working population, these were probably aspirational garments: those at the upper fringes of our group may have tried to own them and would have worn them infrequently (particularly the toga, which was ceremonial gear only). Toga and stola, too, were yet another part of the urban penalty costs for living in cities: Cincinnatus may have left his plow and bundled on his toga, but it's doubtful that most rural dwellers would have bothered. A new plow was a better investment.

Communal Consumption

Adam Smith imagined social inclusion costs as borne by male individuals, at the level of individual consumption. Feminist economic theory has reminded us of other kinds of actors—women and families—while anthropology has exposed the critical consumption acts that take place at the community level.[153] A coffee at the coffeehouse, a shared cigarette or pot of tea: these acts of consumption bind individuals to their communities via small purchases. Weddings, funerals, and religious celebrations are moments of larger-scale consumption, consumption that had been labeled "wasteful" until an anthropological eye pointed out their importance to social functioning. Failure to expend on these moments, big and small, leaves people outside the social group: an Indian family who can't put on a wedding feast for a daughter; a Greek man too poor to afford a coffee at the coffeehouse—all could find themselves outside communal bonds, bonds that are even more critical to its poorer members who rely upon them for work connections and support in times of need.

Roman cities in particular were places where small social expenses formed part of social necessity. Our expense lists repeatedly mention one such outlay: a trip to the baths.[154] Public bathing was a widely shared social ritual in ancient Rome, particularly in cities. But baths were not free: private bathing establishments required an entry fee, and even in public baths a tip was required to guard one's clothes, to pay for soap or oil. Bathing expenses appear in several of our heftier urban lists—some of which, incidentally, may have been kept by slaves. Bathing fees were small but not negligible—something less than half the price of daily expenditures on bread—and would have been a stretch for someone living in true penury. Other kinds of social activities—trips to the theater, the amphitheater and circus games—were free, but almost certainly involved hidden, small-scale spending. New excavations in the drains of Rome's Colosseum have found the remains of glasses, plates and lots of food—from oysters to peaches—the detritus of small expenditures.[155] Many of those expenses were laid out for friends or associates: the Roman world was an "oily, present-giving world"[156] where small gifts of food and objects were part of all social transactions—from a chat with neighbors to getting a day's work. The insistent public sociality that so distinguished Roman towns—their public baths, their spectacles and festivals—together with the Roman gusto for things, would have implanted repeated and required small-scale social spending into the daily lives of all but the truly indigent.

Public religion was also one of the glues that knit communities together. Like all things Roman, this has been often imagined as a top-down arrangement, foisted on an acquiescent population by political elites or Roman occupiers.[157] Only recently, and barely, have we begun to realize that the 90 percent participated in these communal rituals as something other than a passive audience.[158] Because of the expenses involved—some 100 sestertii to join a club of worshipers of Diana and Antinous—there is a tendency to assume that even these gestures were reserved for wealthy freedmen or aspiring elites.[159] But religion need not require membership in a club: acknowledging the gods and by doing so, acknowledging and renewing one's own community, were urgent second-order needs for everyone.

Consumption constituted a key part of those religio-social acts. Animals were sacrificed and eaten; vessels were used and then deliberately broken or placed in wells or ditches. This was a consumption somewhat different than that we've examined thus far, consumption whose purpose was the deliberate removal of objects from the world of human use, so that they might enter the world of the gods.[160] In removing much-needed animals and objects to the divine realm, Romans reaffirmed the bonds that bound them together. This sacrificial consumption was thus another, equally critical component of social inclusion costs.

Some well-preserved examples of such sacrificial consumption, performed seemingly by and for nonelite people, illuminate the costs it entailed. On the occasion of a *lustratio*, or purification ceremony, in second-century BCE Pompeii, a group of what appear to be working, nonelite people sacrificed and consumed multiple cattle, pigs, and sheep, while ritually disposing of around a thousand pots and dishes.[161] While the pots alone might have been worth around 600 sestertii in later Augustan money, the wine, oil and animals would have cost some 1,000 sestertii—almost a year's worth of food consumption at later Pompeiian prices.[162] Similarly, at a temple to Mithras in a rural village in Belgium, the whole village appears to have turned out for a great feast, consuming almost 300 chickens, a dozen lambs and piglets, and discarding some 700 vessels.[163] As it was a village of potters, the ceramics may have been donated, but the chickens, lambs and piglets could have cost around 1,700 sestertii alone, while the imported olive oil could have run to some 1,500 sestertii. These sums approach the yearly food expenditures of middling Pompeiians, or the entire cost of their portable household goods.

One is again struck by the sheer quantity of objects and food with which these people were surrounded, and the sheer quantities they might sacrifice to the gods in a single gesture of spectacular, social consumption. If borne by the group, the cost of these gestures was relatively low. More likely, though, the cost was borne by a handful of more prosperous impresarios who put on these feasts for neighborhood or village.[164] These occasions of lavish expenditure were rare by definition: it was their episodic timing, as well as their huge material and monetary price tag, that made them special.

Unlike the more regular consumption of food and clothing we've discussed in this chapter, consumption for the gods required saving. Like American working households who save up for Christmas, or South African families who save for funerals, the low frequency and high cost of sacrificial consumption required Roman families to squirrel away small sums more regularly, so as to be ready for the big spend.[165] The heaps of broken pots and barbecued meat are thus also proxies for the ability to save. We'll return to savings in chapter 5.

The Costs of Living in a World of Things

The Roman 90 percent were big consumers, both individually and in aggregate. The evidence from expense lists, dowries, and archaeology describes a working majority with historically high levels of consumption. As we have seen, most working Romans consumed a dietary tetrad of cereals, oils, wine, and meat and dairy. They owned a wide range of household goods, from a variety of table and cooking wares in various materials to modest jewelry and religious objects. Those at the very bottom end owned one set of clothes and shoes, while most owned at least two or more sets. Enslaved people, particularly in the countryside, occupied the bottom end of this consumption spectrum, but they too probably consumed more than caloric minima of food. In the upper registers of this spectrum were urbanites who lived in houses with more than one room, decorated with rudimentary painting and furnished with a range of ceramic, glass and metal objects. Many, albeit not all, farmers were also far larger consumers than we have credited, consuming many of the same goods as urbanites, although in more modest materials and spending more on tools than on mirrors.

This is not to deny that some Romans consumed at rock-bottom subsistence—3,000 calories, a single tunic, a single pot. Some rural slaves and mine workers may have come the closest to a coherent—and consistent—group of subsistence consumers. But rather than a permanent state or a class of people, for most of the 90 percent "subsistence" is better imagined as a temporal condition. Like so much food insecurity today, rock-bottom subsistence consumption or even starvation was, for the majority, a specter of intermittent want, punctuation marks of misery experienced alongside moments of sufficiency. The big differences in day-to-day consumption attested in the Pompeiian travelers' list with which we began—a huge splurge one day, literally bread and water the next—was probably typical of the sufficiency and dearth experienced by many of the 90 percent. Instability and volatility are hard to see but were probably as much a part of Roman consumer experience as the sausages and glasses and latest shoe fashions.

This historically high consumption carried a historically high price tag. While basic foods and consumer goods were individually relatively cheap, the sheer quantity consumed—the different kinds of foods and objects of different materials and clothes (not to mention the occasional communal splurges)—added up. Some rough balance sheets, composed from the averages for actual consumption discussed above, give a sense of that price tag (figure 2.15).

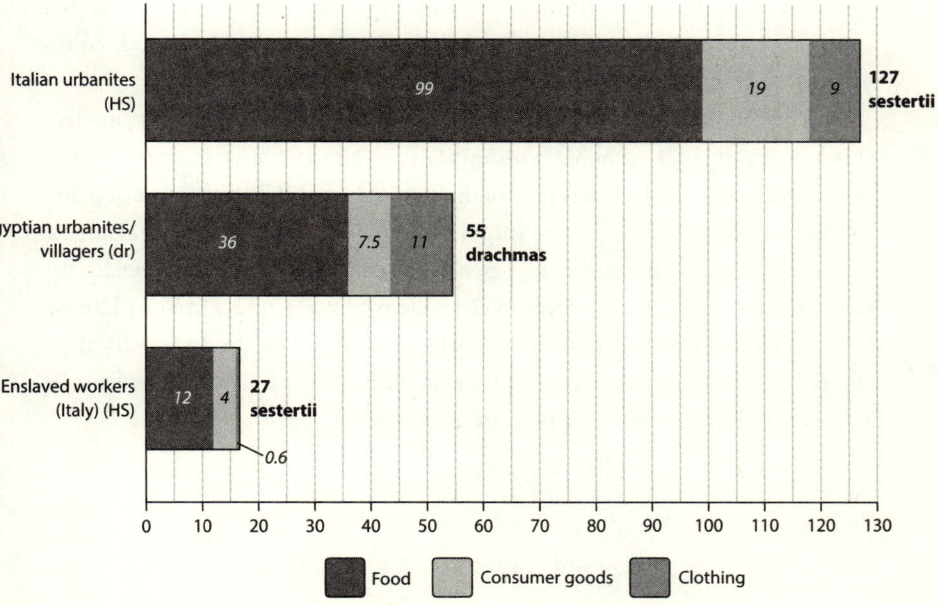

FIGURE 2.15. Roman consumption estimates, per month

These are woefully incomplete: they lack fuel and animal feed and ignore housing and rent. Relative to earlier estimates based on wheat consumption alone, they are unsurprisingly higher. Only the rural enslaved consumed at the levels imagined before. Clearer, too, is the considerable gap between the bottom of the 90 percent and the more prosperous middle-to-top: a sevenfold difference separates the rural slaves of Cato's villa (somewhat confirmed by actual expenditures from their Egyptian brethren) and the sausage-and-wine-consuming workers in Pompeii.

We might construe these higher estimates as evidence for a Galbraith-goes-to-Rome "affluent society" where luxury, not necessities, dominated consumption regimes. This would be wrong. The new evidence finds not only higher consumption, but along with it, a heightened consuming imperative. We can see from the expense lists and house assemblages that more- or less-prosperous working people didn't just have more or less things: they had different things along a spectrum of different quality. Just like elites, the 90 percent were practiced in discernment, and like elites, discernment around objects was a required part of social participation. To participate, one not only had to consume, but had to consume in particular ways, ways that both set one apart and showed one belonged. In a world in which most everyone had different plates for different foods, various types of brooches to fasten one's cloak, and at least two different tunics, it was the specific—of kind, color, origin—that produced distinction, not just having or not having.

But distinction cost and the costs of social inclusion, at least in part, explain this historically high nonelite consumption. Social inclusion is a central part of second-order needs. It was part of the cost of living. While the cost of many individual objects was low, the imperative toward variety and discernment made living in the Roman world expensive—even, and perhaps especially, for working people. Working people in cities were hit particularly hard with these high social inclusion costs—the relentless small outlays on diverse foods, a myriad of objects, gifts for friends. Working Romans lived in what the Roman poet Juvenal lamented as a "pretentious poverty."[166]

3

Farmer Soterichos Goes to Market

AROUND 97 CE, the Egyptian farmer Soterichos died, leaving behind him a mountain of debt.[1] Too poor to own his own land, he rented. The plots he rented were tiny and scattered, leaving him at the mercy of his landlord. His debts were a product of constantly paying his rent in arrears, the inevitable result of too little land and mediocre yields. Soterichos aspired to autarky—producing most everything he needed—but he never achieved it.

This is one story that can be told about Soterichos—the bitter tragedy of ancient smallholder farmers. But the same papyrus archive that gives us this story also tells another one. The small size of their holdings notwithstanding, Soterichos, his wife, Thaisas, and their four children grew a whole range of cash crops—grapes, wheat, dates, castor trees—at one point even specializing in thyme. They rotated their grain crops with fodder crops, weeding and manuring them—practices designed to maximize yields and preserve soil quality. They managed to own some cattle, and thus the means to plow and manure their land. While doomed to rent rather than own, the Soterichoses juggled multiple leases with multiple landlords, staying out of the grip of any one. Above all, the Soterichoses were able to squeak by through selling their crops off the farm: cash crops like wine and thyme and fodder kept them afloat. Selling those crops allowed Thaisas to eventually clear the late Soterichos' debts while supporting her family.

The different stories about the Soterichoses are more than just different stories about one farming family. Today, only a handful of countries on earth still have a majority of farmers.[2] Not so in the ancient world. Most Romans were farmers.[3] The majority of the Roman 90 percent were small farmers of varying degrees of smallness, who, either working their own land, renting from others, or a combination of the two, made a living by making the land produce. The Roman economy was an agrarian economy. The lion's share of its outputs were agricultural products. While the agricultural output of large estates dwarfed that of smallholders, in most parts of the empire, the smallholders were so numerous that their aggregate outputs would have been a major percentage, if not the majority, of all outputs. In short, it is not too much of a stretch to say that Roman smallholders *were* the Roman economy. Thus, whatever stories we tell about families like the Soterichoses will reflect, in aggregate, a bigger story about Roman economic history.

The first story—about a struggling subsistence farmer at the mercy of large landowners—was one told by the Romans themselves. The death of the smallholder at the hands of agribusiness was central to Roman writers' nostalgia for a lost agrarian age. Some modern scholarship has added to it, arguing that Roman smallholders lacked most of the tools—manuring, crop rotation, specialization—to produce anything but mediocre crop yields. In any event, like all premodern smallholders, they were intent on simply growing enough to supply their families, not producing significant surplus for sale off the farm.

The second story has yet to be comprehensively told. Some glimpses were already evident in the previous chapter. Farmers with a gusto for things, purchasing everything from imported wine to glass to finished cloth, hardly fit the image of self-sufficiency. Small farmers must have generated some kinds of surplus, if only to supply their yen for imported wine and the latest footwear. But as we also saw in that chapter, such consumer goods were relatively cheap. Evidence for robust consumption among some, albeit not all, smallholders can't be used as evidence for robust surplus production. This requires its own careful examination—a reckoning with agricultural systems and practices; of land availability and land use; and ultimately, a quantitative reckoning of smallholder farmers' outputs.

It's a delicious irony that more information about the rural Roman 90 percent has emerged from the construction of Euro Disney than from the well-intentioned excavations designed to find them.[4] Large-scale excavations undertaken in advance of modern construction—of airports, trainlines, shopping centers and amusement parks—have transformed what we know about Roman farmers and farming, producing huge amounts of new data upon which a new story can be based. New textual work also plays a role, as papyri, like those describing the Soterichoses, have been revisited from a farmer's-eye view. All of this new data makes it possible to reconstruct the economic status and strategies of Roman smallholders—even many of the very smallest—to a degree unimaginable even two decades ago. And, as one would imagine, that new data has turned most of our previous thinking on its head.

This new data has revealed Roman rural landscapes dominated by smallholders.[5] At the same time, it has exploded the notion of the singular "Roman smallholder," revealing one of the most diverse groups of working people in the Roman world. Many, if not most, of them sold surpluses off the farm: the net-consumer farmer of previous scholarship certainly existed but was probably in the minority in most places for which we have data. All this new work has also revealed another important protagonist in the Roman countryside: animals. Be it the sale of surplus hay through crop rotation, or the breeding and feeding of ever larger cattle, animals were central to growing crops. Finally, all this new data has revealed the combination of incentive and compulsion that drove smallholder production—new urban markets, hyper-dense landscapes, the long hand of the state. Everywhere, though, it was the dense carpet of rural neighbors that constituted one of the biggest sources of demand: surplus tiles and pots, breeding cattle and extra wine—rural farms and villages were major consumers of each other's produce.

This chapter uses three particular Roman farmscapes—Italy, northern Gaul and Britain, and Egypt—to tell this new story of Roman farming. These are arguably the best-understood rural places in the Roman world, and represent the radically different environments—ecological, historical and economic—in which different smallholders got by.[6] Using these regional case studies allows us to play a game of scales, toggling between the evidence for individual farming families like the Soterichoses, the immediate local economic circumstances in which they operated, and the broader regional or provincial forces that impacted their lives. Because the data is now so vast, and studied in such resolutely regional frameworks, it can be easy to forget that an Egyptian farming family like the Soterichoses and one in Cambridgeshire inhabited some shared space, if only one of rent and taxation. But what will emerge, alongside their very different farming landscapes, is a shared set of economic practices—of limited land, of surplus production, of micromanagement of water and soil, of the opportunities and perils of tenancy—to name just a few.

Peasants Past and Farmers Present

As any Roman farmer would tell us, a new crop of ideas requires a thorough clearing of the ground. That ground-clearing starts with the very words we use to talk about our subject. For over a century, our subjects have been referred to as peasants.

Who are peasants?[7] To begin with, they were no one Romans would have recognized. Romans had no term equivalent to peasant: they had words for folks who lived in the countryside (*rustici* or *chorikoi*), for farmers (*agricolae* or *georgoi*), even for people who worked their own land (*autourgoi*). But they had no equivalent to the basket of economic and social habits that scholars mean when they talk about "peasants."

On the one hand, we might imagine peasants are simply folks who live in the countryside and make a living off farming. But this minimalist definition has never been the whole story. Since the origins of the term (from the Latin *paganus* to the Old French *paisant* and Middle English *paissaunt*), peasants have carried other baggage.[8] Baggage about habits of thought: peasants were inherently conservative and slow to change. Baggage about economic practices resultant from those habits of thought: peasants mistrusted markets and coined economies and preferred to restrict their lives as much as possible to their households and at most their villages. All of this has produced the weightiest baggage of all: peasants, no matter when or where they live, carry some of these qualities with them. They are, by virtue of their name, ahistorical creatures. It's not only that they have no histories told about them, as the great historian of peasants Eric Wolf lamented. Worse, because they have a set of fixed properties, all peasants in all times and places are, in fundamental ways, the same. The very name thus already tells us basic things about their economic lives, foreclosing on the very questions with which we ought to begin. "Peasants" are a classic case of a category of analysis thinking for us.

These properties of peasants have made them difficult territory for economic historians. Even Marx tried not to think about them: they weren't really a class, not part of the urban proletariat, and thus a kind of embarrassing throwback, outside the arc of historical materialist history.[9] It fell to subsequent Marxist thinkers like Antonio Gramsci, writing from a nonindustrial, agricultural Italy, to take them more seriously.[10] Roman history has a particularly long, love-hate relationship with peasants. For the nineteenth-century founders of ancient history and many of their successors, the arc of Roman history turned around a doomed Roman peasant: peasants were people to whom things—bad things—happened.[11] New kinds of history writing that grew up after the Second World War—histories not just about great men—returned scholars' attention to ancient peasants. Yet in these new histories, peasants became part of the unchanging historical substrate, their unchanging subsistence agriculture the backdrop of history.[12] Peasants were like the local geology: they constituted the ageless soil that sprouted shorter-term history. Thus, if you interviewed modern Greek or Italian peasants, as many anthropologists and archaeologists in the 1970s and '80s did, you were talking, in some sense, to peasants from the time of Homer or Cincinnatus.[13]

Peasants have proved even more of a problem for Roman economic history's recent performance-centered turn. Finley's vision of the ancient economy was centered on mostly subsistence peasants, their disinterest in market sale and innovation the basis of a whole economy's disinterest in these same things.[14] It is not surprising, then, that the peasant was the baby that got tossed out with Finley's pessimist bathwater.[15] It is hard to imagine a place for peasants in questions about economic performance. They are not included among those with "professions," and the individually small scale of their outputs makes them irrelevant to macroanalysis.

The mishandling of peasants at the hands of Roman history can't all be attributed to the term itself, but too much of it can. "Peasant" appears to be a classic category of analysis, one that has stood in for a series of presumed practices. It won't do here. We will thus refer to our subjects as farmers or smallholders. These terms aren't perfect either: the former exaggerates one part of their portfolio—the farming part—while ignoring other activities—artisanal work, wage labor, trading. Smallholder, a term preferred by modern development economics, emphasizes the size of holdings, leaving open the question of what constitutes "small."[16] But both terms emphasize practices, and both avoid the sense that people who farm belong to some a priori cultural-economic category. "Farmer" and "smallholder" are the best of a bad set of options.

Jettisoning the eternal peasant will allow workers of the land to emerge as more than just victims. For one, we'll be able to see them grappling in complex ways with their environment. Whether they farmed the lands of Egypt or the Île-de-France, Roman farmers—like farmers today—coped with the caprice of weather. While scholars now like to see "climate" as a major driver of history, farmers don't experience climate: they experience the daily and seasonal changes in weather.[17] And despite what appears to have been a climatic period characterized by stability—the so-called Roman climatic optimum—the Mediterranean particularly (and to a lesser extent its northern temperate hinterland) was and still is characterized by major weather volatility. Massive variation in interannual rainfall is one of the region's salient qualities: one of the reasons Egypt was so prized was the relative constancy of the Nile flood compared to precipitation in, say, central Italy. Experience with volatility—and of crop success and failure—together with tools for coping with it were part of all Roman farmers' toolkits. As we shall see, the increasing pressure on the land, together with the greater specialization of crops, meant that weather volatility had more than the usual knock-on effects for smallholders in our period.

Jettisoning "peasant" also means we can dispense with its most unhelpful economic baggage: "subsistence." The concept of subsistence farming was always something of a mirage: no farming family, no matter how modest, aims to produce only enough to survive plus storage for a bad year.[18] Surviving, particularly in the Mediterranean's extreme climatic conditions, requires constant maximizing. Conversely, in economies with market opportunities, surplus sold off the farm may be part of "subsistence": this is precisely how families like Soterichos' appear to have survived. "Surplus" and "subsistence" aren't economic strategies. Instead, we'll be better off sticking to practices themselves—like growing, consuming and selling.[19] Some Roman farmers, as we shall see, ate most of what they grew—they were net-consumers. At the other end of the spectrum were those who sold most of what they grew—net-sellers. And in the middle was a whole world of variations on those extremes. Neither situation—net-consuming or net-selling—was necessarily a proxy for prosperity. Some net-sellers, like Soterichos, were driven by their limited means to convert crop to cash, while some net-consumers, like a family of the smallest holders in Cambridgeshire we shall meet below, appear to have survived for centuries largely on their own production. The majority of Roman smallholders, this chapter will argue, produced more than they consumed and sold those surpluses off the farm.

Farms

There was no such thing as "the Roman farm." From the smallest holders living on tiny allotments, through more complex farms with multiple buildings and animal pens, to the places that start to look like very small villas: everywhere we look, the new evidence reveals the huge diversity of farmers and their productive apparatus.[20]

The smallest farms not only had small buildings and probably small landholdings, but also—and most importantly—very limited apparatus for crop storage or crop processing. In Italy, the farm at Monte Forco north of Rome gives a sense of the type: a single stone building with a hearth, a porch and some outdoor water storage (figure 3.1).[21]

In the northwest provinces, farmers lived in a world of ditches and wooden buildings, very much like their Iron Age predecessors, but the smallest of farms have similar properties to their Italian brethren. Like The Grange in Cambridgeshire, these farms were surrounded by a single ditch to mark the farm boundaries and contain its animals, with a couple of small

FIGURE 3.1. Monte Forco farm, first century BCE–second century CE, Capena, Italy (Illustration: Matilde Grimaldi, after Jones 1963, fig. 18)

wattle-and-daub structures inside (figure 3.2).[22] Not only are the buildings and overall farm small, but the enclosure itself isn't subdivided into different pens, suggesting that these farms had only small animal herds, simply managed. Whether in central Italy or central France, what distinguishes these smallest farms is their limited apparatus for surplus storage or processing: no barns, no granaries, no multiple pens or stalls for large animal herds.

Almost everywhere we find Roman farms, these smallest versions are in the minority.[23] Wherever large-scale excavations have peeled back large sections of the countryside—that is, wherever we can see operations of all different sizes—it is medium-sized farms that are found in the greatest numbers. The building of Euro Disney outside Paris (figure 3.3), a business park near Laon (figure 3.4), a Toyota factory, the expanding town of Cambridge (see figure 3.17): big construction projects have revealed these medium-sized farms by the thousands.[24]

In Italy, where there have been fewer large-scale excavations, medium-sized farms were also probably thick on the ground: a land-reclamation project near Lucca, for example, revealed dozens of them.[25] The hallmark of Roman farming was not the tiny, but the medium-sized, more complex farm.[26]

Whether built of masonry and tiles or of wattle-and-daub, these medium-sized farms share some common features. Not only were they bigger than their

FIGURE 3.2. The Grange farm, second century CE, Cambridgeshire, Britain (Illustration: Matilde Grimaldi, after Wright et al. 2009, fig. 25)

smaller neighbors—bigger farmyards, perhaps bigger buildings—but more of their footprint was dedicated to storage and crop processing. In the northwest provinces, this meant facilities for managing animals: the multiple divisions within those ditched enclosures were presumably for managing stock, and many such medium farms have watering holes.[27] In Britain, many also had grain dryers used for dehusking hulled wheats.[28] Vicar's Farm near Cambridge had all these features (figure 3.5).[29]

In Italy, medium farms are marked by structures for storing grain, for pressing grapes or olives, or for producing artisanal goods. The farm of Pievina, for instance, had a tiny granary, a cistern and a tiny tile kiln (figure 3.6). The farms in the Lucca land-reclamation project also had small granaries, usually added in a second phase. In short, these medium-sized farms were defined by their spaces for processing, storage and, particularly in the northwest provinces, spaces for their many animals.

At the opposite end of the spectrum from the tiny one-room farms are the farms whose investment in something like comfort makes them resemble

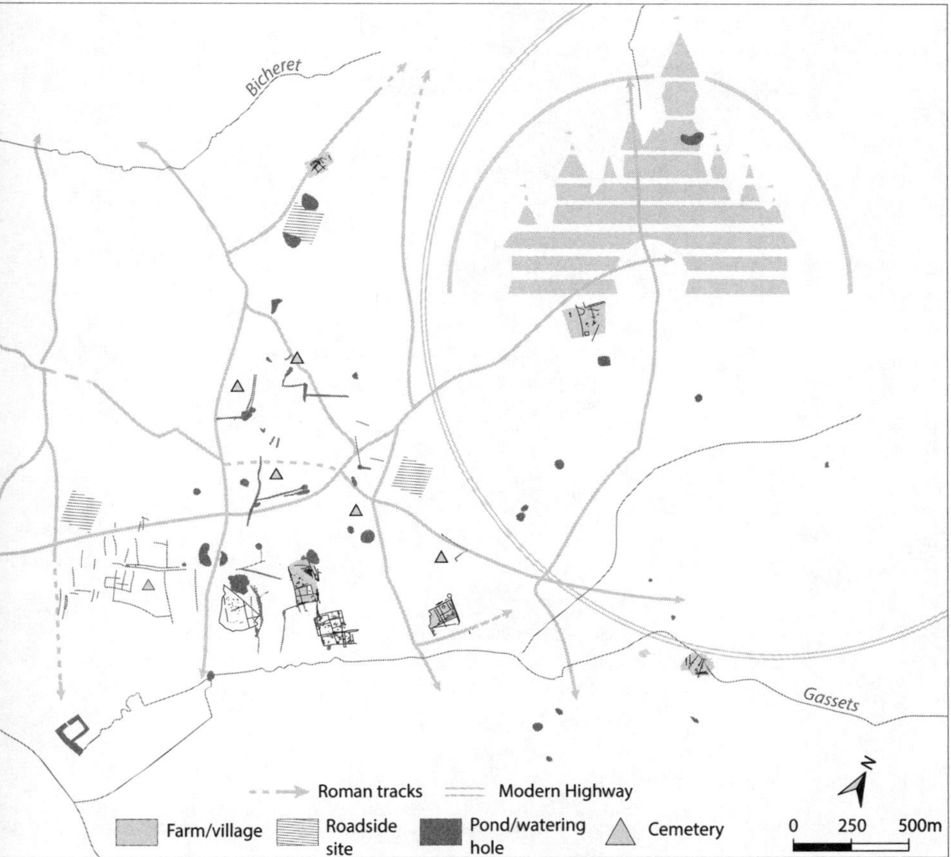

FIGURE 3.3. Roman farmers go to Disney: medium-sized farms found beneath Euro Disney, Île-de-France, France (Illustration: Matilde Grimaldi, after Bernigaud et al. 2017, fig. 36)

small villas. Like an example near Florence, these were larger versions of the medium-sized farms (figure 3.7). Not only were they bigger, but their multiple rooms often had distinctive functions, like the large oil press room shown here, and they often had an identifiable domestic portion with courtyards, masonry or tile floors, here even a rudimentary bath.[30]

In Gaul and Britain, this desire for comfort meant that one or two buildings might be built of stone, not only of wattle-and-daub. The modern workings of an open-pit coal mine near Cologne, on the Rhineland frontier, revealed dozens of these villa-wannabes.[31] Further north along the Dutch portions of the frontier, a farm at Hoogeloon offers a chance to see the evolution from

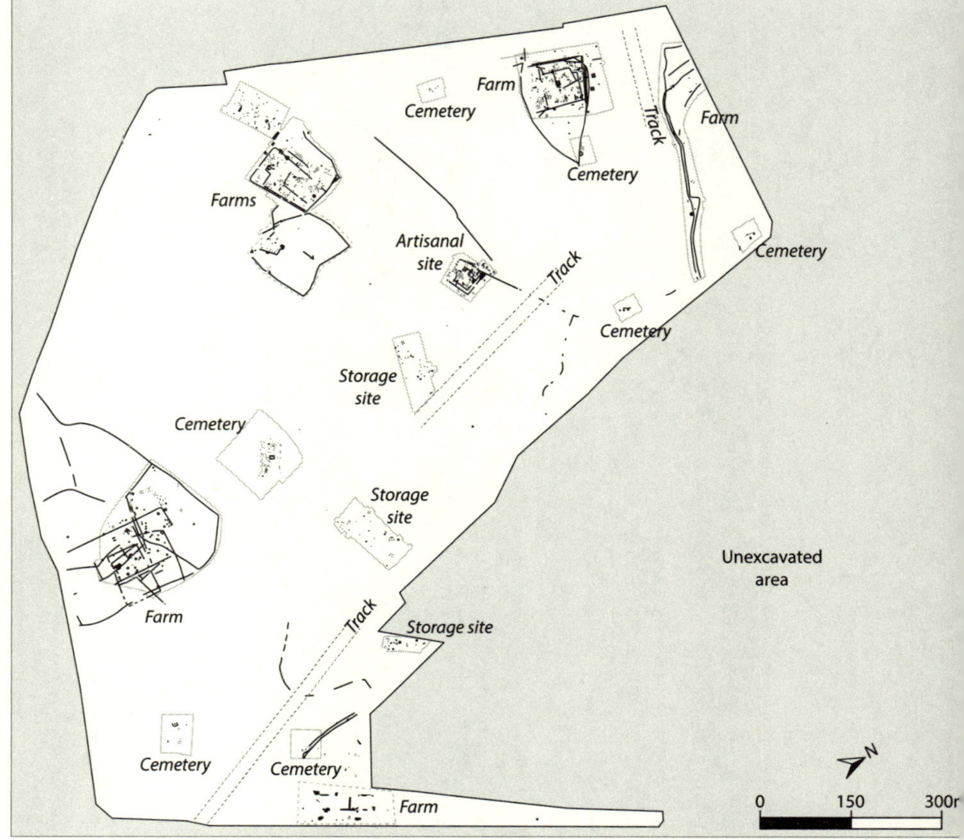

FIGURE 3.4. Roman farmers at the business park: medium-sized farms found beneath the pôle d'activités du Griffon, Hauts-de-France, France (Illustration: Matilde Grimaldi, after Achard-Corompt 2017, fig. 3)

a medium farm into a more luxurious one, seemingly by a local farmer who, having served in the Roman army, returned to expand his cattle farm (figure 3.8).[32] These largest farms have the same or larger storage and processing apparatus as the medium-sized farms. They are chiefly distinguished by their owners' efforts to build particular "domestic" spaces distinct from productive spaces.

These farm categories are useful fictions. There exists much overlap between them, and subsequent modifications, like Hoogeloon, might place them in a new category as the resources of the owner increased or waned. But grouping them this way reveals some important things about Roman farmers and farming. First, it's clear that smallholder production came in different sizes,

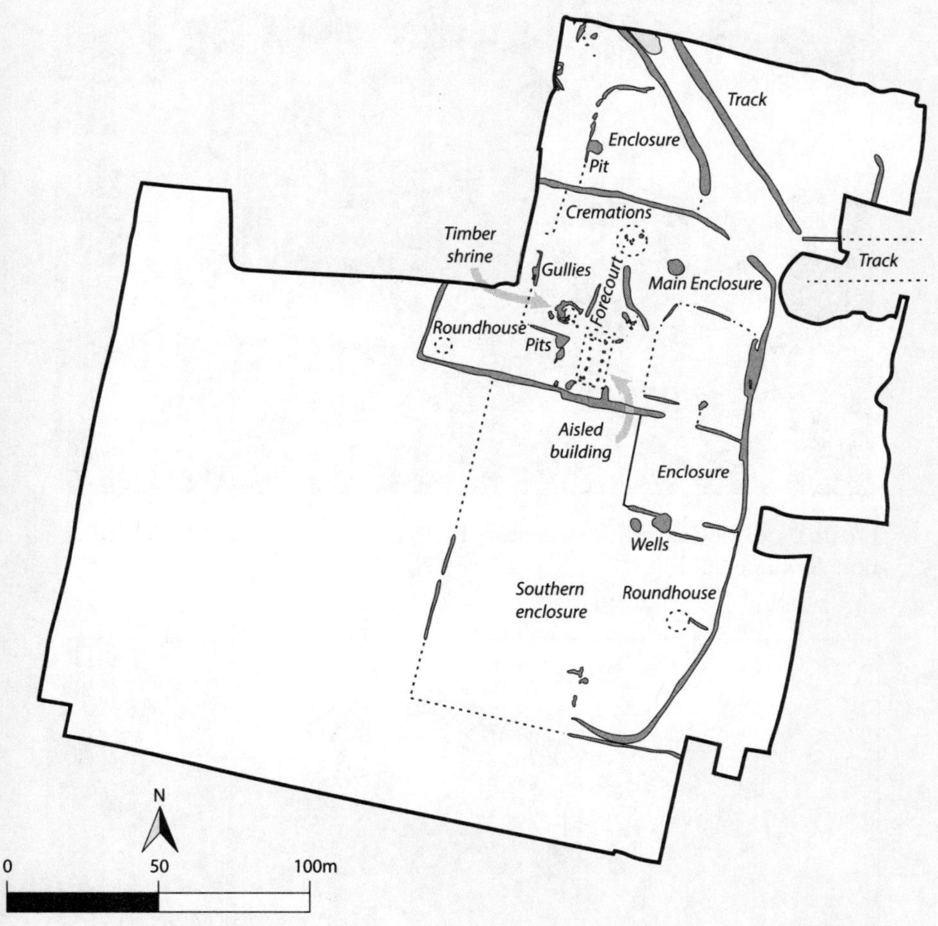

FIGURE 3.5. Vicar's Farm, second-century CE phase, Cambridgeshire, Britain (Illustration: Matilde Grimaldi, after Evans and Lucas 2019, fig. 5.1)

and those different sizes tended to track with increasing facilities for storage and agro-processing.[33] The smallest farms have only limited storage; medium and large farms usually, although not always, have granaries, presses or tile/pottery kilns. In short, farms are thus distinguished by the scale and complexity of production.

Second, farms had to be quite large indeed before their owners bothered to build distinct "domestic" buildings—sleeping or dining quarters, baths.[34] Instead, Roman farmers mostly lived in the same spaces they worked, and, conversely, production and processing everywhere dominate smallholder

FIGURE 3.6. Pievina farm, first century BCE/CE, Grosseto, Italy (Reconstruction: Studio Inklink)

FIGURE 3.7. Ponterotto farm, second- through third-century CE phase, Florence, Italy (Reconstruction: Studio Inklink. By permission of Alderighi and Pittari 2020, fig. 8)

FIGURE 3.8. The successful veteran: Hoogeloon farm/villa, *left to right*, 80 CE and 120 CE phases (Illustration: Matilde Grimaldi, after Roymans and Derks 2015, fig. 11)

dwelling space. This disinterest in the domestic in favor of the productive was, as we shall see, a fact of farming life throughout the empire.

Beyond the Farms

Farms were not the only places that farmers lived and worked. The empires' many ecologies, histories, and cultural habits produced a whole range of non-farm farming spaces. These also have much to tell us about smallholder economies.

The first such space is the land itself. Mediterranean farmers tended to work not single, homogeneous plots of land, but a mosaic of plots: lists of

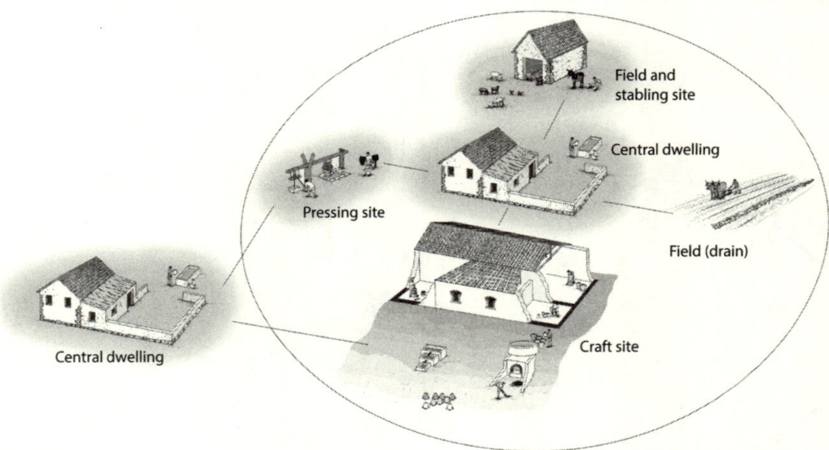

FIGURE 3.9. Distributed habitation and satellite sites among Italian farmers (Illustration: Matilde Grimaldi)

landholdings from central Italy to Egypt and North Africa find families owning multiple pieces of land of varying sizes in a variety of different places.[35] This habit of fragmented landholding was a way of both distributing risk among plots with different characteristics—different soils, rainfall, sunlight—but also of maximizing the use of those different plots. Recent archaeology has shown that smallholders, too, had multiple, fragmented plots. They even built stand-alone satellite sites on them.[36] Shared wine and oil presses, stabling or work sheds, pottery production sites—these satellite sites were highly specialized for herding, pressing or potting (figure 3.9). Why did smallholders build them? Almost certainly to support work at a distance from their "core" farms, doubling down on the properties of individual plots to maximize their usefulness.

Everywhere we find farmers we also find villages. In some parts of the empire—the Dutch river valleys, Egypt, the eastern empire—most farmers lived in villages. Even in places where stand-alone farms were more common, those farms rubbed shoulders with different kinds of agglomerated settlements. For villages were the switching points of the countryside. In most places, they appear to have been home to farming families who worked adjacent lands. But they were also places of artisanal production, animal droving and exchange. Primary products—like grapes or wool—might be bottled or transformed into secondary products—wine or cloth. Tools might be repaired

FIGURE 3.10. Village of Tiel-Passewaaij, second century CE, Gelderland, Netherlands (Reconstruction by M. H. Kriek. By permission of M. H. Kriek and Groot and Kooistra 2009, fig. 8)

or made and sold. And almost everywhere, villages are located on roads or rivers, serving as transport and trade hubs.

In Italy, these villages appear in greatest numbers and size at precisely the moment when their respective farming landscapes are busiest.[37] Virtually none has been thoroughly excavated, but most of those we know about were centers of craft activities—fine pottery, tile, or brick production, iron working, amphorae production, wool working.[38] The roadside versions of these sites (termed *mansiones* in the Roman texts) probably included temporary accommodation for traders or farmers on the move, and they probably hosted periodic markets.[39] In the northwest provinces, some of these villages appear to be principally farming communities. One such village on the Oise River outside Paris, for example, was composed of some 20 farms and their adjacent fields, its residents growing grain, fruits and vegetables and raising sheep for sale out of the village.[40] On the northern reaches of the Rhine, Dutch villages like Tiel-Passewaaij had multiple large houses, multiple granaries and stables, geared toward cattle and barley production for the Rhineland forts (figure 3.10).[41]

But many other northern villages also hosted more specialized functions. One such settlement in Oxfordshire appears to have been a cattle droving site;

others near Cambridge were home to both farmers and artisans. Indeed, pottery kilns and metal and wool production are all more densely concentrated in British villages than on farms.[42] Coin finds are also more plentiful at British village sites, pointing to hot spots of market exchange.[43] And, as we saw in chapter 1, British villages even had a greater concentration of literate people, as writing tools are more plentiful in villages than on farms.[44] These village agglomerations were thus particularly vigorous intermediaries between farm, small town and city, places where things were grown, made and exchanged.

The different sizes and forms of rural settlements raises the question: How "small" were smallholders' properties? How much land did the average Roman farmer have? Archaeology is pretty mute on many of the proprietary and legal questions that kept smallholders up at night. Textual sources, while tantalizing, are only a bit more helpful. Take the land grants given to veteran soldiers. Some Roman veterans were given small plots of land by the state in exchange for their years of military service, kicking out whomever had been living there previously and replacing them with ex-military, presumably loyal to Rome. Literary sources give us some of these land-grant sizes, which in Italy most often ranged between 1.75 and 3 hectares.[45] These are very small indeed, and it's been suggested that these were not intended as a livelihood, but as "starter" grants.[46] As we'll see below, surviving on two or three hectares was a close-run thing, even for the most enterprising.

The size of some plots actually managed by smallholders is indicated, rather vaguely, by a handful of property lists.[47] One such central Italian list, which seems to include some smaller properties, gives a sense of a bottom level—perhaps 2.5 to 5 hectares (10–20 *iugera*), and a more robustly provisioned average—some 20–40 hectares, which is something like the probable size of the Pievina farm we saw earlier. The biggest plots on the list were some 125–250 hectares—several orders of magnitude larger.[48] A sense of the size of more specialized plots is given by one North African register, listing the olive groves of the smallest holders at about a half a hectare, while middling ones ran to perhaps two hectares.[49]

When we bundle together these tantalizingly vague texts, together with the proxy data from archaeology (which we'll do in detail in the final section of this chapter), we can get a sense of the holdings controlled by different gradations of smallholders. The smallest farms in Italy may have been those veteran allotments of two to three hectares. Medium-sized farms may have utilized some 5–15 hectares in Italy and probably somewhat more in the northwest provinces, while larger, cattle-producing quasi-villas near the Rhineland frontier may have held 50 hectares or more. Big villages like Tiel-Passewaaij in that same region probably farmed around 70 hectares. In all cases, these single or multiple plots included arable land, in the Mediterranean areas tree crops like vines and olives, and large swaths of pasture and forest. The problem of land size will return when we try to reconstruct some smallholder balance sheets.

Egyptian Farmers

Egyptian farmers haven't entered the story until now because the kinds of things we know about them are so different—the knowledge that comes from words versus things, from mountains of papyri, not mountains of archaeology.[50] We know the average size of their landholdings, but not the appearance of their farms or fields; we know the value of their land, but not where they kept their animals. We do know that most of them lived in villages. Some of these villages were tiny nuclei of a few families. But most probably lived in larger villages, like the well-known examples from the Fayum, the remains of which have yielded so many papyri—Theadelphia, Tebtunis, Karanis—or those like Kellis from the Western Oases, known from excavations. These are much larger, denser and more organized villages than those from the West. Many were complete with one or more streets, a bath or two, and a temple. Tebtunis, for example, may have had as many as 6,000 inhabitants (including its hinterland) and boasted a large street, a big temple to the crocodile god (Soknebtynis), a bath, and a covered market—a city in miniature (figure 3.11).[51] Even smaller Theadelphia, where the Soterichoses lived, had a population of some 2,300 people.[52]

Along with their communal living, Egyptian farmers had communal agricultural facilities—granaries, barns, presses—shared by village inhabitants for storage and crop processing. But Egyptian farmers did not engage in communal agriculture: they were emphatically individualist, renting and owning their own family plots. A great many people owned varying quantities of land, and everybody, from the largest to the smallest landowners, leased some land.[53] Many people, if not a majority, would have done both—owned and leased. Those leased holdings might include public land (rented from the state) and/or private land, land that was further classified according to a dizzying array of categories, almost all of which had some fiscal rationale. Egyptian farmers thus managed a complex, ever-shifting portfolio of properties.

Farms of all sizes in Egypt were considerably smaller than those in Italy and very much smaller than those in the northwest provinces. This was in large

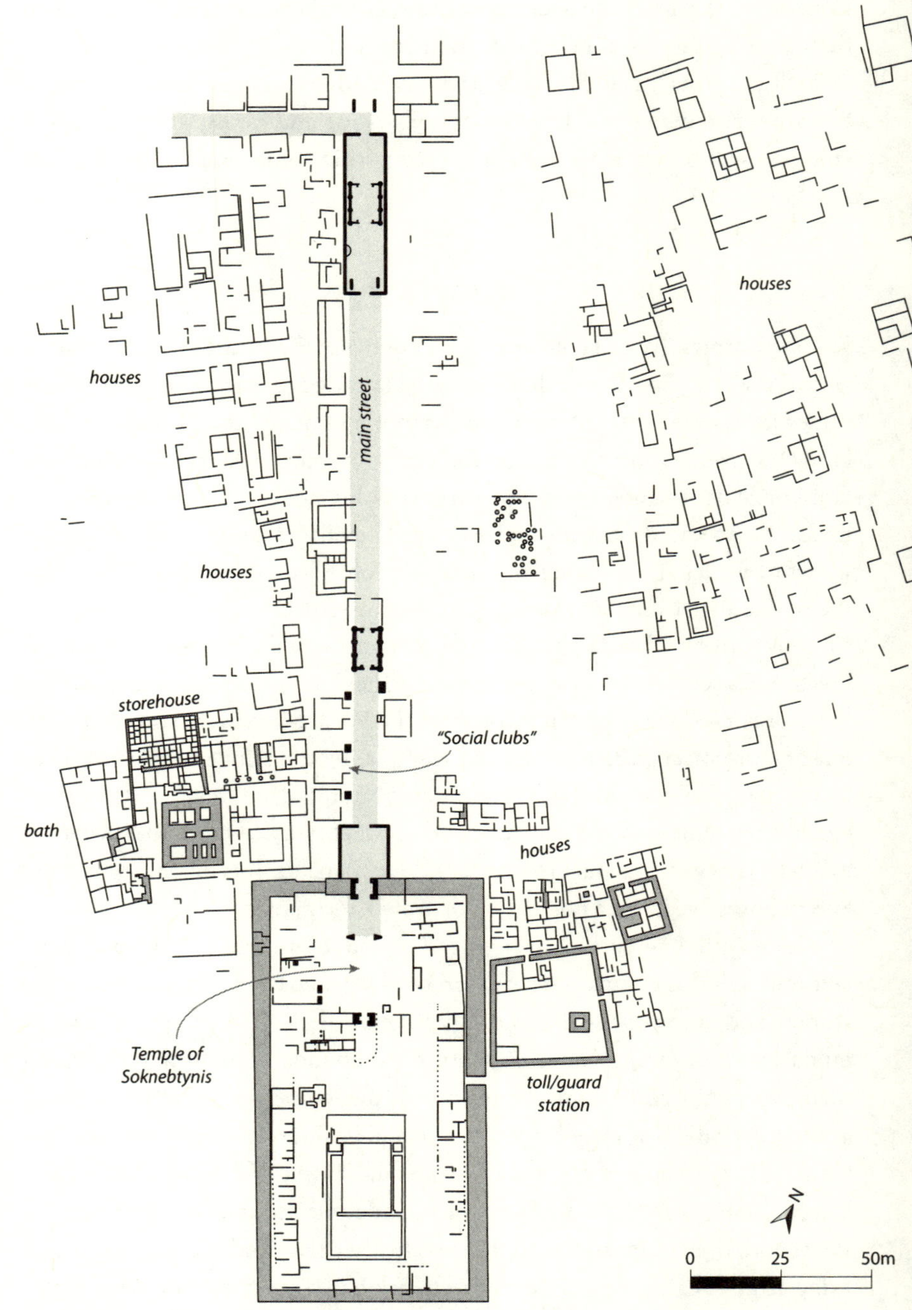

FIGURE 3.11. Village of Tebtunis (Tell Umm el-Baragat, Egypt) (Illustration: Matilde Grimaldi, after Hadji-Minaglou 2007, fig. 1)

part due to the particular—and particularly rich—nature of Egypt's agriculture, carried out principally (although not everywhere) on annually flooded and thus refertilized land.[54] While Egyptian farmers' complex collections of owned and rented land make it difficult to know how much land they farmed in total, most appear to have held total portfolios that, to a western farmer, would have seemed very small. In Tebtunis and Theadelphia, owned plots averaged around three hectares, while rented plots may have been about the same, suggesting a possible total portfolio of around six hectares.[55] In Karanis, another Fayum village, reconstructed total holdings (public leases and private holdings) were in the same ballpark—a median of around seven hectares.[56]

For those leasing land (which was most everyone), it seems to have been common practice to distribute one's lease-holdings among various landlords, in addition to renting state-owned land. Thus, as we shall see, a family like the Kronion family from Tebtunis had to deal with at least four different landlords, while leasing their own land out to their own set of tenants.[57] Even a lessee like Soterichos with no land of his own tended to diversify his tiny leases, holding land simultaneously from as many as three different landowners, plus a state-owned piece of pasture, and moving between landlords over time.[58] While some of these leases were renewed, making for even longer relationships with a given landlord, and state land was probably leased for much longer periods, in general the leasing behavior of Egyptian smallholders speaks to a stubborn independence, staying out of the grip of any one landlord.[59]

To add to the complexity of farmers' portfolios is the clear fragmentation of their holdings into multiple, often noncontiguous plots.[60] We've already seen archaeological evidence for these distributed holdings in Italy. In Egypt, the land rolls and leases describe it everywhere. In the Nile Valley village of Palosis, most landowners owned between two and seven distinct plots of land; in first-century Tebtunis, between one and nine distinct plots. Often these plots were not only noncontiguous, but sometimes even in entirely different villages.[61] In the more verbose leases—like that of Ammonius we saw in chapter 1—one gets a sense of these tiny plots surrounded not only by plots owned by others, but enmeshed in a dense weave of adjacent public and private lands where landowners, lessees and sublessees all rubbed shoulders.[62]

In their dizzying variety of sizes, complexities and productive landscapes, the newly visible farmers of the first and second centuries CE constitute a powerful proxy for economic complexity. From tiny farms with their light material footprint to dispersed farms with a large productive apparatus; from the massive ditched complexes to the varying sizes of farmers' land portfolios: in the diversity of farms and farmers lies the infinitude of different scales of smallholder production. In other words, the complex spectra of dwelling space and landholding all describe an equally complex underlying set of agricultural economies. To which we shall now turn.

Growing: Mixed Agriculture as a System

All too often, we tend to assume that small-scale agriculture equals simple agriculture. In the case of Italian Roman smallholders, we assume they had some wheat fields, a bit of vine, a bit of olives—the so-called Mediterranean triad we examined in chapter 2 made into a farmer's checklist. The history of agriculture writ large has too often been reduced to cereals—as the seeds of civilization, the vehicle of state extraction, the supposed basis for subsistence.[63] The new evidence, above all from the archaeological remains of plants and animals, describes not a checklist but a system, not a triad but a tetrad—cereals, fodder or hay, animals and tree crops, interlinked via an intensive *and* extensive use of the land. This data further shows that there was no such thing as smallholder agriculture—just Roman agriculture. This Roman agriculture was applied by large- and smallholders alike to a locally and regionally specific set of crops, within which individual families—including smallholders—often chose to specialize.

Cereals

Cereal production lies at the imagined heart of peasant agriculture, a picture that is still borne out by the evidence—sort of. Roman grain production throughout the empire included most of the major domesticated varieties: bread wheat and durum wheat (both free-threshing wheats) and emmer, einkorn and spelt (the hulled wheat varieties). Barley was also common and consumed by humans and animals alike. Millet appears to have been much rarer in this period. Each of these grains has different soil, moisture, and temperature optima. The free-threshing wheats require less processing and produce better bread, while hulled wheats must be further roasted and/or milled to free the grain from the hulls but offer better protection in storage.[64]

Each region's farmers—small and large alike—cultivated a different mix of these major cereals. The choices they made, as is now clear, were not entirely

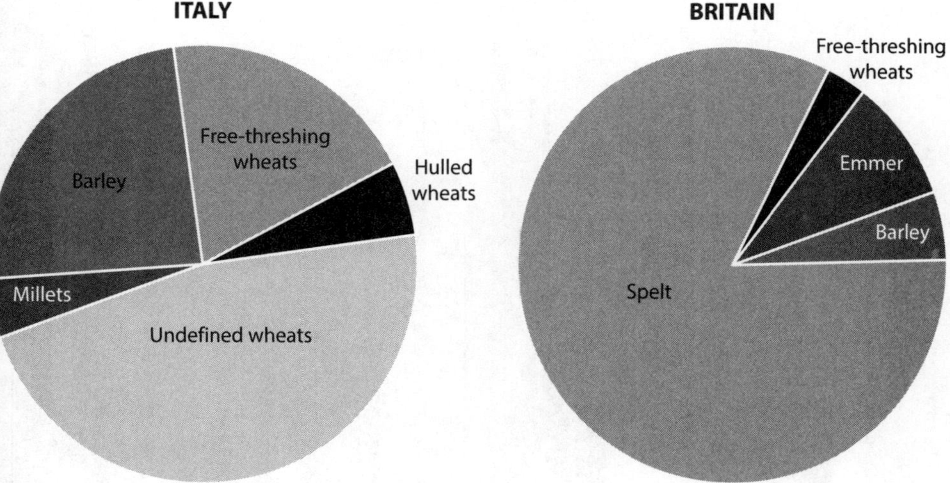

FIGURE 3.12. Major cereal crops produced on smallholder farms: Italy versus Britain (Data: Feito 2022, fig. 5b; Lodwick 2017, table 2.11 [mid-Roman])

environmentally determined, but were shaped by the surplus opportunities presented by local consumers and cities, or by the compulsion of the state.

In Italy, the limited botanical evidence suggests all farmers preferred to grow a mix of cereals—a combination of free-threshing and hulled wheats, plus barley (figure 3.12).[65] It appears that everyone—small- and largeholders alike—cultivated some kind of cereal mix, and even the elite agronomists appear to have viewed a mixed cereal regime as both desirable and profitable.[66]

The farmers of Gaul and Britain, on the other hand, had far more specialized cereal regimes than their Italian comrades. In northern France, there appears to have been a clear geographical divide, with farms north of the Oise River producing mostly spelt and those to the south preferring free-threshing wheats.[67] This specialization was true of most all farms in these areas: small and large farms alike followed the same trends. On the other hand, around some cities, small farms seem to have specialized in specific wheats, seemingly for sale in town. Near Reims, the cellars of one small farm held only free-threshing wheat.[68] This is particularly surprising, as the chalky soils around Reims were not well adapted for nutrient-greedy bread wheats—one of the reasons, perhaps, these farms had relatively short lives.

In Britain, spelt was king (see figure 3.12). Although there is some geographic variability, in the medium-sized farms of the southeast spelt was grown almost as a monocrop.[69] The exceptions to this spelt-over-all trend are the

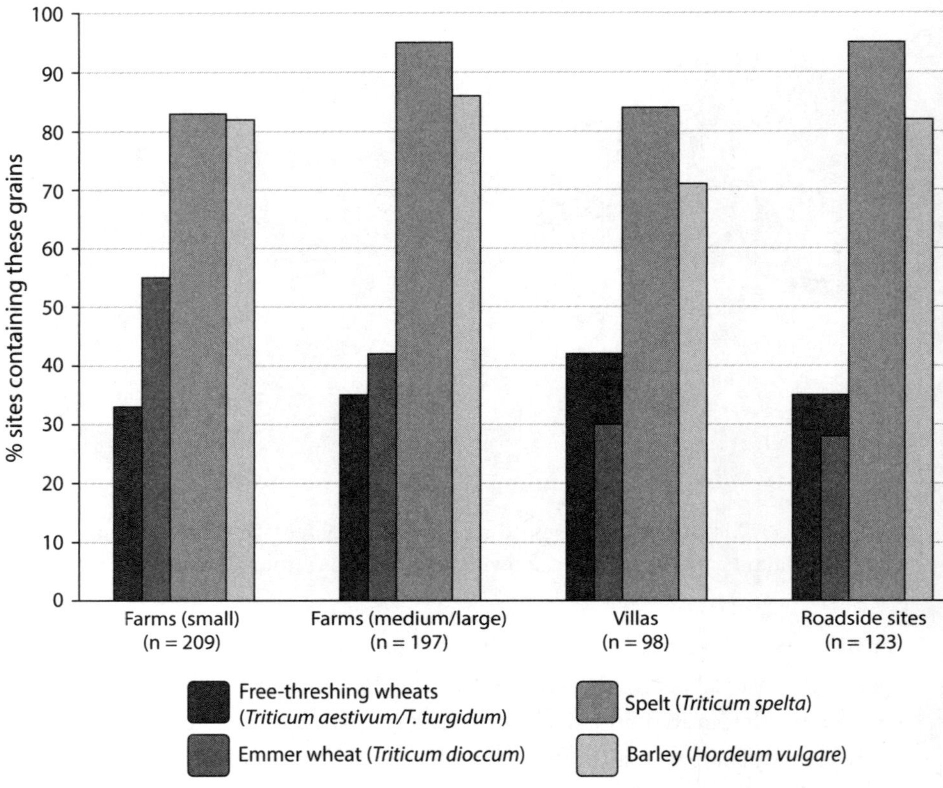

FIGURE 3.13. Everyone's a specialist: frequency of cereal crops by site type in Britain, first through fourth century CE (Data: Lodwick 2017, fig. 2.5)

regions far to the west or the north, places dominated by the smallest farms. These continued the earlier, Iron Age preference for a mix of cereals, including emmer.[70] Otherwise, villas, roadside sites and medium-to-large farms all tended to grow the same mix—a lot of spelt and barley, with lesser amounts of emmer and free-threshing wheats (figure 3.13). All but the smallest smallholders show the same tendency to specialize in spelt as everyone else.

Of all the lands associated with grain agriculture, Egypt sits at the top of the list. Egyptian wheat fed the city of Rome, and taxes and rent were levied in wheat (and occasionally in barley). But we are shockingly underinformed as to what kind of wheat was grown in Egypt. The texts are largely mute on the kind of wheat they so often mention, and the only botanical studies, carried out in the Dakhleh Oasis, point to durum wheat and bread wheat as the principal wheats.[71] Barley is second, and also runs a distant second in the papyrological data.[72] Whether these were the cereals of choice in the Nile Valley and the Fayum, we do not know.

The Other Half of Cereals: Legumes, Fodder and Rotation Strategies

Cereals are often treated as the beginning and end of agricultural production, particularly for smallholders, who are often imagined as cultivating cereals as their principal subsistence crop. But how was cereal cultivation maintained? An older school of Roman agriculture assumed that cereal cultivation was followed by a fallow year, in which the land was simply left alone to recover.[73] Mounting evidence from most—but not all—of the places in our story suggest that more intensive efforts were made to maintain soil fertility while continuing the land's productive capacity, rather than simply leaving it empty. Rotation strategies—alternating nutrient-greedy cereals with legumes, with fodder crops, or with pasture—now appear to lie at the center of Roman cereal agriculture.

In Italy, the evidence for rotational strategies comes both from the archaeological record and, perhaps surprisingly, from the elite Roman agronomists. New data from small farms in Tuscany finds the pollen from leguminous fodder crops appearing in near-equal proportions with that of cereals.[74] This suggests the deliberate rotation of leguminous plants—human edibles like beans and lentils, fodder plants like clover, or both—with cereals. The inclusion of these nitrogen-fixing fodder plants points further to improved pasture—not just land gone wild, but deliberately seeded and coddled pasture for grazing or mowing. The elite agronomists of this period also appear to describe something like such a system, in which land is returned to improved, seeded pasture for a period (what they term *novalis* or *veteretum*), after which it is plowed under and made into arable land for wheat and legumes for a shorter period.[75] The agronomists, too, understood the improved quality of cereal yields after cultivation with legumes, or after a return to pasture.[76] In modern parlance this is termed "ley agriculture," the "ley" comprising the pasture portion of the rotation.

Ley systems have important benefits. Crop yields improve massively under ley systems in temperate climates: the Agricultural Revolution in eighteenth- and nineteenth-century northern Europe was predicated on improved yields due to ley. Yield improvement was probably less impressive in Mediterranean environments due to their more limited water.[77] Nonetheless, if the ley is well-managed—seeded with high-quality pasture plants and drained—it produces high-quality hay *and* returns maximum nutrients to the soil while keeping weeds and pests down.[78] Most critically, it also produces outputs each year: one or two cuttings of hay or pasture for grazing, a bean crop, or a cereal crop. However, the system requires several years of ley to maximize these benefits—something the agronomists also note. Land in ley rotations is a long game, one in which pasture plays as important a role as cereals.

In Gaul and Britain, archaeologists don't agree about the use of rotational strategies. In Gaul, the free-threshing wheat farms of the Île-de-France were clearly rotating cereals with legumes.[79] Evidence for high-quality fodder, including some leguminous-fixing fodder species like vetches, suggests fodder plants may have been used in rotation schemes.[80] In some places, archaeologists actually found Roman-period weeds, their roots still on, pulled from adjacent fields and dumped in nearby ditches.[81] Weeding points to careful crop maintenance in addition to careful field preparation.

In Britain, on the other hand, legumes are less common, and except in Kent and parts of Cambridgeshire, farmers don't seem to have used rotation strategies.[82] A study on nitrogen uptake at a single site found decreasing nitrogen levels in Roman versus Iron Age cereals, suggesting less manuring and potentially no nitrogen return via mechanisms like rotation.[83] Given the knowledge and the incentives, why didn't British farmers rotate their crops? The answer to the riddle may be spelt: even in Gaul, farmers appear to have used rotation less for spelt than for free-threshing wheats. In Britain, where spelt was king, it may have been that rotation with legumes wasn't practiced as assiduously as with the nutrient-greedy bread wheats.

While they may disagree about rotation, archaeologists on both sides of the Channel agree about hay. A major expansion of hay crops took place in the Roman period—what has been termed a "fodder revolution."[84] The species mixes in Gallic sites point to rich hay meadows: these appear to be modest around the Île-de-France, where cattle and sheep are more mixed, and abundant in the east near the Rhine, where larger farms and villages specialized in cattle herding.[85] The evolution of huge Roman scythes (some over a meter in length) from the puny Iron Age sickle also appears to be driven by bigger hay crops and a need for more efficient mowing.[86] In Britain, the expansion of hay meadows also appears to be a largely Roman phenomenon. Hay is found much more commonly on medium-sized farms than on small ones, and all of these sites are concentrated in the southern part of the province, where cereal production (and, as we shall see, cattle production) was at its most intense.[87] Pollen data also shows high levels of improved pasture versus unimproved pasture for the Roman period, particularly in those areas with intensive cattle-spelt production.[88] Fodder and hay crops were thus almost as important as cereals on northern farms, large and small alike.

In Egypt, rotational practices were a regular and required part of smallholders' toolkits. Rotation was required by most multiyear leases in the Nile Valley, with wheat crops followed by mandatory fodder, legume or grass crops.[89] The less abundant evidence from the Fayum mostly suggests the same.[90] For this reason, fodder crops appear almost as often as wheat in the leases from Oxyrhynchus, while in mid-second-century Theadelphia, legumes and fodder together equaled wheat in lists of crops under cultivation.[91]

Fodder was particularly valuable in Egypt owing to some peculiarities of the region's ecology. The Nile flood produced excellent arable soils, but those soils were heavy: they needed animals—particularly cattle—to plow them. That excellent arable land also didn't include a lot of natural permanent pasture to feed the cattle needed to do the plowing. Furthermore, the distance separating those arable fields from the highway that was the Nile River also required a vast herd of donkeys to move crops toward their final fiscal and urban destinations.[92] The upshot was a huge cattle and donkey population, supported by limited pasture and marshland, which, as we'll see, were simultaneously supporting large sheep herds. Fodder and hay, rotated with cereals, was the gasoline that powered this fleet of cattle and donkeys.

If fodder and legumes were cereals' natural partner in soil maintenance, the other obvious means of soil improvement was manuring. The Roman agronomists were fascinated with manure, waxing lyrical on different kinds of dung: pigeon guano was top-class, aged urine was good for new shoots, farmers without compost heaps were lazy sloths.[93] Manure pits have been found in some Italian villas, but smallholder manuring practices are less well known.[94] The best evidence comes from pottery scatters in fields, the remains, perhaps, of collecting manure in messy farmyards and then spreading it on fields before sowing.[95] In Gaul and Britain, the collection of manure was facilitated by the elaborate penning systems in medium and larger farms. Manure pits have been found in many of these pens, and manuring has been detected in moderate to elevated nitrogen levels in cereals on many farms, but not on all.[96] In Egypt, manuring appears as a regular task on farms, carried out after the Nile inundation but before sowing.[97] Egyptian farmers clearly agreed with the agronomists as to the top-class quality of pigeon guano, and dovecotes were built not only to breed and sell pigeons but also to collect and sell their dung.[98] Smallholders thus knew about the value of manure and, when possible, applied it. The question was how much manure their farms could generate. This depended greatly on the other key component of their agriculture—their animals.

Animals: The Missing Link

The silent figures behind ley agricultural strategies and manuring practices are animals. Animals were the "product" of pasture or fodder crops, while their manure returned to the soil a portion of those same consumed nutrients. Scholars have often assumed that Roman smallholders didn't keep animals in any numbers—perhaps a pig or two and a few sheep. Indeed, when one reads that Roman farmers practiced "mixed agriculture," this often refers to a mix of arable and tree crops—not, as is usual in modern parlance, crops *and* animals. But the likelihood that smallholders practiced some form of rotation strategies places animals at the center, rather than the periphery, of their agricultural systems.

Everywhere we find small and medium-sized farms, we find evidence of significant animal herds. And everywhere there were animals, smallholders and elite villas raised more or less the same mix of them. The mix depended on where, not who. Smallholder farmers in Italy, for instance, raised more or less the same mix of cattle, sheep and pigs as their elite villa neighbors, but with somewhat fewer pigs (see figure 2.7). Villas were probably both consuming and exporting more pigs to cities. Small farms, on the other hand, tend to have a more even mix, pointing to less export off the farm and more consumption of animals on it. Some villages on roadsides have particularly high cattle (and horse) populations, suggesting not only a greater use of animals in these places where people were on the move, but also the transshipment of animals through them.

What were Italian smallholders doing with all these animals? Animals' age at slaughter provides some clues. Cattle were slaughtered principally as adults, pointing to their chief use for traction—plowing and hauling—and secondarily for meat and milk. Oxen (castrated males) and cows (females) appear to be equally mixed, suggesting both milk and meat were equally important secondary uses. Sheep were slaughtered at a variety of ages but predominantly as adults, pointing to a mixed use for meat and wool, while pigs were slaughtered at their maximum meat weight of about two years. Thus, Italian smallholder herding strategies were geared toward traction, and probably milk and wool, with meat as a secondary priority.

Animals in Italy were unprecedentedly large.[99] Cattle and pigs get dramatically bigger in the later years of the Roman Republic and the first two centuries of empire, the product of deliberate breeding. The increase in cattle size—in height and/or stockiness—may be specifically related to agricultural needs, as stronger cattle were required to plow the heavy clay soils into which Roman farmers were extending their holdings. Larger pigs, on the other hand, were a product of the increased demand for pork.[100] Importantly, the cattle and pigs raised by Italian smallholders were more or less the same super-sized varieties raised by villa owners: new and improved cattle and bigger pigs were not the province of elites but were being raised and used everywhere.[101]

In the northwest provinces, the choice of what animals to raise was largely determined by what cereals were grown (see figure 2.8). In Britain, and to a certain extent in Gaul, cattle and spelt went together. In places with a heavy preference for spelt—the Rhineland, the Somme valley, the Cambridge fens—cattle were raised in large numbers, almost certainly to pull the plows needed to plant it. Their older age at slaughter tends to support this.[102] The exception was the Dutch river villages, where spelt was less common than barley, but cattle (and horses) were still raised in large quantities. Here younger slaughter patterns and a greater number of female cattle suggests that not only traction but also milk were important drivers of cattle production.[103] Again, in these places where cattle were common, elite villa owners and smallholders alike chose to specialize in them.

The new archaeology has revealed the huge numbers of cattle raised by smallholders in the cattle-spelt system. Indeed, the whole idea of those thousands of medium-sized farms with their multiple pens and watering holes was probably developed to keep cattle. Some roadside villages even appear to be drove-sites, where cattle were collected for onward shipment.[104] Not only did smallholders in the northwest provinces produce lots of cattle, but those cattle were big, too. The large size of British and Gallic cattle, even on smaller farms, have suggested that imported Italian stock was bred with local varieties to produce the same size increases seen in Italy.[105] Again, a need for traction appears to be driving the need for bigger animals, which were then sold for meat once their traction use-life was done.

But cattle weren't king everywhere. In places where other cereals were grown—free-threshing wheat in the Île-de-France or emmer and barley in the Cotswolds—sheep were more common.[106] In Gaul, sheep were slaughtered as adults, pointing to wool/milk or hide production rather than meat.[107] In Britain, on the other hand, the subadult slaughter patterns suggest that milk or meat may have been more important.[108] Roadside villages in particular may have been sites of milk and cheese production, since many of the sheep kept were ewes.

Animals were as central to the Roman Egyptian economy as they were elsewhere, although the proportions raised are less than clear. This is in part due to the lack of archeological evidence, leaving us to fall back on the texts, which describe animals sold (mostly donkeys), leased (sheep), taxed for grazing (sheep again) or cited for trampling other people's crops (sheep and cattle). Animals also fell under the watchful eye of the state—censused, taxed, and requisitioned for state transport when required.[109] Leases on pastureland and the importance of fodder crops are further proxies for a dense animal population. All of this gives us a pointillist, rather than overall, sense of how smallholder families managed their herds.

If you had a modest number of sheep in Roman Egypt, you probably grazed them on public land and paid a tax on them.[110] Herds could have been managed in one of a number of ways that corresponded to their size. Owners of a handful of sheep in the Nile Valley may have been more likely to band together, giving their sheep over to a shepherd to manage.[111] Sheep in the Fayum, on the other hand, appear to have been managed in small to medium-sized herds directly by their owners.[112] Finally, large herds may have been leased to more specialized herders who grazed them on private estate land. The best documented of these were the family of Nilamon, Kalamos and Sons, who made a living by leasing herds of 50 or more animals on the Appianus estate around Theadelphia.[113] In most Egyptian contexts, sheep appear to have been raised principally for wool, while the limited faunal evidence suggest that goats were regarded as a meat source.[114]

Like everywhere else, cattle were the principal plow animal of Egypt.[115] The vast amounts of fodder and hay produced under rotation practices were probably mostly dedicated to their upkeep. Even a very smallholder like Soterichos appears to have owned or leased at least two cattle, as he was fined for allowing them to devour a neighbor's grass.[116] Cattle also appear in large estate records as having been leased during plowing time, presumably from local, smaller farmers who owned them or were subleasing them themselves.[117]

Finally, donkeys, rather than horses, were the chief beast of burden in Egypt, even more so than camels. Whole armies of them were chiefly responsible for the movement of goods and people around the countryside, and to and from cities.[118] Donkeys were fed barley, hay, and undoubtedly straw as well, and thus were cheaper than cattle, but still an important consumer of grass. Despite their cost, many families probably had at least one donkey, which they kept for their own use or rented out.[119] Like cattle and sheep, specialist donkey-herders also existed who either raised them for sale or used them to ferry agricultural surpluses from farm to town.[120]

Roman smallholders were once deemed so poor as to have used their family members as plow animals. The new data suggests otherwise, with animals as central players in a mixed animal-arable system. Supported by rotation regimes and improved pasture, they also provided key land inputs both as plow animals and via their manure. Large cattle and sheep herds were managed by smallholders in the northwest provinces and in Egypt for more specialized uses, while Italian farmers managed their more mixed herds of cattle, sheep and pigs for a combination of outputs—labor, milk, meat. Transport, which, as we shall see, was key to moving surplus off the farm, was almost certainly driving horse and donkey rearing on British and Egyptian farms.

Tree Crops: Another Part of the Smallholder Portfolio

Tree crops—particularly vines and olives—are often presumed to be part of elite villa agriculture, but not so much for smallholders. In part because the elite texts are so obsessed with wine and oil (like Cato's infamous blueprint for a slave-run wine estate), and in part because of the spectacular detritus—amphorae, shipwrecks, presses—of elite investment in these products, smallholders have been largely written out of the histories of wine and olive oil.[121] It remains true that smallholders were less important to wine and oil agribusiness. It is increasingly clear, however, that wine and oil—and other fruit crops—were vitally important to smallholders.

In Italy, the earliest center of Roman wine exports, most known wine and olive presses were located in villas, and the quantification of their outputs forms part of the argument for agricultural expansion in the late Republican and early Imperial period.[122] Yet everywhere we have evidence, we find central Italian smallholders maintaining olive trees and vineyards as well.[123] Grape and olive seeds are standard archaeobotanical finds on smallholder farms.[124] And, as we noted above, many of the medium and larger farms had some kind of pressing apparatus for processing either grapes or olives.[125] Shared presses were another option for farms too small to afford their own. Collective, open-air installations used for grapes, olives or both were places where nearby farmers might bring both grapes and olives for pressing and share the expensive apparatus.[126]

The northwest provinces were too far north to support olive cultivation. But many of the fruits we associate with Britain and northern France today—apples, pears, cherries and grapes, to mention a few—were imported to these areas in the later Iron Age or Roman period, after which time everyone began to grow them.[127] The flourishing of fruit horticulture during the Roman period was not limited to elite villas; smallholders grew and sold fruit with gusto. Among the cluster of medium farms around Reims, one appears to have had a small orchard of at least 1,200 square meters.[128] In Britain, "lazybeds"—deep ridges and furrows for horticulture—have been found near the farms around Cambridge, in one instance attached to wells for seasonal irrigation.[129] But while the expansion of fruit horticulture was embraced by northern smallholders, it's less clear whether they went in for viticulture. A whole range of small amphorae types was developed in the northwest regions of Gaul and even southeast Britain to carry small wine surpluses locally and farther afield.[130] But where the wine was produced remains uncertain: the few grape presses found to date appear in large villas, with only a few in smaller farms.[131] But if the northwest Gallic smallholders were not, perhaps, big wine producers, their cousins to the south were. New work on southern Gallic wine production finds smallholders jumping on the wine-producing bandwagon, specializing in grape production to a remarkable degree.[132]

Like Italy, Egypt's main cash crop was wine. Vineyards were everywhere, although perhaps best known from the Fayum. Unlike Italy, Egyptian wine circulated almost entirely within Egypt itself, moved around in ceramic jars between villages and from the countryside to the cities.[133] Vineyards have been often assumed to be dominated by large metropolitan landowners.[134] This is partially true. Vineyards in Tebtunis, for example, appear to have more commonly been owned by larger landowning families, although even their holdings only amounted to under three hectares—an area Cato would have scoffed at as a mere peasant farm.[135] In Theadelphia, where viticulture was more common, tax rolls suggest that a relatively small group of Romans and Alexandrians (presumably city bigwigs) controlled around half the vineyards, and more as time went on. Nonetheless, small plots owned by locals continued to be an important part of the village's wine output.[136] Tiny vineyard plots form part of the holdings of even the most modest of landholders, like Soterichos, who held a tiny half-hectare of nonirrigated vines.[137]

Tiny crops of fruit and specialized herbs were also critical pieces of Egyptian smallholders' portfolios. Date palm orchards appear regularly among the plots of smallholders, and, as they might be intercropped with arable crops, were a potentially important source of both food and cash.[138] Rents might be paid in dates, and even their stones had a cash value. Garlic was an important crop in the Ptolemaic period, and its importance continued in the Roman Fayum. The farmer Sarapion from Theadelphia grew enough garlic on less than half a hectare of leased land to float a 450-drachma loan.[139] Thyme, cumin, mustard and other herbs may have been similarly cultivated on a larger-than-garden scale.[140] Even a smallholder like Soterichos might opt to invest in herb cultivation, the most specialized of cash crops.[141]

This survey of smallholder agricultural products and practices drives home the fact that there was no such thing as smallholder agriculture—only Roman agriculture. Large landowners and smallholders alike grew largely the same crops, with largely the same techniques—rotation of cereals, with fodder and hay as major second crops. They engaged in both mixed (Italy) and specialized (Gaul, Britain and Egypt) animal husbandry. In the case of viticulture and other tree crops, smallholder and elite cultivation are distinguished principally by the scale of their enterprises. Although it is often claimed that Roman agriculture was characterized by "extensive" practices—an expansion of land under cultivation with minimum labor inputs—it is difficult to characterize smallholder, or even much large-estate agriculture, in this way. The micromanagement of soil and water, the seemingly widespread adaptation of rotation practices and the close integration of animals with those practices—all these describe fairly intensive use of what we will see to be dense, land-limited spaces. How successful these practices actually were raises the critical question of surplus.

Selling: Surplus Production and Places

"Surplus" in smallholder parlance has typically meant quantities sufficient for subsistence, seed, taxes and bad-year storage. What interests us here is surplus over and above those needs—surplus for sale off the farm, substantial tax payments, army requisition, or all of the above. Surplus remains the distinction scholars use to separate so-called peasant production from villa/estate production: peasants don't produce surplus for export off the farm, while villas were largely geared toward it. The new data suggests this binary needs to be revised.[142] Most medium and large farms have evidence for surplus production for export off the farm, and even the smallest farms—like Soterichos'—were sometimes doing so in small ways. The nature and scale of that surplus—and above all its incentives and direction—varied by region and even by individual families' own strategies.

Finding smallholders selling their surplus off the farm, however, requires sailing through the shoals of proxies. Granaries, grain-dryers, amphorae, tax payments we have; account books tallying up own-consumption versus sale-off-the-farm we don't. These surplus proxies aren't always the same as those for elite villas—shipwrecks full of wine, monumental granaries full of grain—but once we start looking for them, they are everywhere.

Selling Cereals

Surplus production in grain is proxied by specialized storage buildings called granaries: grain storage for household consumption could be managed in jars and sheds, while specialized granaries really only made sense if you produced considerably more than you planned to eat and needed to store it before sending it off the farm.[143] Granaries are identified by the lines of piers supporting their suspended floors. While more common in villas, granaries also occur on farms and in villages in both Italy and the northwest provinces. In Britain, where archaeologists have counted them, about 30 percent of the known and possible granaries occur on farms and 10 percent at roadside sites and villages, while 50 percent are found in villas.[144] In Gaul, the numbers are less clear: most of the smaller, simpler types of granaries are to be found on medium farms, while about half of the more complex, buttressed variety were built for the largest "villa-wannabe" farms.[145] We are surely missing some significant grain storage on farms, as granaries are not always easy to detect among the scattershot of post-holes that comprise these northern farmsteads. Everywhere, however, the grain storage capacity of villa granaries mostly dwarfs that of smallholder sites.[146] The granary in the great villa of Settefinestre measured some 500 square meters, while the nearby smallholder versions were probably a quarter or less of the size. But even these small granaries might still be substantial. The Pievina granary in Tuscany (see figure 3.6) may have held some 9,450 kilograms of free-threshing wheat, that at Vicar's Farm in Cambridgeshire (see figure 3.5) some 10,700 kilograms of unhulled spelt and barley.

In Britain and, to a lesser extent, in Gaul, the presence of grain dryers is a signal of surplus grain production.[147] Grain dryers are purpose-built heaters for speeding the dehusking of hulled grains like spelt. An extravagance for household use, they make sense only for larger-scale processing. As hulled

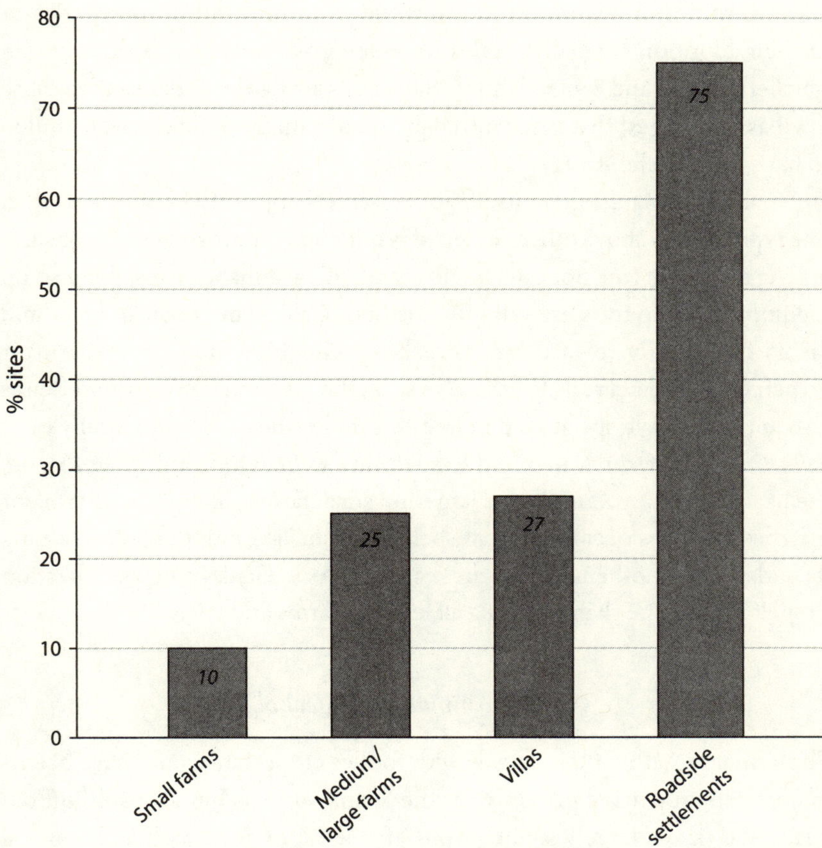

FIGURE 3.14. Distribution of grain dryers, Britain, Central Belt (Data: Lodwick 2017, fig. 2.45)

grains appear to be dehulled before being shipped to cities or the military, grain dryers are also associated with grain export off the farm. Such dryers were also used in malting barley for beer, especially in southeast Britain.[148] In Britain, where we have numbers, these are most common in roadside sites, while medium farms and villas are about equally likely to have them (figure 3.14).[149] As a barometer of surplus production, then, grain dryers appear to be used by smallholders as often as by elite villa owners.

Limited, but still tantalizing, is the evidence for the use of water power to grind grain. Water mills were thought to be limited to urban mills (like the huge mills outside the Roman city of Nîmes with their 16-wheel capacity) or in villas, where larger-scale surplus production made them a more obvious investment.[150] But some very recent discoveries on medium farms might point to their adoption at smaller scales. Wooden post mills have been found in northern France and Switzerland.[151] Such mills are harder to detect than those in villas but suggest that mechanized processing might not have been limited to big estates or the state.

Finally, there is the grain itself. Some farmers appear to be specializing in one type of grain above others, a sign of production for urban or state consumers. Again, this is true not only in villas and villa-wannabe farms, but also on medium farms. In the Oise valley in northern Gaul, some small and medium farms tilt heavily toward free-threshing wheats, which comprise over 90 percent of their cereals.[152] As we've seen, the medium farms around Reims also appear to have specialized in free-threshing wheats, despite locally poor soils. One such farm even opted to specialize in field mustard.[153] In Britain, the heavy shift to spelt impacted large and small farms alike: Vicar's Farm, for instance, registers over 80 percent spelt and a small amount of barley among its finds, just like other farms in the region.[154] As in Gaul, grain specialization in spelt tends to be shared among all kinds of farms and villas.[155]

Selling Animals and Alcohol

For farmers rotating their cereals with fodder crops, hay would have been a major cash crop, used not only for the farm's animals but also sold off the farm. Alas, it is a largely silent surplus, for without good archaeobotanical data, we have only the possible spaces where such hay might be stored—sheds, barns, or satellite sites in the field themselves.[156] Nonetheless, the production of large quantities of fodder is implied by the ley agricultural systems employed by central Italian and central Gallic farmers. Its demand is proxied by the larger, more numerous animal herds, as well as the huge potential markets for hay in villages and cities, where pack animals were in constant use for haulage and communications. The high prices commanded for hay were a talking point in Italy: as we noted in chapter 1, an innkeeper in Isernia could joke that keeping a donkey was far more onerous than paying a prostitute, a claim borne out by the high prices of hay in Pompeii relative to other expenses.[157] Pliny even claimed that one *iugerum* (a quarter hectare) of shrub medick, a much-favored fodder plant, could bring in 2,000 sestertii per year.[158] While we can't yet see it clearly, hay would have been a major potential source of surplus revenue, particularly for farmers living within a day's radius of a town or roadside site.

In Gaul and Britain, many smallholders were quite clearly engaged in surplus animal production, as evidenced by both the scale and specialization in particular species. Specialized droving sites were extreme examples of this specialization in cattle (and horse) agriculture.[159] Indeed, the increase in farm sizes in both provinces is mostly driven by larger animal pens. Not only were British farms getting bigger to raise more cattle, but British farmers in the southeast increasingly specialized in cattle. At Vicar's Farm, as with many Cambridge-area medium farms, cattle constitute over half of the faunal collections. A similar cattle-skew accrues to some farms and villages in the Rhineland regions: in the large farms near Frankfurt and Cologne, and in the villages on the Dutch side, cattle comprised a whopping 80 percent or more of faunal collections. Other regions doubled down on sheep: some farms and villages around Paris have very high (over 60 percent) quantities of sheep, which they appear to be keeping principally for wool or milk production.[160] British roadside villages, even in the cattle-rich southeast, also went for sheep herding, but mostly for milk or meat.[161] Finally, outside Reims, some farmers even opted to specialize in pigs, unusual in this part of the world and clearly destined for the nearby city.[162]

If northwestern smallholders were selling their animals off the farm, central Italian farmers were almost certainly selling their wine. Some recently discovered small, flat-bottomed amphorae of local manufacture appear to have been designed for this purpose (figure 3.15). These had a capacity of perhaps 10–20 liters, were designed to carry wine in carts, and were manufactured seemingly on smallholder sites.[163] Central Italy is home to several flat-bottomed amphorae types, all of small capacity, which began in the heyday of central Italian wine production in the first century BCE.[164] While it is impossible to tie all of these containers to smallholder surplus production, their small capacity, often limited circulation and above all the fact that they were intended to move around on carts, not boats, suggest that smallholders contributed their extra wine production to these containers' contents.

The Road to Market

For smallholders to get any type of surplus off their farms, they needed a transport network. It's now clear that all these expanded farms and villages were everywhere connected to each other and to cities by an astonishingly dense network of tracks. We are accustomed to think of Roman roads as great basalt-paved highways. These smaller tracks constituted the "other" Roman

FIGURE 3.15. Selling smallholder wine: wine amphora, central Italy, first century CE. Large shipboard transport amphora (Dressel 1) for comparison (Reconstruction: Matilde Grimaldi, after E. Vaccaro and Archaeological Data Service)

road system. The small farms around Reims were all connected by trackways.[165] The dense network of farms around Cirencester were all linked by tracks (figure 3.16).[166]

In the Cambridge fens, the dense trackways also linked up to water routes, like the newly built Car Dyke canal.[167] In Italy, tracks have been sensed, rather

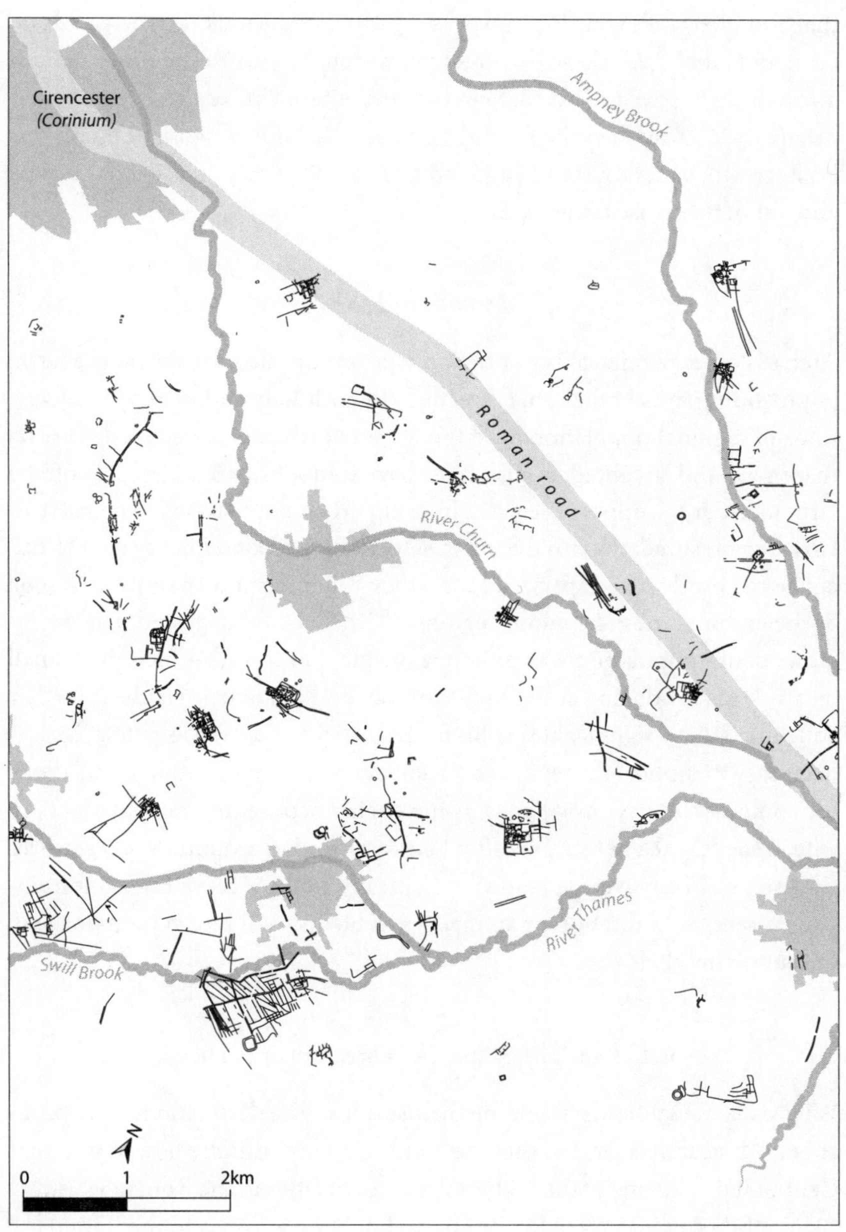

FIGURE 3.16. The road to market: trackways and farms around Cirencester, Oxfordshire (Illustration: Matilde Grimaldi, after Smith 2016b, fig. 3.58)

than found, by following the most likely paths farmers took between field and farm and city.[168] All these dirt tracks connected farms to the more famous arrow-straight paved roads that ran between cities. Unlike those main roads, originally built by the state for military purposes, the network of tracks was homegrown, built by farmers large and small to move crops and people around and out of the dense farmscapes.

Mouths to Feed

Archaeological evidence is not the only proxy for sale of crops off the farm; population points in the same direction. In both Italy and in Egypt, calculations of regional populations and their food needs have persuaded scholars that small- and largeholders alike must have sold substantial surpluses off the farm in order to support their neighboring urban populations. One particularly elegant simulation used Roman settlement and land quality data to calculate the productive capacity of the Tiber Valley, just north of Rome—one of the empire's most populous regions.[169] The results suggested that the region's dense population was only sustainable if everyone—including small farms—was producing at the mid-to-upper end of ancient yields. It further concluded that a significant surplus from small farms as well as elite villas was necessary to support the region's adjacent cities. In Egypt, output calculations for some of the Fayum villages, using their documented tax payments in wheat, suggested a net surplus after taxes and seed of around 28 percent over subsistence for an average family.[170] Critically, none of these calculations included rent, crop rotation or animals—problems we'll return to in our own output models below.

Cities and the State: The Direction of Surplus

Where were smallholders sending their surplus? The destinations were probably both near and far. On the one hand, surplus naturally flowed to cities. Central Italy had one of the highest densities of cities in the Roman world.[171] Many of these cities would have boasted only two thousand inhabitants—some even less. But they constituted a major source of nonproducing mouths to feed. Reconstructions of the Tiber Valley cities and roadside settlements estimated a population of some 18,000 urbanites who had to be fed by their surrounding countryside—and this without including the mega-city of Rome.[172] As noted above, that reconstruction posited significant small-farm surplus to maintain those urban mouths. Even in less urbanized Britain and Gaul, cities would have been natural destinations for smallholder surplus. The farmers around Reims, for instance, were clearly focusing their hard-to-sustain free-threshing wheat production on the city, along with their small orchards and pigpens. While the local supply of Paris is poorly understood, the thicket of farms in the Île-de-France/Val d'Oise may have sent their products cityward.[173] London has been described as an "alien city," wholly cut off from its left-behind rural hinterland and supported by supplies of imported grain and pots.[174] The new discoveries in the Thames Valley estuary with its droving stations, specialization in cattle production, and the beer-producing farms of Kent all show the risks of forgetting smallholders and their contributions to urban staples.[175]

On the other hand, urban markets were not the only source of eager, local consumers. Farmers' biggest customers were probably their neighbors. The sheer rural density of many areas of the British southeast, together with the smallness of the small towns, would have made farm neighbors as important a market as urban ones.[176] In Gaul, the animal and/or grain specialization we've noted in individual farms in the Île-de-France or around Reims, or the hyper-viticulturalists in the south, also made those farms natural purchasers of those things they didn't produce. If all you are growing is spelt or mustard or grapes, you need to buy the rest of what you need from your neighbors. In Italy, small-scale wine surplus clearly circulated among rural neighbors. Everywhere, the increased density of rural settlement, together with increased specialization, made farmers natural consumers of one another's surplus.

Outside of Italy, the state's whip hand may have more forcibly pushed surplus off the farm. Taxation, military supply and the metropolitan food doles were all potential drains on smallholder surplus. The state dealt with these demands in various ways: purchase at market rates, forced sale at below market rates, or, in the case of tax or extraordinary levies, simple requisition without compensation. Again, Britain provides the best-analyzed, perhaps most extreme case. The hand of the state lay heavy in Britain: its restive history and later conquest meant that military presence was thick on the ground. Some 55,000 legionaries and auxiliary soldiers were stationed in the province by the second century, by which time most were located in the north and on Hadrian's Wall, as well as in the Welsh forts to the west.[177] The supply of these troops has long been a matter of puzzlement. The farmscapes near Hadrian's Wall and in Wales were dominated by tiny, net-consumer farms.[178] So where did the supplies come from? As unlikely as it once seemed, it would appear that much of those soldiers' food came from the central belt of medium-sized farms far away from the frontiers in the south, perhaps particularly from Cambridgeshire, which we have mentioned so often above.[179] A possible state-run supply hub and port have been identified among these farms, and perhaps even an imperial estate.[180] If this theory of supply-at-distance is even partially true (and more evidence is required to prove it), then the smallholder families of the British southeast with their surplus of spelt and cattle were, at least in part, producing to feed distant soldiers.[181]

This same kind of supply-in-extreme-depth has also been suggested for northern Gaul. The Rhineland villas, largest farms and Dutch villages were almost certainly supplying the Upper and Lower Rhineland forts, and a number of calculations have been run to determine if they were up to the task.[182] The answer has been—partially. Although, as we've noted above, the villages and farms of the Dutch Rhineland were all producing some surplus, they were still not producing many of the things consumed in these forts—wine, bread wheat and spelt among them. These things were shipped in from some distance. The expansion of wine production in northern Gaul appears to be have been destined for these forts, although, as we've seen, it's not clear smallholders participated in that supply.[183] For the free-threshing wheats, however, the nearest sources of supply were the farmscapes around Paris and Reims—some 500 kilometers distant.[184] The relatively high number of inscriptions left by *negotiatores*—traders on state business—in this province further describes the extent of the state's reach.[185]

In Egypt, the insistent hand of the state siphoned off a portion of smallholders' production to feed Rome, the urban officials, and the (comparatively fewer) local auxiliary soldiers. The great Egyptian cities, clustered in the Nile Valley and much enlarged in the Roman period, were destinations for market surplus. State extraction and urban markets might overlap: the larger cities—Alexandria, Oxyrhynchus and perhaps Hermopolis—had, at various moments, a food dole where the state supplied wheat, wine and/or pork at free or reduced cost to residents.[186] All these needs were met in large part by smallholders' surplus—sold, taxed or requisitioned.

Given the opportunities for and demands on smallholder surplus—and it's rarely possible to disentangle the opportunities from the demands—it's surprising that any small farmer could get by without shipping some products off the farm. But the forces impelling surplus production shouldn't make us blind to the important populations who appear to have been left outside its ambit. The smallest farms—like Monte Forco outside Capena or The

Grange outside Cambridge—have limited evidence for surplus production. Granaries, barns, wine production beyond the household level—are all largely absent. These appear to be classic instances of net-consumers—farmers who consumed almost everything they produced. In Italy, these tiny farms are often found in colonized landscapes and sometimes associated with veterans. In Britain, the immediate hinterland of the military-industrial complexes in the Welsh Marches and along Hadrian's Wall were dominated by these farms, eschewing both surplus and pottery, living much as they had since the Iron Age.[187] The contrast between the economies of these genuinely "subsistence" farms, and those of the neighboring military forts supplied by distant, larger-scale smallholders, could not be starker. We have no idea what percentage of Roman smallholder farms was constituted by these probable net-consumers. Whatever their number, they faced serious challenges to getting by in the long term, challenges to which we shall now turn.

Challenges: Land, Tenancy and Taxes

We've witnessed above the remarkable sophistication and productivity of smallholder agriculture. From rotation schemes to specialization to the evidence for sale off the farm, thanks to new evidence, the Roman small farmer now appears a completely different creature from the autarkic peasant of our earlier scholarship. But the same new evidence that revealed the farmers' sophistication has also revealed the substantial challenges they faced. We might assume that these challenges were largely down to the predatory nature of the imperial state, with its taxation regimes that sucked farmers dry of their surplus. For provincial farmers, taxation was doubtless a problem. But more challenging yet, the new evidence suggests, were the knock-on effects of living in a crowded world.

A Dense World and Its Implications

We do not know how many people lived in the Roman world. Most estimates gravitate to around 50–60 million people, but even these are educated guesses.[188] While the hard numbers are hotly debated, all sides agree that, compared to earlier and later periods, in most parts of its realm the Roman period witnessed an increase, perhaps a significant increase, in population. The possible reasons for this increase can't detain us here, but they certainly included the capacity for greater agricultural surpluses and the ability to move those surpluses around—the very processes we've been discussing here. In part, this bigger population lived in more numerous, bigger cities. But some 70–80 percent of this big population still lived in the countryside, a countryside that, it is now clear, was unprecedently densely occupied.

That density, compared to the periods before and after it, has long been sensed from field surveys. From the South Etruria survey in the Tiber Valley of Italy to the generations of accumulated documentation from Roman Cambridgeshire, in many regions of the Roman West, the Roman period already appeared to have witnessed the densest use of the land until the eighteenth or nineteenth century.[189] But it has only been recently, with the very large-scale excavations carried out in advance of very large-scale building projects, that this density has been truly revealed. In the area around Cambridge, it now emerges, there was a second-century farm every 300 meters; around Cirencester nearly as many (figure 3.17).[190] Parts of the Île-de-France looked similar.[191] The region west of modern Cologne had a large farm every 500 meters.[192] Large-scale archaeology has, in some places, increased by sevenfold the farm density previously estimated from field and aerial surveys.[193] A great many rural regions, even those we had thought were relatively spacious, now look extremely crowded.

The density of farm settlement had major knock-on effects for farmers. Increased density was accompanied by expansion into harder-to-work, harder-to-maintain soils. We see this in the more intensive use of poorer land in the Tiber Valley, the clay bottoms around Cambridgeshire, the chalky soils around Reims, unflooded lands in Egypt.[194] The breeding of bigger cattle to plow those hard-to-work soils, and the development of crop rotation and manuring to maintain them, were thus as much defensive maneuvers driven by a lack of land as they were offensive ones inspired by new markets and the desire for consumer goods.

Drainage was another such defensive/offensive maneuver: drainage brought desperately needed new land into cultivation, even as it maintained the productivity of fertile land. The legal texts of the period resound with water-rights arguments—who was responsible for downslope runoff, who was liable for drains that bisect properties—as well as irrigation and water storage complaints. These complaints were brought to the jurists' attention by angry farmers—small- and largeholders alike.[195] The agronomic texts were similarly preoccupied by drainage, particularly Columella, who provided his readers with detailed advice on field drain construction, cleaning and maintenance—a kind of agro-plumbers' almanac.[196] These are textual echoes of a much broader and louder effort to manage soil water, particularly water in newly arable or indifferently arable soils. The Tuscan countryside has been found to be littered with field drains, built to remove standing water and channel groundwater.[197] In

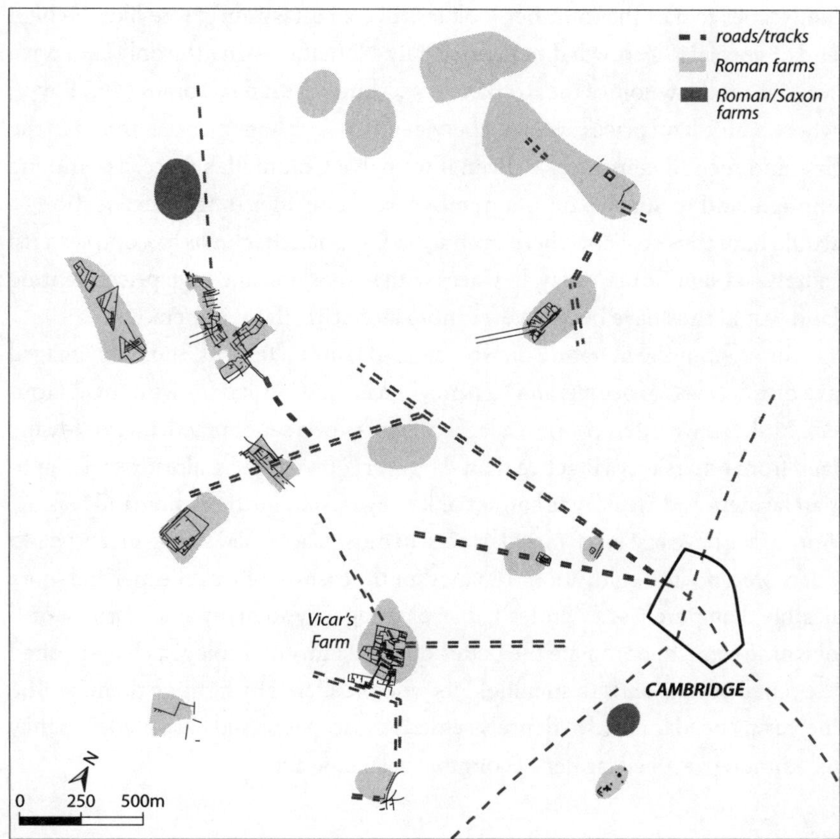

FIGURE 3.17. A dense world: Roman farms northwest of Cambridge, Cambridgeshire, UK, after recent excavations (Illustration: Matilde Grimaldi, after Evans, Aldred and Cooper 2003, fig. 7)

the Île-de-France, the construction of a modern warehouse and office park revealed some 30 hectares of a carefully gridded ditch system: no state hand was at work here, only systematic local efforts to drain the waterlogged soil.[198] The micromanagement of water was on everyone's mind, the product of cheek-by-jowl farms, using every scrap of land, and smallholders appear to have been micromanaging right along with elites and the state.

If land was scarce, scarcer than we had imagined in some regions, then it stands to reason that it was expensive. Columella claimed that one *iugerum* (a quarter hectare) of newly cleared Italian land sold for 1,000 sestertii in the later first century CE. This has long been thought to be a fantasy, for the price is very high indeed, and makes a mockery of most investment calculations that assume relatively low yields.[199] The new archaeological evidence for crowded landscapes makes that number look less like a fantasy and more like the high end of normal in a crowded, expensive Italy. Nonetheless, it's the only land price we have for the whole of the Roman West. More robust data comes from Egypt, where arable land prices averaged between 350–475 drachmas per aroura in the first and second centuries.[200] Even if we halve Columella's price, assembling enough land to survive on—a number we'll consider in the next section—would have thus cost anywhere from 3,500 Egyptian drachmas to 5,000 sestertii in Italy—a significant outlay. In places with scarce land and high prices, renting land would thus have become ever more attractive, if not imperative.

Throughout the literature on Roman land tenure, "tenants" are often imaged as a distinct class of people, and "tenancy" an institution at odds with "free" farmers. In short, we often confuse a legal category for a set of practices. For leasing land from others was a practice shared by everyone.[201] We've already seen Egyptian farmers and wealthy urbanites alike engaged in both owning and leasing. And, as we have just seen, most farmers, in most places, had strong incentives to put more land into cultivation. Tenancy for the cash-poor was cheaper and more flexible than purchase.[202] Indeed, in explaining why so many small farms north of Rome came to dominate the better-quality land, archaeologists have posited the rental of said lands to smallholders who prospered by farming them.[203] The increasing need for land in densely settled landscapes would have made tenancy a common part of all farmers' economic balancing act.

The Hand That Takes

If leasing land was potentially advantageous, it was only so if the rents were reasonable. It has been assumed rents were on par with taxes, as landlords had to compete with the state for farmers' surplus.[204] The sad fact is that we have not one documented land rent from the Roman West. We might deduce them from land prices and from aristocratic expectations of return on their landed investments as being something in the neighborhood of 10–15 percent of expected yields—a guess that amounts to a reasonable percentage of smallholders' surplus.[205]

In Egypt, the only place we have real numbers, rents were not reasonable at all. Rents averaged around seven artabai of wheat per aroura in our period but could often be found in the 10–15 artabai per aroura range.[206] At known yields, Egyptian farmers would have seen 60 percent or even more of their crop vanish into the landlord's pocket in those years. As we shall see in detail below, leasing land at these rates would have made those intensive practices we've described above—rotation, manuring, weeding—absolutely essential in order to increase yields. Renting would have motivated, not discouraged, intensive production.[207] But high rents also meant that what appears to be more than sufficient land to survive was totally insufficient when leased at these rates. High rents—yet another product of the scarcity of land—may have been the biggest challenge faced by Roman smallholders in some areas.

Finally, there was the challenge of taxes. We've already had a short tour of different kinds of Roman taxes in chapter 1, the most complex and comprehensive of which were taxes on provincial land. Italian farmers were exempt from these taxes, although they would have had to pay customs duties on crops shipped to more distant cities. For our British, Gallic and Egyptian smallholders, land taxes might have been owed in cash or in kind, depending on the region and the crop. Again, only in Egypt do we have any hard numbers: here a flat tax of (mostly) one artaba of grain per aroura for arable land amounted to 10 percent or less of likely yields.[208] We have no numbers for anywhere else in the Roman world, only the hint provided by the Latin name for some tax payments—the *decima,* or tenth. Whether tax rates were in fact a tenth of yields on arable land is unknown, but at this point, it's the best guess we have. If this is more or less correct, land tax obligations were a light burden in comparison with some of the high rents charged on some of the empire's most valuable agricultural real estate.

Adding Up: Some Smallholder Balance Sheets

All these findings naturally raise the question of "how much"—how much surplus for how much land did Roman smallholders produce? How much grain, fodder and animals were enough to make a living, and how much might be shipped off the farm as surplus? These may be obvious questions, but they aren't quite the right ones. For smallholders with limited resources of land and labor, "muchness" was necessarily shaped by choices and trade-offs—household consumption versus market sale, rotation versus fallow, animals for milk or hay for cash—an infinitude of exchanges.[209] It's not enough, in short, to ask "how much" surplus a farm might produce. It's necessary first to articulate the system farmers used to grow, rotate, and feed—the "hows." Only then can we get at "how much."[210]

We thus conclude this story of Roman smallholders by estimating the outputs of some of the actual farms or villages we encountered above.[211] Their agricultural systems are based on what we know of that farm's products and practices—its available land, the types of plants and animals grown, and its liabilities like rent and taxes. We can then apply a range of ancient (and some modern) yields for everything from grain to fodder crops to animals to estimate the total outputs produced by each system. We can also estimate the labor required for these farms as a ratio of these outputs. The interested reader can find the details—and the math—in the Appendix.[212]

The purpose of this accounting exercise is twofold. At its most basic, quantification reveals the immense productivity of systems versus cereals, and thus the pathways to survival and flourishing in a land-limited world. At the same time, transforming what is mostly qualitative data into quantitative form gives our story a final sharpness. It transforms the otherwise abstract into the often painfully concrete, throwing the decisions faced by smallholders, and the yawning inequalities that separated them, into stark relief.

Wine, Wheat and Hay on Central Italian Farms

We've already encountered two ends of the Italian farm spectrum in both size and complexity: a possible small veteran farm of seven *iugera* outside Rome near the ancient city of Capena (see figure 3.1) and the medium-sized Pievina in southern Tuscany (see figure 3.6), complete with its small granary and tile kiln.[213] The newest archaeological evidence suggests that farmers like these were not just producers of cereals, but also of hay and fodder through ley rotation systems, as well as grapes and olives. Our reconstructions, then, need to take account of the complex juggling of legume-cereal rotation, a period of ley pasture, the animals raised on this ley, plus small fields of grapes and olives.

The larger Pievina farm, reconstructed at around 70 *iugera* or about 17.5 hectares, was still small compared to estimates for large villas. It would have supported a larger community, sold a substantial surplus off the farm, or some combination of both. Surpluses in grain, hay, or wine were all possible—perhaps 2,600 sestertii per year in wheat alone—depending on the size of the community and what it chose to sell or to consume on the farm. Requiring only a family-sized unit to run, the farm may well have been able to deploy most of these outputs as sold surplus.

The family—possibly a veteran family—at Monte Forco lived in a world apart. The practicality of army veterans subsisting on their tiny seven-*iugera* plots, or Cincinnatus on his four, has attracted an understandable interest.[214] None of these efforts have integrated animals or the land required to feed them. The models run here, which include a short fallow, ley, high yields and maximum use of animals, suggest it could be done—barely. Only with relatively high yields (assisted by rotation, manure and ley) and no disasters could a tiny veteran establishment support a family of four on a seven-*iugera* plot. Putting land into ley rotation would have been a yearly sacrifice, for their holdings were so small that less than a hectare of land could be put into cereal production, while hay output could support perhaps only two head of cattle. The great temptation to sacrifice that ley, particularly in bad years, would have also meant sacrificing yields—and the cattle—in favor of immediate survival.[215] The only way out of this vicious circle was to obtain more land through purchase or lease. Through these grim numbers, one can see how the disappearance of the ancient public grazing lands (the *ager publicus*), combined with the breeding of larger, hungrier cattle, produced a perfect storm of problems for the smallest Italian farmers.[216]

Both Italian farm systems highlight the immense importance of ley strategies and animals, particularly to these smallest farmers. In any given year, roughly the same amount of land might be dedicated to hay as to wheat. That hay was the means by which farmers obtained their higher yields while maintaining cattle for plowing. For a small farm like Monte Forco using rotation strategies, estimated milk and meat production could constitute some 25 percent of human calories produced by the farm—the break-even amounts that could permit the subsistence of another person, the birth of another child. In fact, the animals and the rotation that supported them yielded around 10 percent greater productivity than models run without them, even with more land given over to fodder and less land to wheat.[217] Thus, while the temptation to sacrifice the hay must have been particularly great for the smallest smallholders, it was particularly critical to their survival.

The only positive light for the tiniest farms was the efficiency with which they could be run. A single healthy person could, in theory, do all the tasks required (except at harvest time).[218] Other family members would be free to take up seasonal wage labor opportunities at local potteries or at nearby farms and villas. In the disconnect between subsistence-level outputs and relatively high output/labor ratios lies the prospect, and for the smallest farmers the imperative, for the wage component of farmers' portfolios—opportunities we will examine in the next chapter.

Lots of Cattle, Limited Land: The Dilemma of the British and Gallic Farmer

The extraordinary excavations in Britain and the Dutch Rhineland villages make it possible to model in some detail the very different world of cattle, spelt and barley farming of the northwest provinces of the empire. Neither in Britain nor in the Rhineland is there any strong evidence for ley agricultural practices, but both places were thick with cattle. Sustaining those cattle on limited land was these farmers' principal challenge.

The second-century CE phase at Vicar's Farm near Cambridge (see figure 3.5) was characteristic of the surplus-producing farms of central Britain.[219] Like most farms in its region, the farm was geared heavily toward spelt production (with some barley) and toward cattle (with a significant number of horses). But it had to do all these things with limited amounts of land. The densely settled neighborhood with a farm every 300 meters, together with the size of its granary, suggest a maximum of about 23 hectares of land, around half of which would have been kept in permanent pasture, given the known surplus of cattle. This land scarcity makes the farm's likely surplus in cattle and spelt largely untenable at lower cereal yields: even with half the land in permanent unimproved pasture, 12 hectares couldn't sustain a surplus-producing herd (only 6–7 cattle), while the low-yielding arable land could only just support a family.[220] The high-quality hay grasses (clover, some vetches, Italian rye, medicks) found on the site point to more intensive practices—for fodder and perhaps for spelt—which the land limitations would have made not optional, but imperative. Higher yields for both cereals and pasture would not only have supported the likely population, but the higher output/labor ratios, as well as the huge amounts of unconsumed animal outputs, would have permitted a modest (12–13) cattle/horse herd for sale off the farm. Even with these higher yields, grain sales might have only run around 600 sestertii per year.

The farm family at The Grange, just 10 kilometers down the road from Vicar's Farm, experienced a completely different reality.[221] Despite its prime location off a Roman road, with its old-fashioned round houses, tiny finds assemblages, and no storage, The Grange epitomized a different world from the Vicar's Farm surplus-exporting systems. On the other hand, with evidence for fava and pea crops, the family here was probably rotating their spelt and emmer, and thus could have expected somewhat higher yields. Even so, the limited land available (perhaps only around three hectares given the two farms nearby) could have barely supported a family of four. The difference produced by ley agriculture versus simple rotation, however, is made plain by comparing this family with the veteran's family at Monte Forco. The Italian farm may have been subsisting on a bit more than half the land of the Grange farmers with the added labor burden of cultivating a small vineyard, but their ley system produced as much as five times the outputs per hectare and almost double the output-to-labor ratio. Neither family could have sold a surplus, but the ley system's greater overall productivity provided a greater caloric buffer against deprivation.

A Dutch Rhine Valley village of this period confronted many of the same challenges of land and yield. Some 25–35 people were thought to live in a village like Tiel-Passewaaij during its largest, early-second-century phase (see figure 3.10).[222] They grew a mixture of barley and emmer, raised cattle and horses, and are thought to have exported their surplus to nearby army garrisons.[223] Providing sufficient pasture would have been a challenge in this densely settled valley, which supported dozens of large villages. The actual archaeology—which includes some fava beans—gives some cause for more optimistic yields boosted by rotation strategies. Only with this more intensive system could the probable population have survived, producing both a robust cattle surplus and a modest grain surplus.

The challenges and opportunities presented by animals are obvious in all these models. In the land-limited conditions of most second-century neighborhoods, unimproved pasture made supporting the larger cattle herds described by the archaeological data difficult. When cattle were limited, manure became limited, and manure was doubly necessary to boost yields to survivable quantities. In the land-limited conditions at Vicar's Farm, for instance, only the model with improved pastures permits herd sizes sufficient for surplus and a (barely) adequate manure supply. Only by modestly improving both their grain and their pasture yields could these farmers have supported themselves, their larger cattle and larger herds, and shipped some excess off the farm.

Finally, the limitations of spelt versus free-threshing wheat are also evident in these models. After subtractions for dehulling, seed and losses, only about 35 percent of the spelt or barley crop remained for consumption in these northwestern farms, versus about 60 percent for the Italian, high-yield free-threshing wheat farms. Spelt thus required more land—land that British and Gallic farmers often didn't have.[224] The decision of the Île-de-France and Reims farmers to turn to free-threshing wheats becomes more obvious, and, in the case of the Reims hinterland with its poor soils but dense occupation, the risks were plainly worth it.

Soterichos and Kronion Go to Market: Egyptian Cash-Crops in a Land-Limited World

Lots of math has been aimed at Roman Egyptian farmers, but none of it includes all the variables we have at our disposal—wheat, pasture, vineyards and animals, and, on the minus side, taxes and rents.[225] Reconstructed here are two actual farming families' balance sheets, representing, as elsewhere, the range from the smallest leaseholder to a more prosperous family with a larger portfolio. The Soterichoses, whom we met at the beginning of this chapter, represent the smallest holders, while the Kronion family of Tebtunis represents the more prosperous middle.

Soterichos, his wife, Thaisas, and their four children lived in Theadelphia, where they owned a house but leased all their land.[226] The most they ever leased was a total of around three hectares in 94 and 95 CE: some two hectares of arable land that they had on a long-term lease, a half hectare of vineyard, and a sublease on some state pasture. These are the two years we model here. In 96 CE, Soterichos was forced to pay for grass his cows (and a neighbor's sheep) had devoured, from which we should assume he also had some cattle. Nine times Soterichos paid his rent in arrears, and after his death his family had substantial debts, which they took at least 12 years to repay.

The wildly divergent inputs and rents due in different crop cycles make it necessary to model not one, but two years. However we run these models, the upshot is grim and revealing. The very high, but very normal, rents that the Soterichoses paid for the majority of their leased land ate up huge amounts of their gross yield. At "average" Fayum wheat yields, they could only support one person if they drank their own wine and used all their hay to feed their cattle.[227]

Two overlapping strategies were necessary for the Soterichoses to survive on their small, high-rent plots. The first was to squeeze higher yields from more intensive cultivation. That they had the tools to do so is indicated by the lease itself, which requires them to weed and manure. The second was to sell their wine, not drink it, and to choose their children over their cows. Wine was worth more as cash than as calories, and selling the valuable fodder turned hay into bread. If the hay or wine prices dropped, which they often did, or if the Nile flood failed, they would have had to borrow to survive. The end-of-life debts Soterichos incurred suggest that this happened more than once. Even this scenario doesn't entirely work: the Soterichoses still didn't have quite enough land or money to keep two cattle. Thus, common pasture (which we have no evidence they used), marshland, or "borrowing" the neighbors' pasture grass—their eventual solution—would be key. Soterichos' later loans, his late rent and the fines for cattle grazing are all by-products of too little land, with too high rent, to support a greater-than-average-sized Egyptian family.[228]

If Soterichos epitomized a "modest" leaseholder, the Kronions have been viewed as the typical "prosperous" family, with a larger portfolio of owned and leased land.[229] Over the nearly fifty years we can follow their activities, they owned land, rented land, and used both leased and rented land to back loans.

For the two years of 135 and 136 CE, the family consisted of around eleven persons, including the father, Kronion, his wife, Thenapynchis, two daughters and three sons, plus three grandchildren. This extended family collectively managed three chunks of land, one owned and two leased, planted with wheat and barley in rotation with fodder crops plus pasture. Overall, they had a total of around 17 hectares in cultivation—about the same as the prosperous Tuscan farmers we examined above. The family is not known to have had any vineyards or animals (excepting one donkey who was later lost on a trip to the city).

The Kronion family obviously had more assets than the Soterichoses, but their many outlays for rent and tax also made serious inroads on their surpluses. While they produced enough wheat to feed their eleven family members, the rotation of all that land meant that their real surplus was in hay or fodder crops (worth c. 1,500 drachmas per year at average prices). The family would have used it in part to even out uneven tax/rent obligations, particularly in the second year of the model (136 CE). The seemingly low tax burden (less than a tenth of outputs) on their privately owned land concealed some higher-taxed land among their holdings. More importantly, if they rotated this land, the taxes in wheat would have been due each year—even if those holdings weren't producing wheat. The flexible terms of leased land, where cash rents were due in fodder years and wheat rents in wheat years, didn't accrue to their owned land with its yearly tax burden, and a whopping 100 percent of their wheat crop in year two would have been eaten up with taxes and rents in kind. The rents this family paid were much lower than Soterichos' but, assuming locally average yields, the rent and tax consumed over a third of their total outputs.

Where did all this leave Fayum farmers? Yet again, the very small size of holdings and modest wheat yields seem to have limited farmers' ability to accumulate surplus. The pressure to increase yields by intensive cultivation must have been great. All these difficulties are exacerbated by the huge burden presented by tax and rent. Rent and taxes together were 50–66 percent for leaseholders like Soterichos but averaged 35 percent even for the Kronions, the result of the portfolio quality of holdings—private land taxed at low rates, public land leased at medium rates and private land leased at high rates. It's clear that earlier estimates imagining a simple tax rate of one artaba per aroura everywhere seriously underestimates combined tax/rent drain on even a "prosperous" family like the Kronions.

Most interesting, however, is the role played by the cash market in fodder and hay. It may only have been through selling hay and fodder that all those farmers who were rotating—by which we assume most farmers—could make ends meet. Indeed, depending on current prices, having hay to sell was critical, and abandoning the rotation meant abandoning critical cash resources. In these models, hay or fodder essentially subsidizes the high rents and the taxes.[230] The fact that leases required cash rent both for fodder-rotation years and for pastureland indicates that fodder was imagined as being sold for cash. How much cash—and how critical it was for small and medium holders—is suggested through these models. Finally, the years of debt owed by farmers like Soterichos, which we'll take up further in chapter 6, takes on new importance in light of these calculations.[231] Years with tax owed in wheat but output in fodder, or vice versa, made deficits in one or the other inevitable, even in years of relative plenty. So, too, did the huge annual variation in tax/rent burden (from 15 to 55 percent of gross), as seen in even two years of the Kronion accounts. In short, while the extractive forces of landlord and state may have reduced many Egyptian farmers to a net "subsistence," it may have been markets—in produce and in credit—that enabled them to survive.

It's only in Egypt that we can observe this ruinous impact of modest taxes and high rent: What about our western farmers? We've included a notional land tax of 10 percent for our British/Dutch smallholders, which is frankly a guess.[232] We have no idea of the level of land rents in these provinces or in Italy: if they were as high as the Egyptian rents (unlikely, although possible in Italy), the surpluses we've observed in medium-sized farms in the northwest provinces would have been seriously eroded. Where the Egyptian evidence is blind, however, are all the things we can see in the archaeology-rich West: the positive impact of animals for extra calories, the contents of gardens—all the things that don't get recorded in leases and tax receipts. In other words, for the smallest Egyptian holders like the Soterichoses, it's the things we can't see that may have made the difference.

A Final Harvest

This chapter began by suggesting that the "subsistence peasant" was a poor way to characterize how farmers got by under the Roman empire. It has suggested instead that a majority of smallholders sold crops off the farm on some kind of market—rural, urban or military. The quantified models based on all this new data also suggest that "subsistence" and "surplus" are only the crudest descriptors for how these farmers survived. Multiple parcels of land, often rotated along different rhythms; animals integrated at every turn; consuming some of the land's products and selling the rest, sometimes for critical cash resources required to buy food—these were the categories of practice that lay beyond the analytical categories of "subsistence" and "surplus."

The new evidence thus challenges our notion of so-called peasant agriculture. There was no such thing as peasant agriculture—just Roman agriculture practiced at a variety of scales. A mix of grains and animals in Italy; a specialized, regional division of wheats and cattle or sheep in Gaul; a massive specialization in cattle and spelt in Britain: smallholders participated in and produced regional trends. They didn't occupy a special agricultural sector.

Understanding these different agricultural systems has important implications for our understanding of agricultural yields. In many of the land-limited, high-rent landscapes we've examined, low yields were not an option. These farmers, the new archaeology reveals, had the knowledge to improve their yields—rotation, manuring, weeding, drainage. The output models included here also suggest that higher yields were not necessarily a sign of prosperity but born of need. And it's not just yields for cereals; fodder yields must also have been at the higher end of our assumptions to feed the larger, more numerous animals that all farmers managed. Low yields are an assumption for a different kind of world, where lots of land, modest rents and no seductive consumer goods might permit a kind of "just-enough-ism."[233] This was not that world.

The locus and direction of that surplus production also challenges our notion of market activity. Smallholders often specialized—in sheep or cattle, in free-threshing wheat or barley, in grapes—but at smallish scales. They engaged with distant markets, but their most important markets were probably their neighbors or neighboring towns. Their millions of market activities were rooted in an emphatic local, a local populated by dense neighborhoods of farms and connected by thick networks of minor roads and tracks. The Egyptian farmers like Soterichos who were growing fodder, which they turned around and sold for cash to buy food—the market economy of those transactions took place in the first instance between farmers, or between farmers and local estates. In the second instance, the connective tissues of villages and roadside settlements served as the anchoring points that moved products around these neighborhoods and also out to the wider world. In short, the new evidence ought to put to rest the notion of the Roman city as the sole nexus and destination of market exchange. Exchange, it's now clear, was everywhere.

The major outstanding question about smallholder production remains not whether they produced surplus—most clearly did—but rather, were they able to benefit from it? The models reveal that the grinding loss of surplus was not so much due to tax—normally imagined as the Grim Reaper of smallholder yields—but rent. If rents were as high as they were in Egypt, tenants would have required far more land than someone like Soterichos commanded; they would have had to float constant loans as he did; and they would have had, as he clearly did, an even stronger incentive to convert nonedibles (in his case, hay and thyme, as well as wine) into edibles to avoid starvation. If rents were as high and yields as mediocre as have been assumed, the smallest holders who only rented land had little hope of accumulating sufficient reserves to purchase land. They would have had no choice but to rent yet more land, using their one reserve—their own family labor—to increase their outputs. The knock-on effects of this cleft stick—a much-increased labor regime for everyone but particularly for tenants, the sometimes-necessity for extra wage labor to complement income, and the use of large amounts of credit for everyone but particularly farmers—these are the subjects of the following chapters.

4
Eight Jobs

> Since you have held eight jobs all that is left for you is to hold sixteen: you have worked as an innkeeper, you have worked as a clay man, you have worked as a pickler, you have worked as a baker. You have been a farmer. You have made bronze trinkets. You have been a huckster and now you are a jug-dealer. If you lick cunt, you will have done everything.[1]

The man who was the subject of this Pompeii graffito did many things to get by. While farming may have been the work of most Romans, it was by no means the only work. The explosion of cities and consumer goods meant lots of other kinds of jobs to be done. Those jobs appear under increasingly specialized terms—from pickling to jug-dealing to sexual services of a particular kind. Much of that work—like farming or baking—meant producing a product and selling it. Much of that work, too—like farming or baking or clay-hauling or jug-dealing—might also mean working for someone else, for wages.

Making a living with wages is the first subject of this chapter. It was, as we'll see, one of the most difficult ways of getting by in the Roman world. Some of the poorest people we'll meet in this book survived on wages. But wage earning, as we'll also see, almost always involved doing something else as well—farming, jug-making, innkeeping—and above all, putting the entire family to work. Working for wages throws into high relief one of the central practices of the 90 percent: hustling.

For hustling is the real subject of this chapter: using lots of income streams to make a living. The evidence from Egypt—the only place where we can see wage earning in its full complexity—reveals that those who worked for wages only rarely made a living on them. That is, inside the category of analysis par excellence—"wage labor"—lay the urgent necessity for multiple jobs performed by multiple family members. A great many different kinds of people in the Roman world lived *with* wages, but only the poorest, and some of the more fortunate, actually lived *on* them.

Thus, while we begin with wages as the place where hustling appears as a necessity, we will end with farmers making pots, ironworkers raising cattle, and a family that sold vegetables and pickled fish while prostituting their daughters. It was this normal practice of multitasking that lay behind the specialized job titles and professions of the Roman world. And even as high consumption, low wages, and taxation forced hustling on a working population, it was markets and the spread of money that made hustling possible.

"Wage Labor" Versus Earning Wages

Wage labor seems a self-evident activity, not least to modern academics who make a living from wages. Cicero & Co. appear to confirm the existence of such a category, if only to disparage it. The wage laborer—the *mercennarius* or *misthios*—appears in elite sources as the embodiment of dependence. Cicero was particularly harsh: "the wages of the laborer are the badges of slavery," "no workshop can have anything noble about it" and other jeers appear in his great work on duties.[2] By duties, of course, Cicero meant duties to the state. Cicero (and Seneca and Lucian) harp on the wage laborer not because they were particularly interested in the lives of wage workers. Rather, the wage laborer permitted them to make an important philosophical comment on means and ends. Wages as money intervened between work and its end product and, in so doing, introduced a form of monetary dependence between earner and employer. No longer did work produce a thing: it produced a wage that needed, necessarily, to come from the employer. To the ancient elite mind, all forms of dependence conjured up a language of enslavement: women's dependence on men, children's on their parents, slaves on their masters—all of these dependencies had a family resemblance.[3] The elite mind, then, found the wage worker good to think with.

Cicero & Co. worried about the wage laborer, too, because of what appears to be a genuine increase in the number of wage earners under the empire.[4] The expansion of cities with their new buildings and service apparatus meant a whole array of new jobs to be done—from brick-makers and builders to bath attendants and latrine cleaners. The surging demand for consumer goods—consumer goods that, as we've seen, were increasingly standardized and mass-produced—also produced a demand for specialized work, from clay-hauling to wagon-building to bronze trinket–making to pearl-setting. That specialization also introduced vast numbers of middlemen who further separated the producers of things from their ultimate users—wool dealers, grape dealers, and shopkeepers of every description.[5] The expansion of people who earned money through these channels worried political philosophers like Cicero who were themselves concerned with what they regarded as an increasingly "servile" population.

It's not surprising then that, following Cicero & Co., scholars have seen in the Roman wage laborer a person that Karl Marx would have recognized: a person whose labor was separated from its product, leaving labor itself as their only commodity.[6] Indeed, the evident response of Roman wages to market forces and the increasingly specialized nature of their work—all that pickling and jug-making—would seem to describe the commodification of labor as part and parcel of the Roman economic system.[7]

The capital city of Rome, with its thousands of builders, latrine-cleaners, water-haulers and jug-makers, would seem to be the obvious place to observe the wage earner who so worried Cicero & Co. Alas, not one reliable wage price is known from Rome, and only a couple from the whole of the Roman West.[8] The only place we can really see wages in action is Egypt. Account books, contracts, and pay receipts from Roman Egypt have yielded abundant evidence of folks working for wages, in all sectors of work—agriculture, craft, quarrying, even wet nursing. These sources have long been mined for their cash wage prices.[9] Scholars have organized those prices to produce so-called wage series and "real wages." Wage series are chronologically ordered cash wage prices that reveal changes in wages over time.[10] Real wages, on the other hand, are an expression of what a worker could buy with a wage, calculated by dividing wages by the cost of living. Normalized for what a given wage could buy at the time it was earned, "real wages" are theoretically comparable across time and space, making it possible to compare, say, Roman wages with those in India under the Raj.[11]

And yet, Roman wage series and real wages are less than truly "real."[12] Ripped from their complex contexts, the cash prices of wages are often only half the story.[13] For instance, food was a common part of ancient (and medieval and early modern) wages and is often left out of wage series. A graffito from outside Pompeii—one of the only preserved wage prices from Italy, incidentally—advertises work at the wage of "one denarius and bread."[14] Tax payments on behalf of the employee became part of Egyptian monthly wages. And while the cash part of Roman wages shows fairly clear signs of being driven by supply and demand, the noncash portion appears to have been shaped by tradition, the status of the worker, and, in the case of tax payments, the worker's ability to negotiate. Total wages as experienced by the worker were often more complicated than wage series have allowed.

As any day-laborer knows, wages don't only equal how much you are paid, but how many days you can find work. For the distant (and even not-so-distant) past, we don't know how many days per year workers normally worked.[15] If you want to compare wages across time, this is an important variable, and scholars have been forced to make assumptions. A historical constant of 250 days per year crept its way into many such calculations. Like calorie constants for subsistence, the work-year constant has likewise proved to be mostly wrong when confronted with actual evidence. This chapter will try to unearth some information on the Roman-period "work year," peering past the constants to the realities of how much work was actually available.

At least half the readers of this book will also object to another aspect of wage series and real-wage calculations—their stress on the male wage earner. A relic of both a (still) patriarchal discipline and a (vanishing) postwar world where a male wage earner could actually support a family, earlier wage series were based on male wages only. How the rest of the population—women, children, non-wage-earning men—got by was simply left out. Only recently have new wage series for medieval and early modern Europe included the income contributions of women and children in their models. Their findings are critical, even for this study: from the medieval period through the eighteenth century and beyond, single male wage earners could not support families, even in so-called high performing economies like England.[16] In most times and places, women's and children's contributions were critical parts of family income, in some moments even surpassing male wages. As will be argued here, the same was true in the Roman world. The massive expansion of the textile industry, driven by the gusto for clothes that we saw in chapter 2, meant that women's spinning work probably constituted a major income source for the poorest families.

Economic history's fascination with numbers has also meant that activities that can't be quantified get short shrift. Women's and children's wages fall into this category, but just as important are nonwage sources of income—farming, garden plots, and selling all manner of things from street food to jugs. While historians have long insisted that income from, say, a single cow's milk, a small flock of sheep, or selling extra beer constituted as important an income source as wages, economists often leave these things out, in large part because they are devilishly hard to quantify. As we shall see, we cannot afford to ignore these inputs in the Roman world. They constitute the core of the multiple incomes that lurked behind the too-low male wages.

Despite all their problems, real-wage measurements are enormously important. In laying income against potential expenses, real wages open the door to workers' experience. Diving beneath the employer's perspective to understand what the Roman 90 percent could actually do—and not do—with their wages is the job of this chapter. In doing so, we'll find that "wage worker" and "wage labor" did not mean quite what we—or Cicero & Co.—have implied. Most unskilled wages could not support a single male wage earner. And almost all unskilled wages, and even some skilled ones, were insufficient to support a family, especially the bigger, more complex Roman families. Most Roman wage earners were thus doing multiple things to earn income: eating their farm produce, selling their farm produce or selling their crafts, above all their textile work. Families, particularly landless families, relied heavily on the break-even contributions of women's and children's labor. "Wage labor" as experienced by the laborers themselves breaks down in the face of their many income streams, of which their wage was only a part. Instead of a wage-labor economy, we'll find instead a hustle economy.

The term "hustle" probably demands some explanation. Like many of the other terms in this book, it's a flawed best of worse options. "Makeshifting"—used by historians in other periods—or "informal economy"—the term preferred by economists—both refer to multiple jobs producing multiple income streams.[17] But both assume an outside-the-normal state: makeshifting is a temporary stopgap for an otherwise single "job," while the "informal economy" is the opposite of a "genuine" formal economy. These won't do: the phenomenon we'll unearth here was neither temporary nor abnormal. As this chapter shows, it was the living-wage-producing job that was the aberration. "Hustle" may seem too contemporary: in fact, multiple jobs held by poor and working people is one of the characteristics of our own age, a practice that unites Uber drivers and Nairobi trash recyclers.[18] Contemporary the term may be, but as we'll see, the practices it describes are not. Hustle emphasizes an everyday habit of practice, not limited to wages but including any and all other forms of income—making things and selling them, growing things and selling them, and working several wage jobs simultaneously. Its slightly roguish antecedents avoid romanticizing the lives of those who lived with constant precarity, while at the same time emphasizing their vigor and grit.[19]

A Roman Wage Primer

Whatever its apparent similarities with our own world, Roman wage earning was definitely not ours, and it's worth taking a moment to review some basics, using the one place we can see it clearly—Egypt. The Egyptian papyri preserve not only the most numerous wage records, but also a whole range of job contracts and thus different wage arrangements.[20] Those same sources also include detailed information on the costs of living against which wages must be measured.

As is true of most historical periods, the majority of preserved Roman wage records come from agriculture.[21] Roman Egyptian wages therefore reflect the particular rhythms in a world shaped by the Nile. The different jobs of each season—pumping floodwater onto parched fields in June through September; manuring, plowing and planting as the floods receded in October through December; the harvest from March through June—all had a wage-earning component. Wages could be earned driving oxen for the *saqiya* (water lift), repairing the dikes, spreading manure, harvesting grapes and wheat, even guarding crops from theft. Rural jobs could also be had for carpenters fixing the water wheels, masons building olive presses, even shipwrights building small Nile boats. Outside this world of agricultural wage earning were the wages paid by the state—army account books describe army pay, and pay receipts the remuneration for work in the imperial granite quarries in the Eastern Desert. Sadly, even in Egypt, we have much less information on wages earned in cities and for artisanal work: such sources mostly date to the later Roman empire, in post-inflation currency, and thus after our story ends. The exceptions are apprentice contracts, mostly for placing older children with weavers, and wages paid to wet nurses. Nonetheless, we will encounter people making wages at every job imaginable—from picking up leaves to garlanding statues of the emperor to guarding grain transports as they rumbled from farm to city.[22] Wage-earning work was to be found everywhere there was work, with one possible exception: domestic work remained overwhelmingly the job of slaves. Unlike early modern Europe, where "going into service" allowed women and girls to earn wages, in Roman Egypt women and children appear to have traded domestic service for remission of debt, and we lack any real records for regular wage-paying domestic servants.

While most Roman wages were paid in money, food was also part of wages. Food was not awarded to everyone. Folks paid by the month; those working intensive jobs, like harvesting; those whose workplace made it hard to organize meals—all these tended to include food as part of their pay. Unlike in the Middle Ages or early modern Europe, where full board was often included, in the Roman world food wages mostly meant wheat. Indeed, the "tyranny of cereals" in ancient economic history we noted in chapter 2 is due in part to wheat's frequent appearance in wage packages. One artaba of wheat per month—29.5 kilos and around 3,400 calories per day—was the standard food portion of a male working wage, and is found for soldiers, quarrymen, and monthly workers on larger estates. Women, in the rare instances they received monthly wages, received somewhat less wheat.[23] Workers on shorter-term work—like carpenters working for a week or harvesters for the length of the harvest—might get bread instead of wheat. In addition to wheat or bread, wine and oil might also be included. Finally, the very bottom of the wage-earning spectrum—apprentices, slaves and debt workers—also received clothing as part of their wages. As we've seen in chapter 2, those clothing wages typically consisted of a single tunic per year. Clothing as part of wage thus tends to be a sign not of a generous wage, but its opposite—subsistence and limited freedom.[24]

Egyptian households were composed in particular ways, ways that impacted wage-earning capacities. Most families, particularly in the countryside, were what today we might term "blended," with some combination of older parents, brothers and their wives, plus children, all living together.[25] Those combinations could include everything from all-female families of mothers and aunts to families with only one parent. Average family size ran to around 4.1 persons in the cities and 4.5 in the country, an average bracketed by solitary widows at one extreme, to families like Kronion's, with their 11 people of different ages, at the other. Average *household* (versus family) size was larger—5.3 in cities and 4.8 in the countryside, a result of lodgers and other nonfamily members living under the same roof. Those households might include a domestic slave, but in general there were fewer enslaved people working in Egypt than in other provinces. Census figures, the only ones in the empire that count slaves, suggest only around 11 percent of the population were enslaved, with a modest proportion working in agriculture and the rest concentrated in urban domestic service.[26] In agricultural and mining jobs, we shall meet people—termed *paidaria, oiketai, familiares*—whose labels should describe enslaved workers, but who engage in activities theoretically off-limits to slaves: marrying, paying their own taxes, and earning wages paid to themselves rather than an owner. The difficulty in identifying these individuals as enslaved or free, and their place in the wage-and-hustle economy, forms an important part of our story.

As we saw in the previous chapter, the hand of the state lay heavy on Egypt, and taxes and mandatory labor (called liturgies) were as regular a part of its rhythm as the Nile flood. A variety of taxes were an essential line item on all working people's budgets and an important portion of the costs of subsistence.[27] But the state could also be a source of jobs: by the third century, villages and large estates were tasked with supplying guards for dikes or grain shipments, and they often found it easier to pay a few people to carry out these tasks than to rotate them evenly through the populace.[28] Thus, the hand that took away might also occasionally give back. But as we've already seen, this was no command economy, and a dense web of market exchange connected city and country, a web in which the state played an important, but by no means exclusive, role.

It was a market economy, however, which, particularly in the countryside, ran not only on coin money, but also on account money.[29] So heavily monetized was the Egyptian economic universe, with millions of tiny transactions taking place each day, that people may have found it easier to do without cash money. As we'll see in more detail in chapter 5, many transactions took place in scrip—account money—and everyone from village merchants to the large estates to the village granary (which functioned as a kind of bank) often used the account book, rather than coins, to register monies due and monies paid, including wages earned. It is in part this scrip system that preserves the evidence for wages, and for the hustling that went on around them.

Wages were not static, in Egypt or anywhere else, although they do appear to be mostly stable for long periods of time.[30] Bigger wage changes were almost certainly due to currency adjustments, inflation, plague (fewer workers, higher wages), or all three.[31] We've already noted the slow increase in the price of many goods from the first through the mid-second century CE. Then two inflationary moments—a minor one in the 160s CE and a more major one after 274 CE—produced further jumps in prices. These changes resulted in both cost-of-living increases and wage increases. Wages of the later second and third centuries are 50 percent to 100 percent higher than those prior to the 160s.[32] In the early modern world, cost-of-living increases caused by inflation or crop failure were often compensated with extra food wages; in the Roman world, tax payments on behalf of some employees may have served the same function. To what extent these increases kept pace with rising living costs has been hotly debated.[33] Theoretically they probably did keep up, but the question is somewhat mooted by the fact that it had always been nearly impossible to live on these wages in the first place.

A View from the Accountant's Office

As any small business owner will know, payroll accounting varies from business to business—and Roman payrolls have some peculiarities of their own. It's necessary to descend, for a moment, into the accountant's office and have a glimpse of some payroll accounts in action. As we noted, most work for wages in Egypt was agricultural, and farm payrolls are thus our best source. Some of these farm accounts come from medium-sized farms like the farm of Epimachus, with which we began this book. Epimachus owned some 14 hectares of scattered plots in the area around Hermopolis in the Nile Valley. His accounts that survive cover some nine months between 78 and 79 CE.[34] His are among the most granular daily wage records from the Roman world. The other estates for which we have good records were considerably larger. The descendants of a man called Patron farmed as much as 140 hectares around the village of Tebtunis in the Fayum for at least two or three generations in the 130s–150s CE, while the third-century estate owned by one Appianus included some 110 hectares of large and small parcels around the Fayum villages of Theadelphia and Euhemeria.[35] All these landowners farmed their lands with a combination of tenants, wage workers, and some enslaved labor. We shall get to know these farms and their workers well in the following pages.

As we saw in chapter 1, Epimachus employed a slave, one Didymus, to keep his farm accounts, although he was forced to keep the books himself for a few months while Didymus was sick. Most work on Epimachus' farm was done by daily wage workers, and wage work was a significant part of the later, larger estates' labor force as well.[36] Didymus' account books, organized by day, typically record the task, the number of workers employed, their rate of pay and the total pay given out. Daily wage workers, unless they were skilled, were usually listed as "workmen" (*ergatai*) or "boys" (*paides*): in other words, they were anonymous and mostly males.[37] Two days in September from the account provide a useful glimpse:

September 2

2 men digging manure by the house and loading it on 3 asses of Paos, son of Heracles at 2 obols each. 1 drachma

2 boys driving asses. 2 and a half obols each. 5 obols
Hire of manure carts from Paos, ass driver, as Epimachus ordered. 2 obols
Ambryon, Horus and Epimachus [slave of this name] working the pump on the farm
To Demetrios, son of Pachrates, as wage of a *saqiyah* (pump) man at 3 obols

September 3

2 workers digging manure by the house and loading on 3 asses of Paos, the ass driver, 3 and half obols each. 1 drachma 1 obol.
2 boys driving the asses, 2 and a half obols each. 5 obols.
2 workers carrying clay to the embankment of the two-aroura lot of Indius, 2 and a half obols each. 5 obols.
6 workers digging rushes with mattocks in the 10-aroura lot of Indius and carrying them to the two-aroura lot on the east side as protection against the water. 3 obols each. 3 drachmas.
Ambryon, Horus, Epimachus, and Phibis working the pumps.[38]

Through these accounts we catch a glimpse of the different sorts of people doing the work. Epimachus' accounts, one of the few with named slaves—Ambryon, Horus, Epimachus and Phibis—find them working side by side with the workers, boys and, on occasion, tenant farmers.[39] Boys form a regular part of the workforce here and on other estates, usually paid two-thirds or somewhat more of the adult-worker wage. On the Patron estate, one can sometimes also see a single worker paid an obol more than the others: these may be foremen.[40]

The wages on Epimachus' estate were low. The anonymous workers earned on average only about 3.5 obols per day—enough to pay for a loaf or two of bread. Boys earned a consistent 2.5 obols per day. The accounts for the Patron lands in the 130s through 150s CE generally show higher wages—around a drachma per day—but with enormous variation around that average.[41] On the large estate of Appianus, a century later in the 230s through 250s, daily wages had increased again to a common wage of two drachmas two obols per day.[42] Skilled artisans on both farms earned double these normal wages: masons on the Patron lands earned two drachmas per day, while four drachmas is a consistent wage for carpenters on the Appianus estate.[43]

Above all, though, it is the considerable variation in the number of people working that shines through these accounts. In Epimachus' accounts cited above, on September 2 two men were hired for day labor, while the next day

12 were hired. In May, during the harvest, wage-earning spots varied between two and 20 per day. There are some indications that the more people who turned up to work, the lower their wages. One can see it even in the single day of September wages cited above—the two workers hauling clay made more than the six workers cutting rushes—even on the same plot.[44] All this points to considerable variation in not just the demand for work—for the tasks are usually the same and continue for many days—but also the supply.[45] The variation in both the number of people working and their wages suggests a highly variable pool of workers: some days, lots of people showed up to work; on other days, far fewer.

This shifting supply may be one reason that larger employers opted to bolster their erratic gangs of daily workers with smaller groups of workers paid by the month.[46] But these monthly workers, with some exceptions, were mostly not paid at the daily wage rate times 28 or 30 days. They were mostly paid considerably less, plus some food. On the Patron estate they might be paid simply an artaba of wheat per month (worth around 10 drachmas), or anywhere from four to 24 drachmas in cash. The average monthly wage was 13 drachmas total compensation, whereas a month of daily wage work would have been worth more than twice that.[47] A more complex system was found on the Appianus estate. Some monthly workers, termed *oiketai* (literally, "those of the household"), made a consistent four drachmas plus an artaba of wheat per month. Others, termed *metrematiaioi* ("ration-earners"), had various cash arrangements, ranging from eight to 60 drachmas per month, including or excluding taxes, plus an artaba of wheat and, in some instances, oil.[48] Some jobs done by these monthly workers appear somewhat more specialized than the manure-hauling and reed-cutting carried out by the daily workers, but theirs are by no means skilled jobs. Ox or ass drivers, gardeners, vineyard workers—some monthly wage workers appear to be drawn from the upper end of the unskilled workers.[49] But others—the *oiketai,* for instance, or those working full-time guarding or pumping—are as unskilled as those making daily wages: they differ only in their wage arrangements. Really skilled folks, like carpenters, never get monthly wages, but work either by the day or the piece.

How much does this complex picture of wage earning extend beyond Egypt? Certain aspects of it—the reliance on huge amounts of fluctuating daily wage labor for agriculture, for instance—were probably more prominent in Egypt but also true elsewhere. In the Roman West, the Latin term for wage-laborer—*mercennarius*—appears almost exclusively in contexts associated with farm workers.[50] The relatively low daily wages, however, may be peculiarly Egyptian.[51] Amazingly, we have only three pieces of private-sector wage evidence from the Roman West, and these point to something higher: three or four sestertii (the equivalent of 3–4 Egyptian drachmas) per day, perhaps with bread, in the first century CE. If these were average urban wages, they are perhaps four times what their comrades on Egyptian farms were making.[52] But this is hardly compelling evidence, and in any case, as the breadbasket of the Roman world, Egypt boasted lower food costs than those in central Italy, as we noted in chapter 2.[53] In short, we cannot know how many of the quantitative aspects of the story we're about to tell accrue to the empire as a whole. Traces of its qualitative aspects—in particular, the use of wages as part of a portfolio of hustled income—can be found throughout the empire.

Not Getting By on Wages

How much could Roman Egyptians earn from wages, versus the cost of living? A reckoning with so-called real wages is in order. As will become apparent below, this is an exercise that ultimately reveals its own limitations. But in the process, it will tell us something important about the nature of Roman wage earning. Most of our data speaks to male wages, so we'll begin there.

Previous male real wages for Roman Egypt have been calculated according to the methods used for other historical periods: multiplying an average daily male cash wage by a historical constant for days worked per year (250 days), divided by some estimate of the cost of living.[54] We've already noted the problems with this method above: in particular, the cost of living and days of work.[55]

Here we'll use two sets of monthly cost-of-living estimates, representing both low and sustainable numbers of calories.[56] Even though we argued in chapter 2 that Romans—including rural Egyptians—consumed more calories than previous scholarship had assumed, we also noted that our evidence privileged the middling echelons of that group. For those attempting to live on wages, the spectrum of true neediness is important to capture. Thus, our low-end cost-of-living reconstructions represent survival on a low (1,900) calorie diet, an impracticably tiny amount for housing, clothing, plus basic required taxes. A second, sustainable, but still very basic reconstruction is based on those actual rations given to Egyptian quarry workers, which includes sustainable calories (c. 3,800)[57] for hard work. Taxes are rarely included in real-wage calculations, but, as we noted, they formed an essential and not-insignificant expense in the Roman world.[58] For families, we have assumed something like the "average" Egyptian family of four persons described above—two adults (one male, one female) and two children—with the understanding that this may be impracticably small, and leaves out the myriad of other gender/age configurations that routinely constituted Egyptian families.[59] We'll consider the earnings of these other family members presently.

The ratio between wages earned and costs of living is the so-called real wage or, in the case of total income, "real income." This ratio will be useful in evaluating the life-sustaining—or not—qualities of different kinds of income. When real income equals 1 in these calculations, subsistence—at low or sustainable calories—has been achieved. When real income is less than 1, families or individuals have failed to earn enough to survive, while at more than 1 they have more robust resources or perhaps even savings.

On the vexed question of how many days workers actually worked, we actually have some indications from the account books, but they need unpacking. Accounts like those Didymus kept for Epimachus list X numbers of anonymous individuals earning Y daily wage. Simply multiplying the average wage by 28 or 30 days, or the 250-day/year constant, fails to account for the potentially limited quantity of wage-paying jobs on offer. But some of the account books that include a full month or more of detailed wage data allow us to do somewhat better.[60] Using them, we can produce a best-case scenario for the labor pool of any given month by assuming the numbers who worked were the total supply of workers—an imaginary village at full employment.[61] Understanding take-home pay for monthly workers is infinitely easier: workers' monthly total wage packages (including food) can be divided by our range of subsistence costs—individual or family—to produce a real income estimate.[62]

Examining wages paid in two of the farms mentioned above—Epimachus' and Patron's—provides a sense of what living with daily wages meant in the Egyptian countryside over two centuries of Roman rule. And it mostly meant the same thing: very few people could survive exclusively on daily wage work. In all instances, the rare worker who could find daily wage work 28 days of the month could support himself with sustainable calories and pay both minimal rent and his taxes (figure 4.1). But in every instance, the pool of workers could not (figure 4.2).

Too many workers, too few opportunities, and too low a wage meant that for all the account books where we can track wages over a month or more, most farms did not offer sufficient work for the available casual workers to get by, even under absurdly optimistic employment levels. And while the lucky individual worker with full employment might be able to support himself,

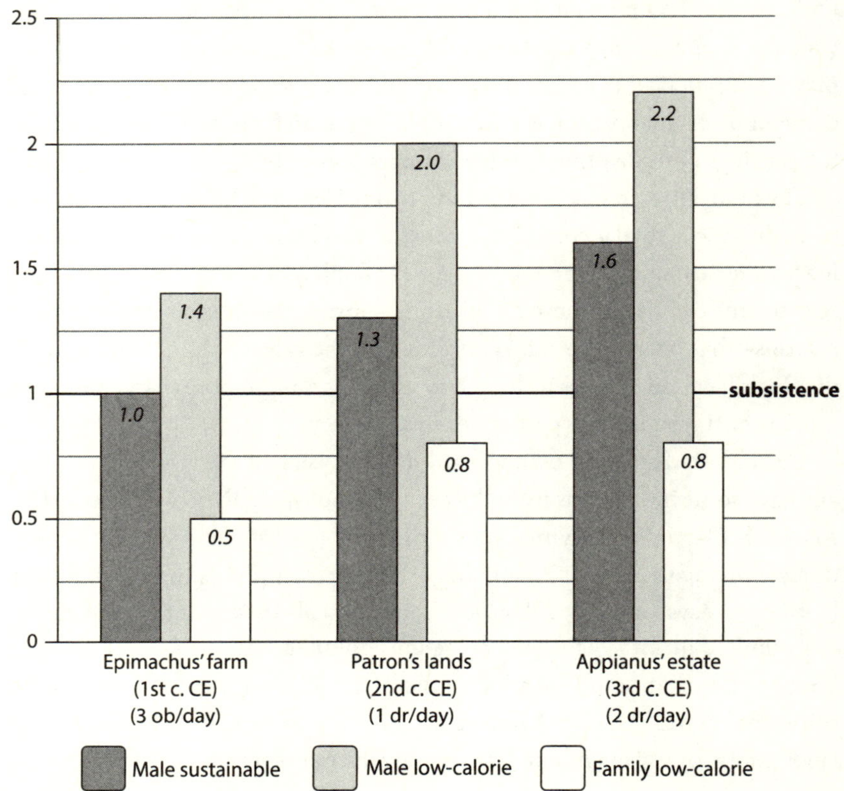

FIGURE 4.1. Hypothetically getting by on full-time labor: male real wages for full-time (28 days) work (Data: *P. Lond.* 131r.; Foraboschi 1991, 28–33; Rathbone 1991, 135–39)

even those wages were nowhere near enough to support the average-sized Egyptian family.

While some monthly wage earners on Egyptian farms apvpear to earn an amount equal to the daily wage multiplied by a full month, on average, monthly wages were considerably lower, even including their food portion (figure 4.3).[63]

Most monthly workers could support themselves on a low-calorie existence; none could survive in a sustainable manner, and none could support a family. Indeed, for most monthly wage workers, their wage—in cash, food, or both—offered a worse living than the lucky (if rare) wage-earning laborer working 28 days per month.[64] On the Appianus estate, the *oiketai* could only have supported a reduced calorie existence at their wages of four drachmas plus

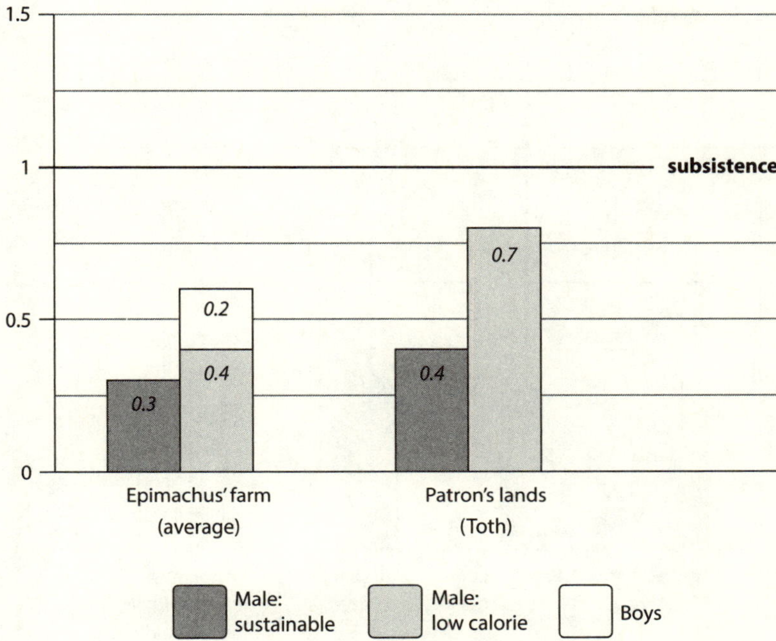

FIGURE 4.2. Not getting by on available labor: ratio of labor pool person/days versus subsistence requirements (Data: *P. Lond.* 131r.; *P. Mil. Vogl.* 302)

one artaba of wheat, but only assuming they were provided free housing.[65] The better-paid *metrematiaioi* suffered more or less the same fate, even with their higher cash wages and their taxes paid: a low-calorie existence was possible, but a more sustainable existence was not. And again, none of these monthly workers could support a family on a single male monthly wage.[66]

In other words, most of the wages in these accounts are quantitatively unable to support the populations—particularly the family units—known to be working for them. This finding is not new to the history of wages. In most of the wage series from the medieval and early modern worlds, prior to the eighteenth century and even much later, most families couldn't survive on single male wages. In many places and times, male wage earners couldn't even support themselves.[67] If the revised male "real wages" presented here are any indication, then Roman real wages were particularly low by historical standards.[68] More to the point, two-thirds or more of the Roman population—women and children—could not be supported by them, even at low-calorie levels.

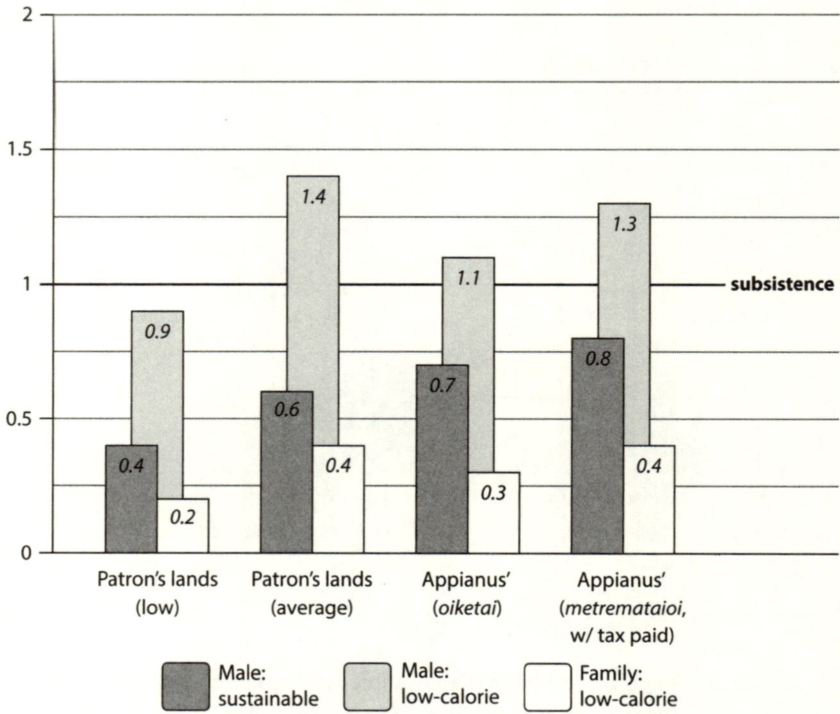

FIGURE 4.3. Not getting by the month: real wages (cash and food), monthly workers (Data: Patron: Foraboschi 1991, 28–33; Appianus: Rathbone 1991, 107–8; table 10)

Hustling with Wages

The unsustainable levels of Roman unskilled wages haven't escaped scholars' notice.[69] But since scholars have been mostly interested in wage formation, rather than the experience of wages, they haven't explored the implications. The first, most obvious implication is that some of these workers were not getting by at all, but were living in a state of malnutrition, homelessness, tax evasion, or all three. Those who were forced to live only on the wages and insufficient workdays produced by the estates or plots in question would have scraped by in true penury. It is they who, in later centuries, would have crowded round the church doors wrapped in rags; it is they whose bodies, as we shall see in chapter 6, bore the signs of insufficient nutrition—rickets, scurvy, stunted growth.

The second implication is that behind the cruel minimalism of the account books, something else is going on. These account books record only wage work on offer in those particular farms, or, in the case of the Patron accounts, plots owned by particular family members. As we saw in chapter 3, the Egyptian agrarian world was a mosaic of small plots and adjacent landowners; other wage opportunities could have been available from any of them. The limited view from the account books opens the first possibility for hustling: working for multiple employers on different days. The anonymity of the workers doesn't allow us to track them as they moved from job to job, but, as will become clearer below, they were clearly doing so.

The third implication is suggested by the identity of the workers themselves. Who were these anonymous "workmen" and "boys" if not "wage laborers"? In the countryside, they were almost certainly smallholder farmers.[70] The Roman agronomists like Cato and Varro advised landowners to hire their occasional labor from among the nearby tenants and smallholders, Cato even supplying a helpful draft of a labor contract.[71] In Egypt, this happened all the time. For instance, in the Epimachus accounts, Demetrios son of Pachrates, who occasionally makes wages or supervises pumping, is also a farmer who shares a plot of land with Epimachus, and evens owns a tiny plot that Epimachus rents from him. His son, Eumenes, also seems to make some wages.[72] Demetrios is thus a landowner, a tenant and a wage worker. On the Patron estate, one Onnophris can be found working for wages, as well as selling some hay to the estate.[73] The hay sale indicates he owns or leases some pastureland: in other words, he's a farmer. Furthermore, the wages he earned are too high for a single person per day: Onnophris is probably acting as a foreman, recruiting and organizing a group of workers while also working himself. Finally, Onnophris is also termed a *karpones*—a contractor responsible for the grape harvest.[74] In other words, Onnophris and many others like him were farmers in their own right. They also organized the grape harvest and, in the off-months, used their grape-harvest connections to organize labor gangs, as well as worked for wages. Many other wage earners in the Patron accounts appear to have had similar kinds of hustles.[75] In short, behind many, if not most, of the anonymous "worker" and "boy" day-laborers were almost certainly a large group of farming families who owned or leased tiny plots.

These were farmers like the Soterichoses, whom we encountered in chapter 3, their leased holdings too small, and leased at too high a rent, to support a family without paying that rent in arrears. They were also like the medieval peasants in northern Spain or early modern serfs in Bohemia, all of whom supplemented their too-small plots with wage work for bigger landowners. But these are also the farming families in modern America, whose too-small farms and too-big debts force adults and teenagers alike to work part-time at Walmart. In monetized economies where land is limited, or rents and debts are high, periodic day-labor formed—and still forms—part of farmers' strategies for survival.[76]

What about those earning monthly wages? A monthly wage conjures up something like a salary, and it's often assumed these monthly-wage earners were doing full-time work for the estates that paid them. But, as is evident from the too-low real-wage calculations (see figure 4.3), they and their families were probably also hustling. Some of the best-remunerated ones may have been working full-time, and those folks may have had a salary based on a full-time multiple of the daily wage.[77] On the Patron estate this would be 28 or 30 drachmas per month—of which there is only one recorded instance. On the later Appianus estate, this would be 56 or 60 drachmas—total compensation (cash, food and tax payments) earned by only six monthly *metrematiaioi*.[78] In other words, monthly compensation at full-time daily wage rates was rare. What, then, of those making less, and probably working less, than full time? Looking carefully, we can see at least some of them hustling.

The first indication of less-than-full-time monthly jobs is the nature of the jobs themselves. On the Patron estate, only guards get monthly wages. Guarding of crops in the fields before they are harvested, or water guards monitoring the flood, are seasonal jobs, and most of these salaries are specified for a month or two. This left lots of time for other activities. On the Appianus estate, the records for monthly workers include several men whose taxes appear to be covered by the estate. This was the fortunate position of Poaris, an ass driver, and Kastor, described as a *prostates*—a vineyard caretaker. Each was paid eight drachmas per month plus an artaba of wheat (worth about 16 drachmas in this period)—a minuscule wage that would barely have supported them as individuals, let alone a family.[79] But in a list of tax payments made to their local village of Euhemeria, the estate also paid 40 drachmas in taxes on their behalf, and then another 20 drachmas, also on their behalf, listed specifically for the *didrachmon*.[80] The 40 drachmas could be 10 months' worth of individual poll taxes. But the *didrachmon* appears some kind of land tax.[81] In other words, what appears to be full-time monthly compensation for Poaris and Kastor may include tax payments on their tiny plots of land.

Why would the estate pay their land taxes? Possibly because the estate was also using their animals. Poaris and his donkeys appear again in a record of hay distributed to animals working on the estate.[82] The estate declared that it owned 13 donkeys, but more than 13 donkeys appear at various jobs over the month recorded, and the extra donkeys are often the four commanded by Poaris. In other words, some of these monthly workers were people who also owned or leased some small plots of land they used to support some animals—and both man and animals were employed by the estate.[83] Indeed, hiring out oneself with one's animals to other farmers was a long-standing hustle in the Egyptian countryside. On the Patron estate, rented cattle come and go as they and their owners are hired to complement those owned by the estate.[84] A great estate like Appianus' could afford to put some of those folks on a monthly wage—a kind of retainer—in order to secure their services when they were necessary. The many varieties of monthly pay on these estates could reflect the number of agreed-upon days in the retainer.[85]

We can't stress enough the importance of these wage-earning farmers. If many, even most agricultural wage earners had access to some kind of land, animals or both, then cash and/or food wages complemented farm production; they didn't replace it. As we have no idea how much land these wage earners owned, we cannot parse the relative importance of wages versus farm production to their income portfolios. Our only indication is a minimum—the gap between wage earning and family requirements—that must have been supplied by other income. A smallholder lessee like Soterichos, whom we met in chapter 3 and whose tiny amounts of high-rent arable land and pasture could not wholly support both his children and his cows if he consumed all his produce, could have been just such a farmer/wage worker. A hypothetical model of the Soterichos family's total real income, including farm production and wages (from adults and/or children), could find them just getting by and maintaining their cattle—but only if they found the equivalent of 22 drachmas of wages or additional income per month (figure 4.4). This reality, that wages complemented smallholder farming rather than replicated its income, would have profoundly shaped both the price and nature of agricultural wages.

Outside of farm work, another way of earning extra income was liturgies—work required by the state. Some liturgies, like work on the dikes, were mandatory: you either paid a fee or did the work. Toward the end of our period, other liturgies were assigned to larger entities like villages and estates, which were responsible for assigning people to do them. In a busy world, it was obviously easier to pay one person to do the work and spread the cost out to the broader community.[86] Liturgies thus came to equal some extra income for those who did them. Guarding was the most commonly assigned liturgy—accompanying

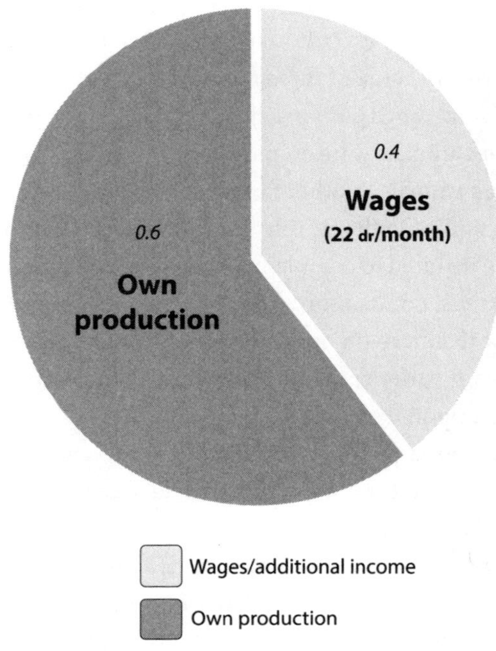

FIGURE 4.4. Real income model for the Soterichos family: own production and wages. Family of six. Assume hay/fodder not sold; Fayum rates/availability (Data: appendix 2, table A.10)

tax collectors, census officials or grain shipments from point A to B. A personal account from one Polion, a tenant farmer on the estate of Appianus, credited him with eight drachmas of liturgic guard duty.[87] Eight drachmas, remember, was the lowest-level monthly cash wage on this estate, so an extra eight drachmas of liturgic work could have made a substantial difference to an underpaid monthly or daily wage worker. The real boost that repeated liturgical work might make to a low income is apparent from a list of such liturgic wage payments from the Appianus estate. Among those making this extra wage were at least three monthly employees of the estate for liturgies including manning watchtowers and accompanying grain transports.[88] One employee, Kastor, together with his brother, made some 158 drachmas through these duties—a huge increase on his eight drachmas and one artaba of wheat monthly salary.

Women and Children at Work

The yawning gap between male wages and family needs, when not filled with farm produce and other wage hustling, must have been filled by other family members' work. In other historical periods, entire wage-earning sectors were dominated by women and older children: household servants, nannies or governesses.[89] In other times and places, too, women's and children's labor is reasonably well documented.[90] None of these is true for the Roman world. As we noted above, household service positions were largely taken by enslaved persons, and the quantifiable traces of child labor are limited to sparse references—the "boys" in farm accounts, a small number of apprentice or debt contracts. In other words, men dominate the evidence for Roman wage earning. Nonetheless, some small but tantalizing pieces of evidence find children and, above all, women making major contributions to household income. Women and girls could make significant income through piecework earned from spinning and weaving, while boys earned wages in the same range of jobs in which we find their fathers.[91]

Textile work was, along with agriculture, probably the most common kind of work in the Roman world.[92] It was practiced in smaller, family-based workshops and in larger-scale operations everywhere. The quantity of tunics and cloaks, socks and hats produced to satisfy what we've already seen was massive consumer demand would have required the full-time efforts of as much as 15 to 50 percent of the total population, and the part-time efforts of many, many more.[93] As we have already noted, most clothing was purchased from small workshops, not made at home, and textile work was a major income stream for many families. Most importantly for our purposes, this massive textile industry was undergirded by women. While both men and women might weave, spinning, one of the most time-intensive parts of cloth-making, was seemingly an all-female activity. Between two and five spinners were probably necessary for every weaver. In short, one of the most widespread cash-earning jobs in the Roman world was done by women and girls.[94]

For the textile-producing world of medieval and early modern England, we know precisely how much a woman might earn spinning, what kinds of families undertook the work, and what their output was. For the much bigger textile-producing world of ancient Rome, we are ill-informed on all these counts.[95] How much a woman or girl might earn through spinning is indicated by a single source, which is worth discussing in some detail. In a second-century CE letter from the city of Oxyrhynchus, one Apollonia lays out the quantities and costs of wool she is assembling for a man's outfit. In it, she details wool that she has spun herself, as well as wool she has let out for spinning. Apollonia paid one obol per stater (around 14 grams) of wool to have three mina spun, and paid just shy of 18 drachmas.[96] While a single source from a private letter, this sounds like a commonly accepted price. One obol per stater or six drachmas per mina is exactly the kind of readily computable, round price that we observed in chapter 1 and that was so prevalent for basic commodities and services. One obol per stater of wool is thus probably the going rate for spinning in the first through third centuries.

How much could a woman or family spin per week? Again, we are in the dark. Some experiments suggest a stater of wool could be spun in about three hours, while historical data suggests much faster times. If a woman could spin half a mina per week, then she could, in theory, earn some 12 drachmas per month.[97] Were these estimates even approximately correct, Roman women's income from spinning rivaled some male monthly wages.[98]

Both women and men might also weave, either paid in wages or by the piece. We find female weavers like Tehat, in the mid-fourth-century Western Oasis village of Kellis, running a small weaving business.[99] At least two women worked for her, making daily wages, while spinning was both done by her household and sent out to others.[100] While these later cash wages are hard to translate into first- through second-century CE equivalents, one barley wage indicates a female weaver might earn an artaba's worth of barley in 12 days—again, the equivalent or higher of male cash wages.[101] In short, lurking behind the consumer revolution in textiles was a revolution in female income earning.

In addition to their textile work, women with young children might also earn very low wages as wet nurses.[102] Women might agree to nurse a child in addition to their own for payment. Unlike in the early modern world, this was not usually a rich woman's child, but an abandoned child who would be raised as a slave. The total wage-plus-food (usually oil) package for this work amounted to the equivalent of some eight drachmas per month in the first century CE, and 12 drachmas per month in the second century CE. These contracts often specify that this sum and/or its food equivalent was intended as maintenance for the nursing woman. Now, eight drachmas were not quite enough to support a nursing woman—her food, clothing and housing—any more than most of the male monthly wages were sufficient to support them. Indeed, some of these arrangements were not intended as wages but often appear to be loans, the woman's nursing and tiny wage in exchange for a cash loan to her husband.[103]

Finally, although women almost never appear to work for wages on the rural estates, they do appear occasionally selling produce. In the Epimachus accounts, the estate buys beans used as chicken feed from one Thallousa on two occasions, earning her eight obols—twice the male daily wage.[104] Another woman, Tanarous, supplied the estate perhaps twice with six artabai—some 240 liters—of carobs (no price given).[105] The wife of the ox driver Maron charged some 42 liters of wine against his estate account at about the same time Maron withdrew money to travel to Arsinoe, the nearest city.[106] That's too much wine for daily drinking, and Maron and his wife may have intended to sell the wine in the city where they could garner a higher price. Again, rather than wages, it was own-production and remarketing of crop surplus where we most often find women's income.

As was true of most of premodernity, what we would term "child labor" was ubiquitous in the Roman world.[107] The quotes indicate a term that no Roman would have recognized. Childhood meant something different in the ancient world than our own, and it was certainly not a life-stage free from labor, as it has come to be enshrined in modern human rights. As we shall see in chapter 6, children's bodies often bear the same signs of hard, physical work that adults do, for the children of working families worked as soon as they were able, doing age-appropriate tasks. It's notable that the wage-earning tasks of the "boys" and even some girls in the account books are often lighter ones—accompanying donkeys, picking up leaves, winnowing grain—than those listed for "workers."[108] But we also find boys hauling manure and girls working on building sites: the children of the working families were not always spared heavy labor.[109]

While children's labor was often critical to their families' survival, the same limited availability of jobs accrued to children as it did to adults. If we look again at Epimachus' accounts and perform the same calculations for the potential child labor supply, we find that even adding "boys'" available income to that of the adult workers didn't overcome the low-wage/limited-availability problem. It did, however, inch those families with working boys closer to subsistence, adding the equivalent of another 35 percent to the estate's total labor income (see figure 4.2).

The accounts of the Appianus estate provide a similarly bleak picture of children's contribution to overall family income. As we've noted in passing, these bigger estates paid many workers on account, rather than in cash, and a handful of individual workers' personal accounts have survived.[110] Maron, the wine-hustling ox driver we met above, was a low-paid monthly worker who earned eight drachmas and an artaba of wheat per month. His accounts find

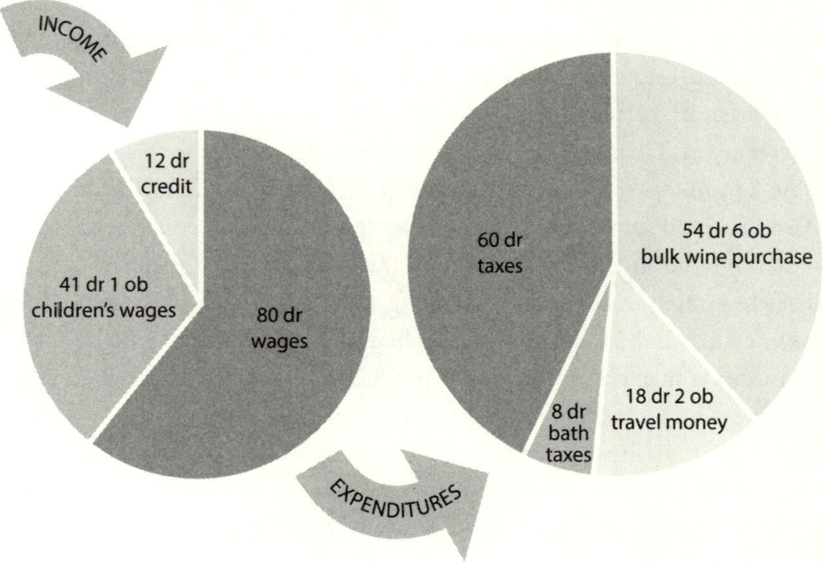

FIGURE 4.5. Account of Maron, ox driver for the Appianus estate, September 247–April 249 CE (Data: *P. Brux* descr.; Rathbone 1991, 125–26)

him leaving his cash wage untouched for 10 months, withdrawing, presumably, only his wheat. To these 80 drachmas in credit, his children also earned 41 drachmas and 1 obol—about half the value of his own wages recorded for the same period (figure 4.5). Even with these combined earnings, however, his family still didn't approach low-calorie subsistence.

Children might also be let out as apprentices.[111] Parents or slaveowners thus shifted most of the child's upkeep onto someone else, while sometimes earning a small income in addition. Apprentice contracts find both free and enslaved children, principally boys but also girls, placed with artisans—mostly weavers.[112] Their masters were usually responsible for their upkeep, with their clothing costs assigned to either master or parent. But "apprenticeship" also concealed a variety of arrangements, quite different from the more regularized medieval versions.[113] Some children were simply placed to learn their trade without a wage, some were placed in exchange for a loan to their parents, while others were paid (or their parents were paid) either from the beginning of their placement or once they reached a certain level of competence. Apprentice wages varied from only around 1–4 drachmas per month if the master provided their food and clothing to 6–14 drachmas per month if the parents (or owner) provided it.[114] Most of the "salary" then, was really upkeep with only a nominal sum paid to the parents or owners.

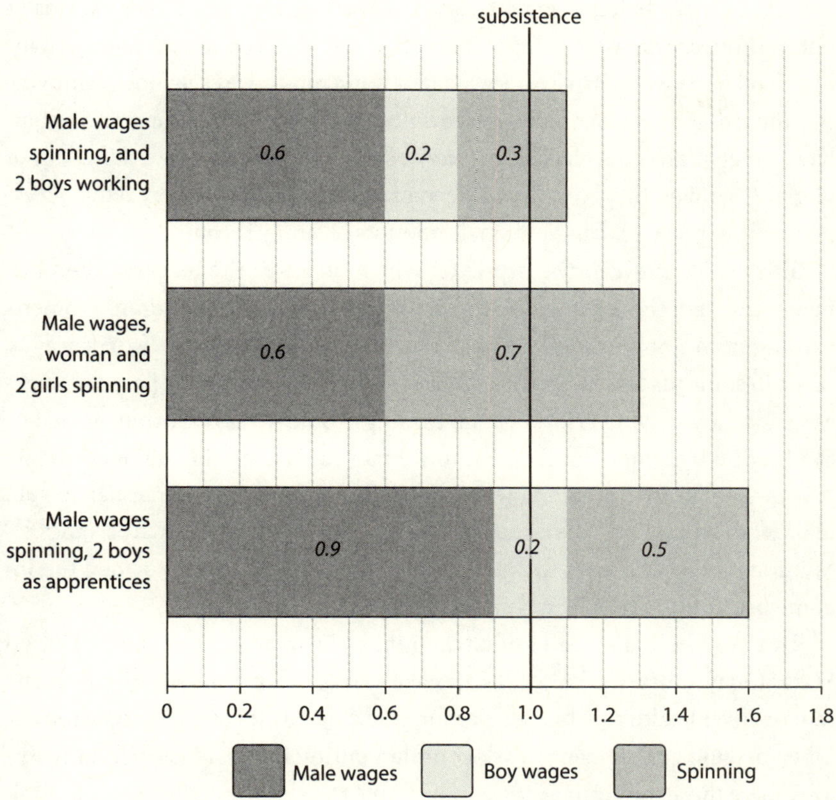

FIGURE 4.6. Three family strategies: reconstruction of hypothetical families, living on wages/apprentice contracts at low-calorie subsistence, Patron estate (Data: Boy wages and availability from *P. Mil. Vogl.* 7.306 [November, 156 CE]; spinning rates: *P. Oxy.* 31.2593; apprentice rates: second-century average from Bergamesco 1995, 162–64)

What did all these potential sources of extra income mean to a struggling family? We can take a stab at reconstructing the whole picture, using a fictitious family with two children on the Patron estate, living solely off wages and piecework (figure 4.6).

A fortunate man with among the highest monthly wages recorded on this estate (the equivalent of 20 drachmas per month) could have put two sons to work for daily wages of four obols per day, but with only limited wage opportunities available, this would still be insufficient for family subsistence at low-calorie levels. His female family members' work at spinning would have tipped them over into survival. If the family had two girls and both spun, their circumstances would have been better than with two boys working for minimal wages. Finally, putting both children out as apprentices at a low (two drachmas per month) wage plus food costs would have improved family circumstances the most, removing two mouths to feed while earning some modest income. Roman apprenticeships have largely been conceived as regimes of skill-building or networking.[115] For working families, they would have been of more immediate use by reducing expenses at home while building small amounts of family income.

This exercise reveals the tripod on which the most the impoverished Romans survived: the earnings of men *and* women, plus their children. Women's earning from spinning might have exceeded poorly paid monthly male wages, while in some places children might have earned up to half their parents' wages at various low-paying tasks. Female earnings could be as important as males', the lifeline by which families without male earners could eke out a living. A widowed mother, pleading with her correspondent to send her flax to spin in order to sell, marked the impoverished end of a spectrum of each earnings.[116] Spinning *and* wage work for varying stretches of time: these formed the income portfolios of the Roman poor.

This story will also be familiar to minimum-wage earners in the United States today, most of whom cannot make enough from a single job to pay the rent or cover health care or even pay for food.[117] Only through multiple jobs—Uber-driving and delivery work complementing low-paid service-industry jobs—are these minimum-wage families able to cobble together a living. Similarly, the Roman "wage" concealed the need for a myriad of family hustles that, for the lucky ones, transformed that nonliving wage into the ingredients for a precarious survival.

Sometimes Getting By on Wages: Artisanal Work

Beyond the hustle of unskilled labor, better opportunities existed for those with some skills. The folks behind the consumer revolution—the skilled workers who made all that fine pottery and glass, all the shoes and tunics—they commanded higher wages, and might also sell their wares by the piece. Could an artisan dodge the low-wage, low-demand trap? In other words, was skill rewarded with a true living wage? The question has been hotly debated. One side sees erratic availability of raw materials, low demand for goods, and a risk-averse mentality as limiting artisanal earnings to not much more than subsistence levels.[118] Another side sees things differently, finding ample evidence for a skill premium, on average about double the unskilled wage.[119]

The same Egyptian accounts we've been examining contain a surprising amount of information about artisans' wages. Potters and masons, carpenters and weavers—even riverboat-builders—all plied their trade in the countryside, perhaps not with the same density or specialization as the city, but they were thick on the ground nonetheless. On the Patron lands, for instance, masons building an olive press made two drachmas per day—around double the unskilled rate.[120] On the Appianus estate, carpenters regularly made four drachmas per day—again, about double the unskilled rate.[121]

Was this enough to make a living on these trades? As we discovered above, the problem facing daily unskilled wage earners wasn't only the low wages, but the availability of enough work for everyone in a crowded labor pool. We have a handful of accounts that, like the unskilled ones, provide a sense of the available work—and thus take-home wages—for a whole month or more of work (figure 4.7). For instance, on the Patron lands, two masons, a stonecutter/quarrier, and some unskilled assistants worked around 39 days over three months to build a new wine press building.[122] For the most part, only two skilled workers were employed on the project—two masons, who worked for between 17 and 20 days. With their 2.3 drachmas per day rate, these masons would have earned between 34 and 40 drachmas from the project—enough to support themselves for a month, but not quite enough for their families.

But the big problem was that, in reality, this pay was stretched out over three months—and so was wholly insufficient for either individual or family survival. In fact, the unskilled laborers on the project, who were paid half as much but had more consistent work, would have been somewhat better off.

Even more highly skilled artisans at considerably higher pay could suffer this same problem. The Appianus estate was so large that it appears to have constructed its own boats—either to convey its crops to market or for fishing and reed-cutting on nearby Lake Mareotis.[123] The accounts include the construction of a largish craft over three weeks of work, employing shipwrights and sawyers, paid seven and eight drachmas per day, respectively. The work again took place intermittently, on 15 days out of 22. Two sawyers, presumably the same two, were employed for a total of eight days, while between four and eight shipwrights were employed for 15 days. Both sawyers and shipwrights could easily support themselves on these generous wages, but neither could support their families at calorie-sufficient wages (see figure 4.7). Even though a much smaller number of workdays was required to achieve subsistence on these higher wages, these highly skilled workers didn't get enough work on this particular project. The case of the sawyers is emblematic: their great skill

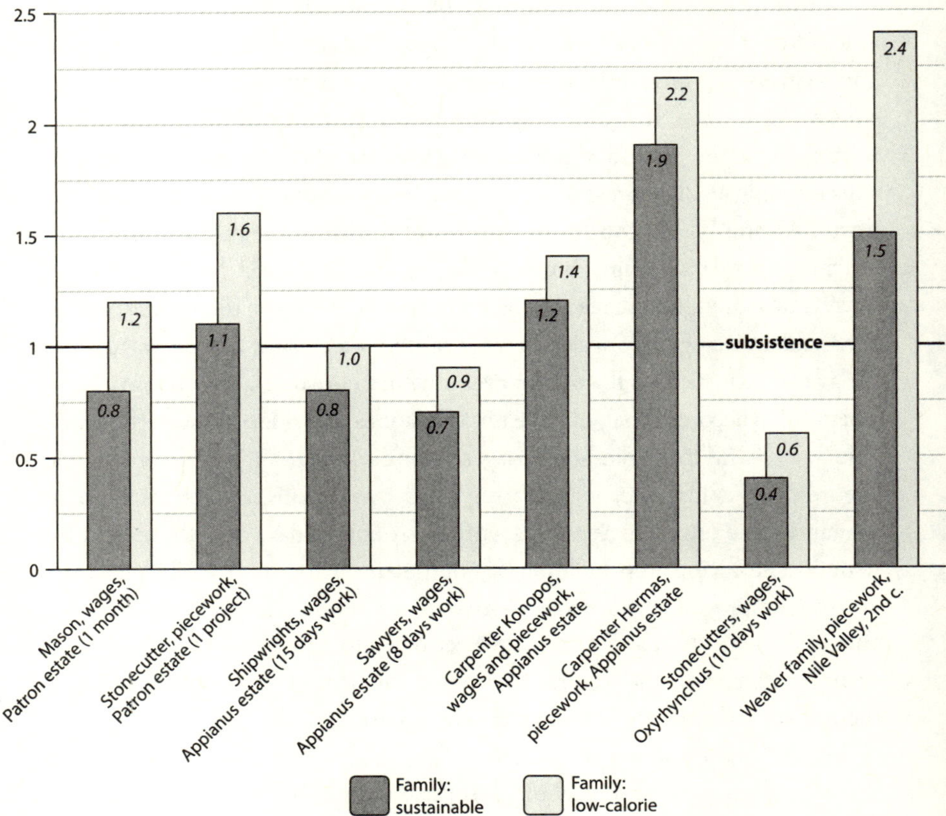

FIGURE 4.7. Some artisan families' real incomes (monthly). Piecework = gross minus 1/3 for raw materials (Data: *P. Mil. Vog.* 7.304; *P. Flor.* 1.69; Rathbone 1991, text 1 and 2; *P. Vindob. G.* 32019; Sijpesteijn 1980, 189096; *P. Oxy.* 3.498; Wild 2002, 31)

in cutting boards to form the ship's hull was needed for only eight days. The lesser-skilled, lower-paid shipwrights not only fitted the frame but were also used to move the scaffolding and were hired for more days. Of course, either set of specialists might have found other work on other projects: had the sawyers found another week of work, they could have supported their families on those wages. The point, again, is that hustle between jobs was necessary even, and perhaps especially, for those doing highly specialized work that was required only for short periods.

The carpenters employed on the Appianus estate illustrate the challenges faced by skilled laborers—and the way out of them. Two sets of accounts find the carpenter Kanopos hired perhaps 17 days in one month, and 30 in another.[124] It's important to note that Kanopos, like many middling-level artisans, made earnings mostly from daily wages but occasionally by the piece, as when he constructed a set of wagon boxes. At the estate-standard skilled rate of four drachmas per day, Kanopos could only maintain his family if he sustained this pace, alternating between half and full time (see figure 4.7). Otherwise, finding other work off the estate, in the local village, would have been critical. Another carpenter, one Hermas, was not paid by the day but by the piece. His specialty seems to have been agricultural machinery, and during the two months for which we have more complete records, he grosses between 200 and 244 drachmas per month building waterwheels and plows. Minus a third of assumed overheads, he netted enough to ensure sustainable provision for his family and some savings. Indeed, Hermas appears again named as a *komarch*—a position in the village council, charged with land matters—a role that had a modest land-owning requirement.[125] In other words, like so many of the hustlers we encountered earlier, Hermas the carpenter was probably also a farmer.

The stonecutter employed on the Patron mill project whom we met above reinforces the higher incomes possible from work paid by the piece (see figure 4.7). If we assume a third of the stonecutter's earnings were eaten up by raw materials and/or transport, he still manages to do somewhat better out of the project than the masons on the same project who were paid by the day. Some other stonecutters in Oxyrhynchus, working perhaps only 10 days and paid by the stone, earned perhaps 20 drachmas per person: while a tidy income for 10 days, they would have needed to work another 10 days at these rates for family subsistence (see figure 4.7).[126]

Textile work was probably the largest Roman industry paid in piecework. Some of that work was paid in wages, as we've already seen. But small-scale weaving businesses proliferated in the villages and cities of the empire, where families of weavers worked more or less full-time at their trade. A second-century weaving family who was able to produce 60 tunics per year (full-time work) might expect to net some 75 drachmas per month—a true family-supporting income, if the family were small enough (see figure 4.7).[127]

In short, for artisans seeking to make a living purely off their craft, piecework was better compensated than wages, even for the same jobs.[128] For wage-earning artisans, their principal challenge was not the wage level, but job frequency. The accounts we have for medium-sized projects, lasting one to three months, suggest that only where such projects might be strung together with just a few days between them could skilled workers make a living on wages alone. Cities were more likely to offer such dense opportunities. A city like Rome or Alexandria, with their huge building projects—those temples and basilicas, baths and streets—provided long-term skilled work for months and years at a time.[129] The higher end of those jobs may have indeed offered a sustainable living: they multiplied the skill premium by its all-critical second factor—time.

Back on the Farm: Craft Hustles

Back in chapter 3, we noted some problems with exchanging the term "peasant" for "farmer." It's time to face those problems here, for "farmers" didn't just farm. In the eighteenth century, farming women were the backbone of the lace-making industry; in medieval England, farmers were the principal brewers of beer; even today, most smallholder families in the Global South have a significant side-hustle outside of agriculture, from which comes the majority of their cash income.[130] In times and places where markets for consumer goods and services are robust, farming families not only hustle for agricultural wages, but they also work outside of agriculture, particularly in artisanal jobs.

This appears to have been particularly true in the Roman world. The gusto for things, which, as we've seen, was driven by the consuming desires of farmers as well as urbanites, meant that the rural world was dense with craft workshops. In Egypt, many people listed as tenant farmers, or as selling fodder to the big estates, also appear to be artisans. So, on the Patron lands, Aunes the builder and Heraklas the surveyor both sold fodder from tiny plots of pastureland, land that they owned or leased.[131] In the village of Tebtunis, we have the names and professions of landowners who performed corvée labor on the dikes—presumably those too poor or unwilling to pay the fee to avoid it. In other words, it's a list of smallholders. That list of smallholders included over fifty people who also identified themselves with a profession outside of farming.[132] In Theadelphia, around four percent of tenants on state land had a secondary, nonagricultural occupation—millers, fishermen, a cattle-breeder, even a musician.[133] Interestingly, it appears that those *leasing* land tended more often to have a secondary occupation in agriculture-adjacent activities—like wool dealer or animal breeder—while those who *owned* land more often had a second occupation in a more highly skilled trade—doctors, smiths, or merchants.[134] Some of these multitaskers may have hired day-laborers to work their land; others will have used family labor to work the land while they pursued their craft. In either case, land plus craft together were the ingredients for these families' total income.

"Farmer" and "artisan" were thus not mutually exclusive categories. Rural people's demand for consumer goods meant many of those consumer-goods industries—potting, iron and glass working—were located in the countryside. Those workshops were therefore also potential sources of income. For those smallholders living on razor-sharp margins, like the Soterichoses or the Monte Forco veterans we met in chapter 3, or for those with some extra land and extra labor, growing things, making things and making wages were mutually supporting hustles.

One of the biggest potential rural hustles was pottery making. Pottery production was everywhere in the countrysides of the Roman world: over half the potteries in Gaul were found in the countryside, and the same was true of Italy.[135] No such survey exists for Egypt, but pottery contracts show in detail the entanglement of potting, farming and local labor. On September 5, 243 CE, one Aurelius Paesis, a potter from a village in the Nile Valley, leased a pottery located on a nearby farm.[136] Aurelius promised to produce a large quantity of wine jars, presumably for bottling the farm's wine, in exchange for a cash price of 32 drachmas per 100 jars (4,800 drachmas in total), plus a modest amount of the wine itself. Aurelius was a local, and he was charged with hiring the remainder of his staff—other potters, assistants, and stokers—presumably from the local village. The payments made to Aurelius give some sense of that labor flow. The bulk (3,600 drachmas) was paid to him during the low point in the agricultural year, from August to May, when presumably the clay digging and cleaning and actual potting took place and when the most labor was available. During the grain harvest time (late May to early July), he was paid much less: the pots were to be fired during these months when the high temperatures were ideal and only smaller kiln crews were needed. The remaining money was paid in July/August, when the jars were to be delivered and the wine harvest was at hand. All the wage labor he must have hired was temporary, and we can't know how many workers were involved.[137] What's clear is the integration of pottery with agricultural production, and the wage-labor opportunities for farming families that it generated.

All those massive excavations in advance of modern trainlines and airports that unearthed the Roman farms we encountered in chapter 3 have also unearthed the remains of farmer-artisans. In Italy and Gaul, the majority of rural potteries were stand-alone specialized centers, producing a whole range of wares for both rural and urban consumers.[138] But individual farms and villages themselves also often had a kiln or two for roof tile and common ware production.[139] These two scenarios—specialized potteries and farm-village potteries—were supported by two labor scenarios. In the specialized potteries, itinerant specialists, like Aurelius Paesis, made the pots, while unskilled wage workers did other jobs—clay digging, water and wood hauling—presumably for wages.[140] The wage workers would have come from local farming families. In the farm-potteries, on the other hand, farmers produced tiles, cooking pots and amphorae for use on the farm, but also sold the surplus to neighbors by the piece. In short, particularly in the countryside, potting and farming were complementary activities, generating either wages, piecework, or both.

Farmers were also part of the vast Roman iron and salt industries. In Britain, iron smelting was emphatically tied to farming: 70 percent of metal production was associated with some kind of farm or village.[141] In the East Midlands—an iron production region not only in the early Industrial Revolution but also in the Roman period—smelting, potting and farming appear to have developed in concert, with iron production often located adjacent to farms, villages and roadside sites.[142] The same might be true of salt-making, another major business. In the salty Cambridge fens or along the north Gallic coast, salting took place seasonally, often in rotation with farming.[143] Iron and salt-making specialists appear to have been members of the farming community, working their trade alternately with agricultural duties.[144]

It's important to emphasize again that this entanglement of artisanal work and farming didn't diminish the specialized skill required by both occupations, or deny that stand-alone professions such as potters, smiths or salt-makers existed. In cities, particularly big cities like Rome and Alexandria, professions could be more single-task-oriented, since, as we've seen above, the work was potentially more frequent, the opportunities denser.[145] In the countryside, multitasking would have been more common, but always anchored around itinerant specialists—potters, smiths, glassblowers—whose outputs were expanded through a whole range of shorter-term, less skilled assistants. It was precisely the increasing specialization and standardization of goods, their expanded production, and the expansion of monetized markets that accompanied them that produced the opportunities for artisan-farmer hustling.

Working for the Man

Thus far, we've found that wage earning mostly involved hustling, with the result that the Pompeiian multitasker with whom we began this chapter, rather than being an oddball, was actually the norm. But there were some wage-earning

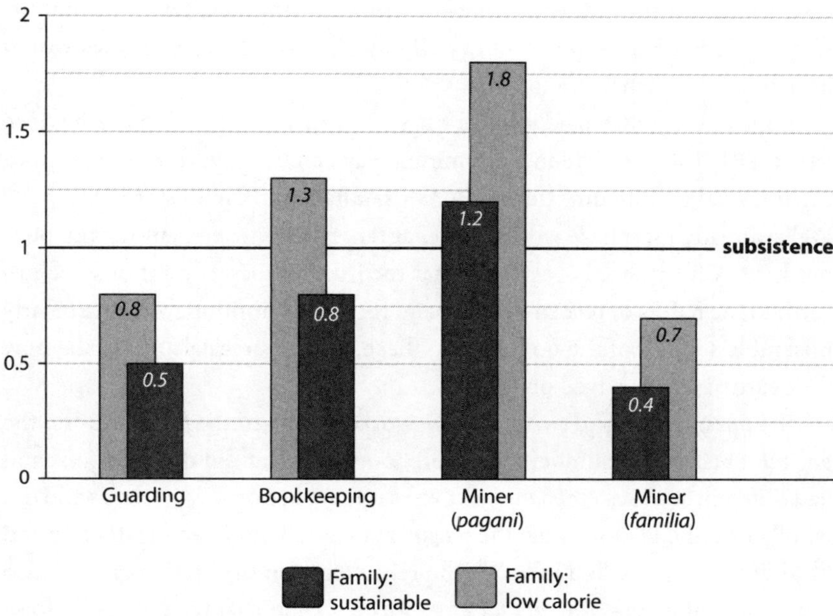

FIGURE 4.8. Working for the man: family real incomes (monthly), state jobs, second/early third century, Nile Valley. Assume miners paying Nile Valley taxes (Data: Freu 2022, 247–48 [averages]; Cuvigny 1996)

jobs where either the pay was sufficient or the hustling opportunities were so limited that one job was all. Many of these jobs involved working for the man—the Roman state (figure 4.8).

In many provinces, the state was a big employer and source of wages. In Egypt, we've already seen agricultural workers getting occasional state pay. But more consistent work for the state was also available—guarding roads or custom houses, maintaining urban infrastructure, even working in the imperial temples.[146] The nonskilled jobs, like guarding, appear to have been paid monthly and garnered similar levels of low cash pay as did monthly agricultural work. The average pay for public guard duty in the second/early third century CE was around 25 drachmas per month; as we only have the cash payments, we don't know if this included food. Other skilled jobs or managerial-level positions were more highly compensated: archivists, secretaries and accountants earned between 30–40 drachmas in cash per month in the second century, more than twice the average monthly unskilled wage.[147] Again, while 30–40 drachmas was a reasonable living for an individual, it was barely sufficient for a whole family. However, as many of these jobs would have been part-time—night guarding and temple account-keeping didn't keep a person busy all day—hustling opportunities would have been abundant.

Some of the better-paid jobs for the state were mining and soldiering (see figure 4.8). The best evidence for mining pay comes again from Egypt, from the imperial granite quarries at Mons Claudianus in the Eastern Desert.[148] We've already met these workers in chapters 1 and 2 where, among the hundreds of pottery sherds (ostraca) that record their pay and rations, we unearthed the habits of record-keeping and food consumption for a particularly miserable section of the 90 percent. These same sources also describe how they earned and survived on wages.

The mines employed two groups of workers, termed the *familiares* and the *pagani*. Each group numbered around 400 strong but did different jobs and had different statuses. The *familiares* were often, but not always, slaves and did wholly unskilled labor, while the *pagani* appear to have been mostly free and have done more skilled jobs.[149] The remuneration of the two groups also took different forms. The *familiares*, as we've seen in chapter 2, received food rations—wheat, lentils, oil—plus a tiny cash wage. The *pagani*, on the other hand, received 47 drachmas per month, plus an artaba of wheat and some unknown wine rations.

In order to convert their wages and wheat to actual edibles in the middle of the desert, the *pagani* designated one of their coworkers to take their pay and orders for food down to the Nile Valley. It's these written orders (*entole*) that are preserved for us. These requests included purchase of a wide range of foodstuffs—vegetables, meat and fish—as well as requests for their families, who lived in the Nile Valley towns, to turn their wheat into bread to be carried back to the quarries.[150] The orders also frequently included the request to sell the worker's wheat ration in order to discharge debts; one such request sees the entirety of the salary—cash and wheat—eaten up by such a debt.[151]

The higher cash wages paid to the *pagani*—the total cash equivalent of around 57 drachmas per month—is important.[152] Why should these mining wages be so high, relative to unskilled rates in the rest of the province? The difficulty of the job could be one reason—quarrying granite in the desert was a miserable task—although plenty of equally miserable jobs were paying much less. Another could be the quarry's isolation in the Eastern Desert and the limitations it put on hustling. While the agricultural workers down in the Nile Valley were, as we've seen, regularly augmenting their low wages with other work, no such opportunities were available to the miners—except, perhaps, getting their children hired by the mines.[153] Their higher wages may thus have been a rare, deliberate subsistence wage: these wages meant that a miner could support a family on sustainable calories with his wages alone.

Some other men earning a (possible) living wage for the state were soldiers. The subject of Roman army pay has vexed whole armies of scholars for over a century.[154] What were legionaries (citizen expeditionary troops) paid versus auxiliaries (mostly noncitizen local garrison troops)? What were foot soldiers paid versus cavalry? All these questions rest on a tiny corpus of sources—hard-to-interpret literary texts and a handful of army paybooks and receipts. In general, most scholars agree that until around 84 CE, pay was made in three installments per year at an empire-wide rate of 750 sestertii per year for the lowest-paid auxiliary foot soldier and 900 sestertii for his legionary equivalent.[155] After that date, rates increased to 1,000 and 1,200 sestertii—83 and 100 drachmas or sestertii per month—respectively.[156] Were this pay fully realized, it would have been a true living wage, with room for savings—a possibility we'll discuss in chapter 5.[157]

At least in the first century, though, that pay wasn't fully realized. Major deductions made major inroads into soldiers' pay. Paybooks from auxiliary units in Egypt, like those for the soldier Quintus Iulius Proclus, begin with what appears to be an unrecorded deduction of 1 percent from the gross pay, followed by deductions for his food, socks and shoes, and (in around two out of three pay periods) a significant expense for clothes and equipment (figure 4.9).[158] On average, these deductions amounted to about 70 percent of soldiers' total pay and, in some instances, 100 percent. The soldiers we have records for were left with only around 15–20 drachmas per month, sometimes less.

The sustainability of these wages depended in large part on whether the soldiers were, as required by law, single men or whether they had families and dependents. The prohibition against soldier marriages has also been much disputed but appears to have remained in effect through much of our period.[159] We catch glimpses of that prohibition precisely because so many soldiers ignored it; many had de facto families, and officials from imperial governors to the emperor himself were forced to reiterate the policy in the face of its being flagrantly disregarded. Soldiers realizing only 20 drachmas per month from their wages could in no way support a family, and hustling—by the soldiers themselves and their families—would have been critical.[160]

Tacitus' complaint that the army was stuffed with soldiers who were nothing but "sleek, money-making traders" was almost certainly a fact of military life.[161] Legions might include among their number soldier-traders—like the

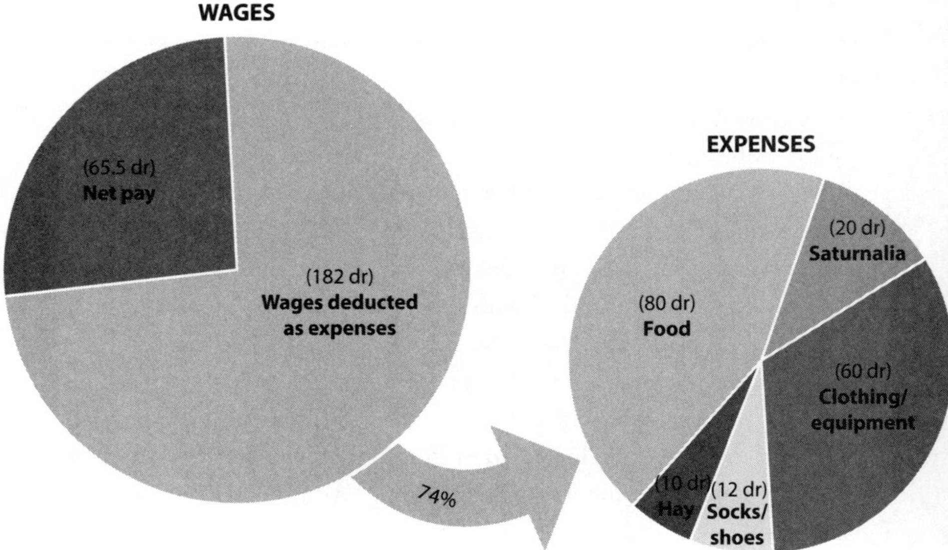

FIGURE 4.9. Wages in—deductions out. Four-month wages for Quintus Iulius Proclus, Egypt, 81 CE (Data: *P. Gen. Lat.* 1 recto 1 [RMR 68], rounded to nearest drachma)

contractor Porcius listed among the troops of the Legio III Cyrenaica, or one Sernus, who calls himself a financial officer (*procurator*) while counting members of a cavalry unit as his "comrades."[162] Two ambitious businessmen at Vindolanda in northern Britain, dealing in large quantities of wheat while at the same time settling small personal debts, may also be soldiers or friends of soldiers, since they refer to them as their "tent mates." The complex mix of state and private sources for military supply meant that the line between soldier and trader was a fine one. For soldiers in long-term postings, this meant various hustling opportunities to augment one's much-reduced take-home pay.[163]

The evidence from the later second century, limited though it is, appears different. Auxiliary soldiers appear to have received the entirety of their pay, with the only deductions made for wheat rations and, for the cavalry, barley for their horses.[164] The soldiers were then responsible for buying their other food—wine, oil, meat, fish and vegetables—from their pay. This appears to have been the situation in the garrisons in the Egyptian Eastern Desert, where we have a number of receipts for soldiers taking delivery of their wheat/barley or hay rations or, almost as frequently, taking the cash value of those rations.[165] Taking cash in lieu of rations was something we can find all ration-earners doing, not just soldiers. Cash was more flexible, and a preference for cash over rations suggests that the urgent need wasn't just subsistence, but debt—something we'll discuss in chapter 5. Selling one's rations was probably also a common hustle.[166]

The army provided a living to more than just its soldiers. Sutlers, or suppliers, of local garrisons were closely entangled with the army itself.[167] Small family businesses arose in supplying soldiers those things not supplied by the army, which, by the second century, may have meant a great many things, including food. Particularly among the auxiliaries, these local sutler families may themselves have had husbands or brothers in the army, and their sutler activities were the hustle that supported their relative's not-quite-sufficient wages. One Zosime, from the Egyptian desert camps, may be emblematic. She appears to be the mother of a soldier, but also seemingly a slave; her husband was a stonecutter, and the two maintained a hustle with her son's soldier friends, to whom they sold wine.[168] Other records are full of the doings of these sutlers—selling bacon and socks, supplying vegetables and poultry—mostly at the tiny quantities that point to family businesses rather than large-scale suppliers.[169] For one such family, we have an ostraca archive of their activities—activities that included supplying not only fruits and vegetables, but also prostitutes.

Philokles, a Greek-speaking Egyptian, together with his relatives and associates, helped supply the garrison at Krokodilo with a variety of goods—everything from onions and wine to poultry and vegetables.[170] He and his family also supplied women, either acting as intermediaries between the owners of enslaved prostitutes and potential clients, or pimping their own prostitutes, including, perhaps, their daughters or wives.[171] Small groups of soldiers appear to have hired pairs of women—perhaps only one of whom provided sexual services while the other acted as a servant—on monthly contracts. Philokles and his family, acting as pimps, collected the payment during their provisioning trips to the camps and delivered it to the owners, sometimes picking up the women as well. An extraordinary set of letters between one Serapias and her pimp, Maximus, finds Serapias having completed her contract but still left at the garrison, where the soldiers continue to molest her.[172]

Monthly "wages" for camp prostitutes like Serapias were relatively high: most documents record somewhere between 60–70 drachmas, while another set were considerably lower (24–40 drachmas).[173] If clients, rather than the pimps, absorbed the food and the passage-tax (*pittakion/quintana*) for the women, this constituted yet another significant income stream for the women's controllers.[174] Cold comfort, though, to the women, stuck in isolation in a repugnant job and also subject, it seems, to constant threats of violence.[175]

Working for the state, at least in some occupations, thus offered some of the only truly subsistence wages we have from the Roman world. And those that didn't quite support a family at sustainable levels—like accounting and guarding—left lots of room for extra hustling. But the generous wages were not without their limitations: leaving aside the dangerous, onerous and isolating circumstances of mining or soldiering, the state often found ways of giving with one hand while taking away with the other. Mining and soldiering wages were, perhaps intentionally, on the knife's edge of family subsistence. The state wasn't interested in supporting families: it was interested in attracting and extracting labor for difficult jobs for which it demanded total dedication. Families—and hustling—were, if not totally excluded, made much harder in these jobs. Indeed, it was left to any family members to do most of the hustling—selling everything from fish to one's body back to the state to make ends meet.

The Enslaved and Their Wages

From the medium-sized farm of Epimachus to the quarries of the Egyptian desert, free and enslaved persons in Egypt worked side by side, often doing the same jobs. Throughout this chapter, we've noted how hard it is to distinguish free from enslaved in wage records. It's worth taking a closer look at this problem, and at those people who ride this boundary. Doing so casts the meaning of "wage" in yet another light, particularly vis-à-vis wages and hustling.

The conundrum can be summarized as a disjunction between labels and activity—a subcategory of the analysis-versus-practice problem we've noted throughout this book. In short, in Egypt, words that should refer to enslaved persons don't correspond with what we assume slaves did. For instance, in the Patron wage records, some women receive subsistence (4/5ths artaba) rations of wheat as wages. Three of them—Athene, Nikes and Kaliopes—have nonlocal, Greek names, and this, paired with their longer-term employment, has suggested they were enslaved domestics.[176] Yet they appear alongside other men and women locals who received similar rations and were seemingly not slaves. On the Appianus estate, some employees termed *paidaria* (the diminutive and derogative "boys") are counted by some scholars as enslaved persons, yet they have a variety of responsible roles—supervisors, carters, carpenters, shepherds—and, in one case, a tenant.[177] Some occasionally receive food payments, and others have families. We've already noted that the *oiketai* (roughly translated as "members of the household") on the same estate also sound like slaves but probably were not: they received monthly low payments in wheat and cash.[178] The *familiares*—another slave moniker—at the Mons Claudianus quarries were distinguished from the *pagani* by their much lower cash pay (probably seven drachmas as opposed to 47 drachmas), their lower water rations, and the fact that instead of a wheat ration, they receive full rations on-site. But it's not clear that even the *familia* are composed entirely of enslaved persons.[179] When it comes to parsing free from slave, words are not always helpful.

The form of their actual salaries tells its own, somewhat different story. Food-only remuneration is most common for people bearing these slave-like labels, while the cash component, when present, is very small—almost like pocket money. The *peculium*, or pocket money given to slaves, seems a possible analogy for these cash payments, but since the *peculium* was not doled out regularly and need not have been small—some slaves' *peculium* was gargantuan—the comparison only works so far.[180]

Rather than trying to force these people into a slave/free binary, it's perhaps more useful to reflect on what their wages tell us about the economic experience of freedom versus slavery for the poorest wage-earning Romans. For those bearing the slave-like labels, their compensation being mostly in food is limiting: wage is equivalent to the physical means of survival. The freedom provided by cash—to determine *how* one survives—is greatly reduced. In the case of the Mons Claudianus *familiares*, providing rations on-site meant very little choice in food. In fact, the archaeological remains of food from a nearby quarry with a *familia*-only workforce had less variety than that from quarries that also employed free workers.[181] While food-only wages could be transformed into cash, as we've seen, workers would probably have relied on their employer for that transaction. Food-only wages thus made a worker doubly dependent on the man. Hustling—the practice we've seen undergirding so much wage activity—may have been much harder for this group. Without hustle, one was left with fewer opportunities to augment those low wages. Perhaps it was this distinction—between the hustlers and those who could not hustle—that separated the earning experiences of the poorest free from the unfree.

A World of Hustlers

The farming, jug-making, trinket-selling, clay-hauling person with whom we began this chapter was ridiculous because he had too many hustles. If he had somewhat fewer, he would have been normal. Hustling is a historically normal condition. Impoverished people in most societies—past and present—have more than one income stream, earned either by multiple family members, or even a single family member. Even the not-so-poor and the prosperous middle had multiple ways of making money. Kronion the village notary was also a farmer; the merchant Nebuchelos in Dura Europos was also a moneylender. Hustling is normal; the industrial-age single job is the aberration.

The hustling done by the Roman 90 percent, however, was particular. As we've already seen, the Roman 90 percent generated a huge demand for consumer goods, industries that, in addition to farming, produced lots of low-wage-paying jobs of a particularly specialized kind—like clay-hauling and trinket-making. They lived, as we shall see more clearly in the next chapter, in a world particularly awash with money with which to pay wages. And while the majority of them lived in the countryside, these were countrysides so dense that they provided a particularly dense landscape of hustling opportunity. The demand for jug-makers, trinket-sellers, and especially spinners, as well as farm work, meant that rural wage-earning opportunities weren't limited to the harvest but extended throughout the year and into many different jobs. Roman hustling was thus, by historical standards, particularly monetized, particularly diverse, and particularly ubiquitous.

The habit of hustling makes us rethink what we mean by "wage laborer." Despite Cicero & Co.'s certainty that such a singular category existed, we've seen that families who survived only on wages were probably in the minority. Making *part* of one's income through wages was, however, especially common. This is not exactly commodified labor as Karl Marx knew it.[182] The highly specialized jobs and payment in money that may look like a prequel to *Das Kapital* conceal a very different reality for workers. It was a more flexible reality than that experienced by the nineteenth-century working class, in that it involved multiple jobs and multiple employers—very often including oneself. It was a much worse reality in that the wages were far lower.

The habit of hustling also makes us rethink what we mean by wages. Roman wages do appear to be historically low. They could be that low because very few people were living on them. Agricultural wages as experienced by agricultural workers are not a living, but a kind of varnish on top of subsistence gained through other means. We can see this in the accounts of the ox driver Maron, who doesn't touch his minuscule eight drachmas monthly wage for a whole 10 months, withdrawing only his wheat. Maron and his family use the wheat wage to supplement their farming while banking the cash wages, probably to pay their taxes. For most, wage is not synonymous with a living, but a complement to a living obtained through other means.

There were some folks living only on their wages. These included the worst-off—malnourished families living on nothing but their too-low, too-infrequent wages. They also included the better-paid—some artisans, soldiers, miners and other specialized jobs in which one's wage was one's living, or mostly. Some artisans were sufficiently compensated for their skill to make enough to support their families, but again, they were better off being paid by the piece rather than in wages. Otherwise, hustling from job to job was required. Soldiers and miners were paid better for hazardous duties—and for not hustling. In compensation for a remote workplace and the requirement to forgo family and other paid work, these people were paid nonhustling rates. This didn't wholly prevent soldiers and miners from sidelines like reselling their rations or equipment. And it certainly didn't prevent the most widespread hustle in the Roman world—moneylending—as we shall see in the next chapter.

5

The 90 Percent and Their Money

FIGURE 5.1. Working people's money: coins from the bar of Vetutius Placidus (Photo: Author. Permission of the Ministero della Cultura, Museo Archeologico Nazionale di Napoli)

WHEN THE Roman 90 percent weren't working, they were sleeping.[1] And when they slept, they dreamed, as often as not about money. Artemidorus, a Roman dream interpreter, appears to have had many of the 90 percent among his clientele—cobblers, farmers and shopkeepers, slaves and free—and he was frequently called upon to interpret their dreams about money.[2] When one of these clients dreamed about taking out a loan, Artemidorus offered this interpretation:

> A loan has the same logic as life. For we owe our life to Universal Nature, just as we owe a loan to a creditor. And a moneylender has the same logic as a loan. For this reason, a moneylender who is standing near sick men and demanding payment signifies danger, and if he takes something from them, it even signifies death. When a moneylender dies, it signifies a release from grief and worry. Moreover, a moneylender and a daughter have the same logic, since one's daughter also demands payment by necessity, since she is raised with much worry and, taking her dowry with her, is let go. For a household slave, a moneylender signifies a master who demands his hire pay.[3]

According to Artemidorus, to dream of borrowing money portends death; to dream of the death of a moneylender portends life. Daughters were like moneylenders—they constituted an outflow of money—while for the enslaved, dreams of borrowing heralded a double death, to work for wages only to see them vanish into the pockets of one's master. The flow of money—of making and borrowing and saving only to spend—is likened to the circle of life.

Artemidorus' dream guide lingers over money, as his poor and working clientele fretted over money. Money worries occupied their sleeping and waking hours. Tellingly, those money worries, as Artemidorus relates them, were complicated. Rather than pots of gold or rags to riches, money dreams involved borrowing and lending, interest and quittances. The money-world of Artemidorus was, even for his poorer working clients, a world of what accountants call financial instruments: tools for doing things with money.

Impoverished and working people are not usually imagined as using financial instruments. Indeed, they are defined by having neither money nor any means of deploying it. The rich have "capital," while the poor have "resources"; the rich use "credit" while the poor incur "debt." Not only is financial activity presumed to break around a jetty of economic class, but the words themselves often shift around those same barriers. Rich people play money games, while the poor suffer from them.

The Roman 90 percent played money games, too. Living in a world saturated with money and credit, they employed most of the same financial tools used by the wealthy. Like hedge fund managers, they lived with huge amounts of risk that they offset by managing a whole range of financial instruments, only at tiny scale. They deployed these tools during not-infrequent moments of shortage, to pass saved wealth to the next generation, and, if possible, to inch forward, using small-scale savings and credit to invest in small-scale capital—a loom, a donkey, a land lease, some seed. The money worries of the 90 percent were bitter and real: their complex portfolios of tiny amounts of saved and borrowed money were simultaneously bulwarks against catastrophe and strategies for getting ahead. Transactional lives lived in a world of money had hard edges, formed by due dates, default clauses, and bottom lines. But those same hard edges might be deployed for gain by the same people who, in other circumstances, could be made to suffer from them. The Roman 90 percent acted as lenders as well as creditors, as agents who shaped—successfully or not—their monetary lives. If the previous chapter began with wages and ended with hustling, this one begins with some other standard categories—savings and credit—and ends with managing—the deployment of a variety of financial tools to plug gaps and make a little go a longer way.

A Bottom-Up History of Roman Money

Making sense of working people's money requires more than the usual words of introduction, for nowhere else is the Roman past a more thoroughly foreign country than in its concept of money. The explanation is doubly necessary, too, as the working majority have occupied a particular and contradictory place in the study of Roman money: they have been assumed to live entirely outside monetary systems, while simultaneously living under the weight of constant, crushing debt. As one of the contentions of this chapter is that neither of these things was true, at least in any useful way, it's important to review not only some basic concepts, but also how they have been deployed.

The problems—and the debates—start with the very definition of money. What was Roman money?[4] Some basics are clear: Roman money was, at least in part, bullion money. Its value depended largely on the value of its precious metal base. The gold aureus was worth its weight in gold, the silver denarius (sort of) worth its weight in silver, while bronze coins were valued by their relationship to the other metals. While Roman coined money may have slowly shed some of this definition over time, with, for instance, silver slowly being removed from the denarius with no appreciable change in its exchange value, nonetheless Roman money—except for bronze—was mostly bullion money.[5]

Beyond this basic definition, for a long time one camp viewed Roman money, as one scholar put it, as "a thin veneer over a subsistence economy."[6] The state, in this view, minted coins for only a very narrow range of uses—to pay its army and as a medium for tax collection.[7] It was only reluctantly and minimally interested in money as an instrument of exchange. The state's seeming ignorance about basic aspects of monetary policy was made plain by some much-cited credit crises, like the one in 33 CE, provoked by cack-handed imperial interventions.[8] The use of coins as army pay, for occasional civilian handouts and little else was seemingly proved by the hundreds of coin hoards of silver or gold in the most militarized parts of the empire—Britain, the Rhineland and Danube frontiers.[9] Farmers, so this theory also goes, had no use for money.[10] The countryside—that is, most of the territories of the empire—was thus a money-free zone. While overall amounts of money increased dramatically under Roman rule, overall use of money remained relatively limited.[11] This meant that not only were transactions in money limited to cities, with the rest of the world using barter, but that monetized thinking was also limited. The Roman 90 percent, in this view, didn't use a lot of money, and didn't think in monetary terms.

This "statist" theory of Roman money has given way in recent years in the face of increasing evidence for both huge amounts of money-centered market exchange and the state's seeming support of it.[12] Under the emperor Augustus, the Roman trimetallic coinage was given a clear and long-lived articulation: the top anchored by the gold aureus, the middle by the silver denarius, and the bottom by the bronze sestertius and its several fractions, including the *as*. It was the bronze sestertius that served as the instrument not only of daily use but also of daily accounting. In the Italian heartland and Roman West, grain, land and other basic costs were expressed in sestertii, while army pay and accounting in the northwest provinces were conducted more in denarii. In Egypt, the bronze drachma assumed the same role, and more or less the same value, as the sestertius.

How much bronze coinage was used by ordinary people, and how much effort the state put into producing it, has been reinforced by archaeology. Excavations of the past half century have found Roman people of all kinds using money—particularly bronze coins—to a degree unthinkable 50 years ago.[13] Even rural dwellers—as will be discussed in detail below—now appear to be consistent, if less intensive, users of coined money.[14] These (generally) abundant amounts of bronze coins were clearly being produced by the state. The state was apparently willing to bear the high cost of minting bronze coins, and its deliberate shipment of bronze issues to the provinces for use in daily exchange suggests that, while its monetary priorities may have lingered on the most important components of its budget—the military and the tax take—it was not ignorant of the importance of money for daily use.[15]

But how much money was available, and who was using it? New work reconstructing Roman monetary output has suggested that the Roman state of the first and second centuries produced quite a lot of money. While early studies were absurdly optimistic, calculating monetization rates at 100–200 percent of GDP, more sober estimates based on die studies have still indicated a robust money supply.[16] But monetization rates are based on the overall value of the money in circulation, not what kind of money or for what purposes. Just as important for our history was the level of "deep monetization"—the amounts of small change available for daily use by ordinary people.[17] While a precise number is currently beyond us, it's clear that, in some moments and places, the Roman world witnessed some of the most widespread use of small change by ordinary people in the premodern world.

This debate between the "statists" and the "marketists" about the state's role in defining money only begs the question of who defines money anyway. The state may mint money, and in the Roman world it was (mostly) only the state or its designated representatives in provincial cities who could mint coins. But what money means, and how it is used, quickly escapes states' control. Money meaning and money use are socially constructed, the product of millions of daily interactions with money by millions of people.[18] Thus, what Roman money "meant" obviously varied depending on which Romans we mean. Newly conquered Romans in the Gallic or British territories, for instance, had a distinctive and long-lived understanding of money as something other than instruments of exchange. Coins in these places were often used as objects of ritual: in Britain, hoards of coins are found in wells and rivers; in the Dutch river valleys, they form part of sacrifices.[19] At the same time, as we shall see, these same people also clearly used coins for daily exchange. Ancient people were capable, as they are today, of multiple kinds of money thinking.

We've already seen in chapter 1 that Roman working people had monetary ways of thinking: they thought and calculated and planned in terms of the money value of things. True barter—exchange not based on monetary values—was rare.[20] But do monetized exchanges always require actual coins? The debates about Roman money have tended to focus on its function—state or market—or the quantity in circulation.[21] Just as important is how money worked as an instrument of daily transaction. Romans had various "modes," or forms in which money-based transactions might take place.[22] The most common mode was coins, used for small-scale daily transactions. But Romans also used commodities like money: we've already seen Egyptian farmers settling their rent or land taxes in artabai of wheat, for example.

In our own world, account money—the transfer of debt claims through accounting, rather than in coin—is the predominant monetary mode: debit cards are everywhere, and cash is increasingly rare. In the Roman world, it was long assumed that coins were the predominant monetary mode: precious metal was the only real source of value, and that value was controlled by the state. But coins are cumbersome, especially for large sums, and both Cicero & Co. and the jurists provide ample evidence that *nomina* (account money) worked just like *pecunia* (coins).[23] Account money, it's quite clear, was used to pay for big-ticket items like land or shipping, where hauling around large quantities of coins was impracticable.[24] And account money, as the transfer of debt claims through accounting, overlaps with credit as a financial instrument—that is, money borrowed on account. Were account money and credit also used by working people? As we'll see, the answer is a resounding yes.

These more complicated definitions of Roman money and the many people who used them runs squarely up against one of the oldest—and newest—paradigms about Romans and their money: the rich creditor and the poor debtor. For Finley, the wealthy borrowed (occasionally) to support their status, while the poor borrowed (frequently) from the rich to survive.[25] The binary can be traced to the Romans themselves. The indebted peasant is a stock figure in histories of the Republic, the demands of constant military service and aristocratic land-grabs forcing Italian farmers into ever more insurmountable debts.[26] Farmers' relationship with credit in these histories is driven by desperation, and the character of the indebted peasant has long been read into all credit transactions involving farmers.[27] David Graeber's monumental book, *Debt: The First 5,000 Years*, depends upon and expands this rich/poor credit binary.[28] The Roman world plays a central role in Graeber's "axial age" of debt, as the expansion of money transformed more reciprocal relationships into debtor/creditor relationships. Graeber's money-war-slavery machine was driven by the need to stave off debt crises through artificial injections of booty or bodies. And as that machine churned along, it deepened the divide between rich and poor, making the state the ultimate creditor.

This rich/poor binary isn't terribly helpful in understanding how not-rich people managed their resources.[29] We'll move beyond it here by, yet again, drawing on a different set of evidence. Much of the earlier understanding of money and credit was informed by literary sources, as well as the records of professional bankers and moneylenders. This chapter draws on other evidence. The coins carried by Pompeii's last inhabitants; the records of a village notary office; graffiti and papyri that track working people's loans to other working people: all this evidence reveals working people as borrowers, lenders and savers—that is, people doing things with money, not simply having things done to them.

While these sources allow us to hear, in their own words, Romans doing things with money, we continue to confront the deafening silence on things we most want to know. While we now have thousands of coin hoards, they tell us even less than we thought about savings. Small-scale credit transactions are mostly preserved in Egypt; how far this world pertains to the Roman West we don't know. We are almost never informed about the reasons for a loan, or the interest rates charged. With all its holes, though, it's nonetheless clear that the Roman 90 percent were immersed in a world of money, and that they deployed it in complex ways for their own survival.

The 90 Percent and Their Monies

Coins may have not been the only form of money, but they were the most fungible and probably the most commonly used. How much and under what circumstances did working Romans use coined money? The statist model of Roman money took it as an article of faith that the daily use of coins was limited. The state didn't care about it, and most people didn't need it. The need to pay taxes may have stimulated the use of coined money in the provinces, but it didn't make coin use a daily habit.[30] But the thousands of recent excavations and enthusiastic work of metal-detectorists have done much to upend this picture. In particular times and places, coins were literally in everyone's pocket.

The time and the place matter.[31] In order for working people to use coins, there needed to be coins for them to use. And it's apparent that the supply of small change in particular times and places was limited, even as the demand for that coinage was high. In second- and even first-century BCE Italy, it is apparent that the state didn't immediately issue lots of bronze coins but relied on preexisting Greek or Oscan mints to do the job.[32] The result was a shortage of small change, for which innovative locals compensated by local minting or importing bronze coins from abroad: Pompeiians of the first century BCE relied on coins from Ibiza, for instance. Only with the advent of empire did the state start to take small-change production seriously, and even then, specific issues might be better or less represented in different places.[33] Outside of Italy, the Roman conquests of its provinces were not immediately followed by a flood of small change produced by local mints.[34] In Britain, locals had to

FIGURE 5.2. Coin box, Herculaneum (Herculaneum, Inv. 3277. Photo by permission of the Ministero della Cultura, Parco Archeologico di Ercolano)

make imitation coins; in Spain, they may have used lead tokens.[35] A similar dearth of small change may have characterized the Egyptian countryside.[36] The state also appears to have preferred to be paid in silver and, in some instances, tacked small fines onto tax payments made in bronze.[37] So while the average Roman may have used coins to a historically unprecedented degree, it's also clear that those high levels of monetization had their limits.

The complex forces of demand and supply also require us to be specific about the context of working people's coin use. Cities and countryside are potentially very different kinds of coined places.[38] Cities constitute sites not only of potentially greater coin supply, but also of more frequent and diverse exchange activities. From small-value exchanges at bars and food sellers, to medium-value exchange around lending and borrowing, to high-value exchange around craft production and the purchase of agricultural surpluses, cities were places where coined exchange potentially happened not only more often but also at a range of different values.

The best place to observe coins in use by urban working people is Pompeii. The coins in savings boxes, cash registers and purses at the moment of Vesuvius' eruption allow a seeming snapshot of coins in use on one day in 79 CE.[39]

The coins from the savings boxes (figure 5.3) and the purses of victims who died in the eruption (figure 5.2) would, at first glance, seem to preserve coins in action—coins as household savings, coins for daily expenses or a mixture of the two. And yet, they don't.[40] The first things fleeing, terrified people grabbed when they left town that day were their valuables, including coins.

FIGURE 5.3. Oplontis Villa B, victim carrying coins and jewelry (Courtesy of the Oplontis Project, by permission of the Ministero della Cultura, Parco Archeologico di Pompei)

Huge amounts of coin would have left the city with the fleeing majority, while what remained were coins on the run—savings boxes rifled for their highest-value items, people running or hiding carrying their most precious portable possessions. The city itself, with its big wine and craft industries and nearby port, probably had a particularly active coined life compared to the more typical Roman town—inland, smaller, more agrarian. Pompeii does not, alas, offer an easy snapshot of typical working people using coins in typical ways.

Nonetheless, Pompeii's coins still tell some important things about how coins functioned in working lives. If we're interested in coin use, it's important to focus on coins where the use context is clearest: coins carried by victims as they fled (see figure 5.3) and coins stored in boxes or jars in houses and shops (see figures 5.1 and 5.2). Both, in different ways, represent coins meant for daily use combined with savings for another day, the two functions hopelessly intertwined.[41]

Pompeiians were well-supplied with—and active users of—coins in all three metals (figure 5.4).[42] The most common coins found on both victims and in savings boxes are bronze issues, attesting to the constant use of small change for everyday exchanges. Bronze coins—even low-value *asses*—are also

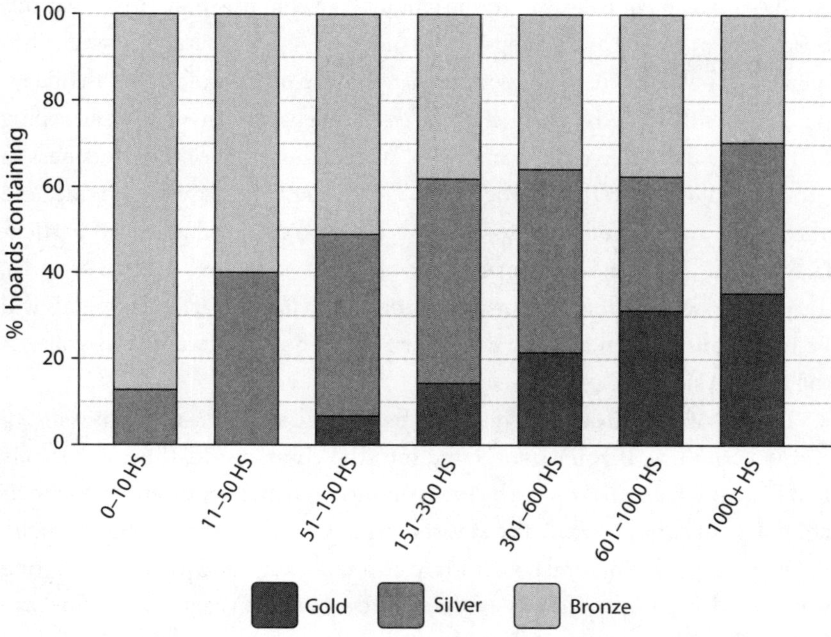

FIGURE 5.4. Metals for all: Pompeii, coin denominations from savings boxes by value range (Bowes 2022b, fig. 4)

found in very high-value hoards dominated by gold, pointing to their use as both small-scale savings *and* coins of daily use. On the flip side, the gold aureus (worth 100 bronze sestertii) is occasionally found beneath shop counters and in smaller hoards. Not simply a ceremonial coin or used purely for savings, it appears that gold was both plentifully supplied (most from the large-scale issues of Nero) and relatively frequently used.[43] Now, Pompeii have may have had an unusually large amount of gold in circulation, a product of Nero's help in reconstructing the town after the earthquake of 62 CE.[44] This caveat in place, we find no indication that the poor lived their lives exclusively in bronze and the rich in gold, as is sometimes supposed. The highest-value coin that did the job was used to do it, and there was sufficient supply and frequency of exchanges to put gold, silver and bronze in the hands of those who needed it.

Pompeii also provides us a sense of what people needed coins to do. Coin finds are particularly dense in places of exchange: the city's most commercial neighborhoods (Regions I, VII and IX) around the forum and major roads were thicker with coins than its more residential neighborhoods.[45] This is hardly surprising but alerts us to the gradients of coin use. Folks in the various businesses of buying and selling—from fullers to shopkeepers, vegetable salesmen to bar owners—used coins more than those in other professions, their days peppered with coined exchange. But even those engaged in buying and selling had diverse coined lives. Bar and shop owners did more of their business in bronze and less with the prestige metals. Resellers of bulk oil and wine, and above all artisans producing for larger-scale markets, used gold and particularly silver.[46] Indeed, silver appears to anchor most savings over 50 sestertii. The ways in which types of transactions partially cling to particular metals will be important to keep in mind as we turn to the quite different coin-scape of the countryside.

The use of coins by countrymen has been regarded as the real litmus test of Roman coin use. If coins penetrated into the countryside, this must surely herald a deep habit of coin use by the farming majority, supported by a deliberate policy of supply. While the statists dismissed rural coin use out of hand, the increasing pace of rural coin finds from archaeology and metal-detectoring was heralded by optimists as evidence for a vast and deep rural monetization.[47] The current state of the evidence reveals a more complex reality, a reality conditioned by the same forces we could observe at work in Pompeii—namely, the different needs for different kinds of coins in different contexts.

As with most things rural, the best data comes from Britain, where coins found in excavations of farms and villages have been systematically collected and analyzed.[48] Britain didn't have a particularly robust supply of small change until the mid-empire. As we noted above, Britons appear to have made local copies of bronze coins to counter this deficit. The fact that some of these counterfeiters appear to have been farmers, and that many of the copies appear in rural contexts, points not only to limited supply, but also to a real demand on the part of rural folks.[49]

In Britain, whether or not you used coins in your daily life depended less on whether you lived in the city or the country, but whether you lived in the north or the south of the province.[50] Coin use was concentrated in the south and eastern part of the island—places we've already observed hosted the majority of surplus agricultural production as well as dense, highly connected rural communities. People living in northern cities, farms and villages were less likely to use coins than their cousins in the south.[51] The north—more heavily militarized, but less highly urbanized and without those surplus-producing farms—showed much less coin use outside of forts and their supply villages. It's interesting here that soldiers—paid in coin and, as we have seen

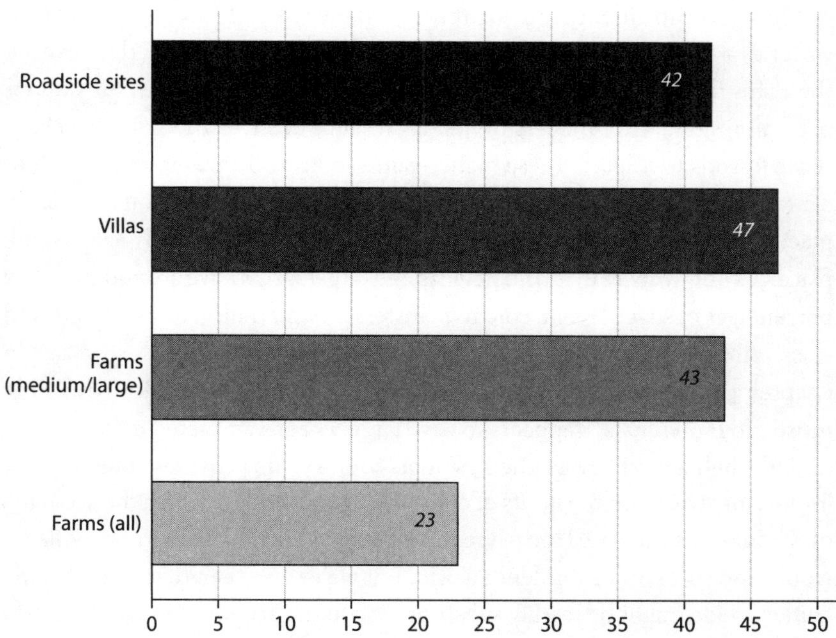

FIGURE 5.5. Coins in the countryside: Roman rural Britain, Central Belt, percentage of rural sites with coins (Reece Period A [1–12], through 260 CE) (Data: Allen et al. 2018)

throughout this book, living money-dense lives—didn't extend their habits of coin use much beyond their barracks.[52]

In the British center and south, places where exchange happened were places that used more coins. British cities were dense sites of coin use and loss; the countryside less so. Considering coin finds of the first through third centuries CE in the most agriculturally rich, central region, just under 50 percent of excavated rural sites produced coins of any kind.[53] But that number conceals important similarities and differences (figure 5.5).

Farmers living on the smallest farms—folks not heavily engaged in surplus production—used coins much more rarely, while those living in larger farms and roadside villages appear to have used them more frequently. It's interesting that the rates for villas, villages/roadside sites and larger farms are more or less the same. In other words, just as with writing and accounting, it's not the class of the occupant that determined coin use as much as the activities that required it: surplus production of agricultural or artisanal goods, exchange for goods and services, or both.

Coins found in excavations tend to skew toward low-denomination varieties—the kind of coins people didn't mind losing. And in this respect, the coins found on British farms are typical: low-value bronze coins dominate rural sites.[54] But the less frequent presence of silver and gold does have some lessons to impart. These higher-value coins, still small in number, concentrate in villas and larger farms.[55] That is, these higher-value coins cluster in places where larger-scale surplus production—and presumably sale—took place. It's noteworthy that British villas and larger farms have around the same percentages of silver. Again, coin use clusters around transactions, not around class. Villages and roadside sites have surprisingly little silver: as we saw in chapter 3, these were places of artisanal production, where sale—probably mostly to individuals—appears to have largely been transacted in bronze.

Although a world away, the Egyptian countryside provides some further important lessons on the limits of coin use in rural settings. From the accounts of Kronion the notary to the payments of wage workers, the Egyptian villages would appear to be a coin-dense world. But we've also seen that in Egypt, the coined mode might be readily substituted with the account mode. The workers on the third-century Appianus estate were probably only occasionally paid in actual coins, their wages, expenses and tax payments occurring through the medium of the account book alone.[56] We've also seen commodities being used in lieu of money: land rents and land taxes were paid in wheat, not coins, and these constituted a big chunk of rural transactions. So while monetary thinking may have been everywhere, money in the Egyptian countryside didn't just mean coins.

The coins we've seen repeatedly in daily use in Egypt were the bronze drachma and its principal fraction, the obol. But bronze was minted only sporadically by the province's only mint in Alexandria and stopped entirely by the early third century.[57] That neglect on the part of the mint is echoed in the finds.[58] The number of pre-260 CE coins from the Fayum villages is astonishingly low—in many cases less than 100 coins.[59] And this from villages of 3,000–6,000 people, who made dozens of daily purchases for centuries. These are the same villages whose financial records have appeared throughout this book, records filled with money transactions. Like the counterfeiting British farmers, Egyptians may have relied in part on lead tokens as substitutes for coinage, but those don't appear to have been terribly plentiful either.[60] It's always possible that this coin-poor world is really a product of poor recording and disinterested archaeology. At the moment, however, the Egyptian countryside appears to be an emblematic example of a robust, highly monetized rural economy running on a minimum of the very coins used in most exchanges. The answer to this conundrum is plain: account and commodity modes must have been major alternatives.

So while money was everywhere among the 90 percent, and monetary thinking even more so, working people used coined money in complex ways. The use of different metals was not determined by wealth or poverty. Coin denominations tracked transaction types, not class. Bronze was used for daily consumption, silver and gold for larger-scale exchanges. Savings were kept in all denominations. Egypt reminds us that a great many major and minor transactions might also be carried out in other monetary modes. In the countryside, rich and poor farmers alike would have recorded their rent and land-tax payments in wheat—the commodity mode—while in shops and on larger estates, many transactions took place on the books alone. As we probe more deeply what coins might tell us about the size of savings, it will be important to keep the Egyptian example in mind.

The 90 Percent and Their Savings

We've already encountered working people saving without commenting upon it. From the farmers in Tuscany who may have produced some 2,600 sestertii per year over subsistence; to Hermas the carpenter, whose wages might have permitted him to put away some 134 drachmas per month; to the auxiliary soldier Quintus Iulius Proclus, who could have saved some 20 drachmas from his monthly pay: some working people could clearly save.

Banks were mostly not how Romans saved. Banks existed, and deposit bankers (*argentarii*) could accept money. We occasionally find wealthy Romans using banks to store their money, but not as often as we might expect.[61] And while we also find working Romans using banks and bankers, they don't appear to have used them to stash their savings.

If we want to know how, and how much, the 90 percent saved, we might turn to the evidence of coin hoards. Coins stored in pots, buried under the floor or hidden in fields, should, in theory, represent somebody's savings. In practice, though, coin hoards represent a whole range of activities. If we want to use coin hoards to find out how much working people saved, it's a fraught business.[62]

First, coins may be hoarded not because they were intended as savings, but for other reasons. Coins with higher metal content may be hoarded, while those with lower content are spent—the so-called Gresham's Law. Our modern pots of pennies illustrate the phenomenon: coins hoarded for their copper value. No one would classify these as significant savings. Moments of inflation may also produce pots of low-bullion coins, as larger quantities are needed for basic purchases. In other words, in a bullion universe, the different values of different hoards might not represent different amounts of savings, but rather the changing levels and perceptions of coins' usefulness as an instrument of exchange. Coins may also be hoarded for entirely noneconomic reasons. Coins were common gifts to the gods and are found in large quantities in temples and shrines.[63] Of course, such hoards still represent a kind of savings, even if they were not intended for spending on a human market. Nonetheless, they may have only a glancing relationship with savings accumulated for other, more mundane reasons.

Finally, there is the problem of value itself.[64] Hoards are more often than not composed of a chronological range of coins whose value on the contemporary "market" in which they were assembled is hard to gauge.[65] More problematic still is what we do with the value once we have it. The purpose of such savings can vary, from daily pocket money (so-called circulation hoards), to hoards produced by the sale of something (transaction hoards), to a month's reserve of salary, a retirement bonus for a soldier, payments received for agricultural surplus, or sums accumulated over the year to pay taxes or rent (savings hoards).[66] Savings for different purposes will obviously differ in their value: rainy-day savings may differ from savings for investment purposes. Distinguishing the tiny savings of poor people from a group of coins simply intended to cover a day's shopping for the wealthier is impossible. Hoards don't come with their owner's names or use labels.

So coin hoards can't tell us exactly how much working people saved. They can, though, tell us something about the monetary modes used for savings. Let us take the best case study we are ever likely to have—the coin hoards from Pompeii.[67] We already noted the problems with even this best-case scenario: most importantly, the fact that lots of coins left the city with the fugitive population. What remained, however, tells us some interesting things about coined savings.

The most important thing it tells us is that coined savings were extremely small (figures 5.6 and 5.7). Around half of the hoards found on victims and 40 percent of the savings box hoards consisted of around only 3–4 sestertii of total coined value. As a reminder, documented food consumption costs in Pompeii as we unearthed it in chapter 2 were around three sestertii per day. Thus, most coined savings could support a day, or at most a week, of such

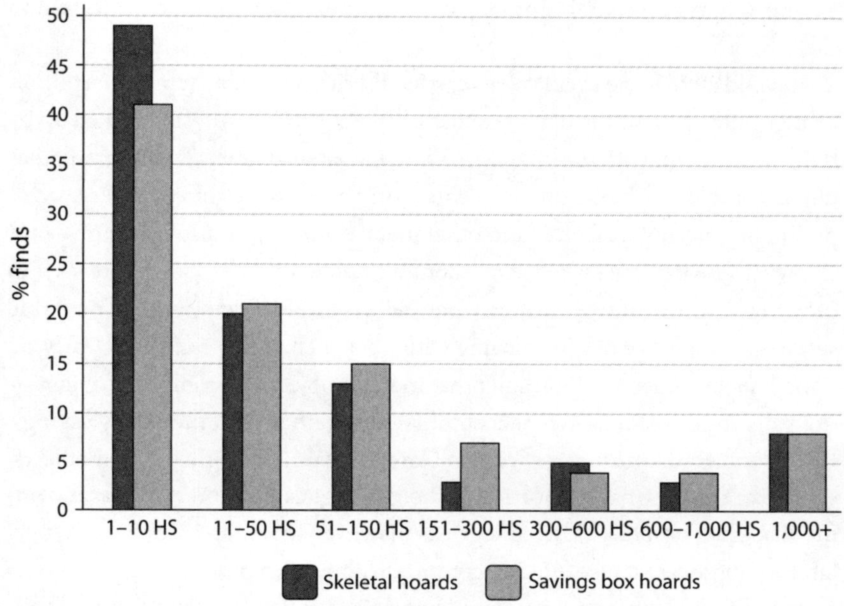

FIGURE 5.6. A savings-poor majority: Pompeii, victim and savings box hoards (n = 431), percentage of hoards by value range (Bowes 2022b, fig. 1)

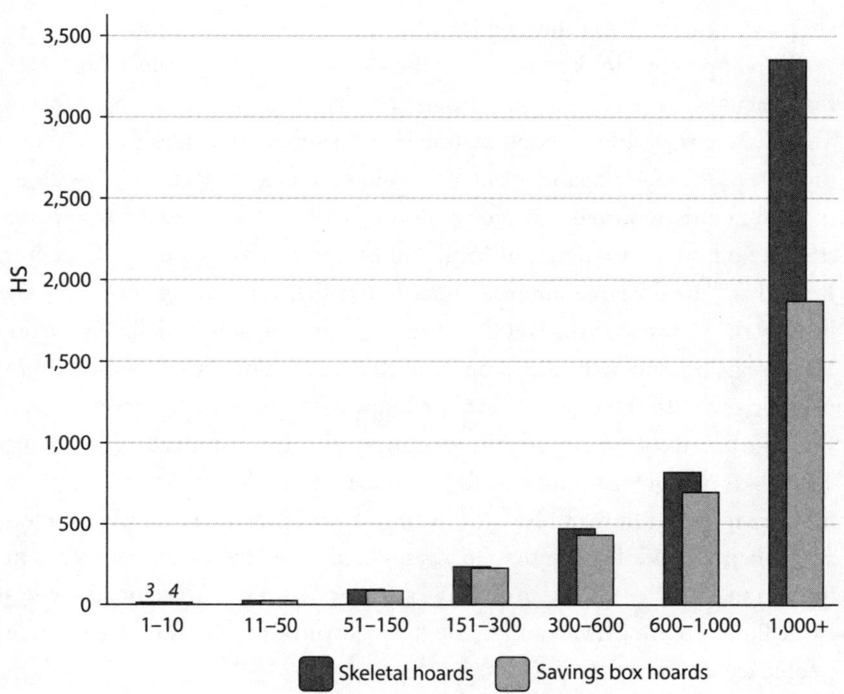

FIGURE 5.7. A low-value majority: Pompeii, victim and savings box hoards (n = 431), average value of hoards by value range (HS) (Bowes 2022b, fig. 2)

expenses and no more. Rainy-day or investment savings are hard to find in these hoards.

It could be that the small values carried by victims simply represents pocket change, intended for the day's expenses. This is possible but isn't backed up by the objects found with the hoards. Around half of the victims' hoards had other objects of value in them. The most common objects were gold or silver jewelry or dining plate, but iron tools and other metal objects were also common—not to mention what appear to be mementoes and keepsakes (see figure 5.3). In other words, not only did many people assemble everything of portable value—and so were not just fleeing with pocket change—but they clearly assigned major value to bullion and other metallic objects. Commodity savings—the value of the metal—were accumulated together with monetary savings. Unfortunately, in most cases we don't know the weight of the bullion objects, so we can't judge what proportion of their savings came from coin versus commodity. The Pompeii evidence suggests that, even in a coin-saturated city, portable savings were constituted of commodity and coin modes.

So we should take the very low coined savings in Pompeii with a grain of salt. We should also worry that even the wealthy's savings appear to be too small. Only a tiny proportion of hoards from the city itself exceeded 1,000 sestertii of value (see figure 5.6). Transactional hoards in the cashboxes of bars and shops are also small in value (figure 5.8).

Even impressive-looking hauls like the 1,450 coins found in the bar of Vetutius Placidus had a value of only around 600 sestertii (see figure 5.1). Most of Vetutius' coins were low-denomination bronzes: his total savings wasn't as impressive as the sheer quantity of coins would indicate. In fact, very few commercial hoards achieved the 5,700 sestertii that was the approximate average transaction value carried out by local middleman and moneylender Caecilius Iucundus.[68] Really large suburban hoards, like the 19,287 sestertii collectively held by the victims at Villa B at Oplontis or the principal Villa della Pisanella/Boscoreale treasure worth 108,400 sestertii in coins alone, were one-offs.[69] In comparison with the cost of things we know elites purchased, however, even the large hoards of the city and the whoppers from the suburbs don't seem big enough. A plot of local land sold for 295,000 sestertii,[70] slaves cost on average 1,800 sestertii per human life,[71] the average transaction carried out by larger-scale financial middlemen ran to 10,945 sestertii,[72] and the wealth requirement for entrance to the equestrian order was 400,000 sestertii. The coined savings from Pompeii are just not big enough to account for the things even rich people were buying.

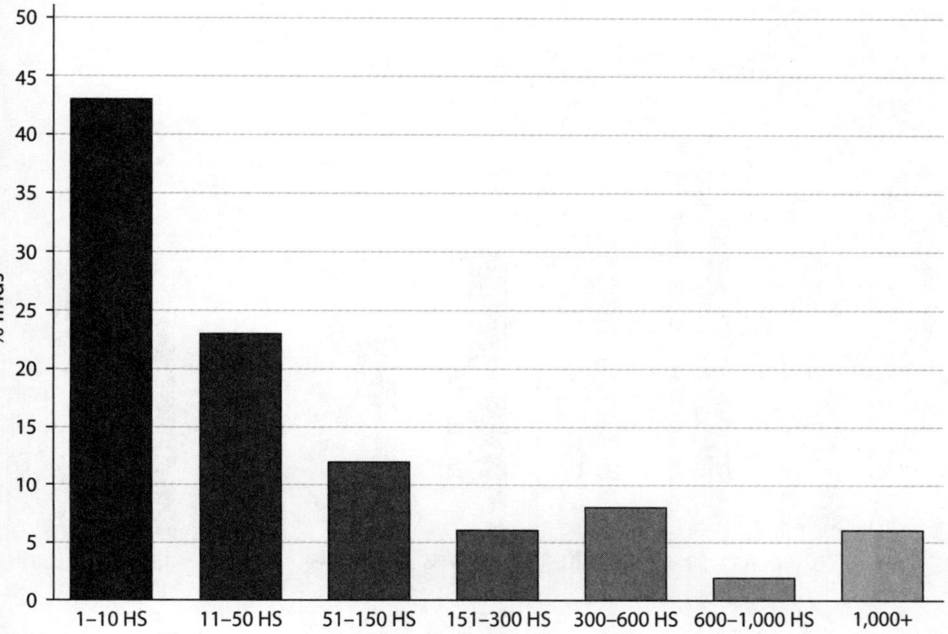

FIGURE 5.8. Shopkeepers with limited savings: Pompeii, savings boxes from commercial spaces (n = 65), average value of hoards by value range in HS. (Data: Bowes 2022b)

Rich people kept their coins in more than one place, and again, it's possible that the real money left the scene during the 18+ hours of the eruption. Much of it must have, and maybe this is the answer to Pompeii's deficit of savings.[73] But the silence of big money, together with the smallness of savings generally, strongly suggests that currency—even currency and bullion objects together—did not constitute all or even the majority of savings for many people, not only the rich but also a portion of the not-rich.[74]

Pompeii may be the best-preserved money environment in the Roman world, but it was hardly a typical one. More representative, in theory, would be the coins hoarded by people around the whole of the empire. But if we examine the coin hoards from the whole empire, we find much the same thing: coin hoards are too small to represent the whole of people's savings. If Pompeii coin hoards need to be taken with a grain of salt, the collected hoards of the empire require a whole bushel.[75] Low-value bronze coins remain horribly undercounted in many places; regional patterns reflect different supply of different kinds of coins to different areas, and very few of the hoards have any recorded

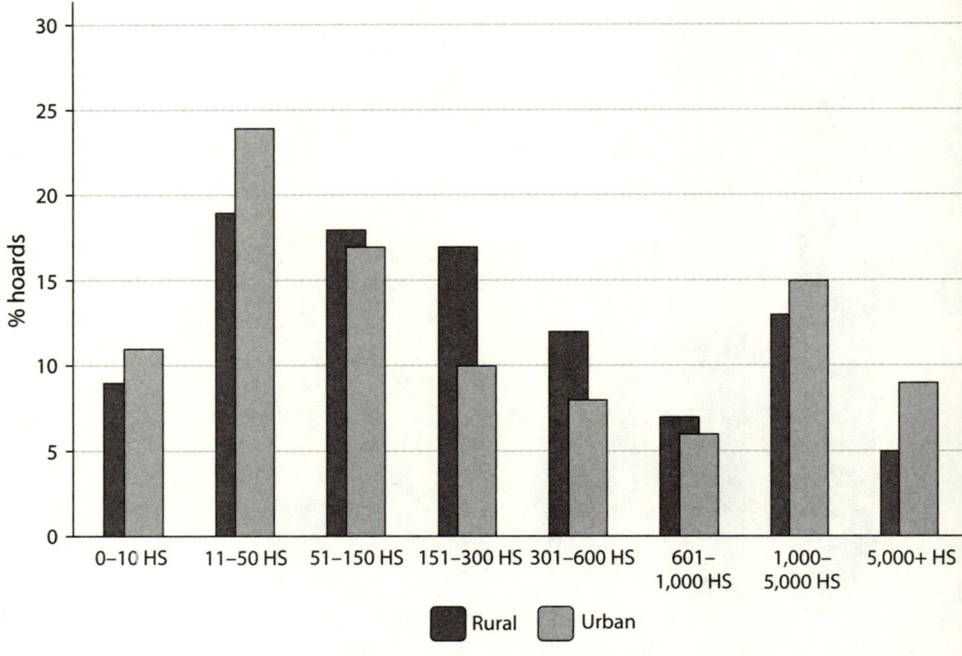

FIGURE 5.9. Coin hoards, Roman empire (n = 1,448), percentage of hoards by value range in HS (Data: Howgego 2019)

contexts, so the circulation hoards of rich people and savings hoards of poor people all look the same.

But the picture, with all its warts, tells the same strange story we found at Pompeii. From a corpus of some 1,448 hoards from around the empire (about a third urban and two-thirds rural), around half of all hoards were worth only 150 sestertii or less (figure 5.9).

These numbers vary a bit for rural versus urban people, with folks in rural contexts having somewhat greater numbers of medium-value hoards. Many rural hoards come from the northwest provinces, where silver denarii and aurei may be the result of military pay and/or bonuses.[76] Nonetheless, and despite these differences, the overall picture is remarkably consistent. Around half of the people represented by these hoards had coined savings of somewhere between 10–150 sestertii or drachmas. Savings of this level would cover the monthly food costs for an individual living in a city like Pompeii or support a family living at low but sustainable subsistence in Egypt for a couple of months. That is, some of these hoards could, theoretically, represent rainy-day savings activities of the 90 percent.

But again, it's the dog that doesn't bark that's most revealing. These empire-wide hoards can't represent the transactional or investment savings that would have also been typical of working people. Seventy percent of the rural hoards are too small to represent the income from a small (seven *iugera*) plot of land; some 80 percent of rural and 75 percent of urban hoards are too small to represent any significant capital expense like the likely cost of a small plot of land. Given the location of so many hoards in highly militarized provinces, a similar problem accrues to the size of those hoards versus the value of an army retirement bonus. From 12,000 sestertii for ordinary legionary soldiers to 20,000 sestertii for a pretorian, the very highest value hoards might represent savings of that magnitude, but the majority do not.[77] And, as with Pompeii, the empire's hoards are just too small to represent the money of the rich: the average value of the very highest value hoards—22–51,000 sestertii—would only barely constitute the yearly income for a member of the equestrian order.[78] In short, even in a collection that probably radically underestimates smaller, bronze-based savings, the hoards are still too small to be representative of values that should have passed through most working peoples' hands, let alone those of elites.

It is, of course, possible that the majority of higher-value hoards have been lost to time and the millennia-long attrition of their precious metal contents. Certainly, the loss of very, very large hoarded savings—like Pliny's mother-in-law's famous cashbox of three million sestertii—certainly suffered from this.[79] But it is hard to imagine that the entire dataset is biased in this way. If anything, it's probably biased in the other direction, by failing to accurately register bronze and lower-value savings. The savings of Pompeii and coin hoards throughout the empire suggest that while working people used coins for daily, small-scale exchanges, and their coined savings were sufficient to support a moderate period of such transactions, significant portions of total savings were not made or held in coins. Other monetary modes—both bullion and agricultural commodities but also credit and account money—must have constituted a sizable chunk of people's savings.[80]

If coins can't give us the whole picture, there is one other place we can look for a more complete picture of working people's savings: dowries. Dowries were gifts of cash, land and commodities—clothes and jewelry—made by the bride's family upon her marriage. Dowries were intended both to support the bride in her new household and to constitute an addition to the new household's property portfolio. They represent, as they do today, poor families' ability to scrimp and save and put aside wealth. For many families, they would have represented the bulk, although not the whole, of their savings.

In most of the Roman world, women retained their dowry if they got divorced, and so it was important to get the details of what was being handed over right—and written down. As a result, we have dozens of dowry agreements from the sands of Roman Egypt. These dowries were complex financial instruments.[81] Most, even small ones, had multiple parts: a part consisting of money, clothes and jewelry that could be accessed by the husband during the marriage (the *pherne*), and a part, mostly in land (and for wealthier families, slaves), that was left in the control of the wife (*parapherna*). An old-fashioned family might include a support contract (*syngraphe trophitis)* consisting mostly of land but expressed as a cash value.[82] It's no accident that Roman Egyptian dowries had the same qualities as Roman savings—they consisted of cash, commodities and land.

The average cash value provided in the *pherne* portion of dowries from Roman Egypt was just shy of 200 drachmas, with a median of 176 drachmas.[83] In the dowries registered in one village, the average was somewhat lower—around 160 drachmas with a median of 80 drachmas.[84] The lower medians here are a product of what appears to be very "sticky" dowry gifts: amounts of 80, 100 and 120 drachmas were probably traditionally gifted sums, which had cultural as well as economic significance—not unlike bar mitzvah gifts today. The smallest dowry recorded was just 16 drachmas. The much larger support contracts (on average around 1,400 drachmas total value) represent the value of land. At average land prices, an average of only about a hectare and a half was reserved for the bride.[85]

Together, these dowry and support contracts indicate the modest quantities of cash, commodity and land that formed part of Egyptian working people's savings. It's notable that the average cash portion in the dowries (c. 160 drachmas) is not too dissimilar from the average savings we found in the empire-wide coin hoards—most commonly 10–150 sestertii. Again, this was only the cash piece: land and clothing were worth more. The cash was enough to buy a donkey, or a loom, or to sustain a new family for a couple of months while children were born. One hundred and fifty sestertii or Egyptian drachmas: it's about as close as we're likely to get to the average cash balance in a working Roman's savings account.

Borrowing and Lending

If coins were only one of a variety of monetary instruments, and coined savings appears to have been pretty modest, how else did working people pay for things? The use of multiple monetary modes—coins, commodities and account money—also generated the need to move between them: sometimes you might have wheat, but you needed to pay rent in coins; sometimes you had coins but needed wheat for seed. In other words, the existence of all these different kinds of "money" made some kind of credit almost essential—not only account money, but also borrowed money. Borrowing was also essential to bridge genuine shortfalls, caused by crop failure, emergency expenses, dowries, the birth of children.

The Roman world, it is now clear, was awash in borrowing. It's been clear for some time that the wealthy lived, unashamedly, on a sea of loans. Cicero's famous house purchases, the younger Pliny's sale of his future grape harvest or his loudly contemplated land mortgages—were all performed at full volume through their (very public) letters.[86] While they may not have bragged about them in the same way, working Romans likewise made vigorous use of credit. Artemidorus the dream interpreter's declaration that loans equaled life spoke to a working clientele whose lives were permeated by borrowing and lending. From the women moneylenders of Pompeii who lent or pawned out of their family workshop, to the Jewish charity regulations insisting that wealth was to be calculated net of debts, to the frenzy of lending and borrowing that took place in army camps—credit activities were everywhere.[87] As we shall see, this ubiquity of borrowing had a very different character than the "profligate rich, indebted poor" of earlier scholarship. That story came mostly from elite literary sources. Looking beyond those sources—above all to the Egyptian papyri and ostraca—reveals more complex motivations for borrowing, and a more complex set of identities for both borrowers and creditors.

Before we examine this complex world in greater detail, it will again be important to clear the air of any contemporary baggage, particularly around vocabulary. Today, credit might take the form of a mortgage, a savings club, or a credit card. Romans' loans were similarly diverse in structure, but quite different in form. The least formal and probably most common loan, among parties who knew each other, was an unwritten agreement. While most of these took place beneath our radar, we might catch some glimpses of them in the lists we examined in chapter 1. For instance, the person we met in the Pompeii gladiatorial barracks recording his expenses for bread, cheese and lots of wine also included a denarius paid to him on the ninth day before the kalends, and a denarius and four semis received from one Lucius Gavius.[88] These instances of monies received are common on expenses lists and may very well reflect those short-term, informal loans for which no written agreement was thought necessary.

Somewhat more formal agreements took place in pawnshops: because an actual object was deposited as security on a loan, a full legal contract was not necessary, but receipts appear to have been given out recording the item pawned, the amount loaned and the date.[89] This constituted proof of both the pawn and also the date around which interest was calculated.

Still more formal arrangements took different forms in different parts of the empire, largely around the different legal traditions that held in the Roman heartland versus those in the Greek East.[90] In the West, formal loan agreements might be drafted by a whole range of people, from the professional deposit bankers (*argentarii*) or moneylenders (*faeneratores*) to multitasking businessmen.[91] In the West there appear to have been no notary offices and thus no way of registering the transaction with the state or checking the security of the loan. Instead, an elaborate contract with multiple witnesses was used. In the Roman West, a loan contract was deemed legally fixed simply by the oral intention to provide a loan and its de facto acceptance: in legal theory, no written contract was necessary. But in practice, in a document-clutching, distrustful world, this system of witnesses and signatures provided a written expression of that oral intention and, presumably, some basis of recourse if things turned sour.[92]

In the East, on the other hand, the written word had long-standing legal force, and whatever Roman law might have dictated, these traditions continued. Aside from the good fortune of preservation, this is one of the reasons we have so many loan documents from Egypt: it formed part of an eastern legal world where writing brought a contract into legal being. A loan contract might take a simple form, usually formed as a letter—X (debtor) greets Y (creditor) and acknowledges receipt of Z loan.[93] We've already seen abbreviated versions of these used by the Egyptian quarry workers. Here is a somewhat more formal example among hundreds:

> Stotoetis, son of Harpagathes, grandson of Harpagathes, to Diogas, greetings. I acknowledge having received from you as a loan two hundred silver drachmas, totals dr. 200, which I shall repay whenever it is required. If I should not repay according to what has been written, I shall pay as a fine . . . [94]

Already before the Roman occupation, notaries might be employed to draft contracts. The notary had many functions: as an intermediary to bring lending and borrowing parties together, to provide writing services to the illiterate and the force of the state to recognize the contract's legality.[95] Under Roman rule, the village notary offices were further expanded. These notary offices comprise some of our best evidence for lending practices, so complete and detailed were their records. These many local notary offices worked together with property archives established in Egyptian district capitals.[96] These latter theoretically kept records of all immovable property transactions—wills, contracts, sales, marriage gifts and loans—and thus helped verify the security used for loans guaranteed with property.

One did not need to use a notary to draft a loan. The letter-format option continued, and notarial fees, just like today, may have kept the poorest borrowers and lenders from registering their transactions in this way.[97] However, those fees, where we can see them, appear to be roughly based on the amount of the transaction, and the fact that some 25 percent of loans registered with the village notary office in Tebtunis were under 50 drachmas suggests that parties involved in even small-scale transactions chose to use it.[98]

Security is one of the bedrocks of credit systems: while we might be willing to lend money to our friends or family based on good faith, having some tangible compensation in the event of nonpayment extends the base of potential creditors to parties who don't know each other. Security guarantees were more common in larger-scale loans, and became increasingly common as time went on.[99] But hints of security are found even in the smallest-scale loans: as we shall see, those whose only asset was their ration payments or their wages pledged future payments or earnings as security, while other security arrangements may be lurking behind the truncated loan lists in the notary's registers.

So, too, poor creditors and borrowers found many ways to insist on and to pay interest on loans. Interest is a vexed question in ancient lending. Very often no interest rate is stipulated, a fact that led previous scholars to assume that no interest was charged and that people lent for altruistic reasons, or to improve their social standing.[100] We're now more skeptical, and scholars have found interest lurking either in separate agreements, or in language that called upon commonly accepted rates. Since the Late Republic, interest rates were legally capped at 12 percent, and 12 percent appears to have been a default, normal rate.[101] However, as we shall see, there is enough variation to suggest, if not an integrated market, at least different levels of perceived risk.[102] What is important to note, however, is the different forms that interest might take, depending on the resources of the borrower. The poorest used their labor or, in the case of women, their nursing bodies to pay interest. Service contracts (*paramone*) were defined as those in which the labor of the borrower or their family member served as interest. For those with tiny amounts of capital, usufruct took the place of interest. Various forms of so-called antichretic loans allowed the creditor the produce of the land (*prodomatic* leases) or the use of a house (*enoikesis*) in lieu of interest. In these cases, what appears to be a lease of land or house is in fact the usufruct agreement, which, rather than paying the lessor a real rent, is actually serving as interest. And many lenders required no interest at all: zero-interest loans are not uncommon, the result of genuine altruism, the expectation of future favors or the building of social capital.[103]

Credit as Survival

In the poorest countries today, those who live on $2 a day or less deploy a complex portfolio of credit, loans and savings to extend their meager earnings into a family existence.[104] Many of these people live with chronic debt—some ultimately devastating, some manageable—while many end their month in the black. In other words, the use of credit need not imply self-destructive indebtedness, nor does poverty mean that credit transactions are simple and one-sided. Even the tiniest amount of food and money can be leveraged in complex ways—as futures, as hedging, to make a very little go further. Similar phenomena can be found in the Roman world among the poorest class of working people—the enslaved and free workers doing the harsh work in the granite quarries in eastern Egypt. These workers constantly used the only things they could control—their rations and their labor—in complex credit arrangements.

We met some of these workers in previous chapters—the so-called *pagani* who were paid a sustainable cash-plus-wheat wage, and another group called the *familiares,* who did the most unskilled labor and were paid in food and clothing rations with a tiny cash wage. Perversely, but as was not uncommon, the *familiares* were paid their food rations after the fact—that is, their rations and wages were delivered at the end of the month to which they pertained.[105] Not unsurprisingly, given the unremittingly hard kinds of work they did, workers sometimes ran out of rations before month's end and needed advances on future rations to make ends meet. Over 200 ostraca requests for such advances have been preserved from the quarries, and it is here we get a glimpse of credit used by those living closet to the bone.

Many of the requests follow the simplest written form described above, with a member of the *familiares* acknowledging, usually to the quartermaster, that they have received rations in advance:

> Didymos, son of Diophantes, to Alexandros, quartermaster, greetings. I acknowledge having received my three *kotyles* of oil and my *mation* of lentils for the month of Mecheir [February] in the 21st year of Hadrian Caesar our lord.[106]

Didymos appears to have used up his rations and has taken an advance on his oil and lentils. Technically, these advances granted to the *familiares* are not loans as properly defined: the "repayment" of the advance is simply taken out of the worker's future rations. In practice, though, the line between advance and loan was constantly blurred, as rations also behaved as commodity money, which might be used as both loan and security. For example:

> I, Philetos, son of Ammonios, acknowledge having received from Ision as an advance three *matia* of wheat [10 liters] which I will reimburse in Phaophi [October].[107]

The Ision from whom Philetos is receiving this advance is not, in fact, the quartermaster, but perhaps a sutler. Ision commonly lent money, oil, wheat and lentils to various of the *familiares*.[108] In short, Philetos has used his future rations as security against which he has taken out a loan of wheat from Ision. These future rations will also be used to repay the loan. In this community of isolated, poorly paid workers, rations serve as a monetized commodity, converted into both security and repayment.

As such, rations might also be used as payment to others besides the worker for whom they were intended:

> Saturninus to Alexandros, quartermaster, greetings. I acknowledge having received my three *kotyles* of oil and my *mation* of lentils, which you will repay to Ision in the month of Phaophi.[109]

Saturninus has also received an advance on his rations from the quartermaster, Alexandros. He has also apparently borrowed from Ision the sutler. Saturninus' future rations, which will be delivered by Alexandros the quartermaster, are to be used to extinguish Saturninus' debt to this third party, Ision. These sorts of "triangular" relationships between a debtor, quartermaster and third-party creditor were common.[110] Neither were they limited to the *familiares*: members of the *pagani*, the free workforce, also used their compensation in this way. One Artemas, son of Artimidorus, gave over the whole of his monthly cash salary, his wheat and his wine to his creditors, not once, but twice.[111]

These transactions raise the question of how workers, who in theory ought to be living hand-to-mouth from wages and/or rations, are doing so when they are paying over part or all of their compensation to creditors. A system that was, in structure, very simple—wages and rations as compensation for work—was modified into one in which present and future wages/rations constituted a set of financial instruments. In short, we can sense behind these triangular credit relationships a world of hustle, using rations and wages, present or future, to underwrite other transactions that lie just outside the purview of the receipts.[112]

What some of these transactions might have been is suggested by the purely cash loans taken out by *familiares*:

> Epithymetos, member of the *numerus* of Porphyrities, *arithmos* [work group] of Claudianus, to Flavius Isidoros of the Alexandrian fleet and the company of Pallas, greetings. I acknowledge to have received from you five drachmas which I will repay without dispute of any kind as soon as my wheat for the month of Thoth has been brought up. The fourth year of Antoninus our lord, 6 Thoth [September 3, 140 CE].[113]

Here Epithymetos, who defines himself by his work group, borrows five drachmas from Flavius Isidoros—a straightforward cash loan. The average amount raised through the *familiares'* cash loans at the quarries was 12 drachmas with a median of eight drachmas.[114] This is significantly more than the *familares'* likely monthly cash wages of around seven drachmas.[115] However, in only two instances is their cash "salary" used as the guarantee; as with Epithymetos, future rations or the clothing allowance serve that purpose. The timing of these loans is also significant. Whenever such cash loans are dated, as in Epithymetos' case, they appear at the beginning of the month in question.[116] Rations and wages have just been paid, so these are unlikely to be loans for survival. Rather, workers flush with rations are using the promise of future rations to raise cash—cash significantly greater than their own cash wages. The planned repayment is either in wheat, or another swap of wheat for cash. Interestingly, though, the debtor didn't, in this instance, sell his rations for cash—that is, he didn't exchange commodity for currency. Rather, he converted commodity into a guarantee for a loan in currency, thereby extending his income.

What did the workers do with this borrowed money? As we saw in chapter 2, the quarries at Mons Claudianus were rich with all kinds of consumer goods—from a wide range of imported foodstuffs to a wider range of clothes and equipment than that likely provided by the *familia*'s yearly clothing ration.[117] To what extent this world of goods was purchased and brought in by the free workers with their generous cash wages, and to what extent it was purchased by the *familiares* with their wages-plus-credit, is unknowable. But the very presence of those goods, and the meagerness of the *familiares'* compensation, attests to some relationship between that gusto for things and credit.

The lenders behind these cash loans are also interesting. When it's possible to know their identities, the lenders appear to be, like Ision, sutlers or traders.[118] Others, like Flavius Isidorus, are soldiers or *pagani*, or have other positions in the quarry administration—the water-manager or a civilian secretary. In short, the lenders are not elites. They are those just a micro-step up the ladder from the bottom-of-the-heap *familiares*, people who had somewhat more resources than their borrowers. What motivated them to lend their own scarce capital again lies just outside the frame of our evidence, as interest is almost never mentioned. They may be reselling the rations used as payment; they may just be looking for future favors. But a world of dimly glimpsed hustle is probably behind these transactions.

The community at Mons Claudianus, with their regular wages, lack of immediate families and isolated location, might seem to be the last place credit would be required. But in practice, the quarries were a natural credit community. A steady supply of minor capital (i.e., wages and rations), distributed unequally between different groups, produced ready-made lenders and borrowers. That steady supply also meant that security, in the form of future wages/rations, was good: moral hazard—the likelihood a debtor would be unable to pay—was low. Finally, the possibility that the state appeared to have purchased wheat at below-market prices may have also provided the basis for earning extra income by commuting commodity into cash.[119] But perhaps the most remarkable thing about this credit community was its apparent need to resort to writing. This isn't how we imagine "informal" credit.[120] Even in a (relatively) small world where debtors and lenders would likely have known one another, the widespread use of written forms literally underwrote credit complexity. Employed overwhelmingly by people with limited literacy, written loans nonetheless made it possible to expand rock-bottom incomes.[121] Written loans allowed these most impoverished of workers to live beyond the quartermaster's monthly system, to engage in triangular debt relationships, to transform commodity into currency. In other words, for this most impoverished group of workers, doing the most miserable work, credit allowed them to transform their restricted earnings into something more.

The Pawnshop: Commodity into Cash

The credit systems in the imperial quarries find complicated lending and borrowing taking place among some of the empire's most marginalized workers. For those a step above, borrowing and lending was rooted in the gusto for things we observed in chapter 2. We examined that phenomenon as a "consumer revolution," as though all those attractive objects—from pots to plows, jewelry to lamps—were wholly consumed through the act of purchase. In reality, of course, buying durable goods merely converted cash into commodity. Those bronze pots and silver earrings, tunics and statuettes, might all be converted back into cash when need called.

Pawnbrokers supplied that need, as did a wider range of people who were willing to supply cash on the security of objects. For instance, at Pompeii, Faustilla, whom we met in chapter 1, lent money without security at interest, but she also pawned objects: a pair of gold earrings for two denarii minus one *as* interest; or two cloaks for 50 denarii minus 12.5 or eight *asses* interest.[122]

The most complete record of pawnbrokering comes, not surprisingly, from Egypt, but, perhaps somewhat surprisingly, from a village.[123] It reminds us that, yet again, the gusto for things extended to the countryside, and that rural people not only consumed along with urbanites, but might need to covert those purchases back to cash at moments of want. The account details the partial records of four customers—all women—over a period of some 14 months. All the women came back to the pawnbroker multiple times. The most complete record—for a woman named Thermouthis—saw her return at least 12 times to the pawnbroker, and in some months, multiple times. A portion of the account reveals her activities:

The 14th year.

September 29th. Thermouthis wife of [—] to pledge 28 drachmas. Security: a tunic [—] without other debts.

October 18th. 8 drachmas. Security: engraved dish, 1 linen [—].

January 11th. 24 drachmas [Security]: Round meal bowl [—].

February 7th. Through her daughter 8 dr. Security: 31 dishes [?] and 1 meal bowl

May 5th. A loan of 8 drachmas and interest 4 obols was paid and she took back the bowls pledged on February 7th.

August 23rd. Through her husband 16 drachmas. Security: 1 [bronze?] bathtub.

August 25th. The same Thermouthis borrowed 11 drachmas. Security: 1 white unwashed tunic.

September 7th. 20 drachmas. Security: 1 red tunic.[124]

Thermouthis pawned a whole range of her possessions—a red tunic, dishes, bowls, a bathtub—but principally vessels and textiles, in exchange for a total of around 125 drachmas in cash over some 13-plus months. She paid back only 32 drachmas over that time, and thus redeemed only a fraction of the objects she pawned. On the rest, she presumably defaulted. The fragmentary records of the other clients show similar records of nonrepayment.

The amounts loaned by first- and second-century pawnbrokers, limited though they are, range from eight to 200 drachmas/sestertii.[125] The average pawn amount from the Fayum pawnbroker was around 17 drachmas. This is somewhat greater than the cash loans made to the Mons Claudianus quarry workers (average 12 drachmas), although not markedly so. While the fragmentary text isn't terribly forthcoming on dates, it is notable, perhaps, that the great majority of dated pawns do not take place during the "hungry season" before the harvest. Rather, they cluster in August through November, during the planning and planting season. To what extent these pawns were used for food, and to what extent their commodity-to-cash exchange was intended to solve liquidity problems during a busy agricultural season, is thus an open question.

Pawnbrokers get a bad rap: infamous for charging ultra-high rates of interest, they are assumed to prey upon those who have only their objects as security.[126] This doesn't quite capture the Roman pawn-universe. Pawnbrokers—today and then—deal in short-term loans. Their annualized interest rates are high, but manageable if paid for only a couple months. This seems to characterize Roman pawning. When we can calculate these rates, they would have been outrageous if annualized—up to 100 percent but averaging around 40 percent.[127] Monthly rates range between one and 10 percent—which is what Thermouthis paid. Another Egyptian account from later in the third century appears to charge around 9–10 percent monthly interest.[128] Faustilla, the Pompeiian woman, appeared to have charged between one and six percent monthly interest. In her case, since the amount was deducted from the loan at the moment of lending, this wasn't "interest" properly defined, just a flat fee.[129] Similarly, a woman from Oxyrhynchus, instructing someone to redeem a whole range of pawned objects—from clothes and textiles to statuettes of Aphrodite—appears to have been charged around four percent of monies lent.[130] In other words, while annualized rates would have been extortionate, it's not clear anyone was using pawns that way. The usurious pawnbroker of modern stereotype exists in these records—although even the 40 percent average per year is reasonable by modern standards—but the experience of the actual borrower was different: a modest sum paid in exchange for a short-term loan.[131]

In fact, we should probably be wary of talking about "pawnbrokers" at all. The term "pawnbroker" doesn't appear in Roman Egypt and very rarely in Roman Italy. There's no common word for it because exchanging consumer goods for cash was done all the time, by all kinds of people.[132] The same people scholars have labeled "pawnbrokers" are, like Faustilla, probably lending money more generally, sometimes around goods left in pledge, and at other times through other means.[133] What we're really observing in the so-called pawnbroker accounts is the fact that a world full of things was not always a world full of cash, and exchanging one for the other marks yet another instance where working Romans used credit to move between monetary modes.

Unlike today, where pawning and pawnshops are overwhelmingly a male world, women appear to dominate our few sources.[134] All of the clients of the Fayum accounts were women. Faustilla and Vettia lent small sums—sometimes on pawn—in Pompeii, while a much later family of Nile Valley moneylenders included several women. Why so many women? It's possible that women found it harder to get more advantageous credit. Only 21 percent of borrowers in formalized Egyptian credit relationships were women, and women were more likely to lend or borrow from other women—suggesting gender restricted both lending and borrowing.[135] But women were also particular custodians of the world of things: their dowries comprised clothes and jewelry they could pawn, while other objects—like plates and bathtubs—were part of their household object universe. Both discrimination and control may have motivated their use of objects for cash.

Money in Action

The problem of the so-called pawnbroker is part of a broader problem of treating "credit" as an isolated phenomenon. This makes sense if you're interested in legal definitions or banks, but it runs aground on people's actual experience. Working people didn't experience "credit." Rather, they deployed small incomes from a variety of sources—including borrowing—together with small amounts of capital and commodities, into an overlapping set of monetary tools. They used those tools to extend their income, and, just as important, to move between different monetary modes. Lending and borrowing, spending and saving—all were entangled in daily life, even if they were legally distinct.

One of the most extraordinary documents from the ancient world preserves a glimpse of these financial instruments in action: the records of the village notary office from Tebtunis. During the 20s through 50s CE, this notary office was run by Kronion and, for a period, his partner Eutuchas.[136] Tebtunis, readers will recall, was one of those large villages inhabited overwhelmingly by farmers, as well as craftsmen and traders. We have already met Kronion in earlier chapters when we examined his private expense accounts. Kronion and Eutuchas produced a wide range of financial documents for the inhabitants of Tebtunis: land leases and dowry agreements, sale receipts and tax declarations. They also produced a huge range of agreements relating to the borrowing and lending of cash and commodities. Their records, which included copies of the actual documents they produced as well as abbreviated registers of document titles, list the transactions as they were carried out, day by day.[137] The registers alone preserve over 1,200 separate transactions over a period of 20 months. In what is one of the most granular financial documents to survive from the ancient world, we can catch a glimpse of the borrowing, lending, saving and spending as entwined in the lives of the 90 percent.[138]

Even so extraordinary a document as this has its limitations. The titles register is, by definition, highly abbreviated: it includes the date, names of the parties, type of transaction, and often the amount of money in question. Interest rates, security, background about the contracting parties—none of these form part of these abbreviated records. Furthermore, how representative is this immense record? While it may be the one of most detailed and sustained record of working people's monetary transactions from the ancient world, the register still only records less than two years of activity from a particular village in Egypt. The lion's share of the register records the transactions of 45 to 46 CE. Allegedly 45 CE was a very bad year, a year with a particularly high and devastating Nile flood.[139] The register has been used to argue that this high flood caused economic disaster among the villages of Egypt, including the Fayum. In other words, the credit transactions—the many loans and, above all, the service and nursing contracts—have been viewed as wholly atypical, a product of an indebted community on the brink.[140] Recent work has questioned this reading of the register: the many transactions of lending and borrowing are increasingly viewed as typical, not atypical, of farming villages, and not necessarily indicative of some disaster.[141] By averaging out the data from the possible "bad year" with "normal" year data, we can compensate for any aberrations and concentrate on what the record reveals about the financial instruments of the rural 90 percent.[142]

Borrowing to Invest

Above all, the Tebtunis records reveal the importance of credit to village life. The notary office drew up dozens of different kinds of agreements, from land leases to wills. Around a third of all transactions were some kind of loan.[143] Loans exceed even land leases in their frequency, and even outside the alleged year of possible agricultural crisis, they also constituted about a third of notarial activity. And Tebtunis was hardly remarkable: some 45 percent of all financial transactions from Roman Egypt were loans of various kinds.[144] Just as notable are the many forms that credit transactions might take: from outright loans to mortgages to deposits (*parathekai*)—where creditors "deposited" their money with lenders—to a whole range of usufruct arrangements where portions of houses, land or labor were used in lieu of interest. Hardly simple arrangements between autarkic farmers, these loans show every sign of having the same complexities as those used by wealthy city dwellers. They also show every intention on the part of the lenders to profit from the transaction.

Houses and land and, to a lesser extent, labor were critical components of these agreements, used either in lieu of interest or as security. That is, not only was lending and borrowing woven into the fabric of village transactional life, but tiny amounts of capital or, in its absence, labor, were used to underwrite that credit network.[145] A portion of a house, a courtyard, a hectare or two of land: these were tiny but valuable commodities in a densely used landscape. Indeed, the frequency with which house usufruct is given over to creditors makes one wonder if principal or secondary residences are being used in these transactions, for surely not all the debtors are giving up their only shelter in exchange for cash. One catches a glimpse of a world of people with modest means and tiny portfolios of land and houses, using portions of them to raise short-term cash or commodities.

We've already seen the importance of security, even of the most modest kind: security makes lending safer and incentivizes lenders to lend.[146] Houses and land were clearly used in place of interest, but were they used as security? Mortgage-backed loans were an urban phenomenon and are rare in Tebtunis, as in other villages.[147] Indeed, security generally is one of the things on which the registers are maddeningly mute, but there may be some clues lurking in the debtors themselves. Around 15 percent of all loans have a husband-wife pair listed as codebtors. Virtually all of these are regular loans (*daneia*) and have the husband's name and "his wife" tacked on—that is, the husband is the principal debtor, but the wife is a cosignatory.[148] Why should she sign? The answer may be because her property, probably from a marriage arrangement or inheritance, is being used as security on the loan. If this were true, it would suggest that even modest security is being used to back modest loans—and that women's property was critical to securing them.

The amounts of cash raised from credit transactions averaged around 160 drachmas, with a median loan of around 100 drachmas. This is somewhat lower on average than that for Egypt as a whole in this period (184 drachmas), but around the same median amount (104 drachmas).[149] This suggests that the rural 90 percent were perhaps making somewhat less use of credit than urbanites, but not dramatically so. Regardless, these are obviously considerably larger sums than those raised by the quarry workers or through pawns. As a reminder, subsistence costs for a male in the Fayum in this period ran around 17 drachmas per month, while those for a family were around 40 drachmas per month.[150] On average, then, these loans, like those for Egypt more broadly, appear too large to be folks borrowing to avoid starvation.[151] Neither do they appear to be loans to cover the poll tax.[152] Poll taxes (which ran around 43–44 drachmas per man per year in the Fayum) were not, as a rule, paid all at once, but in installments perhaps six times per year.[153] Most of these loans are also too large to constitute even very overdue tax payments.

So what were these farmers and artisans doing with their loans? While the records don't tell us, we can find some clues in their timing.[154] Credit transactions tend to cluster in August—at the very end of the calendar year and high point of the inundation—through the planting season of September, October and November (figure 5.10). With some exceptions, these months of planning and planting also tend to see the highest average loan amount. The lowest number of loans, and lowest amounts borrowed, were made during the so-called hungry months—the months of May and June, just before the harvest, when penury stalked the most vulnerable and mortality increased. In other words, not only are most loans mostly too large to be driven by simple food needs, but their timing is not associated with the moments of want in the agricultural calendar.

Instead, the majority of loans appear to be made during the period in which decisions about the next agricultural year were made: when new leases were made, equipment purchased, and land put into cultivation. Loan activity in this Egyptian village was thus closely tied to moments of agricultural investment.[155]

Before we imagine scores of Egyptian smallholders rushing to put more wheat in the ground or buy a new waterwheel, it's important to make clear what "investment" meant to smallholders. First, these loans were principally in cash, not in wheat. So while apparently associated with moments of agricultural investment, they were probably not seed loans. Rather, they appear to be used to raise cash for other purposes. Those purposes probably mixed what we might term "productive" purposes—agricultural investment—and "consumptive" purposes—buying things used by the family. Farmers, like all

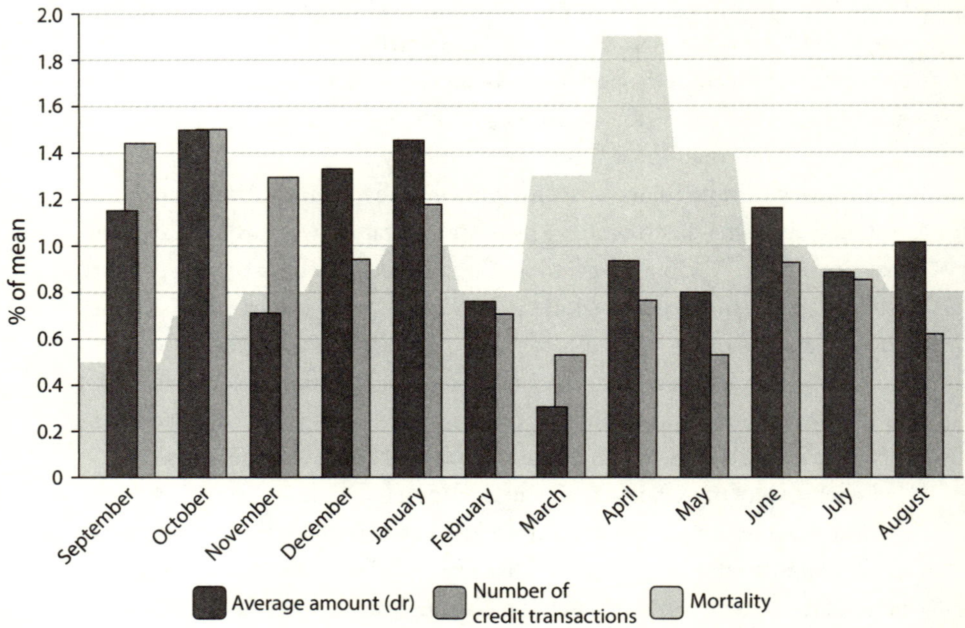

FIGURE 5.10. Borrowing to invest: Tebtunis notary office, credit transactions, number of transactions and average amounts (dr), per month (n = 376. Data: appendix 4, table A.13; mortality data; Scheidel 1998, fig. 3)

self-employed people, constantly muddle these categories. When a loan supports a daughter's dowry so that some saved cash can be put down on a land lease instead, is this productive or consumptive borrowing? The distinction isn't very helpful.[156] The planning-and-planting calendar points to an extra need for cash at the moment when agriculture demanded more of what were limited resources.

The other transactions in the registers hint at what some of those demands could have been. Leases on pastureland were usually paid in cash, and many of the leases made in Tebtunis were, in fact, for pasture.[157] As many of these leases for pastureland were paid in advance, and their timing follows the loan calendar (figure 5.11), these cash loans could have been used to pay the many pasture leases contracted during August, September, and October. Loans could also have been used to buy agricultural equipment, like donkeys.[158] Donkeys were the agricultural machine par excellence in Egypt: they hauled in the manure and seed, helped run the irrigation pumps, then hauled out the harvest. They cost, on average, some 142 drachmas in this period—just under

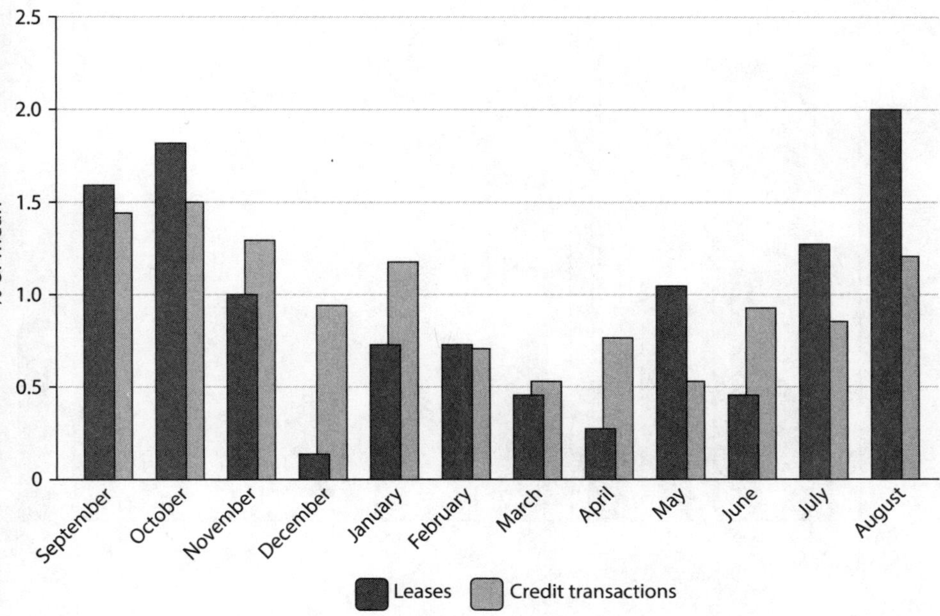

FIGURE 5.11. Borrowing to rent: Tebtunis notary office, leases (n = 229) and credit transactions (n = 376. (Data: appendix 4, table A.13)

the average loan amount—and were principally sold during those same seeding months in October, and to a lesser extent just before harvest in April. Some of these loans could also be donkey investments.

The register records a minority of loans of commodities, principally of wheat. In Tebtunis, loans of wheat had an even stronger timing around the planting season than did the cash loans, heavily concentrated in September, October, November (figure 5.12). This isn't wheat borrowed just to feed hungry mouths: most of it probably went into the ground. The amount of these loans is around or somewhat greater than the amount needed to seed the average land leased in the registers—only around 1.5 hectares.[159] Again, these wheat loans appear to be small-scale efforts to invest in next year's harvest, with some probably used to make the daily bread.

Finally, as we note throughout this chapter, the many loans made during the inundation and planting season at Tebtunis could be driven by the perpetual need to move between monetary modes. During August, September and October, after the harvest, people were rich in grain but potentially poor in cash. Rather than sell their grain so soon after the harvest when prices were

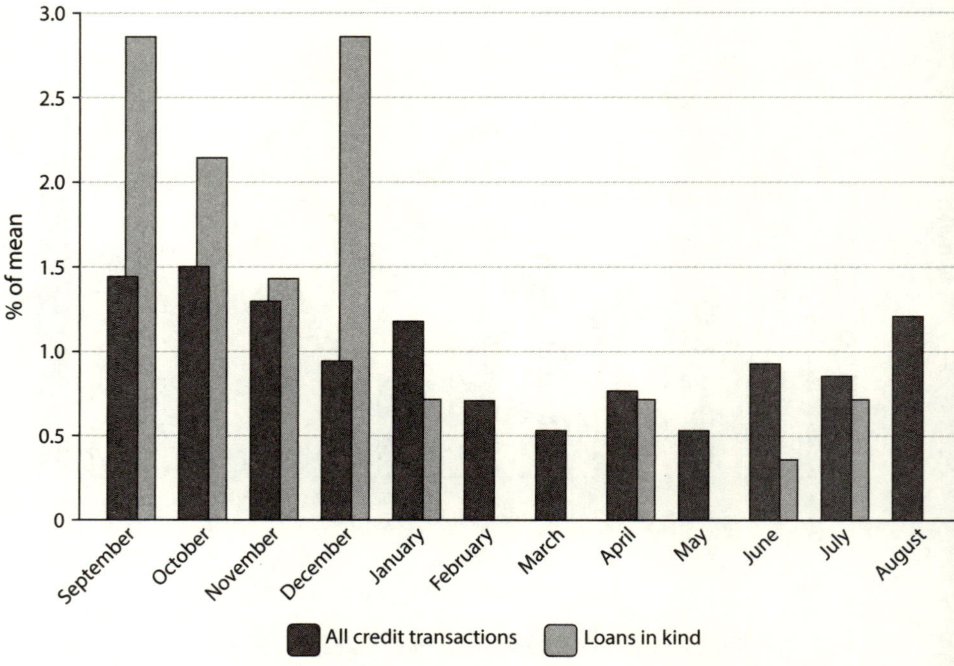

FIGURE 5.12. Cash and seed: Tebtunis notary office, loans in cash and kind (Data: appendix 4, table A.13)

low, they may have elected to hang on to it and borrow the cash. By using their tiny amounts of capital to leverage small-scale loans to make new leases, buy a donkey, pay some wage labor or underwrite other consumption, Tebtunis' 90 percent freed up commodities like seed wheat for agricultural use.[160]

The Neediest Borrowers

Not all borrowing in Tebtunis was driven by agricultural investment. The same calendars that find farmers using loans to invest also reveals other, grimmer realities. A minority of loans were taken out during the "hungry months" of March and April (see figure 5.10). These were also the smallest loans, the loans of March averaging just 45 drachmas. These may be the subsistence loans we miss in the larger averages and broader trends, made by hungry families to tide them over until the harvest. Forty-five drachmas would keep an Egyptian family afloat for a month, and these hungry-month loans may have been taken out to do just that.

These might also be loans for tax payments, for 45 drachmas constituted the approximate yearly tax bill in the Fayum for someone who had failed to make installment payments. An example of such a "tax loan" is preserved in the archive of Tryphon—a weaver from the city of Oxyrhynchus, whose archive preserves a poor family's complex history of borrowing and lending.[161] Among their loans is one that Tryphon's mother, Thamounis, took out from Tryphon himself, for just 16 drachmas. She states that the loan is to pay the delinquent taxes of her other son, Thoonis: 16 drachmas would constitute the likely yearly tax bill for average residents of the Oxyrhynchite region.[162] Neither the mother-son relationship nor the family's illiteracy prevented Tryphon from insisting on a written agreement in proper form, with penalties in the event of nonpayment. Similar overdue taxes may lurk behind those smallest loans from Tebtunis.

The patterns among the most punitive and disadvantageous types of loans are also revealing. These are the loans in which labor, not capital, is used to pay the interest: so-called service (*paramone*) contracts and nursing contracts. In service contracts, a person sells themselves, or more often a child, into service in exchange for a cash loan.[163] Service contracts usually stipulate that the person may not leave the creditor, even for a day, and absence is punished by a fee per day of labor missed. Service contracts are only a hair short of slavery.

One famous, if particularly grim, set of service contracts involved the family of Harthotes.[164] Harthotes was a tenant farmer in nearby Theadelphia, as well as a wage worker, a labor-gang organizer and a village priest—a classic hustler.[165] Despite his priestly office, he appears to have been often in debt. Thus a 24-year-old Harthotes and his mother agreed to contract out Harthotes' 16-year-old brother, Marsisouchos, for four years of labor in exchange for a mere 48 drachmas interest-free loan. Years later, his wife having died leaving him with a small child, Harthotes would send his six-year-old daughter, Tahaunes, out to work in an oil mill for four and a half years. In this case he received an up-front payment of 80 drachmas per two-and-a-half-year period, rather than a loan.[166]

It's not necessary to run the math to see what a bad deal these service contracts are for the debtor, if calculated as either wage or as interest. But that wasn't the math that mattered. Service-contract loans produced immediate cash in hand and, as important, the immediate removal of a hungry mouth from the family's expenses. One might well imagine that a child contracted under these conditions became a de facto slave. But in the case of the Harthoteses, we can also follow these children after their service to some surprising ends. Some 21 years after being placed into service by his brother, Marsisouchos appears as the lessee of some six and a half hectares of land—sufficient for a sustainable living.[167] Tahaunes, the daughter, returned from her service in the olive mill to marry, have a son, send him off to debt service, and then see him return to be a tenant farmer and labor-gang organizer like his grandfather.[168] The brutal math of service-debt was not necessarily a death sentence: rather, it allowed cash-poor, child-rich families to parlay labor for cash, staving off starvation in hopes of better times ahead.

In nursing contracts, a child, most often an abandoned baby to be raised as a slave, is given to a woman to nurse.[169] In all contracts, the woman receives a wage. As we saw in the previous chapter, most nursing "wages" barely pay the subsistence of the nursing woman. In the Tebtunis register, the nursing is often tied to a loan, typically to the woman's husband, in which her nursing pays the interest. Not all nursing contracts are loans, but the frequent co-occurrence in the register of the same parties, one day signing a nursing contract and the next day agreeing upon a loan to the husband, indicate that nursing often underwrote lending. In this way, the woman's nursing body paid the interest on the loan, while earning a small wage in addition.

Service and nursing contracts, while very different kinds of agreements, had important points in common. For one, no capital was required to secure these loans—just labor. They thus were available to the poorest borrowers, those with no third of a house, no half a hectare of land to use as security. Second, the amount of money they secured was small by Tebtunis standards: the loans guaranteed by service contracts are among the smallest at Tebtunis, averaging just 76 drachmas, while the nursing-associated loans were somewhat larger, averaging 125 drachmas. Finally, and most revealingly, lenders sought out these loans at the low point of the agricultural year (figure 5.13). While some service and nursing contracts were agreed upon in the planting season, when extra cash was often needed, most were contracted during April—the hungriest month. In their structure, size and timing, then, service and nursing loans are the best illustration of true survival borrowing. In a world where credit was mostly used for agricultural investment, these loans were an important minority produced by true destitution.

Borrowers and Lenders

We look with horror at the service and nursing arrangements not only because of the use of women's and children's bodies as loan security, but also because of the inequality imagined from these relationships—the cash of the rich

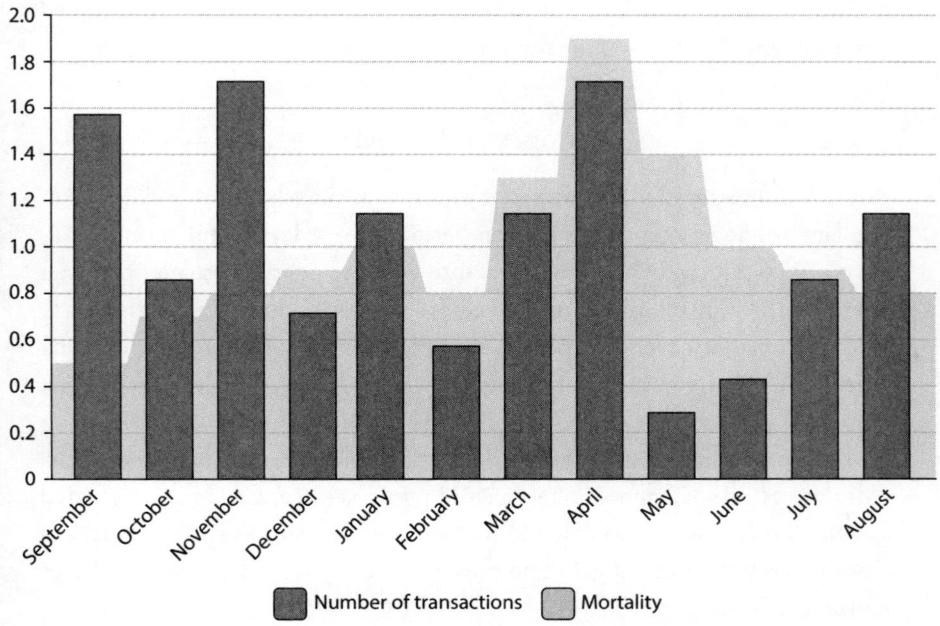

FIGURE 5.13. The most desperate: Tebtunis notary office, nursing and service/loan contracts (n = 69) (Data: appendix 4, table A.13; mortality data; Scheidel 1998, fig. 3)

exchanged for the bodies of the poor.[170] The Tebtunis notary documents are largely mute on the job titles or even geographic origins of their protagonists, making it difficult to unpick the identities of borrowers and lenders. The ethno-geographic origin of names suggests there was a socioeconomic division between borrowers, but of a subtle variety.[171] Around half of the people who appear in creditor roles have Greek-Macedonian names, and thus descend, at least in part, from the Ptolemaic-period colonizers of the Fayum who received grants of land. From all indications, however, these Greeks were also village inhabitants. That is, half of those lending money were higher-status locals. The other half were a mixture of those with Egyptian names, or mixed Egyptian-Greek names: their socioeconomic status is impossible to discern but they, too, were overwhelmingly locals. This situation changed somewhat in the second century, with more lenders being either from the city, of Greek background, or both. Increasingly, too, as the market for credit expanded, creditors and debtors were not necessarily known to one another and hailed from different parts of the province.[172] Even then, though, borrowers and creditors were mostly not separated by a wide gulf. Rather, as we saw at the quarries, the separation appears more like a narrow ditch. Creditors had somewhat greater resources, or, as important, they had resources in the desired mode—mostly cash—at the right time.

Money and the Man

The Tebtunis register presents a very particular snapshot—of one Egyptian village at one moment in its Roman-period history. It is useful because it allows us to put credit activities back into working people's broader financial world. The register allows us to see past categories and their often-binary conclusions—rich lenders, poor borrowers; indebted peasantry, savings-rich urbanites. In its glimpse of ordinary people doing complex things with money, the Tebtunis register reminds us of the many ways that working people put money to work, rather than being passive victims of it. The results of their efforts—a new donkey, a child put in service, a daughter provided with a small dowry—don't lend themselves to easy stories either about economic growth or about grinding poverty. The registers describe instead an insistent doing.

This doing also applies to working people's relationship with institutional powers: the landlord and the state. It's easy to see these powers as a one-way street of oppressive control, and nowhere more so than in matters of money and credit. Rapacious landlords and agribusiness were one of the leitmotifs of Roman Republican history, while the tax collectors' arrival was likened by later Christian authors to the Last Judgment.[173] As we've seen throughout this book, money relationships among working people, landlords and the state were more complicated, with more self-advocacy on the part of the 90 percent than is allowed in the literary historical imagination.

Let's start with the landlord and his account books. The expansion of longer-term monthly labor contracts in Roman Egypt by the third century meant that more workers—although still a minority—had a financial life tied closely to account books rather than daily cash wages.[174] The probable lack of ready cash money in the countryside meant that account money was a significant monetary mode for these wage earners: they were paid on account, and their taxes were paid for them via the estate and/or deducted from their wages—also on account. We've already seen example of this with the ox driver Maron, a monthly worker who, together with his children, was paid on account.

As we also saw in the previous chapter, not only wages and taxes, but also expenses and debts might be put on account. Some workers' accounts from the Appianus estate provide a sense of how working people made this account-world work for them. A portion of the accounts of one Polion, a tenant farmer, here in its original draft format, complete with deletions and occasionally puzzling math, provides a glimpse:

Account of Polion tenant-farmer:

Up to July 26 in the old (accounts)?)
Remainder (in credit) with me [Heroninos the accountant]: 80dr 80b.
20 dr. 4 ob. Through the daughter 8 dr.
September 2: 1 mon. [7.3 liters of wine] 8dr. 80b
2 kot. [0.5 liters] of oil 4dr. 40b
Sept. 1: To the children 2 mon. [14.6 liters of wine] 16dr. 160b
Sept. 10: Through his wife 8dr.
Sept. 19: In the city, of which (he will give) account, to guard 8dr.
Expenses of the village 4dr.
On behalf of the village council 8dr.
And for Sept. 5–27 with the
expenses of the village ~~60~~ 52dr.
Of which, on the same day ~~17~~ 21dr. Remainder ~~31~~ 36dr.
And 2 kot. [0.5 liters] of oil 4dr. 4 ob., 28dr. 24 ob.
To the camel driver of Soterichos 1mon.[wine]. 8dr. 80b.
From Pasis 1 mon. [wine] 8dr. 80b.
Sept. 23: Polion tenant farmer through the city 8dr. Remainder 4dr.
80b. . . .[175]

Polion was not a monthly wage worker: he was a tenant farmer. So his estate account was not driven by the need to pay his wages. It may have derived from the estate's billing him for his tax obligations. But most of these transactions have nothing to do with tax payments. Instead, we find Polion treating the account something like a debit card. He begins the month with a credit; then he, his wife and children use it to debit food and other expenses. He uses it to discharge debts to others (the camel driver), and to credit occasional earnings. And he ends the month with a small credit.

Polion's account performed a variety of functions for him: it allowed him to navigate a coin-poor world by both avoiding the use of cash (the food withdrawals) and drawing cash when needed (while in the city). It allowed him to run up very short-term debts and then discharge them with additional earnings—something that would have been impossible with currency alone. And it allowed his family access to food and money independently of him—for instance, while he was in the city on liturgical guard duty. From the landlord, Appianus', perspective, their financial relationship ran in one direction—Appianus extracted both rent and tax from Polion, forwarding the latter to the state. From Polion's perspective it worked somewhat differently. He parlayed his dependency on Appianus—and the medium of the account book managed by the very accommodating accountant, Heroninos—into a highly flexible monetary medium. He used the account as a credit card, a company store, a bank—purposes far beyond its original purpose of keeping track of Polion's tax payments.

Such accounts could be put to income-earning—or at least income-stretching—purposes. The wage-earning ox driver Maron, it will be recalled, was paid on account.[176] He used his account credit to charge some 42 liters of wine. This is far too much wine for personal consumption, and it is supposed he took it to the nearby city, where he traveled soon after, to resell at a profit.[177] That wine cost him over 54 drachmas, a sum far exceeding his meager eight drachmas and one artaba of wheat salary. Only by using the commodity credit given to him by the estate could he hope to purchase—and then resell—such a quantity.

This use of credit to purchase and resell commodities is precisely what the great businessmen-moneylenders of Pompeii facilitated.[178] Here in these Egyptian accounts we see the same thing at the smaller scale of the 90 percent. Instead of a moneylender, Maron uses the monetary medium of account and the commodities of the Appianus estate. Furthermore, Maron, unlike Polion, ended his month in the red to the tune of some eight drachmas (see figure 4.4). He presumably just kicked this debt to the next month, when it would have been absorbed by his eight drachmas of wages. Indeed, as we saw, Maron rarely seemed to withdraw his cash wages but accumulated them to pay his taxes. As they sat in the account, he used them as a temporary credit against which he leveraged hustles like wine-selling. Again, just like Polion, by extending credit for which no immediate repayment was required, the account mode actually extended income. Of course, in doing so, it also added to the already significant dependency of employees and tenants on their employer/landlord, a dependency that was increased by a reliance on the landholder's account books for so many things. The accounts show the ingenuity to which such dependency and its vehicle—the account itself—could be put.

The use of the account to *not* pay one's debts raises the important question of nonpayment generally. The language of official loan documents makes very clear the fate that awaited defaulters: any and all of their property was eligible for seizure up to the amount of the loan plus interest. But how often did this happen? When we have preserved both the loans and their repayment receipts, it would appear that many borrowers managed to repay their loans on time.[179] The more granular information from personal archives points in the opposite direction. The family of Soterichos the farmer, whom we met in chapter 3, took some 12 years to discharge his debts.[180] So, too, the wealthier Kronion family we met (the farmers, not the notary) also appears to have been in arrears on loans: a large cash loan of 436 drachmas had a very long (11-year) repayment date, while another loan in wheat was paid back many years in arrears.[181]

Default rates on Roman loans are never going to be forthcoming. However common default was, particularly in many cases involving land as security or usufruct, we see a remarkable willingness on the part of the creditor to accept late payments for loans or rent.[182] Either because having the usufruct was more useful than having the cash, or because removing a tenant in rent arrears was harder than letting them stay and eventually pay up, it's remarkable how often we find tardy payers, their tardiness passed over without a comment. Despite a boilerplate legal language that allowed creditors to seize the security or even all the assets of their lenders, it's not clear how often this actually happened.

A creditor who really did need their debtor to pay up, or a debtor faced with rapacious creditors, could ask the law to come to their aid. A lawsuit was always possible but mostly too expensive for working people; even the wealthy avoided it. Arbitration was more common, and wealthy and nonwealthy alike enlisted trusted intermediaries to help the various parties find solutions.[183] But if arbitration failed, really fed-up victims could file a petition. Petitions were official complaints made to state officials—in Egypt, to the *strategos* in the district capitals, or more rarely to the governor of the province.[184] Petitions might be registered for a whole range of transgressions, from magicking away one's crops to illegal grazing to rape and theft. Petitions were very cheap to register: the Tebtunis notary office appears to have charged only around 1–2 obols to register a petition, and sometimes they didn't charge at all.[185] In theory, at any rate, all but the very poorest could register a petition, and it's theoretically possible that working people took advantage of this right in great numbers.[186]

Whether they actually did so is less certain. Relative to their likely population, literate people appear to be better documented as petitioners, as do people with Greek names. Petitioning, then, may have been more aggressively pursued by the middling parts of the 90 percent than the bottom.[187] Even for them, to address an official petition to a state official was probably a last "nuclear" option: most disputes would have been worked out informally without state intervention.[188] Even the petition was probably not intended to send a repo man or a bailiff to the offending party's door, but just to force the opposing party into more serious informal negotiations.

Interestingly, debt issues were a less common motivation for petition than one would think. Although most of our preserved petitions relate to property issues, debt is attested in only around 14 percent of the extant petitions.[189] Theft and violence were far more common reasons to register a petition. The amount for which a person was willing to register a petition is also revealing. Debtors or creditors only petitioned for large amounts—the average is some 6,560 drachmas, and while this number is a product, in part, of some very large alleged debt defaults, even the median of 462 drachmas is far above the average loan of 160 drachmas we found at Tebtunis.[190] Contrast this with the average amount listed in theft petitions—just 292 drachmas on average. One petition for theft listed goods worth only eight drachmas.

This all suggests that involving the state was a kind of last, worst option for credit disputes. Problems between debtors and creditors were mostly worked out by negotiation, and only in the most egregious, large-scale transactions did the parties resort to the law. Theft was a different animal. A theft was already a bigger breach of the social contract, one in which negotiation was less likely to lead to results. A petitioner who had been robbed of eight drachmas, if it cost nothing to petition, had nothing to lose.

The Balance Sheet

The tenant farmer Soterichos we met in chapter 3 was immersed in the Roman world of money. He juggled multiple leases, which he paid in cash and in wheat. He invested in grapes and thyme. And he borrowed quite a lot—both in cash and in wheat. He used his house to pay the interest, while seemingly renting out another house to live in. When he died, leaving many of these debts unpaid, his wife, Thaisas, paid them all back—slowly. Over 12 years or more, she managed to raise nearly 390 drachmas and over 130 artabai of wheat (itself worth over 1,000 drachmas) to discharge Soterichos' debts. She did so, too, about the time her interest payments began to exceed her rent, clearly judging the costs of financing the debt to have finally exceeded the market rental rates.[191]

The story of Soterichos and Thaisas confounds many of the stories we tell about poor people and their money—both today and in the past. Tiny amounts of money didn't—and don't—mean primitive means of using it.

Soterichos and Thaisas' ability to leverage small amounts of capital (their tiny house) to raise money, their ability to gauge the relative costs and advantage of servicing those debts, their ability to save small sums—all these characterize the money world of the Roman 90 percent.

Soterichos and Thaisas' world of cash money and wheat money was part of what we've called Roman monetary modes. Coined money was only one, and perhaps not the most significant, monetary mode used by all Romans. As we've seen, the need to move between these monetary modes—Soterichos' need to convert his hay to cash to buy food, or Maron the ox driver using his credit-wages to buy wine for resale—also generated complex money lives.

Peeping through Soterichos and Thaisas' debt histories are both their use of credit and their ability to save. Credit was a key financial instrument—used by everyone, often backed by some kind of security, and lent at some kind of interest. The most impoverished lived on credit, perhaps wage laborers particularly. The gusto for things we examined in chapter 2 was also entangled in the credit universe. In pawnshops, we find the same objects that featured in the "consumer revolution" being used to secure cash in need. Farming families like the Soterichoses particularly commingled borrowing for consumption with borrowing for investment. Like the farmers in nearby Tebtunis, the Soterichoses' seed and cash loans permitted them to put land into cultivation, pay cash leases on pastureland, even buy a share on donkeys.[192] All at the cost of a sizable portfolio of debt.

But the Soterichos' debts also presuppose the ability to save. Although it may have taken her twelve years of putting money by, Thaisas' repayment of their cash and wheat loans are quiet testimony of working people's ability to save. Saving was hard: the gusto for things, high rents, and unpredictable incomes all made saving a long slog. As we've seen, savings in cash were limited. Other forms of stored value—bullion, land, real estate and animals—were as important as coins.

The debt and saving portfolios of the Roman 90 percent were small. The average cash value of both loans and savings were both around 150–200 drachmas or sestertii. In Egypt, that would have been anywhere from two to four times a poor family's monthly expenses. In Pompeii, it would have represented barely a month. These small figures were, again, only part of the story: loans in wheat or savings in land—all probably dwarfed the coin transactions we can see.

The smallness of debt and savings, relative to the cost of living, tells three different stories. On the one hand, debts are not excessively large relative to the costs of scraping by.[193] A debt of 200 drachmas for a year at 12 percent interest rate meant finding an extra 18 drachmas per month to pay it off. For an Egyptian family living at a sustainable but base level, their debt/income ratio was only about 30 percent—a pittance compared to the millions of Americans whose debts run to more than twice their monthly income.[194]

But debt and savings had harder edges for a family like the Soterichoses compared to a more indebted American family. Food, taxes and, in their case, high land rents required all their income to stave off starvation. We've already seen that Soterichos and his family probably needed to work for wages in order to keep their cows, and they paid their rent in arrears. If the Nile flood failed, or the price of wine or hay collapsed, they went hungry. Saving even three months of income—the equivalent of one of their debts or an average-sized dowry for their daughter—would have been hard indeed. The difficulty of saving meant that rainy-day funds were small, at least ones in cash. While not necessarily encumbered by huge amounts of unmanageable debt, neither were working families protected with large amounts of liquid savings.

The final lesson from this broader history of money-managing is that savings—small savings—were possible. The fact that in a rural village like Tebtunis average savings (in the form of dowries) and average loans were about equal finds rural families putting small sums by. Thaisas, too, managed to slowly save, even after the death of her husband. By juggling debt and income, negotiating late payments with their landlords and lenders, and parlaying their multiple tiny assets, working families like the Soterichoses could save small sums, one drachma at a time.

6

The Load-Carrying Mother

FIGURE 6.1. Herculaneum, victims of the eruption of Vesuvius sheltering near the beach (Photo: Bruno Rijsman. Wikimedia Commons. Creative Commons A-SA 2.0 License)

ONE MORNING in the summer of 79 CE, a young woman began her working day in Herculaneum. She was particularly short for her twenty-odd years and had already borne a child. Despite having suffered a series of childhood illnesses, she had a stout frame. Her work involved carrying heavy loads up and down the streets and stairs of the city. By the time she died in the eruption of Mount Vesuvius later that year, this work had already taken a toll on her still-young limbs: carrying heavy burdens had damaged the cartilage of her right shoulder, while her back already had at least one herniated disc. The scientists who studied her remains named her "the Load-Carrying Mother."[1]

While the Roman 90 percent may have relied on credit and markets for survival, their most important economic tool was their body. A time-traveler to ancient Herculaneum or Tebtunis would have found Romans' money savvy and acquisitiveness recognizable, even impressive. That same traveler would have been appalled and uncomprehending at the uses to which Romans put their bodies. The human body was the principal productive machine of the Roman world.[2] The hoeing and herding and scything we observed in chapter 3, the digging and hammering and hauling of chapter 4: these and thousands of other tasks were carried out by human bodies—enslaved bodies and free, male and female bodies, children's bodies. The relentless drive to surplus production, the borrowing and lending that supported it, and the gusto for things were sustained by, and took their toll on, all these bodies.

Economic activities' most visceral impacts are on the body. The very poor are at greater risk of malnutrition; miners are at risk of cancer; farm kids have more broken bones. Human skeletons, like those of the Load-Carrying Mother, tell us something of how the economies of the Roman world impacted what it meant to live and labor in that world. New data on these bodies, some of which is analyzed here for the first time, makes this possible.

Unlike other kinds of evidence for the 90 percent, where we must excavate the working majority out from under an overburden of elites, Roman skeletons are overwhelmingly those of nonelite, working people. These skeletons come from scores of Roman-period cemeteries, large and small, located outside cities and villages or at the edges of farms. Farmers and artisans, haulers of salt and shapers of clay, enslaved and free, the individuals buried in these cemeteries were mostly laid to rest in simple graves. No inscriptions give us their names. Our knowledge of them comes from their bodies and the signs they bear of stresses and trauma, survivorship and ultimately death.

These bodies make clear the enormous toll that Roman surplus production took on the bodies of those who did the producing. Whether mining, weaving, hoeing or scything, surplus-producing labor was quite literally embodied by its agents. What's also clear is the price these people paid for their densely settled environments. Whether they lived in the world of cities like Herculaneum, or the incredibly dense countrysides we examined in chapter 3, heightened population density and proximity to one's neighbors took a toll in the form of an increased burden of disease. These disease regimes were mostly democratic, impacting poor and rich, but targeting children above all. These children would become laboring adults, having survived multiple bouts of childhood disease. Labor and disease, as much or more so than nutrition, were the biggest challenges to working people's physical flourishing.

Although they shared a high disease burden, the Roman rural majority were impacted differently than their urban neighbors. We've already seen that farmers had slightly different diets. We'll see here that those diets may have been somewhat poorer. These differences shine through particularly from a comparison of the heavily urban world of Italy versus the more rural world of Roman Britain.

And what of those whose labor was fused by law to their bodies—the enslaved? Aristotle termed enslaved people "speaking tools," their lives defined and limited by the work they performed. And yet the physical remains of the Roman enslaved are practically indistinguishable from the working free. Why this should be so—that is, why a legal category fails to reveal itself in the skeleton—sheds yet further light on what it meant to work in the Roman world, as well as the limitations of physical remains to speak to the daily experience of labor.

The difficulties of distinguishing slave versus free, and the worn bodies that produced the world full of things, force us, yet again, to set aside analytical categories in favor of practice. This is practice at its most tangible: the work as literally embodied in the workers. Here we come face-to-face with the context of that work and its toll on physical well-being. We'll also confront working people's extraordinary resilience, living with bodies racked by injury and illness and continuing to push them to days and years of labor. We will thus have particularly tough choices about what story to tell with and about these bodies: a history of the oppression of market forces, a predatory empire, and a "slave economy"—or of the triumph of human grit and will. All of these stories are borne out by the evidence.

Body Counting

Two different disciplines address the intersection of human health and economics. The first is the subdiscipline of anthropology termed bioarchaeology, which has developed the principal scientific techniques for recording and analyzing human skeletal remains. The second is economic anthropometrics, the use of the body, particularly body stature (height), as a proxy for economic performance. These two apparatuses meet around some of their methods and systems of measurement but part company in what they think those measurements mean.

Anthropologists study ancient bodies by cataloging their various characteristics, particularly lesions and other pathologies that appear to denote physical stress or impairment. Some of these skeletal characteristics are straightforward manifestations of a trauma or pathology. Caries (or cavities), for instance, are pits in the dental enamel that make the tooth weaker; fractures are skeletal breaks, cracks or compression caused by physical trauma. Many skeletal metrics, however, are phenomena whose impact on the body's ability to function, and thus on health outcomes, is less clear: these are termed nonspecific stresses. Pitting found in the ocular orbits of the skull, termed cribra orbitalia, is observed in both animal and human populations. Its cause, or etiology, is unknown. Linear enamel hypoplasia, or linear inconsistencies in the tooth enamel, is probably caused by nutrient deficits at the moment the tooth was growing; related to stress caused by weaning, poor diet and/or disease, its exact physiological mechanisms remain poorly understood. Both phenomena have been correlated with but not observed to cause poor health and higher mortality.[3] Both phenomena form only after the stress in question is survived. These multiple and murky causes and outcomes are true of many of the health-related markers that bioarchaeologists document on the skeleton. What all these skeletal markers actually meant, and what it meant that they were found on people who were, by definition, *not* part of the community of the living but dead in a cemetery, began to raise worrying questions for the field.

These doubts culminated in the 1990s, a moment of self-reckoning when the discipline of bioarchaeology realized that it had been reading skeletal indices with complex causes as straightforward metrics for "health."[4] Using dead people to reconstruct the health of the living also began to appear worryingly paradoxical. After all, cemeteries might preferentially contain those who failed to survive, or, if it contained older adults, those who were particularly resilient. Anthropologists realized, too, that different metrics reflected health or stress at different moments of the life course.[5] Cribra orbitalia records stresses experienced in childhood; stature is largely a product of later childhood and adolescence; osteoarthritis appears in later adulthood, and so on. The deceased adult body, bioarchaeologists realized, contains a layered record of a whole life's physiological experience, experiences that must be unpacked to understand the whole.

This moment of self-reckoning, when bioarchaeology realized there was no health Santa Claus, largely missed the economists. Economic anthropometrics was born out of economics' turn to numbers. At the same moment when bioarchaeologists were still making confident pronouncements about past human health, economists were busily searching for quantitative datasets on which to do economic history. The human body seemed to be an excellent proxy for economic well-being, particularly human stature. Economic history bestsellers like *Time on the Cross* prompted a new industry on the height and nutrition of American slaves, then branched out to long-term studies of British and American height and economic growth.[6] Taller adults seemed to be found in economies with higher wages and GDP, while shorter ones were associated with stagnating economies. A series of big-data projects, first around stature and now around a wider range of skeletal observations, have laid out a sweeping, millennia-long health and economic history.[7] These studies argue that, prior to the advent of modern economic growth and modern medicine, human health had been mostly on the decline since the Stone Age. The Roman period, in these accounts, constituted a particularly bleak period of short stature and high stress, its unequal, slave-owning society producing short, sick people, ultimately conquered by taller (no joke), healthier Gothic barbarians.[8]

Anthropologist David Graeber has described this brand of scholarship as a kind of wistful pessimism made into statistically verified common sense. As Graeber has also quipped, it doesn't make very good or very interesting history.[9] Leaving aside the "everything-has-been-miserable-since-we-left-the-jungle" paradigm that has such a current vogue, both the data and the methods raise serious questions about Roman health and how to read it. The "big data" in most of these projects is often very small, verging on the statistically insignificant.[10] More worrisome is that the multiple causes for everything from stature to pits in the skull are swept away in favor of single causes—usually nutrition.[11] Nutrition is the go-to cause of most nonspecific stress for economists, as nutrition can be more readily mapped onto economic variables like production or wages. Poor people have less food, so they are shorter. Disease—which also impacts overall height—tends to get sidelined because it's much messier.[12]

The Roman empire is a tempting place to read sweeping histories off of the body, or to use the body to justify particular histories of empire. It's been tempting to go shopping in the supermarket of historical "facts," culled from secondary literature, in order to explain skeletal phenomena with multiple possible causes. The result is a growing body of literature that argues from effects to causes, in which contradictory aspects of history can be made to explain the same data, or contradictory results can be explained away with the same historical facts. The short Romans vanquished by the tall barbarians, an explanation that fails to explain how those same short Romans maintained an empire by conquest, is just the tip of a wobbly interpretive iceberg. Equally tempting is to linger on stress and nonfunctioning. How adults who died bearing markers of what are mostly childhood stresses survived, often for decades, isn't part of the Roman conversation, nor is the fate of those whose bodies are free from such stress markers.[13] Resilience is downplayed in a Roman-period literature that can often read like a jeremiad of misery.

Ironically, economists interested in the body have a certain blind spot when it comes to labor. The enormous impact of labor regimes—on the calories required to survive, on final adult stature, on work-related fractures, on musculoskeletal stress—tend to be shunted to the side. In a world before mechanization made labor easier, labor was dangerous, and it took an immense toll on the body. Labor, this chapter will emphasize, strongly impacted Roman bodies: most fractures, for instance, are probably a product of work injury; childhood stress levels leap up when kids start to work; and so on. Putting labor back into histories of the body allows us to see past a list of skeletal metrics—past the jeremiad of misery, past proxies for GDP or wages—to actual lives lived. By admitting that people did things with the bodies they had, rather than cataloging them against the (nonexistent but tacitly modern) "healthy" bodies they didn't have, we come closer to meeting the Roman 90 percent where they were, while also learning something about their work.[14]

So here we use the bodies of the 90 percent to tell a different story. A large corpus of data, much of which is synthesized here for the first time, informs it.[15] To get at the very different impact of labor on very different bodies, it uses working people from two extremes of the empire. Italy was the imperial center and thick with cities; Britain was at its periphery and, despite many new cities, more rural. The people who lived and died in these two regions between the first and third or fourth centuries CE make up this story. The cemeteries in which they were buried were dominated by working people—farmers and potters, water carriers and fullers. Most were buried in modest graves. In Italy they were buried "a cappuccina"—not with a coffee, but in a simple tomb made with reused tiles. In Britain they were buried in wooden coffins if they were lucky, and in the earth if they were not. Very often the dead were laid to rest with modest objects—a pot or two, a glass, and, most interestingly, their tools—almost certainly placed there by the family or community who buried them.

This story of working bodies is assembled from the many different observations made from human skeletons—from lesions and cavities to height and bone isotopes. Many of these observations are indices of stress—from nonspecific stresses whose causes are unclear to very specific ones like bone breaks or herniated discs. As we reveal the stories beneath these metrics, it's important to underline yet again that many of the people we are examining did not die of these things—they died *with* them. We aren't analyzing causes of death here, but the layers of stresses that individuals accumulated throughout their lives, some of which may have had a negative effect on their functioning and mortality—and some of which didn't. Anyone looking for easy answers about the health of past people should not expect to find it in their bones, and no such easy answers will be found here.[16]

One final, expanding body of information will help us put these body-histories in context: ancient genomics. The growing study of ancient DNA—both of humans and of their microbe predators—has helped to crack open the broader world with which these working bodies had to contend. Ancient DNA is starting to reveal the extraordinary ethnic diversity of Roman families and neighbors: in Roman cities especially, people from Asia and Africa regularly rubbed shoulders with people from Italy and Gaul.[17] Ancient DNA is also driving home those diverse Romans' enormous diversity of biological functioning: their very different biological backgrounds meant that Romans had unusually diverse vulnerability to and resistance from disease. And above all, these new explorations have exposed an entirely new community—the community of microbes.[18] The ability to extract from human and animal bones the genetic residues of the diseases they fought has admitted new characters into the historical drama. It has revealed the power of these characters to wipe out whole communities, to shape seasons of death. It has also revealed the role that Romans themselves played in shaping the very disease communities that challenged them. The unprecedented connectivity of the Roman world not only connected people but also their diseases. Its unprecedented density brought greater challenges still. From the hyper-dense farming neighborhoods of rural Britain to the urban high-rises of Italy, we've already seen working Romans living cheek by jowl. We've also seen the equally dense animal landscapes they sustained, animals that were often the vectors of disease. We'll now see the impact those densities had, both on children and on the laboring adults those children would become.

Adult Workers, Childhood Stress

Stress experienced in childhood would have resonated through adulthood. It's increasingly clear that disease, malnutrition and other stresses of childhood have—and perhaps had in the past—adverse effects later in life.[19] This

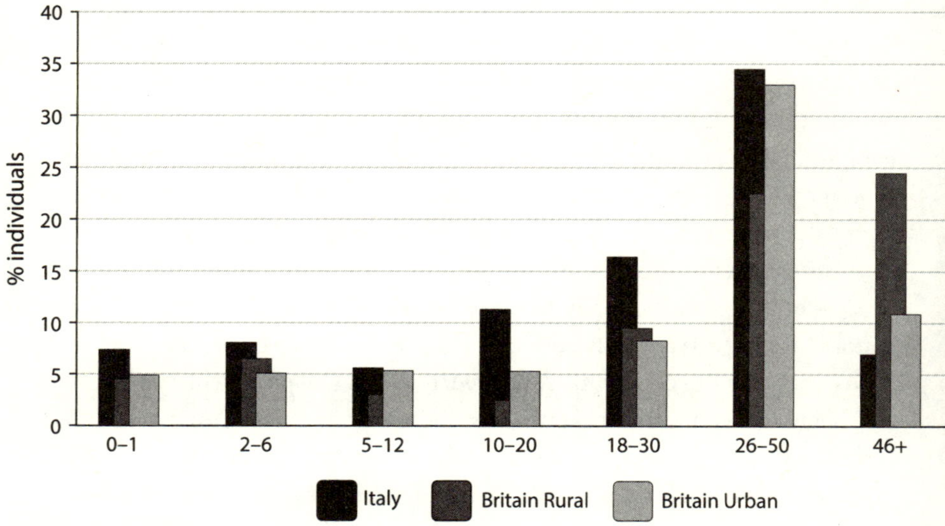

FIGURE 6.2. The missing children: age at death, Italian and British cemeteries (Data: Italy: appendix 5, table A.14; Britain rural: Rohnbogner 2018, average fig. 7.6, 7.10 [early Roman]; Britain urban: Bonsall 2013, appendix, tables 102, 105–11. Overlapping age categories due to diverse age parameters)

research also suggests that those who survive such stresses may carry with them particular toughness.[20] The contradictory forces of frailty and resilience are particularly important for working people, people who periodically lived at the edge of nutritional deficits and whose jobs demanded hard labor. Any effort to understand working adults' bodies must thus begin with their child selves. Unfortunately for the scholar, most Roman cemeteries have a serious lack of small children (figure 6.2). We are probably not wrong to assume that the mortality of infants was around 30 percent, while that of all children through five years of age as high as 50 percent or more.[21] Where, then, are all the deceased children under five? It is assumed that they were buried elsewhere—in infant-only cemeteries, beneath the floors of houses, at the edges of farms.[22] Romans did not have modern ideas about childhood. While they mourned their dead little ones, those little ones weren't treated as fully fledged members of the community. Their absence from adult cemeteries is a result.

But some remnants of those missing children are preserved in the bones and teeth of adults. In particular, the linear patterns in teeth termed linear enamel hypoplasia, and the pits and groves in the skull termed cribra orbitalia or porotic hyperostosis, were laid down in childhood. As we mentioned above,

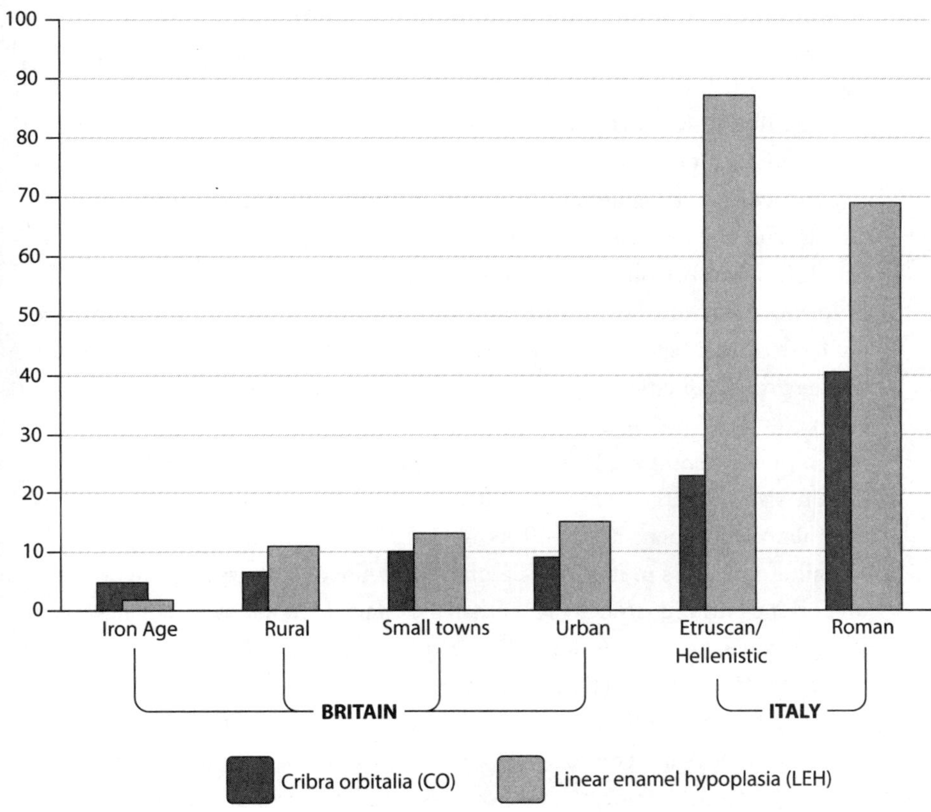

FIGURE 6.3. A hazardous childhood: pre-Roman and Roman childhood stress markers (crude prevalence rates) (Data: appendix 5, table A.14)

both of these stress markers only formed when the stress was survived, and adults who survived them bear the signs of that struggle. Diseases of vitamin deficiency like scurvy or rickets, respiratory diseases like bronchitis, and the most incapacitating and feared of infectious diseases—tuberculosis—all were commonly experienced in childhood and are also sometimes preserved in the skeleton. Thus, from our adult-majority cemeteries, we may find the traces of the stresses of Roman childhood.

These childhood stress markers tell two stories that may ultimately be the same story. For the individuals buried in British cemeteries, the stresses represented by cribra orbitalia increase dramatically with the advent of Roman rule (figure 6.3). The number of adult individuals showing signs of tooth hypoplasia also increased significantly.[23] The harder-to-read signs of metabolic and infectious diseases were very low, but also appear to have been on the rise during the Roman period.[24] In Roman Britain, at any rate, Roman rule appears to have made for tough childhoods.

One reason for this may have been the growth of cities. While around 11 percent of adults in the British countryside had signs of hypoplasic stresses experienced in early childhood, that number jumps considerably for individuals (adults and children alike) who died in British cities (see figure 6.3). Cribra orbitalia levels in British urban adults also appear to be higher than those in the British countryside. So, too, do infectious disease and vitamin deficiencies, as we'll see further below. Childhood stress thus may have been increased in part by the growth of cities, cities that in Britain were only really built under the Romans.[25]

Central and southern Italy was relatively thick with cities prior to the Roman conquests, and by the Roman period the region had more people living in cities than almost anywhere on earth. This may partially explain the much higher levels of childhood stress in Italian skeletons (see figure 6.3). Both tooth hypoplasia and orbital pitting are much higher than in Britain. Hypoplasia was high already prior to the Roman expansion, while cribra orbitalia prevalence increased dramatically.[26] Signs of infectious disease and diseases of vitamin deficiency again appear to be rare, but the cases we have are concentrated in cities.[27] As we noted above, the Italian data comes mostly from cities, so we have no way to rigorously test urban/rural differences. The one well-studied, truly rural cemetery—at Vagnari in southern Italy—had hypoplasia levels somewhat lower than the mean but still very high. So at least some of these childhood stresses may be a product of Italians living such high-density lives.

Life in cities may not be the only culprit behind Italian urban stress for kids. Malaria may also be to blame. Cribra orbitalia appears to be caused by some type of anemia, and in Mediterranean contexts anthropologists often assume it was caused by malarial diseases, since malaria may produce iron-deficient anemia.[28] While mosquito-borne malaria probably existed even in Britain, it was almost certainly more common in warm, Mediterranean Italy, impacting children above all.[29] Italian seasonal mortality patterns known from tombstones show a spike in mortality in the summer months, mortality that might be driven by summer's mosquitoes.[30] Some big-data projects have also noted a statistically significant relationship between altitude and cribra orbitalia—lower-elevation populations report more cribra orbitalia across the 1,500 years of European history.[31] Lower elevation and marshy, coastal sites are, of course, more likely to have the standing water where malarial mosquitoes breed. All these factors may have increased the risk to Mediterranean children versus their northern cousins.

But the risks from malaria are hard to disentangle from those caused by living in dense worlds. Recent work suggests a more subtle set of causes for cribra orbitalia than iron-deficient anemia. Hemolytic and megaloblastic anemias, the kind that result from diarrheal diseases and high parasite load, may cause that characteristic pitting. These are precisely the kinds of waterborne illnesses common in dense cities.[32] Cities are more often situated at lower altitudes than higher ones; thus urbanism may be driving the association between cribra orbitalia and altitude. New tests for identifying malaria in human remains using DNA and biochemical signatures may soon resolve this question.[33] Regardless, multiple causes, not a singular one, probably produced the phenomenon of orbital pitting. And whether associated with cribra orbitalia or not, malaria was almost certainly a major stressor, if not killer, of Roman children.

Why should Roman cities, in Britain or in Italy, have been so dangerous for the young? While the Romans may be famous for their aqueducts and sewer systems, Roman cities still carried a particularly high disease load.[34] Perhaps a fifth of the Roman population lived in cities, cities that were bigger and denser than we previously thought.[35] High population densities meant high disease densities, densities that even today particularly impact the young. Even cities with good drainage, sewer systems, public latrines, and aqueduct water—as some, but not all, Roman cities had—would have had higher levels of waterborne illnesses like diarrhea and dysentery. Respiratory diseases, from bronchitis and pneumonia to the feared tuberculosis, are also increased with higher population densities. The Roman period sees a big jump in periostitis on the ribs—lesions produced by respiratory illness—as well as indications of sinusitis.[36] The thousands of indoor fires and increase in smoke pollution seems to have vastly increased respiratory illnesses of all kinds. Very large cities like Rome and Ostia, with apartment buildings that might have been five stories tall or more, may have been unusually dark, particularly for the working poor living in small apartments or in the back of shops, thereby increasing the risk for vitamin D deficiency and rickets.[37] It is important to remember that all of these diseases were also found in the countryside. Indeed, animals were an important vector of disease, and people and their animals moved back and forth between city and country, field and abattoir, both of them carrying diseases as they went.[38]

If we want to put the Roman disease threat to city kids in perspective, there's no better comparative case than that most infamous of historical cities—Victorian London. Mid-nineteenth-century London was a city undergoing massive change—a huge population rise, immigration from the countryside, combined with the rise of industry and limited sanitary infrastructure.

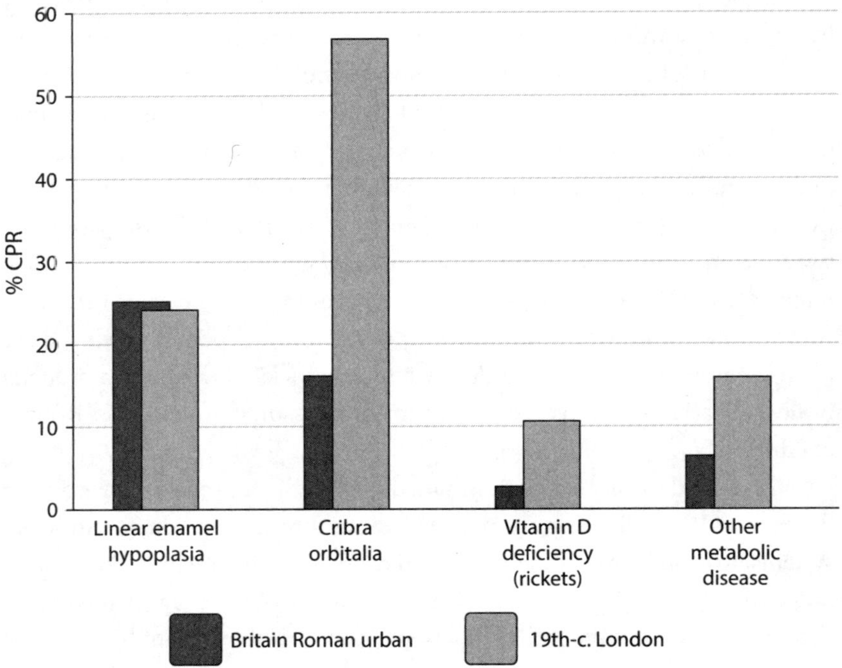

FIGURE 6.4. Oliver Twist had it worse: childhood stress and infectious/metabolic disease indicators (crude prevalence rates), child populations (0–16 years old): Roman British urban sample versus Christ Church Spitalfields, London, late 18th–mid-19th c. (Data: Rohnbogner 2022, fig. 5.37)

One need only read Charles Dickens' novels, or peruse the reports of the Poor Law Commission, to get a sense of the dangers this new megalopolis presented to children.[39] London's cemeteries are just as eloquent. Middle-class—not even poor—children who died in Victorian London have cribra orbitalia, rickets and other metabolic diseases at levels that dwarf those of children who died in Roman British cities (figure 6.4). Cribra orbitalia alone is around twice as high.[40] As bad as the urban disease environment was for Roman children, Oliver Twist had it worse.

If cities were dangerous places for Roman children, they may have produced particularly resilient adults. We can see this in Britain, the only place scholars have studied a reasonable number of both child and adult skeletons. Children who died in the British countryside displayed mostly higher levels of childhood-related stresses than their peers in the city.[41] Signs of infectious disease are also more common in those rural children.[42] But the children who survived and reached adulthood still retaining traces of those stresses were more commonly found in cities.[43] What should we make of this seeming paradox?

The answer may be that cities were not only hazardous for the young, but also breeders of the strong. The extraordinary genetic diversity of Roman cities, whose different populations brought with them not only diseases, but also a whole soup of immunities, may have helped produce urban resilience. More homogeneous, largely native-born country folks may have been more vulnerable.[44] Working adult Romans who died in cities may represent the resilient who survived this panoply of childhood stresses, while in the countryside, more vulnerable children simply died of them.[45]

Tall or Short

The Roman 90 percent who survived early infancy would begin to grow. Their final adult height, or stature, was a product of their health and nutrition in their next life-phase: later childhood and adolescence.

Economic historians think height is a really important mirror of human health—and wealth. Bioarcheologists are much less sold on it. Why the difference? Early economic anthropometric studies found such a powerful correlation between stature and things like wages and GDP that it engendered confidence in stature's validity as a proxy for economic well-being. The Power of a Single Number phenomenon, which we've already observed for GDP, is particularly alluring with stature. Height is a number; we don't have to quibble about its relative presence, its qualities or character—it's deceptively straightforward.[46] Bioarcheologists, on the other hand, understand stature as a product of so many different factors that, as a health indicator, they find it pretty crude. As bioarcheologists also work on historically short but healthy populations, like hunter-gatherers, they may be less likely to assume that "tall is good."

Adult stature is a product of three principal factors: childhood consumption of protein, calcium and vitamins A and D; childhood disease and labor burdens that sap gross nutrition; and genetics.[47] Which of these has the biggest impact on stature is unclear. Calculating stature from skeletons is also tricky. A skeleton is much shorter than a living human; how much shorter depends on the various regression formulae used to reconstruct living height from the length of skeletons. These regression formulae are an object of much contention, and even avoiding them and simply measuring the length of femurs—our longest, most height-sensitive bones—ignores potential shifts in overall body proportions.[48] We, unfortunately, shall have to make use of reconstructed height here in order to include the majority of Italian studies, which don't report femur length consistently.[49]

The debate about physical well-being in the Roman world has raged largely around stature. A series of "big data" projects on the western empire have come to conflicting conclusions. Four such studies, including a very large one based on femur length alone, concluded that stature mostly decreased during the Roman period, only to increase in later Roman antiquity.[50] An exception appeared to be Roman Britain, where men were somewhat taller than their Iron Age predecessors. A fourth study, carried out for Italy alone, concluded that height increased in the Roman period.[51] The consensus from the big data projects, insofar as there is one, thus appears to be that stature declined during the Roman period, but maybe not in Britain.

All of these studies have their problems.[52] The data used here has problems, too. On the one hand, it's based on a larger number of individuals than previous studies, and it's more place- and date-specific.[53] On the other hand, much of that data is of uneven quality.[54] Again, given the doubts about how to calculate living height from skeletons, these shouldn't be regarded as actual heights: it's the variation—over time, between provinces and above all between genders—that is most significant.

The most interesting story revealed by Roman stature is probably not about men—who are most often studied—but women (figure 6.5). In both Britain and in Italy, Roman working men were about the same height as, or somewhat taller than, their Iron Age predecessors, but women appear to be quite a bit shorter—perhaps some three centimeters. It's also revealing that the data here suggest only a small height difference between British and Italian Roman men (169 versus 168.5 centimeters) but a pretty big one between British and Italian Roman women (159 versus 155 centimeters, respectively).[55] Living under the Roman empire may have produced somewhat shorter men, but it appears to have produced significantly shorter women, pointing to particular challenges for girl children and teenagers.

What could be causing these gendered differences in height? It's probably not those early childhood stresses we saw above. Were they to blame, those particularly high Italian stresses should have produced particularly shorter Italian men, which wasn't the case, and the stresses should have been higher among Italian women, which they weren't. The much shorter Italian women are a puzzle, one that has a couple of possible answers. The first could be catch-up growth in Italian boys but not in girls: stresses experienced in early

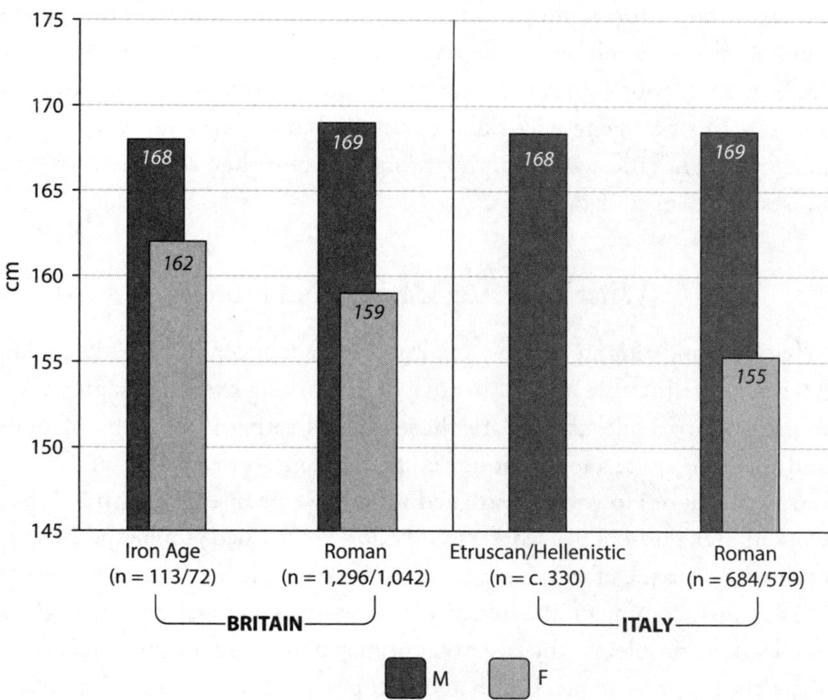

FIGURE 6.5. Stature, pre-Roman and Roman populations (Data: appendix 5, table A.14)

childhood might have been compensated for with better nutrition and living conditions for boys later on, resulting in later adolescent growth spurts.[56] The second, which is implicit in the first, is better adolescent nutrition for boys than for girls. While boys and girls appear to have suffered equally from childhood disease, boys could have been compensated later with better food, while girls were not. As we'll see in a moment, there is some data to suggest that Italian boys and adult men had better access to protein than Italian girls and women.

Finally, there's the oft-sidelined problem of genetics. Different populations have different genetic maximum heights. It's usually assumed that this genetic maximum only comes into play once disease and malnutrition have been eliminated, as in many modern wealthy nations. This is probably an exaggeration. Genetic predispositions make themselves felt even in children and adolescents without those advantages, as new ancient DNA work is suggesting.[57] The extraordinary amounts of immigration from the Roman

East into Italy—forced migration through slavery and voluntary movement through trade—is only now becoming apparent through ancient DNA studies. Eastern populations appear to have been—and continue to be—somewhat shorter. This new genetic cocktail could not but impact overall heights—particularly in cities, where immigration concentrated and from whence most of our Italian data comes.

What They Ate: Cavities and Protein

What boys and girls ate in later childhood and adolescence drove their adult height. What they ate as adults drove their working lives. In chapter 2, we found working adults, particularly those in cities, eating a wide range of foods and spending quite a lot of money on them. Here we are asking a more detailed question: How well nourished were these people? Poorly nourished workers aren't productive workers, and poorly nourished families perpetuate cycles of poverty. Unfortunately, as we've also seen, the human skeleton is not terribly forthcoming on the nutrition that produced it: stature is a good example of the problems. The two other principal metrics for nutrition are also still only proxies—dental health and isotopes in bones. Both tend to reflect diet in the later, adult phases of life.

People's mouths carry histories of what they ate. Caries (cavities), calculus (tartar) and antemortem tooth loss (tooth loss before death) provide a sense of diet's impact on teeth. Higher caries and calculus, with resultant tooth loss during life, are caused by diets higher in sugar and carbohydrates, genetic susceptibility and poor oral hygiene.[58] Dental health is thus a crude measurement of diet, mostly useful when used comparatively—men versus women, different regions or different periods. Major shifts in diet—like that from hunter-gatherers to settled agriculture in the Neolithic, or to industrial foods in the early 20th century—are well documented through dental health, but nuanced changes probably not so much.

There's a lot of data on working Romans' teeth, but it isn't terribly revealing.[59] There are no major differences between men and women's oral health, although British men may have had more cavities than women. In Britain, cavities, calculus and antemortem tooth loss all increase dramatically with the Roman conquest. Dental health is somewhat better in the countryside than in the cities—a finding that is puzzling, as we'll see. In Italy, as with most other metrics, no great change distinguishes Roman-period dental health from earlier periods and over half of people died with at least one cavity. Interestingly,

British urbanites had the same or perhaps even worse dental health as the mostly urban Italian sample. Living in cities may have meant a wider variety of foods, but those foods, it appears, weren't always good for your teeth.

The frustrations of distinguishing disease versus nutrition's impact on the body, together with new technologies, have led scientists to turn to stable isotopes for better answers.[60] Our bones contain the residue of the various sources of protein that went into building them. Those protein sources can be partially traced through the ratios of carbon and nitrogen isotopes ($^{13}C/^{12}C$, $^{15}N/^{14}N$) ingested with food and then laid down in bone, particularly the collagen in bone. Isotope evidence thus provides a partial map of the sources and levels of protein consumption. Protein, as we've seen, helps determine stature, and it impacts disease immunity and bone robustness—all things that matter for health. By sourcing protein, isotopes also gesture to, but don't directly describe, the rest of the diet.[61]

But isotope values are not a food diary. Isotopes record specific aspects of dietary intake over some portion of a lifetime. They are best at capturing the trophic level of the food consumed (where that food is on the food chain) and much poorer at capturing other components of dietary protein, particularly plant proteins. Thus, while broadly speaking a grain- and vegetable-rich diet should yield lower ^{13}C and ^{15}N values, and a fish-rich diet higher ^{13}C and ^{15}N values, there are lots of exceptions. Like all proxies, isotopes are best used comparatively—between different places, genders and contexts.

Some of the most significant isotope differences may be between farmers and city folk (figure 6.6). Country people in Italy have lower ^{13}C and ^{15}N values than their comrades in cities. To a certain extent, this can be attributed to differences in fish consumption, since fish raises both ^{13}C and ^{15}N. This isn't a huge surprise. As we saw in chapter 2, farmers almost never ate fish and only rarely fish sauce (*garum*). And, as we also saw, urbanites, like those in Pompeii and Herculaneum, consumed a wide range of fish. But the isotope data further shows us that not all urbanites, even those living on the coast, were that lucky. The inhabitants of the city of Velia, south of Naples, had relatively low ^{13}C and ^{15}N values compared to another seaside town, the port city of Ostia.[62] The exceptions were a handful of men with higher levels of carbon and especially nitrogen. These same men were also found to have auditory exostoses—surfer's ear—produced by long-term exposure to cold water.[63] In other words, these folks with higher ^{13}C and ^{15}N values were almost certainly fishermen who spent time on the stormy seas and who had ready access to fish. The rest of this seaside population seemingly did not.

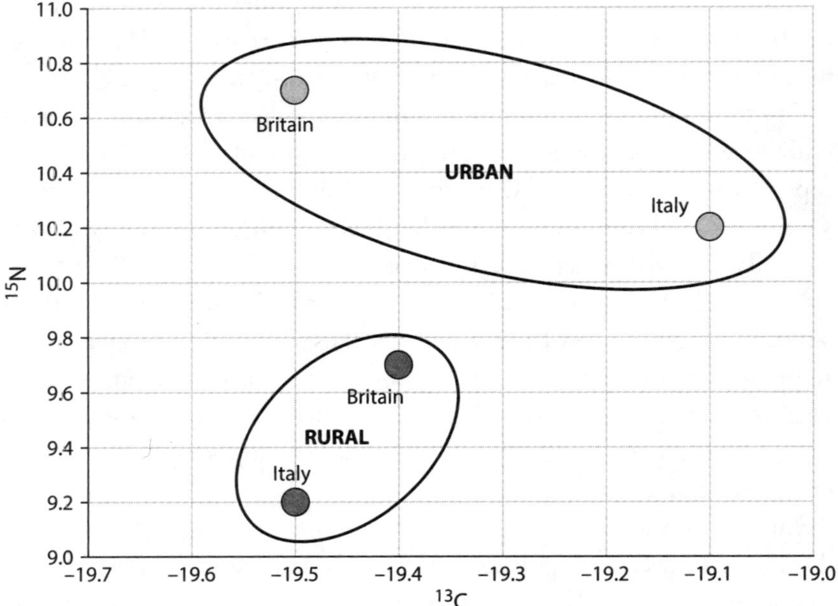

FIGURE 6.6. City and countryside diets: average dietary isotope values from British and Italian sites (Data: Bowes and Pearson, forthcoming)

In Britain, farmers and city folk had virtually identical ^{13}C values, but rural people had significantly lower ^{15}N values, pointing to less consumption of protein from higher trophic sources.[64] This cannot be attributed solely to different availability of fish. Rather, it tentatively suggests that those British farmers we examined in chapter 3 were not consuming that much of the milk and beef surplus they produced, but rather shipping much of it off the farm to the city or the military. Their diets would have relied more heavily on plant proteins—beans and other legumes—as well as some meat and dairy. The fact that these farmers had fewer cavities also point to their eating plant proteins, rather than simply lots of grain.

Finally, while it's also unsurprisingly clear that Britons and Italians had different diets (they certainly do today), from an isotope perspective those differences are only significant among city dwellers. Farmers' diets in both places appear to be relatively similar. As we already saw in chapter 2, the countryside experienced a muted version of the pan-Roman increase in dietary variety. As far as their isotopes are concerned, farmers' diets tended to have more in common, while regional differences would have been more apparent among those living in cities.

A new effort to reconstruct a total Roman diet using isotope data reinforces this sense that cities were not only hot spots of dietary variety, but also of robust meat and fish consumption. Using a small number of adults from Herculaneum who perished in the eruption of Vesuvius, the study specifically analyzed the amino acids from bone collagen, producing a more detailed breakdown of those proteins' origins. It concluded that marine fish contributed some 5–15 percent of calories consumed by these individuals, cereals around 50 percent, and terrestrial protein (meat, oil, dairy and legumes) around 40 percent.[65] It included one plant source—olive oil—which it estimated to be as much as 29 percent of total dietary calories. Not all of these numbers derived from the isotopes themselves (the olive oil number is largely a guess). Nonetheless, it points to an urban diet richer in terrestrial protein—meat, cheese and legumes—than was once supposed.

Rich Bodies, Poor Bodies, Men and Women

Today the bodies of poor and working people are visibly different from those of the wealthy. In wealthy countries, poor people suffer higher levels of obesity and tooth decay, and are often, but not always, shorter than richer people.[66] A word about the bodies of richer versus poorer is in order here, not least because the relative nature of the skeletal data might seem to demand it. High stress compared to what? Lower nitrogen compared to what? This same data also turns out to be a cautionary tale about the places where wealth inequality matters—and where it doesn't.

Two efforts to sort out health inequalities in Roman Britain examined the graves of those who appeared to be of higher status than others, comparing a whole range of stress markers and different means of measuring status and/or wealth. One study determined that inequality (measured by grave goods and coffins) didn't track most stress or pathology markers, with some possible exceptions between urban and rural cemeteries.[67] Another found that juveniles buried in coffins had a somewhat lower mortality risk than those without coffins, but that adults exhibited no such distinctions.[68] In short: no smoking gun showing healthy rich people and sick poor people.

In Italy, our data again is terrible, a pity given other evidence for massive wealth inequality in and around the city of Rome. At the port city of Ostia, a study compared various dietary isotope values with different types of burial—from those laid in the plain earth to those buried in a mausoleum. It uncovered no real differences between those with only rudimentary burial and those in a fine mausoleum.[69] Similar results came from a small mausoleum and surrounding burials from the edge of Rome: no major differences in isotope values indicating different diets, or for childhood stress markers between the mausoleum population versus the folks in modest burials.[70] In both places, the only real differences were in dental hygiene: the poorest had worse dental health than the possibly-rich—a result that continues to hold true today.[71]

These unspectacular results are important. They highlight the difficulty of knowing who is rich and who is not from burial alone. Grave goods and even coffins were relatively inexpensive in a world full of things and aren't necessarily a good way of distinguishing wealthy from poor. But mostly this negative result highlights a broadly shared world of disease—particularly childhood disease. Although larger houses with better light and ventilation probably gave the rich some health advantages, the thick miasma of waterborne and respiratory disease in which all ancient people, particularly those in cities, lived seems to have been only slightly thinned by wealth. One could not buy one's way out of the greatly increased disease burden of the Roman world with better insurance or better healthcare, as the rich do today. As we've seen, even middle-class kids in Victorian London suffered the urban disease burden. Rich and poor Roman kids appeared to have suffered more or less equally.

Gender appears to have made a bigger difference in bodily experience, although not necessarily in childhood stress markers. Although individual cemeteries sometimes show gendered differences in dental health or other stress markers, at the larger, regional level these differences disappear.[72] Levels of nonspecific stress experienced in childhood (enamel hypoplasia and cribra orbitalia) appear to be broadly equal between men and women.[73] Oral health is also roughly the same, with caries and antemortem tooth loss at similar levels.

It's in diet, as revealed by isotopes, that more consistent, if subtle, gender divisions can be found (figure 6.7). In Britain, men and women have similar isotope values for nitrogen (women's are slightly lower), while for carbon, women's values are somewhat lower. Indeed, a much-heralded discovery of dietary class differences in one British cemetery is, upon more careful analysis, a product of gender differences: the "rich" folks are mostly men, and it's the men who have the higher carbon and nitrogen.[74] In Italy, gender differences in diet are much more pronounced, with women having significantly lower values for both nitrogen and carbon.[75] The total diet reconstruction based on those few folks from Herculaneum points in the same direction, suggesting women were getting fewer calories from fish and more from grain and meat/dairy. If this translated into girls getting consistently less protein than boys,

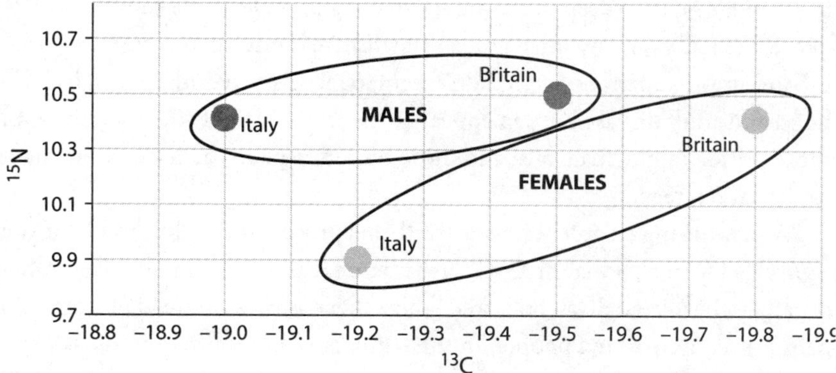

FIGURE 6.7. Different male and female diets? Average dietary isotope values, Britain and Italy (Data: Bowes and Pearson, forthcoming)

this could help explain why Italian women of the Roman period were so short, compared to both Italian men and their pre-Roman predecessors.

Finally, one of the most important differences between working men and women is longevity. Everywhere we have them, the age-at-death statistics suggest that young women died in greater numbers than young men. Roman cemeteries everywhere have far more young women who died between the ages of 13 and 30 than young men.[76] These higher levels of female mortality are almost certainly a result of complications around pregnancy and childbirth. Women were married relatively young in the Roman world, probably in their late teens in the cities of the Roman West, perhaps somewhat later in the countryside.[77] Adolescent mothers are at greater risk in childbirth than those in their twenties. Mothers who may not have had great adolescent nutrition were at even higher risk. Thus, while men and women appear to have experienced similar levels of childhood stress, childbirth took a harsh toll among adolescent and young women.

Bodies at Work

Roman working adults lived in a complex, even contradictory health environment. In general, they experienced much higher levels of childhood stress than their historical predecessors. If they were born and lived in a city, they probably had access to a diet with more protein, or at least more fish protein, but suffered the so-called urban penalty in the form of a higher disease burden. If they were born and lived in the country, they may have consumed less fish, meat and/or dairy (despite raising it), making them less able to weather less dense, but still grim, disease regimes. The disease burden may have recognized urban/rural distinctions, but it didn't seem to recognize wealth: the high childhood and adult disease burden appears to have been largely democratic, with those buried in fine mausolea and those buried in plain earth experiencing it to similar degrees.

Most working people who survived this precarious childhood bear the signs of a life of heavy labor. Osteoarthritis, degenerative joint disease, enthesopathies, herniated discs, fractured limbs: these are the jeremiad of stress and pain borne by working people. In the Roman world, these musculoskeletal stresses have received far less attention than diet or disease. We have forgotten the physical toll that labor used to take on the body. The working majority in a modern wealthy country sits at a desk: they are at risk of verbal abuse and carpal tunnel syndrome. We forget that labor used to mean, and for many still means, a normalcy of spinal compression, the erosion of ligaments and tendons, and an expectation of broken bones. This goes beyond what philosophers imagine constitutes "the embodiment" of a working class—as though embodiment were just posture and dress. These were bodies that served as tools, worn until they wore out.[78]

The causes of these musculoskeletal stresses are just as complex as the other phenomena we've been discussing. Polishing on the joints, bony spurs, and/or pitting that are the signs of osteoarthritis, or the bulging of herniated discs (termed Schmorl's nodes)—these are principally due to the heavy use of joints and bones over a lifetime, although genetic predisposition, gender and, above all, age also play a role.[79] How they are counted by bioarchaeologists, and whether they are counted by body part or in gross, constitutes the biggest challenge to analyzing and comparing them.[80] An earlier generation's overenthusiasm in tying specific joint stress to specific occupations has largely been tamped down: you can't, as it turns out, tell a shoemaker by his knees.[81] The biggest limiting factor behind this data is the age profile of the individuals in question: the older you are, the more wear and tear on your joints you will have, even if you sit at a desk. Musculoskeletal stress is cumulative, and thus an aged person or older population with high stress scores can't be easily compared with a younger one. Usefully for us, the age profiles of most of the cemeteries included in this study are more or less the same: few children, a majority of people who died aged between 20 and 40 years of age, and far fewer individuals over 50 (see figure 6.2 above). We thus have some grounds for comparing gross numbers, while remaining alert to any especially old populations.

Broken bones, or trauma, deserve a special note here. The current interest in violence in the archaeological and historical record has sometimes obscured the fact that most broken bones in most past populations came from accidents, and most of those accidents were incurred while working.[82] Only injuries to the upper parts of the head and so-called parry fractures to the forearm are more likely to derive from interpersonal violence.[83] These kinds of interpersonal trauma register only around 2–5 percent of all traumatic injuries in most Roman communities.[84] Far more common are injuries related to accidents, probably work-related. In all periods—and the Roman is no exception—men experience higher levels of work-related broken bones than women, and the location of those breaks can be revealing of gendered work differences.[85] Indeed, labor-related trauma was one of the hallmarks of Roman working bodies.

Musculoskeletal stresses and work trauma appear to have massively increased in the Roman period in our two regions (figure 6.8). Metrics for herniated discs (Schmorl's nodes), osteoarthritis in all limbs, and trauma all increase two- to tenfold in the Roman period.[86] This is even more marked than the increase in nonspecific stress indices or stature, although the quantity of pre-Roman data is still not what we might wish. Here is the stark price paid for a world awash with things and agricultural surplus, a price paid with the worn bodies of the people who did the producing.

Farmers laboring at hoeing and herding have skeletal stresses particular to their world. In Britain, while osteoarthritis was probably around the same in city and country, joint degeneration of the lower body—the hips and knees—was more common in the countryside. These are patterns that seem to hold true in Europe until the Industrial Revolution: farming produced preferential stress on the hips, knees and legs.[87] Broken bones in the countryside also tended to occur in the lower limbs, particularly among men, who incurred most of them. These are almost certainly the result of hoeing and plowing but also of animal droving: animals kick, and those kicks preferentially impact the lower limbs. More intensive agriculture, more animals—all of which we saw in chapter 3—are evident in the bodies of these British farmers. Finally, the hallmark injury of farmers, left on their flesh if not their bones, was the left-handed pinky scar—the vestige of seasons of wielding a scythe.[88] An overwhelming number of signatories on Egyptian documents were identified by this hallmark of rural labor.

At Vagnari, in southern Italy, a population of farmers and craftspeople on an imperial estate displayed many of those same trends. Some 20 percent of

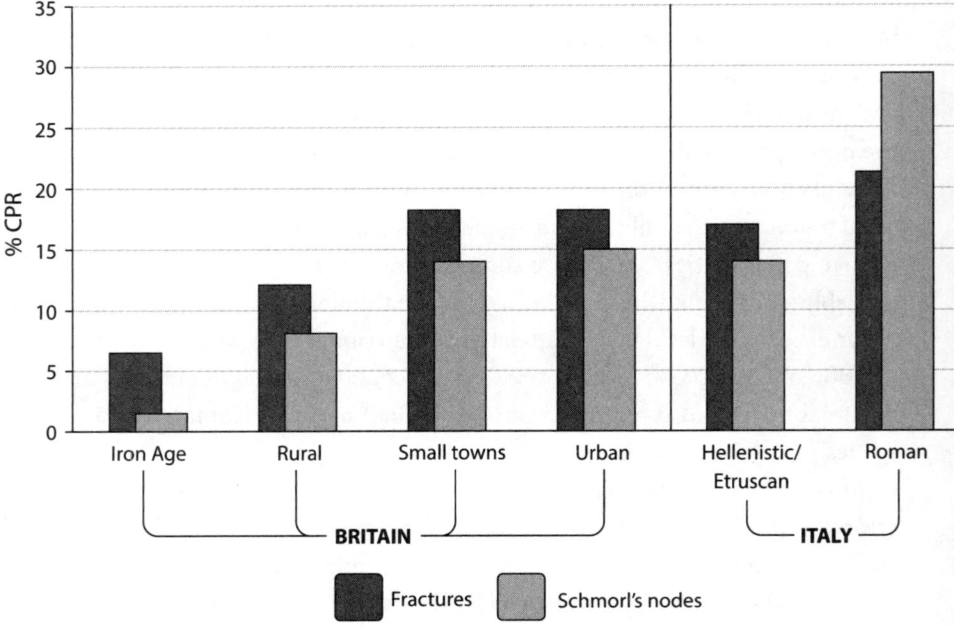

FIGURE 6.8. The worn working body: musculoskeletal stress markers, crude prevalence rates (Data: appendix 5, table A.14)

the community had osteoarthritis; 25 percent had herniated discs; some 30 percent had broken bones. Men showed more fractures and stress on the lower limbs; women tended to have fractures on the upper body.[89] Interestingly, these working people also buried their dead with an unusually large and diverse array of objects, including tools.[90] Pruning hooks, punches, knives or scrapers might be laid outside the grave as well as in it. Tools were particularly likely to be deposited alongside older men whose bodies showed the signs of a long life of hard labor—osteoarthritis, herniated discs and fractures.[91] A lifetime of labor—male labor at any rate—was commemorated with the tools of that labor.

If we dig into the rural sample a bit more and look specifically at those same southeastern British countrysides we examined in chapter 3, we get yet more detail about the activities that were hardest on the body. The farmers and artisans of central and southern Britain are impacted by musculoskeletal stress at about the average level for rural Britain generally—over a third had some kind of degenerative joint disease, mostly in the spine; around a tenth had herniated discs and broken bones—all of which are notably lower than at the

Italian Vagnari. However, the highest levels of musculoskeletal stress are not in the surplus-producing farms—although they are high there, too—but in roadside and industrial sites. Roadside sites have osteoarthritis at twice the levels of farms for almost every limb, and the highest levels of herniated discs. Unusual, too, is the fact that the women in these settlements were impacted by arthritis almost as often as men.[92] Broken bones were also most prevalent in these sites. If we recall, roadside sites and villages in Britain were sites not only of farming, but also of craft production and animal droving. This more specialized work appears to have taken a greater toll—in terms of arthritis and trauma—than plain intensive farming alone.

The bodies of those who died in urban Italy, at the edges of the city of Rome, bear stark testament to the cost of specialized work. It's worth remembering that the Italian data comes overwhelmingly from the great suburban cemeteries around Rome, where the levels of arthritis, herniated discs and broken bones are much higher than in Britain (see figure 6.8). The fact that these stresses are counted by overall rates, rather by specific limbs, makes comparison with the British data a bit difficult. Nonetheless, the more straightforward numbers of herniated discs (a third of individuals), spinal osteoarthritis (well over half) and overall signs of joint degeneration (ditto) are very high indeed. Not all cemeteries have such high levels of bodily stress. For instance, a group of individuals in and around a fine mausoleum in the Roman suburbs had much lower levels, while a population of workers from a fullery right next door had far higher.

The kind of work that really wore out workers' bodies is also evident from these Roman suburban cemeteries. Some of the highest levels of musculoskeletal stress in the Roman world come from cemeteries in and around specialized work sites: a fullery and a possible saltworks. These sites and their cemeteries deserve a special look, as the rates of musculoskeletal stresses and trauma are remarkable (figure 6.9).[93]

Osteoarthritis, herniated discs and broken bones are all off the charts. They appear at higher-than-normal levels in women as well as men. The age data for the saltworks in particular points to an older-than-normal population, so some of the high numbers are a result of an aged, work-worn population. But even young adults have high levels of stress in these cemeteries, as we'll see in a moment. In the fullery, osteoarthritis impacted the lower body, while in the saltworks, the upper body bore the brunt of stress—the result, perhaps, of squatting and carrying heavy loads, respectively. Over half the people in the saltworks cemetery had at least one broken bone, and over half had herniated

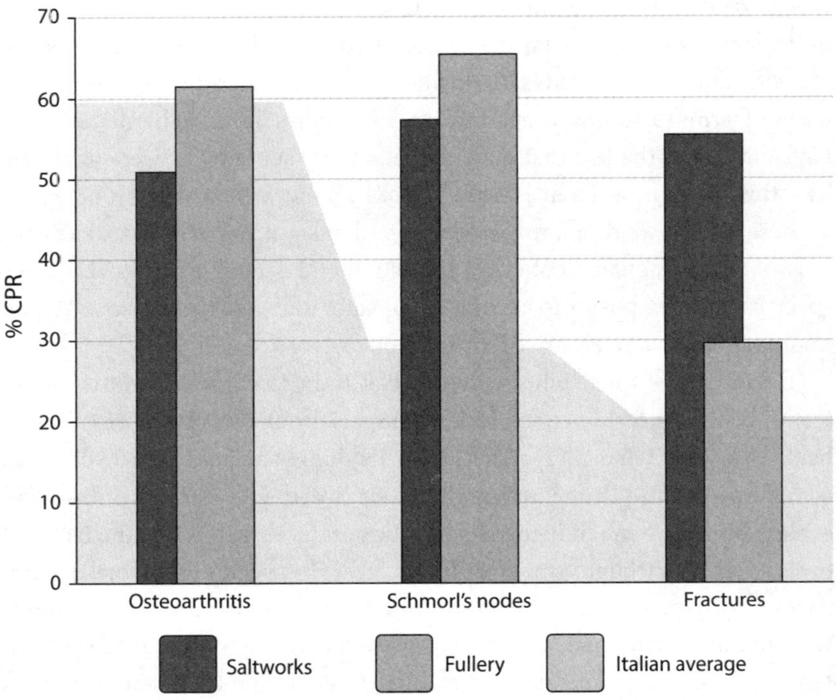

FIGURE 6.9. The bodies of salt workers and fullers (Data: Castel Malnome: Minozzi et al. 2012; Piccioli et al. 2015; Caldarini et al. 2015; Casal Bertone Fullery (Area Q): Caldarini et al. 2015)

discs. One is struck both by the immense wear and tear on these workers' bodies and by their extraordinary resilience—nearly 10 percent of the individuals at the saltworks were over 50 years old when they died, a big accomplishment for a premodern world.[94]

We can't be sure the people buried near these specialized industries necessarily worked in them.[95] We don't have to, for the whole city of Rome and its suburbs boasted not only the largest city in the Roman world but the highest density of specialized work in the Roman world. Brick and tile works, fulleries, foundries, bakeries, potteries, quarries: all were found in profusion in and around the city, and all required heavy labor.[96] The very high levels of physical stress evident in many of Rome's urban and suburban populations may be related to Rome and central Italy's status not only as *caput mundi* but as *caput fabricae*—the center of making things.

These same labor regimes did not spare children, either in specialized industry or in the countryside. As we already noted when we discussed child wages, there was no such thing as "child labor" in the Roman world, simply because childhood was not imagined as a particular labor category. Children worked as soon as they were able, at whatever task they were able to do. Younger children herded geese and weeded and swept leaves; older children herded larger animals and ran errands and carried water.[97] We've already seen children around 12–14 years given over as apprentices—as weavers or smiths or potters.[98] Thus, it should come as no surprise that, when they died young, children's bodies also bore the signs of heavy labor.

Such labor is somewhat harder to detect in child bones. Osteoarthritis, herniated discs and other indicators are the result of years of labor—years that those who died young did not have the chance to accumulate. Nonetheless, the signs of child labor are there, everywhere there are children. In Britain, some two percent of children studied had fractures, mostly to their shoulders.[99] In those surplus-producing countrysides of the British southeast, some 20 percent of teenagers and young adults already had degenerative joint disease, the product of heavy labor.[100] In the cemeteries around Rome, enthesopathy—inflammation around the connection points for tendons and ligaments—impacted a majority of children, from around a third in some cemeteries to 100 percent of children at the fullery site.[101] These children's shoulders were most impacted by stress, followed by their legs, the results of carrying heavy loads. At Herculaneum, too, some 11 percent of children had enthesopathy at the shoulder; two of them, only eight or nine years old, had serious lesions.[102]

In most cemetery populations, the majority of children do not bear these markers of heavy labor. This doesn't mean that most children did not work. It means that the places we can see joint disease and enthesopathy and fractures mark the extreme end of a spectrum of working children, an extreme where the bodies of children had already begun to resemble the worn bodies of adults. Outside these extremes lay labor which is less visible. A study of Roman British children found that rates of mortality substantially worsen after six years of age, with six- to ten-year-olds showing increased hypoplasia, cribra orbitalia and other nonspecific stress indicators. These may be the less obvious signs of children now put to work.[103]

These historically high levels of musculoskeletal stress, even among some of the young, may shed further light on Roman stature and nutrition. We've seen throughout this book that gross calorie intake among even the enslaved appears to have been pretty robust. *Gross* is the key word here: all this hard work soaked up those calories. Those doing the particularly onerous, heavy labor that took such a toll on their backs, hips and knees needed more than the 3,700 calories we've identified as the "subsistence" bottom. If working adolescents didn't get those calories—in particular the protein and vitamins that promote long-bone growth—their adult stature would have been limited. If girls were doing similar work but getting less protein, their growth would have been particularly limited. Labor and disease—those vampires of gross calories—may have taken some of those low-end but reasonably robust diets and reduced them to barely enough.

Enslaved Bodies

The worn bodies near the industrial sites of suburban Rome, or the Herculaneum children's bodies worn beyond their years, raise the question—were these enslaved people? Treading in urine, wading through salt pans, or making children carry heavy loads certainly seems like work that would be forced upon slaves. And yet the answer is—maybe. The difficulties in answering the question are perhaps more revealing than the ambiguous answer.[104] For in trying to identify enslaved labor through the body, we have to confront the particular nature of that labor and thus a particularly thorny instance of the difference between categories of analysis versus categories of practice.

We've followed in the steps of the enslaved throughout this book, noting the entanglement of slaves and the poorest free labor—working at the same jobs, receiving indistinguishable wages, eating similar foods. Above all, we've seen that Roman slavery, as a distinct and brutalizing legal category, doesn't readily map onto a distinct category of practice. With the possible exception of domestic service, most types of work—even mining—were done by enslaved and free alike. Mining or fulling or smithing were practices that didn't always map onto legally grounded categories of analysis—enslaved, free, freed, apprentice. It's not surprising, then, that the bodies of slaves are mostly indistinguishable from those of the free. The worn bodies of those buried near the fullery or the saltworks could very well be those of the enslaved. Genetic studies suggest that some of these individuals were of North African and eastern Mediterranean origin.[105] But we need more than their high levels of stress and diverse backgrounds to prove their enslaved status.

Instead, we should ask—what aspects of the legal category of being enslaved might be manifest in ways that are distinct from the heavy labor shared by working people more generally? What bodily experiences were specific to enslavement? One such experience was violence. Violence is a corollary of ownership, its perpetual, evil twin.[106] In Latin, owning and dominating used the same root word (*domino*).[107] Roman slave owners could and did beat, crucify and rape their slaves as a matter of course. An inscription that sets out the duties of public undertakers in one Roman city even included a fee-scale for slave whippings and crucifixions: the undertaker had to provide the whipping post, while the slave owner was obliged to pay the floggers (four sestertii each).[108] In the gold mines of Spain, an inscription sets out the rules of the mines and fines and punishments for breaking them. It's clear that the work—and the rules—were the same for slaves and free, but only the slaves were whipped for breaking them.[109] Perhaps, then, finding enslaved labor on the body requires looking for signs of interpersonal violence.

Yet for all this sense of a quotidian, even casual violence against the enslaved, we have no idea how often Roman slave owners beat their slaves. There is no ancient corollary to the whipping diaries kept by American plantation owners.[110] We've also seen that most trauma in Roman skeletal communities appears to be caused by work: blunt force trauma to the upper head or parry fractures to arms are pretty rare. Interestingly, the very high number of fractures at the Rome saltworks and fullery don't appear to include any of these skull or parry wounds.

We can find some individuals who bear the signs of multiple violent injuries suffered at the hands of others. One example stands out, for the signs of both hard work and violent trauma.[111] A woman buried in the Collatina necropolis in the Roman suburbs was over 50 years old when she died. Her skull displays multiple blows to the head, which may have produced swelling in the brain. Her jaw had been fractured, and parry fractures to her right arm describe her attempts to defend herself. All of these injuries showed different degrees of healing, suggesting not one, but multiple episodes of violent attack. Her shoulder had been dislocated, while Schmorl's nodes and osteoarthritis in her back describe a life bearing heavy loads. She had borne multiple children. She was buried in an only partially covered grave, devoid of any grave goods.

The archaeologists who excavated her speculate that this woman may have been a slave, but they note, too, that poor working women of all legal statuses would have been—and continue to be—susceptible to violence at the hands of the people around them. The Collatina woman, while helping us imagine the violence suffered by the enslaved, reminds us of the others who may have suffered it as well.

There is one other population of Roman bodies that should contain a majority of enslaved persons: the victims in Herculaneum, including the

Load-Bearing Mother, who have played such an important role in our body histories (see figure 6.1). Calculations from a partially preserved list of city residents reckon that some 40 percent of the population of Herculaneum were slaves.[112] The 200-plus individuals who failed to escape the eruption of Vesuvius, and whose skeletons have been the object of so many studies, ought to at least mirror this demographic or, more likely, exceed it. For during the twelve hours between Vesuvius' initial eruption and the town's final devastation, most inhabitants were able to escape.[113] Why didn't these individuals? Remaining behind to look after a master's belongings would have been well within the duties of slaves. The several hundred victims found sheltering on the beach, including the young woman with the worn back with whom we began this chapter, may well have been predominately domestic slaves, left behind by their masters.[114]

Needless to say, there is nothing in the bodies of the Herculaneum dead to distinguish slave from free. Even the children with high levels of musculoskeletal stress described above could be working free children. The likelihood that the Herculaneum dead count the enslaved among them is really owed to texts and the demographics they provide. In a world of entangled labor practices, the bodies of the enslaved are often mute about their status.

Their muteness is even more noteworthy when we compare the difficulties of distinguishing slave bodies in ancient Rome with the much clearer, grimmer picture from the Americas. Slave cemeteries in the Caribbean and the American South have the worst metrics for childhood disease from the eighteenth and nineteenth centuries. The tiny, stunted bodies of slave children describe the toll both rampant disease and poor infant nutrition took on stature.[115] In the Americas, the widespread practice of chaining slaves also appears to have left permanent signs on neck and shoulders, weighted down by heavy metal collars.[116] But even this more brutal and segregationist slave regime didn't always result in adult bodies distinguishable from the poor working free.[117] Even the horrors of the American slave experience were embodied in ways we can't always see in skeletons.

The Final Bill

The anonymous Herculaneum woman with whom we began epitomized the toll that living through the Roman empire took on the bodies that made it run. Her teeth and bones showed the signs of childhood stresses born of years struggling with disease. Disease, as evidenced by the lines in her teeth, would have been a constant companion, but one that ultimately may have made her stronger. Women like her may not have eaten as much fish as their male neighbors and may have had a poorer diet more generally. Her food fueled a lifetime of heavy work—of loads hauled, floors swept, water carried—that was already taking a toll on her bones. When she died, overwhelmed by the final heat and fumes of Vesuvius, beside her lay children who already bore those same signs of hard work.

The huge amount of new data from human skeletons has revealed the particular challenges of living in—and producing—a pan-Mediterranean, surplus-producing, consumer-goods-loving economy. It was a hazardous world, particularly for those new to its hazards. Those hazards came less from getting enough to eat—although some, particularly girls and women, may have had less—and more from living with historically high levels of disease and historically high amounts of work.

The increased population density with which people lived—in new or bigger cities or even in densely packed countrysides—brought with it an increased burden of disease. From dysentery to malaria, tuberculosis to bronchitis, heightened levels of disease were the price of living cheek by jowl with others. Density was not just an urban phenomenon. In chapter 3 we saw that the Roman period witnessed some of the densest use of the countryside before modernity. The expansion of agricultural surplus production, which, as we saw, pulled most farmers into its wake, also led to increased mobility—going to town to sell crops, traveling to the nearby village to buy cloth. To an extent unmatched perhaps until the nineteenth century, city and countryside were more densely populated and more connected. As we've also seen, that density included not only people but their greatly increased number of animals—animals that carried tuberculosis and plague and parasites. It was this density of humans and animals, probably even more than long-distance trade and travel, that produced an environment in which disease flourished. And it was disease, more than gross nutrition, that probably constituted the biggest challenge to working people's physical well-being.[118]

Cities were particularly densely populated, and particularly hazardous. The data from urban cemeteries are eloquent on the higher disease burden in cities. For places like Britain that didn't really have cities prior to Roman rule, the hazards were particularly stark. That disease hazard hit the young the hardest. Like our Herculaneum woman, those who survived urban living bear the signs of a childhood of sickness. But while living in cities carried an urban penalty for the 90 percent, it also carried an urban advantage. Whether in ancient

London or Rome, living and working in a city seems to have meant greater dietary variety, and perhaps more constant and frequent sources of protein. We've seen this in the urban expense lists, full of sausages and cheese. Cities were also testing grounds for resilience: those who grew up and survived their rigors may have carried not only the scars but the protection brought about by continual bouts of illness.

Workers in the countryside experienced their own set of hazards. The miasma of disease was a bit thinner here: even the dense farmscapes of Cambridgeshire had more space, and less stress, than the town itself. Food, as in cities, appears to have been reasonably plentiful but less varied, and perhaps more likely to miss key proteins. Those nutritional deficits, plus the more sporadic encounter with disease, may have left rural kids more vulnerable than their urban neighbors. Farm families saw their children die of the diseases that tougher, perhaps better-nourished urban kids survived.

Working women, like the anonymous Herculaneum mother, faced particular challenges. While girls confronted the same burden of disease as boys, their growth appears to have been somewhat stunted. Subtly different diets, particularly as adolescents, could have been to blame. And they alone undertook the most difficult and dangerous labor—bearing children, a labor that resulted in shorter lifespans than their brothers'.

Those who survived to adulthood bear the toll paid for surplus and specialization. The bodies of farmers and urbanites, men and women are subtly different, reflecting the different work and its strains. Farmers had bad hips and broken legs, urbanites bad shoulders and broken arms. And everyone had herniated discs and arthritic backs. The price of specialization—of fine-ware pots and dyed clothes and preserved meat—was particularly high. People who did specialized labor had particularly worn bodies, worn according to the nature of the repetitive, hard work that worked particular limbs literally to the bone. Again, the spread of that work and its punishing labor was not limited to cities, but with the expansion of the consumer-goods apparatus, it extended into the countryside. As the most important machines in the Roman world, the bodies of workers bear the signs of unprecedentedly high levels of stress, the high price that workers paid for a world full of things.

7

The Bottom Line

EPIMACHUS THE tenant farmer; Faustilla the workshop manager-cum-moneylender; Aurelius Paesis the potter; the anonymous young mother with the worn back. The previous pages have introduced us to people who have long stood on the sidelines of history. We have met farmers who made pots, herders speculating on wool, and families willing to let out their children for a loan. We've met, in short, the ordinary working Romans who went to extraordinary lengths to survive, and sometimes thrive, under the world's first "global" economy. Women, children and men, enslaved and free: in their complex strategies for getting by, they challenge the categories to which they've been confined—subsistence farmers, wage laborers, the poor. Through their passion for things, their manically intensive farming and their juggling of loans and hard-won small savings, this history of the Roman 90 percent is instead a thousand stories of emphatic, insistent doing.

This has been a history that has deliberately failed to launch, forgoing both macroeconomic performance metrics and the comparisons with other economies they engender to linger instead on the hows and how muches that mattered to Roman working people. But having gathered these stories of farmers and potters, spinners and slaves, it seems apropos in conclusion to zoom out slightly, to see what kind of new macro is revealed from this micro. Rather than a wide zoom back to categories of analysis—to the high altitude of per capita GDP or household final consumption expenses—a low hover seems more fitting, a reflection on a macro of practice. What do all these very particular practices of growing and hustling and borrowing tell us about the bigger challenges and opportunities working families faced? And how did those practices cocreate Romans' very particular economic world? Here, at the bottom line, we reflect on how the practices of households helped make history, even as they suffered through it.[1]

Gross Performance Metrics Were High . . .

We can start by reflecting on the distance between the high altitude and the ground—that is, between the aggregate measurements and what we've learned about performance from practices. Readers will recall that per capita gross domestic product has been estimated for both Roman consumption and Roman income. Unlike modern such estimates, which are the result of millions of transactions, these ancient performance metrics are acts of radical reduction, compensating for a lack of deep data by using a few data points from the bottom end of subsistence and extending them to the entire Roman population.

Our journey through Roman farms and expense lists, from ancient crop remains to ancient leases, all suggest that these estimates are too low. Food consumption, for one, appears to be considerably higher than the cost of 1,940 calories of food used in these reconstructions. Subsistence rations for enslaved workers were both imagined and delivered at almost twice this caloric amount. Expense lists kept by urbanites with more middling or higher resources describe food expenses at some four to twenty times the per capita estimates. This quantitatively higher consumption was a product of a very different qualitative approach to eating. Urbanites spent only 30–50 percent of their food budget on cheap cereals, and the rest on other things: meat, fish, cheese, wine, oil and pungent vegetables—but above all, on a robust variety of foods. The origins of their calories may have been similar, with only the enslaved and really poor subsisting on the 70-percent-cereal diet of previous imaginings, while others ate more calories and more different things, things like meat, wine and various fats.

Food consumption constituted the biggest chunk of consumption, but it was accompanied by a similar gusto for things. Cups and pots and incense and purple thread and children's toys and shoes and earrings—the gusto for an abundance of things pushed per capita consumption even higher. Those things came in both cheap and more expensive versions. The enslaved (?) vineyard workers outside Pompeii ate off ceramic plates while the freedman (?) Habonius Primus used glass plates; the workers lit their quarters with clay lamps, Habonius Primus' family had bronze lamps.[2] The overall contents of their houses were worth about or just over yearly per capita food consumption, but were, of course, the result of years of accumulated purchases.

We still are no wiser quantitatively about what rural farmers consumed. But the archaeological and skeletal data points in the same direction as the urban folks: a calorically robust diet composed of many things other than plants, minus some of the variety and quantities of meat and fish. That minus may have been particularly tough on farmers' children, leaving them vulnerable to disease. Farmers had the same gusto for things, albeit with fewer lamps and mirrors and more tools and wagons.

On the income side, we've seen that unskilled wages, which were very low indeed, were also a very bad proxy for income. Wages were usually part of a portfolio of income, a portfolio that all family members contributed to, but one still centered on own-production—either farming or textile/artisanal work. Unskilled wages supplemented own-production; they mostly weren't equivalent to it. Roman wages, unlike modern wages, can't be used as a proxy for income.

Gross income from own-production, particularly farming, appears to have been much higher than previously supposed. Rotation strategies practiced by Italian and Egyptian farmers meant that per-hectare outputs were many times greater than alternate fallow models predicted, since outputs included not only wheat but also significant quantities of fodder and animals. In the northwest provinces, where rotation was less common, outputs per hectare were lower but still included some hay and larger animal herds. And everywhere, high settlement densities and shrinking amounts of land would have urged farmers to achieve higher yields—in some places three or more times greater than previously supposed. We can't be sure they managed this, only that low yields would have been mostly untenable and that farmers had the tools—rotation, manuring, weeding—to achieve higher ones.

In uncovering this considerably greater consumption and production, we've also uncovered the Roman world's real inequality—the enormously different consumption and production experienced by different portions of the 90 percent. The farm outputs and consumption patterns of a tiny farm like The Grange outside Cambridge in Britain were only marginally greater than earlier subsistence estimates might have had them, while those of the neighboring Vicar's Farm, with its animal pens and small granary and impressive haul of consumer goods, were much bigger. Ditto the difference between a tiny Pompeiian household and a merely medium one down the street at Habonius Primus'.

The rub is: we still have no way of estimating this spectrum's demographic breakdown—how many Granges, how many Vicar's Farms, how many Soterichoses barely scraping by, how many Hermases with a thriving carpentry business. The previous estimates assumed a very large group—perhaps 90 percent—living at subsistence, and a tiny middling group. It is possible that some of the stories outlined in the previous chapters applied only to this tiny group of middling and larger artisans, farmers and merchants. It is possible, but it's unlikely. If we take just farmers, the majority of the 90 percent, the huge and comprehensive commercial excavations in Gaul and Britain have uncovered far more of the medium, Vicar's Farm-type installations than the tiny, Grange-sized ones. Indeed, the increased size of "small" farms is one of the hallmarks of the Roman period in these places. If the rural majority is any indication, then it would appear that not only did the bottom—the smallest farmers, or the rural and urban enslaved—consume and produce more, but that the middle of the 90 percent were more numerous and bigger consumers than we had assumed.

This is all pretty vague. "Middling," "bottom," and "more than we assumed" are not the stuff of quantitative economic history. We're beginning to have the data—and the tools—to expand the consumption picture for a city like Pompeii over the whole of the city's diverse neighborhoods, or to extend the output models for small farms over whole regions. That's a job for another book.

For those eager for numbers, it would appear that the poorest farmers, manual laborers and laboring enslaved may have consumed around 200 sestertii per year, a majority middle anywhere from 900 to 1,500 sestertii, while a medium-sized farmer in Italy could have made some 2,500 sestertii in surplus grain sales in a good year. Those readers keen for numbers can excavate many more from the appendixes of this book; hopefully those readers will refine and improve them. But hopefully, too, we've shown that one set of numbers—for consumption or income—misses the point.

. . . Did It Matter?

On the one hand, all this new evidence has suggested that the majority of Romans were consuming a relatively robust caloric package. This meant a lot more energy to do work, and thus a lot more work could be done. The Colosseum was not built on 1,900 calories per day. All those consumer goods likewise point to a majority living something more than an animal existence. With a couple of sets of clothes, and plates and glasses, and cheap jewelry, a great many achieved some degree of comfort. The Colosseum was not built by workers scraping their porridge out of a single pot.

On the other hand, one of the goals of this book has been to highlight the disconnect between measurements of economic performance and the economic practices and precarities of daily life. The Roman 90 percent had many minuses to count against these imputed positives. As we saw in chapter 6, their robust caloric consumption had to support a punishing amount of work. Those seemingly generous caloric allowances of 3,700 calories for enslaved workers would have been quickly depleted by what appear to be historically high amounts of physical labor. The Colosseum could have been built on 3,700 calories per day—barely—but such a diet would have left its workers physically depleted.

So, too, the minus of rent and tax would have eaten away at income, leaving seemingly high levels of consumption but nothing else. If even moderate Egyptian rents were typical for the rest of the empire, tenants would have watched perhaps half or more of their cereal outputs vanish into the pockets of their landlords. Of course, the 90 percent included both landlords and tenants, and the hand that took away might very well be one's farmer-neighbors. Nonetheless, the increasing pressure on land revealed by all the new archaeology describes a world where owning probably got harder and renting became the principal path to expand one's land portfolio.

Roman tax rates have long been viewed as pretty low, stimulating investment and trade.[3] While the Heritage Foundation might have found much to love about Roman taxation, the experience of working people was more complicated. Land tax, as we'll discuss further below, was clearly designed to privilege land owning and landowners. The burden of poll tax on the poorest, however, was substantial. For an Egyptian male living in the Fayum, some 20–30 percent of subsistence-level living costs went to poll tax alone. Indeed, lurking behind those higher-than-supposed gross output numbers was the need to grow or earn more to pay tax. As we saw in chapter 4, tax drains mattered more the poorer you got.

Other drains on income were self-driven. The gusto for things that resulted in such high consumption levels resulted from two combined forces—working families' desire for such things, together with the particular importance of consumption in Roman social belonging. Belonging and distinction—the flip sides of the same social substance—were minted in the coin of stuff. As we've seen, objects from lettuce to glass, imported wine to earrings, were the particular Roman currency by which social status was produced, reinforced, and critiqued. This wasn't just a rich man's game of distinction-via-things: everyone had to play. But all that stuff—both desired and required—also cost, and that cost resulted in historically high expenditure. The result, income net of expenditures, was something less than affluence, and certainly something less than economic security. The results were something that resembled, albeit for very different reasons, the high-wire act performed by working families in places like America and China today—awash with TVs and sneakers and iPhones while simultaneously vulnerable to hunger and homelessness. The results were what the poet Juvenal bemoaned as a "pretentious poverty."[4]

It's this flow of income and expenditure, rather than aggregate performance measurements, that not only better captures the experiences of the Roman 90 percent, but also reveals their peculiarity. Because despite some superficial similarities with other consuming cultures, those flows were quintessentially Roman.

The Family Goes to Market

Throughout this book, we've found working families deeply entangled with markets. While we would expect the innkeeper and vegetable vendor with whom we began to live via markets, a great many people we didn't expect needed them as well. Roman small farmers in particular appear to have survived via a complex negotiation with markets. Whether it was the Soterichoses' sale of thyme, wine and hay to keep their family afloat; the grain dryers in British farms that gesture to sale of spelt off the farm; or the small, flat-bottomed wine amphorae produced by central Italian farmers to sell their wine to their neighbors: smallholders the empire over appear to have sold their products off the farm on various kinds of markets. Wage earning and the hustling required to make enough wages were predicated on markets: wages appear to have fluctuated on daily supply, wage earners negotiated with their employers for perks, while the ability—and necessity—to move from job to job all took place on a great canvas of rural and urban labor markets. The credit critical to agricultural investment and bridging income gaps was bought and sold through markets. If we imagine a spectrum of market interaction from the sporadic contact of the stereotypical peasant to the deliberate orientation of early modern artisans, Roman working families appear to have sat somewhere closer to the latter.[5]

As we've also seen, market interaction lay in pools: deep in some places, shallow in others. That uneven topography was regional—the difference, say, between central Italian farmers with their thick carpet of neighborhood and city markets for hay, cereals and wine, versus the largely self-contained farmers of northern Britain, growing, making and consuming most of what they needed. But market engagement was ruled by more than geography: it could also be the product of individual family circumstances. The difference between

Vicar's Farm near Cambridge, with its spelt-cattle monocultures apparently oriented toward sale off the farm, and The Grange, just ten kilometers down the road, which appeared to have pursued net-consumption rather than net-selling, speaks to families' intentions being as important as geography. Nor was market orientation a simple factor of wealth: think of the Soterichos family, who were only able to survive through a combination of crop sales, credit and probably wages—all of which were provided by markets. In some times and places, poor farmers may have been more dependent on markets than wealthier ones.

Agricultural surplus, wage and credit all moved around in quite different kinds of markets. The market in hay, largely unappreciated by historians but critical to smallholders, was probably most driven by the forces of supply and demand. The credit market was more complex, framed around by custom, law and social relationships. But what makes the Roman case so interesting is the constant recourse to extra-household exchange for the very basis of survival. Roman working families of all kinds were the opposite of autarkic islands: they needed markets at every turn.

To say that the Roman 90 percent "needed" markets is a deliberate turn of phrase. It steps out of a particular binary to which premodern people have often been assigned: risk-avoiding or profit-seeking.[6] "Risk" was the framing device most beloved by an earlier generation of historians and anthropologists: premodern people, it was assumed, were focused on "bad year economics," reducing their risks, not maximizing their gains, and markets were inherently risky things to be avoided.[7] Profit-seeking, on the other hand, is the tacit assumption of much recent work. Markets were the means by which people got ahead, a little spark of protomodernity. Markets, of course, can be used for both risk mitigation *and* profit seeking. Wage labor markets, as they were used by hustling farmers, eased risks—the risk of bad agricultural years, of large families and of too many seductive consumer goods. Growing a field of thyme to sell for cash, as the Soterichoses did, was patently a risk designed to make cash to stave off starvation. Roman working people's use of—and need for—markets was, like so much of their existence, a both/and proposition.

All Change

Roman families' reliance on markets had a big impact on the volatility of their household finances. This volatility was experienced not only as uneven income, but also as changing consumption and labor. We've noted throughout this book that the Roman 90 percent lived in a daily context of particularly felt change—change in where they lived versus were they worked, in the different things they did to get by, in the fashions they followed and the goods they consumed. Their dependence on markets both produced and deepened that change-filled environment in subtle and not-so-subtle ways.

On the one hand, exogenous forces like weather were a force of constant change.[8] The Mediterranean's massive variability in rainfall alone—from year to year, from microregion to microregion—meant that farming from Spain to Egypt involved living with boom-bust cycles of plenty and failure. Roman smallholders' integration with markets probably deepened that volatility, for those interactions drove them to a gentle, if insistent, specialization. The farm-distant satellites of Roman-period Italian smallholders are the residues of doubling down on the particular qualities of particular plots, while even the smallest Egyptian smallholders like the Soterichoses included highly specialized crops like thyme among their holdings. When they succeeded with a specialized cash crop, a pile of cash was the result; too much or too little rain meant serious dearth. In the temperate northern climes, specialization is even more marked: those spelt-and-cattle monocultures of Britain and parts of Gaul would have been particularly subject to weather- and disease-driven ups and downs. Weather-driven volatility meant volatile prices—another mainstay of Roman agriculture. But smallholders, with their limited land and razor-thin margins, were more exposed to those price variations, an exposure proportionate to their degree of market engagement.

Volatility also impacted the demand for labor. The same weather forces that occasionally reduced fields to swamps likewise made road travel difficult, ceramic production challenging and urban building construction a nightmare. The particular Roman unskilled labor market, concentrated in consumer goods and building trades, would, in wet years particularly, coincide with bad agricultural years. As the labor pool was largely the same—the surplus labor from farming families—the dip in income would have been doubly felt.[9] Indeed, the potting, glass-making and other artisanal businesses we've discussed in the previous chapters appear to have been volatile regardless of weather. While big installations continued for centuries, even huge ceramic facilities had ups and downs, while smaller manufactories appear to have lasted only decades or operated sporadically.[10] At least some of the consumer-goods income stream thus also appears to be subject to big volatility.

But families themselves were also volatile economic entities. The high-fertility, high-mortality regime under which Roman families lived meant that families were always changing.[11] The death of wage earners and the birth of children all strained family finances; the growth of children into working adults improved them. Marriages with their attendant dowries increased one family's wealth while reducing another's. Families were the backdrop of internal instability against which the particular witch's brew of weather, specialization and wage-labor ebbs and flows took place.

Hustling was one response to this constant volatility. By juggling their own-production of crops and/or artisanal goods with wage labor, textile work and child labor, families pushed back against the forces of volatile income. Trickles of wages could, in theory, help even out the ups and downs of poor harvests or poor sales. But Roman hustling was market-driven and market-dependent. It relied upon the markets for day-laborers, for textiles, for the jug-making and baking and all the other eight jobs juggled by our much-mocked Pompeiian multitasker. Roman hustling thus bred its own volatilities. Family members moved around in response to labor opportunities—to the neighboring farm to the next city. Hustling opportunities often clashed with the agricultural cycle: potting, building and farming were all summer-intensive jobs. The need to toggle between the world of growing and the world of making forced particularly hard choices on families as to how to use their labor: getting it wrong meant double disaster, getting it right meant a really good year. Instead of leveling out income, hustling could also exacerbate its ups and downs.

A Dense World

The carpet of Italian cities, the cheek-by-jowl farms of Cambridgeshire, the big villages of the Egyptian Fayum, the heaving agro-industrial belt around the city of Rome: the Roman 90 percent lived in an unprecedently dense world. We've mostly dodged the debates about the size of the Roman population here, preferring to examine people in their contexts rather than use assumptions about those contexts to make sense of people.[12] But throughout this book, we've found working people impacted by—and cocreating—their thickly populated environments. And those environments shaped economic practice in ways both obvious and not.

The go-to model for the impact of population on economic practice is that of the eighteenth-century demographer Thomas Malthus. Living in an increasingly dense late-eighteenth-century world, Malthus and his followers regarded population as a grim and inexorable wheel. Unchecked fertility regimes, encouraged by higher wages, would drive population up faster than food production, with lower wages, famine and misery for the poor the inevitable result—the so-called Malthusian trap. Malthus has been much invoked by demographers, even before the mounting evidence for very large Roman populations. Whether or not Romans found themselves in a Malthusian trap, or managed to escape it through increased agricultural productivity, has been much debated.[13]

The impact of living in a high-density world can't be easily reduced to a thumbs-up or thumbs-down. On the one hand, we've seen that wages were, indeed, very low. On the other hand, we've also seen that very few people lived exclusively on wages.[14] Those low wages may very well have been pushed down by inflated supply caused by high population and further devalued by enslaved labor. But wage formation was also driven by what workers actually did with wages—which in the Roman case mostly meant using them as a supplement, not a living.

Harder to surmount was the limited land confronted by at least some farmers. Land limitation—even in places like Britain that we long assumed were less densely settled—had all the knock-on effects we modeled in chapter 3. Not only would land have been dearer, and rents higher, but decisions around its use became more fraught. Animals, as we saw, were hugely important to all kinds of Roman activities. Animals, especially cattle, require lots of land, land that had to be balanced with other arable uses. Roman smallholders living in a dense world were constantly confronted by arable-pastoral trade-offs when managing their limited plots. The use of ley systems by smallholders in Italy and Egypt was clearly intended to make limited land do this both/and work.

Population density is usually imagined to be a human problem and an urban problem. We've seen in chapter 6 that the growth of cities, more than the lack of food, presented the biggest challenge to physical flourishing. If a fifth of the Roman population lived in cities, the disease density produced by urban density was obviously a big problem. But in the Roman world, density was also an animal problem and a rural problem. Those dense farmscapes unearthed by the bulldozers in Gaul and Britain were not only dense with humans, but also dense with cattle and sheep. Animal-dense farms and urban agriculture brought those animals into increased contact with humans. From tuberculosis to brucellosis to respiratory illness, dense human-animal interactions heightened the already increased disease pool produced by bigger cities and lots of moving people.[15] That vastly increased disease burden that sapped net-nutrition and challenged productivity was a product of this dense human and animal, rural and urban world.

But if Malthus might have found his theories proven correct in ancient Rome, so, too, could have Ester Boserup. Boserup, a Danish economist, identified a set of more positive responses to high population, among them increased productivity and greater specialization.[16] In the Roman world, a density of farms and farm consumers made the countryside a viable and valuable place for both the production and sale of everything from iron tools to fine wine. Dense cities drove specialization that produced ever more diverse goods but also ever more standardized ones. And the shorter distance between places made possible a living for a whole swath of the people we've met here, from small-time traders like Sotas with his donkey-loads of fodder to village weavers like Tehat making tunics for local farmers and distant urban consumers alike.

Critics of Malthus, like Boserup, have countered that people don't just suffer through higher population—they respond and change.[17] But their responses are multiple and don't always result in clear positives or negatives in economic well-being. In the Roman case, some of those responses probably exacerbated the problem, while others improved quality of life. But they were all linked in a daisy chain of cause and effect—land, production, disease, and movement.

The Cheap Goods Trap

As we've seen, the Roman 90 percent lived among and perpetuated a world of relatively cheap things. Vessels in ceramic, glass and even metal were inexpensive by historical standards; clothing was probably less so.[18] Habonius Primus was able to fill his house with bronze pots and glass jugs at less than the annual cost of food for a single adult family member because many of those things could be had for comparatively little money. This world of cheap things, accessible to a wide swath of the population, constituted a minor portion of their food-majority budgets but lent their lives comfort and pleasure. Anyone who visits a museum with Roman objects is struck by the seeming affluence of a society in which even farmers might dine on fine plates and use perfume.

Those cheap goods were built on cheap labor. As we've seen, these goods were highly standardized, and standardization, particularly for ceramics, glass and other vessels, allowed economies of scale and production in bulk. As we've also seen, these goods were made everywhere, from large regional centers to smaller, local workshops. Workshops were often not part of households, but rather located in stand-alone, specialized production centers where those economies of scale and standardization could be put into practice. All this cumulatively large-scale production was supported by dense demand, demand from the denser carpet of cities as well as demand from the cheek-by-jowl farms. But it was also supported by a combination of low unskilled wages and, particularly in Italy and the East, slave labor. Through all these means, the kilns of a great ceramic production site might produce as many as 30,000 fine ceramic vessels per batch, vessels that sold for only some 5–20 *asses* each.[19]

For many consumer goods, the value of labor as a percentage of the object's value was low. Value resided in the substance—the amount of clay, glass, metal—not the work required to transform it. We can see this most clearly in Diocletian's Price Edict, where the prices of raw materials, labor and finished products and labor are all listed, and all consistently undervalue labor in favor of material.[20] This was particularly true for valuable objects like silver: the work of the silversmith in some work contracts was valued at as little as a quarter of a percentage of the value of the raw metal.[21] For less valuable substances like clay or glass, the relative value of labor would naturally have been greater, but was still very low. Aurelius Paesis the potter's labor and that of his unknown number of employees together was only compensated at two obols per 19-liter jar.[22]

Roman women's particular role in the cheap-goods trap is worth highlighting. Spinning, perhaps even more than farming, was probably the most common cash income–earning activity in the Roman world, and spinning was largely a female occupation. Like other parts of the cheap-goods world, the clothing revolution took place courtesy of poorly compensated piecework. But spinning work, unlike wage labor, was more constantly available. As we've also seen, spinning earnings provided a solid grounding to erratic men's wages, sometimes even out-earning them. The millions of Roman spinners, wearing the tunics and headscarves and cloaks produced by their own cheap labor that nonetheless provided break-even income for the poorest families, epitomize the contradictory experience of a cheap-goods world.

The result was a world in which objects were inexpensive and both desired and required, and thus consumption of them was high. But that consumer-driven world of goods didn't necessarily give back in income-earning opportunity what it elicited in expenditure. The very low wages earned by many artisans, particularly the unskilled backbone of large-scale production, were, as we've seen, only rarely enough to live on. And the enslaved, of course, often earned no income at all. Unskilled artisanal wages were mostly a supplement to farming, spinning and other hustles, not a living on their own. The cheap-goods world was thus underwritten by own-production, by farming.[23] Or, from the workers' perspective, farming plus wage-hustling was the only way to have your goods and eat, too.

Deficit Finance

The combination of volatile income, high consumption and the limited ability of wage earning to completely fill the gaps produced a paradox: a world of high consumption supported by barely sufficient or insufficient income. In this, the Roman world joins other societies, like eighteenth-century Europe or contemporary America, with a similar paradox: high-calorie diets combined with a desire for things like tea and pocket watches or hamburgers and iPhones, all of which is barely supported (and frequently not supported at all) by total household income.[24] In each of these societies, households depend on deficit financing.

In the case of the Roman world, we can see the world of goods both driving this gap and being used to fill it in. High consumption was, in part, fueled by the purchase of lots of consumer goods—goods that, in a pinch, might be used as security to borrow money to plug income gaps. This is the story told by the Egyptian pawnshop we examined, the red tunics and bronze bowls and lamps turned into cash, occasionally redeemed but often sacrificed. In other contexts, these actions have been decried as "legalized plunder," people stripped of their goods to satisfy their creditors.[25] But the creditors in the Roman world were not always faceless wealthy moneylenders: they were often neighboring artisans and retailers who also lent money on the side. People like Faustilla the Pompeiian pawnbroker-cum-shop manager were fellow members of the 90 percent, themselves making a living through the debt-plugging qualities of things.

Debt was also used to extend income. As in the early modern world, this debt might take the form of store or wage credit. The ox driver Maron, who used his credited wages to underwrite the purchase of a wholesale lot of wine—a purchase his wages alone could not have supported—is a good example of this income-extending quality of credit. In Maron's case, he used the "extended" income for a small investment. The mine workers at Mons Claudianus, borrowing off future rations, may simply have been trying to survive another day. Either way, both used credit to temporarily increase their income, kicking the ball to another month in hopes that other income—from debts owed, crops due, wages earned—might cover both principal and interest.

This ball-kicking behavior would appear to be feckless and irresponsible, the Roman 90 percent running up debt after debt through an inability to rein in their outgoings to match their income. But what appears to have been a propensity toward deficit financing was only a real problem if interest rates were high and/or if volatile incomes went down more often than they went up. The former appears to have been less of a problem than the latter. Even if the legal cap of 12 percent was not always obeyed, interest rates were (mostly) not terribly high. We've also noted anecdotally a tendency for creditors to wait, often years, for repayment rather than pursue their debtors' property as was their legal right. Most of the women who pawned objects at the village pawnshop likewise never redeemed them. The overspending only really appears to have caught up with those who experienced a succession of bad years—particularly, but not limited to, bad harvests.[26] In other words, financial catastrophe appears to be driven more by erratic income than by profligate consumption.

Enter, again, the hustling opportunities of wage earning. While wholly insufficient as a living, hustling would appear an opportune, if gradual, debt-eraser.[27] Day wages or unskilled artisanal wages like spinning were probably very useful as savings income, the kind of income that could be put by, bit by bit, to pay off a debt, a seed loan or a store credit. While they rarely provided a total income on their own, wages may have chipped away at debt burdens, rendering them more bearable.

Finally, it's important to recognize the kind of financial flows that farming—the majority of all income—produced. Farming income is experienced in sudden rushes of large income, followed by no income. During the various harvests, even smallholders see thousands of sestertii in money or commodities pass through their hands. These moments are centered on the late spring through fall and are followed by the fall and winter months when no income comes in, and then by winter-spring moments of huge expenditure—in seed and in animal and human labor. Credit greases the wheels of this farming cycle, providing seed or money inputs when income is at its lowest and expenditure its highest—which is precisely when we saw Egyptian Roman farmers borrowing. The more volatile that agricultural income is—and we've seen above why it may have been particularly volatile in the Roman world—the more credit is necessary to keep the farming cycle ticking over. In other words, the deficit-finance tendencies of the 90 percent were due not only to erratic income and high consumption, but also to the experiences of their intensified, specialized agricultural world.

Not Our Revolution

This book has revealed a world where working families consumed more, ate more and worked more, their household activities increasingly bound up with markets. This is a story that's been told before—but about early modern Europe.[28] The eighteenth century witnessed a similar transformation in the lives of working people. Their tastes and desires—for pocket watches and teacups and lace—spawned the expansion of new industries, from comb-making to spinning to brewing. Their longer, more intensive workdays, involving all family members, resulted in more artisanal work being done and more crops being grown. And as a consequence of the latter, they ate more calorie-saturated diets. All these things were facilitated through families' use of and orientation toward markets. Sometimes termed the "Industrious Revolution," this century-plus moment is thought to have provided the momentum—in consumer demand, skills, labor and markets—that would ultimately give rise to the Industrial Revolution. It was, in short, the prequel to our own modernity.

This eighteenth-century moment would appear eerily similar to the picture we've painted of the Roman world, one of the reasons it has made cameo appearances throughout this book. But it isn't really similar. The reasons it isn't, and the reasons why the experiences of a working Roman like Soterichos were fundamentally different from, say, an eighteenth-century British farm servant, are worth unraveling.[29]

One of the critical differences was wages. We've seen that Roman real wages were relatively low by historical standards. Expanded consumer goods and consumption were not compensated with life-sustaining wages. This is one of the reasons that wage labor remained relatively limited, a supplementary means of earning income. In the eighteenth century, by contrast, wage earning was already the single largest source of income—something that could never be said of the Roman world. And in northwest Europe, those wages were historically high.[30] Even if they weren't family-sustaining as we once thought, wages were much closer to break-even, particularly when women's and children's income were included. Many of those folks earning wages were doing so at consumer-good-producing jobs, as well as in agriculture. In other words, the expansion of consumption in early modern Europe was not only driven by the demands of working households, but that demand was much closer to being self-sustaining, generating jobs that paid higher wages. Early modern Europe appears to have avoided the cheap-goods trap that made high consumption ultimately more punitive for Roman families.

Early modern families, like Roman ones, did a lot of hustling.[31] Increasingly, though, this was wage-only hustling—men making farm and weaving wages, women making textile wages. More and more left farming altogether. Roman low wages, on the other hand, forced Roman families to hustle, which mostly meant a continued reliance on farming as well as small-scale artisanal production and textile work. The Roman low-wage universe thus continued to privilege own-production over wage earning. As we'll see momentarily, that meant a much greater privileging of those with capital, no matter how small, over those with only their own labor.

Another practice distinguishing the economic lives of working Romans from their successors was the paths to savings. The eighteenth-century Industrious Revolution was partially fueled by savings, savings produced in part by delaying marriage.[32] Instead of marrying young, teenage girls in northern Europe often went into service or worked at cottage textile industries, only getting married in their mid-twenties. This enabled them to save small sums before starting a family. Their savings, together with those of their husbands, in part paid for all the teacups and linen shirts. Savings produced by later marriage and combined with more industriousness helped drive higher consumption and supported them through the challenges of erratic incomes.

None of these things accrued to the Roman world. Roman girls got married considerably younger than their European sisters, nonelite girls probably in their later teens.[33] Domestic service, as we've seen, was not a wage-earning option in the Roman world, as service jobs were overwhelmingly done by enslaved persons. Instead, Roman marriage strategies concentrated on moving girls out of the household while, as we've seen, keeping tight control over their dowries. This protected girls' assets, but didn't really add to them. The Roman marriage and dowry pattern had the economic effect of guarding wealth, not really growing it.

All these differences meant that some of the critical paths of "industriousness" pursued by eighteenth-century people—somewhat more robust wage earning and potential savings from delayed marriage—were less available to working Romans. While superficially similar in their high-consumption economies, working Romans had fewer opportunities to expand their income and buffer risk. As a consequence, those high levels of consumption were, in theory anyway, less firmly supported. For all their shared gusto for consumer goods and new foods, Roman working families probably found themselves more precariously situated than their early modern descendants.

Capital: The Inequality That Mattered

Belaboring the contrast with early modern Europe is more than just touching the brakes on a too-easy game of historical comparison. Using the Industrious Revolution, not as a decoder ring, but as a foil, throws some of the Roman world's peculiarities into higher relief. Through the contrast with our own pre-modernity, we can see more clearly the ingredients for precarity and success among the Roman 90 percent.

Soterichos the tenant farmer's challenges, as we exposed them in chapter 3, reveal one of those ingredients: capital. Capital is usually imagined as something the rich have and the poor lack, and the gap between those with capital and those without is simply the gap between rich and poor. But we've seen lots of owners of capital among the 90 percent: shop-owners and weaver owner-operators, owners of tiny quarter-hectare plots and owners of a yoke of cattle. The capital-driven inequalities we're interested in—and which constituted the real inequalities among the 90 percent—were the inequalities between those with tiny amounts of capital and those with none.

The Soterichoses, paying between 60 and 70 percent of their outputs in rent, exemplify the disadvantages of renting over owning. As the reader will remember, we have no idea of agricultural rents outside of Egypt. The assumption for the Roman West—10–15 percent of wheat outputs—appears too low in comparison with the 50 percent or higher paid by Egyptian farmers like Soterichos. Most of our farm output models in chapter 3 were for owners. If, on the other hand, those same farmers were renting rather than owning and paying even a midpoint 30 percent of their yields, the results would have been quite different. The smallest farms would have been wholly untenable, while the medium-sized ones would have seen their solid surplus reduced to something more precarious.

For those who owned their own land, land taxes, presumed to run around 10 percent of yields, were far less punitive. This advantage of owning over renting was eroded somewhat, at least in Egypt, by the many other taxes paid by owners of land, not to mention the liturgical obligations they owed to their villages and the state. We saw the toll these took on the Kronions' family income. Nonetheless, for the farmers who worked their own land, owning even a small chunk was better than having to rent it all.

There were some exceptions to the rent disadvantage. Tenants on imperial land appeared to have paid lower rents than those on private land. Land under pasture had very low rents and could generate a considerable return—hence the major importance of the hay market for smallholders.[34] And cobbling together a portfolio of owned land with lower-return rented land—especially if you could plant it with cash crops like fodder or mustard—would have made the rent-drain more bearable. In general, though, if the Egyptian situation accrued elsewhere in the empire, the imperial tax structure assigned considerable advantage to land owning over land renting.[35]

A more complex set of capital advantages was found in artisanal businesses. Aurelius Paesis, whom we met in chapter 4, ran his pottery workshop in the typical way: he rented it from a landowner.[36] Artisanal businesses of all kinds were often rented from property owners, or from the state as part of the control of craft monopolies.[37] Artisans or entrepreneurs would rent out the workshop, supplying the labor, while the owner would supply the infrastructure and some of the raw materials. The actual work was done by the artisans themselves for small operations, and artisans plus wage-laborers and/or enslaved persons for larger ones. Owners of infrastructure—usually landowners—raked in relatively risk-free rent. Artisans or artisan-entrepreneurs assumed the lion's share of the expenses and all the risk—and manufacturing fine pottery and glass was hugely risky—but often owned the final product (although not always, as was the case for Aurelius Paesis).[38] At the bottom of the pyramid were the enslaved or wage-working laborers, skilled and unskilled, who owned nothing but their low wage, if that. Artisanal business income thus probably tracked capital, with the lion's share going to the owner of the land and infrastructure, the proceeds minus costs and taxes to the lessee-craftsman, and the least to the laborers.

Within the artisanal capital pyramid, Roman goods taxes also appear to have been specially aimed at artisans, avoiding the owners of productive capital.[39] Thus, there were personal taxes on specific professions—like weavers—but seemingly not on weaving studios. Taxes on mills and bakeries appear to have been borne by the millers or bakers as a portion of their output. The owners of the facilities presumably paid land or real-estate tax—which we've already seen was relatively low—while the artisans, at least in Egypt, were hit by various taxes on themselves or their products.

The result of all this was a probable net earnings gap between those with small amounts of capital and those without. Unknown tax rates make it impossible to quantify this gap precisely, for taxes on land and real estate may have narrowed it. But the existence of the gap helps explain why "wage labor" as such was rare, and wage earning mostly existed to plug gaps in own-production, particularly own-production on rented land.

The Challenge of Savings

From the modest coin hoards around the empire and the modest dowries assembled by Egyptian villagers, to the occasional big spend on religious celebrations, we've found working Romans making savings. Since savings were assembled in many forms—coins, commodities, real estate—we only have a fragmented sense of their average overall size. As we saw in chapter 5, average cash savings from the coin hoards more or less maps onto a month or two of food expenses. The cash component of dowries in an Egyptian village was somewhat larger—perhaps three months of bottom-end sustainable expenses.

These savings are actually pretty robust as a backstop. Given the expenses that eroded working families' incomes, the ability of at least some families to reserve enough cash for a month or two of food is remarkable. To put this in context, only around 50 percent of American families today have enough in the bank to meet three months of expenses.[40] But as we've seen, Roman savings were wholly insufficient for the investments necessary to get ahead. The cash value of dowry savings was less than half the cost of an aroura of land, and the same was probably true, if not worse, of the relationship between average cash savings from hoards and land prices in Italy. Even were we to add in the wholly unknown quasi-liquid savings—in commodities, jewelry and clothing—it's unlikely to amount to enough to make up such sums. In short, most families struggled to assemble enough savings to transform it into capital.

So how did a working family make the jump? How did they escape the savings-to-capital trap? We've already seen some of the ingredients for success in the practices of Roman farmers: low-cost, land-intensive cash crops. Hay may not have brought in as much as wheat per land area, but with two cuttings per year (possible in some places in some years) and the high-quality grasses and seeding practices we know they used, hay had the big advantage of low costs and a constant market. A quarter hectare of high-quality fodder crop might earn anywhere from 200 to 2,000 sestertii or drachmas per year with two cuttings. Greater income was possible with crops like viticulture or fruit, but they required up-front investment with no return in the initial years. Hence why a family like the Soterichoses chose to rent a vineyard: even paying two-thirds of their outputs as rent, they could still make more with grapes than selling hay, while avoiding the upfront capital costs. The tiny crops of specialized products—the farmers near Reims with their field mustard and orchards, the Cambridge farmers with their lazybed terraces, the small batches of

Tuscan wine—these are the detritus of folks trying to break the savings-to-capital trap.

There were some occupations that yielded real cash windfalls—albeit at a steep price. One was soldiering. Retirement bonuses for ordinary legionary soldiers amounted to some 12,000 sestertii. If you survived a career of some twenty years of service, mostly far from home, and hadn't eroded your salary through deep-seated debt—as some soldiers on Hadrian's Wall appeared bent on doing—real money awaited at the end. This was sufficient to actually buy land or set up a business. And indeed, as we've noted, some veterans, like the proprietor of Hoogeloon or the sutlers supplying the northern armies, returned home and did just that.

The odds of securing this pension were not great: many hazards over many years separated the poor young recruit from the prosperous middle-aged veteran-turned-cattle farmer. Even worse odds were faced by those whose escape from the savings-to-capital trap was perhaps most meteoric, and most loathed: the freed slave.

As we've seen throughout this book, there was no single type of enslaved worker, nor were the laboring enslaved and the poorest free always remarkably different from each other in their day-to-day consumption and earnings. Those slaves who worked in household jobs may have eaten well, been well-clothed and taken trips to the baths, like the slaves (?) who jotted down their expenses on a dining room wall in Ephesus.[41] Others, like Cato's agricultural slaves or the workers at the imperial quarries, had to maintain small gardens and flocks to augment their solid yet still insufficient rations. Whatever their circumstances, most enslaved workers had at least a contribution toward their overall upkeep from their masters, lowering their overall consumption costs and allowing them to squirrel away any incidental income. As we've seen, slaves received gifts from their owners—like a young woman who died in Pompeii still wearing the gold bracelet given her by her owner.[42] They might, like the *familiares* at the imperial quarries, get tiny cash wages that they were allowed to keep. Some enslaved, then, may have had a leg up on the savings problem, even if they were deprived in every other respect.

A few particularly fortunate enslaved people had a major advantage: the advantage of their master's capital. Enslaved men might be put to work as their master's business representatives. They might be set up in businesses of their own. Thousands of these freedmen- or slave-run businesses dotted the streets of Rome particularly, and it is from them that we know as much as we do about crafts and retail in the Roman world. Slaves might be given these business responsibilities while still enslaved, or be set free and then set up in a business.

But the money behind these businesses was overwhelmingly derived at first or second hand from their master.[43] Slowly hoarded gifts and tiny wages were not enough to rent a whole ceramics workshop or start a dry-goods store. From ceramics entrepreneurs to goldsmiths, enslaved and freed men of business were made so courtesy of their master's capital, capital that, together with custom, continued to harness them to their master's will.

That capital, as we've seen, often flowed through the strange legal device known as the *peculium*. The *peculium*—the savings and property of those who theoretically could own no property and were property themselves—was a legal fiction.[44] It allowed the enslaved to control money and property on behalf of a master. The *peculium* outsourced to enslaved intermediaries the grubby work of moneymaking of the kind that Cicero & Co. so despised but that constituted so much of their fortunes. In the process, the institution of the *peculium* also created a group of enslaved and free people—a limited group to be sure—who leapfrogged over the savings-to-capital trap.

It was this ability to accumulate and deploy real savings—savings that were big enough to become capital—that carved huge and angry chasms between the enslaved or freed set up in business by their master, and the free-born. For as we've seen throughout this book, savings was a hard-won fight. It slipped away with every new cloak or bad harvest or rent payment. It slipped away as a percentage of every donkey-load and every paycheck. Those who didn't have to endure the excruciating years of putting by small sums but could plunk down the full cost of a lease or pay for a consignment of produce—these were envied creatures.

Enslaved, and above all freedmen's, escape from the savings-to-capital trap lurks behind the extraordinary vitriol piled on them by the wannabe-rich free. The chattering classes famously derided wealthy slaves and freedmen, sneering at their "five shops that bring in 400,000 sestertii," or their "sweating finger(s) bearing a ring of gold," jealously remarking upon the "savings of well-groomed slaves."[45] Now chattering writers like Juvenal and Martial were not the poverty-stricken poets they claimed to be,[46] but neither did they have the bulletproof fortunes of the senatorial elite. Those of their status—equestrians, provincial landowners—had not only newly built fortunes, but fortunes grafted out of a mixed portfolio of income from ceramics, trade and farming.[47] Theirs was more precarious wealth, built on newer, more volatile foundations. The savings to invest in more stolid and solid things like rural estates came through a combination of good luck and generational grit. Their teeth-grinding rage at the parvenu freedman was not only disgust at huge wealth held by nonpeople. It bubbled up from the wellsprings of the struggle to save, to convert savings into capital, and the slow slog of building ever-greater bulwarks between flourishing and disaster.

The Bottom Line

This alien Roman world—where capital might cling to fortunate slaves, where exchanging children for loans was common, and where five-year-olds worked if they managed to survive at all—was ineluctably different from our own. Its low life expectancies, and the low value it assigned to human life and to human labor, drive home the enormous improvements in economic well-being experienced by many, but still not all, of the 90 percent over the twentieth century.

Where this world resembles our own is in the relentless persistence and shrewdness with which working Romans of all kinds squeezed a living out of their circumstances. Their hustles and money-maneuvers and crop-juggling are echoed in the perseverance and ingenuity with which contemporary poor and working people, from Bangladesh to the Bronx, wring a living from their own expensive and uncompromising economies. It's this grit and hustle that passes unacknowledged—unacknowledged in premodern people relegated to historical categories, and unacknowledged in modern working people obliterated by economists' aggregates.

That grit and hustle characterized, as it does today, an enormous and diverse group of people, people who defy the categories in which they are too easily placed. "Underclass," "poor," "subsistence majority" flatten the radically different resources and capabilities of the 90 percent, then and now. Those categories also erase the practices—the rotating, managing, and borrowing—that united, and continue to unite, this group. Both a struggling tenant farmer like Soterichos and a reasonably well-off notary like Kronion experienced income ups and downs, found themselves in the red, borrowed to get to another month. Hustle, and the economic precarity that motivates it, also increasingly characterizes a wide swath of modern Americans, from single mothers earning minimum wage to college graduates with low-income jobs and massive debt.[48]

This book has tried to raise up a working majority from the detritus of a distant and very foreign past, and with them a sense of their emphatic doing. Theirs were not the heady days when a self-conscious class organized for better circumstances.[49] They had no organizers or spokesmen. Their accomplishment, like so many of the 90 percent today, was their ability to wrest a living from a hard and complex world.

WEIGHTS AND MEASURES OF THE ROMAN WORLD

THE ROMAN world used a variety of different measurement systems, and these mattered to the 90 percent. Throughout, ancient units are converted to modern. Curious readers may find the below cheat-sheet useful. These are also the conversions used in the appendixes.

Land measurements

aroura (ar.) (Egypt) = 0.276 hectares
iugerum (Roman West) = 0.25 hectares

Dry measure

artaba (art.) (Egypt) = 38.8 liters = 29.5 kg
mation (Egypt) = 3.3 liters
modius (Roman West) = 8.6 liters = 6.55 kg
1 kilogram wheat = 3,400 calories

Wet measure

keramion monochoron (Egypt): 7.3 liters
kotyle (Egypt): 0.25 liters
sextarius (Roman West) = 0.54 liters

Weights

libra = 0.329 kilos
stater (Egypt) = 14 grams

Currency (30s BCE through 260s CE):

Roman West: 1 denarius = 4 sestertii (HS) = 16 *asses* = 32 semi
Roman Egypt: 1 denarius = 1 Egyptian tetradrachma = 4 drachma (dr) = 24–28 obols (ob) (silver standard)
Roman East/Ephesus (260s–270s CE): 1 denarius = 21 assaria= 10+ (?) obols (ob)

APPENDIX 1

A World Full of Things: Consumption Data

BLE A.1. Expense lists

	Egypt (in dr)						
	Total expenses pp/day (low)*	Total expenses pp/day (high)	Food expenses pp/day (low)	Food expenses pp/day (high)	Bread % of cost	Consumer goods per day (dr)	Meat % days
t–2nd c. CE							
Oxy. 4.736	2.5	3.8	0.7	1		1.1	23%
Oxy. 4.739	5.8	8.8	1.3	2.2		2.6	50%
Mich. 2.127 (Kronion, 45–46 CE) daily average	1.6	2.4	1.2	1.8		0.5	
Bern. 2.210	0.5	0.8	0.4	0.7	47%	0	60%
verage 1st c.	**2.6**	**4.0**	**0.9**	**1.4**		**1.05**	
ate 2nd–3rd c.							
Mich. 11.619	11.9	20	9.5	9%	0.7	50%	
Corn. 35r.	7.8	23.3	13.8		1.8	100%	
verage late 2nd/3rd c.	**9.9**	**21.7**	**11.7**		**1.25**		
ombined averages				**24%**		**57%**	

Continued on next page

TABLE A.1. (*continued*)

	Pompeii (HS)						
	Total expenses pp/day (low)*	Total expenses pp/day (high)	Food expenses pp/day (low)	Food expenses pp/day (high)	Bread % of cost	Consumer goods (HS)	M… % da…
CIL 4.8566	3.4	6.8	3.4	6.8	7%	0.0	
CIL 4.8561	2.3	4.5	1.7	3.4	19%	0.0	
CIL 4.5380**	3.0	3.0	2.9	2.9	40%	0.3	
CIL 4.4422***	2.7	5.4	2.4	4.8	29%	0.6	
CIL 4.4888	2.0	4.0	1.5	3.0	50%	0.5	
Averages	**2.7**	**4.7**	**2.4**	**4.2**	**29%**	**0.3**	**28**

* Low-end hypothetical reconstructions: Egypt: minus 1/3 expenses for poss. dependents; Pompeii: minus 1/2 expenses fo two people

**Calculated for 2.5 persons for 5 days, and 1.5 persons for 3 days

***Reconstructed total

	Ephesus (denarii) (late 3rd c. CE)				
	Total expenses pp/day	Food expenses (pp/day)	Bread % of cost	Consumer goods (den)	Meat % days
GR 158 (per day)	3.7	5.2	41%		67%
GR 158 (per day w/out lawyer)	2.4			0.5	
GR 181	1.1	0.9		0.1	0%
GR 138	1.3				–
GR 50*	3	1.6	62%	0.1	100%
GR 51	3	2.7	32%	0	100%
GR 53	3.2	2.9	8%	0	100%
GR 357	4.3	2.7	16%	0.7	100%
GR 370	7.2	7.1	28%	0.1	100%
Hang 3.16	14.6	12.9	93%	0	0%
Averages	**4.60**	**4.5**	**40%**	**0.2**	**71%**

Note: All graffiti references to Taeuber 2005, 2010, 2016.

*Assuming 1 denarius = 1K = 1assarius = 0.5 obols

TABLE A.2. Costs for household contents, sacrificial deposits and clothing reconstructions

Durable goods costs		
	Low (HS)	**High (HS)**
Ceramics (small, coarse only)	0.25	0.5
Ceramics (small, fine only)	2.5	5
Ceramics (coarse and fine)*	1.25	2.5
Glass and small bronze utensils*	3.75	7.5
Small bronze vessels/larger glass vessels*	7.5	15
Jewelry/larger bronze vessels*	12.5	50
Silver/marble	by weight	
Wagon**	500	500

Clothing	
Average cost of tunic, Egypt 1st–2nd c. CE (Drexhage 1991, 368)	23 dr
Pompeii, tunic (*CIL* 4.10664)	1 den, 8 ass
Pompeii, tunic (Étienne 1966, 230)	15 HS
Vindolanda, tunic (*Tab. Vind.* 181)	3 den
Pompeii, 2 (?) cloaks security for 50 HS (*CIL* 4.8204)	6.25 den

Food costs (for sacrifice reconstructions)	
Oil (per libra) (*CIL* 4.4000)	1 HS
Wine (per sextarius) (*CIL* 4.1629)	0.25 HS
Chicken (per)*	4 HS
Cattle (per)*	250 HS
Pig (per)*	25 HS
Lamb/sheep*	25 HS

*Costs reconstructed from cost ratios from the *Edictum de pretiis rerum venalium*, checked by costs for similar goods from Drexhage 1991, 379–84, 396–401.

**Cost of 4-wheel wagon is 1.5 times cost of 2-wheel wagon.

TABLE A.3. Household goods, Pompeii houses and Villa Regina Boscoreale

	House of Habonius Primus (I 11, 5, 8) (350 m^2)	House of L. Caelius Ianuarius (I 11 ,17) (140 m^2)	House I 10, 1 (85 m^2)	Villa Regina Boscoreale (450 m^2 farm)
Class 1 goods: highest-value goods: larger vessels in silver/gold; machinery (number)	2 plain silver cups, 1 silver ladle*	silver mirror**	terra-cotta sculpture	wagon***
Functions: luxury tableware; major machinery				
Value (HS)	576	180	13–39	500
Class 2 goods: jewelry in silver/gold; lamps/larger vessels in bronze, incl. paterae (number)	**15**	**26**	**1**	**2**
Functions: personal adornment; personal hygiene; food preparation; tableware; light; writing; religion				
Value (HS) (assume 12.5–50 HS per object)	188–750	325–1,300	13–39	25–100
Class 3 goods: large glass vessels; tools in iron; smaller bronze vessels (number)	**11**	**31**	**4**	**4**
Functions: food preparation; tableware; storage; tools; personal adornment; personal hygiene; sculpture				
Value (HS) (assume 7.5–15 HS per object)	83–165	233–465	38–75	30–60
Class 4 goods: small/medium vessels in glass; small bronze utensils (number)	**8**	**22**	**27**	**0**
Functions: tableware; personal adornment; personal hygiene; small tools; writing				
Value (HS) (assume 3.75–7.5 HS per object)	30–60	83–165	79–158	0
Class 5 goods: ceramics; small glass objects/vessels (number); game pieces	**25**	**33**	**31**	**59**
Functions: cooking ware; storage; tableware; personal adornment; light, entertainment; bronze coins at value				
Value (HS) (assume 1.25–2.5 HS per object)	31–63	41–83	19–38	74–148
Total number of goods	*63*	*113*	*63*	66
Total value (HS)	**907–1,608**	**861–2,192**	**166–334**	**629–807**
Average value per good	14–26	8–19	3–5	10–12 (2–5 w/out wagon)

Source: Peña in press; Allison 2006

*Silver cups assumed to be 0.5 libra with 96 silver denarii/libra; ladle assumed to be 0.5 libra.

**Silver mirror assumed to be 0.5 libra.

TABLE A.4. Minimum clothing and costs

Men's Clothing				
Cato's slave clothing rations (*De Agr.* 59) (using lowest prices from Vesuvian cities)	**HS**	**Minimum male working clothing**	**Vesuvian cities (HS)**	**Egypt (dr)**
Cloak	8	Tunics (two)	50	63
Short tunic	6	Mantle	25	33
Wooden shoes		Cloak	25	33
Total	**14**	Scarf	8	8
		Total	**108**	**137**
Apprentice contracts, Egypt, 2nd c. CE	**dr**			
Tunic, 1 per year	23			

Women's Clothing			
Nonna's dowry, 3rd c. (*SB* 14.11575)	**dr**	**Clothing from the household inventory of Paulus, c. 266 CE (*P. Tebt.* 2.406)**	**dr**
Linen dress/tunic with purple border	62	Tunic new from the fuller, with Lakonian stripe worth a stater	46.2
Face cloth		White veil with a Lakonian stripe and a didrachm	40
Head cloth	24	Tunic half worn out	46
Tarsian bath towel	6	New linen shirt with two stripes	46
Sandals	4	New linen kerchief	30
Total	96	12 linen cloths	96
Converted to 2nd c. prices (dr)	**32–48**	Total	304
		Converted to 2nd c. prices (dr)	**100–152**

APPENDIX 2

Smallholder Farms and Their Outputs

TABLE A.5. Farm types, Italy

Type	Characteristics	Area	Surplus storage/ built	Surplus storage/ dolia	Agro-processing	Other features	Domestic quarters	Examples
Type A Small	Single building, 1–2 rooms; hearth; use of outdoor space/ porch	50–200 m^2	No	Yes	No	External pits: clay/rubbish	Nondistinguished	Monte Forco, Ager Capena, Rome; Podere Cosciano, Pisa; Podere S. Mario
Type B Medium	EITHER: Single building, 3 or more rooms, linear or square arrangement; OR multiple separate buildings with specific functions; hearth	110–1,000+ m^2	Often	Yes	Often	Occasionally foot press or tanks; granary; sheds; hearths	Nondistinguished	Farmstead 9, Luni; Fossa Nera A and B (Phase 1), Luca; Pievina, Grosseto

Type C Large	Single building; central courtyard; possible second story; separation between residential and agro-processing/ storage spaces	600–1,200 m^2	Yes	Yes	Yes	Press; cistern; kiln; granary	Distinguished	Villa Sambuco, Luni; Selvasecca; Mulino San Vincenzo(?), Florence; Ponterotto, Florence
Satellites	Agro-processing, stabling, field management	50–100 m^2	No	No	Some	Seasonal/short term use: no cooking facilities, no storage	Nondistinguished	San Martino stabling shed; Poggio dell'Amore stabling shed; Colle Massari field drain; Case Nuove collective press

TABLE A.6. Farm types, Gaul and Britain

	Characteristics	Total Area	Surplus storage/Built	Agro-processing	Domestic quarters	Examples
Type A Small	Single enclosure, undivided; 1–3 buildings	0.25–0.5 ha	Rare	Rare	Nondistinguished	**Gaul**: Villiers-sur-Seine "Le Gros Buisson" **Britain**: The Grange; Stubbs Farm
Type B Medium	Multiple linked enclosures, subdivided; watering holes for stock; 3+ buildings	0.75+ ha	More common	Common (Britain)	Sometimes distinguished	**Gaul**: Chevrières "Bois Madame;" Montévrain; Bezannés: Le Griffon **Britain:** Vicar's Farm; Langdale Hale; Cotswold Community

Type C Large	As per Type B, but with one or more stone buildings, typically for domestic use; **no** decorative/luxury architecture (i.e., mosaics, paintings)	1+ ha	Common	Common	Probably distinguished	**Gaul**: Venette "Le Bois de Plaisance" Zone 4; Palaiseau "Les Trois Mares"; Hambach; Hoogeloon; **Britain**: Orton Hall Farm
Villages/roadside settlements	Multiple, adjacent ditched enclosures; multiple buildings for storage and/or residence; roadside sites have longitudinal arrangement	5–40 ha	Common	Common	Rarely distinguished	**Gaul**: Longueil-Sainte-Marie; Tiel-Passewaaij; **Britain**: Longstanton; Site IV, NW Cambridge; Gill Mill

Farm Outputs

The three biggest variables in smallholder outputs are cereal yields, farm size and cattle grazing needs, and all of them are fenced round with uncertainties. The question of ancient cereal yields is a particularly vexed one: a handful of ancient yields, expressed as the ratio of seeds sown to grains grown, provide such a huge range—from 4:1 to 100:1—as to be totally unsatisfying.[1] The models here are run on a range of yields drawn from the most recent consensus for each region. While it is not their purpose, the models often cast some doubt on that consensus. A similar approach is taken for estimating available land: a series of possible farm sizes is modeled based on the local settlement pattern and/or proxy data (granary size, likely herd size, etc.).[2] Finally, because so little thought has been given to the relationship between animal herds and agricultural output, one of the biggest questions remains cattle feed requirements. Nobody can agree on how much cows ate. Columella's feed recommendations roughly match modern smaller-breed cattle requirements, assuming they had adequate free grazing—an important and limiting assumption, as these models demonstrate.[3]

The following numbers are used in all models:

Cattle feed requirements: 4,000 kg/head (Columella, *Rust.* 6.3 extended to 12 months = low end from Lepetz and Zech-Matterne 2018, 373; Ouzoulias 2006, 189, n. 130).

Manure production: 40 kg/day for cattle; 7 kg/day for pigs; 2.3 kg/day for sheep (Alcock, Cherry and Davis 1994, 154).

Manure application: 40 m^2/ha (Spurr 1986, 129 = low end of modern Italian numbers and somewhat less than Columella, *Rust.* 2.14).

Milk yields: Goodchild 2007, 289.

Meat weight, all animals: MacKinnon 2004, 190, *except* pigs: Goodchild 2007, 284 for 40 kg pig, applied to 50 kg pig.

Taxes on provincial land: assume 10 percent (Hopkins 1980, 119).

Losses: from threshing floor and storage: 30 percent (Forbes and Foxhall 1995, 73–74), except Egypt.

Manpower requirements: Unless otherwise noted, Columella, *Rust.* 2.12.2–6; converted into hectares in Goodchild 2007, 300.

All models run on 3,500 kcal/pp calorie requirements (cf. chapter 2).

1. Pievina (Tuscany), first century BCE/CE *(Ghisleni et al. 2010; Bowes et al. 2021, 63–105)*

Crops (local comparanda): Bread wheat (*Triticum aestivum*); olives; grapes

Local faunal % NISP averages: 34 cattle; 27 sheep; 45 pigs

Farm size calculated from maximum granary capacity of 9,450 kg (method: Martin 2017), assuming bread wheat contents. At below yields and ley system, total land = 16.5 ha arable. Assume 0.5 ha for vines and 1 ha for olives. Total: 18 ha/72 *iugera*

System: Ley system (Arnoldus et al 2021; Kron 2000) with one year fallow, improved pasture and legume rotations. For ease of calculation, assumed six fields of 2.75 ha each: two (5.5 ha) in cereals, one in fallow, one of legumes, two of fodder crops, plus separate vineyard and olives.

Yields:

Wheat: 15:1, 10:1, from Goodchild 2007, 252, 383, assuming yields descending after ley rotation.

Hay: 5,600 kg/ha, with lower yields immediately after cereals. Lepetz and Zech-Matterne 2018, 373.

Olive oil: assuming 120 trees/ha with alternating bad (720 kg/ha) and good (2,400 kg/ha) years, with a 25 percent oil yield. Osborne 1987, 45.

Wine: Goodchild 2007, 260, using Columella's low-ceiling yields (6,288 L/ha) and his very lowest yields (2,096 L/ha) in alternation for bad years.

Fava bean: 1,100 kg/ha. Modern yields in smallholder farms: FAO: https://www.feedipedia.org/node/4926, lowest end with deductions for seed.

Straw and chaff: Wheat: 20 percent of seed yield; legume straw: 100 percent of seed yield.

Seeding rate: 5 modii/*iugerum* = 135 kg/ha (Goodchild 2007, 250); fava = 6 modii/*iugerum* (Pliny *HN* 18.55).

Manpower requirements: Olives assumed to be 1/5 of cereal requirements. Fallow assumed to be 1 plowing/year + seeding, two cuttings per year = 1/2 labor of grain.

Surplus sale: Assume wheat = 60 percent of diet and thus 0.63 kg/day/pp; 6 people). Modius = 6.55 kg; Price: 3 HS/modius.

2. Monte Forco (Lazio), first century BCE–CE (*Jones 1963*)*: 2 models*

Crops: (assumed) bread wheat; olives, grapes

Regional faunal % NISP averages (small farm sites): 34 cattle; 27 sheep; 45 pigs

Farm size: 10 *iugera* (2.5 ha) veteran settlement, of which only 7 (1.75 ha) were usable given topographic constraints (cf. Jones 1963, 147, who suggests this may be as small as 5–6 *iugera*).

Model 1: Ley system (Arnoldus et al. 2021; Kron 2000) with continuous plantings, 0.21 ha plots: three in cereals, one in legumes, three in ley, with 0.28 ha vineyard.

Model 2: Alternate fallow in 0.73 ha plots, with 0.28 ha vineyard.

Yields:

Wheat: Model 1: 15:1, 10:1, 7:1: from Goodchild 2007, 252, assuming yields descending after ley rotation. Model 2: 10:1 (presumed lower yields with no rotation).

Hay (Model 1 only): 5,600 kg/ha, with lower yields immediately after cereals (Lepetz and Zech-Matterne 2018, 373).

Wine, both models: Goodchild 2007, 260, using Columella's low-ceiling yields (6,288 L/ha) and his very lowest yields (2,096 L/ha) in alternation for bad years.

Fava beans (Model 1 only): 1,100 kg/ha. Modern yields in smallholder farms: FAO: https://www.feedipedia.org/node/4926, lowest end, lowest end with deductions for seed.

Straw and chaff: Wheat: 20 percent of seed yield; legume straw: 100 percent of seed yield.

Seeding rate: 5 modii/*iugerum* = 135 kg/ha (Goodchild 2007, 250); fava = 6 modii/*iugerum* (Pliny *HN* 18.55).

Manpower requirements:

Model 1: Columella, *Rust.* 2.12.2-6; converted into hectares in Goodchild 2007, 300.

Model 2: Multiplied by 2, assuming no cattle for plowing.

TABLE A.7. Farm output models, Italy: Pievina (Grosseto, Tuscany) and Monte Forco (Capena, Lazio)

	Pievina	Monte Forco (Model 1: Ley)	Monte Forco (Model 2: Alternate Fallow)
SYSTEM			
Determinants	Land required to fill 60 m^2 granary = 5.5 ha, ley system, 15% fallow, avg. 12:1 yields	1.75 ha (7 *iugera*); family of 4; ley system, 15% fallow; avg. 12:1 yields	1.75 ha (7 *iugera*); family of 4; 50% fallow yields 10:1
Total land (ha)	18	1.75	1.75
Arable crops			
Wheat	5.5	0.45	0.73
Ley	5.5	0.45	0
Fallow	2.75	0.245	0.73
Legumes	2.75	0.245	0
Grapes	0.5	0.28	0.28
Olives	1	–	–
Animals			
Total cattle supported	11	1	0
Pigs (P); sheep (S) goats (S)	P: 14; S: 30; G: 5	P: 4; S: 10; G: 2	P: 4; S: 10; G: 2
Total manure produced by system (ha)	12	2.1	1.2

Continued on next page

TABLE A.7. *(continued)*

	Pievina		Monte Forco (Model 1: Ley)		Monte Forco (Model 2: Alternate Fallow)	
NET OUTPUTS (net of seed, loss)	**KG**	**KCAL**	**KG**	**KCAL**	**KG**	**KCAL**
Total outputs from arable	10,406	31,178,888	2,028	3,626,077	1,765	2,913,950
Total outputs from hay	36,960		3,293		0	
Total outputs animal (consumed)	5,590	6,500,337	1,115	1,211,352	542	966,252
Total animal outputs (live)	12,143		1,247		1,275	
Total outputs (live/hay [kg]/consumable [kcal])	59,509	37,679,225	6,596	4,837,429	3,040	3,858,202
OVERALL OUTPUTS						
Output per ha (kg)	**3,306**		**3,769**		**1,737**	
Total adults supported at above outputs @ 3,500kcal/day	**29**		**4**		**3**	
Sale of surplus (HS)	**2,656**		**0**		**0**	
LABOR REQUIREMENTS						
Total persons required at 265/year	4		1		3	
Ratio of output to labor inputs	7.8:1		5.8:1		3.3:1	

Data: Appendix 2

3. *Vicar's Farm (Cambridgeshire), 180–270 CE* (*Evans and Lucas 2019*)

Crops: majority spelt with minority barley
Site faunal % NISP: 59 cattle; 23 pigs; 21 sheep; 16 horses

Farm size: Max: from local settlement pattern, open land to NW, bounded on E and S by tracks, 20 ha. Enclosure =1.5 ha. Min: from 9 } 18m aisled hall, possible use as granary. 10,700 kg (using Martin 2017) for unhulled spelt. With 5:1 yields of spelt (with some barley,) c. 14 ha under cultivation in cereals per year.
Model: 10 ha arable (1.6 each, two in spelt, one in barley); 12 ha permanent pasture; 1.5 ha enclosure = 23.5 ha.

System: Alternate fallow

Model 1: Spelt/barley yields: 4:1; unimproved pasture yields 2,000 kg/ha (Ouzoulias 2006, 183).
Model 2: Spelt/barley yields 12:1; improved pasture yields 4,000 kg/ha; **no** deliberate seeding of vetch, etc.

Seeding rate: 10 modii per *iugerum* = spelt 150 kg/ha (Ouzoulias 2006, 179); barley 147 kg/ha.
Losses: Hulling (spelt only): 30 percent (Ouzoulias 2006, 176) + storage: 30 percent.
Grain prices: assume 2 HS/modius (lower than Italian prices of 3 HS/modius).

4. *The Grange (Cambridgeshire), 2nd–3rd centuries CE* (*Wright et al. 2009*)

Crops: majority spelt with minority emmer; Celtic bean (fava).
Local average faunal % NISP: 47 cattle; 29 sheep; 3 pigs; 6 horses.

Farm size: enclosure = 0.35 ha. Max: from local settlement pattern radius of 100 m = 3.1 ha.

System: Rotation: spelt/emmer (0.67 ha); bean (0.67 ha); fallow.

Model: 2 ha in arable (3 fields of 0.67 ha each), 1 ha in permanent pasture.

Yields: Spelt/emmer 12:1 (averaged); improved pasture yields 4,000 kg/ha.
Seeding rate: 10 modii/*iugerum* = spelt/emmer 150 kg/ha (Ouzoulias 2006, 179); 6 modii/*iugerum* (Pliny, *HN* 18.55) = beans 87 kg/ha.
Losses: Hulling (spelt/emmer): 30 percent (Ouzoulias 2006, 176) + storage: 30 percent.

TABLE A.8. Farm output models, northwest provinces

	Vicar's Farm Model 1 (low yields)	Vicar's Farm Model 2 (high yields)	The Grange
SYSTEM			
Determinants	land req'd to fill granary = 10 ha arable; majority spelt @ 4:1 yields; 50% fallow; unimproved permanent pasture; surplus cattle; 1.5 ha enclosure	land req'd to fill granary = 10 ha arable; majority spelt @ 12:1 yields; 50% fallow; improved permanent pasture; surplus cattle; 1.5 ha enclosure	locally available land 3.1 ha; spelt and emmer @ 12:1 yields; 30% fallow rotated with pea/bean; improved pasture; 0.35 ha enclosure
Total land (ha)	23.5	23.5	3.35
Arable crops			
Spelt/emmer	Spelt: 3.3	Spelt: 3.3	Spelt/emmer: 0.67
Barley	1.6	1.6	–
Fallow	5	5	0.67
Permanent pasture	12	12	1
Legumes	0	0	0.67
Animals			
Total cattle/horse supported	6	12	1
Cattle (C); pigs (P); sheep (S); goats (S); horses (H)	C: 4; P: 2; S: 10; G: 2; H: 2	C: 10; P: 2; S: 10; G: 2; H: 2	C: 1; P: 1; S: 5
Total manure produced by system (ha)	6.3	15	1

NET OUTPUTS (net of seed, loss, tax)	**KG**	**KCAL**	**KG**	**KCAL**	**KG**	**KCAL**
Total outputs from arable	975	337,190	3,177	10,873,980	708	2,424,257
Total outputs from hay	24,358		49,221		4,214	
Total outputs animal (consumed)	1,975	2,831,106	1,975	2,726,811	764	785,126
Total animal outputs (live)	2,567		4,805		664	
Total outputs (live/hay [kg]/consumable [kcal])	**27,900**	**6,168,296**	**57,203**	**13,600,791**	**5,568**	**3,209,383**
OVERALL OUTPUTS						
Output per ha (kg)	**1,268**		**2,600**		**1,862**	
Total adults supported at above outputs @ 3500 kcal/day	**5**		**11**		**3**	
Sale of surplus (HS)	0		**689**		0	
LABOR REQUIREMENTS						
Total persons required at 265/year	**2**		**2**		**1**	
Ratio of outputs to labor inputs	**2.0:1**		**4.5:1**		**5:1**	

Data: Appendix 2

5. Tiel-Passewaaij (Gelderland), 100–150 CE *(Groot 2009, supplemented by Groot and Kooistra 2009)*

Village: 25–35 people, 9 houses.

Crops: majority barley with minority emmer.

Site faunal % NISP: 39 cattle; 7 pigs; 42 sheep; 12 horses.

Farm size: estimated from landscape archaeology 32 ha arable; 40 ha pastures = 72 ha total.

System:
Model 1: Alternate fallow: three fields of 5.3 ha each: two of barley (10.7 ha); one of emmer (5.3 ha); fallow (16 ha).
Model 2: Rotation: barley (10.8 ha); emmer (5.3 ha); bean (5.3 ha); fallow (10.6 ha).

Yields:
Model 1: barley/emmer: 4:1; pasture yields 4,000 kg/ha
Model 2: barley/emmer: 12:1; pasture yields 4,000 kg/ha

Seeding rate: 10 modii/*iugerum* = spelt/emmer 150 kg/ha (Ouzoulias 2006, 179); beans: 6 modi per *iugerum* (Pliny, *HN* 18.55).

Losses: Hulling (spelt/emmer): 30 percent (Ouzoulias 2006, 176) + storage: 30 percent.

Grain prices: assume 2 HS/modius (lower than Italian prices of 3 HS/modius).

TABLE A.9. Farm output models: Tiel-Passewaaij (Gelderland, Netherlands)

	Teil-Passewaaij Model 1 (low yields)	Teil-Passewaaij Model 2 (rotation, high yields)
SYSTEM		
Determinants	Locally available land; 25–35 people; barley majority with some emmer @ 4:1 yields; 50% fallow; improved pasture; cattle surplus	Locally available land; 25–35 people; barley majority with some emmer @ 8:1 yields; 30% fallow, rotated with beans; improved pasture; cattle surplus
Total land (ha)	72	72
Arable crops		
Spelt/emmer	Emmer: 5.3	Emmer: 5.3
Barley	10.7	10.7
Fallow	16	10.7
Permanent pasture	40	40
Legumes	0	5.3
Animals		
Total cattle/horse supported	40	40
Cattle (C); pigs (P); sheep (S); goats (S); horses (H)	C: 38; P: 4; S: 20; H: 2	C: 38; P: 4; S: 20; H: 2
Total manure produced by system (ha)	37	37

Continued on next page

TABLE A.9. (*continued*)

	Teil-Passewaaij Model 1 (low yields)		Teil-Passewaaij Model 2 (rotation, high yields)	
NET OUTPUTS (net of seed, loss, tax)	**KG**	**KCAL**	**KG**	**KCAL**
Total outputs from arable	5,849	20,168,866	12,522	43,102,426
Total outputs from hay	160,000		160,000	
Total outputs animal (consumed)	12,223	10,989,502	12,223	10,989,502
Total animal outputs (live)	8,935		8,935	
Total outputs (live/hay [kg]/consumable [kcal])	**174,784**	**31,518,368**	**181,457**	**54,091,928**
OVERALL OUTPUTS				
Output per ha (kg)	**2,428**		**2,520**	
Total adults supported at above outputs @ 3500 kcal/day	**24**		**42**	
Sale of surplus (HS)	0		**2,068**	
LABOR REQUIREMENTS				
Total persons required at 265/year	**6**		**6**	
Ratio of outputs to labor inputs	**4.3:1**		**7.4:1**	

Data: Appendix 2

6. Soterichos family, 94–5 CE (Theadelphia): 6 persons (2 adults, 4 children of various ages) (P. Soter.)

Crops: bread wheat, wine, fodder.
Animals: at least two cattle (Elgenedy 2022).
Farm size in 94–95 CE: 8 ar (2.2 ha) in arable; 1.5 ar (0.41 ha) vineyard (plus orchard not modeled) (*P. Soter.* 3), 1.75 ar (0.48 ha) prodomatic lease of state pastureland (*P. Soter.* 5) = 11.5 ar (3.1 ha).

System:
Rotation presumed for 8 ar (2.2 ha) of arable land with fodder plant (*chortos*).

Models:
Model 1: All fodder consumed by cattle; wine and wheat consumed by family.
Model 2: All wheat consumed by family; alternate-year fodder consumed by cattle; state land fodder and wine sold to buy additional food.

Yields:
Wheat: Model 1: 11.5 art:1 aroura (Rathbone 1991, 243–45; median yields from Theadelphia in 3rd c.).
Model 2: 16 art:1 aroura (Rathbone 1991, 243–45: high yield from Theadelphia in 3rd c.).
Hay: calculated from 3,000 bundles/ar (Rathbone 1991, 242) about 3,260 kg/ha
Wine: 2,500 L/ha (Rathbone 1991, 247).

Cattle requirements: c. 40 bundles/day (if donkeys are 10) = 4.9 ar/head (1.3 ha).

Seeding rate: 1 art/ar (standard for Egypt: Rathbone 1991, 243). Assume seed is provided by owner for 8 ar plot.
Losses: Storage: 5 percent (Rathbone 1991, appendix 2, 465–66).[4]

Prices:
Hay: 64 dr/art. Average of 138 CE prices (*P. Mil. Vogl.* 2.52) (low) and 140–142 CE prices (*P. Ross. Georg.* 2.8; *P. Oxy* 4.728; *P. Lond.* 3.1165) (high) (Drexhage 1991, 321–24).
Wheat: 8 dr/art. Average price (Rathbone 1997, 191–92).
Wine: 5 dr/monochoron= average of late 1st/mid-2nd-century wine prices (Kelly 2021, supplemental data 2).

TABLE A.10. Farm output models: Soterichos family (Theadelphia, Egypt, 94–95 CE)

	Model 1 (low yields)		Model 2 (high yields, crop sales)	
SYSTEM				
Determinants	3.1 ha land; wheat (11.5 yields), rotated with fodder; vineyard; permanent pasture		3.1 ha land; wheat (11.5 yields), rotated with fodder; vineyard; permanent pasture	
Total land	3.1		3.2	
Arable crops				
Wheat	(2.2)		(2.2)	
Fodder rotation	(2.2)		(2.2)	
Grapes	0.42		0.42	
Pasture	0.48		0.48	
Animals				
Total cattle supported by pasture	1		1	
Total manure produced by system (ha)	1.0		1.0	
NET OUTPUTS (net of seed, loss, rent)	**KG**	**KCAL**	**KG**	**KCAL**
Total outputs from arable/vineyard (per year over two years)	724	2,382,756	1,236	3,243,250
Total outputs from hay (pasture and fodder/year for 2 years)	4,861		4,861	
Total outputs animal (consumed)	0	0	0	0
Total animal outputs (live)	635		635	
Total outputs (per year over two years)	**6,040**	**1,511,881**	**5,917**	**3,243,250**

OVERALL OUTPUTS				
Output per ha (kg) over two-year rotation	**438**		1,909	
Total adults supported at above outputs @ 3,500 kcal/day	**1**		2.5	
Sale of surplus (dr/KCAL)	0	351		4,319,292
Total adults supported with crop sales included		**6**		
RENT				
Percent paid to rent (average)	68%		60%	

Data: Appendix 2

Rents:

8 ar plot: 8 art/ar (*P. Soter.* 3)
Vineyard: 2/3 crop + 1/10th (*P. Soter.* 3)
State pasture: just seed (*P. Soter.* 5)

7. Kronion family 135–6 CE (Tebtunis): 11 persons, adults and children, ages unknown (P. Kron.)

Crops: bread wheat, barley, fodder.

Animals: none.

Farm size in 135–136 CE: Renting: 12.5 ar arable; 12.5 ar permanent pasture (*P. Kron.* 34); 3 ar arable (*P. Kron.* 35); owned: 34.75 ar. Total land: 62.75 ar (17.3 ha). (*P. Kron.* 10, 17, 18, 19, 20).

System: 25 ar rented land, 12.5 arable in rotation with fodder + 12.5 permanent pasture; 3 ar arable assumed in rotation with barley; 34.75 ar owned land assumed in full rotation each year with fodder.

Yields:
Wheat: 11.5 art:1 aroura (Rathbone 1991, 243–45; median yields from Theadelphia in 3rd c.)
Fodder: calculated from 3,000 bundles/ar (Rathbone 1991, 242) about 3,260 kg/ar.
Hay: presumed unimproved permanent pasture = 2,000 kg/ar.

Cattle requirements: c. 40 bundles/day (if donkeys are 10) = 4.9 ar/head (1.3 ha).

Seeding rate: 1 art/ar (standard for Egypt: Rathbone 1991, 243). Assume Kronions are seeding all plots.

Losses: Storage: 5 percent (Rathbone 1991, appendix 2, 465–66).

Prices:
Wheat: 8 dr/art. Average price (Rathbone 1997, 191–92).
Hay: 64 dr/ar. Average of 138 CE prices (*P. Mil. Vogl.* 2.53) (deemed particularly low) and 140–142 CE prices (*P. Ross. Georg.* 2.8; *P. Oxy.* 4.728; *P. Lond.* 3.1165) (deemed particularly high) (Drexhage 1991, 321–24).

TABLE A.11. Farm output model: Kronion family (Tebtunis, Egypt, 135–36 CE)

SYSTEM		
Determinants	3 plots (17.3 ha); wheat/fodder + permanent pasture; barley/fodder; wheat/fodder; family of 11	
Total land		17.3
Arable crops		
Wheat rotation		13.05
Fodder rotation		13.88
Barley		0.828
Pasture		3.45
NET OUPUTS (net of seed, loss, rent, tax)	**KG**	**KCAL**
Total outputs from arable/year over 2 years	4,537	15,154,215
Total outputs from fodder/year for 2 years	31,268	
Total outputs/year over 2 years	35,806	15,154,215
OVERALL OUTPUTS		
Total adults supported at above outputs @ 3,500 kcal/day		12
Sale of fodder (dr)/year		1,560
RENT/TAX		
Percent paid to tax/rent (average)		34%

Data: Appendix 2

Rents/taxes

Rent: **25 ar plot**: For years 1, 3, 5, 7: taxes of 1.1 art/ar (26.8 art) + *naubion* (9 dr) +

thallos (11 dr); for years 2, 4, 6: 80 art + 240 (silver) dr + *thallos* (11 dr)

3 ar plot: rent unknown. Assume 7 art/ar (barley years) + 20 dr/art (fodder years)

Tax: **34.75 ar owned land**: assume 1 art/ar, but 9.5 ar of which is *epibole*: assume 4 art/ar (Rowlandson 1996, 292, appendix table 3)

22.25 katoecic land: assume 1 art/ar (Wallace 1938, 13)

APPENDIX 3

Cost of Living Calculations

TABLE A.12. Subsistence cost calculations used in chapter 4

Base Food/Clothing Costs (Miner's food + clothing per month, 2nd c. Mons Claudianus)					
	Quantity: ancient	Quantity: modern	kcal	Cost equivalent (dr)	Cost notes
Wheat	1 art	29.5 kg/38.8l	100,300	10	Rathbone, 1991, table A8.112, average of 100–150 prices
Lentils	1 mation	1/12 of artaba = 3.3l (Cuvigny 2021a, 334)	3,104	0.4	5dr/art (Drexhage 1991, 35)
Oil	3 kotyle	0.75l (Cuvigny 221d,.423 n. 47)	6,000	2.64	0.88/kot (Drexhage 1991, 46)
Tunic	1 per year			1.9	Drexhage 1991, 368
Totals (kcal/day; cost) per month			**3,647**	**15.0**	cf. Cuvigny 2000, 47, 3,857 kcal

1st c. CE food/clothing costs per month			
		Cost (dr)	Cost notes
Wheat	1 art	8	Wheat prices: *P. Lond.* 131v.
Lentils	1 mation	0.4	Drexhage 1991, 35
Oil	3 kotyle	1.98	Drexhage 1991, 46
Tunic	1 per year	1	Drexhage 1991, 355
Totals per month		**11**	

3rd c. CE food/clothing costs per month

		Cost (dr)	Cost notes
Wheat	1 art	16.6	Rathbone 1991, 464, average price on Appianus estate
Lentils	1 mation	0.4	Drexhage 1991, 35
Oil	3 kotyle	5.46	Drexhage 1991, 46
Tunic	1 per year	4.0	Rathbone 1991, 109
Totals per month		**26**	

Individual sustainable costs

	Epimachus' farm	Fayum 1st c. CE	Patron's Lands	2nd c. Nile Valley	Appianus' estate	Cost notes
Food/clothing	11	11	15	15	26	
Housing	1.7	1.7	2.5	2.5	4.5	Drexhage 1991, 92 (1st–2nd c. CE; Rathbone 1991, 109 [half], Appianus estate)
Taxes (poll + dike or village)	1.9	4.3	4.3	1.9	4.2	*
Totals	**15**	**17**	**22**	**19**	**35**	

Continued on next page

TABLE A.12. (*continued*)

Individual low-calorie costs						
Food/clothing/ housing	9	9	9	9	22	Scheidel 2010, 432
Taxes (poll + dike or village)	1.9	4.3	4.3	1.9	4.2	*
Totals	**11**	**13**	**13**	**11**	**26**	
Family sustainable costs						
Woman						
Food/clothing	9	9	12.0	12.0	21	Food at 80% of male costs
Child						
Food/clothing	7	7	9.0	9.0	16	Food at 60% of male costs
Family totals (2 adults, 2 children)	**37**	**40**	**52**	**49**	**88**	
Family low-calorie costs						
Food/clothing/ housing	30	30	30	30	70	Scheidel 2010, 432
Taxes (poll + dike or village, 1 man)	1.9	4.3	4.3	1.9	4.2	*
Totals	**32**	**34**	**34**	**32**	**74**	

Source: Cuvigny 2000, 41

*Taxes: Wallace 1938, 1, 123, 126, 140–41 (Arsinoite [using the combined συντάξιμοι] and Hermopolite nomes, and χωματικόν, respectively; Rathbone 1991, 125 (Appianus estate).

APPENDIX 4

Tebtunis *grapheion*: Transaction Types and Averages

TABLE A.13. Tebtunis *grapheion*, transaction types and averages used in chapter 5

	n	n (w/ dr preserved)	Mean (ar, dr or art)	Median (ar or dr)
Total transactions	**1,235**			
Land		221	7.5 ar	5.0
Cash		481	229	100
Total creditary transactions (loans, deposits, *hypothekai*, *enoikesis*, *paramone*, nursing contracts [all]) (30%)	**376**	**304**	**160**	**100**
[cf. totals for other creditary contracts, outside the grapheion, 30 BCE–69 CE; Lerouxel 2016, 49–50]*	72	53	184	104
Creditary transactions 50 dr and under		80		
Loans (*daneia*)	131	111	147	100
Deposits (*paratheke*)	96	90	240	100
Loans/deposits in kind or mixed		32	7.8 art	
Paramone	38	31	76	60
Nursing contracts (loans associated with)	31	24	125	105
Antichretic rental contracts (*enoikesis*) and mortgages (*hypothekai*)	80	67	115	80
Loan transactions with husband/wife debtors	51	46	123	100
Leases (land) (19%)	**229**	**203**	**5.6**	
Cession (*parachoresis*/*enchoresis*)	16	13	5.0	
Total sale transactions (9%)	**110**			
Dowries (*pherne*) only (no alimentary contracts [*syngraphe trophitis*])	**77**	**68**	**161**	**80**
[cf. 1st-c. CE dowry, *pherne* only, outside the Tebtynis registers (Yiftach-Firanko 2003, appendix 4C)**	23	23	193	176

Data: *P. Mich.* 2. 121v; 132r.; 5.238

*Average without 2 exceptionally high loans, one from Tebtynis of 13,500 dr and one from Ptolomais Euergetes of 3,000 dr.

APPENDIX 5

Human Skeletal Remains, Italy and Britain: Data and Bibliography

Central/South Italy Data Sources: Bibliography

Hellenistic/Iron Age

Chiusi (urban): Capasso 1984; Capasso and Di Tota 1995; Masotti et al. 2013.

Ferrone/Tolfa (urban): Rubini et al. 1999; Masotti et al. 2013.

Gildone (rural): Petrone 1994.

Metaponto (urban/rural): Henneberg and Henneberg 1998.

Monte Belvedere (Matera) (rural): Marchi and Borgognini Tarli 2002.

Pontecagnano (urban): Sonego and Scarsini 1994.

Potenza (rural?): Henneberg and Henneberg 1998.

Riofreddo (rural): Rubini and Coppa 1991.

Selvaccia (rural?): Pardini and Mannucci 1981.

Tarquinia (urban): Henneberg and Henneberg 1998.

Timmari (Matera) (rural): Marchi and Borgognini Tarli 2002.

Volterra (urban): Capasso 1984; Capasso and Di Tota 1995; Masotti et al. 2013.

Roman

Casal Bertone (mausoleum and necropolis) (Rome: near suburbium): Killgrove 2010; Killgrove and Tycot 2013; Killgrove and Montgomery 2016; Killgrove 2019.

Casal Bertone fullery/Area Q: Caldarini et al. 2015.

Castallaccio Europarco (Rome, far suburbium): Kilgrove 2010; Killgrove 2019.

Castel Malnome (Rome, far suburbium): Catalano et al. 2010; Minozzi et al. 2012; Piccoli et al. 2015; Calderini et al. 2015; Varano et al. 2020.

Gabii: Killgrove 2021.

Grottaperfetta (Rome, far suburbium): Macchiarelli 2002–3.

Herculaneum (catastrophic death assemblage; urban): Capasso 2001; Torino and Fornaciari 2000; Petrone et al. 2002; Martyn et al. 2018; Soncin et al. 2021.

Isernia/Quadrella (urban): Bonfiglioli et al. 2003; Belcastro et al. 2007; Giannechini and Moggi-Cecchi 2008; Terzani and Matteini Chiari 1997.

Isola Sacra (urban): Manzi et al. 1999; Prowse 2001; Prowse et al. 2005.

Lucus Feroniae (urban/rural): Manzi et al. 1989; Manzi et al. 1999; Salvadei, Ricci and Manzi 2001.

Muracciola Torresina (urban): Baldoni et al. 2020.

Musarna (urban): Rebillard 2009; Caldarini 2009; Glieze 2009.

Osteria del Curato I and II (far suburbium): Egidi, Catalano and Spadoni 2003; Buccellato et al. 2003; Minozzi et al. 2012.

Pompeii (catastrophic death assemblage, urban): Lazer 2009, 2017; Gowland and Garnsey 2017.

Quadraro (near suburbium): Killgrove 2010, 137, 95; Catalano, Minozzi and Pantano 2001.

San Vittorino (rural): Killgrove 2010; Catalano 2001, 128, 362.

Vagnari (rural): Prowse, Nause and Ledger 2014; Brent and Prowse 2014; Gilmour 2017; Semchuk 2016; Brent and Prowse forthcoming.

Vallerano (far suburbium): Bedini, Testa and Catalano 1995; Catalano, Minozzi and Pantano 2001; Cucina et al. 2006; Bucellato and Catalano 2003.

Velia (urban): Craig et al. 2009; Bondioli et al. 2016; Sperduti et al. 2018.

Via Basiliano (Collatina) (near suburbium): Buccellato and Catalano 2003; Buccellato et al. 2008.

TABLE A.14. Human skeletal metrics, Britain and Italy

	Britain Iron Age (Roberts and Cox 2003, 96–103, n = 398)	Britain Roman rural (1st–4th c.) (Rohnbogner 2018, n = 1,759)	Britain Roman small towns (2nd–4th c.) (Pitts and Griffin 2012, n = 824)	Britain Roman urban (2nd–4th c.) (Pitts and Griffin 2012, n = 3,347)	Central/So. Italy Iron Age (n = 920)	Central/So. Italy Roman (1st–3rd) (n = 3,007 [aged], 1,887 [dental/cranial])
	% adults	% adults	% juveniles and adults	% juveniles and adults	% juveniles and adults; weighted averages	% juveniles and adults; weighted averages
Childhood stress indicators						
Cribra orbitalia	4.8	6.6	10	9	23	40.5
Porotic hyperostosis/cribra crania	0	1.6				26.9
Linear enamel hypoplasia	1.8	10.9	13	15	87.2	69/41.7
Infectious disease and nutrient deficiency indicators						
Subperiosteal new bone formation	1.0	7.1				
Endocranial lesions	0.5	0.9				
Osteitis	0.5	0.3				

Continued on next page

TABLE A.14. (*continued*)

Osteomyelitis	0	0.7				
Sinusitis	0	1.1				
Rib periostitis	0.3	0.9		3		
Tuberculosis	0.3	1.0				
Vitamin D deficiency	0	0.4				
Vitamin C deficiency	0	0.3				
Musculoskeletal indicators						
Trauma	6.5	12.1	[0.07]	[0.15]		21.3
Interpersonal trauma (crania/ulna)	2.6 (skull only)	1.8				5.6
Schmorl's nodes	1.5	8.1	14	15	14	29.4
Spondylolysis	1.3	1.5	3.70	2		
Joint-specific rates of degeneration						
Shoulder	0.5	5.9	2.9	4.8		
Spine	32.7	25.6	23	18	64	62.3
Hip	1.0	7.0				
Knee	0.5	4.9				
Lower body		12	6.6	4.5		
Joint degeneration/ OA total/extraspinal (Roberts and Cox 2003)					40	59.6

	Britain Iron Age (Roberts and Cox 2003, 96–103, n = 398)	Britain Roman rural (1st–4th c.) (Rohnbogner 2018, n = 1,759)	Britain Roman small towns (2nd–4th c.) (Pitts and Griffin 2012, n = 824)	Britain Roman urban (2nd–4th c.) (Pitts and Griffin 2012, n = 3,347)	Central/So. Italy Iron Age (n = 920)	Central/So. Italy Roman (1st–3rd) (n = 3,007 [aged], 1,887 [dental/cranial])
Dental disease						
Calculus	4.1 (CPR)	25.4 (CPR)	19	29		
Caries	4.8 (CPR)	26.9 (CPR)	6 (TPR) [36–42 est. CPR]	12 (TPR) [est. 72 TPR]	48.7	52.5/6.4
AMTL	3.5 (CPR)	20.4 (CPR)	13(TPR)	12 (TPR)	11.3	9.1
Abscess/PAL	6.8 (CPR)	10.4 (CPR)	4 (TPR)	1 (TPR)		
Stature (M/F)						
	Iron Age Britain (Roberts and Cox 2003, 396; n = 113/72)	**Roman Britain (Roberts and Cox 2003, 396; n = 1,296/1,042)**			**Central/ So. Italy Iron Age (n = c. 400)**	**Central/So. Italy Roman (n = 684/579)**
	168/162	169/159			167.5 (M only)	168.5/155.3

Data: Appendix 5

NOTES

Introduction: Getting Down to Work

1. This story is extracted from the account books of Epimachus, son of Polydeuces (the landlord, not the tenant), preserved in *P. Lond.* 131v and r, in the British Museum. For the circumstances surrounding the discovery of the papyrus and thus the possible location of the farm, see Budge 1920, 2:148–50; and Sayce 1923, 332–34. This is explained in more detail in chapter 3.

2. An earlier historical literature (e.g., Weber 1891; Rostovsteff 1926) was passionately interested in something like our subject. The difference between their efforts to winkle a system of history out of farmers or "the working classes" versus the project of this book will become apparent throughout. Distinct, too, is the important effort to identify working people and their economic struggles as impellers of history, in particular the decline of the Roman Republic (Brunt 1968, 1971a, 1971b). Actual working people from the 19th century onward found much to admire in the Roman world, as Edith Hall and Henry Stead have discovered: Hall and Stead 2020.

3. Cicero, *Off.* 1.150.

4. See Veyne 2000; Berrendonner 2007; Lis and Soly 2012; Flohr and Bowes 2024 for more nuanced dissections of what Cicero & Co. meant when they disparaged work and workers. See Bond 2016 for a different perspective.

5. On Finley, his background and his impact, see the papers collected in Harris 2013; Jew, Osborne and Scott 2016. On the stubbornness, particularly the reluctance to admit that new data pointed to a new model, see the preface to the second edition in Finley 1985 and Finley's interview with Keith Hopkins (Hopkins 2014).

6. Finley 1973, with a second edition in 1985, and a third edition published posthumously in 1999. On Finley's complex background in economics (from Schumpeter to Polanyi) and the conclusions he drew from it regarding ancient economic thinking, see Saller 2013. Finley's certainty that ancient people had no use for laboring wasn't new: he bundled up and popularized a series of earlier 20th-century certainties, e.g., Vernant 1955; Veyne 1961; Visscher 1965.

7. A view recently reiterated through a reading of Pliny the Elder's *Natural History*: Saller 2022.

8. If Finley's work epitomized previous generations' certainties, he defined a subsequent generation's approach, emphasizing the socially embedded qualities of economic behavior: e.g., Garnsey and Saller 1987. The French tradition, rooted in the Annales school, had different origins but arrived in many of the same places: e.g., Veyne 1985. More explicitly Marxist approaches that emphasized slave economies emerged from British but mostly emphatically Italian intellectual settings: e.g., De St. Croix 1981; Giardina and Schiavone 1981; Carandini 1988.

9. The shoe example comes from Aristotle, *Pol.* 1257a, as part of a longer discussion on man's relationship with things and labor as part of the proper functioning of the city. See also Plato,

Rep. 590c, where the author compares the dependence of the laborer on others, and thus his inability to govern himself. These deep waters were plumbed in part by Vernant (1955, 1966, 274–94); on the Roman side by Thomas 2004; Berrendonner 2007, and more generally by Lis and Soly 2012, reviewed and critiqued by Verboven 2014.

10. For a fuller discussion of this narrative, see Bowes 2021a, 2021b. On Weber, Rostovtzeff and the 19th and early 20th centuries' arc of agrarian-centered history, see Momigliano 1982. Peter Brunt (1968, 1971a, 1971b), using the largely imperial-period sources on the late Republic, made a passionate case for the causes of peasant decline.

11. Finley 1999, 105–11.

12. The work of Andrew Wilson and the Oxford Economy Project is particularly noteworthy here. Early work includes Wilson 2002; Bowman and Wilson 2009. For the scholarly fisticuffs between this emphasis on scale and complexity versus Finley's model, see Morris 1999, xxvii–xxviii; Morley 2007, 1–16.

13. E.g., Andreau 1987, 1999a; Lerouxel 2016; Harris 2019a; Erdkamp, Verboven and Zuiderhoek 2015.

14. The twin emphasis on the state and performance comes courtesy of the precepts of New Institutional Economics (NIE), as pioneered in the 1980s–90s by Douglass North (e.g., North 1981). For the Roman economy, the shift toward cliometrics was anticipated by the at-the-time unheralded work of Duncan-Jones, whose data-gathering on prices, costs, wages and a host of other variables has proven so essential: Richard Duncan-Jones 1974, 1990, 1994. Keith Hopkins' (e.g., 1980, 1995) insistence that social scientific models were useful for making sense of ancient economic activities marked another milestone. Data and modeling were united in the groundbreaking work of Walter Scheidel, who, more than any other, helped usher in the application of NIE and economic theory to the Roman economy: e.g., Scheidel 1996a, 2001, 2009, 2010. The introduction to Scheidel, Morris and Saller 2007 was the culminating programmatic statement of this shift and the embrace of NIE. For other perspectives on the state's relationship to the market: Temin 2012; Kay 2014 (from whom the "economic revolution" claim); Lo Cascio 2020; Elliot 2020. For an overview of NIE as applied to the Roman economy, see Verboven 2015.

15. Baking: Monteix 2016; wine and oil production: Brun 2003, 2004; De Sena 2005; Marzano 2013; retail: Holleran 2012; Ellis 2018; Flohr and Monteix 2020; fulling: Flohr 2013; ceramics: Peña and McCallum 2009; Murphy 2016; Van Oyen 2016. Textile making is harder to find archaeologically, but the papyri have helped: Gällnö 2013; Larsson Lovén 2013; Woodworking (Ulrich 2007) and ironworking (Lang 2017) also have their studies.

16. Cam Hawkins' (2016) book on artisans and their role in the Roman economy, and Miriam Groen-Vallinga's on families and labor (2022) are exceptions, both of which depart from a set of comparativist and NIE foundations.

17. One important effort to do so relied heavily on comparative models: Hawkins 2016.

18. The political/ideological rationale for this focus is beautifully dissected in Terrenato 2005. Some canonical villa projects: Settefinestre (Carandini 1985), which, in part via Marxism and in part via a reliance on Columella, paid unusually equal attention to the productive quarters; the excavations in the British villa-cum-governor's residence at Fishborne (Cunliffe 1971), driven by an interest in the Roman conquest of Britain. More recent villa studies have examined the elite sociocultural habitus (e.g., Bodel 1997; Van Oyen 2019) and now as elements in Roman economic growth (e.g., Aubert 2009; Marzano 2015).

19. The canonical Roman landscape project was the South Etruria Survey in central Italy, begun after the Second World War, published in short reports and a longer popular summary (Potter 1979), and restudied and definitely published only recently (Patterson, Witcher and Di Giuseppe 2020). Landscape archaeology's aims and methods (see Witcher 2006a; 2012 for critiques) aren't well adapted for understanding people's lives, but rather examine the broader categories of settlement and topographic change.

20. All discussed in detail in chapter 3. Major studies: Smith et al. 2016; Allen et al. 2017; Reddé 2017–18; Bowes 2021c. Hollander 2020 provides a new view drawn principally from the texts.

21. The term is Roger Bagnall's (2011), whose book on graffiti and ostraca from the Roman East laid out the agenda. Collected papers on graffiti published that same year (Baird and Taylor 2011; Corbier and Guilhembet 2011) share a similar set of goals. For an integration of "everyday writing" with the everyday world of things in Roman Egyptian households, see Boozer 2021, who similarly insists on a bottom-up narrative.

22. Skepticism that bottom-up economic history can be done for the ancient world: Scheidel 2020.

23. Thompson 1963, 9–12, on definitions.

24. Marxist histories (e.g., De Ste. Croix 1981) and the French and Italian traditions (e.g., Veyne 1976, 2000; Giardina and Schiavone 1981) didn't share the class allergy and were happy to explore the concept's applicability in ancient contexts.

25. Finley 1999, 49–50.

26. Finley 1999: 51, as clarified in Morris' (1999, xx) excellent foreword to the third edition.

27. Veyne (2000) was of the opinion that when elites talked about "the poor" they were mostly describing the *plebs media*—something like a middle class. Emanuel Mayer's (2012) more recent book on the Roman middle classes embraces the English term. The class allergy is not limited to ancient history: Sayer (2005) makes a persuasive case that contemporary society shares that class allergy—to its detriment. Indeed, class as a heuristic has returned somewhat to Roman history: Zuiderhoek 2013; Harris 2019b; Bond 2025.

28. For the pejoratives, see Bond 2016.

29. On which, Courrier 2014.

30. The seminal study by Joshel (1992) on occupational inscriptions in Rome is still fundamental for seeing the distortions in the epigraphic data. Groen-Vallinga (2022) has elucidated the great households of workers and their particular identities, drawing on parallels from 18th-century great houses. Ruffing (2008) provides comprehensive catalogs of occupational titles from the eastern empire.

31. As work and profession have become of greater interest, *collegia* have been taken from the world of religion and legal status, where earlier scholarship had assigned them, and careful assessments made of their economic character and function. Liu's in-depth studies of the Gallic textile worker *collegia* have been groundbreaking in this regard (Liu 2008, 2009, 2013); Terpstra and Verboven have made the most trenchant efforts to see them as economic entities (Terpstra 2013, 2019; Verboven 2016), contested by Liu 2016, while Tran (2006) has assessed the social networks and hierarchies of the members themselves. See also Dondin-Payre and Tran 2012. In a very different approach, Bond (2025) has recently viewed them as proto–labor unions.

32. *CIL* 2.1167; *CIL* 14.4365; 4382.

33. For the majority as "poor," Harris 2011; Liu 2017. On the destitute, Rosillo-Lopez 2021. Whittaker (1993), Woolf (2006) and Morley (2006) are thoughtful about the category and its constructedness.

34. Cicero: *Off.* 2.71; mock trials: e.g., Seneca, *Controv.* 1.1; 2.1; Juvenal: *Sat.* 3.239–40. Woolf (2006) summarizes some of the literary evidence and describes its sociopolitical utility. As Veyne (2000) notes, the "poor" in many elite sources are actually something like a *plebs media*—working people, not the destitute. This dichotomy takes on new forms in early Christian writing: Brown 2012.

35. On which the seminal article is Brubaker and Cooper 2000, a critique of the concept of identity as used in literary and historical studies. It takes a page out of Bourdieu (1977) but addresses more explicitly the analytical/praxis muddle. Certeau's "practices" describe resistance

to or deviation from cultural production by its consumers (Certeau 1994). For some applications of the practice/analysis distinction: Reed 2018.

36. Finley's definition of status admits that legal category and practice might be fundamentally different: Finley 1999, 45–51. See more forcefully on the nonoverlap of practical and legal category for rural workers, Grey 2011, 27–28.

37. A series of volumes address the economic aspects of mostly artisanal occupations: Stewart, Harris and Lewis 2020; Hawkins 2016; Verboven and Laes 2016; Wilson and Flohr 2016; Monteix and Tran 2011. On the social aspects: Tran 2013; Lytle 2019. On details of workshop practices in individual professions, see above, n. 15. For professional titles, Drexhage (2004) and Ruffing (2008) provide helpful lists.

38. As described now for the Roman world by Groen-Vallinga 2022.

39. On the butcher shop: a relief depicting a scene from a butcher's shop with a seated woman holding a writing tablet: Staatliche Kustsammlungen, Dresden: Hm 418; children of farmers sweeping leaves: see chapter 4.

40. An earlier Italian Marxist tradition framed whole parts of Roman society in this way: e.g., Giardina and Schiavone 1981; Carandini 1985. More recently, on slave demographics and their place in the Roman economy: Scheidel 2005; Roth 2007, 2010; Harper 2011. Attempts to recreate slaves' lived experience (Lenski 2012; Joshel and Petersen 2014; Padilla Peralta 2017) and, conversely, ideologies of slave owning on the Roman political imagination (Lavan 2013) address the particularized perception of the enslaved. Vlassopoulos (2021) pushes back against this tendency to assume a singular identity tied to an ahistorical definition of slavery, advocating the kind of practice-based, historically particularized study of Roman or Greek slavery proposed in the present volume.

41. The linguistic shift is reparative in ambition, generated from histories of American enslavement. See Rinehart 2019 for a short, nuanced discussion. For the ancient world, Vlassopoulos 2022, 92–112, reiterates the noncorrespondence between slave categorical and practical identities.

42. Cohen 2023, 49–82.

43. On slaves as part of the labor market: Holleran 2017, 89–90. The literature on slave *peculia*—gifts given to slaves by their masters—reveals the complexity of slaves' own economic practices: Roth 2005; Gamauf 2009; Cohen 2023; and chapter 6.

44. Petronius makes much of this transition from labor to leisure among freedmen (and also back to labor again when fortunes are lost): Petronius, *Sat.* 37–38, 43, 57, 71, 74–77.

45. The result is not too dissimilar from Harris' more recent effort to parse Roman "class" into three groups, principally on the basis of capital and labor: those who didn't need to work and supported themselves on rents and investments; those who probably needed to work but had enough assets to produce some kind of security; and those who had very few or no assets. See Harris 2019b. The 90 percent here include his second and third groups, with the understanding that the boundary between them was porous.

46. Brent Shaw tells the harvester's story in a rich history of harvesting and harvesters: Shaw 2013, esp. 281–98.

47. Fisherman: Rowlandson 2013, 223; herders: Schwartz 1964; priest: Claytor, Litinas and Nabney 2016; salt workers: Caldarini, Zavaroni and Benassi 2015; Morelli and Forte 2014.

48. For a history of development economics and the challenges posed by gross performance measurements: Ravallion 2016, 111–127.

49. Lepenies 2016. To be fair, Simon Kuznets, who came up with the concept of GDP, was rightly worried about what it actually represented and how it might be used.

50. Stiglitz, Sen and Fitoussi 2009, 12.

51. The winners were Angus Deaton, Michael Kremer, Ester Duflo and Abhijit Banerjee, building on decades of work by economists on household-based approaches to development

problems. Their approach is summarized for the nonspecialist in Collins et al. 2009; Rutherford and Arora 2009; Banerjee and Duflo 2011; Morduch and Schneider 2017.

52. The debates are usefully summarized in the heterodox King 2012, 1–46.

53. This debate lay at the heart of the raison-d'être of microhistory when it arose in the 1970s, as set out by Ginzburg and Poni 1979 and debated by many: Revel 1995; De Vries 2019.

54. The issue of aggregates lurks behind the structure/agency debate, micro- and macrosociology, micro- and macrohistory and many other questions in social theory of the second half of the twentieth century: Mouzelis 2008 (sociology); Christian 2005; Armitage and Guldi 2015 (history); Peltonen 2014 (more broadly).

55. Finley 1999, 17–19; family as institutionalist firm: Becker 1981.

56. Italian Roman family structure: Saller 1984; Shaw 1984, critiqued by Martin 1996; Britain: Allason-Jones 2004, 273–74; Egypt: Huebner 2013; eastern villages: Thoneman 2023, 146–93.

57. As well as many of the more avowedly Marxist ancient historians: e.g., Capogrossi Colognesi, Giardina and Schiavone 1978; De Ste. Croix 1981; Banaji 2003.

58. E.g., Hobsbawm 1968 (including "vulgar Marxism," by which the present study could be classed), 1988, 1997.

59. Piketty 2014. Piketty's *Capital* inspired Scheidel's longer excursus on historical inequality and violence (Scheidel 2017), which in turn suggested a set of collected papers on capital and *Capital* in ancient history: Koedijk and Morley 2022. See also Scheidel 2020; Weisweiler 2021; Cohen 2023. For a summary of inequality measurements as applied to past societies, see Jackson 2023. For a critique, Bowes 2022a.

60. So says Seneca (*Ep.* 95.42), for whom the outrageously pricey mullet emblematized what Jeff Bezos' yacht stands for to us: outrageous wealth and its moral contagion.

61. A recent, nuanced defense for the study of long-term inequality: Jackson 2023, with an aside (283) that such studies may incidentally reveal something about the lives of the poor. Less persuasively, Milanovic 2007.

62. The insistence on the nastiness of Roman rule has been less addressed by economics per se and has concentrated on the rule of the provinces, e.g., Mattingly 2006, 2013; and on the archaeology of violence: Fernández-Götz, Maschek and Roymans 2020; Fernández-Götz and Roymans 2019. Mascheck 2023 provides a bridge to economics by examining proposed predatory real estate practices.

63. A useful critique of agency, in the context of enslaved and freed people's ability to bring lawsuits in the American South, can be found in Welch 2018, 19.

64. Boldizzoni 2011, 11.

65. One exception was Morris' (2011) project to build a social-development index from 16,000 years of archaeological data, which escaped some of these pitfalls by "measuring" a whole range of variables from energy use to knowledge networks. Other methods model that uncertainty: Danon, Jew and Lavan 2022.

66. Most notably, the work of Angus Maddison (2001, 2003, 2007, 2010), which underlies much of Milanovic 2005; Milanovic, Lindert and Williamson 2007; Galor 2011; and Piketty 2014. A current database on world inequality now eschews the premodern world and extends only to the mid-19th century (Alvaredo et al. 2022).

67. See Milanovic, Lindert and Williamson 2007, appendix 2; Piketty 2014, 92; Scheidel and Friesen 2009, 66.

68. Maddison's invented data: Clark 2009. Data-laundering using comparative data: Bowes 2021e, 16–23.

69. Cf. Morris's (2010, 161–70) clever deconstruction of a similar graph for social development. His observations on what one chooses to measure driving sameness and difference (e.g., 2010, 143–57; 2011, 25–52) are also germane here.

70. The bibliography presuming a subsistence living for the Roman 90 percent is vast. It lay at the heart of Finley's original model (1973, 105–8), although his thinking on peasant practices was somewhat more maximalist than he is often given credit for (Saller 2002, 225). Forbes and Foxhall's seminal work on this subject is also often misread, mined for crop yields and the composition of the "subsistence diet": Foxhall and Forbes 1982; Forbes and Foxhall 1995. Similarly, Garnsey's seminal work on food supply that gave subsistence greater color and depth (and some numbers) is often mined for those numbers rather than its nuance (Garnsey 1988). Ligt (1990, 1991) was one of the first to push on the assumption of peasant subsistence. Nonetheless, it appears regularly in everything from surveys of Roman production (Kehoe 2007) to inequality estimates (Scheidel and Freisen 2009) to the GDP calculations (see above).

71. Some examples: Dyer 1989, 2002; Muldrew 1998, 2011; Banerjee and Duflo 2011; Collins et al. 2009; Anderson and Ahmed 2016. A'Hearn, Amendola and Vecchi's work on historical household budgets is somewhat more macro-oriented: A'Hearn, Amendola and Vecchi 2016.

72. The shift in economics, as lamented by Debreu 1991; in economic history, as lamented by Boldizzoni 2011. Wages: Allen 2001, questioned by Hatcher and Stephenson 2018; slaves and others' development and stature: Steckel 1979; Flogel et al. 1983, questioned by Deaton 2007. Age-heaping: Duncan-Jones 1977; A'Hearn, Baten and Crayen 2009; questioned by A'Hearn, Delfino and Nuvolari 2022.

73. Poetics of muchness: Flandreau 2019, 3, adopted from the great gadfly of economists and their use of numbers, Deirdre McCloskey (1985).

74. Some brilliant work in the stochastic line: Kelly 2022, 2023; Collins-Elliot 2018 and forthcoming.

1. Let's Settle Up

1. *CIL* 9.2689. Translation Fagan 2017, on which also the interpretation of the relief as the sign for an inn.

2. Rieche 1986, 180 and Minaud 2006, 8–9 for the hand-counting gestures on this relief, with alternate readings of the numbers being displayed. The relief is so worn that a precise reading isn't possible.

3. On which, Giraudeau 2017.

4. The debate, which is often short-handed as a debate between the so-called modernists and substantivists, was highlighted by the work of Karl Polanyi and his followers: Polanyi 1944, more explicitly laid out in Polanyi 1992. For an overview of the debate and its impact on anthropology and sociology, see Beckert 2009.

5. Graeber 2009, 2012.

6. On status, economic thinking and accounting in his *Ancient Economy*, Finley 1999, 35–64, 108–22, 181. Finley, of course, was not alone in his conclusions on ancient accounting: Mickwitz 1937 (on agriculture); De Ste. Croix 1956 (on accounting).

7. This kind of thinking was particularly attributed to peasants. Chayanov's (1966) work on early 20th-century Russian peasants was highly influential, together with Kula's (1976) study of early modern Polish peasants. Ethnographic accounts (e.g., Du Boulay 1974, 35–38) appeared to confirm the same picture. The ethnography, together with Finley's more elite-centered story, lead many scholars to assume that Greek and Roman peasants shared these same habits of thought: e.g., Gallant 1991, 98–101. For a call to return to these concepts, see Boldizzoni 2011, 84.

8. E.g., Rathbone 1991, more recently articulated through the prism of New Institutional Economics: Temin 2001; Broekaert and Zuiderhoek 2015; Zuiderhoek 2016; Lo Cascio 2020; Arruñada 2020. Associations: Hawkins 2016, 78–138; Terpstra 2013; Hoyer 2018b; cf. Andreau and Maucourant 1999; Verboven 2015; Liu 2016; Elliot 2020 for debate. For some rare work on the older question of social status and economic behavior, see Shaw 2020 on the *equites*. Saller's

(2022) analysis of Pliny the Elder's *Natural History* as an economic text finds plenty of modern economic thinking, and an equal dose of disinterest in innovation, à la Finley.

9. On New Institutional Economics' concealment of rational-actor theory in the guise of institutions, see Boldizzoni 2011, 18.

10. On which Polanyi 1992; Hodges 1998.

11. Finley on markets: Finley 1999, 29, 34, 138–40; see also Bang 2008. For bigger scale: Hopkins 1980; Kay 2014. For market integration, see now Reden and Rathbone 2014; cf. Temin 2020. For important debates on what is meant by "market" as applied to the Roman Egyptian estates, see Andreau and Maucourant 1999, 53–54; 85–89.

12. For development economics' disinterest in people's practice, Hill 1986; Sen 1983, 1985. Practices, as understood through household surveys, now increasingly guide policy: Deaton 1997.

13. Pleading for flax to spin: *SB* 14.11881; peach speculation: *SB* 7242.

14. Pohl (2022, 3–7) explains the concept of pragmatics as it has been applied to the study of literacy.

15. Readers can find Roman monetary equivalencies in "Weights and Measures of the Roman World."

16. In the Eastern cities, the obol value of the assarius is not always clear, nor the value of the assarius to the denarius, which appears to have been different in different cities. Bronze coinage in the East had a long history before the arrival of the Romans and it appears to have carried on, particularly at the level of daily exchange, with only glancing reference to the Roman denarius.

17. Pompeiian loaves appear to have weighed between 2–3 *librae* and cost around three *asses* (Bowes 2021d); portions of unknown weight in Egypt cost a consistent one obol (Drexhage 1991, 29); the cheapest bread in Ephesus cost two obols per libra (*SEG* 4.518).

18. On price formation and change, the best overview of the Egyptian data is still Rathbone 1997. For the timing of these price increases and their differential impact on wheat versus other goods, see now Kelly 2021.

19. On numeracy as distinct from literacy: Overmann 2022. On the spectrum of numeracy: Cuomo 2012. Economic historians have been convinced that numeracy rates, and thus human capital, in different societies could be reconstructed from people's ability to accurately record their age—so-called age-heaping. This method has been applied to the Roman world using tombstones (Duncan-Jones 1977; Baten and Priwitzer 2015) and census declarations (Scheidel 1996b; Bagnall and Frier 1994, 20). Tombstones turn out to be heavily, if not entirely, conditioned by the particular cultural meaning of age in the context of commemoration (Laurence and Trifilò 2022; cf. A'Hearn, Delfino and Nuvolari 2022 for modern critique) and probably have very little to do with numeracy. Census declarations probably better represent the genuinely higher levels of Egyptian numeracy produced in part by the census itself. We'll consider this latter phenomenon further below.

20. For the Roman finger-counting system, see Alföldi-Rosenbaum 1971; Rieche 1986; Minaud 2006; Laurence and Trifilò 2023, 70–71.

21. Cicero, *Ad Att.* 5.21.31.

22. See Kifleyesus 2009.

23. On the contexts in which Roman finger-counting appears in images, see Minaud 2006.

24. Netz 2002.

25. A catalog of extant Greek abaci can be found in Schärlig 2001. For some images of the abacus in use, see Rieche 1986; Schärlig 2004.

26. Bailey 2011, 47–48.

27. For the lists from Pompeii, see Bowes 2021d. See also Bandi 1937 and Bailey 2011, 108–34, which include discussions of some Egyptian expense lists, in addition to other kinds of similar accounts. On the logic of Roman lists more generally, Riggsby 2019, 10–48.

28. *O. Berenike* 2.210. See Bagnall, Helms and Verhoogt 2005, 90. Translation: APIS. Here and elsewhere in the book, an attempt has been made to reproduce the formatting of the original documents, including spacing and columnar format (when it exists). Some uncertainties of preservation or translation have been removed, punctuation added and abbreviations expanded to make these sketchy documents more legible to the modern reader.

29. Pompeii: *CIL* 4.8566; Berenike ostracon: *O. Berenike* 2.210.

30. *Tab. Lond. Bloomberg* 72.

31. *CIL* 4.4528. Alternate readings: Clauss et al. 2023: EDSC 26000099.

32. *O. Claud.* 541.

33. On which see Cuvigny 2000, 56.

34. See e.g., Rowlandson 1996, including appendix 2, for a study of a large group of leases from Oxyrhynchus.

35. *P. Oxy.* 3.499; adopted from translation in Grenfell and Hunt 1914, vol. 3, 218.

36. For the discovery and edition of the documents, Lewis, Yadin and Greenfield 1989. On Babatha's property, Lewis 1985–88; Cotton 1997. Babatha is sometimes described as a wealthy woman, but her many disputes over child support for her son, and the size of her property as declared (24.5 *bet se'ah* or around two hectares), suggest more modest means.

37. *P. Yadin* 16. Translation adopted from Lewis, Yadin and Greenfield 1989, 67–68.

38. Le Teuff 2012, 138.

39. On the meaning of Greek literacy in Babatha's world, see Charlesworth 2014. More generally, on what it meant to navigate financial and legal worlds in languages other than Greek and Latin, see Harris 1989, 175–90; Bowman 1994; Woolf 1994; Cooley 2002; Tomlin 2018.

40. On illiteracy in the Egyptian papyri, Calderini 1950; examples of slow-writers, Youtie 1971 (Egypt) and Tomlin 1988; 87–101 (Britain). See also Schubert 2018, on how documents might be formatted to make it easier for semiliterate people to navigate.

41. Priest/bookkeeper: Ruffing 2018, 228; clerks: Youtie 1971.

42. The debate was begun by Harris (1989, 2018) who, responding to the unsubstantiated optimism of a previous generation, proposed very low (i.e., less than 10 percent) literacy levels. The increasing publication of what has been termed "everyday writing"—graffiti, wooden tablets, ceramic labels and the like—and the emphasis on a spectrum of literacy linked to particular social contexts, led to a substantial pushback against Harris' pessimistic scenario (e.g., Beard 1991; Bowman and Woolf 1994; Cooley 2002; Corbier and Guilhembet 2011; Baird and Taylor 2011; Bagnall 2011; Benefiel and Keegan 2016; Kolb 2018a). No one, however, has rebutted Harris' claim that mass literacy was nonexistent in the ancient world.

43. On reading/writing: Overmann 2022; Thomas 2011; on numeracy: Netz 2002; on accounting: Basu and Waymire 2006.

44. As long ago noted by Hopkins 1991.

45. Harris 1989, 202–211; Hopkins 1991.

46. Netz 2002; Kallet 2022.

47. Harris (1989, 202) notes the taxation bureaucracy's impact on literacy. On Roman fiscal assessment generally, Neesen 1980; Brunt 1981; Lo Cascio 1986; Scheidel 2015, 234–42. Unsurprisingly, Egypt's tax assessment and collection is the best understood of all the Roman provinces: for the many taxes of Egypt, Wallace 1938.

48. For toll taxes, De Laet 1949; for Egypt, see Sijpesteijn 1987. On the literacy demands on large-scale traders, Morley 2007, 77. For a bottom-up view of smaller-scale traders' interaction with officialdom through the toll tax, Sancinito 2023, 23–25.

49. For an overview of innovation and tradition in Roman taxation systems, see Neesen 1980; Brunt 1981; Lo Cascio 1986, esp. 36–39 for the decreasing use of tax farmers (*publicani*) and increasing reliance on the census; for Egypt, Monson 2012. For a comprehensive overview of what we know about the mechanics of the Roman census and tax assessment, see Le Teuff

2012, esp. 93–148 on the land tax (*tributum soli*) and the probable need to provide yield estimates or relative soil quality. See also Brunt 1981. The Roman agronomist Hyginus Gromaticus (*De limitibus constituendis* 167–69) and the jurist Ulpian (*Digest* 50.15.4) also indicated that land was assessed not only on its area but also on its quality, number of trees, etc. For the mechanics of the Egyptian census, which was geared principally toward the collection of the head/poll tax, not land tax, see Bagnall and Frier 1994, 1–30; Le Teuff 2012, 325–38. For the northwest provinces in particular see France 2001, esp. 375 on revolts linked to taxation.

50. Such declarations were made only in the event of poor yields, in which case the taxpayer made a declaration of previous tax paid and requested a revision.

51. Emigh 2002.

52. Silverman 1975, 57–58.

53. Davies 1994.

54. The relatively more abundant documentation relating to army accounting and its impact on literacy and numeracy has resulted in a rich bibliography, among which: Harris 1989, 217; Bowman 1994; Haynes 2002, 2013, 312–36. See also Verboven 2007b, 2009, 118 on account money used in the army. The tablets from the British fort at Vindolanda have been beautifully illuminated by Bowman 1998.

55. Soldiers' pay: *RMR* 68–70; Masada: *P. Yadin* 722; sutler's account: *Tab. Vindol.* 181, 182, 184; ration receipts: *RMR* 76, 78–81; Cuvigny 2021a, 2021f.

56. On which see particularly *Tab. Vind.* 180–144.

57. On auxiliary veterans and their spread of literacy and numeracy, Haynes 2013, 312–36; Verboven 2007. While they may have returned home to spread accounting thinking, they didn't necessarily swell the ranks of citizens: Lavan 2019.

58. Hopkins 1991; Morley 2007, 77–78; Aubert 2004; Ruffing 2018.

59. Amphorae: Molina Vidal and Mateo Corredor 2018; Wallace-Hadrill 2011; the camel teamster Sotas: Sijpesteijn 1971, plus *P. Mich.* 6182e, 6177c, 6152, 6161a; bulk clothing tags from Bordeaux: France and Laurin 2009.

60. Aubert 2004 on accounting and surplus production in the elite villa, but the observations apply to smaller surplus producers as well.

61. A recent nuanced account of chattel slave accounting in the Caribbean and American South is Rosenthal 2018.

62. Cato, *Agr.* 56–58.

63. As observed by Forbes and Foxhall 1982, 63–64.

64. Bagnall and Frier 1994, 70.

65. On which Harris 1989, 34–35 on what he terms "second-hand literacy." On enslaved estate manager/accountants, some of whom seemingly can't read, see Aubert 2004. On slaves and legal status in banking and business, Cohen 2023; Broakaert 2016, 2017 (on freedmen for conflict resolution); Verboven 2008; Andreau 1987, 359–438.

66. On the slave *peculium* as a legal conundrum, see Cohen 2023, 49–82; Silver 2016; Gamauf 2009.

67. On the history of numeracy and accounting mentalities in pre-Roman Egypt, see Golet, Hudson and Wunsch 2004; Muhs 2016, 5–10 and throughout, for the profound changes in accounting practices and motivations over two millennia. On Ptolemaic taxation systems and changes under the Romans, see Monson 2012.

68. Using Scheidel 1996b, 26. The so-called Whipple's Index of age-heaping is a scale of 100 (perfect reporting of age) to 500 (all persons report an age of 0 or 5) that measures societies' tendency to report ages in multiples of 5—so-called age-heaping. Scheidel calculates a Whipple's Index of 123.8. See Bagnall and Frier 1994, 20, for a slightly different number, and the explanation.

69. As discovered by Kelly 2023, 12–14.

70. The data is drawn from Yiftach 2016. On a more positive view of women's engagement with written language, see Kolb 2018b.

71. Cf. Cribiore 2001, 167–68 on "signature literacy."

72. Hailwood 2022.

73. On the pre-Roman experience of written language: Mullen 2014. On tribute—its existence and mechanisms—the problems are summarized in Creighton 2000, 4–21.

74. Mattingly 2006, 130–31.

75. Tomlin 2016, 36, 55 (date), 54 (soldiers), 180–81 (Batavian soldier).

76. On which, Mattingly 2006, 174, 354–55, 361. The early evidence comes from Tacitus, *Agr.* 19.4–5. See also France 2001, 373–74.

77. Data gathered from Allen et al. 2018. Analysis of writing implements published by Smith 2018 arrives at slightly different results, although the general patterns are the same. For earlier studies on the archaeology of writing in the British countryside, see Hanson and Conolly 2002; Mullen 2014; Tomlin 2018; Eckhardt 2018.

78. Minaud (2005, 33–68). See also the thesis by LaGroue 2014, 5–30, and Riggsby 2019, 62–66.

79. Sombart (1902, v. 1, 394–95) and Weber (1922) identified the intellectual and bureaucratic processes behind double-entry bookkeeping as crucial for the development of capitalism, a thesis that was influential among ancient historians, who dismissed the absence of such systems in the ancient world as brakes on economic development (Mickwitz 1937; De Ste. Croix 1956). The causal link between capitalism and double-entry systems has long been contested (Yamey 1947, 1949; Goody 1996, 49–81; Todeschini 2006), as has the notion that ancient bookkeeping practices stifled economic development(Macve 1984; Bresson and Bresson 2004; LaGroue 2014). For some things that double-entry systems are good at, and why they came to be preferred: Basu and Waymire 2021.

80. On which Macve 1984; LaGroue 2014; Minaud 2005, which are principally concerned with elite or institutional accounts. Bailey's (2011) excellent thesis covers nonelite accounting practices.

81. And in Egypt, principally only in one estate, that of Appianus, whose accounts have been brilliantly elucidated in Rathbone 1991, esp. 331–87. The present book returns to Rathbone's rendition of these accounts at various parts of its narrative.

82. Bagnall and Jones 2019.

83. See also Bailey 2011, 2013. On Roman versus other ancient and medieval accounting systems, LaGroue 2014, 78–86. On the backward-looking quality of the best-preserved Egyptian estate accounts and their redaction and final composition at year's end, see Rathbone 1991, 369–87. On the concreteness and reference to actual spoken or visual practices in many Roman information systems, see Riggsby 2019.

84. Verboven 2009.

85. Bailey 2013. See also Rathbone 2013, 129–36.

86. *CIL* 4.8566. The reconstruction here follows Benefiel 2013–24, AGP-EDR128734.

87. On the list-like quality of columns that appear to be tabular, see Riggsby 2019, 46–50, 62–66.

88. As emphasized by Bailey 2013.

89. See Rathbone 2013, 129–36, for this tendency in the account of Kronion, one of the longest personal expense accounts preserved from the Roman period.

90. *P. Oxy.* 4.739. Translation Grenfell and Hunt 1914 v. 4, 236.

91. *P. Oxy.* 4.520. Translation Johnson 1936, 385.

92. Shop: *P. Oxy.* 14.1727; pawnbroker: *P. Lond.* 2.193v.; beer: *Tab. Lond. Bloomberg* 72. See also *P. Prag.* 3.240 for employees' accounts kept by a large estate, with similar third-party type organization.

93. *P. Oxy.* 14.1731, the accounts of a baker, one Onnophris, are an exception, and even these don't include things like rent.

94. On microbusiness accounting (businesses with less than 10 employees), see Ahammed 2019; Ramli et al. 2017.

95. *P. Lond.* 131r (v) and r*(r). See Johnson 1936, 177–207; and Świderek 1960 for commentary on the size and structure of the estate. On Didymus, his (possible) slave accountant, *P. Lond.* 131r. 1.3.

96. See Bailey 2011, chapter 2. Riggsby (2019) has found similar impulses to verify in other Roman information technologies.

97. On the use of financial and audit accounting in small family businesses today, see Sognini, Gnan and Maalmi 2013, 74.

98. One of the best-preserved accounts of someone on the move is that of the wealthy Theophanes, a lawyer who traveled from Hermopolis to Antioch and back. Most of what we know about the journey is probably the result of Theophanes' slaves paying for expenses and recording them. On the scribal hands and redactions: Roberts and Turner 1952, 123, 133; for the recent study, Matthews 2008.

99. Rathbone 1991, 369–87. The fact that unit accounts were only submitted to the central administration at year's end precluded any real-time planning at a central level.

100. Cf. Riggsby 2019, 42–46.

101. What constitutes a document archive, particularly a papyrus archive, has been subject to intense debate. Most agree that deliberate collection and retention distinguish archives from mere dossiers or random assemblages. Since most archives were discovered in early, haphazard excavations, often in rubbish heaps where they had been deposited after no longer being needed, deciding what was "deliberately" kept is often tricky. On definitions, see Pestmann 1990, 51; Jördens 2001; Vandorp 2011; Fournet 2018, 174–83. For an effort to return to old excavations to find archives in rooms or houses, Minnen 1994, with doubts registered by Terpstra 2014.

102. For Tryphon the weaver's family archive, Biscottini 1966; for the tenant farmer, Harthotes, who rented out his children, Claytor, Litinas and Nabney 2016. See also chapter 5 in this book.

103. On which, Omar 1979, and Elgenedy 2022, for the newly discovered cattle-damage compensation. *P. Soter.* 5 attests to Soterichos' illiteracy.

104. On the pleasant fictions spun by Seneca and Horace, among others, see MacRae, forthcoming. I'm grateful to the author for sharing this work in advance of publication.

105. *SB* 7242. Translation Johnson 1936, 387.

106. *SB* 16.12607.

107. Jakab 2009, whose corpus of Egyptian documents reflects the much later (i.e., 4th c. and later) date of many sales-on-delivery agreements. On the *karponai* and contracting out of grape harvests: Rathbone 1991, 193–95; on sales of wine for future delivery, see Kruit 1992.

108. Andreau 1987, 585–86, although he doubts that Caecilius Iucundus, the freedman *affairiste* of Pompeii, was much into wine auctions (1974, 268). Shaw (2019) vividly describes Pliny's sale of his own future grapes and subsequent, very public, forgiveness of the speculators' losses. Rathbone (2011) wonders if a future wine sale from a tenant to his landlord in a later document might describe smallholders using futures as additional income. On the work of *karponai*, see also Rathbone 1991, 193–95.

109. *P. Sakaon* 95. For this family of sheep lessees, Schwartz 1964; Rathbone 1991, 209–11.

110. On sales on delivery and the puzzles they pose: Packman 1975; Bagnall 1977; Jördens 1993; Blouin 2010; and now Silver 2014, who regards these not as simply means of managing inflationary futures but as actual hedges.

111. Sometimes the interest only is paid by commodity, rather than being deducted from the cash paid: Blouin 2010.

112. For the use of arbitration in cases involving money, Broekaert 2017. For a recent view of the lived experience of law in the provinces, including the blurriness of Roman and local legal systems and their employment by working people of a range of legal status, see the collected papers in Czajkowski, Eckhardt and Strothmann 2020. See also Richardson 2015, 51–57.

113. *P. Mich.* 11.619 and Shelton 1971, 48–57 (freedman); Taeuber 2010, GR 158; 2022 (possible slave from Ephesus).

114. *Tab. Lond. Bloomberg* 51.

115. On petitions, petitioners and expectations of justice in Roman Egypt, see Kelly 2011.

116. Quigley has termed the ancient expectation that gods were themselves economic agents "theo-economics": Quigley 2021.

117. Tomlin 1988, 60–71 (theft and legal language), 79–81 (theft), 84–101 (abilities and identity of writers). Plow: *Tab. Sullis* 31; gloves: *Tab. Sulis* 5; five denarii: *Tab. Sulis* 34.

118. On 18th–19th-century farm accounts in England: Turner, Beckett and Afton 2001, 36–39; Hoyle 2013, 28–36. The accounting practices of modern family businesses, on the other hand, is still poorly understood: see Sogni, Gnam and Maalmi 2013. On microfirms: Malaysia; Ramli et al. 2017; Scotland: Ahammed 2019. The modern poor as hedge fund managers: Banerjee and Duflo 2011, chapter 6; see also Rutherford and Arora 2009, 132. American household budgets: Gallup Analytics 2013. Document-keeping: Northcott and Doolin 2000; Carnegie and Walker 2007; Ramlugun, Ramdhony and Poornima 2016. American short-term budget thinking: Morduch and Schneider 2017, esp. 87–109.

2. A World Full of Things

1. The graffito is *CIL* 4.5360. Identification of house IX 7.25 as an inn: Mau 1882; Della Corte 1965, 197. The date is one of three suggested by Solin and Caruso 2016, 13–14. The family's occupation is suggested by food payments to a "domator" or trainer, and the large expense for "montana" (probably fodder). For more bibliography on the list and its context, see Bowes 2021d, 553–56.

2. The apostle of using household consumption data in development economics context is Angus Deaton: 1992, 1997. On the importance of consumption measurements to estimates of economic performance: Stiglitz, Sen and Fitoussi 2009, 13; importance of consumption measurements and data to welfare in the past: A'Hearn, Amendola and Vecchi 2016.

3. Originally so termed by Woolf 1998, 174, who was reprising McKendrick, Brewer and Plumb's (1982) description of consumer culture in 18th-century England. See also Greene 2008; Wallace-Hadrill 2008. Morris (2011, table 3.1) posited a similar increase in consumption, albeit measured in overall energy capture that included principally food and fuel but also consumer goods.

4. Galbraith 1958, 124.

5. Particularly among midcentury economists confronted with the vast expansion of the consumer economy in the postwar period (Duesenberry 1949; Galbraith 1958; Scitovsky 1976). For a review, see De Vries 2023.

6. Commodity fetishism of the Veblenian rather than the Marxist variety. Edwards (1993) unpacks the political valence elite Roman elites ascribed to different kinds of consumption; see Morley (2007, 35–54) for the impact of those valences on trade.

7. On the 5,000 HS fish: Seneca *Ep. Mor.* 9.42; on women's jewelry: Juvenal *Sat.* 6.457; on eels with jewelry: Aelian, *NA* 8.4.

8. Finley 1999, 124–25.

9. On urban production; Wilson 1990, and more recently Wilson and Flohr 2016. Whittaker (1990) posited the vicus as a kind of third space mediating between city and country, but without imagining any peasant consumption. On "the city" as including its hinterland, Morley 1996. For a critique of the continued assumption of urban/rural binaries, Van Oyen 2015.

10. Working urbanites' consumption dismissed: Hawkins 2016. Nonelite consumption as theoretically large in the aggregate but hampered by low GDP: Scheidel and Friesen 2009, 89–90, cf. Maiuro 2012, 117–45. On peasant nonconsumption, the argument is made largely through silence, with the locus of consumption as centered on cities/elites: e.g., Jongman 2007; Wallace-Hadrill 2008. The two large projects on Roman rural economies in Britain and Gaul almost entirely ignore rural consumption: Allen et al. 2017; Reddé 2018. Luuk de Ligt's work constitutes a major exception: Ligt 1990, 1991.

11. On which Hopkins 1980, 118; Goldsmith 1984; Scheidel and Friesen 2009; Maiuro 2012, 117–45. Temin (2006) eschewed consumption-based measurements on the grounds that they were too hard to estimate for the Roman world. Morris' "energy capture" measurement (2011, 53–114) is more all-inclusive and reflects some sense of the historically high numbers proposed here. What it lacks in granularity it makes up for by including fuel—which is not included here.

12. The proportion of wheat in the diet has often been derived from Foxhall and Forbes 1982. The proportion of food to total expenditure is largely derived from modern (and some early modern) economies: Goldsmith 1984, 266–67; Scheidel and Freisen 2009, 67–69.

13. Early efforts were undertaken by those interested in prices and consisted of adding up the costs of a notional assemblage of goods: Prell 1996; Drexhage 1991, 440–54. Allen 2009, revised by Scheidel 2010, reconstructed ancient commodity baskets in the more traditional economic sense. Scheidel and Friesen 2009, 68–69, applied them to GDP calculations. Debate: Bowes 2021e; Scheidel 2020. Critique of the method for another historical period: Muldrew 2011, 6–10: "The numerical abstraction of such series often masks the difficulties in collecting evidence robust enough to be used in comparative terms." This critique is even more true of the ancient world.

14. Ranging from an annual 86 to 200 sestertii per person for food alone and 153 to 380 sestertii for total annual consumption: see principally Hopkins 1980; Goldsmith 1984; Maddison 2007, 11–68; Scheidel and Friesen 2009.

15. Jongman 2007; Jongman, Jacobs and Klein Goldewijk, 2019; Kron 2014, 2019.

16. On standardization and homogenization of goods: Morel 2008; Wallace-Hadrill 2008; Wilson 2009; Mayer 2012, 166–212; Van Oyen 2016; Pitts 2014, 2018; Jiménez 2017; Collins-Elliot in press.

17. Contra Wallace-Hadrill 2008, see Mayer 2012; Collins-Elliot in press. This is also part of an extended critique about the nature of "Romanization," begun by Woolf (1998) and refined by Greene 2008; Dietler 2010; Pitts 2014, among others.

18. Clarke 2003 on the art of "ordinary Romans"; Mayer 2012, chapter 5, on the different meanings the "middle class" gave to standard subjects; Petersen 2006, demolishing the notion of a specific "freedman" style, emphasizing its shared features with elites and nonelites alike. On the so-called taberna culture of brash and successful artisans and merchants, see Ellis 2018; Flohr 2020. On the loudly proclaimed value assigned to work by some freedmen, George 2006.

19. See, respectively, Fulford et al. 2017, 336–55; Pitts 2018, 215.

20. The rise of consumption studies in history and anthropology in the 1990s witnessed the widening gap between economic models and approaches centered on questions of identity and agency. For an early critique, see Pennell 1999, and more recently De Vries 2008.

21. Discussed in Ravallion 2016, 108–9; 139–40, 200.

22. The observations are drawn from Stallybrass 1998.

23. On social inclusion costs, see Atkinson and Bourguignon 2000.

24. They are, as Bakhtin might have put it, heteroglossic: Bakhtin 1981. Bourdieu's *Distinction* (1979), which used statistical surveys to document the use of objects (among other things) to make social distinctions, is also fundamental.

25. Atkinson and Bourguignon 2000, working from Sen's concept of capabilities: Sen 1985.

26. First- and second-order needs: Roche 2000, 12–14.

27. The bibliography on the calculation of poverty lines, and the costs—and goods—of social inclusion, is immense. For an introduction, Ravallion 2016, 191–218.

28. Roche 2000, 7.

29. I've borrowed this phrase from Ago 2013, who uses it to describe a taste for things—not only as newly purchased but also passed down through generations.

30. Farmers: Muldrew 2011, 29; Aristocrats and merchants: Weatherill 1988, table 6.4.

31. On the elasticity of food and calories, see Subramanian and Deaton 1996; Deaton and Drèze 2009.

32. E.g., Allen 2001, more specifically tailored to UN guidelines in Allen 2013.

33. Cato, *Agr*. 56. Trans. Roth 2007, 27.

34. Cato, *Agr*. 56–58 on food rations; 59 on clothing.

35. On the performance of knowledge in the agronomic and other Roman "technical" texts, see Thibodeau 2018.

36. Roth 2005; 2007, 32–39 on slave gardens, animals and other foods consumed as let slip by Cato and other authors.

37. 3,000 kcal wheat; 450 wine; 134 oil; 115 olives. Roth (2007, 30) arrives at a somewhat lower reconstruction of 3,500 kcal.

38. See Muldrew 2011, tables 3.7 and 3.9, respectively. Cf. Roth 2007, 38–39, who assumes the rations provided by Cato were too large to be plausible and assumed that they must be intended for entire families.

39. The caloric total of Cato's diet is similar to some of Polybius's equally truncated and rhetorical discourse on Roman army rations. See Foxhall and Forbes 1982, 63.

40. Collected and studied by Cuvigny 2000; see also Cuvigny 1996. These rations pertain to the so-called *familiares*, the lowest group of quarry workers, composed mostly of enslaved but also some seemingly free workers.

41. The nearby quarry of Domitianè/Kaine Latomia was worked almost entirely by *familia* workers and constitutes the best evidence for what they, versus their wholly free coworkers, ate: Leguilloux 2018; Van der Veen et al. 2018.

42. The tiny wages of 7 dr per month were probably intended to cover incidentals and food of the worker's choosing. On the wages of the *familiares*, Cuvigy 2000, 41.

43. *Tosefta,* tractate *Pe'ah* 4:8a–c. Translation Gardner 2014, 255, along with the caloric reconstructions.

44. Foxhall and Forbes 1982 is the classic study on cereals, while Garnsey (1988) laid out an influential model for the meat-poor, protein- and nutrient-deficient dietary package.

45. Smith, *Wealth of Nations* 11; Weber 1976, 41; Marx, *Capital,* 3.6.39; Scott 2017; Graeber and Wengrow 2021.

46. Roche 2000, 59.

47. Pushback against the tyranny of wheat in Roman diets has already begun. On the higher nutritional value of ancient cereals versus modern ones: Heinrich 2019; arguing for a more limited role of cereals: Jongman 2007, 604–5; Heinrich and Erdkamp 2019; Kron 2019; Van Limbergen 2018.

48. Listed and described in detail in appendix 1. The problems with the Pompeiian lists, which mirror the problems attendant to the lists from Egypt and Asia Minor, are discussed in some detail in Bowes 2021d.

49. On Gemellus and what we know of his status and history, see Shelton 1971.

50. Rathbone's suggestion: Rathbone 2013, 127. Kronion's meat-eating isn't included in the meat-frequency tallies here, as his otherwise carefully documented expenses aren't always easy to pin to specific days.

51. Rowan 2016, 2017.

52. Lepetz and Oueslati 2003.

53. Davies 1971.

54. *Tab. Vindol.* 182.

55. For a general discussion from the isotopic evidence from Britain, see Cummings 2009; for Italy, Soncin et al. 2021.

56. Soncin et al. 2021.

57. Otter 2020.

58. On the definition of luxury foods, and their periodic consumption around moments of social cohesion/distinction, see Van der Veen 2003.

59. *Tosefta* tractate *Pe'ah* 4:8, on which see Gardner 2014, 263–64, who assumes fish is a luxury.

60. *Tab. Vindol.* 182.6.

61. On the sausages: Bodel 1989.

62. See Bowes 2021d, 568–69.

63. https://ourworldindata.org/grapher/share-of-energy-from-cereals-roots-and-tubers-vs-gdp-per-capita?tab=table.

64. On which Subramanian and Deaton 1996.

65. On the autarkic and/or vegetarian peasant: Jongman 1988, 79; Garnsey 1988, 14–15; 45ff.; Corbier 1989, 224; Ligt 1990, 43–47. Even more recently, MacKinnon (2019) isn't optimistic about peasant meat consumption.

66. The details are provided in chapter 3. In brief for Italy: Bowes, MacKinnon et al. 2021, 519–20; Gaul: Lepetz and Zech-Matterne 2018; Britain: Lodwick 2017.

67. Italy: vegetables: Bowes, MacKinnon et al. 2021, 520–21; fruit: Bowes, MacKinnon et al 2021, 520–21; Motta 1997. Britain: vegetables: Van der Veen 2008; Lodwick 2017, 77–79. Egypt: Thanheiser, Walter and Hope 2002.

68. Bakels and Jacomet 2003; Van der Veen 2008, table 2; Reddé et al. 2018, 530–31.

69. Bowes, Vaccaro et al. 2021, 550–51.

70. Timby in Fulford et al. 2017, fig. 7.11.

71. The farm is Cotswold Community: see Biddulph in Smith, Powell and Booth 2010, 22–24.

72. Fulford et al. 2017, 355. See more generally Perring and Pitts 2013.

73. MacKinnon 2004, 145–47.

74. Data on chickens: Britain: Allen 2017, 135–36; Italy: cities, villas, roadside settlements: MacKinnon 2013 and personal communication; farms: MacKinnon, Vaccaro and Bowes 2021.

75. For Britain, Locker 2007; Italy, MacKinnon 2004, 54–56.

76. A detailed discussion appears in chapter 6. See also Müldner 2013 on tentative urban/rural differences.

77. On standardization of pottery: Van Oyen 2016; Pitts 2014, 2018.

78. On dietary and cooking homogenization, Cool 2006, with an emphasis on regional inflections. See also Collins-Elliot in press. On shoes and clothing: Driel-Murray 2016; Radicke 2023. For an extraordinary exposition of Egyptian households through their things, see Boozer 2021.

79. Bang (2008) made a bold argument for the fragility of consumer supply networks. As more archaeological data mounts for stable, medium-distance exchange of everything from basic foodstuffs to consumer goods (e.g., Van Horn 2025), this caution now appears somewhat overblown.

80. As shown now for grain by Rathbone and Reden 2014, contra Kessler and Temin 2008. See also Adams 2007 on the myriad of ways that transport costs might be absorbed by producers, middlemen and the state. On long-distance traded cooking pots: Montana et al. 2007.

81. For a critique, see Fulford et al. 2017, 281–82.

82. On the structure of the glass making industry, see Stern 1999, 454.

83. Glass is typically studied separately from pottery, making comparative study difficult. On its ubiquity in the well-preserved assemblages at Pompeii, see Ray 2017.

84. Ray 2017. The undercounting of metal objects in archaeological versus testamentary contexts for the medieval period has been examined for England: Jarvis, Briggs and 2015.

85. Brilliant new work has revealed this world: Holleran 2012; Ellis 2018; Flohr 2020.

86. See appendix 1. The Egyptian lists are skewed by those of Kronion, who included many larger-scale wool purchases, almost certainly for spinning by his female family members.

87. E.g., Weatherill 1998; Dyer 1989; Overton et al. 2004; Smail 2016.

88. The evidence for abandonment and out-of-position objects has come most clearly from the extraordinary study of the so-called Insula of Menander—its architecture, decoration and house contents. That project also documented the major lacunae in the recording of certain objects—like plain pottery—by the early excavators. The findings are published in three volumes (Ling 1997), of which Allison 2006 provides the most complete account of these issues. See also Allison 2004.

89. Interestingly, the early modern probate inventories often fail to itemize the same things—common pottery, for instance—that the Pompeiian excavators omitted: Overton et al. 2004, 14–18. At Pompeii, the Pompeii Artifact Life History Project has worked to rectify many of these problems, recording the complete household contents of poor and middling houses: see Peña, in press. New excavations in the House of the Lararium have also targeted a small-to-middling house and its contents: http://pompeiisites.org/en/comunicati/the-discovery-of-furnishings-from-the-house-of-the-lararium-in-regio-v-a-snapshot-of-middle-class-pompeii/.

90. Flohr 2017. Also the general contention of Mayer 2012, 53–56, who argues that various members of the commercial classes occupied small and larger houses alike. Cf. Simelius 2022.

91. *House of Habonius Primus* (I 11, 5/8) (350 m^2): The very brief excavation reports from 1913 are summarized in Peña, in press, but the house was never fully published. The household population and house contents are from Peña, in press. *House of L. Caelius Ianuarius* (I 11, 17) (140 m^2); Pugliesi Caratelli and Baldassari 1990, 666–83; contents: Peña, in press. *House I 10, 1* (1 10, 1) description and contents: Allison 2006. My thanks to Ted Peña for sharing his and his team's unpublished work on the contents of I 11, 5/8 and I 11, 17 as well as the Villa Regina (see below).

92. Rarely considered, even in the literature on the Pompeiian middle classes, but discussed in the newer literature on slave experience in these houses: Joshel and Petersen 2014, 24–86. For the house-painting business and the people who did it: Esposito 2017.

93. Room rental costs are almost nowhere given. The evidence is reviewed by Frier 1977, 34; Santomato 2014, 326. The absurdly inexpensive 1 *as* per night room in Petronius' *Satyria* (Petron. *Sat.* 8.4) is almost certainly rhetorical exaggeration.

94. Pompeii is thought to have a particularly robust rental market, with one estimate putting some 40 percent of households as living in rented accommodation: Pirson 1999, 174. The amount Caecilius Iucundus pays for a fullery (1,652 HS/year) seems too small to be rent and may be tax (Andreu 1974, 69–70).

95. Data is found in appendix 1, table A.1.

96. The value of objects was calculated from some known costs from the Vesuvian cities, and for the majority of objects for which we have no price, an estimate from the ratios of value preserved in the much later Edict of Maximum Prices of Diocletian, checked against those ratios as found in the Egyptian price corpus. Specifics are found in appendix 1, table A.2.

97. Indeed, the relative cheapness of ceramic objects makes their likely undercounting in the earlier excavations less of a problem for this exercise.

98. Thirsk 1978; Weatherill 1988; McKendrick, Brewer and Plumb 1992; Pennell 1999; Overton et al. 2004 (on Britain); Roche 2000 (on France); Ago 2013 (Rome); De Vries 2011 (economic implications). For the data: 18th-century working urbanites: Muldrew 1998, tables 1.1–1.5; 18th-century tablewares: Overton et al. 2004, 107. The inventories, like the early Pompeiian

excavators, tend to undercount nonmetal and nonfurniture items, like wood or earthenware pots, so these comparisons shouldn't be extended too far: see Jervis, Briggs and Tompkins 2015, 178; Overton et al. 2004, 14–18.

99. The autarkic peasant is a staple of the earlier historiography, a trope that has slowly been dismantled by both historical and anthropological literature. For an early critique, see Aymard 1983.

100. Perring and Pitts 2013; Pitts 2014; Fernández-Götz, Maschek and Roymans 2020.

101. De Caro 1994.

102. The names Secundus, Hilarus and Masculus were found etched on the villa and may be the names of free or enslaved workers on the farm. De Caro 1994, 87, 125–26.

103. Data from Peña, in press. Again, thanks to Ted Peña for sharing this work prior to publication.

104. Data from Camin 2005.

105. Data from Smith, Powell and Booth 2010.

106. Pontine survey: Haas 2011, tables 3.1, 3.3, 4.1, 4.3, 5.1, 5.3, for 62 surveyed sites.

107. Arguing for rural landscapes cut off from Roman goods: Perring and Pitts 2013. For the statistics on rural sigillata (in Britain termed Samian Ware), see now Fulford et al. 2017, fig. 7.1, from 3,652 excavated sites.

108. The data is gathered and analyzed by Dossey 2010, 48–54, cf. 62–97 on the fourth-fifth centuries. It should be noted that, as in Italy, the data comes only from field survey, which probably underrepresents the presence of fine wares.

109. Cool 2006, 191, on the limited number of forms in British rural sites versus urban and military ones.

110. Cool 2006, 202, on some British cities. More broadly, particularly on African Red Slip forms: Carandini 1981, 15; Hudson 2010; Durham and Hawthorne 1999.

111. Fulford and Clarke 2011, 100–203.

112. Data from Allen et al. 2018.

113. Smith 2018, fig. 3.12.

114. Dossey 2010, 43–54.

115. For value calculations, see appendix 1, table A.2.

116. On Britain, see Brindle 2017a. Most preserved collections of metal tools come from villas, almost certainly because metal objects were too precious to be abandoned by farmers: only some 2 percent of farms sites in Britain preserve remains of plows, for instance, compared to 5 percent for villas, and the few larger assemblages of tools in the province are virtually all from villas. For an example from Gestingthorpe villa with its assemblage of plows, billhooks, knives and many, many keys, see Manning 1985.

117. For Ponterotto, see chapter 3 and Alderighi and Pittari 2020.

118. Similarly, probate inventories of farmers versus merchants in 18th-century England demonstrate this same locus of value in tools and apparatus: Overton et al. 2004, 88.

119. On which, see Otter 2007, 223.

120. Goldberg 2008; Overton et al. 2004, 161–62.

121. Turner 1980.

122. *Wealth of Nations* 2.2.4. On Smith's linen shirt as an early historical example of social inclusion costs, see Ravallion 2016, 106–8.

123. Miller 2009, 24–65; Fisk 1989, 1–22.

124. Turner-Bowker 2001.

125. Sebesta and Bonfante 1994; Edmonson and Keith 2008. The tide is changing, however, as witnessed by new studies on later Roman working people's dress: Pennick Morgan 2018; Jørgensen 2021. Swift, Stoner and Pudsey 2021, chapter 1, discuss the range of nonperishable dress items—jewelry, belts, etc.—that were likewise important for women but not included here.

126. E.g., Martial 1.92, 6.11; Cato, *Agr.* 59. See also Radicke 2023 for a robust collection of these sneering texts.

127. Wild 2009 (northern provinces); Droß-Krüpe 2011 (Egypt).

128. Jones 1960; seconded by Carrié 2004, 25; Radman-Livaja 2013, and upheld by the signs of professionalization and standardization even in villagers' clothing in the Egyptian Oases: Hope et al. 2022, 121–28. Contra Droß-Krüppe 2011, who sees Egyptian textile production as heavily home-based, most other assessments conclude that while spinning took place at home, weaving finished cloth tended to take place in larger, more specialized (although still often home-based) workshops: Carrié 2004; Carrié and Freu 2019, 44–49.

129. On the Gallic cloth production industry, see Liu 2009, 2013; on Egypt: Minnen 1986; Droß-Krüpe 2011; North Africa: Wilson 1990. It's important to note that most clothes were probably woven to shape—tunics, cloaks, and the other major articles of clothing being relatively simple forms—not cut out of bolts of cloth (Granger-Taylor 1982).

130. The adoption of the larger, more expensive two-beam vertical looms during the Roman period may have prompted this shift toward specialized weavers. See Wild 2002, 11. On the increasing specialization of rural textile work in Britain, Smith 2017, 229.

131. Tehat and her weaving business: *P.Kellis Copt.* 44.8; local and imported clothes: Hope et al. 2022, 127.

132. On the *centonarii*: Liu 2009. For a fascinating examination of some actual used clothing from the later Roman world: Pennick Morgan 2018, 80–96.

133. As shown through the various studies of Carol van Driel-Murray: 2001, 2016.

134. Driel-Murray 2016.

135. Cato, *Agr.* 59. *Dig.* 34.2.23.2 provides Ulpian's less precise but also somewhat longer list of clothing for the slave *familia*: tunic, cloak and poncho. See also Radicke 2023, 375.

136. Sources for apprentice clothing are collected in Drexhage 1991, 368.

137. Radicke 2023, 264–76.

138. See also Radicke 2023, 254; Hamel 1990, 60–62, 68–74, on the early Jewish and New Testament sources, also describing the destitute or those deliberately placing themselves outside society (philosophers, prophets) as having only a single tunic. The fourth-century Jewish sources stipulate that every man must have two sets of clothing, although this is to preserve a clean set for Shabbat: *Jerusalem Talmud*, tractate *Pe'ah* 8:7. John Chrysostom, who, after Martial, was one of antiquity's most clothing-conscious writers, likewise defined the poor man as one who had but one inner tunic (*Homily 10, on Philippians* [*PG* 62.259]). Nonetheless, many scholars use the single tunic to calculate normal, basic clothing requirements: Scheidel 2010, 431, 434; Huebner 2013, table 3.1; Menten-Plesters 2017, 115.

139. *Babylonian Talmud*, tractate *Shabbat*, 120a.

140. Jørgensen 2021; on purple stripes, formerly thought to be the province of elites, as common on working people's clothing: Cardon et al. 2012. For the Judean material, Yadin 1963, chapters 10–12; Shamir and Sukenik 2011; Shamir 2017.

141. *SB* 14.11575.

142. On the dalmatic, Pennick Morgan 2018, 17.

143. Radicke 2023, 264–76.

144. Rothe 2009, 45–46. In the 1st century a tunic and overtunic; by the 2nd century a tunic-like slip and a tunic. A mantle is requisite throughout.

145. *Mishnah Kethuboth* 5.8–9. See also Hamel 1990, 65–66.

146. Hamel 1990, 75–76.

147. For some Roman-Egyptian footwear: Hope et al. 2022, 85–89; for the Rhineland bargeman: Driel-Murray 1996.

148. Appendix 1, table A.4.

149. This is in the ballpark for the few testamentary annuities for clothing we know of, mostly from the jurists: *Dig.* 34.3.28 pr (25 denarii per year for the descendants of one Aurelius

Symphorus); *Dig.* 10.2.39.2 (25 denarii per year for a freed slave); *Dig.* 34.1.20.3 (50 [denarii?] for a freed slave); *CIL* 13.5708 (the so-called testament from Lingon, Germania superior, 20 [or 30] denarii). See Frier 1993. The minimum clothing allowance of 50 dinars/*zuz* (50 denarii) to be supplied by a husband to his wife according to the late second-/third-century Mishnah Ketubot (5:8) is around the same but may reflect the increased prices of the 3rd century. On Jewish poverty and its sources, Gardner 2022.

150. In Britain, the fibulae and other ornaments found in the countryside are demonstrably distinct from those in cities: Brindle 2018.

151. On toga/stola requirements and discourse, see Edmundson 2008. Citizens in first-century BCE Rome and some other places were, in theory, required to wear a toga to get into the forum. But the reiterated imperial dicta around toga-wearing suggests many ignored the requirements. On the stola, see Radicke 2023, 270ff.

152. In one instance, Martial claims a cheap one could be had for three denarii (9.100.6); his later estimate of 60 (HS?) seems somewhat more plausible (4.26.4).

153. On the bias toward the male individual, England 1993. On the importance of consumption that takes place at the border of family and community, Banerjee and Duflo 2007.

154. Bath fees: Ephesus: GR 158 (3 instances); GR 50 (1 instance); GR 51 (1 instance); GR 53 (1 instance); GR 357 (1 instance); Taeuber 2002, 97 (1 instance). Egypt, Oxyrhynchus (?): *P. Mich.* 11.619 (3 instances).

155. Maida 2022.

156. MacMullen 1965, 126.

157. The so-called civic compromise model of religion, by which religious functions were placed in the hands of political elites as the appropriate representatives of the *res publica*. For an overview and critique, see Gordon 1990.

158. Padilla Peralta 2020, for a revised model of quasi-voluntary compliance together with ritual reiterations of civic cohesion. On the religious practices and identities of slaves, freedmen and neighbors, see Padilla Peralta 2017; Flower 2017.

159. On the *cultores* of Diana and Antinous: *CIL* 14.2112. On the high costs and social exclusion of *collegia*: Tran 2006, 105–9; Liu 2016, 209.

160. Cf. Ago 2013, 4.

161. The data is found in Bustamante-Álvarez et al. 2017; 2020. The occasion is unknown; a *lustratio* is only a guess based on species sacrificed—a so-called *suovetaurilia* (a cow, sheep and pig), said to be sacrificed for these rituals. Shortly after, the neighborhood would be developed as a series of workshops, including (eventually) perfumeries.

162. See appendix 1, table A.2. Transplanting first-century CE prices and the Augustan monetary system onto a world of about a century earlier is perilous. It's possible, even likely, that costs rose between the later Republic and early empire. However, coin supply and ceramic outputs also increased, and the impact of all these things on prices is entirely unknown. On wheat price shifts over this period, see Rathbone and Reden 2014, 176–77.

163. Martens, Ervynck and Gordon 2020; Martens 2004. For the costs used, see appendix 1, table A.2.

164. As suggested for the Pompeiian *lustratio* by Bustamante-Álvarez et al. 2017, 109.

165. On American families and Christmas: Morduch and Schneider 2017, 81; on South African families and funerals, Case and Menendez 2009.

166. Juvenal, *Sat.* 3.182–3.

3. Farmer Soterichos Goes to Market

1. The Soterichos family archive is described and translated in Omar 1979. A newly discovered piece of the archive tells us about the cows: Elgenedy 2022.

2. https://ourworldindata.org/grapher/employment-in-agri-vs-urban-pop.

3. See Hanson 2016, 72 for a bigger urban population than we thought, but still leaving a big (75–80 percent) rural majority.

4. British archaeologists have thought most deeply about the role of developer-funded archaeology in changing our view of the Roman world: Fulford and Holbrook 2011; Evans, Aldred and Cooper 2023.

5. See for northern Gaul, Ouzoulias 2007–8; Kasprzyk 2019; for Britain, Allen and Smith 2016; for Italy, Bowes, Collins-Elliot and Grey 2021.

6. For other farming regions, like those in North Africa, we still lack the granular details that only excavation can provide. Roman North African farmscapes have been largely mediated through field survey (e.g., Leveau 1984; Barker et al. 1996; Dietz, Ladjimi and Ben Hassan 1995; Fentress, Drine and Holod 2009), the study of the great olive-oil agribusinesses (Mattingly 1998), or the feeding of its frontier armies (e.g., Fentress 1979; Guédon 2018). Only a handful of farms have been excavated and published, and correspondingly very little archaeobotanical or faunal data exists (recent exception for a later period: De Vos Raaijmakers and Maurina 2019). Assessments of smallholder economies thus proceed from very different data (e.g., Dossey 2010; for a later period, Tedesco 2018).

7. On the origins of the term and its baggage, see Wolf 1966, 1982; Shanin 1980, 1988, 1990; Grey 2011, 32–33. An overview of more recent trends with accompanying bibliography: Bernstein and Byers 2001.

8. Midcentury scholarship, most of which was based on ethnographic work in modern agricultural communities, both reified and complicated the picture: among many, Chayanov 1966; Dalton 1972 (tribal versus peasant economies); Dalton 1971, especially 143–92 (markets); Scott 1977, with an overview and critique in Bernstein and Byers 2001; Narotsky 2016.

9. An aside in the *Eighteenth Brumaire*—French peasants *not* to be considered a class—was about all the time Marx gave them. Engels was more convinced that the urban proletariat and peasants might make common cause (his book on the 16th-century German peasant rebellions, *The German Peasant War*, and articles on the "Peasant Question in France and Germany" were all published during or just after the revolutions of 1848–49). For the complex relationship between Marxism and peasants, see Levien, Watts and Yan 2018.

10. E.g., Gramschi's *Operai e contadini* of 1920.

11. Momigliano 1982, provides the road map. Brunt (1971a, 1971b) fleshed out this vision with more robust economic data. See also Bowes 2021a, 4–6; and Bowes 2021b, 123–24.

12. The historians of the Annales school were above all interested in the peasants and peasant economies of medieval and early modern France: Block 1931; Duby 1962. It was Braudel's work on the Mediterranean, however, that drove home the timeless, "geological" peasant: Braudel 1972, 25–102.

13. E.g., Gallant 1991; Halstead 2014, inspired by an earlier generation of Mediterranean peasant ethnography: e.g., Banfield 1958; Silverman 1975. Forbes and Foxhall (1995) provide a counterpoint, also informed by ethnography, but more cautiously applied. See also Garnsey 1988, 44–56. Conversely, modern peasants might be made sense of through ancient comparanda: Delano-Smith 1979.

14. Finley 1999, chapter 4 and throughout. Finley is somewhat conflicted about the "nonprimitive" quality of ancient Mediterranean peasants—he recognized that they engaged with the broader economy (1999, 105), but he didn't allow that they sold anything significant off the farm or produced cash crops (106–7). See Saller 2002.

15. For the exception, see Kron 2000, 2002, 2005b, 2008, 2012, 2015.

16. On the definition of modern smallholders, see Lowder, Skoet and Raney 2016, 26–27.

17. The advocates for climate as a major historical and economic agent in the Roman world have acknowledged the climate-weather distinction, while accepting granular dating for what are still broad chronologies and, for the most part, assigning climate a greater role than human

agency: e.g., Harper 2017; J. Manning 2018, 137–72; McCormick and Harper 2018. For a still-relevant critique as regards regionalism and chronological granularity, see S. Manning 2013; on causality, see Grey 2025. On the Roman climatic optimum, first observed in Bianchi and McCave 1999, it's now clear that climatic periods (again, very broadly dated) were highly regional, not global or even hemispheric: Neukom et al. 2019.

18. The anthropological interest in subsistence met Roman peasants in part through the nuanced and groundbreaking work of Peter Garnsey (1976, 1979, 1988), himself influenced both by the Annales school and by comparative anthropology (e.g., Scott 1977). See also Veyne 1979; Aymard 1983.

19. On which, see Andersen and Ahmed 2016. For an application, concentrated on selling and consumption in a medieval context, see Marfany 2018. In an early modern context, see Hoffman 1996.

20. For details on the three size categories used here, see appendix 2, tables A.4 and A.5.

21. Jones 1963, 147–58.

22. On these smallest farms, a consolidated discussion in Allen and Smith 2016, 23–28 (enclosed farms). For Gaul, the discussion is not so consolidated (unlike for the Iron Age: see Malrain and Lorho 2015), but some efforts may be found in Malrain et al. 2017, 323 (Level 4); Bernigaud et al. 2017, 399. For The Grange, Wright et al. 2009. For Italy, see examples collected in Bowes, Collins-Elliot and Grey 2021.

23. Some exceptions include northern and southwestern Britain: Brindle 2016a, 2016b.

24. Euro Disney at Montévrain: Bernigaud et al. 2017, 435–40; Reims: Bezannés: Achard-Corompt 2012: Laon/Le Griffon: Achard-Corompt et al. 2017, 499–504. Toyota Factory at Vallée de l'Escaut: Clotuche et al. 2017, 186–91. Gravel quarry at Cotswold Community: Powell, Smith and Laws 2010.

25. Ewell and Taylor 2003; Ciampoltrini 2004; Ciampoltrini and Zecchini 2005.

26. As suggested for an earlier Roman period in Italy by Roselaar 2019, 85–93.

27. Allen and Smith 2016, 28–33; Nüsslein and Bernigaud 2018, 133–39.

28. On the presence of grain dryers and granaries in medium farms, see further below.

29. Vicar's Farm: Evans and Lucas 2019, 251–434; Langdale Hale: Evans 2013, 21–178. On the Cambridge-area farms more generally, Smith 2016b, 192–206.

30. On Ponterotto (Florence), Alderighi and Pittari 2020: the authors alternately identify the site as a farm or a *mansio*/waystation. See also Forin 2017 on the same distinction around domestic space in northern Italian farms.

31. Heimberg 2002; Brüggler et al. 2017: 34–38, with dimensions of various Hambach farms in table 1. For a different, architecturally driven way of categorizing these farms, see Habermehl 2013. For a British version at Orton Hall, Mackreth 1996.

32. Hoogeloon: Roymans, Derks and Heddink 2015; Roymans and Derks 2015.

33. For similar conclusions on farm plot sizes, see Goodchild 2007, 78–120.

34. Also tacitly assumed in the categories developed for northern Italian farms by Forin (Forin 2017; Busana and Forin 2020).

35. Distributed landholding: as revealed in allotment lists from the Trajanic alimentary schemes, as found in Ligures Baebiani (*CIL* 9.1455; Duncan-Jones 1976, 1990, 126–42); and an irrigation plan from Lamasba (Shaw 1982); as well as Cicero, *Rosc. Am.* 7.20; Pliny, *Ep.* 3.19.2. Generally: Garnsey 1988, 47–50. Egyptian evidence discussed below. On the central role played by microregional variability in ancient Mediterranean environments, Horden and Purcell 2000, especially 77–79.

36. Bowes, Collins-Elliot and Grey 2021. In Greece: Foxhall 2020.

37. Long examined through textual or epigraphic evidence, the legal category of these places was more interesting to scholars than what they actually did. Todisco (2011) and De Francesco (2014) provide useful catalogs of the *vici*, Corsi (2000) on the state-designated way stations (*mansiones* and *stationes*).

38. On the role of crafts and trade: Johnson, Keay and Millett 2004 (Tiber Valley); Tol et al. 2014 (Pontine Plain); Santoro 2017 (more northerly examples). Forum Appi: Tol, de Haas and Anastasia 2016. Another partially excavated example at Torrita di Siena: Pucci 1992. See also Witcher 2020, 144–50 on the Tiber Valley roadside and port sites; De Francesco 2014, 190–91 on productive installations in Lazio *vici*.

39. The importance of these intermediary market spaces (*nundinae*), known from texts in Italy if not from archaeology, has long been recognized: Whittaker 1990; Ligt 1993. Morley (2000) notes that elites appear to be disinterested in *nundinae*, although many potential periodic market sites seem to attract elite euergetism.

40. Malrain et al. 2017, 318–19 and throughout.

41. Groot et al. 2009; Groot 2016. Doubts on the volume of surplus expressed by Martin 2017. On which more below.

42. Gill Mill: Booth and Simmonds 2012. Other examples in Cambridgeshire: Longstanton: Evans, MacKay and Appleby 2006; Site IV: Evans and Newman 2010. Artisanal and other specialized work in British villages: Smith 2017. On the same characteristics of artisanal specialization and export in Gallic villages, see Kasprzyk 2019.

43. Brindle 2017b.

44. Smith 2018, 69–76.

45. For a summary of the various land sizes given away in different colonial moments and enterprises, see Roselaar 2009.

46. On the nonsustainability of many veteran grants: Garnsey 1988, 46; Erdkamp 2005, 322–23. Others have been more optimistic, e.g., Roselaar 2009; 2010, 204–7, who has maintained that seven iugera, at the higher productivity we now know from Italian farms, was viable. Review of the models: Goodchild and Witcher 2010. The models produced below for Monte Forco address this issue.

47. Often wrongly termed land registers, some of these lists were made to record tax levies or participants in alimentary programs and are given in land value, leaving scholars to puzzle over the size of the plots: see Duncan-Jones 1964, 1976. Another such list, from Lamasba in Numidia, records plots in an unknown unit, perhaps number of olive trees (Shaw 1982, 87).

48. The Ligures Baebiani register (*CIL* 9.1455): see Duncan-Jones 1976, 14–16, who uses Columella's price of 1000 HS/*iugerum*, noting it may be two times too high. Numbers here assume a range from 500 to 1000 HS/*iugerum*.

49. *CIL* 8.2.18587; Shaw 1982, 87.

50. There are many Egypts: the hyper-fertile, hyper-dense Nile Valley; the Fayum fed by its great artificial canal; and the distant Western Desert oases. This account focuses on the Fayum, where the majority of quantified documentation clusters, touching more briefly on the Nile Valley and the Dakhleh Oasis. It leaves out almost entirely the important and distinctive mixed agro-pisciculture of the Nile Delta, on which see the brilliant Blouin 2014.

51. Langellotti 2020.

52. Rathbone 1990, 134; Sharp 1999, 164.

53. Detailed studies on property and leasing: Oxyrhynchite nome: Rowlandson 1996; Theadelphia: France 1999; Sharp 1999; and, for somewhat later, Rathbone 1991; Tebtunis: Bagnall 1974; Rowlandson 1999; Langellotti 2020; Takahashi 2021; Karanis: Bagnall 1992, 132–36; Mendasian nome: Blouin 2014, 193–207; Hermopolite nome and generally (fourth century): Bowman 1985, with corrections from Bagnall 1992.

54. This was particularly true in the Nile Valley, but not necessarily so for the Fayum, where water was delivered via the great Bahr Yussef canal, prone to salinization and ultimately breakage: Monson 2012, 36ff.; Haug 2015. The oases were supplied from huge wells and missed the effects of the floodwaters altogether, relying on fertilizer: Hope 2022; Bagnall, Thanheiser and Bowen 2022.

55. Tebtunis: data based on Langellotti 2020, table 5.2, corrected. This figure is similar to the plot sizes attested in land transactions (leases and sales): Langellotti 2020, 157. Theadelphia: France 1999, 334–36; Sharp 1999. Some farmers had much less land: farmers in one village in the Nile Valley had on average only one and a half hectares in total: *P. Oxy.* 7.1044. Rowlandson 1996, table 7, with discussion 98, 128–30.

56. Bagnall 1992, 135 and table 2, reconstructed on the basis of tax payments.

57. Kronion's lease-holdings are detailed by Foraboschi 1971.

58. Omar 1979.

59. Kehoe 1992, 144; Rowlandson 1999.

60. Rowlandson 1996, 124–38.

61. Takahashi 2021, 39–41.

62. The complexity of these abutting properties is made wonderfully clear in Rowlandson 1996, fig. 2, with the example of the properties of a woman in the Oxyrhynchite nome.

63. E.g., Scott 2017.

64. Foxhall and Forbes (1982) offer a useful overview.

65. On which now see Feito 2022; Arnoldus et al. 2021; Stirn, Sgorous and Carroll 2022.

66. Columella, *Rust.* 2, ostensibly on soils, is principally dedicated to soil selection, plowing and seeding for a wide variety of cereals and legumes. See also Cato, *Agr.* 34–37; Varro, *Rust.* 9, 42–53; Bowes et al. 2017.

67. Lepetz and Zech-Matterne 2018.

68. On the Reims farms, Achard-Corormpt et al. 2017; Toulemonde et al. 2017.

69. Lodwick 2017. Why spelt: Van der Veen and Palmer 1997; see also Van der Veen and O'Connell 1998.

70. Lodwick 2017, 16–17; 26–27.

71. Thanheiser et al. 2002; Thanheiser and König 2008. Less convincing is Cappers 2016.

72. Barley in the Oxyrhynchite leases: Rowlandson 1996, 237. For Theadelphia, Sharp 1999, 173–74.

73. White (1970) proposes a dry or naked fallow norm, which was occasionally breached in densely used areas with some (reluctant) legume rotation. Delano-Smith (1979, 35–36, 174–76) was even more pessimistic. Spurr (1986) was more confident that a range of practices existed, including a real rotation option. See also Evans 1981; Marcone 1997, 63. Jongman (1988, 80–82) doubled down on the dry-fallow norm in his early (and very pessimistic) reconstructions of Pompeii's economic hinterland.

74. Arnoldus et al. 2021, 492–98. Erdkamp 2005, 77 had expressed similar reservations that smallholders had sufficient land to commit to ley systems.

75. Kron 2000.

76. Columella, *Rust.*, 2.10.

77. Modern studies on rotation of rain-fed wheat crops with legumes in the Mediterranean have been split on its benefits: Ryan et al. 2010 (no yield increases); Pisante et al. 2013 (21 percent increases); Stagnari et al. 2017 (improved weed control).

78. The argument of not only Kron (2000, 2004) but also the European Union's Common Agricultural Policy (CAP) as of 2021: Art. 12, GAEC 7, Annex II: http://data.europa.eu/eli/reg/2021/2115/oj.

79. Lepetz and Zech-Matterne 2018, 353–58, 381–84.

80. The evidence is collected in Lepetz and Zech-Matterne 2018, 376–84.

81. Malrain et al. 2017, 335–36.

82. Limited evidence for legumes and leguminous fodder as signs of poor soil fertility: Lodwick 2017, 33–41.

83. Lodwick et al. 2021.

84. Lepetz and Zech-Matterne 2018, 366–84.

85. Lepetz and Zech-Matterne 2018, 377.

86. Grapin and Marbach 2016.

87. Lodwick 2017, 80–81.

88. Rippon, Smart and Pears 2015, table 3.2 and fig. 3.4.

89. Rowlandson 1996, 236–38. Legumes were principally lentils and fava, while fodder crops included vetches, perhaps clover (*lotos* or *lotinon*), or a generic grass/hay crop (*chortos, chlora*). See Rowlandson 1996, 20–22; Thanheiser et al. 2002, 302–8. As most of our lease data pertains to private land, it is impossible to know if rotation requirements also accrued to public land.

90. Tebtunis: Langellotti 2020, 176; Theadelphia: fewer leases, collected in French 1999, 325–27.

91. Oxyrhynchite nome: leases collected in Rowlandson 1996, 236–38; Fayum: the land-use records are in *P. Berl. Leihg.* II.32. For commentary, Sharp 1999, 173; France 1999, 326.

92. On which, see Adams 2007.

93. Columella, *Rust.* 2.14; Cato *Agr.* 5; 29; 36.

94. Manure pits: Marzano 2007, 387.

95. The meaning of the resultant so-called off-site scatters of pottery, particularly for Roman landscapes and manuring, is hotly debated: Bintliff and Snodgrass 1988; Pettegrew 2001; Ikeguchi 2006; Haas 2012.

96. Ditched farms facilitating manure collection: Adam 2017; manure pits: Rouppert 2017. Isotopic evidence for manuring in the Île-de-France but perhaps not elsewhere: Aguilera et al. 2015, 2018. Likely variation in practice: Lepetz and Zech-Matterne 2018, 387–93.

97. See *P. Lond.* 131v, many entries for transportation and spreading of manure in the month of Toth/Augustus (September).

98. See Delia 1986. For the thousands of pigeons kept in tower-like dovecotes in the Great Oasis, see Hope 2022, 8–9.

99. On the increase in cattle size: MacKinnon 2010. For beginnings in the Iron Age: Trentacoste et al. 2021.

100. MacKinnon 2001.

101. MacKinnon, Vaccaro and Bowes 2021, 513 and table 13.16.

102. Malrain et al. 2017, 342; Reddé et al. 2018, 553–54 for variability.

103. Grau-Sologestoa, Groot and Deschler-Erb 2022, 12.

104. Booth and Simonds 2012.

105. Cattle size increase: Gaul and Germany: Groot 2016; Lepetz and Zech-Matterne 2018, 359–69; Grau-Sologestoa, Groot and Deschler-Erb 2022; Britain: Albarella, Johnstone and Vickers 2008; Rizzeto, Albarella and Crabtree 2017; Allen 2017, 99–104.

106. Bernigaud et al. 2017, 403; Allen 2017, 91–92.

107. For example, the village at Longueil-Sainte Marie: Malrain et al. 2017, 308–9.

108. Allen 2017, 114–18.

109. Adams 2007, 119–34.

110. On sheep herding, see Langellotti 2012. On the tax, Wallace 1938, 79, 86–88.

111. Keenan 1989, 178–79.

112. Langellotti 2012, 123.

113. See Schwartz 1964; Rathbone 1991, 209–11. For all their sheep and goat leasing activities, it's important to note that this family also owned a tiny amount of grain land (some 3.1 ar [0.8 hectares] by the mid-fourth century) and may have sold reeds in addition to their sheep's wool.

114. Keenan 1989; Langellotti 2012; Churcher 2002.

115. Adams 2007, 62–64.

116. Elgenedy 2022.

117. For instance, the Patron lands: Bagnall 1974, 159–62.

118. Adams 2007, 56–58.

119. Jördens 1995, 58, disputed by Adams (2007, 102–3), who claims they were too expensive to purchase for very small holders.

120. Jördens 1995; Adams 2007, 93–100; Rathbone 1991, 268–69.

121. E.g., Marzano 2013, 2015. More recently, however, Marzano 2020.

122. De Sena 2005; Marzano 2013.

123. As recognized by Goodchild's (2007, 2013) models for agricultural production in the Tiber Valley. While distant in space, the Lamasba land list, possibly describing olive groves, suggests that even in a place where oleiculture was big business, smallholders had some piece of the action: Shaw 1982.

124. Arnoldus et al. 2021, 482; Motta, Camin and Terrenato 1993; Perkins and Attolini 1987.

125. Motta, Camin and Terrenato 1993; Camin and McCall 2002–3; Ewell and Taylor 2010.

126. Case Nuove: Vaccaro et al. 2013; Corsica: Raux and Vidal 2017. Olives and perhaps grapes might also be grown in the same fields as cereals—so-called intercropping—or in separate plots. A thorough discussion can be found in Goodchild 2007, 262–66.

127. Van der Veen 2008.

128. Achard-Corompt et al. 2017, 521.

129. Smith 2016b, 183.

130. Laubenheimer and Marlière 2010; Schmitz 2013; Castle 1978.

131. Hervé-Montiel et al. 2011.

132. Rice 2024.

133. Rathbone (1997, 198–200) has a useful summary of the business.

134. Clarysse and Vandorpe 1995, 72–73; Rowlandson 1999, 149.

135. Langellotti 2020, 5.5. The second-century Laches family owned some vineyards, but it's not clear how many: Bagnall 1974, 135–40.

136. These documents are particularly hard to interpret: see Sharp 1999, 174–76; France 1999, 373–440.

137. *P. Soter.* 3 on Soterichos; see also *SB* 6.9109 on Kronion son of Zoilos, who held a similarly sized plot.

138. On dates, abundantly listed in the Kellis Agricultural Account book, see Bagnall 1997b, 42–43, 54–55. The prices for dates here are subject to fourth-century inflation. In Theadelphia, see Sharp 1999, 184.

139. *P. Oslo* 3.133. See also Crawford 1973.

140. Cumin appears in the Kellis account book in the Dakhla Oasis as a traded foodstuff (*P. Kell.* 4 Gr.96.1267); for the rest, see France 1999, 327–28. Safflower was controlled by a government monopoly: aside from prohibitions from growing it on many leases (including that of Soterichos, on which more below), it's not clear to what extent smallholders engaged in safflower cultivation.

141. *P. Soter.* 14 and Omar 1979, 29.

142. As recognized now for Italy: Kron 2008; Hollander 2020. For the northwest provinces: Ouzoulias and Van Ossel 2009; Lodwick 2017, 202; Lepetz and Zech-Matterne 2018; Reddé 2017; Reddé et al. 2018, with some reservations on the role of "the market." For Egypt: Minnen 2000; Monson 2012.

143. On the problems with using granaries as proxies for grain surplus, see Huitorel 2017, who notes that the raised-floor granary was used for very short terms and specific uses—to hold fully processed grain prior to its onward shipment off the farm. During the multiple prior processing steps, grain was stored in barns or other covered areas. On the rhetorical statements that elite made through their granaries, Van Oyen 2019.

144. 51 farms with aisled buildings (out of 168 sites with aisled buildings); 13 farms with granaries (out of 41 sites). Smith 2016a, 58 and 67–68.

145. Ferdière 2015: of his Type 1, on posts, some 26 of 35 examples are found in farms. Since that article, many more Type 1 granaries have been documented in the villages of the Dutch river valleys. Of his Type 2, with buttresses, some 23 of 50 examples are in Type C farms. See also Clotuchet et al. 2017, 190–91 on the frequency of buttressed granaries in the Flemish farms.

146. In Gaul: Ferdière 2015, 39, Type 2 are often found in villas with areas of c. 100–200 m^2. In Italy, the size of known medium-farm granaries in northern and central Italy ranges from 25–325 m^2 (see Ghisleni et al. 2010; Ciampoltrini 2000; Garanzini and Mordeglia 2022; Zamboni 2022, 120–21; Forin 2017, 154–56).

147. Lodwick 2017, 55.

148. Lodwick 2017, 55.

149. Britain: Lodwick 2017, 55. In Gaul, the function of these "dryers" remains unclear—grain, meat smoking or other artisanal activities. A catalog can be found in Van Ossel and Huitorel 2017, but without indication of the types of rural sites where they are found. That they appear in farms is suggested by their appearance in the farms around Reims: Achard-Corompte et al. 2017; Dumas-Lattaque and Arnaud 2015.

150. Catalog in Brun 2016.

151. See examples in Brun et al. 2017, 121–24, plus wooden paddle wheel mills in farms in Sorigny (Indre-et-Loire): Sarreste 2017; and in Lucciana (Corsica): Longepierre 2020.

152. Malrain et al. 2017, 333.

153. Achard-Corompte et al. 2017, 548–49; on mustard at Champ Drillon: Dumas-Lattaque 2017.

154. Lodwick 2017, fig. 2.17; Evans and Lucas 2019, 386.

155. Lodwick 2017, fig. 2.12.

156. E.g., Bowes 2021c, 163–82.

157. Isernia innkeeper's tab: *CIL* 9.2689; Fagan 2017. Pompeii: *CIL* 4.4000 (hay and fenugreek); and possibly *CIL* 4.5380 (*montana* may be hay).

158. Pliny *HN* 13.130.

159. Allen 2017, 91–93; Rouppert 2017.

160. Malrain et al. 2017, 341.

161. Strid 2009. On roadside-site sheep production more generally, see Allen 2017, 117.

162. Achard-Corompt et al. 2017.

163. In Tuscany: Pecci, Vaccaro and Cau Ontiveros 2015; Bowes, Vaccaro et al. 2021, 557–8; Van Horn 2025. Capacity: E. Vaccaro, personal communication. In Corsica: Raux and Vidal 2017.

164. Cherubini, Del Rio and Menchelli 2006; Menchelli and Picchi 2016.

165. Achard-Corompt et al. 2017, 512–15.

166. Powell, Smith and Laws 2010, 138–44.

167. Smith 2016b, 176–79.

168. Grey et al. 2015. Geophysics also reveals these tracks: see Campana 2017.

169. Goodchild 2007; Goodchild and Witcher 2010; Goodchild 2013.

170. Bowman 2013, 240–43, using and modifying Bagnall 1985a.

171. See generally Hanson 2016, figs. 45–53. On Tiber Valley urbanism and suggested demographics, see Witcher 2020, 138–47.

172. Witcher 2020, 172–76; Goodchild and Witcher 2009.

173. On cattle production for London: Allen 2017, 89–91.

174. Perring and Pitts 2013.

175. Thames Valley: Allen 2017, 90–92; beer in Kent: Lodwick 2017, 21.

176. Fulford et al. 2017, 336–52 on rural-oriented pottery industries.

177. Mattingly 2006, 130–36.

178. Brindle 2016a (north); Brindle 2016b (Wales).

179. Allen and Lodwick 2017, 173–75.

180. On the imperial estate: Malim 2005, 127; Fincham 2002. For the notion of an *ager publicus* around here: Mattingly 2006, 385–86.

181. An ongoing isotope study of cattle remains is intended to clarify if cattle supplying the Welsh and northern forts did indeed come from the southeast: Madgwick et al. 2019.

182. Kooistra et al. 2013; Dinter et al. 2014; Verhagen, de Kleijn and Joyce 2021.

183. The regional supply of wine to the forts from the Schedlt Valley and the Tongres/Bavay area: see Laubenheimer and Marlière 2010. At the moment, wine surplus appears to be largely dominated by villas.

184. The arguments and complexities are laid out in Reddé 2018b; Reddé et al. 2018.

185. On the *negotiatores*, see Verboven 2007; Schmidts 2011.

186. Carrié 1998.

187. Brindle 2016a (north); Brindle 2016b (Wales).

188. The fundamental study on ancient demography was Beloch 1886. More recent efforts to calculate the population of Italy: Scheidel 2007a, 2008; Ligt 2012; Hin 2013; the whole empire: Frier 2000; Lo Cascio and Malanima 2005; Scheidel 2007a. New models for Roman urbanization rates have reinvigorated the debates: Hanson 2016, 2022. Rising population and possibility of overpopulation: Frier 2001. Much higher urban populations and their rise through the third century CE: Hanson 2016, 69–72.

189. Density estimates for the Tiber Valley: Witcher 2020, 163–76; for Cambridge: Evans, Aldred and Cooper 2022.

190. For a specific discussion on the density as revealed by commercial archaeology, see Evans, Aldred and Cooper 2022; Reddé 2016. On Cirencester, Powell, Smith and Laws 2010, 138–41. On the extraordinary and increased density of Roman landscapes in these regions more generally: Smith and Fulford 2016, 386–92 (Britain); Reddé 2018a (northern Gaul, with discussion of already dense Iron Age landscapes).

191. Île-de-France: Bernigaud et al. 2017, and for the implications, Ouzoulias 2014.

192. Wendt and Zimmerman 2008, table 1; Brüggler et al. 2017, 22–27.

193. Evans, Aldred and Cooper 2022 compare the results from early-century surveys through aerial and fieldwalking surveys to large-scale commercial archaeology around Cambridge.

194. The clays around Cambridge had been breached already in the later Iron Age, but the processes expanded under Roman rule: Mills 2007. Reims: Achard-Corompt et al. 2017, 495–97. Tiber Valley: Goodchild 2007, 207.

195. Ronin 2018. The Lamasba land list, discussed above, is a product of just such a water dispute—the right to irrigated water: Shaw 1982.

196. Columella, *Rust.* 1.5, 2.4.

197. Arnoldus et al. 2021, 495–96; Bowes 2021c, 68–69; 207–20; 225; and probably located by Campana 2015.

198. Desrayaud 2008; Bernigaud, et al 2017, 450–56; Blanchard 2012.

199. Columella, *Rust.* 3.8, in the context of a debate over how much to pay for a slave vinedresser. Columella's price too high: Duncan-Jones 1974, 49–52, 1976, 11.

200. Averages prices (37–160 CE) from the Oxyrhynchite nome: 475 dr/ar; Arsinoite nome (Fayum): 258 dr/ar. Prices from Kelly 2021, appendix 2.

201. Foxhall 1990, Kehoe 1997 generally and 140 on the juridical corpus dominated by cases between landowners and wealthy tenants; Lo Cascio 2009, 91–113.

202. Kehoe 1988, 1992, and 1997 stresses the risk-aversion and stability of tenancy relationships. I'm not convinced the Egyptian leases, at any rate, point to either risk-reduction or stability, e.g., Rowlandson 1996, 295.

203. Goodchild and Witcher 2009.

204. Principally by Hopkins 1995–96, 202, 207–8.

205. Duncan-Jones 1974, 209, lays out the guesstimates based on investment income.

206. Rents: Nile Valley: Rowlandson 1996, fig. 4; Fayum: Rowlandson 1999; France 1999, 399; Langellotti 2020, chapter 5. Average yields, based on little data, are thought to be 11.5:1, while better ones are to be found at 16:1: Rathbone 1991, 243–45. These high rents have been explained by the fact that they are due only every other year in a rotational system where wheat alternated with fodder crops. This would have made little difference to the smallholders who had to subsist for two years on half their crop or less.

207. Foxhall 1990.

208. Wallace 1938, 13–19.

209. Not unlike Sen's "exchange entitlement mapping," but applied to agricultural outputs: Sen 1983.

210. To date, ancient agricultural production models have mostly run on a macro-scale, to answer macro-questions—the carrying capacity to feed cities, the surplus required to feed military garrisons. A sampling: Erdkamp 2005, 47–49; Goodchild 2007 (a rare and excellent example that includes nonwheat outputs); Goodchild and Witcher 2009. Gaul: Ouzoulias 2006; Rhineland: Kooistra et al. 2013; Dinter et al. 2014; Verhagen, de Kleijn and Joyce 2021. Egypt: Bowman 2013. Other landscapes: Anatolia: Bikoulis 2018; Palmyra: Campmany Jiménez, et al. 2022.

211. I've deliberately eschewed the use of contemporary agricultural simulation software to make these calculations. Although industrial agricultural simulation programs like APSIM have been redesigned to model smallholder farms, in particular taking into account the critical role played by animals—CLEM is one example (https://research.csiro.au/foodglobalsecurity/data-and-tools/models/clem/)—the chronological granularity required by these simulations means that one risks simulating a highly sophisticated systems view that masks huge amounts of guesswork.

212. Appendix 2 details the archaeological and comparative additional data brought to bear and lays out the detailed results.

213. Monte Forco: Plot size: Jones 1963, 130, 147 (grape cultivation), 144. Pievina's holdings were derived from the capacity of its granary, presumed to be built to hold the maximum yield from one year's free-threshing wheat harvest. Bowes 2021c, 104.

214. See above and summarized in Roselaar 2010, 204–7. All but the last are run on cereal crops alone, without wine, oil, fodder and animals. Identification of some veteran farms in Tuscany: Cambi 2002.

215. As foreseen by Erdkamp 2005, 77. See table A.7, model 2 in appendix 2.

216. The *ager publicus* in this region was long gone by the time the Monte Forco farmers came to their plot: Roselaar 2010, 278 on the *ager publicus* in Etruria.

217. Cf. Goodchild 2007, 326.

218. Also noted by Rosenstein 2004.

219. The data is drawn from Evans and Lucas 2019.

220. Model 1 in appendix 2.

221. The data is drawn from Wright et al. 2009; Hamilton-Dyer 2009; and Stevens 2009.

222. The data is drawn from Groot et al. 2009; Groot and Kooistra 2009. My model did not rely on granary sizes, and thus did not make specific use of the critique presented in Martin 2017, although it arrives at a similar result.

223. Original model: Groot et al. 2009, critiqued by Martin 2017. Both model and critique neglected to account for cattle feed.

224. As noted by Ouzoulias 2006, 183, spelt required 25 percent more land for subsistence than free-threshing wheat. Under higher yield conditions produced by rotation or deliberate manuring, net spelt yield might have improved somewhat to around 45 percent of the crop—yet another impetus for even modestly improving practices.

225. Rowlandson 1996, 119–22, using Baer 1962; Bowman 2013, using tax and available land data. The most sophisticated effort to date is Kelly 2022, who produces a stochastic model for

a hypothetical tenant family living on 20 ar, including fodder and income. He also models variable yields due to Nile flood failure, wage labor (presented here in chapter 4) and child mortality, as well as interest payments on debt. His results are more nuanced and more fine-grained, although they don't include the all-critical animals.

226. Data is drawn from Omar 1979 and Elgenedy 2022. Soterichos' archive has served as a kind of Rorschach test for different perspectives on the Egyptian economy and has thus elicited many comments: e.g., Bagnall 1985a, 307; Kehoe 1992, 144; France 1999, 453.

227. Model 1, table A.10, appendix 2.

228. Kelly's (2022) more sophisticated model, which is run on 20 ar of arable alone, without animals or vineyard, lower rents, lower hay prices, and a variable family size, comes to similar conclusions, although with considerably greater financial stability owing to both a larger land portfolio and lower rents.

229. Data is drawn from Foraboschi 1971, corrected by Kehoe 1992, 149–58; Rowlandson 1999, 153–55; Smolders 2011.

230. This is sort of the idea of Rowlandson 1996, 249–51, although she assumes that very low cash rent in fodder years acted to essentially lower overall rents. The fact that wheat-rent years often wiped out much of a smallholder family's food source makes the "lowering" entirely notional.

231. As indicated in Kelly's (2022) models, albeit for different reasons.

232. Hopkins' guess; Hopkins 1980, 119, which is broadly supported by the Egyptian data: low/average yields of 10:1 and tax at 1 art/ar.

233. See Garnsey 1998, 27; cf. Hopkins 1995–96, 198–200, whose revised model didn't allow much space for higher yields or higher rent.

4. Eight Jobs

1. *CIL* 4.10150. Trans. after Mayer 2012, 57. The graffito was scratched on the walls of a stairway leading to a small second-story apartment over the Praedia Julia Felix (II 4,10).

2. Cicero, *Off.* 1.150. See also Varro: *Ling.* 7, 105; Seneca, *Ben.* 3.22.2; and *Ep.* 80.7; Lucian *Merc. Cond.* 4. This elite view parsed: Lis and Soly 2012, 58–63; Freu 2024. On the use of the term "mercenarius" in Latin literature, see Berrendonner 2007.

3. On the ubiquitous language of slavery in Roman thinking, see Lavan 2013.

4. Freu 2022. On specialization and its causes, Erdkamp 2015; Ruffing 2016.

5. Flohr 2016b, 159–62, has noted how specialization and scale increasingly separated those who made things from the end consumers of those things.

6. See Freu 2022, 2024; Banaji 1997, 2001, 206. Cf. Freu 2013.

7. On the commodification of wages: Harper 2016; Freu 2022, 2024. On market forces: Temin 2004.

8. For the tiny collection of non-Egyptian wages, see the summary in Rathbone 2009, 315, to which can be added two graffiti from Pompeii: *CIL* 4.6877; 10606.

9. Drexhage's (1991, 412–39) collection of wages used in Scheidel 2002; Harper 2016, 822–28. Wage series critiqued in Freu 2016b and replaced now by the comprehensive and brilliantly nuanced work of Freu 2022. See also Rathbone 2009.

10. Roman wage series used to argue for the impact of various plagues on wage prices: as debated by Bagnall 2002; Scheidel 2002, 2012; Harper 2016.

11. Real wages: Allen's (2001) original model for a long series of real European wages was followed by real wages generated for particularly Roman contexts: Allen 2009; Scheidel 2010; Harper 2016.

12. As argued for later periods in the collection of essays by Hatcher and Stephenson 2018.

13. As noted by Freu 2016b. For other historical periods, Muldrew 2011, 210; Muldrew 2018; Humphries and Weisdorf 2019, 2871.

14. *CIL* 4.6877.

15. Allen 2001; 2009 uses the 250-day constant, which has been adopted by others. For a critique of the constant, see Humphries and Weisdorf 2019, 2868-71.

16. Humphries and Weisdorf 2019; Horrell, Humphries and Weisdorf 2022.

17. "Makeshifting" is used by Muldrew and King 2003 to describe the many forms that compensation took in coin-poor economies. Definitions of the "informal economy": Elgin 2020, chapter 2. "Gig work" tends to refer to independent contractor-type work—defined in the Roman world by *locatio conductio operis* arrangements. While gig work describes the layered and multiple strands of income observed here, it includes those on a much higher economic level, as well as those close to the bottom of the 90 percent, on which see Rani and Gobel 2023; Ravenelle 2019.

18. For the rise of the what the United States Census refers to as "multiple jobholding" since the mid-1990s, see Bailey and Spletzer 2021. Overwhelmingly multiple jobholding is characteristic of women, Black Americans, and families with lower incomes. Cf. Ravenelle 2019.

19. On the utility of the term "hustle" described in these terms, see Thieme 2018; see also MacMillan Cottom 2020. *Débrouillardise*, or System D, is an analogous concept, similarly value neutral, with an emphasis on daily practice: Neurwirth 2012.

20. Roman law clearly defined wage labor as the free exchange of labor for recompense, one unbound by the status of the parties involved (Thomas 2004). This makes it possible to understand how a slave, for instance, could work for wages, on which see Bürge 2023. But wage in exchange for payment on a debt (*paramone*), in exchange for maintenance (*opsonion*), and in exchange for service (*misthos*) were all regarded as different, and each had their own language. Work in exchange for a product, such as a potter producing a specific number of pots, or stonemasons a number of stones, was governed by a different arrangement—independent contracting (*locatio conductio operis*)—but might overlap with wage work. On the definitions used in Egyptian contracts, see Freu 2022.

21. There is one major source of Roman wage data not used here: Diocletian's Edict on Maximum Prices (*Edictum de pretiis rerum venalium*). Issued in 301 CE, the edict included maximum allowable prices for a whole range of commodities, but also a whole range of different kinds of wage-labor jobs. It would seem a rich source of wage data particularly for those jobs—like artisanal work—we are missing from the Egyptian corpus. We will not use it here. A top-down effort directed mostly at state (principally military) suppliers, the Edict is a record of what people should have been paid, not what they were actually paid. While the ratios paid to different jobs is useful for those interested in wage formation (Frézouls 1977; Groen-Vallinga and Tacoma 2016), and the astonishingly little value accorded to work versus commodity reflects some of the findings here (Frézouls 1978), the absolute numbers are impossible to compare with the earlier, first to third-century wages that are our subject.

22. The different kinds of wage-paying work in Egypt are now thoroughly reviewed and cataloged by Freu 2022.

23. E.g., *P. Mil. Vogl.* 2.58; 7.302.

24. On clothing as part of remuneration, see Freu 2022, 234–36.

25. Bagnall and Frier 1994, 67–69, and more recently Huebner 2013, on the temporal and geographic variation in Egyptian households.

26. On the census figures, see Bagnall and Frier 1994, 70–71. On slavery in Egypt more generally see Bagnall 1993, 123–27. A maximalist view is found in Harper 2011, 517, who believes the rural *oiketai* might have been enslaved.

27. The best catalog of these many taxes remains Wallace 1938.

28. On liturgies generally, Lewis 1999, 156–84; on wages earned from liturgy distribution: Rathbone 1991, 122. For the third-century date of the assignment of liturgies to village or estate groups for allocation, see Rathbone 1996, 339.

29. As argued by Rowlandson 2001. See also Rathbone 1991, 112–13; Rathbone 2013. More generally on account money, see Verboven 2009.

30. Wages are generally sticky, now as then: Bewley 1999 on contemporary wage rigidity; Hatcher 2018, 23, on historical wage stickiness. Cf. Bernard 2023 on the particular reasons for Roman wage stickiness.

31. Rathbone 1996; Harper 2016.

32. Rathbone 1996, 1997.

33. Rathbone 2009; Scheidel 2010.

34. *P. Lond.* 131r.(v.) and r.*(r.). See Johnson 1938, 181–87; and Świderek 1960 for commentary. The find spot of the accounts is unclear, but they came from somewhere in the Hermopolite nome: Budge 1920, 2: 148–50; Sayce 1923, 332–34.

35. Lands owned by the descendants of Patron, previously (and erroneously) termed the lands of Laches: for an overview see Bagnall 1974; further commentaries on its management by a group of different managers representing different family members can be found in Foraboschi 1981; Kehoe 1992, 74–92; Smolders 2013. On the Appianus estate, Rathbone 1991.

36. Estimated as about half the labor force on the Appianus estate, more during the harvest: Rathbone 1991, table 11 assumes that the *oiketai* and *metremaitaioi* were working full-time for the estate, which, as we'll see, may not be entirely true. If they weren't, then the proportion of daily wage labor would be higher. On the Patron lands, casual labor also appears to be the majority: Takahashi 2021, 128–29.

37. *Paides* is also a word used for slaves. "Children," not "slaves," is the most common meaning in the papyrological corpus: Mirković 2005, 140–41.

38. *P. Lond.* 131r., 27–40.

39. Nowhere are these individuals named as slaves, and their status is based on the fact that they never receive wages or other remuneration. Johnson was certain they were slaves (1938, 177, 186); Świderek (1960, 103) had her doubts; Freu (2022, 69) assumed they were.

40. See instance in *P. Mil. Vogl.* 7.302.175-277; *P. Mil. Vogl.* 7.305.

41. Variation: some persons not named as boys paid only two or three obols, some boys paid four obols and some boys paid the same rate as adult workers. See, e.g., *P. Mil. Vogl.* 7.302, 305, 306; and Foraboschi 1981, 28–33.

42. Rathbone 1991, table 12. The average conceals a low of 1 dr. 5 ob. and a high of 4 dr. for some heavy or harvest work.

43. Patron: *P. Mil. Vogl.* 7.304 and Foraboschi 1981, 28–33; Appianus: Rathbone 1991, 171 and table 12.

44. For other instances among many, see *P. Mil. Vogl.* 302.179–82: on the 27th of Mesore one worker raising the canal banks made 7 ob., while on the 28th, 10 workers made only 6, while a possible foreman made 7.

45. Takahashi 2021, 125. For more general observations on labor supply, and how workers may have gotten jobs in the city of Rome, see Holleran 2017.

46. Freu has suggested a shift toward monthly wages over time (2013, 199), pointing to the greater presence of monthly workers in third- and fourth-century estate accounts.

47. Payments in food, e.g., *P. Mil. Vogl.* 2.58; payments in cash: collected in Foraboschi 1981, 28–33; and summarized by Freu 2022, 244, who emphasizes the higher salaries.

48. Rathbone 1991, 91–147.

49. Freu (2022, 101–23) notes the more specialized jobs of those who get monthly wages versus day-laborers.

50. Berrondonner 2007.

51. Rathbone 2009, 315–16.

52. See Cicero, *Pro. Rosc. Com.* 28 (3 HS per day) for Rome, in a rhetorical context. More reliable are two graffiti from the Vesuvian cities: *CIL* 4.6877; 10606 cite broadly similar amounts.

From an earlier age, second-century BCE wages for a cattle driver, including cattle rental, cited at 2 HS per day, while a skilled constructor of olive mills cited at 8 HS: Cato, *Agr*. 22.3; 21.21.5, respectively. On western wages generally, Rathbone 2009, 314–17. On wages in the Vesuvian cities, see Santomato 2014, 324–25; Verboven 2017, 369–70.

53. See also chapter 2 and Rathbone 2009, 314–16.

54. Robert Allen, who introduced the method to comparative historical economics, originally termed this a "welfare ratio": Allen 2001, 2009, 2013, 2015.

55. Most previous estimates for bare-bones costs of Roman-Egyptian living land on around 8–10 drachmas per month in the first through second centuries, and double this for the first half of the third century. Different calculative bases have been used: using wheat prices as a placeholder: Rathbone 2009 (1 artaba or 4–5 modii of wheat; around 8 dr/month); Huebner 2013 (price of 1 artaba of wheat + 20 percent); calculation of more complex consumption baskets: Scheidel 2010, who used Allen's original, lower-calorie bare-bones basket (1940 kcal for a male, multiplied by 3 for a family). Drexhage's (1991, 444) more granular accounting includes the cost of 1.16 artabai of wheat, 2 kotyle of oil and 0.87 keramia of wine to arrive at 12–18 dr per month in the first and second centuries, and some 33 after the 160s. None includes taxes.

56. See appendix 3 for the numbers.

57. Low-calorie costs of living: taken from Scheidel 2010, 432, with rationale at 430–32. Scheidel's list, drawn from Allen's original, low-calories version (Allen 2009, 421, cf. Allen 2015, table 2), includes principally foodstuffs, with a small amount for lamp oil, and a notional add-on of 5 percent for housing. The 5 percent add-on appears too low, as preserved housing costs, even in the rural villages, were mostly somewhat higher (Drexhage 1991, 92; Rathbone 1991, 109–10; cf. Kelly 2023, 58–59, where housing is reversed calculated based on Scheidel's numbers). Sustainable costs of living: listed in appendix 3. Taxes included in both costings are poll and dike (*komatikon*) taxes, or for the Appianus estate, the *isophorion*. Because of the tax requirements (which fell on adult men only), the family basket is not an even multiplier of the male basket. As a reference, these sustainable costs are around two times the costs of a wheat-only equivalent for a male individual, and about 1.6 times that for a family.

58. These estimated taxes are probably too low, as they include only poll and dike taxes: there might also be taxes for the baths, drinking water, and other services. Indeed, an indebted weaver who agreed to work for free in exchange for tax payments listed some six types of tax he owed: *PSI* 8.902; duplicated in *P. Mich*. 5.355. See Montevecchi 1950, 31–33.

59. Scheidel's "bare-bones" costs for a family equal individual costs multiplied by 3—thus, a somewhat larger family. Scheidel 2010, 432.

60. The Epimachus accounts are the best, as they include nine months of almost complete data. The Patron lands have a handful of months of almost-complete data, although these were accounted by plot, not the whole estate.

61. The cost of subsistence divided by the average wage provides the minimum number of days required to make subsistence. Multiplying the minimum labor pool by those days provides the number of person-days that would be required for that labor pool to make a subsistence living. The average number hired per day times 30 provides the number of worker-days actually provided by the estate in that month. Comparing these two numbers—person-days required and person-days produced—reveals an absurdly optimistic estimate of the subsistence-supporting labor opportunities in any given month. The emphasis here is on "optimistic": all of the assumptions used to produce the estimates imagine full employment for a minimum number of people, a fantasy that's good to think with. Estimates of the probability of an individual worker earning enough for subsistence can also be made using a cumulative probability on a binomial distribution: $\mathrm{p}\,(\mathrm{X}+\mathrm{k}) = ({}^{\mathrm{n}}/_{\mathrm{k}})\mathrm{p}^{\mathrm{k}}\,(1-\mathrm{p})^{\mathrm{n}-\mathrm{k}}$, where *n* is the total number of days, *k* is the number of days a worker is hired, and *p* is the probability of being hired on any given day.

62. The principal challenge is distinguishing those who had taxes paid on their behalf, and those who didn't: Rathbone 1991, 121–47 wrestles with this question for the employees of the Appianus estate.

63. Freu 2022, 270, and Rathbone 1991, 135–39 on possible relationships between daily and some *metrematiaioi* monthly rates. See also below.

64. As has been long noted: Rathbone 1991, 109 (on the *oiketai* monthly wages); Cuvigny 1996, 144; Takahashi 2021, 125 (for those on the Patron lands).

65. As noted by Rathbone 1991, 109.

66. Freu, relying on Scheidel and Bagnall's estimates for living costs, comes to somewhat different conclusions, arguing that only those in her first salary bracket of 12–15 dr in total monthly compensation would have been unable to support themselves, with around 30 dr as the threshold past which family labor was less necessary (Freu 2022, 263–71). It's important to note, too, that overall high compensation for some employees on her list includes taxes paid on behalf of the employee. Some would have been just *isophorion* (i.e., the per capita portion of village tax burden), but others, as we'll see below, were probably land taxes.

67. See Allen 2001; Humphries and Weisdorf 2019, 2873; Horrell, Humphries and Weisdorf 2021, fig. 1, for England.

68. As argued long ago by Allen 2009, on the basis of Diocletian's Price Edict.

69. Historians reading these wages in their local contexts have long noted that they appear too low to be a whole income: Foraboschi 1981, 35; Rathbone 1991, 165–66 (who calculates a monthly subsistence cost of c. 35 dr with taxes); Drexhage 1991, 440–54; Freu 2022, 198, 265–67. Cf. Allen (2009) and Scheidel (2010), who assume they constituted the majority of a whole livelihood and that their unsustainability left the majority of the populace in total penury.

70. As long noted by those who have studied these accounts: Rathbone 1991, 164 on the casual laborers on the Appianus estate; Takahashi 2021, 129, on the Patron lands. For other historical periods, the practice is also ubiquitous: Dyer 1989, 133, 2002, 159–60; Muldrew 2011, 246–57.

71. Cato *Agr.* 4, 13, 66–67, 144–45; Varro, *Rust.* 1, 17. See also Tietz 2020.

72. *P. Lond.* 131r. 32, 55, 81, 273, 312, 497, 505–11, 523–25, 566–72.

73. *P. Mil. Vogl.* 2.52.25, 37, 46, 76 (from 138 CE). See also Bagnall 1974, 171–72.

74. Other examples of similar hustlers from the Patron archives include: Ammonas: *P. Mil. Vogl.* 2.52.22; Orseus: P. *Mil. Vogl.* 2.52.50, 87, 117. Bagnall 1974, 171.

75. E.g., one Ankolis: *P. Mil. Vogl.* 2. 52.2, 14, 17, 43.

76. Medieval Spain: Marfany 2018; Bohemia: Ogilvie 2001; America: Wright 1988 (addressing mostly off-farm wage-labor); Chang, Huang and Chen 2012 (on the decisions about family labor deployment).

77. As noted by Rathbone 1991, 135–39 and Freu 2022, 270.

78. Rathbone 1991, 136–38.

79. Their wages are ascertained by multiple months' wage records, collected in Rathbone 1991, 99.

80. Tax payments are collected by Rathbone 1991, table 9, 130–31.

81. On the *didrachmon*, see Wallace 1938, 67–68; Gara 1979.

82. Rathbone 1991, Text 1r. 241; Text 1v. 55, 62, 72, 77, 82.

83. Rathbone 1991, 268–69, thinks the animals of Poaris' and all the others named as having teams of asses or cattle were owned by the estate.

84. *P. Mil. Vogl.* 3.147. Bagnall 1974, 160.

85. Takahashi 2021, 124–25.

86. Rathbone 1991, 121–22.

87. *P. Prag.* 3.240.ii.18.

88. *P. Flor.* 375.1, 7, 13, 21, 27–29. See also Rathbone 1991, 122, and table 6 for Kastor. On the liturgies, Lewis 1997, μαγδωλοφυλακία (37); διεραματίτης (21). In theory, some grain-transporting liturgies had a minimum wealth requirement of 200–600 dr (φυλακία, Lewis 1997, 49), although not, seemingly, the διεραματίτης.

89. To give some sense, in early modern England, some 60 percent of the English population aged 15–24 was "in service" at any given time—a huge migration of younger workers out of their homes and into income- and subsistence-bearing positions. See Cooper 2005.

90. On which, for England, see Humphries and Weisdorf 2015; Horrell and Humphries 2019; Horrell, Humphries and Weisdorf 2021; Sweden: Molinder and Pihl 2022; Spain: Drelichman and González Agudo 2020.

91. For the predominance of piecework versus wages for Roman women, Freu 2022, 198.

92. Minnen 1986; Carrié 2004, 38.

93. Carrié 2004, 38–39 on the total population involved in textile work. He calculates two spinners necessary for every weaver, while Wild (2002) assumes five spinners and thus that up to half the population of Roman Britain was engaged in textile production. For some calculations on the number of textile workers required to clothe the city of Alexandria, Menten-Plesters 2017, 118.

94. On spinning in Roman Egypt generally, Gällnö 2013, although without discussion of income. For a rare woman and her daughters who declare their profession for the census as spinners: *P. Kellis* P99.2a and 2d. See also *BGU* 10.1942 for another private list of female textile workers, probably mostly enslaved women.

95. *PSI* 6.599, a letter from the Ptolemaic period, describes four weavers taking six days to produce a linen garment, charging either around 4 dr per piece or 1.5 obols per day for men, and 0.5 obols per day for a woman. This reflects the much lower prices of the third century BCE. Most other weaving contracts and wage data come from late antiquity, with its much higher, postinflationary wages and price: Freu 2022, 144–55.

96. *P. Oxy.* 31.2593. Apollonia also claims she had 30 staters of wool spun for a stater, i.e., 4 dr, which comes out to about the same thing—1 ob per stater.

97. Spinning rates depend on the weight of the spindle whorl and the thickness of the resultant yarn. See Andersson et al. 2008 for experimental rates using Bronze Age spindle replicas: 40 g (or 40 m)/hour is average. Other experiments and some 18th-century spinning rates were about twice this rate, but for the latter, it's not clear if the spinners were using wheels or spindles: Harlow 2021, table 8.2 (ancient rates); 18th-century rates: Muldrew 2012, 505–7.

98. For the similar importance of women's spinning income in early modern England, Muldrew 2011, 234–46; Muldrew 2012.

99. *P. Kell. Copt.* 18.7; 58. For other family weaving businesses in the same house, *P. Kell. Copt.* 76; 96. See also Hope and Bowen 2022, 46–47.

100. *P. Kell. Copt.* 44; cf. 48 from the same house. The rates indicated here (1616 nummi for 3 mina of weft and 2 of warp) is hard to translate into time or pieces. Wages in these documents distinguish between "weaving wages" and "wool wages," perhaps wool preparation and spinning. On spinning carried out by the family or sent out, see *P. Kell. Copt.* 18, 58B.

101. Cash wages: *P. Kell. Copt.* 48. 18ff.: 13 weaving days are paid at 800 talents, or 60 talents per day. Barley wages: *P. Kell. Copt.* 48.20: Lo receives 3 maji (1/12 artaba) of barley for three days of weaving. See also Gardner, Alcock and Funck 1999, 270.

102. Collected in Manca Masciadri and Montevecchi 1982. See also Freu 2022, 228–30, 249, 266.

103. See Manca Masciadri and Montevecchi 1982. Hobson (1984) suggested the increase in these contracts during some poor harvest years in the 40s CE, as women used their lactating bodies in exchange for loans of cash to their families. Most of the nursing-for-loan contracts

included a loan of 100–120 dr (see chapter 5 in this book), roughly equivalent to the yearly value of the nonloan contracts.

104. *P. Lond.* 131r. 202, 291.

105. *P. Lond.* 131r.* 9 (?), 13.

106. *P. Brux.* desc. Bingen 1951. See also Rathbone 1991, 126–27.

107. On which Bradley 1985; Laes 2008; Porena 2016, the latter two of which are focused mostly on enslaved children.

108. On which, see Lewit 2022. For girls winnowing grain, *P. Fay.* 102.

109. Boys hauling manure: *P. Lond.* 131r. 12; girls on building sites: *BGU* 3.894.

110. See *P. Brux.* desc. On which, see Bingen 1951. Another such account, for Aunes, a daily-wage worker, had his own labor credit augmented by that of his father, who seemed to have worked for a day cutting sesame: *P. Prag.* 3.240.iii.36–49.

111. On which, see Bradley 1985; Freu 2011, 2016a; Vuolanto 2015; Hawkins 2016, 192–267.

112. While it was mostly boys and enslaved girls who were apprenticed out to learn the textile trade, free-born girls would occasionally be sent out as well but would have also been readily trained at home: Minnen 1998.

113. On the variety of arrangements we have labeled "apprenticeship," see Freu 2011.

114. Averages calculated from data collected by Bergamesco 1995, 162–64, seven apprentice contracts from the first and second centuries CE.

115. On apprenticeships building knowledge capital, Freu 2016. Vuolanto (2015) sees apprentice families as "middling" in wealth and thus motivated by needs other than survival.

116. Letter pleading for flax to spin: *SB* 14.11881.

117. Nadeau and Glasmeier 2016. The same has been true in many historical periods: see Muldrew 2011, table 5.19 for 16th–17th-century England.

118. Hawkins 2016.

119. Some work has been based solely on Diocletian's Edict on Maximum Prices: see *Edictum de pretiis* 7.1.9; 7.1.32; Groen-Vallinga and Tacoma 2016; Frézouls 1977, 1978. For a skill premium based on broader data, see Bernard 2023. Thanks to Seth Bernard for sharing this article prior to its publication.

120. E.g., *P. Mil. Vogl.* 7.304; Foraboschi 1981, 28–33.

121. Rathbone 1991, table 12.

122. *P. Mil. Vogl.* 7.304; also Foraboschi 1981, 65.

123. *P. Flor.* 69. See Casson 1990. The possibility that this boat construction belongs to the Appianus estate comes from the fact that accounts of the estate appear on the document's verso (*P. Flor.* 2.123–124). For the navigability of the Bahr Yussef: Derda 2006. The Appianus estate lies far from both the Nile and the Bahr Yussef, adjacent to the Bahr El-Nazla feeder canal, and near Lake Mareotis.

124. For Kanopos and Hermas: *SB* 9408.2 & 9409.7 = Rathbone 1991, text 1, ll. 68–78; 84–93; 160; *SB* 9409.2 and 12382 = Rathbone 1991, text 2, ll. 67–68, 76; *SB* 16.12381.4.

125. On Hermas' role as *komarch*: *SB* 20.14645. On Hermas as the same person as the carpenter in the accounts: Rathbone 1991, 130. On the role of the *komarch*: Thomas 1975; in Theadelphia, France 1999, 189; on the wealth requirement, Lewis 1997, 35. Land required perhaps only some 2–3 arourae: for the land prices in the Arisinoite nome in the early third century, Drexhage 1991, 131.

126. *P. Oxy.* 3.498.

127. After Wild 2002, 31, based on *PSI* 6.599 (the third-century BCE letter, describing four persons producing a linen sheet in six days of weaving, cited above), 23 dr average tunic price (Drexhage 1991, 109) and a third deducted for raw materials. This also assumes they are doing their own spinning. Cf. Carrié 2004, 39, who argues that a single weaver plus a couple of

assistants could produce 55 tunic/cloak combos per year, considerably more than assumed in the model here.

128. As also suggested by *PSI* 6.599, where the per-piece option presented by the weavers probably earned them somewhat more income per month than the per-day wage option. See Clarysse and Vandorpe 1995, 64–65.

129. The massive demand for building labor—free as well as enslaved—in the city of Rome: Brunt 1980; DeLaine 1997, 175–94; Bernard 2017. These observations are necessarily qualitative, as we have very little idea how much these workers in Rome were paid. More generally, see Erdkamp 2015.

130. Lace making: Thirsk 1961; beer brewing: Dyer 2002, 170–71; modern smallholders: Anderson and Ahmed 2016, 29–35; Banerjee and Duflo 2007, 152–54. See also Sterling 1965, 88 (20th-century Turkish farmers/artisans); Hill 1986, 10 (West African and Indian artisan/farmers).

131. *P. Mil. Vogl.* 2.52.24, 26.

132. *SB* 1.5124. France 1999, 461–62. On the *naubion* tax, see Wallace 1938, 69–71.

133. *BGU* 9.1900. French 1999, 461.

134. France 1999, 461.

135. For the stats, see Ferdière 2006 (Gaul): Olcese 2011–12, now somewhat out of date with many new rural sites discovered (Italy).

136. See the edition in Cockle 1981.

137. Cockle 1981, 96–97, took a stab at a calculation based on wheat prices and Hopkins' subsistence models, and landed on a maximum of nine families employed.

138. In Italy, see for instance the sites at Marzuolo: Vaccaro, Capelli and Ghisleni 2017; Bowes, Vaccaro et al. 2021; Van Oyen 2020; Vignano: Menchelli and Picchi 2016; Scopietto: Bergamini 2011. On Gaul: Ferdière 2006, 15–18; and Goodman 2013, 127–30 on production in *vici*.

139. For instance: Pievina: Ghisleni et al. 2010; Il Cotone: Schörner 2020; Selvasecca: Berggren 1969. As particularly common in first-century CE Britain: Smith 2017, 203–7. On the potter-farmers of Addenbrooke: Evans 2008, 128ff.

140. As noted for Gaul by Deru and González Villaescusa 2014; Goodman 2013, 125; Van Oyen 2016; Italy: Bowes, Vaccaro et al. 2021. On the seasonal workshop practices of ceramic *officinae*, see Murphy 2016.

141. Smith 2017, 183–86.

142. Smith 2017, 185; Schrüfer-Kolb 2004.

143. Britain: Smith 2017, 212–16; Gaul: Dekoninck and De Clerq 2022.

144. In Gaul, specialized ironworking villages appeared to be less connected with farming: Ferdière 2006, 11–13.

145. See Ruffing 2016, for urbanization and specialized work.

146. Guarding: e.g., *P. Customs* 573–96 (archers at a customs post); water systems: *P. Lond.* 3.1177; Bruun 2003; Capitoline temple in Arsinoe: *BGU* 2.362. For the collection of imperial wages in Egypt, Freu 2022, table 6 and 276–78. Freu sees imperial jobs as better remunerated, which, compared to the lowest-level agricultural jobs, they surely were. On average, though, the difference for unskilled (guarding) work isn't remarkable until the later empire.

147. For private sector managerial salaries, we have only one other datapoint: *P. Theon.* 3; 13. It's not until the early third century that Heroninos, one of the accountants for the Appianus estate, made 40 dr/month.

148. The standard study for pay at Mons Claudianus is Cuvigny 1996. Since then, see corrections and additions in Cuvigny 2000, 2021g. The only other mining wage data is much more fragmentary and comes from the gold mines in Dacia (modern Romania): Noeske 1977 presents the evidence from the wooden tablets. See also Hirt 2010, 270–72.

149. For the organization of the quarry workers, see Cuvigny 2021g.

150. See Cuvigny 2021g and 2021b.

151. *O. Claud.* 8867; Cuvigny 2021h.

152. It has been argued that these constituted an empire-wide wage rate for imperial mining jobs, on the basis of comparison with gold-miner wages in Romania: Cuvigny 1996, 142–45. On the three Romanian Alburnus Major tablets with miner wages: *CIL* 3, pp. 944–49, with commentary by Noeske 1977, 396–404.

153. Occasional children's wages are preserved at both Mons Claudianus (Cuvigny 1996, 140–41) and Alburnus Major (*CIL* 3, p. 948; Noeske 1977, 402–3), but it doesn't seem to have been common practice.

154. For the texts: literary texts: Tacitus, *Ann.* 1.17.4; Suetonius, *Iul.* 26.3; *Dom.* 7.3; papyri: *RMR* 68–72 (= Roman Military Records; Fink 1971). For the arguments, Brunt 1950; Watson 1958; Speidel 1971; Duncan-Jones 1990, chapter 4; Speidel 1992, 2014; versus Alston 1994; Rathbone 2008; and see now Cuvigny 2021a and 2021f.

155. For a brief time, under the emperor Domitian, it was increased to four.

156. As per Speidel 1992. Alston (1994) argues that auxiliaries and legionaries were paid the same.

157. As we'll discuss, other records for money on deposit find some soldiers with significant savings, and many with significant debts: see *RMR* 70, 71, 73–74.

158. *P. Lat. Gen.* 1 and 4 (*RMR* 68, 69). Even higher deductions are to be found in the Masada paybooks to legionaries: *P. Yadin* 722, one of the reasons Alston read them as accounting for only part of soldiers' pay.

159. Phang 2001, with the relevant texts, including the Cattaoui papyri that contain excerpts of cases brought before the prefect of Egypt on the subject.

160. As noted by Rathbone 2009, 312, who wonders how soldiers appear to have accumulated the savings to purchase lavish funerary monuments.

161. Tacitus, *Ann.* 13.35, who further suggests that these soldiers were not above selling their armor for profit.

162. *RMR* 58.5; 80.1–3. See also Roth 1999, 91 on *immunes*. On the overlapping activities and difficulty of distinguishing civilian and military suppliers, see Whittaker 2002, 207–19.

163. For the question of state-management versus private outsourcing of military supply during the Principate, see Erdkamp 2002b; cf. Whittaker 2002. The problem looks different depending on the sources one reads: the literary sources preferentially discuss the former, while the local, on-the-ground records, like the Vindolanda tablets and Eastern Desert ostraca, preserve the latter.

164. A conclusion reached by Speidel 1992, 78–79, on the basis of records like *RMR* 70, and further confirmed by ostraca from the Eastern Desert forts: Cuvigny 2021a, 2021f.

165. Cuvigny 2021a; 2021f; *RMR* 76 (for hay); 78.

166. As alleged by Sallust, *Iug.* 44.5; 45.2, during the Jugurthine War. Cuvigny (2021f, 352–53) notes that some ostraca attest to low (i.e. 5 dr/art) grain prices in army camps, something the soldiers could have potentially profited from when they left camp. The *pagani* at Mons Claudianus also regularly sold their wheat: *O. Bahira* 20; Cuvigny 2021h.

167. On sutlers and their entanglement with the army, see Whittaker 2002; Roth 1999, 96–101. On the family relationships between sutlers and the soldiers, see Verboven 2007b, especially 304; Kolbeck 2018. Most of these authors are concerned with the larger-scale supply of the army by *negotiatores*. Cuvigny 2003 and Bowman 1998, examining the records from the Eastern Desert and Vindolanda, respectively, parse the detailed evidence for sutler families.

168. On Zosime, see Cuvigny 2003, 395.

169. Vindolanda: see *Tab. Vindol.* 2.181, 182, 184.

170. The ostraca archive of Philokles is published by Bülow-Jacobsen 2019. See also Redon 2019; Cuvigny 2003, 376–83.

171. On prostitution in the circle of Philokles, Cuvigny 2003, 383–89; Cuvigny 2021d; 2021e. Bülow-Jacobsen 2019, 38–41 discusses the prostitute Iulia and possible prostitute/madam Tiberia, who may be daughters of Philokles or his wives.

172. *O. Dios.* 439. Cuvigny 2021c.

173. Collected in Cuvigny 2003, 388.

174. On the *pittakion* and *quintana* passage taxes, see Cuvigny 2003, 374–75, 2021d. In *O. Krok.* 219 and 221, it appears that the clients paid the 12 dr *quintana.*

175. *O. Krok.* 2.218.

176. *P. Mil. Vogl.* 2.58; see also *P. Mil. Vogl.* 7.302 for some of the same women. Takahashi 2021, 120–21.

177. Rathbone 1991, 89–91, lays out the case for their having been freeborn. On slave tenants, see Vlassopolous 2021, 58–59 with previous literature. Bürge (2023) makes the case, largely on the basis of Roman legal evidence, that wage labor was dominated by hired slaves, a finding that seems dubious for Egypt, if not more generally.

178. Rathbone 1991, 106–16, argues convincingly for their free status. Harper (2016, 513–18) leaves open the door for their being slaves, at least by the later empire.

179. Cuvigny 2000, 33–36. The pay terminology for these people is not much more helpful. None of these possible slaves are listed as receiving a *misthos,* a wage in exchange for service, but rather only an *opsonion,* a subsistence. But many other people who are clearly not enslaved only receive *opsonia* as well, for the term could sometimes be a synonym for *misthos.* On which Freu 2013, 292, 2016, 168.

180. See Gamauf 2009; Silver 2016; Cohen 2023; *TPSulp.* 45, 51, 52, 67.

181. Van der Veen et al. 2018; Leguilloux 2018.

182. Marx actually imagined a form of hustling as part of his ideal communist society—the dream of escaping from the division of labor and doing something different each day (*Die deutsche ideologie,* 1.A.4). This is patently not the hustling we're talking about here.

5. The 90 Percent and Their Money

1. Brown 1971, 49 drew our attention to the sleeping and dreaming of the historical subject.

2. On Artemidorus as having an all-class clientele, see Thoneman 2020, 177–89.

3. *Oneirocritica* 3.41. Adopted from translation of Harris-McCoy 2012, 281.

4. Some useful overviews of the question: Lo Cascio 1996; Aarts 2005; Harris 2006, 2008; Verboven 2009; Reden 2010, 3–8; Hoyer 2018b, 63–67; Elliot 2020, 20–50.

5. On the importance of the fiduciary value of Roman money as visible particularly during the moments of major debasement, see Rathbone 1996; Verboven 2007a; Harl 2015. This fiduciary system broke down in the later third century: Haklai-Rotenberg 2011.

6. The quote is from Hopkins 1980, 104, who actually imagined a far greater supply and use of money than the traditional statist model had supposed. But even he thought that supply and use met its limits in the countryside, where coin would only be used to pay rent or tax.

7. The classic statist works are Finley 1999, 196: "money was essentially coined metal and little else"; Crawford 1970; Rodewald 1976; Duncan-Jones 1994.

8. On the crisis of 33 CE, see the historiography laid out in Elliott 2015; cf. Crawford 1970, 46; Duncan-Jones 1994, 23–25.

9. For hoards as evidence for army pay and other fiscal handouts termed *congiaria,* Duncan-Jones 1994, 67–94. The more recent data for the hoards in the northwest provinces is summarized in Mairat, Howgego and Wilson 2022.

10. Crawford 1970, 43–45.

11. Hopkins (1980, 104) argument, based on Crawford's (1974) study of Republican coins.

12. For instance, Howgego 1992, 1994; Harl 1996; Andreau 1999a, 107–10.

13. New evidence from hoards is summarized by the articles in Mairat, Howgego and Wilson 2022. Regional studies on overall levels of monetization from coin finds: Africa: Hoyer 2018; Britain: Reece 2004; Walton 2012.

14. First suggested by Ligt 1990, 1991; more expansively argued by Howgego 1992. Hollander (2007, 122–35) sees rural monetization in the Republic as characterized less by supply than by diminished need and frequency of use.

15. Hoyer 2018, 64–72; Katsari 2008. See also Reece 2016 for some data on denarii, sestertii and lower-value bronzes in western Roman provinces.

16. On the calculation of coin output on the basis of die studies: first efforts: Crawford 1974, 640–707; Hopkins 1980; pessimism: Buttrey 1994. Early high estimates: Duncan-Jones 1994. Critiques and revisions: De Callataÿ 1995; Lockyear 1999; Albarède et al. 2021; Bransbourg 2022; Mayer forthcoming. Thanks to Emanuel Mayer for sharing drafts of this work prior to publication.

17. Deep monetization: Lucassen 2014; as applied in Roman contexts in its original broader sense of broadly based monetized thinking: Verboven 2009, 105.

18. As emphasized by Ingen 2000.

19. Millett 1995; Brindle 2017, 263–64; Howgego and Wilson 2022, 13; Aarts 2005.

20. On barter, cf. Aubert 2014.

21. Verboven 2009, 124.

22. For similar comments on different monetary modes, see Hopkins 1980 (monetary planes); Hollander 2007, 7 ("variety of objects"); Elliot 2018, 20–50 (importance of "embedding contexts" for understanding coin versus other monetary instruments). This account follows the basic definitions set out in Verboven 2009.

23. Harris 2006, 2008, 2019.

24. The jurists on the uses of the credit (having to do with ship loans): *Dig.* 12.1; 14.1.8–11; and *Dig.* 14.1.7. See also Harris 2006.

25. Finley 1952, 79–87; Finley 1999, 115–19.

26. E.g., Livy 2.23. On debt among the Republican peasantry occasioned by conscription, poor harvests, and land grabs, see Rosenstein 2004, especially 54–55; Bernard 2016.

27. Foraboschi 1971, xxix–xxxiii; 1982; Foraboschi and Gara 1981, 340–43, whose elegant model for the difference between interest rates on cash versus wheat loans runs aground on these assumptions; Gara 1988, 946.

28. Graeber 2014, especially 228–32 on the ancient Mediterranean. For an analysis of some of Graeber's concepts as applied to the "axial age" of the ancient world, see Weisweiler 2022.

29. As recognized by Kelly 2023, whose data-driven study of Egyptian financial relationships comes to many of the same conclusions as this one.

30. Hopkins 1980.

31. The Roman monetary system underwent major changes in the third century CE that had a huge impact on coin use. In short, some combination of debasement (minting coins with less precious metal content) and the revaluation of the relationship between gold, silver and bronze resulted in the eventual demolition of the silver denarius. The result was the introduction of huge numbers of tiny bronze coins (*nummi*), because huge quantities—measured now in weight, not number—were now needed to pay for even small purchases. For these reasons, this chapter focuses only on the period up to around 260 CE, the point at which these changes began to be felt. For the origins and impacts of the third-century monetary crisis, there is a sizable bibliography: Bagnall 1985b; Rathbone 1996, 1997, 2009; Lo Cascio 1997; Verboven 2007a; Harl 2015; Butcher 2015. For the impact of the need for all those tiny bronze coins on rural coin finds and supply, see Reece 2004.

32. Stannard 2018, 2021.

33. Two of the best places to see these ups-and-downs of supply are Britain (Reece 1991, and for the copies Walton 2012, 79–80), and the Vesuvian cities (Duncan-Jones 2003; cf. Bransbourg 2022, 147–51; Talierico Mensitieri 2012; cf. earlier shortage of small change: Stannard 2018, 2019).

34. See the articles published in the 2024 issue of the *Revue Belge de Numismatique*. Thanks to Lucia Carbone for conversations on this issue.

35. Walton 2012, 79–80; Carbone 2018.

36. Rowlandson 2001; cf. Rathbone 2013, 135–36.

37. E.g., in Egypt, see Maresch 1996; and more broadly Bresson 2017b.

38. As emphasized particularly by Hollander 2007; 122–35, 2008. See also Katsari 2008.

39. This discussion of Pompeii is taken in part from a longer article on coined savings from that town: Bowes 2022. Earlier discussions include Breglia 1950; Duncan-Jones 2003; Taliercio Mensitieri 2012; Depeyrot 2016.

40. The many problems with the atypical moment preserved in the Pompeii coinage are summarized by Andreau 2008; Bransbourg 2022, 144–47; Bowes 2022, 3–7. Depeyrot 2016, 64, on the other hand, viewed the coin finds as representative, not only of a typical Pompeiian scene but of all Italian towns of its size.

41. The Keynesian division of monetary demand—transactions, precautionary and speculative—seems overly determined and, in the latter two kinds of demand, impossible to disentangle. Cf. Hollander 2007.

42. Taliercio Mensitieri 2012.

43. Cf. Duncan-Jones 1994; Jongman 2003, who assumed gold functioned principally as a vehicle for savings. See Lo Cascio 2008, who takes a more nuanced view, and Mayer forthcoming for Nero's aureus outputs. See Bresson 2017 for a broader discussion of how metal differences and the exchange taxes on bronze impacted economic inequality in the ancient world.

44. Bransbourg 2022, 147–51.

45. Taliercio Mensitieri 2007, 2012.

46. Taliericio Mensitieri 2012, 201–3.

47. Ligt 1990; Howgego 1992, 19–22; Hollander 2007, 122–35 on arguments for varying levels of rural monetization and/or demand.

48. The data here comes from the most recent effort to do so, paying particular attention to different kinds of rural places: Brindle 2017. However, this effort rests on a long tradition of tracking rural money use: Reece 1991, 2004; Walton 2012.

49. On the rural origins of copies, see Brindle 2017, 260–61. For a similar phenomenon in Spain, see Carbone 2018.

50. Walton 2012.

51. Brindle 2017, 237–39.

52. Cf. Katsari 2008, who, although she argued that urbanization was the driver of monetization in the Danube provinces, similarly observed that it was the density of exchange opportunities, not presence/absence of the military, that drove monetization.

53. Brindle 2017, 238–46.

54. Brindle 2017, fig. 6.23.

55. Brindle 2017, 258–60.

56. Rathbone 1991. Rathbone 2013, using the accounts of the notary Kronion, argues for thicker use of coins in village life.

57. The Egyptian monetary system was largely a closed one: coins minted in the province circulated inside the province and imperial coins, or even those of the adjacent Greek provinces, didn't circulate widely within it: Christiansen 2004, 40–46; cf. Andreau 2005. Thus, the outsized importance of the Alexandria mint.

58. Christiansen's (2004) compete account of the hoards, for instance, leaves out bronze almost entirely (a brief discussion at 48–52).

59. Milne 1900, 69–71; Alston 1998, 176: 76 coins from Tebtunis, some 36 from Euhemeria, only 20 in Theadelphia.

60. On the lead tokens of the high empire, Milne's (1900, 71–74, 1908, 1933, 1938, 213–14 [on Tebtunis]) studies remain fundamental. On their debated function and importance: Christiansen 2004, 52, 2014, 6; Faucher 2022, 229.

61. For the contested role and legal limitations on *argentarii*, Andreau 1987, 61–167, 1999a, 39; Verboven 2008, 211; Rathbone and Temin 2008.

62. On the many challenges of interpreting hoards, Reece 1988; Guest 2015; Howgego and Wilson 2022.

63. On which in Britain, which has a great many such religious coin finds, see Reece 1996. On the difficulty of parsing ritual hoards, particularly in rural contexts, see Mairat, Howgego and Wilson 2022, 13; Millett 1995; Brindle 2017, 263–64, respectively. See also Aarts 2005.

64. Most studies of coin hoards have been largely disinterested in value: minting patterns, coin circulation, and the use of hoards to proxy military maneuvers or periods of insecurity have dominated the literature. A major noteworthy exception was Duncan-Jones' (1994, 67–94) empire-wide value-based study, discussed further below.

65. Howgego and Wilson 2022, 9–10, acknowledge the importance of value studies, and the methodological challenges attending them, although there are no studies based on value in their volume.

66. On the distinction between savings and circulation hoards, see Duncan-Jones 1994, 67 n. 1.

67. Again, a more detailed version may be found in Bowes 2022.

68. For the Caecilius Iucundus' average, see Andreau 1974, 89.

69. On these hoards see Taliercio Mensitieri 2012.

70. Camodeca 2003, 94. High-quality land, according to Columella, *Rust.* 3.3.3, ran 1000 HS/ *iugerum*. Duncan-Jones (1976, 11) thinks this number accrued to particularly expensive land, although productive vineyards would have cost even more.

71. Average price from Vesuvian cities: Duncan-Jones 1974, 348.

72. Lerouxel 2016, 215.

73. Bransbourg (2022, 144–15) drew attention to the small number of preserved coins (c. 40,000 by an earlier catalog) for a population of some 7,500 to 13,500 people, and Verboven assumed that about six times that would have constituted the original coin supply. All of these studies were concerned with coin supply, not the coined value possessed by individuals—our interest here.

74. As already noted by Cantilena 2005, regarding Pompeii, and Harris 2006, 2008 more generally.

75. This exercise draws on the collected hoards in the Coin Hoards of the Roman Empire (CHRE) database: Howgego 2019, including imperial hoards (defined as a collection of two or more coins, whatever their value) through 260 CE. The earlier effort to do this was published by Duncan-Jones 1994, 67–94, who studied 230 Roman-period hoards, restricting his study only to those of 400 HS or greater. He concluded that they represented either military pay or civilian handouts, not the savings of average people. Criticism levied at the time: Creighton 1997. For the radical and important undercounting of bronze coins in the present dataset, both due to antiquarian and metal-detectorist disregard: Howgego and Wilson 2022, 11; Brindle 2017, 259–60. Regional variations—lots of silver- and bronze-majority hoards in Britain and the Balkans, more gold in Gaul, very little bronze in Egypt—are due again to recording issues, but also supply of different metals to different regions as well as the use of some metals (especially gold) in ritual deposits.

76. Rural hoards are also more likely to conceal ritual and perhaps collective ritual activities. For instance, in western Britain, the fact that many rural hoards are found some distance from settlements, not inside them, may suggest some ritual function, if not a determined desire for secrecy: Brindle 2017, 263.

77. On the value of discharge payments as established by Augustus: *Dio* 55.23.

78. Assuming a 400,000 HS threshold wealth requirement, and a six percent yearly yield on that interest. Many equestrians had much larger fortunes and incomes: Scheidel and Friesen 2009, 75–78.

79. Pliny, *Ep*. 3.19.

80. Substantially the same conclusions reached qualitatively by Howgego 1992 and Verboven 2009.

81. The technical details are parsed in Yiftach-Firanko 2003, which is followed below.

82. Montevecchi 1936, 16–20, who, although overly attached to the idea that the *syngraphe trophitis* marks a marriage between two "indigenous" people, nonetheless provides a useful overview of the evidence.

83. Yiftach-Firanko 2003, appendixes 4C and 4D.

84. See appendix 4.

85. Average value of *synagraphe trophitis* contracts in the Tebtynis register. First-century CE land prices in the Arsinoite nome: Kelly 2021, appendix 2: average 276 dr/aroura.

86. Cicero: e.g., *Ad Fam*. 5.6.2, with Verboven 2002; Pliny: *Ep*. 8.2.1–4; 3.19.8, with Shaw 2019; Duncan-Jones 1974, 20–21.

87. Female lenders at Pompeii: *CIL* 4.4528; 8203; 8204. Jewish maximum wealth requirements for charity: *Pe'ah* 8:8–9; borrowing at army camps: *Tab. Vind*. 181, 182.

88. *CIL* 4.8566, and see chapters 1 and 2. See similar expenses registered in *CIL* 4.4888 (4 *asses* for an "procurator" or agent). One reading of *CIL* 4.5380 sees "sittuae/Sittiae" as a family name and thus a debt owed to a person or persons by this name: Solin and Caruso 2016, 111 and 123.

89. A collection of which, all from Egypt, can be found in Husselman 1961, and see more below.

90. For the legal forms used in Egypt and the Vesuvian cities, see Lerouxel 2016.

91. The identities and job descriptions of different kinds of bankers and moneylenders is detailed in Andreau 1987, 1999a; cf. Verboven 2008.

92. Birks 2014. On the written forms, see the Herculaneum tablets, many of which preserve the separate pages for witness signatures: Camodeca 2017; and the Bloomberg tablets in London: Tomlin 2016, especially nos. 27, 44, 53, 54, 55, 56, 58, 61, 76.

93. Wolff 1978, 106–13. On the changes to *cheirographa* between the Ptolemaic and Roman periods, Yiftach-Firanko 2007.

94. *P. Leid. Inst*. 1.26. Trans. Hoogendijk and Minnen 1991, 133.

95. Wolff 1978, 34–44.

96. On the *bibliotheke enkteseon*, Lerouxel 2015; 2016, 145–91.

97. Lerouxel 2016, 20–21.

98. Langellotti 2020, appendix 1 on the fees (*grammatikon*) charged by the Tebtunis grapheion.

99. Lerouxel 2016, 112–20.

100. On the lack of information on interest rates and its possible meaning: Millett 1991 (ancient Greece: personal relationships motivating interest-free loans); Pestmann 1971 (lack of a specified rate didn't mean interest-free); Camodeca 1992, 173–77 (lack of stated rate due to illegal usurious rates charged by deducting from the amount loaned); Andreau 1999a, 98–99; Lerouxel 2012, 2016, 110–12, 238 (use of a default rate of 12 percent). The absence of contractually stipulated interest, and the use of commonly accepted rates, need not be a sign of a lackluster market for credit: see e.g., Hoffman, Postel-Vinay and Rosenthal 2019. Similarly, assuming that trust and personal relationships guide the poor's use of credit isn't always helpful: Guinnane 2005.

101. On the vexed question of whether or not the Twelve Tables already capped interest rates at 12 percent—a claim we know about only from Tacitus—see the summary of the debates in Silver 2012, 224–26.

102. A list of attested rates that provides some sense of the variability can be found in Foraboschi and Gara 1981, 337.

103. On zero-interest loans and the importance of reciprocity as a motivator for lending, Kelly 2023, 118–44. Cf. Guinnane 2005 in other historical contexts.

104. Collins et al. 2009. For the Roman world, Kelly 2023, 7 on modern portfolio theory.

105. Cuvigny 2000, 46.

106. *O. Claud.* 420. On the chirographic form, Cuvigny 2000, 81–82.

107. *O. Claud.* 456.

108. Cuvigny 2000, 150–51.

109. *O. Claud.* 425.

110. For a list, Cuvigny 2000, 78.

111. *O. Bahira* 20; Cuvigny 2021h.

112. As also noted by Cuvigny 2000, 49.

113. *O. Claud.* 540.

114. Data drawn from Cuvigny 2000, 47–48.

115. See Cuvigny 2000, 41–43.

116. Cuvigny 2000, 49.

117. Van der Veen 1998; Van der Veen et al. 2018; Jørgensen 2021.

118. Cuvigny 2000, 78.

119. On the evidence for lower wheat prices among the fort communities of the eastern desert, *O. Xer.* inv. 464; *O. Max.* inv. 45; Cuvigny 2021f, 350–51. The price of wheat at the quarries is unknown.

120. On which Guinnane 2003.

121. The c. 200 ostraca are mostly not written by the debtors but by one of some 25 different hands, including some of the quartermasters, as well as others—presumably other literate members of the community. See Cuvigny 2000, 95–96.

122. *CIL* 4.4528; 8203; 8204. See also Andreau 1974, 119–22.

123. *P. Lond.* 2.193v. See also Sakellaridou-Soutiroudi 1979. The find spot is imprecise but appears to come from the Arisinoite nome in the Fayum.

124. *P. Lond.* 2.193v., 2.17–23. Trans. Johnson 1936, 458–59.

125. *CIL* 4.8203; 8204; *P. Lond.* 2.193v. The other pawnbroker accounts from antiquity date from late antiquity or don't preserve loan amounts: Husselman 1961; Welles 1933, 273. Of particular interest are a family of seventh/eighth-century moneylenders from Jême, near Luxor in the Nile Valley, who included several women and who lent at interest and also pawned objects: Wilfong 1990; 2002, 117–249. See also Papaconstantinou 2020.

126. For a more sympathetic treatment in an early modern context, see Fontaine 2008, 105–9.

127. Kelly 2023, 123–24; 154–55.

128. *P. Mich.* Inv. 1950. Husselman 1961, 253–56.

129. Monthly rate: Mau in *CIL* 4.4528, 8203, 8204). See Andreau 1974, 119–22, who calculated much higher annualized rates.

130. *P. Oxy.* 1.114: one stater per mina (4 dr/100 dr). Rowlandson (1998, 257) calculates this as 48 percent interest, assuming that it extended for a year. The loan length is nowhere stated.

131. On modern pawn loan rates in the United States, Caskey 1991.

132. The term ἐνεχυραστής doesn't appear in the papyrological or literary corpus as such (*TLG* 'ἐνεχυριαστής'), and only two Latin inscriptions mention individuals identified as *pigneratori* (*TLL* 10.1.2118–9). Martial's Claudius (2.56) may be one such person but is not labeled as a *pignerator*. In general, the term is rarely used and when it appears is more associated with seizure of property (e.g., Cicero, *Ver.* 2.37). "Pawnbrokers" largely have been identified by scholars by virtue of lists of objects labeled as "pledges" (*enechura/pigna*).

133. The seventh/eighth-century pawnbroker/moneylenders from Jême are another example, Wilfong 1990, 173–74.

134. The Jême moneylenders were also women, as were many, but not all, of their clients.

135. Kelly 2023, 153–54. Cf. early modern Europe, Fontaine 2008, 136–66.

136. On Kronion's archive, its discovery and contents, see Langellotti 2020, 31–55, and Toepel 1973. Original publication of the registers: Boak 1933; Husselman, Boak and Edgerton 1944.

137. The registers were made in different forms: registers of titles (*anagraphai*), which include only a very brief summary of the documents produced by the office, and registers of abstracts (*eiromena*) that provide longer descriptions and essential elements of the agreements in question but cover a shorter period. The present analysis is based on the longest two preserved sections of the title registers—a four-month period from May to August in 42 CE and sixteen months from September 45 CE through December 46 CE: *P. Mich.* 2.121v. (42 CE) and *P. Mich.* 2.123r. (45–46 CE) and *P. Mich.* 5.238 (46 CE), respectively.

138. Lerouxel's (2016) broader study on credit in Egypt and Kelly's (2023) big-data analysis of Egyptian financial relationships both provide important context for this single-village analysis and are cited throughout.

139. The primary evidence comes from Pliny, *HN* 5.10, who describes a particularly high flood under the emperor Claudius. Pliny's testimony is expanded upon by Gapp 1935 and Bonneau 1971.

140. The registers were strongly interpreted in light of this event by Toepel 1973, and subsequent readings tended to see the loan evidence in this light, particularly the nursing and *paramone* contracts: Manca Masciardi and Montevecchi 1982; Montevecchi 1987; Hobson 1984. Tenger 1993, 252–59, extends the level of the Nile flood to the study of all loans, claiming to see a pattern between particularly high and low flood levels and numbers of loans. Correlation and noncorrelation seem to me to be equally evident.

141. Bagnall 1997a, 137; Rowlandson 1999, 149–50; Langellotti 2020, 68–73, 102–37.

142. This was done by averaging all duplicate months' records—that is, the May to August 42 CE with the May to August of 46 CE, and the September through December of 45 CE with those same months in 46 CE. This provides some balance to eight months of a twelve-month combined record, running from September to August (Toth to Mesore). Epagonal days have been added to the end of Mesore.

143. See appendix 4 for the data on the Tebtunis register.

144. From the study of some 4,367 transactions by Kelly 2023, 16.

145. Cf. Lerouxel 2016, 56–59, who notes a similar tendency in the broader Egyptian loan records of the period. Kelly 2023, 135, sees the antichretic loans as evidence of reciprocal relationships—a swap of money for housing—rather than the deployment of capital to pay interest.

146. Lerouxel 2016, 112. By the second century CE, security had become even more common in all kinds of loans, particularly larger ones.

147. Kelly 2023, 141.

148. Under Roman law, most women were required to have a "guardian" approve and cosign any financial transactions. Women as principal debtors thus would have been required to have a male signatory, whether security was involved or not.

149. Lerouxel 2016, 49–50 (average); Kelly 2023, 110–11 (median). Kelly's (2023, 95) rural average (probably derived substantially from the Tebtunis archive) substantially agrees with my own (168 dr).

150. See appendix 4.

151. *Contra* Kelly 2023, 130–31, in more substantial agreement with Lerouxel 2016, 52–54.

152. *Contra* Tenger 1993, 240.

153. The poll tax receipts collected by Maresch 1996, 217–35, with the Fayum at 232–35, provide a useful indication of poll-tax paying habits. Other receipts that list a whole year of payments provide other installment options: Claytor, Litinas and Nabney 2016.

154. Kelly 2023, 113–14, finds no seasonal patterns in the Egyptian loan corpus as a whole, with the exception of an uptick in August. His corpus included a sizable number of urban loans (particularly from Oxyrynchus) and a sizable corpus of mid-fourth-century loans—none of which are included in this village study, and which may account for the difference. His quite different conclusions as to the function of these loans is impacted by these findings.

155. Cf. Tenger 1992, 13–16, 32, 51, who analyzed each type of loan separately, attributing many loans to seed loans without indicating why the loan should be in cash. Kelly 2023, 130–31, finding no seasonal trends in his pan-Egyptian study, also concluded that loans were driven by consumption needs.

156. As argued by Hoffman, Postel-Vinay and Rosenthal 2019, 35–36, in their study of 18th-century French credit activities among farmers. Cf. Kelly 2023, 130–32, who cites the productive/consumptive binary. In the absence of an overall seasonal pattern for Egyptian loans as a whole and the absence of frequently cited investment purposes, he views these loans as consumptive.

157. On cash for pasture leases, see Rowlandson 1999.

158. On donkey sales and prices generally, see Rathbone 1997, 207–10. For donkey prices, Kelly 2021, supp. 2.

159. Seeding rates at 1 art/ar. See appendix 2 for seeding rates, appendix 4 for loans in kind from the register.

160. Foraboschi and Gara 1981, suggest something similar to explain how interest rates on loans in kind (often 50 percent) could be so much higher than rates for cash (12 percent), citing price differentials between harvest and sowing. While there isn't enough data to support the radical shifts in price they suggest (Rathbone 1997, 190–98), their observation that farmers used cash and kind loans to move between different monetary modes is an important one.

161. On the archive of Tryphon, see Biscottini 1966, especially 215–17, for the loan in question (*P. Oxy*. 315, 37 CE).

162. Urban residents of Oxyrhynchus paid lower taxes than those in the Arsinoite nome: Wallace 1938, 127.

163. Paramone contracts: a partial list at Johnson 1936, 452–54 and, more recently and completely, Freu 2022, 25–43, with a list at 241–42.

164. The following account follows the chronology and editions of the relevant papyri published in Claytor, Litinas, and Nabney 2016.

165. Public farmer: *P. Oslo* 2.32 and Claytor, Warga and Smith 2016, texts 3 and 4; wage work and labor gang: *P. Mich*, inv. 4436g + 4344; priest: *SB* 20.14440.

166. *P. Mich*. 4346 + 4446f, with renewal for a further two and a half years: *P. Mich*. 931 + *P. Col*. 10.249. The 80 dr wage is known from the second agreement only.

167. *P. Mert*. 1.8 + *P. Mil*. 2.43 and *P. Col*. 8.209. Claytor, Litinas, and Nabney 2016, 87.

168. *SB* 14.11279. Claytor, Litinas, and Nabney 2016, 86.

169. An updated list can be found in Freu 2022, 249. Manca Masciardi and Montevecchi 1982 and Hobson 1984 both associate what they view as the unusually high number of nursing contracts in the 45–46 CE portions of the Tebtunis register with parents selling their newborns into slavery, occasioned by famine caused by the high flood of 45 CE. As Freu notes (165–66), Augustan-period Alexandria also saw many nursing contracts signed—more indications of economic hardship, or business as usual for poor families? Bagnall (1997, 137–38) thinks the latter, adding that the infants in Tebtunis may well have come from Arsinoe, where girls are underrepresented in the census records, to be raised by poor ruralites in exchange for cash and some rations.

170. Foraboschi 1971, xxix–xxxiii, emphasizing the Kronion family's borrowing from the wealthier Herakleides-Lourios family, whom he nonetheless terms a Hellenized "rural middle class." For nursing contracts, there may be an important majority of urban creditors: Freu 2022, 168, n. 373 has the data for the phenomenon, which Bagnall (1997a) had already supposed on demographic grounds.

171. Langellotti 2020, 102–37. Cf. Tenger 1993, who, although noting the problems in deducing the identity from a reluctant source corpus, nonetheless forces them into a grid of eight identity categories.

172. Lerouxel 2016, 126–43.

173. Brown 1971, 36.

174. The best demonstration for the importance of account money for these people comes from the Appianus estate, and Rathbone's masterful study thereof: Rathbone 1991 is used throughout.

175. *P. Prag.* 3.240, 10–27. Trans. Rathbone 2011, 116; 119 for commentary.

176. The account remains unpublished, summarized as *P. Brux.* descr. in Bingen 1951. Discussed and contextualized in Rathbone 1991, 112–13.

177. Rathbone 1991, 126.

178. Andreau 1999a, 150–52.

179. Tenger 1993, 40–41 for a list of *chresis*-type loans and their repayment.

180. *P. Soter.* 24, 25.

181. Cash: *P. Kron.* 8 repaid in *P. Kron.* 11; wheat: *P. Kron.* 9 repaid in *P. Kron.* 12.

182. Tenger 1993, 121–23 (loans); Rowlandson 1996, 254 (rent).

183. On the use of mediation and slaves and freedmen's important role in it, see Broekaert 2017.

184. The most recent study is Kelly 2011.

185. See e.g. *P. Mich.* 2.123r.; 3.44; 4.22, 35, 44; 6.21.

186. As alleged by Ruffini 2013; skepticism about the numbers echoed here: B. Kelly 2023.

187. B. Kelly 2011, 143–53; B. Kelly 2023, 175–91.

188. B. Kelly 2011.

189. B. Kelly 2023, 170, with some reservations about the numbers on 170–74.

190. The data here comes from a corpus of petitions assembled by Ben Kelly (and used in B. Kelly 2011 and 2023), who kindly shared it with me for my own calculations.

191. On the debts, *P. Kron.* 22–25; house rental: *P. Kron.* 26; house as interest: *P. Kron.* 25. The usufruct/interest began to exceed the 8 dr house rental rate around the time that loan was repaid.

192. On the donkey, *P. Kron.* 27. There are some questions whether the son of Soterichos mentioned here is the same as the protagonist in this archive: Omar 1979, 136.

193. Cf. Lerouxel 2016, 51–52, comparing an unsustainable subsistence cost with average loan values.

194. See appendix 3 for family sustainable subsistence costs. American household debt/income ratios: https://www.federalreserve.gov/releases/z1/dataviz/household_debt/state/table/.

6. The Load-Carrying Mother

1. The description is taken from the remains known as E76. She was found in the vaulted substructures near the beach in Herculaneum, where she and hundreds of others sheltered from and were eventually killed by the eruption of Vesuvius. Capasso 2001, 630–33.

2. An enthusiastic account of the levels of mechanization in the Roman world can be found in Wilson 2002, 2006. The human body remained the principal machine and food the principal energy source.

3. On these multiple, contested etiologies, see below, although a summary can be found in Sperduti et al. 2018.

4. Wood et al. 1992.

5. On which see Agarwal 2016; Glencross 2011; for Mediterranean examples, Prowse 2011; Robb 2019.

6. The scholars working in early cliometric history and anthropometrics also substantially overlapped, particularly around the figures of Robert Fogel, Roderick Floud and later Richard Steckel. Many of the key arguments in *Time on the Cross* (Fogel and Engerman 1974)—around slave nutrition, for instance—were subsequently investigated by Steckel (e.g., Steckel 1979, 1986), while these three scholars, together with others, began the first large projects on human stature: Fogel et al. 1983; Steckel and Floud 1997. For some important anomalies, particularly around the apparent decrease in heights during industrialization: Komlos 1998 (for a "biological standard of living" distinct from a strictly economic one); Craig 2015 (inequality); A'Hearn 2015 (genetics); Bodenhorn, Guinnane and Mroz 2019 (data problems).

7. Steckel and Rose 2002; Steckel at al. 2019a.

8. On the barbarians, Meinzer, Steckel and Baten 2019, 238.

9. Graeber and Wengrow 2021, 3, 7.

10. On the former, Steckel et al. 2019 helpfully put their data online: https://economics.osu.edu/european-module. A rummage reveals that what counts as "ancient" or "pre-medieval" are c. 1,100 individuals dating mostly from the fourth through sixth centuries CE, virtually none of them from the Mediterranean and some from outside the empire entirely. For the height project, Koepke and Baten 2005. More on not-very-big datasets below. For a critique of the composition of even the modern data, see Bodenhorn, Guinnane and Mroz 2019.

11. This tendency is on display most particularly in the introduction and conclusions of these big projects: Steckel, Sciulli and Rose 2002; Steckel, Roberts and Baten 2019; Baten et al. 2019.

12. See particularly Baten et al. 2019; Meinzer, Steckel and Baten 2019. A critique: Bowes 2024.

13. An otherwise excellent study of Roman British children (Rohnbogner 2022) found that over 60 percent of all children had no pathological markers on their skeletons, a finding that goes largely unremarked upon in the remainder of the book focused on pathologies.

14. Again, bioarchaeologists have long been gathering data on resilience (Temple and Goodman 2014; Temple and Stojanowski 2019), care (Tilley 2015), and individuals (Stodder and Palkovich 2012), not necessarily fully utilized in Roman-period discussions.

15. Data is provided in appendix 5. For Britain, the data has already been well collected and analyzed. The principal analyses and data collections are Rohnbogner 2022 (children); Rohnbogner 2018 (rural); Pitts and Griffin 2012 (urban data); Redfern et al. 2015 (urban and rural data from Dorset); Roberts and Cox 2003 (Iron Age and Roman data). For Italy, the data is much more diffuse, of varying quality and mostly not analyzed. The sources for the Italian data are given in appendix 5 and an overview in Bowes 2024. Some analyses of smaller collections of this data can be found in Scheidel 2003; Killgrove 2017; Kron 2019. The isotope data was collected by myself and Jessica Pearson: Bowes and Pearson in preparation. Most of the Italian data represents people who lived and died in the later first through third centuries CE, the British data those from the second through fourth centuries CE.

16. The challenges as applied to Roman Italian populations are usefully and honestly laid out in Killgrove 2019 and Flohr 2019.

17. Antonio et al. 2019; Prowse et al. 2010.

18. As emphasized by Harper 2017, 2021. On plague bacilli, among a large literature, Harbeck et al. 2013; Keller et al. 2019. On malaria plasmodia: Marciniak et al. 2016, 2018.

19. The so-called Developmental Origins of Health and Disease (DOHaD) paradigm, an overview of which can be found in Agarwal 2016, 135.

20. As emphasized by Wood et al. 1992.

21. On child mortality estimates: Bagnall and Frier 1994, 32–35, 87–88; Scheidel 2001, 21–24.

22. On which, see Carroll 2011; Gowland, Chamberlain and Redfern 2014; Millet and Gowland 2015.

23. While weaning is one of the stresses registered by LEH, this trend doesn't appear to be driven by a change in weaning age. Roman and Iron Age weaning ages appear to be similar at

around two-plus years of age. For variable weaning ages in Britain: London: Redfern et al. 2018; rural Oxfordshire: Fuller et al. 2006; Nehlich et al. 2011; Dorset: Redfern et al. 2012. On the Iron Age, only a single site has been studied in detail: Jay et al. 2008.

24. See appendix 5.

25. Also the conclusions of Rohnbogner's (2022, 165) study of children only.

26. These higher levels conceal a huge amount of variety: see the discussion in Killgrove 2017, who analyzes some Rome cemeteries with quite low CO and LEH. Higher Italian LEH levels do not appear to be driven by substantially different weaning ages, with babies in Britain and Italy being weaned between 2.5 to 3 years of age: Prowse et al. 2008; De Angelis et al. 2020.

27. E.g., Minozzi et al. 2012, 274–79 on a handful of identified cases of tuberculosis, scurvy and rickets, together with rates of general periostitis in the Rome cemeteries. Very little, if any, periostitis is specifically reported for the ribs in Italian cases, but rather for the lower legs, probably the result of injuries: Paine et al. 2009; Baldoni et al. 2020; Kilgrove 2010, 108. On rickets: Mays et al. 2018.

28. Gowland and Garnsey 2010. See also Scheidel 2003, 2014. A recent study on CO in ancient Egyptian populations, including Roman ones, interprets it as a straightforward marker of malaria: Smith-Guzmàn 2015.

29. See Sallares 2002; Sallares, Bouwman and Anderung 2004. For a late Roman children's cemetery in central Italy where infants may have died of malaria, see Wilson et al. 2022.

30. Shaw 1996, 2006.

31. Papathanasiou et al. 2019, 214–17.

32. Walker et al. 2009; McIlvaine 2015. As accepted in studies on the Roman British material: Rohnbogner 2022, 105.

33. Marciniak et al. 2016. Traces of the DNA of the malarial parasite *Plasmodium falciparum* are often elusive in friable ancient human remains. Hemozoin, a biocrystal synthesized by the parasite, may be more readily identified: Inwood 2017. Traces of either DNA or hemozoin have been found in Roman individuals, but the spread of the disease, its mortality profiles and specific populations' exposure and resilience are all yet to be understood.

34. A lengthy, not always evidence-based literature has discussed the disease burden brought about by Roman urbanization: Scobie 1986 is wholly pessimistic and now not entirely accurate; Scheidel 2003, 2014 are more evidence-based, including a précis of the skeletal material. Oerlemans and Tacoma (2014) provide a careful if qualitative unpacking of the ancient and modern data for malaria, tuberculosis and typhoid as they impacted the city of Rome.

35. Hanson 2016, 72.

36. See appendix 5: data for Britain only. On respiratory illness in the Roman period and its causes: Rohnbogner 2018, 332, 335–36; Bresson 2017a.

37. As suggested by the research of Mays et al. 2018 for the Ostian skeletal population.

38. For example, there is evidence for brucellosis carried by contaminated milk or meat in the Vesuvian cities: Capasso 2002.

39. For example, the groundbreaking 1842 Chadwick Report that detailed the disease burden suffered by working people: Chadwick 1842.

40. As detailed in Rohnbogner 2022, 87–91.

41. Rohnbogner 2022, especially 65, 114. The exception is enamel hypoplasia, which is higher among children who died in the city.

42. Rohnbogner 2022, 65.

43. Rohnbogner 2018, table 290, on a relatively small urban sample. Redfern et al. (2015) came to some of these same conclusions examining cemeteries from Dorset only: while they found higher mortality risk to urban children, they noted higher survivorship and lower mortality for urban adults.

44. On the particular genetic diversity of cities versus the countryside, see Antonio et al. 2021; Martiniano 2016 (cities); cf. Prowse et al. 2010; Scheib et al. 2023 (countryside).

45. As also suggested by Bonsall 2013, 281, who observed similar patterns at work in her sample of urban and rural adults and children in Britain.

46. Power of a Single Number: the eponymous study by Lepenies (2016) on the history of GDP as a measurement. For the data pointing to this correlation between height and economic variables, see n. 6 above.

47. Bogin 2021.

48. The debates are summarized in Gowland and Walther 2018. For the changing proportions of bodies in Roman and post-Roman Britain, see Walther 2017.

49. The large study of Italian and other Roman femur lengths did not report individualized or even averaged data by province and those could not be used here: Jongman, Jacobs and Klein Goldewijk 2019. It also appears that much of the city of Rome data—by far the largest dataset for Italian individuals of the second through third centuries—was not included in that femur study. It is included in the present study, again, in weighted-average form. Only populations reported with Trotter and Gleser formulae are included, but which version of that regression is not always stated.

50. Koepke and Baten 2005; Giannecchini and Moggi-Cecchi 2008 (Italy); Jongman, Jacobs and Klein Goldewijk 2019; Quade and Gowland 2021 (Gaul). A very broad study on classical and Roman Greece (Koukli et al. 2023) found that stature increased during the Roman period. A study using the more exacting Fulley method found that stature was higher in post-Roman Britain than during Roman rule, but with no comparison with pre-Roman data: Walther 2017.

51. Kron 2005a.

52. The different regression formulae used to reconstruct total "living" height produce different, incomparable results. The "big" data also often turns out to be not very big: fewer than 300 individuals of Roman date comprise two of the studies: Koepke and Batten (2005): 165 individuals; Giannecchini and Moggi-Cecchi: 283 individuals. Kron's 2005a study is dominated by Hellenistic and Etruscan sites, but as dates are only occasionally provided, the actual number of the Roman-period sample is unclear. In the femur study (Jongman, Jacobs and Klein Goldewijk 2019), the most for any given 50-year period is 400 (from late antique Britain), while for the western Mediterranean (mostly Italy), it is mostly around 10–20 individuals or less. Most of those come from 500–200 BCE—that is, before the Roman period—and from late antiquity; see Jongman, Jacobs and Klein Goldewijk 2019, fig. 3. Finally, the pan-empire studies also tend to be swamped by a huge British dataset for later antiquity (i.e., 300–700 CE). As British individuals were found to be taller in all periods than the southern and western Mediterranean folks, it could be that the putative rising stature in later antiquity is really a relic of all those tall Brits.

53. 2,338 first- through fourth-century CE male and female individuals for Britain, and 1,263 first- through third-century CE male and female individuals for central/southern Italy.

54. This dataset relied on total height calculated using Trotter and Gleser's regression formula only, not because this formula is more accurate (it probably isn't), but simply because it was used the most often.

55. These differences in female height were also found, although not discussed, in the femur study: Jongman, Jacobs and Klein Goldewijk 2019, 8. Walther's (2017) study of Roman versus early medieval stature found that female stature changed only slightly after the end of Roman rule, while male height increased significantly (some 6 cm).

56. Bogin 2021, 119–20. On possible catch-up growth in Roman children, see Watts 2013. A larger study of British children found those over five falling behind their 19th-century successors on growth: Rohnbogner 2022, 98–99.

57. Cox et al. 2022.

58. Buikstra 2019, chapter 21.

59. See appendix 5.

60. For a useful overview of stable isotope analysis, its possibilities and limitations, see Sperduti et al. 2018.

61. Some canonical studies include for Italy: Prowse et al. 2004; Craig et al. 2009; Craig et al. 2013; Killgrove and Tycot 2013; Martyn et al. 2018; Soncin et al. 2021; Britain: Richards et al. 1998; Müldner 2013. Some recent overenthusiasm: Leggett 2022; Cocozza et al. 2022, centered on the Roman–medieval transition using big datasets.

62. Already observed by Craig et al. 2009.

63. Crowe et al. 2010.

64. As tentatively observed from a smaller dataset by Müldner 2013.

65. Soncin et al. 2021.

66. Van Rossem et al. 2019; Chiu et al. 2013; Deaton 2007.

67. Pitts and Griffin 2012.

68. Redfern et al. 2015.

69. Prowse 2001, 117.

70. Killgrove 2010, 173. The biggest difference between the two populations was variability—those in the mausoleum had a more consistent diet, while those buried in humbler settings in the surrounding necropolis had more variation. As the mausoleum population was considerably larger and may have been interred over a longer period of time, this isn't surprising.

71. Prowse 2001, 153.

72. On gendered dental health differences at Vagnari see Prowse, Naus and Ledger 2014.

73. Summarized, but not tallied, in Rohnbogner 2018, 334–35.

74. Richards et al. 1998. While the authors claim to have found no significant gender differences in the population they studied, this appears to be a result of agglomerating all Iron Age and Roman individuals in the gender analysis. Male later Roman averages = $^{13}C = -18.9$; $^{15}N = 10.0$. Female: $^{13}C = -19.1$; $^{15}N = 8.7$. The mausoleum population: M = 7; F = 3.

75. Also noted at Ostia: Prowse 2011, 420; and at Herculaneum: Soncin et al. 2019.

76. Rural Britain: Rohnbogner 2018, 334. In Italy, we have age-at-death data broken down by gender for only a handful of the Roman necropoles: e.g., Minozzi et al. 2012, 270; Catalano et al. 2010, 115; Prowse 2001.

77. Shaw 1987; Scheidel 2007b. See Bagnall and Frier 1994, 111–16 on the somewhat earlier Egyptian pattern, which includes the Egyptian countryside.

78. Charlesworth's dissection of the working class in northern England closes in on this visceral embodiment of labor as a daily practice (Charlesworth 2000, 241–43) but veers off in the end toward class embodiment as analytical category. On which see Bourdieu 1979.

79. Waldron 2012; Weiss and Jurmain 2007.

80. Waldron and Rogers 1991.

81. E.g., Bisel and Bisel 2002; cf. Waldron 2009, 29.

82. For the current fascination with interpersonal violence over labor, see Redfern 2017; Baten and Steckel 2019.

83. On the difficulties of identifying interpersonal versus accidental trauma, see Judd and Redfern 2012, 365.

84. Appendix 5. Most of these numbers are taken from overall cranial fractures, which aren't distinguished by their location. Upper cranial fractures are more likely to be the result of interpersonal violence. Thus, even these numbers may include accidental fractures and thus be too high.

85. Glencross 2011; Judd and Redfern 2012.

86. The only exception to this increase is spinal osteoarthritis, which appears to have remained relatively constant. Spinal arthritis appears to be a misery all humans share—a product

of an erect posture and walking on two legs—and thus is pretty constant through the ages. See Knüsel, Göggel and Lucy 1997.

87. For the longer-term patterns of osteoarthritis among farmers, see Williams, Meinzer and Larsen 2019. For farming trauma in the medieval and early modern periods, Redfern 2017, 74–76.

88. Kelly 2023, 12–13.

89. Prowse, Nause and Ledger 2014, 219–20. For a more detailed discussion, see Gilmour 2017.

90. Brent and Prowse 2014.

91. Brent and Prowse 2024.

92. Rohnbogner 2018, 316–22.

93. The two cemeteries have seen focused, if not statistically robust, studies on musculoskeletal stress. Musco et al. 2008; Catalano et al. 2010; Benassi et al. 2011; Caldarini, Zavaroni and Benassi 2015. On the presence of salt carriers in this area, see *CIL* 14.4285; *AE* 2014, 264; Cébeillac-Gervasoni and Morelli 2014; Morelli and Forte 2014.

94. Earlier methods of estimating age at death probably underestimated the old (Chamberlain 2006). The dataset certainly suffers from this, and thus older Romans may have been more common than we assumed.

95. At least some of the people buried at Casal Bertone were fullers: De Angelis et al. 2022.

96. This is not to argue for some kind of industrial belt around Rome: as Allison Emmerson (2020) has shown, the suburbs were a heterogeneous space where tile works might rub shoulders with elite villas, tombs and shops.

97. On "child labor" in antiquity and tasks children are known to have done from the literary and legal evidence, see Bradley 1985; Laes 2008 (particularly on enslaved children); Lewit 2022 (farm children). On task levels and child age, the comparison with the enslaved populations of the Americas is illuminating, as slave owners discussed the nature of tasks set to different aged children: see Turner 2017.

98. On apprenticeship, see Freu 2011, 2016. On the age at which children were apprenticed, based on the Egyptian papyri, Bradley 1985.

99. Rohnbogner 2022, 82–85.

100. Rohnbogner 2018, 338.

101. Caldarini, Zavaroni and Benassi 2015; Benassi et al. 2011, 296–97.

102. Capasso and Di Domenicantonio 1998.

103. Rohnbogner 2022, 66–75.

104. On the technical difficulties of finding slaves in the Roman archaeological record, Redfern 2018.

105. From Casal Bertone: De Angelis et al. 2022.

106. Patterson 1982. For Baptist (2014), the violence that defined the transatlantic slave system also defined the origins of capitalism.

107. As emphasized by Lenski 2016, 277.

108. As described in the so-called *Lex Libitinae*, found near Puteoli: EDR075111/TR 250398. Bodel 1994, 72–80; Castagnetti 2012.

109. Vipasca II (HE 19992) ll. 10, 13, 15.

110. For what we do know, Lenski 2016: for the American plantation whipping diaries, Baptist 2014.

111. The data is given in Minozzi et al. 2012, 273–74.

112. Ligt and Garnsey 2012.

113. Luongo et al. 2003, 182.

114. As also tentatively suggested of the Pompeii victims by Bowes 2022b.

115. Among many, Corruccini et al. 1982; Rathbun 1987; Rathbun and Steckel 2002; Blakey and Rankin-Hill 2009, 157–254; Shuler 2011.

116. Bemko and Monge 2018.

117. Rathbun and Steckel 2002; De La Cova 2010; 2011.

118. Cf. Jongman, Jacobs and Klein Goldewijk 2019; Komlos 1998, albeit for different reasons.

7. The Bottom Line

1. On households making history, Hartman 2004.

2. Peña, in press, table 3.

3. Hopkins 1980 and Monson 2012. Kelly 2023, 101, on the other hand, compares rentier and tenant income, leading him to conclude that Roman poll taxes were progressive—the tenant paying mere poll tax and the rentier elite only slowly realizing their investment. Comparing owner-operators with tenants rather than rentiers would make more sense. At a flat c. 4 dr/month, the poll tax clearly hit the poorest hardest.

4. Juvenal, *Sat.* 3.182–83.

5. Finley distinguished Greek and Roman families from "primitive" producers on the one hand, and "entrepreneurs" on the other. His insistence that farmers were not market oriented appears to have left them as incidental and occasional, rather than purposeful and frequent, users of markets. Finley 1999, 106–11.

6. The binary has been regularly challenged in the work of Laurence Fontaine (2008, 2014) on early modern working people.

7. On the risk paradigm, see Halstead and O'Shea 1989; Gallant 1991. Modern risk studies take a somewhat different approach, focused on responses to uncertainty, particularly among the vulnerable: for an application to the ancient world, see Grey 2025.

8. The vagaries of Mediterranean weather are discussed in chapter 3, where the difference between climate—so much in vogue in ancient history—and weather are plumbed.

9. On the entanglement of city-country labor pools, see Erdkamp 2015.

10. On production ups and downs at La Graufesenque, Vernhet 1981. On other ceramic production, Goodman 2013; Van Oyen 2023.

11. Emphasized in Heubner 2013, and economically in Kelly 2022.

12. See chapter 3 for a summary.

13. On the Malthusian side: Scheidel 2009; invocation of Ester Boserup: Erdkamp 2016. Debates usefully summarized and analyzed in Morley 2011.

14. Cf. modern Malthusians like Galor 2011 and his unified growth theory, which is predicated on the value of the "wage" in premodern societies as the sole source of income, and thus perpetually tamped down by population increase.

15. The ONE-pathology model recently proposed by Jane Buikstra emphasizes the importance of this human-animal relationship to past human functioning: Buikstra and Uhl 2023. Many thanks to the author for sharing this work.

16. Boserup 1965.

17. See Morley 2011, 31 for the Roman case and the importance of multiple responses.

18. In the Roman world, a cooking pot at one obol cost one sixth of daily wage; in medieval Britain, by comparison, a cooking pot at around half pence cost half of daily wage. On the medieval costs, see Dyer 1989, 173 and 215.

19. Vernhet 1981 on the production capacities at La Graufesenque in southern Gaul. For the costs, see chapter 2.

20. Frézouls 1978.

21. Burkhalter 1998.

22. As calculated from the contracts published in Cockle 1981.

23. Cf. Erdkamp 2015, who views the phenomenon of farmer-artisans as a byproduct of population growth.

24. On this paradox for the early modern world, see particularly Muldrew 1998. On the increased but still often insufficient estimates for household income, see Humphries 2013; Horrel, Humphries and Weisdorf 2022.

25. Smail 2016.

26. As argued by Kelly 2023, 92–96, on the basis of financial simulations run on a hypothetical Egyptian tenant farming family. His model is driven by his biggest variable—the hypothetical changes in the Nile flood—which produces the income volatility.

27. Thanks to Seth Bernard for a discussion about this use of wage labor.

28. The story was first told by De Vries 2008, elaborated for food (in Britain) by Muldrew 2011, and for other countries outside northwest Europe by many others, e.g., Marfany 2018; Ogilvie 2010. For a different story told about the role of consumer goods, credit and markets among the early modern poor, Fontaine 2008, 2014.

29. So, too, concludes Hawkins 2016, 61, albeit for very different reasons.

30. The contention of Allen 2001 and reiterated in 2015, despite argument around the constitution of consumption baskets, and the calculus' single male-wage basis: Humphries 2013. Even Horrel, Humphries and Weisdorf's (2022) most recent reconstruction of total family income still finds many families unable to subsist on likely wages, let alone the higher consumption packages documented by Muldrew (2011).

31. Muldrew and King 2003.

32. Central to De Vries' hypothesis, and derived from Hartman 2004, now elaborated by Zanden, Carmichael and De Moor 2018, and given a central role in Bateman 2019.

33. As discussed in chapter 6. See Shaw 1987; Scheidel 2007b; Bagnall and Frier 1994, 111–16.

34. For lower rents on imperial land: Kehoe 1988; Rowlandson 2005, 180–81. Cf. Monson 2012, who compares higher "rents" on imperial land in Egypt with the lower taxes on private land—on the principle that they are all somehow tax. This is not a comparison any farmer would have made: rents on imperial land were lower than rents on private land, whatever the final destination of the money. See Rowlandson 1996, 71–76. On low rents for pasture: Rowlandson 1996, 249–51; Rowlandson 1999, 144–45.

35. Kelly 2023, 101, comparing a landlord's income with that of a tenant farmer's, argued for the higher relative tax burden from land taxes relative to land prices, versus poll taxes (?) relative to leased income. This is a comparison of rentier versus tenant tax burden: it might be more apropos to compare owner-farmer with tenant-farmer burdens.

36. See the lease published in Cockle 1981. For the leasehold and income structure in the Roman sigillata pottery business, see Fülle 1997. On the particular legal nature of the Egyptian contracts, see below.

37. On the craft monopolies in Egypt, Wallace 1938, 181–90.

38. The Egyptian pottery contracts are complex: some second-century examples are clear examples of facilities rental (*locatio conductio rei*) where the lessee owns the final product. The third-century examples, like Aurelius Paesis', are a combination of such a lease arrangement with an independent-contractor-type contract (*locatio conductio operis*) in which the landowner owned the final product, and a labor contract (*locatio conductio operarum*) in which the contractor is paid a wage. See Fülle 1997, 121–22 for a summary of the problems.

39. On which see Wallace 1938, 191–213, 222–27.

40. Durante and Chen 2023.

41. Taeuber 2002, 93.

42. Costabile 2001; Baird 2013.

43. Garnsey 1981 assumed that freedmen were just that—free to run their own businesses. More recent assessments have found freedmen were either directly controlled by or strongly linked to their former masters: Mouritsen 2011, 206–47; Broekaert 2016.

44. Discussed in chapter 5 and most especially Cohen 2023, whose term I use.

45. This particular vitriol may be found in Juvenal's *Satires* (1.105, 28; 3.188–189) but there's plenty more: Martial 5.13; 3.4, 5.56, 3.16, 3.59, 9.73; Petronius, *Sat.* especially 37–38.

46. Tennant 2000.

47. On the heterogeneous nature of equestrian money-making, see Shaw 2020; Bodel 2015, 41–42; Andreau 1999b.

48. As described by Morduch and Schneider 2017; Ravenelle 2019.

49. Cf. Bond 2025.

Appendix Two: Smallholder Farms and Their Outputs

1. The 100:1 yields from literary sources are clearly overexcited rhetoric, and even the more monotone accounts from the Fayum papyri appear either too low for those scholars who point to super-high rents paid on those lands, or too high to those who see the Fayum's hind-end irrigation and high soil salinity as necessarily limiting. On yields: Italian data is summarized in Goodchild 2007, appendix V with a long discussion at 246–62, including wheat, grapes and olives. Egyptian data: Rathbone 1991, 242–48 (including wheat, hay and viticulture). Gaul: Ouzoulias uses the agronomists' data, plus some historical French data, for cereals only: Ouzoulias 2006, 179–83. Modern experiments on the Butser Ancient Farm also failed to resolve the problem, critics claiming their relatively high yields—30:1—were the result of anachronistic seed drilling and too-careful cosseting of the crops: Reynolds 1992; critique at Lang 2009.

2. For fragmented plots (Italy), sufficient land of the correct type for the crop in question is identified in the vicinity, without assuming that any particular plot was being used in perpetuity.

3. Columella's instructions at *Rust.* 6.3 provide for about 12 kg/day of hay for cattle for six months, with six months of largely cut woodland forage—elm, ash, poplar, etc. always being supplemented by vetch, beans, mast, etc.—about 4,000 kg of hay equivalent per year. Cato, *Agr.* 60, describes only around 600 kg of feed per head (part of the text is missing), seemingly just for winter, nongrazed feed, which is still only about a third of what Columella describes. Ouzoulias (2006, 189, n. 130) and Lepetz and Zech-Matterne (2018, 371 and 373–74) using modern rations, assumes 15 kg/day or 1.5 ha of pasture/head, assuming two cuttings. I'm grateful to Angela Trentacoste for conversations about this issue.

4. Thanks to Dominic Rathbone for drawing my attention to this measure.

BIBLIOGRAPHY

Aarts, Joris. 2005. "Coins, Money and Exchange in the Roman World: A Cultural-Economic Perspective." *Archaeological Dialogues* 12: 1–28.

Achard-Corompt, Nathalie. 2012. "La fouille d'un petit établissement gallo-romain de la seconde moitié du 1er s. ap. J.-C. à Bezannes, en périphérie de Reims (Marne)." *Revue Archéologique de l'Est* 61: 337–49.

Achard-Corompt, Nathalie, Alexandre Audebert, Marion Dessaint, Raphael Durost, and Vincent Le Quellec. 2017. "Les modes d'occupation du sol chez les Rèmes." In *Gallia Rustica 1. Les campagnes du nord-est de la Gaule, de la fin de l'âge du Fer à l'Antiquité tardive*, edited by Michel Reddé, 495–553. Bordeaux: Ausonius Éditions.

Adam, Stéphane. 2017. "Les structures fossoyées de Flamanville-Motteville: Contribution à la question du parcage des animaux d'élevage en Normandie au Haute-Empire." In *Produire, transformer et stocker dans les campagnes des Gaules romaines*, edited by Frédéric Trément, 549–65. Aquitaine: Fédération Aquitania.

Adams, Colin. 2007. *Land Transport in Roman Egypt: A Study of Economics and Administration in a Roman Province*. Oxford: Oxford University Press.

Agarwal, Sabrina. 2016. "Bone Morphologies and Histories: Life Course Approaches in Bioarchaeology." *American Journal of Physical Anthropology Supplement: Yearbook of Physical Anthropology* 159: 130–49.

Ago, Renata. 2013. *A Gusto for Things: A History of Objects in Seventeenth-Century Rome*. Chicago: University of Chicago Press.

Aguilera, Mónica, Marie Balasse, Sébastien Lepetz, and Véronique Zech-Materne. 2015. "Fertilisation des sols de culture par les fumiers et rôle potentiel des céréales dans l'affouragement du bétail: L'éclairage des analyses isotopiques sur restes carpologiques et archéozoologiques." In *Méthodes d'analyse des différents paysages ruraux dans le nord-est de la Gaule romaine*, edited by Michel Reddé, 41–46. Paris: HAL.

Aguilera, Mònica, Véronique Zech-Matterne, Sébastien Lepetz, and Marie Balasse. 2018. "Crop Fertility Conditions in North-Eastern Gaul during the La Tène and Roman Periods: A Combined Stable Isotope Analysis of Archaeobotanical and Archaeozoological Remains." *Environmental Archaeology* 23 (4): 323–37.

Ahammed, Shaif Uddin. 2019. "An Examination of Accounting Practices and Business Relationships of Micro-Businesses in Scotland." PhD thesis, University of West Scotland.

A'Hearn, Brian, Nicola Amendola, and Giovanni Vecchi. 2016. "On Historical Household Budgets." *Rivista di storia economica* 32 (2): 132–76.

A'Hearn, Brian, Jörg Baten, and Dorothee Crayen. 2009. "Quantifying Quantitative Literacy: Age Heaping and the History of Human Capital." *The Journal of Economic History* 69 (3): 783–808.

A'Hearn, Brian, Alexia Delfino, and Alessandro Nuvolari. 2022. "Rethinking Age Heaping: A Cautionary Tale from Nineteenth-Century Italy." *Economic History Review* 75: 111–37.

Albarède, Francis, François De Callataÿ, Pierluigi Debernardi, and Janne Blichert-Toft. 2021. "Model for Ancient Greek and Roman Coinage Production." *Journal of Archaeological Science* 131 (July): 105406. https://doi.org/10.1016/j.jas.2021.105406.

Albarella, Umberto, Cluny Johnstone, and Kim Vickers. 2008. "The Development of Animal Husbandry from the Late Iron Age to the End of the Roman Period: A Case Study from South-East Britain." *Journal of Archaeological Science* 35: 1828–48.

Alcock, Susan, John Cherry, and Jack Davis. 1994. "Intensive Survey, Agricultural Practice and the Classical Landscape of Greece." In *Classical Greece: Ancient Histories and Modern Archaeologies*, edited by Ian Morris, 137–70. Cambridge: Cambridge University Press.

Alderighi, Lorella, and Agnese Pittari. 2020. "The Settlement of Ponterotto (San Casciano in Val Di Pesa/FI)." In *The Vienna Orme and Pesa Valley Project. Proceedings of the International Workshop Held at Vienna, June 22–23, 2018*, edited by Günther Schörner, 237–61. Vienna: Projektinitiative Roman Rural Landscapes am Institut für Klassische Archäologie der Universität Wien.

Alföldi-Rosenbaum, Elizabeth. 1971. "The Finger Calculus in Antiquity and the Early Middle Ages." *Fruhmittelalterliche Studien* 5: 1–9.

Allason-Jones, Lindsay. 2004. "The Family in Roman Britain." In *A Companion to Roman Britain*, edited by Malcolm Todd, 273–87. Hoboken: Wiley Blackwell.

Allen, Martyn. 2017. "Pastoral Farming." In *New Visions of the Countryside of Roman Britain. Volume 2. The Economy of Roman Britain*, edited by Martyn Allen, Lisa Lodwick, Tom Brindle, Michael Fulford, and Alexander Smith, 85–141. London: Society for the Promotion of Roman Studies.

Allen, Martyn, Nathan Blick, Tom Brindle, Tim Evans, Michael Fulford, Neil Holbrook, Lisa Lodwick, Julian Richards, and Alex Smith. 2018. "The Rural Settlement of Roman Britain: An Online Resource." https://doi.org/10.5284/1030449.

Allen, Martyn, and Lisa Lodwick. 2017. "Agricultural Strategies in Roman Britain." In *New Visions of the Countryside of Roman Britain. Volume 2. The Economy of Roman Britain*, edited by Martyn Allen, Lisa Lodwick, Tom Brindle, Michael Fulford, and Alexander Smith, 142–77. London: Society for the Promotion of Roman Studies.

Allen, Martyn, Lisa Lodwick, Tom Brindle, Michael Fulford, and Alexander Smith. 2017. *New Visions of the Countryside of Roman Britain. Volume 2. The Economy of Roman Britain*. Britannia Monograph Series, 30. London: Society for the Promotion of Roman Studies.

Allen, Martyn, and Alexander Smith. 2016. "Rural Settlement in Roman Britain: Morphological Classification and Overview." In *New Visions of the Countryside of Roman Britain: Volume 1. The Rural Settlement of Roman Britain*, edited by Alexander Smith, Martyn Allen, Tom Brindle, and Michael Fulford, 17–43. Britannia Monograph Series, 29. London.

Allen, Robert. 2001. "The Great Divergence in European Wages and Prices from the Middle Ages to the Second World War." *Explorations in Economic History* 38: 411–47.

———. 2009. "How Prosperous Were the Ancient Romans? Evidence from Diocletian's Price Edict (301 AD)." In *Quantifying the Roman Economy: Methods and Problems*, edited by Alan Bowman and Andrew Wilson, 327–45. Oxford: Oxford University Press.

———. 2013. "Poverty Lines in History, Theory and Current International Practice." *Economic Series Working Papers*, University of Oxford, 685.

———. 2015. "The High Wage Economy and the Industrial Revolution: A Restatement." *The Economic History Review* 68 (1): 1–22.

Allison, Penelope. 2004. *Pompeii Households: Analysis of the Material Culture*. Los Angeles: Cotsen Institute of Archaeology.

———. 2006. *The Insula of the Menander at Pompeii. Volume III: The Finds, A Contextual Study*. Oxford: Oxford University Press.

Alston, Richard. 1994. "Military Pay from Augustus to Diocletian." *Journal of Roman Studies* 84: 113–23.

Alston, Richard. 1998. "Trade and the City in Roman Egypt." In *Trade, Traders and the Ancient City*, edited by Helen Parkins and Christopher Smith, 168–202. New York: Routledge.

Alvaredo, Facundo, Lucas Chancel, Thomas Piketty, Emmanuel Saez, and Gabriel Zucman. 2022. "World Inequality Database." https://wid.world/.

Anderson, Jamie, and Wajiha Ahmed. 2016. "Smallholder Diaries: Building the Evidence Base with Farming Families in Mozambique, Tanzania, and Pakistan." *Perspectives. CGAP* 2. https://www.cgap.org/sites/default/files/CGAP_Persp2_Apr2016-R.pdf.

Andersson, Eva, Linda Mårtensson, and Marie-Louise Nosch. 2008. "New Research on Bronze Age Textile Production." *Bulletin of the Institute of Classical Studies* 51: 171–74.

Andreau, Jean. 1974. *Les affaires de Monsieur Jucundus*. Rome: École française de Rome.

———. 1987. *Le vie financière dans le monde romain: les métiers de manieurs d'argent*. Rome: École française de Rome.

———. 1999a. *Banking and Business in the Roman World*. New York: Cambridge University Press.

———. 1999b. "Intérêts non agricoles des chevaliers romains (IIe siècle av. J.-C.—IIIe siècle ap. J.-C.)." In *L'ordre équestre. Histoire d'une aristocratie (IIe siècle av. J.-C.—IIIe siècle ap. J.-C.)*, edited by Ségolène Demougin, Hubert Devijver, and Marie-Thérèse Raepsaet-Charlier. https://www.persee.fr/doc/efr_0223-5099_1999_act_257_1_5498.

———. 2005. "Le système monétaire partiellement 'fermé' de l'Égypte romaine." In *L'exception égyptienne? Production et échanges monétaires en Égypte hellénistique et romaine*, 329–38. Cairo: Institut français d'archéologie orientale.

———. 2008. "The Use and Survival of Coins and of Gold and Silver in the Vesuvian Cities." In *The Monetary Systems of the Greeks and Romans*, edited by W. V. Harris. Oxford: Oxford University Press. https://doi.org/10.1093/acprof:oso/9780199233359.003.0011.

Andreau, Jean, and Jérôme Maucourant. 1999. "À propos de la rationalité économique dans l'Antiquité gréco-romaine: Une interprétation des thèses de D. Rathbone (1991)." *Topoi. Orient-Occident*, 47–102.

Antonio, Margaret L., Ziyue Gao, Hannah M. Moots, Michaela Lucci, Francesca Candilio, Susanna Sawyer, Victoria Oberreiter, et al. 2019. "Ancient Rome: A Genetic Crossroads of Europe and the Mediterranean." *Science* 366 (6466): 708–14.

Armitage, David, and Jo Guldi. 2015. "Le retour de la longue durée: Une perspective anglo-américaine." *Annales: Histoire, Sciences Sociales* 70: 289–318.

Arnoldus, Antonia, Kim Bowes, Michael MacKinnon, Anna Maria Mercuri, Eleonora Rattighieri, and Rosella Rinaldi. 2021. "Agriculture and Land Use." In *The Roman Peasant Project 2009–2015: Excavating the Roman Poor*, edited by Kim Bowes, 2: 471–516. Philadelphia: University of Pennsylvania Museum of Archaeology and Anthropology.

Arruñada, Benito. 2020. "The Institutions of Roman Markets." In *Roman Law and Economics: Volume II: Exchange, Ownership, and Disputes*, edited by Giuseppe Dari-Mattiacci and Dennis P. Kehoe, 247–98. Oxford University Press.

Atkinson, Tony, and François Bourguignon. 2000. "Pauvreté et inclusion dans une perspective mondiale." *Revue d'économie du développement* 8 (1–2): 13–32.

Aubert, Jean-Jacques. 2004. "De l'usage de l'écriture dans la gestion d'entreprise à l'époque romaine." In *Mentalités et choix économiques des Romains*, edited by Jean Andreau, Jérôme France, and Sylvie Pittia, 127–47. Bordeaux: Ausonius Éditions.

———. 2009. "Productive Investments in Agriculture: *Instrumentum fundi* and *peculium* in the Later Roman Republic." In *Agricoltura e scambi nell'Italia tardo-repubblicana*, edited by Jesper Carlsen and Elio Lo Cascio, 167–85. Bari, Italy: Edipuglia.

———. 2014. "For Swap or Sale: The Roman Law of Barter." In *Les Affaires de Monsieur Andreau: Économie et Société du Monde Romain*, edited by Catherine Apicella, Marie-Laurence Haack, and François Lerouxel, 109–21. Bordeaux: Ausonius Éditions.

Aymard, Maurice. 1983. "Autoconsommation et marchés: Chayanov, Labrousse ou Le Roy Ladurie?" *Annales. Economies, sociétés, civilisations* 38: 1392–1410.

Baer, Gabriel. 1962. *A History of Landownership in Modern Egypt 1800–1950*. London: Oxford University Press.

Bagnall, Roger. 1974. "The Archive of Laches. Prosperous Farmers in the Fayum in the Second Century." PhD thesis, Duke University.

———. 1977. "Price in 'Sales on Delivery.'" *Greek, Roman and Byzantine Studies* 18: 85–96.

———. 1985a. "Agricultural Productivity and Taxation in Later Roman Egypt." *Transactions of the American Philological Association* 115: 289–308.

———. 1985b. *Currency and Inflation in Fourth Century Egypt*. Chico, CA: Scholars Press.

———. 1992. "Landholding in Late Roman Egypt: The Distribution of Wealth." *Journal of Roman Studies* 82: 128–49.

———. 1993. *Egypt in Late Antiquity*. Princeton, NJ: Princeton University Press.

———. 1997a. "Missing Females in Roman Egypt." *Scripta Classica Israelica* 16: 121–38.

———. 1997b. *The Kellis Agricultural Account Book (P. Kell. IV Gr. 96)*. Oxford: Oxbow.

———. 2002. "The Effects of Plague: Model and Evidence." *Journal of Roman Archaeology* 15: 114–20.

———. 2011. *Everyday Writing in the Greco-Roman East*. Berkeley: University of California Press.

Bagnall, Roger, and Bruce Frier. 1994. *The Demography of Roman Egypt*. Cambridge: Cambridge University Press.

Bagnall, Roger, Christina Helms, and Arthur Verhoogt. 2005. *Documents from Berenike: Vol. 2. Texts from the 1999–2001 Seasons*. Brussels: Fondation Égyptologique Reine Élisabeth.

Bagnall, Roger, and Alexander Jones, eds. 2019. *Mathematics, Metrology, and Model Contracts: A Codex from Late Antique Business Education (P. Math.)*. New York: Institute for the Study of the Ancient World and New York University Press.

Bagnall, Roger, Ursula Thanheiser, and Gillian Bowen. 2022. "The Economy." In *Kellis: A Roman-Period Village in Egypt's Dakhleh Oasis*, edited by Colin Hope and Gilllian Bowen, 135–68. Cambridge: Cambridge University Press.

Bailey, Keith, and James Spletzer. 2021. "A New Measure of Multiple Jobholding in the U.S. Economy." *Labour Economics* 71: 102009. https://doi.org/10.1016/j.labeco.2021.102009.

Bailey, Melissa. 2011. "To Separate the Act from the Thing: Technologies of Value in the Ancient Mediterranean." PhD thesis, Stanford University.

———. 2013. "Roman Money and Numerical Practice." *Revue Belge de Philologie et d'Histoire* 91 (91): 153–86.

Baird, J. A. 2013. "On Reading the Material Culture of Ancient Sexual Labor." *Helios* 42 (1): 163–75.

Baird, J. A., and Claire Taylor, eds. 2011. *Ancient Graffiti in Context*. New York/London: Routledge.

Bakels, Corrie, and Stefanie Jacomet. 2003. "Access to Luxury Foods in Central Europe during the Roman Period: The Archaeobotanical Evidence." *World Archaeology* 34 (3): 542–57.

Bakhtin, Mikhail. 1981. *The Dialogic Imagination. Four Essays*. Translated by Caryl Emerson and Michael Holquist. Austin: University of Texas.

Baldoni, Marica, Angelo Gismondi, Michelle Alexander, Alessia D'Agostino, Domitilla Tibaldi, Gabriele Di Marco, Giuseppina Scano, et al. 2020. "A Multidisciplinary Approach to Investigate the Osteobiography of the Roman Imperial Population from Muracciola Torresina (Palestrina, Rome, Italy)." *Journal of Archaeological Science: Reports*, 102279. https://doi.org/10.1016/j.jasrep.2020.102279.

Banaji, Jairus. 1997. "Lavoratori liberi e residenza coatta: Il colonato romano in prospettiva storica." In *Terre, proprietari e contadini dell'impero romano*, edited by Elio Lo Cascio, 253–80. Rome: Nuova Italia scientifica.

———. 2001. *Agrarian Change in Late Antiquity: Gold, Labour and Aristocratic Dominance*. Oxford: Oxford University Press.

———. 2003. "The Fictions of Free Labour: Contract, Coercion, and So-Called Unfree Labour." *Historical Materialism* 11 (3): 69–95.

Bandi, Lydia. 1937. "I conti privati nei papiri dell'Egitto greco-romo." *Aegyptus* 17 (4): 349–451.

Banerjee, Abhijit, and Esther Duflo. 2007. "The Economic Lives of the Poor." *Journal of Economic Perspectives* 21 (1): 141–67.

———. 2011. *Poor Economics: A Radical Rethinking of the Way to Fight Global Poverty*. New York: Public Affairs.

Banfield, Edward. 1958. *Moral Basis for a Backward Society*. New York: Free Press.

Bang, Peter. 2008. *The Roman Bazaar*. Cambridge: Cambridge University Press.

Baptist, Edward. 2014. *The Half Has Never Been Told: Slavery and the Making of American Capitalism*. New York: Basic Books.

Barker, Graeme, David Gilbertson, Barri Jones, and David Mattingly, eds. 1996. *Farming the Desert: The UNESCO Libyan Valley Archaeological Survey*. 2 vols. Paris/Tripoli/London: UNESCO Publishing; Department of Antiquities: Libyan Studies.

Basu, Sudipta, and Gregory Waymire. 2006. "Recordkeeping and Human Evolution." *Accounting Horizons* 20 (3): 201–29.

———. 2021. "The Evolution of Double-Entry Bookkeeping." SSRN. https://ssrn.com/abstract=3093303 or http://dx.doi.org/10.2139/ssrn.3093303.

Bateman, Victoria. 2019. *The Sex Factor: How Women Made the West Rich*. Medford, MA: Polity.

Baten, Joerg, and Stefan Priwitzer. 2015. "Social and Intertemporal Differences of Basic Numeracy in Pannonia (First Century BCE to Third Century CE)." *Scandinavian Economic History Review* 63 (2): 110–34.

Baten, Joerg, and Richard Steckel. 2019. "The History of Violence in Europe: Evidence from Cranial and Postcranial Bone Trauma." In *The Backbone of Europe: Health, Diet, Work and Violence over Two Millennia*, edited by Richard Steckel, Clark Spencer Larsen, Charlotte Roberts, and Joerg Baten, 300–324. Cambridge: Cambridge University Press.

Baten, Joerg, Richard H. Steckel, Clark Spencer Larsen, and Charlotte A. Roberts. 2019. "Multidimensional Patterns of European Health, Work, and Violence over the Past Two Millennia." In *The Backbone of Europe: Health, Diet, Work and Violence over Two Millennia*, edited by Richard Steckel, Clark Spencer Larsen, Charlotte Roberts, and Joerg Baten, 381–96. Cambridge: Cambridge University Press.

Beard, Mary, ed. 1991. *Literacy in the Roman World*. Ann Arbor, MI: Journal of Roman Archaeology Supplementary Series.

Becker, Gary. 1981. *Treatise on the Family*. Cambridge, MA: Cambridge University Press.

Beckert, Jens. 2009. "The Great Transformation of Embeddedness: Karl Polanyi and the New Economic Sociology." In *Market and Society: The Great Transformation Today*, edited by Chris Hann and Keith Hart, 38–55. Cambridge: Cambridge University Press.

Bedini, Alessandro, Carla Testa, and Paola Catalano. 1995. "Roma–Un sepolcreto d'epoca imperiale a Vallerano." *Archeologia Laziale* 12: 319–31.

Belcastro, Giovanna, Elisa Rastelli, Valentina Mariotti, Chiara Consiglio, Fiorenzo Facchini, and Benedetta Bonfiglioli. 2007. "Continuity or Discontinuity of the Life-Style in Central Italy During the Roman Imperial Age–Early Middle Ages Transition: Diet, Health, and Behavior." *American Journal of Physical Anthropology* 132: 381–94.

Beloch, Karl Julius. 1886. *Die Bevölkerung der Griechisch-Römischen Welt*. Leipzig: Duncker & Humblot.

Bemko, Zhenia, and Janet Monge. 2018. "Cotton Marks My Body, Cotton Marks My Soul." Lecture, African American Museum of Philadelphia.

Benassi, Valentina, Anna Buccellato, Carla Caldarini, Paola Catalano, Flavio DeAngelis, R. Egidi, Simona Minozzi, et al. 2011. "La donna come forza lavoro nella Roma Imperiale: Nuove prospettive da recenti scavi nel Suburbio." *Medicina nei secoli* 22: 291–302.

Benefiel, Rebecca. 2013. "Ancient Graffiti Project." http://ancientgraffiti.org.

Benefiel, Rebecca, and Peter Keegan, eds. 2016. *Inscriptions in the Private Sphere in the Greco-Roman World*. Leiden: Brill.

Bergamesco, Marco. 1995. "Le διδασκαλικαί nella ricerca attuale." *Aegyptus* 75 (1/2): 95–167.

Bergamini, Margherita, ed. 2011. *Scoppieto II: I materiali*. Florence: All'Insegna del giglio.

Berggren, Eric. 1969. "Blera (località Selvasecca): Villa rustica etrusco-romano con manifattura di terrecotte architettoniche." *Notizie degli Scavi di Antichità* ser. 8.23: 51–59.

Bernard, Seth. 2016. "Debt, Land, and Labor in the Early Republican Economy." *Phoenix* 70 (3–4): 317–38.

———. 2017. "Workers in the Roman Imperial Building Industry." In *Work, Labour, and Professions in the Roman World*, edited by Koenraad Verboven and Christian Laes, 62–86. Leiden: Brill.

———. 2023. "Premium for Skilled Labor in the Roman World." *Explorations in Economic History* 88. https://doi.org/10.1016/j.eeh.2023.101516.

Bernigaud, Nicolas, Alain Berga, Johann Blanchard, Olivier Blin, Muriel Boulen, Lionel Boulenger, Marie Derreumaux, et al. 2017. "L'Île-de-France." In *Gallia Rustica 1: Les campagnes du nord-est de la Gaule, de la fin de l'âge du Fer à l'Antiquité tardive*, edited by Michel Reddé, 389–494. Bordeaux: Ausonius Éditions.

Bernstein, Henry, and Terence Byers. 2001. "From Peasant Studies to Agrarian Change." *Journal of Agrarian Change* 1 (1): 1–56.

Berrendonner, Clara. 2007. "*Mercennarius* dans les sources littéraires." In *Vocabulaire et expressions de l'économie dans le monde antique*, edited by Jean Andreau and Véronique Chankowski, 211–31. Bordeaux: Ausonius Éditions.

Bewley, Truman. 1999. *Why Wages Don't Fall During a Recession*. Cambridge, MA: Harvard University Press.

Bianchi, Giancarlo, and Nicholas McCave. 1999. "Holocene Periodicity in North Atlantic Climate and Deep-Ocean Flow South of Iceland." *Nature* 397 (6719): 515–17.

Bikoulis, Peter. 2018. "The Countryside." In *Archaeology and Urban Settlement in Late Roman and Byzantine Anatolia: Euchaïta-Avkat-Beyözü and Its Environment*, edited by Hugh Elton, James Newhard, and John Haldon, 97–133. Cambridge: Cambridge University Press.

Bingen, P. 1951. "Les comptes dans les archives d'Héroninos." *Chronique d'Égypte* 26: 378–85.

Bintliff, John, and Anthony Snodgrass. 1988. "Off-Site Pottery Distribution: A Regional and Interregional Perspective." *Current Anthropology* 29: 506–13.

Birks, Peter. 2014. *The Roman Law of Obligations*. Oxford: Oxford University Press.

Biscottini, Maria Valentina. 1966. "L'archivio di Tryphon tessitore di Oxyrhynchos." *Aegyptus* 46 (3/4): 60–90, 186–292.

Bisel, Jane, and Sara Bisel. 2002. "Health and Nutrition at Herculaneum: An Examination of Human Skeletal Remains." In *Natural History of Pompeii*, edited by Wilhelmina Jashemski and Frederick Mayer, 451–75. Cambridge: Cambridge University Press.

Blakey, Michael, and Lesley Rankin-Hill. 2009. *Skeletal Biology of the New York African Burial Ground*. Washington, DC: Howard University Press.

Blanchard, Johann. 2012. "Un réseau de fossés antique original au nord-ouest du plateau briard: Nouvelles observations réalisées à Bussy-Saint-Georges (Marne-la-Vallée, Seine-et-Marne)." *Revue archéologique du Centre de la France* 52: 191–230.

Bloch, Marc. 1931. *Les caractères originaux de l'histoire rurale française*. Paris: Librairie Armand Colin.

Blouin, Katherine. 2010. "An Arsinoite Loan of Money with Interest in Kind." *Bulletin of the American Society of Papyrologists* 47: 93–109.

———. 2014. *Triangular Landscapes: Environment, Society and the State in the Nile Delta under Roman Rule*. Oxford: Oxford University Press.

Boak, Arthur. 1933. *Papyri from Tebtynis. Vol. 1*. Michigan Papyri, 2. Ann Arbor: University of Michigan Press.

Bodel, John. 1989. "Missing Links: *Thymatulum* or *Tomaculum*?" *Harvard Studies in Classical Philology* 92: 349–66.

———. 1994. "Graveyards and Groves. A Study of the *Lex Lucerina*." *American Journal of Ancient History* 11: 1–119.

———. 1997. "Monumental Villas and Villa Monuments." *Journal of Roman Archaeology* 10: 5–35.

———. 2015. "Status Dissonance and Status Dissidents in the Equestrian Order." In *Social Status and Prestige in the Graeco-Roman World*, edited by Annika Kuhn, 29–44. Stuttgart: Franz Steiner Verlag.

Bodenhorn, Howard, Timothy Guinnane, and Thomas Mroz. 2019. "Theory and Diagnostics for Selection Biases in Historical Height Samples." *Research in Economic History* 35: 59–89.

Bogin, Barry. 2021. *Patterns of Human Growth*. 3rd ed. Cambridge: Cambridge University Press.

Boldizzoni, Francesco. 2011. *The Poverty of Clio: Resurrecting Economic History*. Princeton, NJ: Princeton University Press.

Bond, Sarah. 2016. *Trade and Taboo: Disreputable Professions in the Roman Mediterranean*. Ann Arbor: University of Michigan Press.

———. 2025. *Strike. Labor, Unions, and Resistance in the Roman Empire*. New Haven, CT: Yale University Press.

Bondioli, Luca, Alessia Nava, Paola Francesca Rossi, and Alessandra Sperduti. 2016. "Diet and Health in Central-Southern Italy during the Roman Imperial Time." *Acta Imeko* 5 (2): 19–25.

Bonfiglioli, Benedetta, Patricia Brasili Gualandi, and Giovanna Belcastro. 2003. "Dento-Alveolar Lesions and Nutritional Habits of a Roman Imperial Age Population (1st–4th c. AD): Quadrella (Molise, Italy)." *Homo* 54 (1): 36–56.

Bonneau, Danielle. 1971. *Le fisc et le Nil: Incidences des irrégularités de la crue du Nil sur la fiscalité foncière dans l'Égypte grecque et romaine*. Paris: Cujas.

Bonsall, Laura. 2013. "Variations in the Health Status of Urban Populations in Roman Britain: A Comparison of Skeletal Samples from Major and Minor Towns." PhD thesis, University of Edinburgh.

Booth, Paul, and Andrew Simmonds. 2012. *Gill Mill, Ducklington and South Leigh, Oxfordshire: Post-Excavation Assessment and Project Design*. Oxford: Oxford Archaeology.

Boozer, Anna Lucille. 2021. *At Home in Roman Egypt: A Social Archaeology*. Cambridge: Cambridge University Press.

Boserup, Ester. 1965. *The Conditions of Agricultural Growth*. London: George Allen & Unwin.

Bourdieu, Pierre. 1977. *Outline of a Theory of Practice*. Translated by R. Nice. Cambridge: Cambridge University Press.

———. 1979. *La distinction: Critique sociale du jugement*. Paris: Les Éditions de Minuit.

Bowes, Kim. 2021a. "Introduction: Inventing Roman Peasants." In *The Roman Peasant Project 2009–2015: Excavating the Roman Rural Poor*, edited by Kim Bowes, 1: 1–18. Philadelphia: University of Pennsylvania Museum of Archaeology and Anthropology.

———. 2021b. "Roman Agriculture from Above and Below: Words and Things." In *Ancient History from Below: Subaltern Experiences and Actions in Context*, edited by Cyril Courrier and Julio Cesar Magalhães de Olivera, 122–54. London: Routledge.

———, ed. 2021c. *The Roman Peasant Project 2009–2015: Excavating the Roman Rural Poor*. 2 vols. Philadelphia: University of Pennsylvania Museum of Archaeology and Anthropology.

———. 2021d. "Tracking Consumption at Pompeii: The Graffiti Lists." *Journal of Roman Archaeology* 34: 552–84.

———. 2021e. "When Kuznets Went to Rome: Roman Economic Well-Being and the Reframing of Roman History." *Capitalism: A Journal of History and Economics* 2 (1): 7–40.

———. 2022a. "Beyond *Capital*." In *Capital in Classical Antiquity*, edited by Max Koedijk and Neville Morley, 339–54. Cham, Switzerland: Palgrave Macmillan.

———. 2022b. "Tracking Liquid Savings at Pompeii: The Coin Hoard Data." *Journal of Roman Archaeology* 35 (1): 1–27.

———. 2024. "The 'Health Problem' in Roman Economic History: A Prolegomenon." In *Morality and Models: Assessing Modern Approaches to the Greco-Roman Economy*, edited by Seth Bernard and Sarah Murray, 345–80. Cham, Switzerland: Palgrave Macmillan.

Bowes, Kim, Stephen Collins-Elliot, and Cam Grey. 2021. "Where Did Roman Peasants Live?" In *The Roman Peasant Project 2009–2015: Excavating the Roman Rural Poor*, edited by Kim Bowes, 2: 435–70. Philadelphia: University of Pennsylvania Museum of Archaeology and Anthropology.

Bowes, Kim, Michael MacKinnon, Anna Maria Mercuri, Eleonora Rattighieri, and Rosella Rinaldi. 2021. "Diet, Dining and Subsistence." In *The Roman Peasant Project 2009–2015: Excavating the Roman Poor*, edited by Kim Bowes, 2: 517–42. Philadelphia: University of Pennsylvania Museum of Archaeology and Anthropology.

Bowes, Kim, Anna Maria Mercuri, Eleonora Rattigheri, Rossella Rinaldi, Antonia Arnoldus-Huyzendveld, Mariaelena Ghisleni, Cam Grey, Michael MacKinnon, and Emanuele Vaccaro. 2017. "Peasant Agricultural Strategies in Southern Tuscany: Convertible Agriculture and the Importance of Pasture." In *The Economic Integration of Rural Italy: Rural Communities in a Globalizing World*, edited by de Timn Haas and Gijs Tol, 165–94. Leiden: Brill.

Bowes, Kim, and Jessica Pearson. In preparation. "Dietary Isotopes of the Roman Empire."

Bowes, Kim, Emanuele Vaccaro, Stephen Collins-Elliot, and Cam Grey. 2021. "Non-Agricultural Production, Markets, and Trade." In *The Roman Peasant Project 2009–2015: Excavating the Roman Rural Poor*, edited by Kim Bowes, 2: 543–66. Philadelphia: University of Pennsylvania Museum of Archaeology and Anthropology.

Bowman, Alan. 1985. "Landholding in the Hermopolite Nome in the Fourth Century AD." *Journal of Roman Studies* 75: 137–63.

———. 1994. "The Roman Imperial Army: Letters and Literacy on the Northern Frontier." In *Literacy and Power in the Ancient World*, edited by Greg Woolf and Alan Bowman, 109–25. Cambridge: Cambridge University Press.

———. 1998. *Life and Letters from the Roman Frontier: Vindolanda and Its People*. London: Routledge.

———. 2013. "Agricultural Productivity in Roman Egypt." In *The Roman Agricultural Economy: Organization, Investment and Production*, edited by Andrew Wilson and Alan Bowman, 219–53. Oxford: Oxford University Press.

Bowman, Alan, and Andrew Wilson, eds. 2009. *Quantifying the Roman Economy: Methods and Problems*. Oxford: Oxford University Press.

Bowman, Alan, and Greg Woolf, eds. 1994. *Literacy and Power in the Ancient World*. Cambridge: Cambridge University Press.

Bradley, Keith. 1985. "Child Labour in the Roman World." *Historical Reflections/Réflexions Historiques* 12 (2): 311–30.

Bransbourg, Gilles. 2022. "Roman Coinage under the Antonines Revisited: An Economy of Silver, Not Gold." In *The Uncertain Past: Probability in Ancient History*, edited by Myles Lavan, Daniel Jew, and Brent Danon, 135–94. Cambridge: Cambridge University Press.

Braudel, Fernand. 1972. *The Mediterranean and the Mediterranean World in the Age of Philip II*. New York: Harper & Row.

Breglia, Laura. 1950. "Circolazione monetale a Pompeii." In *Pompeiana: Raccolta di studi per il secondo centenario degli scavi di Pompeii*, 41–59. Naples: Gaetano Macchiaroli.

Brent, Liana, and Tracy Prowse. 2014. "Grave Goods, Burial Practices and Patterns of Distribution in the Vagnari Cemetery." In *Beyond Vagnari: New Themes in the Study of Roman South Italy*, edited by A.M. Small, 99–109. Bari, Italy: Edipuglia.

———. 2024. "Rural Labor and Identity at Vagnari in Southern Italy." In *Valuing Labour in Antiquity*, edited by Miko Flohr and Kim Bowes, 264–86. Leiden: Brill.

Bresson, Alain. 2017a. "Anthropogenic Pollution in Greece and Rome." In *Pollution and the Environment in Ancient Life and Thought*, edited by Orietta Dora Cordovana and Gian Franco Chiai, 179–202. Stuttgart: Franz Steiner Verlag.

———. 2017b. "Money Exchange and the Economics of Inequality in the Ancient Greek and Roman World." In *Economy and Inequality: Resources, Exchange and Power in Classical Antiquity*, 271–308. Geneva: Fondation Hardt.

Bresson, Alain, and François Bresson. 2004. "Max Weber, la comptabilité rationnelle et l'économie du monde gréco-romain." *Les Cahiers du Centre de Recherches Historiques* 34: 1–21.

Brewer, John, and Roy Porter, eds. 1993. *Consumption and the World of Goods*. New York: Routledge.

Brindle, Tom. 2016a. "The North." In *New Visions of the Countryside of Roman Britain: Volume 1. The Rural Settlement of Roman Britain*, edited by Alexander Smith, Martyn Allen, Tom Brindle, and Michael Fulford, 308–30. London: Society for the Promotion of Roman Studies.

———. 2016b. "The South-West." In *New Visions of the Countryside of Roman Britain: Volume 1. The Rural Settlement of Roman Britain*, edited by Alexander Smith, Martyn Allen, Tom Brindle, and Michael Fulford, 331–58. London: Society for the Promotion of Roman Studies.

———. 2017a. "Ards or Ploughs in Arable Farming, Plant Foods and Resources." In *New Visions of the Countryside of Roman Britain. Volume 2. The Economy of Roman Britain*, edited by Martyn Allen, Lisa Lodwick, Tom Brindle, Michael Fulford, and Alexander Smith, 42–43. London: Society for the Promotion of Roman Studies.

———. 2017b. "Coins and Markets in the Countryside." In *New Visions of the Countryside of Roman Britain. Volume 2. The Economy of Roman Britain*, edited by Martyn Allen, Lisa Lodwick, Tom Brindle, Michael Fulford, and Alexander Smith, 237–80. London: Society for the Promotion of Roman Studies.

———. 2018. "Personal Appearance in the Countryside of Roman Britain." In *New Visions of the Countryside of Roman Britain: Volume 3. Life and Death in the Countryside of Roman Britain*, edited by Alexander Smith, Martyn Allen, Tom Brindle, Michael Fulford, Lisa Lodwick, and Anna Rohnbogner, 6–47. London: Society for the Promotion of Roman Studies.

Broekaert, Wim. 2016. "Freedmen and Agency in Roman Business." In *Urban Craftsmen and Traders in the Roman World*, edited by Andrew Wilson and Miko Flohr, 222–53. Oxford: Oxford University Press.

———. 2017. "Conflicts, Contract Enforcement and Business Communities in the Archive of the Sulpicii." In *The Economy of Pompeii*, edited by Miko Flohr and Andrew Wilson, 387–414. Oxford: Oxford University Press.

Broekaert, Wim, and Arjan Zuiderhoek. 2015. "Society, the Market, or Actually Both? Networks and the Allocation of Credit and Capital Goods in the Roman Economy." *Cahiers du Centre Gustave Glotz* 26: 141–90.

Brown, Peter. 1971. *The World of Late Antiquity: From Marcus Aurelius to Muhammad*. London: Thames & Hudson.

———. 2012. *Through the Eye of a Needle: Wealth, the Fall of Rome, and the Making of Christianity in the West, 350–550 AD*. Princeton, NJ: Princeton University Press.

Brubaker, Rogers, and Frederick Cooper. 2000. "Beyond 'Identity.'" *Theory and Society* 29 (1): 1–47.

Brüggler, Marion, Karen Jeneson, Renate Gerlach, Jutta Meurers-Balke, Tanja Zerl, and Michael Herchenbach. 2017. "The Roman Rhineland: Farming and Consumption in Different Landscapes." In *Gallia Rustica 1. Les campagnes du nord-est de la Gaule, de la fin de l'âge du Fer à l'Antiquité tardive*, edited by Michel Reddé, 19–95. Bordeaux: Ausonius Éditions.

Brun, Jean-Pierre. 2003. *Le vin et l'huile dans la Méditerranée antique: Viticulture, oléiculture et procédés de transformation*. Paris: Errance.

———. 2004. *Archéologie du vin et de l'huile dans l'Empire romain*. Paris: Errance.

———. 2016. "Les moulins hydrauliques dans l'Antiquité." In *Archéologie des moulins hydrauliques, à traction animale et à vent des origines à l'époque médiévale et moderne en Europe et dans le monde méditerranéen.*, 21–50. Besançon: Presses universitaires de Franche-Comté.

Brun, Jean-Pierre, Luc Jaccottey, Florent Jodry, Stéphanie Lapareux-Couturier, Paul Picavet, and Boris Robin. 2017. "Pistes pour l'identification des activités de mouture sur les sites ruraux de la Gaule romaine." In *Produire, transformer et stocker dans les campagnes des Gaules romaines*, edited by Frédéric Trément, 113–37. Bordeaux: Éditions de la Féderation Aquitania.

Brunt, P. A. 1950. "Pay and Superannuation in the Roman Army." *Papers of the British School at Rome* 18: 50–71.

———. 1968. "The Army and the Land in the Roman Revolution." *Journal of Roman Studies* 52: 68–86.

———. 1971a. *Italian Manpower 225 B.C.–A.D. 14*. Cambridge: Cambridge University Press.

———. 1971b. *Social Conflicts in the Roman Republic*. London: Chatto & Windus.

———. 1980. "Free Labour and Public Works at Rome." *Journal of Roman Studies* 70: 81–100.

———. 1981. "The Revenues of Rome." *Journal of Roman Studies* 71: 161–72.

Bruun, Christer. 2003. "*Medius fidius . . . tantam pecuniam Nicomedenses perdiderint!*" Roman Water Supply, Public Administration, and Private Contractors." In *Tâches publiques et entreprise privée dans le monde romain*, edited by Jean-Jacques Aubert, 305–25. Geneva: Université de Neuchâtel.

Buccellato, Anna, Carla Caldarini, Paola Catalano, Stefano Musco, Walter Pantano, Carlo Torri, and Federica Zabotti. 2008. "La nécropole de Collatina." *Dossiers d'Archéologie* 330: 28–37.

Buccellato, Anna, and Paola Catalano. 2003. "Il comprensorio della necropoli di via Basiliano (Roma): un'indagine multidisciplinare." *Mélanges de l'École Française de Rome* 115 (1): 311–76.

Budge, E. A. Wallis. 1920. *By Nile and Tigris: A Narrative of Journeys in Egypt and Mesopotamia on Behalf of the British Museum Between the Years 1886 and 1913*. 2 vols. London: J. Murray.

Buikstra, Jane, ed. 2019. *Ortner's Identification of Pathological Conditions in Human Skeletal Remains*. London: Academic Press.

Buikstra, Jane, and Elizabeth Uhl. 2023. "21st Century Paleopathology: Integrating Theoretical Models with Biomedical Advances." *Asian Journal of Paleopathology* 5: 1–7.

Bülow-Jacobsen, Adam. 2019. "The Archive of Philokles." In *Ostraca de Krokodilo II. La correspondance privée et les réseaux personnels de Philoklès, Apollôs et Ischyras: O. Krok. 152–334*, edited by Adam Bülow-Jacobsen, Jean-Luc Fournet, and Bérangère Redon, 33–128. Cairo: Institut français d'archéologie orientale.

Bürge, Alfons. 2023. *Die Lohnarbeit in der Antike*. Munich: C.H. Beck.

Burkhalter, Fabienne. 1998. "La production des objets en métal (or, argent, bronze) en Egypte hellénistique et romaine à travers les sources papyrologiques." In *Commerce et artisanat dans l'Alexandrie hellénistique et romaine*, edited by Jean-Yves Empereur, 125–33. Suppléments au Bulletin de Correspondance Hellénique, 33. Paris: Boccard.

Busana, Maria Stella, and Claudia Forin. 2020. "Economy and Production Systems in Roman Cisalpine Gaul: Some Data on Farms and Villae." In *Villas, Peasant Agriculture, and the*

Roman Rural Economy: Archaeology and Economy in the Ancient World—Proceedings of the 19th International Congress of Classical Archaeology, Cologne/Bonn 2018, edited by Annalisa Marzano, 17–30. Heidelberg: Heidelberg University Library.

Bustamante-Álvarez, Macarena, Francisco Javier Heras, Esperança Huguet Enguita, Adrien Malingas, Jordi Principal, and Albert Ribera i Lacomba. 2017. "Via degli Augustali VII, 4, 28: Una fosa singular de mediados del siglo II a.C. en Pompeya." *Empúries* 57: 85–118.

———. 2020. "Via degli Augustali VII 4.28: Las evidencias cerámicas de una fosa singular de mediados del siglo II a.C." In *Fecisti Cretaria. Dal frammento al contesto: studi sul vasellame ceramico del territorio vesuviano*, edited by Luana Toniolo and Masimo Osanna, 281–96. Rome: L'Erma di Bretschneider.

Butcher, Kevin. 2015. "Debasement and the Decline of Rome." In *Studies in Ancient Coinage in Honor of Andrew Burnett*, edited by Dario Calomino and Roger Bland, 181–205. London: Spink.

Buttrey, Theodore V. 1994. "Calculating Ancient Coin Production II: Why It Cannot Be Done." *Numismatic Chronicle* 154: 341–52.

Caldarini, Carla. 2009. "Analisi antropologica dei reperti scheletrici e dentali." In *Musarna 3: La nécropole impériale*, edited by Eric Rebillard, 89–99. Rome: École française de Rome.

Caldarini, Carla, Federica Zavaroni, and Valentina Benassi. 2015. "Indicatori scheletrici di lavoro: Marcatori muscolo-scheletrici, artropatie e traumi." *Medicina nei secoli* 27 (3): 905–68.

Calderini, Rita. 1950. "Gli ἀγράμματοι nell'Egitto greco-romano." *Aegyptus* 30 (1): 14–41.

Cambi, Franco. 2002. "La casa del colono e il paesaggio (II–III secolo a.C.)." In *Paesaggi d'Etruria. Valle dell'Albegna, Valle d'Oro, Valle del Chiarone, Valle del Tafone. Progetto di ricerca italo-britannico seguito allo scavo di Settefinestre*, edited by Andrea Carandini, Franco Cambi, Maria Grazia Celuzza, and Elizabeth Fentress, 137–44.

Camin, Lorenza. 2005. "Un affibbiaglio, una gemma e un bronzetto dal sito romano di Podere S. Mario." *Ostraka* 14 (1): 7–14.

Camin, Lorenza, and Walter McCall. 2002. "Settlement Patterns and Rural Habitation in the Middle Cecina Valley between the Hellenic to Roman Age: The Case of Podere Cosciano." *Etruscan Studies* 9 (March): 19–27.

Camodeca, Giuseppe. 1992. *L'archivio puteolano dei Sulpicii*. Naples: Università Napoli Federico II.

———. 2003. "Il credito negli archivi campani: Il caso di Puteoli e di Herculaneum." In *Credito e moneta nel mondo romano*, edited by Elio Lo Cascio, 69–98. Bari, Italy: Edipuglia.

———. 2017. *Tabulae Herculanenses: Edizione e commento*. Rome: Quasar.

Campana, Stefano. 2017. "Emptyscapes: Filling an 'Empty' Mediterranean Landscape at Rusellae, Italy." *Antiquity* 91 (359): 1223–40.

Campmany Jiménez, Joan, Iza Romanowska, Rubina Raja, and Eivind Seland. 2022. "Food Security in Roman Palmyra (Syria) in Light of Paleoclimatological Evidence and Its Historical Implications." *PLoS ONE* September 21, 2022. https://doi.org/10.1371/journal.pone.0273241.

Cantilena, Renata. 2005. "Monete d'oro a Pompei." In *XIII Congreso Internacional de Numismática – Actas (Madrid, 15–19 settembre 2003)*, edited by Carmen Alfaro Asins, Carmen Marcos Alonso, and Paloma Otero Morán, 673–79. Madrid: Ministerio de Cultura, Secretaría General Técnica.

Capasso, Luigi. 1984. "Dental Pathology and Alimentary Habits Reconstruction of the Etruscan Population: Proceedings of the 5th European Meeting of the Paleopathological Association." In *Proceedings of the 5th European Meeting of the Paleopathological Association*, 59–67.

———. 2001. *I Fuggiaschi di Ercolano: Paleobiologia delle vittime dell'eruzione vesuviana del 79 d.C.* Rome: L'Erma di Breschneider.

———. 2002. "Bacteria in Two-Millennia-Old Cheese, and Related Epizoonoses in Roman Populations." *Journal of Infection* 45 (2): 122–27.

Capasso, Luigi, and Luisa Di Domenicantonio. 1998. "Work-Related Syndesmoses on the Bones of Children Who Died at Herculaneum." *The Lancet* 352 (9140). https://doi.org/10.1016/S0140-6736(05)61104-X.

Capasso, Luigi, and Gabriele Di Tota. 1995. "Malattie infettive degli Etruschi." In *Aspetti della cultura etrusca di Volterra Etrusca tra l'età del ferro e l'età ellenistica*, 551–57. Florence: Olschki.

Capogrossi Colognesi, Luigi, Andrea Giardina, and Aldo Schiavone, eds. 1978. *Analisi Marxista e Società Antiche*. Rome: Istituto Gramsci.

Cappers, R.T.J. 2016. "Modelling Shifts in Cereal Cultivation in Egypt from the Start of Agriculture until Modern Times." In *News from the Past: Progress in African Archaeobotany. Proceedings of the 7th International Workshop on African Archaeobotany in Vienna, 2–5 July 2012*, edited by Ursula Thanheiser, 27–35. Groningen: Barkhuis.

Carandini, Andrea, ed. 1981. *Atlante della forme ceramiche. I. Ceramica fine romana nel bacino mediterraneo (medio e tardo impero)*. Rome: Istituto della Enciclopedia Italiana.

———, ed. 1985. *Settefinestre, una villa schiavistica nell'Etruria Romana*. 3 vols. Modena: Panini.

———. 1988. *Schiavi in Italia: Gli strumenti pensanti dei Romani fra tarda Repubblica e medio Impero*. Rome: Nuova Italia Scientifica.

Cardon, Dominique, Witold Nowik, Hero Granger-Taylor, Renata Marcinowska, Katarzyna Kusyk, and Marek Trojanowicz. 2010. "Who Would Wear True Purple in Roman Egypt? Technical and Social Considerations on Some New Identifications of Purple from Marine Molluscs in Archaeological Textiles." In *Textiles y tintes en la ciudad antigua*: *Purpureae vestes III*, edited by Carmen Alfaro, Jean-Pierre Brun, Philippe Bordard, and Rafaela Pierobon Benoît, 197–214. Valencia: Centre Jean Bérard.

Carnegie, Garry, and Stephen Walker. 2007. "Household Accounting in Australia." *Accounting, Auditing & Accountability Journal* 20 (1): 41–73.

Carrié, J. M. 1998. "Archives municipales et distributions alimentaires dans l'Égypte romaine." In *La mémoire perdue: Recherches sur l'administration romaine*, 271–95. Collection d'École française de Rome 243. Paris: École française de Rome.

———. 2004. "Vitalité de l'industrie textile à la fin de l'Antiquité: Considérations économiques et technologiques." *Antiquité Tardive* 12:E 13–43.

Carrié, J. M., and Christel Freu. 2019. "Les métiers et leur organisation dans l'Antiquité tardive: Une introduction" In *Mestieri e Professioni Della Tarda Antichità: Organizzazione, lessico, norme*, 7–79. Naples: Edizioni scientifiche italiane.

Carroll, Maureen. 2011. "Infant Death and Burial in Roman Italy." *Journal of Roman Archaeology* 24: 99–120.

Case, Anne, and Alicia Menendez. 2009. "*Requiescat in Pace*? The Consequences of High-Priced Funerals in South Africa." W14998. NBER Working Paper. DOI 10.3386/w14998; http://www.nber.org/papers/w14998.

Caskey, John P. 1991. "Pawnbroking in America: The Economics of a Forgotten Credit Market." *Journal of Money, Credit and Banking* 23 (1): 85–99.

Casson, Lionel. 1990. "Documentary Evidence for Graeco-Roman Shipbuilding (*P. Flor.* I 69)." *Bulletin of the American Society of Papyrologists* 27 (1): 15–19.

Castagnetti, Sergio. 2012. *Le leges libitinariae flegree: Edizione e commento*. Naples: Satura editrice.

Castle, S. A. 1978. "Amphorae from Brockley Hill." *Britannia* 9: 383–92.

Catalano, Paola, Valentina Benassi, Carla Caldarini, Laura Cianfriglia, Romina Mosticone, Alessia Nava, Walter Pantano, and F. Porreca. 2010. "Attività lavorative e condizione di vita della comunità de Castel Malnome (Roma, I–II sec. D.C.)." *Medicina nei secoli* 22 (1–3): 111–28.

Catalano, Paola, Carla Caldarini, Flavio De Angelis, and Walter Pantano. 2017. "Funerary Complexes from Imperial Rome: A New Approach to Anthropological Study Using Excavation and Laboratory Data." In *Death as a Process: The Archaeology of the Roman Funeral*, edited by John Pearce and Jake Weekes, 208–25. Oxford: Oxbow.

Catalano, Paola, Carla Caldarini, Romina Mosticone, and Federica Zavaroni. 2013. "Il contributo dell'analisi traumatologica nella ricostruzione dello stile di vita della comunità di Castel Malnome (Roma, I–II sec. D.C.)." *Medicina nei secoli* 25 (1): 101–18.

Catalano, Paola, Simona Minozzi, and Walter Pantano. 2001. "Le necropoli romane di età imperiale: Un contributo all'interpretazione del popolamento e della qualità della vita nell'antica Roma." In *Urbanizzazione delle campagne nell'Italia antica*, edited by S. Quilici Gigli and Lorenzo Quilici, 127–37. Atlante tematico di topografia antica 10. Rome: L'Erma di Bretschneider.

Cébeillac-Gervasoni, Mireille, and Cinzia Morelli. 2014. "Les *conductores* du *Campus Salinarum Romanarum*." *Melanges de l'École Française de Rome - Antiquité* 126 (1): 9–21.

Certeau, Michele de. 1994. *The Practice of Everyday Life*. Berkeley: University of California Press.

Chadwick, Edwin. 1982. "Report on the Sanitary Conditions of the Labouring Population of Great Britain." UK: House of Commons Sessional Paper.

Chamberlain, Andrew. 2006. *Demography in Archaeology*. Cambridge: Cambridge University Press.

Chang, Yang-Ming, Biing-Wen Huang, and Yun-Ju Chen. 2012. "Labor Supply, Income, and Welfare of the Farm Household." *Labor Economics* 19: 427–37.

Charlesworth, Scott. 2014. "Recognizing Greek Literacy in Early Roman Documents from the Judaean Desert." *Bulletin of the American Society of Papyrologists* 51: 161–89.

Charlesworth, Simon. 2000. *A Phenomenology of Working-Class Experience*. Cambridge: Cambridge University Press.

Chayanov, Alexander. 1966. *The Theory of Peasant Economy*. Homewood, IL: American Economic Association.

Cherubini, Linda, Antonella Del Rio, and Simonetta Menchelli. 2006. "Paesaggi della produzione: Attività agricole e manifatturiere nel territorio pisano-volterrano in età Romana." In *Territorio e produzioni ceramiche: Paesaggi, economia e società in età romana*, edited by Simonetta Menchelli and Margherita Pasquinnuci, 69–76. Pisa: Università di Pisa.

Chiu, Sheau-Huey, Marguerite A. Dimarco, and Jessica L. Prokop. 2013. "Childhood Obesity and Dental Caries in Homeless Children." *Journal of Pediatric Health Care* 27 (4): 278–83.

Christian, David. 2005. "Macrohistory: A Play of Scales." *Social Evolution & History* 4 (1): 22–59.

Christiansen, Erik. 2004. *Coinage in Roman Egypt: The Hoard Evidence*. Aarhus: Aarhus University Press.

Churcher, Charles. 2002. "Faunal Remains from Kellis." In *Dakhleh Oasis Project: Preliminary Reports on the 1994–1995 to 1998–1999 Seasons*, edited by Colin Hope and Gillian Bowen, 105–13. Oxford: Oxbow.

Ciampoltrini, Giulio. 2004. "Insediamenti e strutture rurali nella Piana di Lucca tra tarda repubblica e prima etá imperiale." *Journal of Ancient Topography* 14: 8–24.

Ciampoltrini, Giulio, and M. Zecchini, eds. 2005. *Le dimore dell'Auser: Archeologia, archittetura, ambiente dell'antico lago di Sesto*. Lucca: Istituto Storico Lucchese.

Clark, Gregory. 2009. "Review: Contours of the World Economy, 1–2030 AD: Essays in Macro-Economic History. By Angus Maddison." *Journal of Economic History*, 1156–61.

Clarke, John. 2003. *Art in the Lives of Ordinary Romans: Visual Representation and Non-Elite Viewers in Italy, 100 B.C.–A.D. 315*. Berkeley: University of California Press.

Clarysse, Willy, and Vandorpe, Katelijn. 1995. *Zénon, un homme d'affaires grec à l'ombre des pyramides*. Louvian: Louvian University Press.

Clauss, Manfred, Anne Kolb, Wolfgang Slabey, and Barbara Woitas. 2023. "Epigraphik-Datenbank." http://www.manfredclauss.de/.

Claytor, Graham, Nikos Litinas, and Elizabeth Nabney. 2016. "Labor Contracts from the Harthotes Archive." *Bulletin of the American Society of Papyrologists* 53: 79–119.

Claytor, Graham, Richard Warga, and Zachary Smith. 2016. "Four Poll Tax Receipts on Papyrus from the Early Roman Fayum." *Bulletin of the American Society of Papyrologists* 53: 121–54.

Clotuche, Raphaël, Marie Derreumaux, Fabienne Pigière, Gaëtan Jouanin, Sidonie Preiss, and Jean-Hervé Yvinec. 2017. "Les campagnes du territoire nervien: Approches croisées." In *Gallia Rustica 1. Les campagnes du nord-est de la Gaule, de la fin de l'âge du Fer à l'Antiquité tardive*, edited by Michel Reddé, 179–210. Bordeaux: Ausonius Éditions.

Cockle, Helen. 1981. "Pottery Manufacture in Roman Egypt: A New Papyrus." *Journal of Roman Studies* 71: 87–97.

Cocozza, Carlo, Enrico Cirelli, Marcus Groß, Wolf-Rüdiger Teegen, and Ricardo Fernandes. 2022. "Presenting the Compendium Isotoporum Medii Aevi, a Multi-Isotope Database for Medieval Europe." *Scientific Data* 9 (1): 354. https://doi.org/10.1038/s41597-022-01462-8.

Cohen, Edward. 2023. *Roman Inequality: Affluent Slaves, Businesswomen, Legal Fictions*. Oxford: Oxford University Press.

Collins, Daryl, Jonathan Morduch, Stuart Rutherford, and Orlanda Ruthven. 2009. *Portfolios of the Poor*. Princeton, NJ: Princeton University Press.

Collins-Elliot, Stephen. 2018. "A Behavioral Analysis of Monetary Exchange and Craft Production in Rural Tuscany via Small Finds from the Roman Peasant Project." *Journal of Mediterranean Archaeology* 31: 155–79.

———. Forthcoming. *The Rise of Rome and the Culture of Mass Consumption, ca. 400 BCE–50 CE*.

Cool, Helen. 2006. *Eating and Drinking in Roman Britain*. Cambridge: Cambridge University Press.

Cooley, Alison, ed. 2002. *Becoming Roman, Writing Latin? Literacy and Epigraphy in the Roman West*. Journal of Roman Archaeology Supplementary Series, 48. Portsmouth, RI: Journal of Roman Archaeology.

Cooper, Sheila McIsaac. 2005. "Service to Servitude? The Decline and Demise of Life-Cycle Service in England." *The History of the Family* 10 (4): 367–86.

Corbier, Mireille. 1989. "The Ambiguous Status of Meat in Ancient Rome." *Food and Foodways* 3 (3): 223–64.

Corbier, Mireille, and Jean-Pierre Guilhembet, eds. 2011. *L'Écriture dans la maison romaine*. Paris: De Boccard.

Corruccini, Robert, Jerome Handler, Robert Mutaw, and Frederick Lange. 1982. "Osteology of a Slave Burial Population from Barbados, West Indies." *American Journal of Physical Anthropology* 59 (4): 443–59.

Corsi, Cristina. 2000. *Le strutture di servizio del cursus publicus in Italia*. BAR International Series, 875. Oxford: Archaeopress.

Costabile, Felice. 2001. "Ancilla Domni: Una nuova dedica su armilla aurea da Pompei." *Minima Epigraphica et Papyrologica* 6: 447–74.

Cotton, Hannah M. 1997. "Land Tenure in the Documents from the Nabataean Kingdom and the Roman Province of Arabia." *Zeitschrift für Papyrologie und Epigraphik* 119: 255–65.

Courrier, Cyril. 2014. *La plèbe de Rome et sa culture (fin du IIe siècle av. J.-C.–fin du ier siècle ap. J.-C.)*. Rome: École française de Rome.

Cox, Samantha, Hannah Moots, Jay Stock, Andrej Shbat, Bárbara Bitarello, Nicole Nicklisch, Kurt Alt, et al. 2022. "Predicting Skeletal Stature Using Ancient DNA." *American Journal of Biological Anthropology* 177 (1): 162–74.

Craig, Lee A. 2015. "Antebellum Puzzle: The Decline in Heights at the Onset of Modern Economic Growth." In *The Oxford Handbook of Economics and Human Biology*, edited by John Komlos and Inas Kelly, 751–64. Oxford: Oxford University Press.

Craig, Oliver, Marco Biazzo, Tamsin O'Connell, Peter Garnsey, Cristina Martinez-Labarga, Roberta Lelli, Loretana Salvadei, et al. 2009. "Stable Isotopic Evidence for Diet at the Imperial Roman Coastal Site of Velia (1st and 2nd Centuries AD) in Southern Italy." *American Journal of Physical Anthropology* 139: 572–83.

Craig, Oliver, Luca Bondioli, Luciano Fattore, Tom Higham, and Robert Hedges. 2013. "Evaluating Marine Diets through Radiocarbon Dating and Stable Isotope Analysis of Victims of the AD 79 Eruption of Vesuvius." *American Journal of Physical Anthropology* 152: 345–52.

Crawford, Dorothy. 1973. "Garlic-Growing and Agricultural Specialization in Greco-Roman Egypt." *Cronique d'Egypt* 48 (96): 350–63.

Crawford, Michael. 1970. "Money and Exchange in the Roman World." *Journal of Roman Studies* 60: 40–48.

———. 1974. *Roman Republican Coinage*. Cambridge: Cambridge University Press.

Creighton, John. 1997. "Money, Hoards and the Roman State." *Journal of Roman Archaeology* 10: 423–25.

———. 2000. *Coins and Power in Late Iron Age Britain*. Cambridge: Cambridge University Press.

Cribiore, Raffaela. 2001. *Gymnastics of the Mind: Greek Education in Hellenistic and Roman Egypt*. Princeton, NJ: Princeton University Press.

Crowe, Fiona, Alessandra Sperduti, Tamsin C. O'Connell, Oliver E. Craig, Karola Kirsanow, Paola Germoni, Roberto Macchiarelli, Peter Garnsey, and Lucca Bondioli. 2010. "Water-Related Occupations and Diet in Two Roman Coastal Communities (Italy, First to Third Century AD): Correlation between Stable Carbon and Nitrogen Isotope Values and Auricular Exostosis Prevalence." *American Journal of Physical Anthropology* 142 (3): 355–66.

Cucina, Andrea, Rita Vargiu, Domenico Mancinelli, Riccardo Ricci, E. Santandrea, Paola Catalano, and Alfredo Coppa. 2006. "The Necropolis of Vallerano (Rome, 2nd–3rd Century AD): An Anthropological Perspective on the Ancient Romans in the Suburbium." *International Journal of Osteoarchaeology* 16: 104–17.

Cummings, Colleen. 2008. "Meat Consumption in Roman Britain: The Evidence from Stable Isotopes." Edited by Mark Driessen. *TRAC 2008: Proceedings of the Eighteenth Annual Theoretical Roman Archaeology Conference*, 73–83.

Cunliffe, Barry. 1971. *Fishbourne: A Roman Palace and Its Garden*. Baltimore: Johns Hopkins University Press.

Cuomo, Serafina. 2012. "Exploring Ancient Greek and Roman Numeracy." *BSHM Bulletin: Journal of the British Society for the History of Mathematics* 27 (1): 1–12.

———. 2019. "Mathematical Traditions in Ancient Greece and Rome." *HAU: Journal of Ethnographic Theory* 9 (1): 75–85.

Cuvigny, Hélène. 1996. "The Amount of Wages Paid to the Quarry-Workers at Mons Claudianus." *Journal of Roman Studies* 86: 139–45.

———. 2000. *Mons Claudianus. Ostraca graeca et latina. III. Le reçus pour avances à la familia*. Cairo: Institut français d'archéologie orientale.

———. 2003. "La société civile des praesidia." In *La route de Myos Hormos: L'armée raomaine dans le désert Oriental d'Égypte. Praesidia du désert de Bérénice. Vol. 1*, edited by Hélène Cuvigny, 361–95. Cairo: Institut français d'archéologie orientale.

———. 2021a. "A Receipt for Military Rations in Exchange for Payment of Publica." In *Rome in Egypt's Eastern Desert: Volume 2*, edited by Hélène Cuvigny, 325–35. New York: New York University Press.

———. 2021b. "Kaine, a New Town: An Experiment in Familial Reunification in the Second Century AD." In *Rome in Egypt's Eastern Desert: Volume 1*, edited by Hélène Cuvigny, 227–32. New York: New York University Press.

———. 2021c. "'Me Too' in the Praesidia, or When Reality Meets Theatrical Fiction." In *Rome in Egypt's Eastern Desert: Volume 2*, edited by Hélène Cuvigny, 389–94. New York: New York University Press.

———. 2021d. "Quintana, a Woman Transformed into a Tax." In *Rome in Egypt's Eastern Desert: Volume 2*, edited by Hélène Cuvigny, 375–78. New York: New York University Press.

———. 2021e. "Rotating Women: Remarks on Prostitution in the Roman Garrisons of the Desert of Berenike." In *Rome in Egypt's Eastern Desert: Volume 2*, edited by Hélène Cuvigny, 379–88. New York: New York University Press.

———. 2021f. "The Monthly Ration of a Cavalryman and His Horse According to an Ostracon from the Praesidium of Dios." In *Rome in Egypt's Eastern Desert: Volume 2*, edited by Hélène Cuvigny, 337–53. New York: New York University Press.

———. 2021g. "The Organization Chart of the Personnel of an Imperial Quarry According to an Ostracon of Mons Claudianus." In *Rome in Egypt's Eastern Desert. Vol. 1*, edited by Hélène Cuvigny, 181–212. New York: New York University Press.

———. 2021h. "Two Ostraca from Mons Claudianus: *O. Bahria* 20 and 21." In *Rome in Egypt's Eastern Desert: Volume 1*, edited by Hélène Cuvigny, 175–180. New York: New York University Press.

Czajkowski, Kimberley, Benedikt Eckhardt, and Meret Strothmann, eds. 2020. *Law in the Roman Provinces*. Oxford: Oxford University Press.

Dalton, George. 1971. *Economic Anthropology and Development: Essays on Tribal and Peasant Economies*. New York: Basic Books.

———. 1972. "Peasantries in Anthropology and History." *Current Anthropology* 13 (3): 385–415.

Danon, Bart, Daniel Jew, and Myles Lavan, eds. 2022. *The Uncertain Past: Probability in Ancient History*. Cambridge: Cambridge University Press.

Davies, R. W. 1971. "The Roman Military Diet." *Britannia* 2: 122–42.

Davies, Siriol. 1994. "Tithe-Collection in the Venetian Peloponnese 1696–1705." *Annual of the British School at Athens* 89: 443–55.

De Angelis, Flavio, Marco Romboni, Virginia Veltre, Paola Catalano, Cristina Martínez-Labarga, Valentina Gazzaniga, and Olga Rickards. 2022. "First Glimpse into the Genomic Characterization of People from the Imperial Roman Community of Casal Bertone (Rome, First–Third Centuries AD)." *Genes (Basel)* 13 (1). https://doi.org/10.3390/genes13010136.

De Angelis, Flavio, Virginia Veltre, Sara Varano, Marco Romboni, Sonia Renzi, Stefania Zingale, Paola Ricci, et al. 2020. "Dietary and Weaning Habits of the Roman Community of Quarto Cappello Del Prete (Rome, 1st–3rd Century CE)." *Environmental Archaeology* 30 (2): 1–15.

De Callataÿ, François. 1995. "Calculating Ancient Coin Production: Seeking a Balance." *Numismatic Chronicle* 155: 289–311.

De Caro, Stefano. 1994. *La villa rustica in località Villa Regina a Boscoreale*. Rome: Centro di Studi della Magna Grecia dell'Università di Napoli Federico II.

De Francesco, Daniela. 2014. *Ricerche sui villaggi nel Lazio dalle età imperiale alla tarda antichità*. Rome: Edizioni Quasar.

De la Cova, Carlina. 2010. "Cultural Patterns of Trauma among 19th-Century-Born Males in Cadaver Collections." *American Anthropologist* 112 (4): 589–606.

———. 2011. "Race, Health, and Disease in 19th-Century-Born Males." *American Journal of Physical Anthropology* 144: 526–37.

De Laet, Sigfried. 1949. *Portorium: Étude sur l'organisation douanière chez les romains, surtout à l'époque du haut-empire*. Bruges: De Tempel.

De Sena, Eric. 2005. "An Assessment of Wine and Oil Production in Rome's Hinterland: Ceramic, Literary, Art Historical and Modern Evidence." In *Roman Villas around the Urbs: Interaction with Landscape and Environment. Proceedings of a Conference Held at the Swedish Institute in Rome, September 17–18 2004*, edited by Barbro Santillo Frizell and Allan Klynne, 135–49. Rome: Swedish Institute.

De Ste. Croix, G.E.M. 1956. "Greek and Roman Accounting." In *Studies in the History of Accounting*, edited by A. C. Littleton and Basil Yarney, 14–74. New York: Arno Press.

———. 1981. *The Class Struggle in the Ancient Greek World: From the Archaic Age to the Arab Conquests*. Ithaca, NY: Cornell University Press.

De Vos Raaijmakers, Mariette, and Barbara Maurina, eds. 2019. *Rus Africum IV: La fattoria Bizantina di Aïn Wassel, Africa Proconsularis (Alto Tell, Tunisia): Lo scavo stratigrafico e i materiali*. Oxford: Archeopress.

De Vries, Jan. 2008. *The Industrious Revolution: Consumer Behavior and the Economy, 1650 to the Present*. Cambridge: Cambridge University Press.

———. 2019. "Playing with Scales: The Global and the Micro, the Macro and the Nano." *Past & Present* 242: 23–36.

———. 2023. "Whatever Happened to the Affluent Society? Or, the Dynamics of Consumer-Driven Capitalism Revealed." *Capitalism: A Journal of History and Economics* 4 (2): 215–57.

Deaton, Angus. 1992. *Understanding Consumption*. Oxford: Oxford University Press.

———. 1997. *The Analysis of Household Surveys: A Microeconomic Approach to Development Policy*. Washington, DC: World Bank. https://openknowledge.worldbank.org/handle/10986/30394.

———. 2007. "Height, Health, and Development." *Proceedings of the National Academy of Sciences* 104 (33): 13232–37.

Deaton, Angus, and Jean Drèze. 2009. "Food and Nutrition in India: Facts and Interpretations." *Economic and Political Weekly* 44 (7): 42–65.

Debreu, Gerard. 1991. "The Mathematization of Economic Theory." *American Economic Review* 81 (1): 1–7.

Dekoninck, Michiel, and Wim De Clerq. 2022. "Settling the Salinaria? Evaluating Site Location Patterns of Iron Age and Roman Salt Production in Northern Gaul." In *Reframing the Roman Economy*, edited by Dimitri Van Limbergen, Adeline Hoffelinck, and Devi Taelman, 267–303. Cham, Switzerland: Palgrave Macmillan.

DeLaine, Janet. 1997. *The Baths of Caracalla: A Study in the Design, Construction, and Economics of Large-Scale Building Projects in Imperial Rome*. Portsmouth, RI: Journal of Roman Archaeology.

Delano-Smith, Catherine. 1979. *Western Mediterranean Europe: A Historical Geography of Italy, Spain and Southern France since the Neolithic*. London: Academic Press.

Delia, D. 1986. "Carrying Dung in Ancient Egypt: A Contract to Perform Work for a Vineyard." *Bulletin of the American Society of Papyrologists* 23: 61–64.

Della Corte, Matteo. 1965. *Case ed abitanti dei Pompeii*. Naples: Fausto Fiorentino.

Depeyrot, Georges. 2016. *Currency, the Pompeiians and Vesuvius*. Wetteren, Belgium: Moneta.

Derda, Tomasz. 2006. "Waterway Fayum–Alexandria. A Note on *P. Lille* I 1 (= *P. Zen. Pest.*, Appendix A)." *Journal of Juristic Papyri* 36: 9–20.

Deru, Xavier, and R. González Villaescusa, eds. 2014. *Consommer dans les campagnes de la Gaule romaine*. Revue du Nord, 21. Lille: Université Charles-de-Gaulle Lille 3.

Desrayaud, Gilles. 2008. "Parcellaires fossoyés du Haut Empire des plateaux de Brie: Jossigny/Serris et Moissy-Cramayel (Seine-et-Marne). Approche méthodologique de l'étude des réseaux." *Revue archéologique du Centre de la France* 47. http://journals.openedition.org/racf/1161.

Dietler, Michael. 2010. *Archaeologies of Colonialism: Consumption, Entanglement, and Violence in Ancient Mediterranean France*. Berkeley: University of California Press.

Dietz, S., L. Ladjimi Sebaï, and B. Ben Hassen, eds. 1995. *Africa Proconsularis: Regional Studies in the Segermes Valley of Northern Tunisia*. Vol. 1. Copenhagen: Aarhus University Press.

Dinter, Marieke van, Laura I. Kooistra, Monica K. Dütting, Pauline van Rijn, and Chiara Cavallo. 2014. "Could the Local Population of the Lower Rhine Delta Supply the Roman Army? Part II. Modelling the Carrying Capacity Using Archaeological, Palaeo-Ecological and Geomorphological Data." *Journal of the Archaeology of the Low Countries* 5: 1–50.

Dondin-Payre, Monique, and Nicolas Tran, eds. 2012. *Collegia: Le phénomène associatif dans l'Occident romain*. Scripta Antiqua, 41. Bordeaux: Ausonius Éditions.

Dossey, Leslie. 2010. *Peasant and Empire in Christian North Africa*. Berkeley: University of California Press.

Drelichman, Mauricio, and David Agudo González. 2020. "The Gender Wage Gap in Early Modern Toledo, 1550–1650." *Journal of Economic History* 80 (2): 351–85.

Drexhage, Hans-Joachim. 1991. *Preise, Mieten/Pachten, Kosten und Löhne im römischen Ägypten bis zum Regierungsantritt Dioketians*. St. Katharinen: Scripta Mercaturae.

Driel-Murray, Carol van. 1996. "'Die Schuhe aus Schiff I und ein lederner Schildüberzug' in J. K. Haalebos, Ein römisches Getreideschiff in Woerden." *Jahrbuch des Römisch-Germanischen Zentralmuseums Mainz* 43: 493–98.

———. 2001. "Footwear in the North-Western Provinces of the Roman Empire." In *Stepping through Time: Archaeological Footwear from Prehistoric Times until 1800*, edited by Olaf Goubitz, W. Groenman van Waateringe, and Carol van Driel-Murray, 337–75. Zwolle: SPA Uitgevers.

———. 2016. "Fashionable Footwear: Craftsmen and Consumers in the North-West Provinces of the Roman Empire." In *Urban Craftsmen and Traders in the Roman World*, edited by Andrew Wilson and Miko Flohr, 132–52. Oxford: Oxford University Press.

Droß-Krüpe, Kirsten. 2011. *Wolle–Weber–Wirtschaft: Die Textilproduktion der römischen Kaiserzeit im Spiegel der papyrologischen Überlieferung*. Wiesbaden: Harrassowitz Verlag.

Du Boulay, Juliet. 1974. *Portrait of a Greek Mountain Village*. Oxford: Clarendon Press.

Duby, Georges. 1962. *L'économie rurale et la vie des campagnes dans l'occident médiéval (France, Angleterre, Empire, IX-XV siècles): Essai de synthèse et perspectives de recherches*. Paris: Aubier.

Duesenerry, James. 1949. *Income, Saving and the Theory of Consumer Behavior*. Cambridge, MA: Harvard University Press.

Dumas-Lattaque, Pierre. 2017. "Une production de céréales et de moutarde sur l'établissement rural du 'Champ Drillon' à Bezannes (Marne)." In *Produire, transformer et stocker dans les campagnes des Gaules romaines*, edited by Frédéric Trément, 323–28. Bordeaux: Fédération Aquitania.

Dumas-Lattaque, Pierre, and Mathilde Arnaud. 2015. "Le site du 'Champ Drillon,' un établissement agricole antique à Bezannes (Marne)." *Revue archéologique de l'Est* 64: 275–99.

Duncan-Jones, Richard. 1964. "The Purpose and Organisation of the Alimenta." *Papers of the British School at Rome* 32: 123–46.

———. 1974. *The Economy of the Roman Empire: Quantitative Studies*. Cambridge: Cambridge University Press.

———. 1976. "Some Configurations of Landholding in the Roman Empire." In *Studies in Roman Property*, edited by M. I. Finley, 7–33. Cambridge: Cambridge Philological Society.

———. 1977. "Age-Rounding, Illiteracy and Social Differentiation in the Roman Empire." *Chiron* 7: 333–57.

———. 1990. *Structure and Scale in the Roman Economy*. Cambridge: Cambridge University Press.

———. 1994. *Money and Government in the Roman Empire*. Cambridge: Cambridge University Press.

———. 2003. "Coin Circulation and the Cities of Vesuvius." In *Credito e Moneta Nel Mondo Romano*, edited by Elio Lo Cascio, 161–80. Bari, Italy: Edipuglia.

Durante, Alex, and Lisa Chen. 2019. "Report on the Economic Well-Being of U.S. Households in 2018." Washington, DC: Federal Reserve Board.

Durham, Peter, and J. J. Hawthorne. 1999. "Quantifying Shape: African Red Slip Ware and Eating Habits." In *Archaeology in the Age of the Internet: CAA 97 : Computer Applications and Quantitative Methods in Archaeology: Proceedings of the 25th Anniversary Conference, University of Birmingham, April 1997, Volume 750*, edited by Lucie Dingwall, Sally Exon, Vince Gaffney, Sue Laflin, and Martijn van Leusen, 280-1-280–84. Oxford: Archaeopress.

Dyer, Christopher. 1989. *Standards of Living in the Later Middle Ages: Social Change in England, c. 1200–1520*. Cambridge: Cambridge University Press.

———. 2002. *Making a Living in the Middle Ages: The People of Britain 850–1050 AD*. New Haven, CT: Yale University Press.

Eckardt, Hella. 2018. *Writing and Power in the Roman World: Literacies and Material Culture*. Cambridge: Cambridge University Press.

Edmondson, Jonathon. 2008. "Public Dress and Social Control in Late Republican and Early Imperial Rome." In *Roman Dress and the Fabrics of Roman Culture*, edited by Jonathon Edmonson and Allison Keith, 21–46. Toronto: University of Toronto Press.

Edmonson, Jonathon, and Allison Keith, eds. 2008. *Roman Dress and the Fabrics of Roman Culture*. Toronto: University of Toronto Press.

Edwards, Catharine. 1993. *The Politics of Immorality in Ancient Rome*. Cambridge: Cambridge University Press.

Egidi, Roberto, Paola Catalano, and Daniela Spadoni, eds. 2003. *Aspetti di vita quotidiana dalle necropoti della via Latina–Osteria del Curato*. Rome: Ministero per i beni e le attività culturale.

Elgenedy, Walaa Abdel-Hameed Ahmed. 2022. "A New Document of the Soterichos Archive from Cairo Museum: Receipt for Grass-Price." *International Journal of Advanced Studies in World Archaeology* 5 (1): 83–88.

Elgin, Ceyhun. 2020. *The Informal Economy: Measures, Causes, and Consequences*. London: Routledge.

Elliott, Colin. 2020. *Economic Theory and the Roman Monetary Economy*. Cambridge: Cambridge University Press.

Ellis, Steven. 2018. *The Roman Retail Revolution: The Socio-Economic World of the Taberna*. Oxford: Oxford University Press.

Emigh, Rebecca Jean. 2002. "Numeracy or Enumeration? The Uses of Numbers by States and Societies." *Social Science History* 26 (4): 653–98.

Emmerson, Allison. 2020. *Life and Death in the Roman Suburb*. Oxford: Oxford University Press.

England, Paula. 1993. "The Separative Self: Androcentric Bias in Neoclassical Assumptions." In *Beyond Economic Man: Feminist Theory and Economics*, edited by Marianne Ferber and Julie Nelson, 37–53. Chicago: University of Chicago Press.

Erdkamp, Paul. 2002. "'A Starving Mob Has No Respect': Urban Markets and Food Riots in the Roman World, 100 BC–400 AD." In *The Transformation of Economic Life under the Roman Empire*, edited by Lukas De Blois and John Rich, 93–115. Leiden: Brill.

———. 2005. *The Grain Market in the Roman Empire: A Social, Political, and Economic Study*. Cambridge: Cambridge University Press.

———. 2015. "Agriculture, Division of Labor and the Paths to Economic Growth." In *Ownership and Exploitation of Land and Natural Resources in the Roman World*, edited by Paul Erdkamp, Koenraad Verboven, and Arjan Zuiderhoek, 18–39. Oxford: Oxford University Press.

———. 2016. "Economic Growth in the Roman Mediterranean World: An Early Good-Bye to Malthus?" *Explorations in Economic History* 60: 1–20.

Esposito, Domenico. 2017. "Economics of Pompeian Painting." In *The Economy of Pompeii*, edited by Miko Flohr and Andrew Wilson, 263–89. Oxford: Oxford University Press.

Étienne, Robert. 1966. *Le vie quotidienne a Pompéi*. Paris: Hachette.

Evans, Christopher, ed. 2008. *Borderlands: The Archaeology of the Addenbrooke's Environs, South Cambridge*. Cambridge: Cambridge Archaeological Unit.

———. 2013. *Process and History: Romano-British Communities at Colne Fen, Earith*. Cambridge: Oxbow.

Evans, Christopher, Oscar Aldred, and Anwen Cooper. 2023. "Dense Pasts: Settlement Archaeology after Fox's *The Archaeology of the Cambridge Region* (1923)." *Antiquity* 97 (395): 1–19.

Evans, Christopher, and Gavin Lucas, eds. 2019. *Hinterlands and Inlands: The Archaeology of West Cambridge and Roman Cambridge Revisited*. Cambridge: MacDonald Institute for Archaeological Research.

Evans, Christopher, Duncan Mackay, and Grahame Appleby. 2006. *Longstanton, Cambridgeshire. A Village Hinterland (I, II and III). 2004, 2005 and 2006 Investigations*. Cambridge: Cambridge Archaeological Unit. https://doi.org/10.5284/1021795.

Evans, Christopher, and Richard Newman. 2010. *North West Cambridge, University of Cambridge: Archaeological Evaluation Fieldwork*. Cambridge: Cambridge Archaeological Unit Report. https://doi.org/10.5284/1016790.

Evans, J. K. 1981. "Wheat Production and Its Social Consequences in the Roman World." *Classical Quarterly* 31: 428–42.

Ewell, Charles, and Laurel Taylor. 2010. "Excavations at the 'Project of 100 Roman Farms,' Lucca, Italy: The 2006–2008 Seasons at Palazzaccio." *FOLD&R Italy* 173.

Fagan, Garreth. 2017. "The Traveler's Bill (*CIL* IX 2689 = *ILS* 7478 = *AE* 1983.329)?" *Zeitschrift für Papyrologie und Epigraphik* 204: 246–50.

Faucher, Thomas. 2022. "Roman Coin Hoards from Egypt: What Next?" In *Coin Hoards and Hoarding in the Roman World*, edited by Jerome Mairat, Andrew Wilson, and Chris Howgego, 221–34. Oxford: Oxford University Press.

Feito, Jessica. 2022. "Plant Use and Agriculture in Roman Italy." *Archaeology of Food and Foodways* 1 (2): 123–53.

Fentress, Elizabeth. 1979. *Numidia and the Roman Army: Social, Military and Economic Aspects of the Frontier Zone*. BAR International Series, 53. Oxford: Archaeopress.

Fentress, Elizabeth, Ali Drine, and Renata Holod, eds. 2009. *An Island Through Time: Jerba Studies*. Portsmouth, RI: Journal of Roman Studies.

Ferdière, Alain. 2006. "La place de l'artisanat en Gaule romaine du Centre, Nord-Ouest et Centre-Ouest (province de Lyonnaise et cités d'Aquitaine septentrionale)." *Revue archéologique du Centre de la France* 45–46 (July): 1–35.

———. 2015. "Essai de typologie des greniers ruraux de Gaule du Nord." *Revue archéologique du Centre de la France* 54. http://racf.revues.org/2294.

Fernández-Götz, Manuel, Dominik Maschek, and Nico Roymans. 2020. "The Dark Side of the Empire: Roman Expansionism between Object Agency and Predatory Regime." *Antiquity* 94 (378): 1630–39.

Fernández-Götz, Manuel, and Nico Roymans, eds. 2019. *Conflict Archaeology Materialities of Collective Violence from Prehistory to Late Antiquity*. New York: Routledge.

Fincham, Garrick. 2002. *Landscapes of Imperialism: Roman and Native Interaction in the East Anglian Fenland*. BAR British Series 338. Oxford: British Archaeological Reports.

Fink, Robert. 1971. *Roman Military Records on Papyrus*. Ann Arbor, MI: American Philological Association.

Finley, Moses. 1952. *Studies in Land and Credit in Ancient Athens, 500–200 BC*. New Brunswick, NJ: Rutgers University Press.

———. 1973. *The Ancient Economy*. Berkeley: University of California Press.

———. 1985. *The Ancient Economy*. 2nd ed. Berkeley: University of California Press.

———. 1999. *The Ancient Economy*. 3rd ed. Berkeley: University of California Press.

Fiske, John. 1989. *Understanding Popular Culture*. London: Routledge.

Flandreau, Marc. 2019. "Border Crossing." *Capitalism: A Journal of History and Economics* 1 (1): 1–9.

Flohr, Miko. 2013. *The World of the Fullo: Work, Economy and Society in Roman Italy*. Oxford: Oxford University Press.

———. 2016. "Constructing Occupational Identities in the Roman World." In *Work, Labour and Professions in the Roman World*, edited by Koenraad Verboven and Christian Laes, 147–72. Leiden: Brill.

———. 2017. "Quantifying Pompeii: Population, Inequality and the Urban Economy." In *The Economy of Pompeii*, edited by Miko Flohr and Andrew Wilson, 53–84. Oxford: Oxford University Press.

———. 2019. "Skeletons in the Cupboard." In *The Routledge Handbook of Diet and Nutrition in the Roman World*, edited by Paul Erdkamp and Claire Holleran, 273–80. London: Routledge.

———. 2020. "Commerce and Architecture in Late Hellenistic Italy: The Emergence of the Taberna Row." In *Shops, Workshops and Urban Economic History in the Roman World*, edited by Miko Flohr and Nicolas Monteix, 1–11. Heidelberg: Propylaeum.

Flohr, Miko, and Kim Bowes. 2024. *Valuing Labor in Greco-Roman Antiquity*. Leiden: Brill.

Flohr, Miko, and Nicolas Monteix, eds. 2020. *Shops, Workshops and Urban Economic History in the Roman World*. Heidelberg: Propylaeum.

Flower, Harriet. 2017. *Dancing Lares and the Serpent in the Garden: Religion at the Roman Street Corner*. Princeton, NJ: Princeton University Press.

Fogel, Robert. 1974. *Time on the Cross*. Boston: Little Brown.

Fogel, Robert, Stanley Engerman, Roderick Floud, Gerald Friedman, Robert Margo, Kenneth Sokoloff, Richard Steckel, T. James Trussell, Georgia Villaflor, and Kenneth W. Wachter. 1983. "Secular Changes in American and British Stature and Nutrition." *Journal of Interdisciplinary History* 14 (2): 445–81.

Fontaine, Laurence. 2008. *L'économie Morale: Pauvreté, crédit et confiance dans l'Europe préindustrielle*. Paris: Gallimard.

———. 2014. *Le Marché: Histoire et usages d'une conquête sociale*. Paris: Gallimard.

Foraboschi, Daniele. 1971. *L'archivio di Kronion*. Milan: Cisalpino-La Goliardica.

———. 1981. *Papiri della Università degli studi di Milano. (P. Mil. Vogliano 301–308). Vol. 7. La contabilità di un'azienda agricola nel II sec. d.C.* Milan: Istituto Editoriale Cisalpino.

———. 1982. "L'economia dei crediti in natura (Egitto)." *Athenaeum (Pavia)* 60: 69–83.

Foraboschi, Daniele, and Alessandra Gara. 1981. "Sulla differenza tra tassi di interesse in natura e in moneta nell'Egitto greco-romano." In *Proceedings of the XVI International Congress of Papyrology*, 335–43. Chico, CA: Scholars Press.

Forbes, Hamish, and Lin Foxhall. 1995. "Ethnoarchaeology and Storage in the Ancient Mediterranean: Beyond Risk and Survival." In *Food in Antiquity*, edited by John Wilkins, F. D. Harvey, and Mike Dobson, 69–86. Exeter: University of Exeter Press.

Forin, Claudia. 2017. "Ville e fattorie nell'Italia settentrionale in epoca romana (II sec. a.C.–V sec. d.C.): Architettura, economia e società." PhD thesis, Università di Padova.

Fournet, Jean-Luc. 2018. "Archives and Libraries in Greco-Roman Egypt." In *Manuscripts and Archives: Comparative Views on Record-Keeping*, edited by Alessandro Baussi, Christian Brockmann, Michael Friedrich, and Sabine Keinitz, 171–200. Berlin: De Gruyter.

Foxhall, Lin. 1990. "The Dependent Tenant: Land, Leasing and Labour in Italy and Greece." *Journal of Roman Studies* 80: 97–114.

———. 2020. "The Village beyond the Village: Communities in Rural Landscapes in Ancient Greek Countrysides." *Journal of Modern Greek Studies* 38 (1): 1–20.

Foxhall, Lin, and Hamish Forbes. 1982. "Σιτομετρεία: The Role of Grain as a Staple Food in Classical Antiquity." *Chiron* 12: 41–90.

France, Jacques. 1999. "Theadelphia and Euhemereia: Village History in Greco-Roman Egypt." Katholieke Universiteit Leuven.

France, Jérôme. 2001. "Remarques sur les 'tributa' dans les provinces nord-occidentales du Haut Empire romain (Bretagne, Gaules, Germanies)." *Latomus* 60 (2): 359–79.

———. 2003. "Les rapports fiscaux entre les cités et le pouvoir impérial dans l'Empire romain: Le rôle des assemblées provinciales (à propos d'une dédicace de Tarragone, CIL, II, 4248)." *Cahiers du Centre Gustave Glotz*, 209–25.

France, Jérôme and Laurin, Louise. 2009. "Une liste comptable sur plomb découverte à Bordeaux." *Zeitschrift für Papyrologie und Epigraphik* 170: 247–64.

Freu, Christel. 2011. "Apprendre et exercer un métier dans l'Egypte romaine (Ie–IVe siècles ap. J.-C.)." In *Les savoirs professionnels des gens de métier*, edited by Nicolas Montiex and Nicolas Tran, 27–40. Paris: Centre Jean Bernard.

———. 2013. "Les salariés de la terre dans l'antiquité tardive." *Antiquité Tardive* 21: 283–98.

———. 2016a. "*Disciplina, Patrocinium, Nomen*: The Benefits of Apprenticeship in the Roman World." In *Urban Craftsmen and Traders in the Roman World*, edited by Andrew Wilson and Miko Flohr, 183–99. Oxford: Oxford University Press.

———. 2016b. "Labor Status and Economic Stratification in the Roman World: The Hierarchy of Wages in Egypt." *Journal of Roman Archaeology* 28: 161–77.

———. 2022. *Les salariés de l'Égypte romano-Byzantine*. Paris: Association des Amis du Centre d'Histoire et Civilisation de Byzance.

———. 2024. "Who's Afraid of Wage Labor? Analyzing Some Texts of the Second Sophistic." In *Valuing Labor in Greco-Roman Antiquity*, edited by Miko Flohr and Kim Bowes, 150–68. Leiden: Brill.

Frézouls, Edmond. 1977. "Prix, salaires et niveaux de vie: Quelques enseignements de l'Édit du Maximum." *Ktèma* 2: 253–68.

———. 1978. "Prix, salaires et niveaux de vie: Quelques enseignements de l'Edit du Maximum (II)." *Ktema* 3: 289–300.

Frier, Bruce. 1977. "The Rental Market in Early Imperial Rome." *Journal of Roman Studies* 67: 27–37.

———. 1993. "Subsistence Annuities and Per Capita Income in the Early Roman Empire." *Classical Philology* 88 (3): 222–30.

———. 2000. "Demography." In *The Cambridge Ancient History. Vol. 11. The High Empire, A.D. 70–192*, edited by Alan Bowman, Peter Garnsey, and Dominic Rathbone, 2nd ed., 787–816. Cambridge: Cambridge University Press.

———. 2001. "More Is Worse: Some Observations on the Population of the Roman Empire." In *Debating Roman Demography*, edited by Walter Scheidel, 139–59. Leiden: Brill.

Fulford, Michael, Tom Brindle, Paul Bidwell, Jane Timby, Stephen Rippon, and J.R.L. Allen. 2017. "Movement of Resources." In *New Visions of the Countryside of Roman Britain. Volume 2. The Economy of Roman Britain*, edited by Martyn Allen, Lisa Lodwick, Tom Brindle, Michael Fulford, and Alexander Smith, 281–357. London: Society for the Promotion of Roman Studies.

Fulford, Michael, and A. Clarke, eds. 2011. *Silchester: City in Transition: The Mid-Roman Occupation of Insula IX, c. A.D. 125–250/300*. London: Society for the Promotion of Roman Studies.

Fulford, Michael, and Neil Holbrook. 2011. "Assessing the Contribution of Commercial Archaeology to the Study of the Roman Period in England, 1990–2004." *The Antiquaries Journal* 91: 323–45.

Fülle, Gunnar. 1997. "The Internal Organization of the Arretine Terra Sigillata Industry: Problems of Evidence and Interpretation." *Journal of Roman Studies* 87: 111–55.

Fuller, B. T., T. I. Molleson, D. A. Harris, L. T. Gilmour, and R.E.M. Hedges. 2006. "Isotopic Evidence for Breastfeeding and Possible Adult Dietary Differences from Late/Sub-Roman Britain." *American Journal of Physical Anthropology* 129 (1): 45–54.

Galbraith, John Kenneth. 1958. *The Affluent Society*. Boston: Houghton Mifflin.

Gallant, Thomas. 1991. *Risk and Survival in Ancient Greece*. Stanford, CA: Stanford University Press.

Gällnö, Sophie. 2013. "(In)Visible Spinners in the Documentary Papyri from Roman Egypt." In *Making Textiles in Pre-Roman and Roman Times: People, Places, Identities*, edited by Margarita Gleba and Judit Pástókai-Szeőke, 161–70. Oxford: Oxbow.

Gallup Analytics. 2013. "Gallup's Annual Economy and Personal Finance Survey." https://news.gallup.com/poll/162872/one-three-americans-prepare-detailed-household-budget.aspx.

Galor, Oded. 2011. *Unified Growth Theory*. Princeton, NJ: Princeton University Press.

Gamauf, Richard. 2009. "Slaves Doing Business: The Role of Roman Law in the Economy of a Roman Household." *European Review of History: Revue Européenne d'histoire* 16 (3): 331–46.

Gapp, Kenneth Sperber. 1935. "The Universal Famine under Claudius." *Harvard Theological Review* 28 (4): 258–65.

Gara, Alessandra. 1979. "Tre papiri dalla Collezione Michigan." *Zeitschrift für Papyrologie und Epigraphik* 35: 115–27.

———. 1988. "Aspetti di economia monetaria dell'Egitto romano." *ANRW* 10 (1): 912–51.

Garanzini, Francesca, and Lucia Mordeglia. 2022. "Biandrate (NO), un nuovo insediamento rustico di età romana: Note preliminari." In *Edifici rustici romani tra Pianura e Appenino: Stato della ricerca*, edited by Stefano Maggi, Manuela Battaglia, and Lorenzo Zamboni, 37–47. Florence: All'Insegna del giglio.

Gardner, Gregg. 2014. "Let Them Eat Fish: Food for the Poor in Early Rabbinic Judaism." *Journal for the Study of Judaism* 45 (2): 250–70.

———. 2022. *Wealth, Poverty and Charity in Jewish Antiquity*. Berkeley: University of California Press.

Gardner, Iain, Anthony Alcock, and Wolf-Peter Funk. 1999. *Coptic Documentary Texts from Kellis. Vol. 1*. Oxford: Oxbow.

Garnsey, Peter. 1976. "Peasants in Ancient Roman Society." *Journal of Peasant Studies* 3: 221–35.

———. 1979. "Where Did Italian Peasants Live?" *Proceedings of the Cambridge Philological Society* 205, n.s. 25: 1–25.

———. 1981. "Independent Freedmen and the Economy of Roman Italy under the Principate." *Klio* 63: 359–71.

———. 1988. *Famine and Food Supply in the Graeco-Roman World: Responses to Risk and Crisis*. Cambridge: Cambridge University Press.

———. 1999. *Food and Society in Classical Antiquity*. Cambridge: Cambridge University Press.

Garnsey, Peter, and Richard Saller. 1987. *The Roman Empire: Economy, Society and Culture*. Berkeley: University of California Press.

George, Michele. 2006. "Social Identity and the Dignity of Work in Freedmen's Reliefs." In *The Art of Citizens, Soldiers and Freedmen in the Roman World*, edited by Eve D'Ambra and Guy Métraux, 19–30. Oxford: Oxford University Press.

Ghisleni, M., E. Vaccaro, and Kim Bowes. 2011. "Excavating the Roman Peasant: Excavations at Pievina." *Papers of the British School at Rome* 79: 95–145.

Giannecchini, Monica, and Jacopo Moggi-Cecchi. 2008. "Stature in Archeological Samples from Central Italy: Methodological Issues and Diachronic Changes." *American Journal of Physical Anthropology* 135: 284–92.

Giardina, Andrea, and Aldo Schiavone, eds. 1981. *Società romana e produzione schiavistica*. 3 vols. Bari, Italy: Edipuglia.

Gilmour, Rebecca. 2017. "Resilient Romans: Cross-Sectional Evidence for Long-Term Functional Consequences of Extremity Trauma." PhD thesis, McMaster University.

Ginzburg, Carlo, and Carlo Poni. 1979. "Il nome e il come: scambio ineguale e mercato storiografico." *Quaderni storici* 14 (40 (1)): 181–90.

Giraudeau, Martin. 2017. "The Farm as an Accounting Laboratory: An Essay on the History of Accounting and Agriculture." *Accounting History Review* 27 (2): 201–15.

Gleize, Yves. 2009. "Étude archéo-anthropologique des inhumations." In *Musarna 3: La nécropole impériale*, edited by Eric Rebillard, 67–87. Rome: École française de Rome.

Glencross, Bonnie. 2011. "Skeletal Injury across the Life Course: Towards Understanding Social Agency." In *Social Bioarchaeology*, edited by Sabrina Argarwal and Bonnie Glencross, 390–409. Malden, MA: Wiley-Blackwell.

Goldberg, Jeremy. 2008. "The Fashioning of Bourgeois Domesticity in Late Medieval England: A Material Culture Perspective." In *Medieval Domesticity: Home, Housing and Household in Medieval England*, edited by Jeremy Goldberg and Maryanne Kowaleski, 124–44. Cambridge: Cambridge University Press.

Goldsmith, Raymond. 1984. "An Estimate of the Size and Structure of the National Product of the Early Roman Empire." *Review of Income and Wealth* 30: 263–88.

Golet, Ogden, Michael Hudson, and Cornelia Wunsch. 2004. "Accounting Practices and Economic Planning in Ancient Egypt before the Hellenistic Era." In *Creating Economic Order: Record-Keeping, Standardization, and the Development of Accounting in the Ancient Near East*, 215–86. Bethesda, MA: CDL Press.

Goodchild, Helen. 2007. "Modelling Roman Agricultural Production in the Middle Tiber Valley, Central Italy." PhD thesis, University of Birmingham.

———. 2013. "GIS Models of Roman Agricultural Production." In *The Roman Agricultural Economy: Organization, Investment and Production*, edited by Alan Bowman and Andrew Wilson, 55–83. Oxford: Oxford University Press.

Goodchild, Helen, and Robert Witcher. 2010. "Modelling the Agricultural Landscapes of Republican Italy." In *Agricoltura e scambi nell'Italia tardo repubblicana*, edited by Jesper Carlsen and Elio Lo Cascio, 187–220. Bari, Italy: Edipuglia.

Goodman, Penelope. 2013. "The Production Centres: Settlement Hierarchies and Spatial Distribution." In *Seeing Red: New Economic and Social Perspectives on Terra Sigillata*, edited by Michael Fulford and Emma Durham, 121–36. London: Institute of Classical Studies.

Goody, Jack. 1986. *The Logic of Writing and the Organization of Society*. Cambridge: Cambridge University Press.

———. 1996. *The East in the West*. Cambridge: Cambridge University Press.

Gordon, Richard. 1990. "Religion in the Roman Empire: The Civic Compromise and Its Limits." In *Pagan Priests: Religion and Power in the Ancient World*, edited by Mary Beard and John North, 235–55. Ithaca, NY: Cornell University Press.

Gowland, Rebecca, A. T. Chamberlain, and Rebecca Redfern. 2014. "On the Brink of Being: Re-Evaluating Infanticide and Infant Burial in Roman Britain." *Journal of Roman Archaeology* 96: 69–88.

Gowland, Rebecca, and Peter Garnsey. 2010. "Skeletal Evidence for Health, Nutritional Status and Malaria in Rome and the Empire." In *Roman Diasporas: Archaeological Approaches to Mobility and Diversity in the Roman Empire*, edited by H. Eckardt, 131–56. Portsmouth, RI: Journal of Roman Archaeology.

Gowland, Rebecca, and Lauren Walther. 2018. "Human Growth and Stature." In *The Science of Roman History: Biology, Climate, and the Future of the Past*, edited by Walter Scheidel, 174–204. Princeton, NJ: Princeton University Press.

Graeber, David. 2009. "Debt, Violence and Imperial Markets: Polanyian Meditations." In *Market and Society: The Great Transformation Today*, edited by Keith Hart and Chris Hann, 106–32. Cambridge University Press.

———. 2012. *Debt: The First 5,000 Years*. Brooklyn: Melville House.

Graeber, David, and David Wengrow. 2021. *The Dawn of Everything: A New History of Humanity*. London: Allen Lane.

Granger-Taylor, Hero. 1982. "Weaving Clothes to Shape in the Ancient World: The Tunic and Toga of the Arringatore." *Textile History* 13 (1): 3–25.

Grapin, Claude, and André Marbach. 2016. "Identification d'un fer de faux droite à coupe latérale gallo-romain à Alésia (Côte-d'Or): Une Découverte Importante." *Revue Archéologique de l'Est* 65: 371–81.

Grau-Sologestoa, Idoia, Maaike Groot, and Sabine Deschler-Erb. 2022. "Innovation and Intensification: The Use of Cattle in the Roman Rhine Region." *Environmental Archaeology*, 1–19. https://doi.org/10.1080/14614103.2022.2090094

Greene, Kevin. 2008. "Learning to Consume: Consumption and Consumerism in the Roman Empire." *Journal of Roman Archaeology* 21: 64–82.

Grenfell, Bernhard and Hunt, Arthur. 1914. *Oxyrhynchus Papyri*. Oxford: H. Hart.

Grey, Cam. 2011. *Constructing Communities in the Late Roman Countryside*. Cambridge: Cambridge University Press.

———. 2025. *Living with Risk in the Late Roman World*. Philadelphia: University of Pennsylvania Press.

Grey, Cam, James Mathieu, Antonia Arnoldus-Huyzendveld, Andrea Patacchini, and Mariaelena Ghisleni. 2015. "Familiarity, Repetition, and Quotidian Movement in Roman Tuscany." *Journal of Mediterranean Archaeology* 28 (2): 195–219.

Groen-Vallinga, Miriam. 2022. *Work and Labour in the Cities of Roman Italy*. Liverpool: Liverpool University Press.

Groen-Vallinga, Miriam, and Laurens Tacoma. 2016. "The Value of Labor: Diocletian's Price Edict." In *Work, Labour and Professions in the Roman World*, edited by Koenraad Verboven and Christian Laes, 104–32. Leiden: Brill.

Groot, Maaike. 2016. *Livestock for Sale: Animal Husbandry in a Roman Frontier Zone*. Amsterdam: Amsterdam University Press.

Groot, Maaike, Stijn Heeren, Laura Kooistra, and Wouter Vos. 2009. "Surplus Production for the Market? The Agrarian Economy in the Non-villa Landscapes of Germania Inferior." *Journal of Roman Archaeology* 22 (1): 231–53.

Groot, Maaike, and Laura Kooistra. 2009. "Land Use and the Agrarian Economy in the Roman Dutch River Area." *Internet Archaeology* 27. http://intarch.ac.uk/journal/issue27/groot_toc.html.

Guédon, Stéphanie. 2018. *La frontière romaine de l'Africa sous le Haut-Empire*. Madrid: Casa de Velázquez.

Guest, Peter. 2015. "The Burial, Loss and Recovery of Roman Coin Hoards in Britain and Beyond: Past, Present and Future." In *Hoarding and the Deposition of Metalwork from the Bronze Age to the 20th Century: A British Perspective*, 101–16. Oxford: Archaeopress.

Guinnane, Timothy. 2003. "Informal Credit." In *Oxford Encyclopedia of Economic History Vol. 3*, edited by Joel Mokyr, 68–70. Oxford: Oxford University Press.

———. 2005. "Trust: A Concept Too Many." *Jahrbuch Für Wirtschaftsgeschichte/Economic History Yearbook* 46 (1): 77–92.

Haas, Tymon de, ed. 2011. *Fields, Farms and Colonists: Intensive Field Survey and the Early Roman Colonization in the Pontine Region, Central Italy*. 2 vols. Groningen: Barkuis.

———. 2012. "Beyond Dots on the Map: Intensive Survey Data and the Interpretation of Small Sites and off-Site Distributions." In *Comparative Issues in the Archaeology of the Roman Rural Landscape: Site Classification between Survey, Excavation and Historical Categories*, edited by Peter Attema and Günther Schörner, 55–79. Portsmouth, RI: Journal of Roman Archaeology.

Habermehl, Diederick. 2013. *Settling in a Changing World: Villa Development in the Northern Provinces of the Roman Empire*. Amsterdam: Amsterdam University Press.

Hailwood, Mark. 2023. "Rethinking Literacy in Rural England, 1550–1700." *Past & Present* 260 (1): 38–70.

Haklai-Rotenberg, Merav. 2011. "Aurelian's Monetary Reform: Between Debasement and Public Trust." *Chiron* 41: 1–40.

Hall, Edith, and Henry Stead. 2020. *A People's History of Classics: Class and Greco-Roman Antiquity in Britain and Ireland 1689 to 1939*. Abingdon, UK: Routledge.

Halstead, Paul. 2014. *Two Oxen Ahead: Pre-Mechanized Farming in the Mediterranean*. Malden, MA: Wiley Blackwell.

Halstead, Paul, and John O'Shea, eds. 1989. *Bad Year Economics: Cultural Responses to Risk and Uncertainty*. Cambridge: Cambridge University Press.

Hamel, Gildas. 1990. *Poverty and Charity in Roman Palestine, First Three Centuries CE*. Berkeley: University of California Press.

Hamilton-Dyer, Sheila. 2009. "Animal Bone." In *Cambourne New Settlement Iron Age and Romano-British Settlement on the Clay Uplands of West Cambridgeshire. Volume 2: Specialist Appendices*, edited by James Wright, Matt Leivers, Rachael Seager Smith, and Chris J. Stevens, 82–133. Salisbury, UK: Wessex Archaeology.

Hanson, J. W. 2016. *An Urban Geography of the Roman World, 100 BC to AD 300*. Oxford: Archaeopress.

———. 2022. "New Approaches to the Urban Population and Urbanization Rate of the Roman Empire, AD 1 to 200." In *The Uncertain Past: Probability in Ancient History*, edited by Bart Danon, Daniel Jew, and Myles Lavan, 271–96. Cambridge: Cambridge University Press.

Hanson, William, and Richard Conolly. 2002. "Language and Literacy in Roman Britain: Some Archaeological Considerations." In *Becoming Roman, Writing Latin?*, edited by Alison Cooley, 151–64. Portsmouth, RI: Journal of Roman Archaeology Supplementary Series.

Harbeck, Michaela, Lisa Seifert, Stephanie Hänsch, David M. Wagner, Dawn Birdsell, Katy L. Parise, Ingrid Wiechmann, et al. 2013. "*Yersinia pestis* DNA from Skeletal Remains from the 6th Century AD Reveals Insights into Justinianic Plague." *PLoS Pathogens* 9 (5): e1003349. https://doi.org/10.1371/journal.ppat.1003349.

Harl, Kenneth. 2015. "From Aurelian to Diocletian: Financing Imperial Recovery by Coinage Debasements and Fiduciary Currencies." In *Money in the Pre-Industrial World: Bullion, Debasements and Coin Substitutes*, edited by John Munro, 33–44. London: Routledge.

Harlow, Mary. 2021. "Spinning, the Invisible Profession." In *The Value of Making: Theory and Practice in Ancient Craft Production*, edited by Helle Hocsheide and Ben Russell, 123–38. Turnhout, Belguim: Brepols.

Harper, Kyle. 2011. *Slavery in the Late Roman World, AD 275–425*. Cambridge: Cambridge University Press.

———. 2016. "People, Plagues and Prices in the Roman World: The Evidence from Egypt." *Journal of Economic History* 76 (3): 803–39.

———. 2017. *The Fate of Rome: Climate, Disease and the End of an Empire*. Princeton, NJ: Princeton University Press.

———. 2021. *Plagues upon the Earth: Disease and the Course of Human History*. Princeton, NJ: Princeton University Press.

Harper, Kyle, and Michael McCormick. 2018. "Reconstructing the Roman Climate." In *The Science of Roman History: Biology, Climate, and the Future of the Past*, edited by Walter Scheidel, 11–52. Princeton, NJ: Princeton University Press.

Harris, William V. 1989. *Ancient Literacy*. Cambridge, MA: Harvard University Press.

———. 2006. "A Revisionist View of Roman Money." *Journal of Roman Studies* 96: 1–24.

———. 2008. "The Nature of Roman Money." In *The Monetary Systems of the Greeks and the Romans*, edited by William V. Harris, 242–66. Oxford: Oxford University Press.

———. 2011. "Poverty and Destitution in the Roman Empire." In *Rome's Imperial Economy: Twelve Essays*, 27–54. Oxford: Oxford University Press.

———, ed. 2013. *Moses Finely and Politics*. Leiden: Brill.

———. 2018. "Literacy in Everyday Ancient Life: From Gabii to Gloucestershire." In *Literacy in Ancient Everyday Life*, 143–58. Berlin: De Gruyter.

———. 2019a. "Credit-Money in the Roman Economy." *Klio* 101 (1): 158–89.

———. 2019b "Social Class in the Roman World." In *Uomini, istituzioni, mercati: Studi di storia per Elio Lo Cascio*, edited by Marco Maiuro, 117–28. Bari, Italy: Edipuglia.

Hartman, Mary. 2004. *The Household and the Making of History. A Subversive View of the Western Past*. New York: Cambridge University Press.

Hatcher, John. 2018. "Seven Centuries of Unreal Wages." In *Seven Centuries of Unreal Wages: The Unreliable Data, Sources and Methods That Have Been Used for Measuring Standards of Living in the Past*, edited by John Hatcher and Judy Stephenson, 15–69. Cham, Switzerland: Palgrave Macmillan.

Hatcher, John, and Judy Stephenson, eds. 2018. *Seven Centuries of Unreal Wages: The Unreliable Data, Sources and Methods That Have Been Used for Measuring Standards of Living in the Past*. Cham, Switzerland: Palgrave Macmillan.

Haug, Brendan. 2015. "Environment, Adaptation, and Administration in the Roman Fayyūm." In *Von der Pharaonenzeit bis zur Spätantike: Kulturelle Vielfalt im Fayum*, edited by Nadine Quenouille, 55–71. Wiesbaden: Harrassowitz Verlag.

Hawkins, Cameron. 2016. *Roman Artisans and the Urban Economy*. Cambridge: Cambridge University Press.

Haynes, Ian. 2002. "Britain's First Information Revolution: The Roman Army and the Transformation of Economic Life." In *The Roman Army and the Economy*, edited by Paul Erdkamp, 111–26. Amsterdam: Gieben.

———. 2013. *Blood of the Provinces: The Roman Auxilia and the Making of Provincial Society from Augustus to the Severans*. Oxford: Oxford University Press.

Heimberg, Ursula. 2002–2003. "Römische Villen an Rhein und Maas." *Bonner Jahrbücher* 2002–3 (February–January): 57–148.

Heinrich, Frits. 2019. "Cereals and Bread." In *The Routledge Handbook of Diet and Nutrition in the Roman World*, edited by Paul Erdkamp and Claire Holleran, 101–15. London: Routledge.

Heinrich, Frits, and Paul Erdkamp. 2017. "The Role of Modern Malnutrition in Modelling Roman Malnutrition: Aid or Anachronism?" *Journal of Archaeological Science: Reports*, June. https://doi.org/10.1016/j.jasrep.2017.06.011.

Henneberg, Maciej, and Renata Henneberg. 1998. "Biological Characteristics of the Population Based on Analysis of Skeletal Remains." In *The Chora of Metaponto. Vol. 2. The Necropoles*, edited by J. C. Carter, 503–59. Austin: University of Texas Press.

Hervé-Monteil, Marie-Laure, Dagmar Lukas, Martial Monteil, Marie-France Dietsch-Sellami, Antoine Archer, Élisabeth Lecler-Huby, Serge Le Maho, and Maxime Mortreau. 2011. "La viticulture dans l'ouest de La Gaule Lyonnaise: Les pressoirs de Parville (Eure) et de Piriac-sur-Mer (Loire-Atlantique)." *Gallia* 68 (1): 163–214.

Hill, Polly. 1986. *Development Economics on Trial: The Anthropological Case for a Prosecution.* Cambridge: Cambridge University Press.

Hin, Saskia. 2013. *The Demography of Roman Italy: Population Dynamics in an Ancient Conquest Society 201 BCE–14 CE.* Cambridge: Cambridge University Press.

Hirt, Alfred. 2010. *Imperial Mines and Quarries in the Roman World: Organizational Aspects.* Oxford: Oxford University Press.

Hobsbawm, Eric. 1968. "Karl Marx's Contribution to Historiography." *On History* 64: 37–56.

———. 1988. "On History from Below." In *History from Below: Studies in Popular Protest and Popular Ideology*, edited by Frederic Kranz, 13–28. Oxford: Oxford University Press.

———. 1997. "British History and the Annales: A Note." In *On History*, 178–85. London: Abacus.

Hobson, Deborah. 1984. "The Role of Women in the Economic Life of Roman Egypt: A Case Study from First Century Tebtunis." *Echos Du Monde Classique: Classical Views* 28 (3): 373–90.

Hodges, Richard. 1988. *Peasant and Primitive Markets.* Oxford: Blackwell.

Hoffman, Philip. 1996. *Growth in a Traditional Society: The French Countryside 1450–1815.* Princeton, NJ: Princeton University Press.

Hoffman, Philip, Gilles Postel-Vinay, and Jean-Laurent Rosenthal. 2019. *Dark Matter Credit: The Development of the Peer-to-Peer Lending and Banking in France.* Princeton, NJ: Princeton University Press.

Hollander, David. 2007. *Money in the Late Roman Republic.* Leiden: Brill.

———. 2008. "The Demand for Money in the Late Roman Republic." In *The Monetary Systems of the Greeks and Romans*, edited by William V. Harris, 112–36. Oxford: Oxford University Press.

———. 2020. *Farmers and Agriculture in the Roman Empire.* London: Routledge.

Holleran, Claire. 2012. *Shopping in Ancient Rome: The Retail Trade in the Late Republic and the Principate.* Oxford: Oxford University Press.

———. 2017. "Getting a Job: Finding Work in the City of Rome." In *Work, Labour, and Professions in the Roman World*, edited by Koenraad Verboven and Christian Laes, 87–103. Leiden: Brill.

Hoogendijk, Francesca, and Peter van Minnen. 1991. *Papyri, Ostraca, Parchments and Waxed Tablets in the Leiden Papyrological Institute.* Leiden: Brill.

Hope, Colin. 2022. "Kellis in Context." In *Kellis: A Roman-Period Village in Egypt's Dakhleh Oasis*, edited by Colin Hope and Gillian Bowen, 1–14. Cambridge: Cambridge University Press.

Hope, Colin, and Gillian Bowen. 2022. "Houses, Households, Household Activities." In *Kellis: A Roman-Period Village in Egypt's Dakhleh Oasis*, edited by Colin Hope and Gillian Bowen, 15–56. Cambridge: Cambridge University Press.

Hope, Colin, Gillian Bowen, Marie-Dominique Nenna, and Roseanne Livingstone. 2022. "Crafts." In *Kellis: A Roman-Period Village in Egypt's Dakhleh Oasis*, edited by Colin Hope and Gillian Bowen, 79–128. Cambridge: Cambridge University Press.

Hopkins, Keith. 1980. "Taxes and Trade in the Roman Empire (200 B.C.–A.D. 400)." *Journal of Roman Studies* 70: 101–25.

———. 1991. "Conquest by Book." In *Literacy in the Roman World*, edited by Mary Beard, 133–58. Ann Arbor, MI: Journal of Roman Archaeology Supplementary Series.

———. 1995. "Rome, Taxes, Rents and Trade." *Kodai* 6–7: 41–75.

———. 2014. "Keith Hopkins Interviews Sir Moses Finley: October 1985 Transcript." *American Journal of Philology* 135 (2): 179-201.

Horden, Peregrine, and Nicholas Purcell. 2000. *The Corrupting Sea: A Study of Mediterranean History.* Oxford: Oxford University Press.

Horrell, Sara, and Jane Humphries. 2019. "Children's Work and Wages in Britain, 1280–1860." *Explorations in Economic History* 73: 101272. https://doi.org/10.1016/j.eeh.2019.04.001.

Horrell, Sara, Jane Humphries, and Jacob Weisdorf. 2022. "Beyond the Male Breadwinner: Life-Cycle Living Standards of Intact and Disrupted English Working Families, 1260–1850." *Economic History Review* 75 (2): 530–60.

Howgego, Chris. 1992. "The Supply and Use of Money in the Roman World 200 B.C. to A.D. 300." *Journal of Roman Studies* 82: 1–31.

———. 1994. "Coin Circulation and the Integration of the Roman Economy." *Journal of Roman Archaeology* 7: 7–21.

———. 2019. "Coin Hoards of the Roman Empire." Oxford: Ashmolean Museum. https://chre.ashmus.ox.ac.uk/.

Howgego, Chris, and Andrew Wilson. 2022. "Introduction: Coin Hoards and Hoarding in the Roman World." In *Coin Hoards and Hoarding in the Roman World*, edited by Jerome Mairat, Andrew Wilson, and Chris Howgego, 3–22. Oxford: Oxford University Press.

Hoyer, Daniel. 2018a. "An Overview of the Numismatic Evidence from Imperial Roman Africa." *Institute for the Study of the Ancient World, Papers* 13. http://doi.org/2333.1/76hdrfz3.

———. 2018b. *Money, Culture, and Well-Being in Rome's Economic Development*. Leiden: Brill.

Hoyle, Richard. 2013. "Introduction: Recovering the Farmer." In *The Farmer in England, 1650–1980*, edited by Richard Hoyle, 1–42. Farnham, UK: Ashgate.

Hudson, Nicholas. 2010. "Changing Places: The Archaeology of the Roman Convivium." *American Journal of Archaeology* 114 (4): 663–95.

Huebner, Sabine. 2013. *The Family in Roman Egypt: A Comparative Approach to Intergenerational Solidarity and Conflict*. Cambridge: Cambridge University Press.

Huitorel, Guillaume. 2017. "Stocker les céréales dans les établissements ruraux du nord de la Gaule à l'époque romaine: Essai d'identification des modes de stockage entre le Ier et le IVe siècle ap. J.-C." In *Les céréales dans le monde antique: Regards croisés sur les stratégies de gestion des cultures, de leur stockage et de leurs modes de consommation*, edited by Adeline Bats, 217–38. Nehet, 5. Paris: Sorbonne Université–Université Libre de Bruxelles.

Humphries, Jane. 2013. "The Lure of Aggregates and the Pitfalls of the Patriarchal Perspective: A Critique of the High Wage Economy Interpretation of the British Industrial Revolution." *Economic History Review* 66 (3): 693–714.

Humphries, Jane, and Jacob Weisdorf. 2015. "The Wages of Women in England, 1260–1850." *Journal of Economic History* 75 (2): 405–47.

———. 2019. "Unreal Wages? Real Income and Economic Growth in England, 1260–1850." *The Economic Journal* 129 (623): 2867–87.

Husselman, Elinor. 1961. "Pawnbrokers' Accounts from Roman Egypt." *Transactions and Proceedings of the American Philological Association* 92: 251–66.

Husselman, Elinor, Arthur Boak, and William Edgerton. 1944. *Papyri from Tebtynis. Vol. 2.* Michigan Papyri, 5. University of Michigan Press.

Ikeguchi, Mamoru. 2006. "A Method for Comparing and Interpreting Field Survey Data." In *Ancient Economies, Modern Methodologies: Archaeology, Comparative History, Models and Institutions*, edited by Peter F. Bang, Mamoru Ikeguchi, and Harmut G. Ziche, 137–58. Bari, Italy: Edipuglia.

Ingen, Geoffrey. 2000. "'Babylonian Madness': On the Historical and Sociological Origins of Money." In *What Is Money?*, edited by John Smithin, 16–41. London: Routledge.

Inwood, Jamie. 2017. "Identifying Malaria in Ancient Human Remains: A Molecular and Biochemical Approach." PhD thesis, Yale University.

Jackson, Trevor. 2023. "The New History of Old Inequality." *Past & Present* 259: 262–89.

Jakab, Éva. 2009. *Risikomanagement beim Weinkauf: Periculum und Praxis im Imperium Romanum*. Munich: Beck.

Jarvis, Ben, Chris Briggs, and Matthew Tompkins. 2015. "Exploring Text and Objects: Escheators' Inventories and Material Culture in Medieval English Rural Households." *Medieval Archaeology* 59: 168–92.

Jay, Mandy, B. T. Fuller, Michael Richards, Christopher Knüsel, and Sarah King. 2008. "Iron Age Breastfeeding Practices in Britain: Isotopic Evidence from Wetwang Slack, East Yorkshire." *American Journal of Physical Anthropology* 136 (3): 327–37.

Jew, Daniel, Robin Osborne, and Michael Scott, eds. 2016. *M. I. Finley: An Ancient Historian and His Impact.* Cambridge: Cambridge University Press.

Jiménez, Alicia. 2017. "Standard Time: Typologies in Roman Antiquity." In *Materializing Roman Histories,* edited by Astrid Van Oyen and Martin Pitts, 75–84. Oxford: Oxbow.

Johnson, Alan Chester. 1936. *Roman Egypt to the Reign of Diocletian.* An Economic Survey of Ancient Rome, Vol. 2. Baltimore, MD: Johns Hopkins Press.

Johnson, Paul, Simon Keay, and Martin Millett. 2004. "Lesser Urban Sites in the Tiber Valley: Baccanae, Forum Casii and Castellum Amerinum." *Papers of the British School at Rome* 72: 69–99.

Jones, A.M.H. 1960. "The Cloth Industry under the Roman Empire." *Economic History Review* 13: 83–92.

Jones, G.D.B. 1963. "Capena and the Ager Capenas: Part II." *Papers of the British School at Rome* 31, n.s. 18: 100–158.

Jongman, Willem. 1988. *The Economy and Society of Pompeii.* Amsterdam: J. C. Gieben.

———. 2003. "A Golden Age: Death, Money Supply and Social Succession in the Roman Empire." In *Credito e moneta nel mondo romano,* edited by Elio Lo Cascio, 181–96. Bari, Italy: Edipuglia.

———. 2007. "The Early Roman Empire: Consumption." In *Cambridge Economic History of the Greco-Roman World,* edited by Walter Scheidel, Ian Morris, and Richard P. Saller, 592–618.

Jongman, Willem, Jan Jacobs, and Geertje Klein Goldewijk. 2019. "Health and Wealth in the Roman Empire." *Economics and Human Biology* 34: 138–50.

Jördens, Andrea. 1993. "Kaufpreisstundungen (Sales on Credit)." *Zeitschrift für Papyrologie und Epigraphik* 98: 263–82.

———. 1995. "Sozialstrukturen im Arbeitstierhandel des kaiserlichen Ägypten." *Tyche* 10: 37–100.

———. 2001. "Papyri und private Archive: Ein Diskussionsbeitrag zur papyrologischen Terminologie." In *Vorträge zur griechischen und hellenistischen Rechtsgeschichte,* edited by Eva Cantarella and Gerhard Tür, 253–67. Cologne: Böhlau.

Jørgensen, Lise Bender. 2021. "Dress in the Desert: Archaeological Textiles as a Source for Work Clothes in Roman Egypt." In *Dress in Mediterranean Antiquity: Greeks, Romans, Jews, Christians,* edited by Alicia J. Batten and Kelly Olson, 1st ed., 109–25. London: T&T Clark.

Joshel, Sandra. 1992. *Work, Identity and Legal Status at Rome: A Study of the Occupational Inscriptions.* Norman: Oklahoma University Press.

Joshel, Sandra, and Lauren Petersen. 2014. *The Material Life of Roman Slaves.* Cambridge: Cambridge University Press.

Judd, Margaret A., and Rebecca Redfern. 2012. "Trauma." In *A Companion to Paleopathology,* edited by Anne L. Grauer, 359–79. Oxford: Blackwell.

Kallet, Lisa. 2022. "A Counting People: Valuing Numeracy in Democratic Athens." In *Numbers and Numeracy in the Greek Polis,* edited by Robert Sing, Tazuko van Berkel, and Robin Osborne, 27–57. Leiden: Brill.

Kasprzyk, Michael. 2019. "Production et commerce, quelques aspects dans le nord de la Gaule romaine (Ier–IIIe siècle de notre ère)." *Archéopages* Hors-séries 5: 97–108.

Katsari, Constantina. 2008. "The Monetization of Rome's Frontier Provinces." In *The Monetary Systems of the Greeks and Romans,* edited by William V. Harris, 242–66. Oxford: Oxford University Press.

Kay, Philip. 2014. *Rome's Economic Revolution*. Oxford: Oxford University Press.

Keenan, James. 1989. "Pastoralism in Roman Egypt." *Bulletin of the American Society of Papyrologists* 26 (3/4): 175–200.

Kehoe, Dennis. 1988. *The Economics of Agriculture on Roman Imperial Estates in North Africa*. Hypomnemata, 89. Göttingen: Vandenhoeck u. Ruprecht.

———. 1992. *Management and Investment on Estates in Roman Egypt*. Bonn: R. Habelt.

———. 1997. *Investment, Profit and Tenancy: The Jurists and the Roman Agrarian Economy*. Ann Arbor: University of Michigan Press.

———. 2007. "The Early Roman Empire: Production." In *Cambridge Economic History of the Greco-Roman World*, edited by Walter Scheidel, Ian Morris, and Richard P. Saller, 543–69. Cambridge: Cambridge University Press.

Keller, Marcel, Maria Spyrou, Christiana Scheib, Andreas Kröpelin, Brigitte Haas-Gebhard, Bernd Päffgen, Jochen Haberstroh, et al. 2019. "Ancient *Yersinia Pestis* Genomes from across Western Europe Reveal Early Diversification during the First Pandemic (541–750)." *Proceedings of the National Academy of Sciences* 116 (25): 12363–72.

Kelly, Benjamin. 2011. *Petitions, Litigation and Social Control in Roman Egypt*. Oxford: Oxford University Press.

———. 2023. "Accessing Justice in Roman Egypt: Quantitative Methods and Their Limitations." In *Seeking Justice in and out of Court: Dispute Resolution in Greco-Roman and Late Antique Egypt*, edited by Sofie Waebens, Katelijn Vandorpe, and Nick Vaneerdewegh, 159–92. Leuven: Peeters.

Kelly, Paul V. 2021. "Third-Century Price Inflation Reassessed." *Theoretical Roman Archaeology* 4 (1): 1–22.

———. 2022. "Children and Their Impact on Family Finances in Roman Egypt." In *The Uncertain Past: Probability in Ancient History*, edited by Myles Lavan, Daniel Jew, and Bart Danon, 197–230. Cambridge: Cambridge University Press.

———. 2023. *The Financial Markets of Roman Egypt*. Liverpool: Liverpool University Press.

Kessler, David, and Peter Temin. 2008. "Money and Prices in the Early Roman Empire." In *The Monetary Systems of the Greeks and Romans*, edited by William Harris, 137–59. Oxford: Oxford University Press.

Kifleyesus, Abbebe. 2009. "Jeberti Women Traders' Innumeracy: Its Impact on Commercial Activity in Eritrea." *L'Homme* 189: 49–80.

Killgrove, Kristina. 2010. "Migration and Mobility in Imperial Rome." PhD thesis, University of North Carolina, Chapel Hill.

———. 2017. "Imperialism and Physiological Stress in Rome, First to Third Centuries A.D." In *Colonized Bodies, Worlds Transformed: Toward a Global Bioarchaeology of Contact and Colonialism*, edited by Melissa S. Murphy and Haagen D. Klaus, 247–77. Oxford: Oxford University Press.

———. 2019. "Using Skeletal Remains as a Proxy for Roman Lifestyles: The Potential and Problems with Osteological Reconstructions of Health, Diet, and Stature in Imperial Rome." In *The Routledge Handbook of Diet and Nutrition in the Roman World*, edited by Paul Erdkamp and Clair Holleran, 245–58. London: Routledge.

Killgrove, Kristina, and Janet Montgomery. 2016. "All Roads Lead to Rome: Exploring Human Migration to the Eternal City through Biochemistry of Skeletons from Two Imperial-Era Cemeteries (1st–3rd c AD)." *PLoS ONE* 11 (2). https://doi.org/10.1371/journal.pone.0147585.

Killgrove, Kristina, and Robert Tycot. 2013. "Food for Rome: A Stable Isotope Investigation of Diet in the Imperial Period (1st–3rd Centuries AD)." *Journal of Anthropological Archaeology* 32: 28–38.

King, J. E. 2012. *The Microfoundations Delusion: Metaphor and Dogma in the History of Macroeconomics*. Cheltenham, UK, Edward Elgar.

Knüsel, Christopher, Sonia Göggel, and David Lucy. 1997. "Comparative Degenerative Joint Disease of the Vertebral Column in the Medieval Monastic Cemetery of the Gilbertine Priory of St. Andrew, Fishergate, York, England." *American Journal of Physical Anthropology* 103 (4): 481–95.

Koedijk, Max, and Neville Morley, eds. 2022. *Capital in Classical Antiquity*. Cham, Switzerland: Palgrave Macmillan.

Koepke, Nikola, and Jörg Baten. 2005. "The Biological Standard of Living in Europe during the Last Two Millennia." *European Review of Economic History* 9 (1): 61–95.

Kolb, Anne. 2018a. "Frauen und Schriftlichkeit im Römischen Ägypten." In *Literacy in Ancient Everyday Life*, edited by Sabine Hübner, 163–78. Berlin: De Gruyter.

———, ed. 2018b. *Literacy in Ancient Everyday Life*. Berlin: De Gruyter.

Kolbeck, Ben. 2018. "A Foot in Both Camps: The Civilian Suppliers of the Army in Roman Britain." *Theoretical Roman Archaeology Journal* 1. https://doi.org/10.16995/traj.355.

Komlos, John. 1998. "Shrinking in a Growing Economy? The Mystery of Physical Stature during the Industrial Revolution." *Journal of Economic History* 58 (3): 779–802.

Kooistra, Laura I., Marieke van Dinter, Monica K. Dütting, Pauline van Rijn, and Chiara Cavallo. 2013. "Could the Local Population of the Lower Rhine Delta Supply the Roman Army? Part 1: The Archaeological and Historical Framework." *Journal of the Archaeology of the Low Countries* 4: 1–23.

Koukli, Marianna, Frank Siegmund, and Christina Papageorgopoulou. 2023. "Stature Estimation in Ancient Greece: Population-Specific Equations and Secular Trends from 9000 BC to 900 AD." *Archaeological and Anthropological Sciences* 15 (5): 53. https://doi.org/10.1007/s12520-023-01744-1.

Kron, Geoffrey. 2000. "Roman Ley Farming." *Journal of Roman Archaeology* 13: 277–87.

———. 2002. "Archeozoological Evidence for the Productivity of Roman Livestock Farming." *Münstersche Beiträge zur antiken Handelsgeschichte* 21 (2): 53–73.

———. 2004. "A Deposit of Carbonized Hay at Oplontis and Roman Forage Quality." *Mouseion* Ser. III, 4: 275–330.

———. 2005a. "Anthropometry, Physical Anthropology, and the Reconstruction of Ancient Health, Nutrition, and Living Standards." *Historia: Zeitschrift Für Alte Geschichte* 54 (1): 68–83.

———. 2005b. "Sustainable Roman Intensive Mixed Farming Methods: Water Conservation and Erosion Control." In *Concepts, pratiques et enjeux environnementaux dans l'empire romain*, edited by Robert Bedon and Ella Hermon, 285–308. Limoges: Presses Universitaires de Limoges et du Limousin.

———. 2008. "The Much-Maligned Peasant: Comparative Perspectives on the Productivity of the Small Farmer in Classical Antiquity." In *People, Land and Politics: Demographic Developments and the Transformation of Roman Italy, 300 BC–AD 14*, edited by Luk de Ligt and Simon Northwood, 71–119. Leiden: Brill.

———. 2012. "Food Production." In *The Cambridge Companion to the Economic History of the Roman World*, edited by Walter Scheidel, 156–74. Cambridge.

———. 2014. "Comparative Evidence and the Reconstruction of the Ancient Economy: Greco-Roman Housing and the Level and Distribution of Wealth and Income." In *Quantifying the Greco-Roman Economy and Beyond*, edited by François De Callataÿ, 123–46. Bari, Italy: Edipuglia.

———. 2015. "Agriculture." In *A Companion to Food in the Ancient World*, edited by John Wilkins and Robin Nadeau, 160–72. Chichester, UK: John Wiley & Sons.

———. 2019. "Comparative Perspectives on Nutrition and Social Inequality in the Roman World." In *The Routledge Handbook of Diet and Nutrition in the Roman World*, edited by Paul Erdkamp and Claire Holleran, 259–72. London: Routledge.

Kruit, Nico. 1992. "Local Customs in the Formulas of Sales of Wine for Future Delivery (A Supplement to *P. Heid* V)." *Zeitschrift für Papyrologie und Epigraphik* 94: 167–84.

Laes, Christian. 2008. "Child Slaves at Work in Roman Antiquity." *Ancient Society* 38: 235–83.

LaGroue, Lance. 2014. "Accounting and Auditing in Roman Society." PhD thesis, University of North Carolina, Chapel Hill.

Lang, F. 2009. "Ernteträge nördlich der Alpen in römischer Zeit: Überlegungen zur Leistungsfähigkeit der Landwirtschaft und zu den Auswirkungen des Butser Ancient Farm Project." *Archäologisches Korrespondenzblatt* 39: 393–407.

Lang, Janet. 2017. "Roman Iron and Steel: A Review." *Materials and Manufacturing Processes* 32 (7–8): 857–66.

Langellotti, Micaela. 2012. *L'allevamento di pecore e capre nell'Egitto romano: Aspetti economici e sociali*. Bari, Italy: Edipuglia.

———. 2020. *Village Life in Roman Egypt: Tebtunis in the First Century AD*. Oxford: Oxford University Press.

Larsson Lovén, Lena. 2013. "Female Work and Identity in Roman Textile Production and Trade: A Methodological Discussion." In *Making Textiles in Pre-Roman and Roman Times: People, Places, Identities*, edited by Margarita Gleba and Judit Pástókai-Szeőke, 109–25. Oxford: Oxbow.

Laubenheimer, Fanette, and Élise Marlière. 2010. *Échanges et vie économique dans le Nord-Ouest des Gaules. (Nord/Pas-de-Calais, Picardie, Haute-Normandie): Le témoignage des amphores du IIe s. av. J.-C. au IVe s. ap. J.-C.* Besançon: Institut des Sciences et Techniques de l'Antiquité.

Laurence, Ray, and Francesco Trifilò. 2023. *Mediterranean Timescapes: Chronological Age and Cultural Practice in the Roman Empire*. Abingdon, UK: Routledge.

Lavan, Myles. 2013. *Slaves to Rome: Paradigms of Empire in Roman Culture*. Cambridge: Cambridge University Press.

———. 2019. "The Army and the Spread of Roman Citizenship." *Journal of Roman Studies* 109: 27–69.

Lazer, Estelle. 2009. *Resurrecting Pompeii*. New York: Routledge.

———. 2017. "Skeletal Remains and the Health of the Population at Pompeii." In *The Economy of Pompeii*, edited by Miko Flohr and Andrew Wilson, 135–59. Oxford: Oxford University Press.

Le Teuff, Béatrice. 2012. "Census: Les recensements dans les provinces de l'empire romain d'Auguste à Dioclétien." PhD thesis, Université Bordeaux 3.

Leggett, Sam. 2022. "A Hierarchical Meta-Analytical Approach to Western European Dietary Transitions in the First Millennium AD." *European Journal of Archaeology*, 1–21.

Leguilloux, Martine. 2018. "The Exploitation of Animals in the Roman *Praesidia* on the Routes to Myos Hormos and to Berenike: On Food, Transport and Craftsmanship." In *The Eastern Desert of Egypt during the Greco-Roman Period: Archaeological Reports*. Paris: Collège de France. https://books.openedition.org/cdf/5245.

Lenski, Noel. 2012. "Working Models: Functional Art and Roman Conceptions of Slavery." In *Roman Slavery and Roman Material Culture*, edited by Michele George, 130–57. Toronto: University of Toronto Press.

———. 2016. "Violence and the Roman Slave." In *The Topography of Violence in the Greco-Roman World*, edited by Werner Reiss, 275–98. Ann Arbor: University of Michigan Press.

Lepenies, Philipp. 2016. *The Power of a Single Number: A Political History of GDP*. New York: Columbia University Press.

Lepetz, Sébastien, and Tarek Oueslati. 2003. "La consommation de viande dans les villes romaines d'Île-de-France au Ier siècle: Les cas de Meaux et de Paris (Seine-et-Marne et Seine)." *Revue archéologique du Centre de la France* 42: 41–59.

Lepetz, Sébastien, and Véronique Zech-Matterne. 2018. "Systèmes agro-pastoraux à l'âge du Fer et à la période romaine." In *Gallia Rustica 2. Les campagnes du nord-est de la Gaule, de la fin de l'âge du Fer à l'Antiquité tardive*, edited by Michel Reddé, 327–400. Bordeaux: Ausonius Éditions.

Lerouxel, François. 2012. "Des prêts sans intérêt? Le taux d'intérêt dans le nome oxyrhynchite avant 79 après J.-C." *Zeitschrift für Papyrologie und Epigraphik* 181: 161–72.

———. 2015. "The Biblioteke Eukteson and Transaction Costs in the Credit Market of Roman Egypt (30 B.C.E. to ca. 170 C.E.)." In *Law and Transaction Costs in the Ancient Economy,* edited by Denis Kehoe, David Ratzan, and Uri Yiftach-Firanko, 162–84. Ann Arbor, MI: University of Michigan Press.

———. 2016. *Le marché du crédit dans le monde romain (Égypte et Campanie).* Rome: École française de Rome.

Leveau, Philippe. 1984. *Caesarea de Maurétanie: Une villa romaine et ses campagnes.* Rome: Éditions de l'École Française de Rome.

Levien, Michael, Michael Watts, and Hairong Yan. 2018. "Agrarian Marxism." *Journal of Peasant Studies* 45 (5–6): 853–83.

Lewis, Naphtali. 1988. "A Jewish Landowner in Provincia Arabia." *Scripta Classica Israelica* 8–9: 132–37.

———. 1997. *Compulsory Public Services of Roman Egypt.* Florence: Edizioni Gonnelli.

———. 1999. *Life in Egypt under Roman Rule.* Atlanta: Scholars Press.

Lewis, Naphtali, Yigael Yadin, and Jonas Greenfield. 1989. *Documents from the Bar Kokhba Period in the Cave of Letters.* Jerusalem: Hebrew University.

Lewit, Tamara. 2022. "Children in the Roman Farming Economy: Evidence, Problems and Possibilities." In *Reframing the Roman Economy,* edited by Dimitri Van Limbergen, Adeline Hoffelinck, and Devi Taelman, 81–122. Cham, Switzerland: Palgrave Macmillan.

Ligt, Luuk de. 1990. "Demand, Supply, Distribution, I: Rural Monetization and Peasant Demand." *Münstersche Beiträge zur antiken Handelsgeschichte* 9 (2): 24–56.

———. 1991. "Demand, Supply, Distribution, II: Rural Crafts, Distribution and a Comparative Perspective." *Münstersche Beiträge zur antiken Handelsgeschichte* 10 (1): 37–77.

———. 1993. *Fairs and Markets in the Roman Empire.* Amsterdam: J. C. Gieben.

———. 2012. *Peasants, Citizens and Soldiers.* Cambridge: Cambridge University Press.

Ligt, Luuk de, and Peter Garnsey. 2012. "The Album of Herculaneum and a Model of the Town's Demography." *Journal of Roman Archaeology* 25: 69–94.

Ling, Roger, ed. 1997. *The Insula of the Menander at Pompeii.* 3 vols. Oxford: Oxford University Press.

Lis, Catharina, and Hugo Soly. 2012. *Worthy Efforts: Attitudes to Work and Workers in Pre-Industrial Europe.* Leiden: Brill.

Liu, Jinyu. 2008. "The Economy of Endowments: The Case of the Roman *Collegia.*" In Pistoi Dai Tèn Technèn. *Bankers, Loans and Archives in the Ancient World,* edited by Koenraad Verboven, Katelijn Vandorpe, and Véronique Chankowski, 231–56. Leuven: Peeters.

———. 2009. Collegia Centonariorum*: The Guilds of Textile Dealers in the Roman West.* Leiden: Brill.

———. 2013. "Trade, Traders and Guilds (?) in Textiles: The Case of Southern Gaul and Northern Italy (1st–3rd Centuries AD)." In *Making Textiles in Pre-Roman and Roman Times: People, Places, Identities,* edited by Margarita Gleba and Judit Pástókai-Szeőke, 126–41. Oxford: Oxbow.

———. 2016. "Group Membership, Trust Networks, and Social Capital: A Critical Analysis." In *Work, Labour and Professions in the Roman World,* edited by Koenraad Verboven and Christian Laes. Leiden: Brill.

———. 2017. "Urban Poverty in the Roman Empire: Material Conditions." In *Paul and Economics: A Handbook,* edited by Raymond Pickett and Thomas Blanton, 23–56. Minneapolis: Augsburg Fortress.

Lo Cascio, Elio. 1986. "La struttura fiscale del impero romano." In *L'Impero Romano e le strutture economiche e sociali delle provincie,* edited by Michael Crawford, 29–59. Como: New Press.

———. 1996. "How Did the Romans View Their Coinage and Its Function?" In *Coin Finds and Coin Use in the Roman World*, edited by Cathy E. King and David Wigg, 271–87. Berlin: G. Mann.

———. 1997. "Prezzi in oro e prezzi in unita di conto tra il III e il IV sec. d.C." In *Économie antique: Prix et formations des prix dans les économies antiques*, edited by Jean Andreau, Pierre Briant, and Raymond Descat, 161–82. Saint-Bertrand-de-Comminges: Musée archéologique départemental.

———. 2008. "The Function of Gold Coinage in the Monetary Economy of the Roman Empire." In *The Monetary Systems of the Greeks and Romans*, edited by William V. Harris, 160–73. Oxford: Oxford University Press.

———. 2009. *Crescita e declino: Studi di storia dell'economia romana*. Centro Ricerche e Documentazione Sull'antichità Classica, 32. Rome: L'Erma di Bretschneider.

———. 2020. "Setting the Rules of the Game: The Market and Its Working in the Roman Empire." In *Roman Law and Economics: Institutions and Organizations Volume I*, edited by Giuseppe Dari-Mattiacci and Dennis P. Kehoe, 111–36. Oxford: Oxford University Press.

Lo Cascio, Elio, and Paolo Malanima. 2005. "Cycles and Stability: Italian Population before the Demographic Transition (225 B.C.–A.D. 1900)." *Rivista di storia economica* 21: 5–40.

Locker, Alison. 2007. "*In Piscibus Diversis*: The Bone Evidence for Fish Consumption in Roman Britain." *Britannia* 38: 141–80.

Lockyear, Chris. 1999. "Hoard Structure and Coin Production in Antiquity—an Empirical Investigation." *Numismatic Chronicle* 159: 215–43.

Lodwick, Lisa. 2017. "Arable Farming, Plant Foods and Resources." In *New Visions of the Countryside of Roman Britain. Volume 2. The Economy of Roman Britain*, edited by Martyn Allen, Lisa Lodwick, Tom Brindle, Michael Fulford, and Alexander Smith, 11–84. London: Society for the Promotion of Roman Studies.

Lodwick, Lisa, Gill Campbell, Vicky Crosby, and Gundula Müldner. 2021. "Isotopic Evidence for Changes in Cereal Production Strategies in Iron Age and Roman Britain." *Environmental Archaeology* 26 (1): 13–28.

Longepierre, Samuel. 2020. "Un moulin hydraulique au sein d'une ferme antique à Lucciana-Procojo (Haute-Corse)." INRAP: Actualités. 2020. https://www.inrap.fr/un-moulin-hydraulique-au-sein-d-une-ferme-antique-lucciana-procojo-haute-corse-15378.

Lowder, Sarah K., Jakob Skoet, and Terri Raney. 2016. "The Number, Size, and Distribution of Farms, Smallholder Farms, and Family Farms Worldwide." *World Development* 87: 16–29. https://doi.org/10.1016/j.worlddev.2015.10.041.

Lucassen, Jan. 2014. "Deep Monetisation: The Case of the Netherlands 1200–1940." *Tijdschrift voor Sociale en Economische Geschiedenis* 11 (3): 73–121.

Luongo, Giuseppe, Annamaria Perrotta, Claudio Scarpatia, Ernesto De Carolis, Giovanni Patricelli, and Annamaria Ciarallo. 2003. "Impact of the AD 79 Explosive Eruption on Pompeii, II: Causes of Death of the Inhabitants Inferred by Stratigraphic Analysis and Areal Distribution of the Human Casualties." *Journal of Volcanology and Geothermal Research* 126: 169–200.

Lytle, Ephraim, ed. 2019. *A Cultural History of Work in Antiquity*. London: Bloomsbury.

Macchiarelli, Roberto. 2002. "Analisi antropologica dei resti scheletrici." *Notizie degli Scavi di Antichità* ser. 9 13–14 (March): 444–51.

MacKinnon, Michael. 2001. "High on the Hog: Linking Zooarchaeological, Literary, and Artistic Data for Pig Breeds in Roman Italy." *American Journal of Archaeology* 105 (4): 649–73.

———. 2004. *Animal Production and Consumption in Roman Italy: Integrating the Zooarchaeological and Textual Evidence*. Journal of Roman Archaeology Supplementary Series, 54. Portsmouth, RI: Journal of Roman Archaeology.

———. 2010. "Cattle 'Breed' Variation and Improvement in Roman Italy: Connecting the Zooarchaeological and Ancient Textual Evidence." *World Archaeology* 42 (1): 55–73.

———. 2013. "Pack Animals, Pets, Pests and Other Non-Human Beings." In *The Cambridge Companion to Ancient Rome*, edited by Paul Erdkamp, 110–28. Cambridge: Cambridge University Press.

———. 2019. "Meat and Other Animal Products." In *The Routledge Handbook of Diet and Nutrition in the Roman World*, edited by Paul Erdkamp and Claire Holleran. Abingdon, UK: Routledge.

MacKinnon, Michael, Emanuele Vaccaro, and Kim Bowes. 2021. "Cooking and Diet in 'Diet, Dining and Subsistence.'" In *The Roman Peasant Project 2009–2015: Excavating the Rural Poor*, 527–33. Philadelphia: University of Pennsylvania Museum of Archaeology and Anthropology.

Mackreth, Donald. 1996. *Orton Hall Farm: A Roman and Early Anglo-Saxon Farmstead*. Manchester, UK: Nene Valley Archaeological Trust.

MacMillan Cottom, Tressie. 2020. "The Hustle Economy." *Dissent*, September. https://www.dissentmagazine.org/article/the-hustle-economy/.

MacMullen, Ramsay. 1965. *Corruption and the Decline of Rome*. New Haven, CT: Yale University Press.

MacRae, Duncan. Forthcoming. *Roman Futures: An Essay in Cultural History*.

Macve, Richard H. 1985. "Some Glosses on 'Greek and Roman Accounting.'" *History of Political Thought* 6 (1/2): 233–64.

Maddison, Angus. 2001. *The World Economy: A Millennial Perspective*. Paris: Development Centre of the Organisation for Economic Co-operation and Development.

———. 2003. *The World Economy: Historical Statistics*. Paris: Development Centre of the Organisation for Economic Co-operation and Development.

———. 2007. *Contours of the World Economy, 1–2030 AD*. Oxford: Oxford University Press.

———. 2010. "Statistics on World Population, GDP and Per Capita GDP, 1–2008 AD." http://www.ggdc.net/MADDISON/oriindex.htm.

Madgwick, Richard, Jamie Lewis, Vaughan Grimes, and Peter Guest. 2019. "On the Hoof: Exploring the Supply of Animals to the Roman Legionary Fortress at Caerleon Using Strontium (87Sr/86Sr) Isotope Analysis." *Archaeological and Anthropological Sciences* 11 (1): 223–35.

Maida, Desirée. 2022. "Le fogne del Colosseo svelano usi e costumi degli antichi Romani. Ecco cosa è emerso dagli scavi." *Artribune*, November. https://www.artribune.com/arti-visive/archeologia-arte-antica/2022/11/fogne-colosseo-scavi-scoperte/.

Mairat, Jerome, Andrew Wilson, and Chris Howgego, eds. 2022. *Coin Hoards and Hoarding in the Roman World*. Oxford: Oxford University Press.

Maiuro, Marco. 2012. *"Res Caesaris": Ricerche sulla proprietà imperiale nel Principato*. Bari, Italy: Edipuglia.

Malim, Tim. 2005. *Stonea and the Roman Fens*. Stroud, UK: Tempus.

Malrain, François, and Thierry Lorho. 2015. "Base de données sur les établissements ruraux du Second âge du Fer: Quelques résultats sur le monde rural laténien." In *Méthodes d'analyse des différents paysages ruraux dans le nord-est de la Gaule romaine*, edited by Michel Reddé, 47–62. Paris: HAL.

Malrain, François, Denis Maréchal, Marjolaine de Muylder, Sébastien Lepetz, Patrice Méniel, and Véronique Zech-Matterne. 2017. "La Vallée de l'Oise." In *Gallia Rustica 1. Les campagnes du nord-est de la Gaule, de la fin de l'âge du Fer à l'Antiquité tardive*, edited by Michel Reddé, 303–52. Bordeaux: Ausonius Éditions.

Manca Masciadri, Maria Adele, and Orsolina Montevecchi. 1982. "Contratti di baliatico e vendite fiduciarie a Tebtynis." *Aegyptus* 62 (1/2): 148–61.

Manning, J. G. 2018. *The Open Sea: The Economic Life of the Ancient Mediterranean World from the Iron Age to the Rise of Rome*. Princeton, NJ: Princeton University Press.

Manning, Sturt. 2013. "The Roman World and Climate: Context, Relevance of Climate Change, and Some Issues." In *The Ancient Mediterranean Environment between Science and History*, edited by William V. Harris, 103–70. Leiden: Brill.

Manning, W. H. 1985. "Ironwork." In *Excavations at Hill Farm, Gestingthorpe, Essex*, edited by Jo Draper, 45–60. Chelmsford, UK: East Anglian Archaeology.

Manzi, Giorgio, Laura Censi, Alessandra Sperduti, and Piero Passarello. 1989. "Linee di Harris e ipoplasia dello smalto nei resti scheletrici delle popolazioni umane di Isola Sacra e Lucus Feroniae (Roma, I–III sec. d.C.)." *Rivista di Antropologia* 67 (January): 129–48.

Manzi, Giorgio, Loretana Salvadei, Alessandro Vienna, and Piero Passarello. 1999. "Discontinuity of Life Conditions at the Transition from the Roman Imperial Age to the Early Middle Ages: Example from Central Italy Evaluated by Pathological Dento-Alveolar Lesions." *American Journal of Human Biology* 11: 327–41.

Manzon, Vanessa, and Emanuela Gualdi-Russo. 2016. "Health Patterns of the Etruscan Population (6th–3rd Centuries BC) in Northern Italy: The Case of Spina." *International Journal of Osteoarchaeology* 26: 490–501.

Marchi, Damiano, and Silvana Borgognini Tarli. 2002. "The Skeletal Biology of Two Italian Peninsular Magna Graecia Necropoles, Timmari and Montescaglioso." *Homo* 53 (1): 59–78.

Marciniak, Stephanie, D. Ann Herring, Alessandra Sperduti, Hendrik N. Poinar, and Tracy L. Prowse. 2018. "A Multi-Faceted Anthropological and Genomic Approach to Framing *Plasmodium falciparum* Malaria in Imperial Period Central-Southern Italy (1st–4th c. CE)." *Journal of Anthropological Archaeology* 49: 210–24.

Marciniak, Stephanie, Tracy L. Prowse, D. Ann Herring, Jennifer Klunk, Melanie Kuch, Ana T. Duggan, Luca Bondioli, Edward C. Holmes, and Hendrik N. Poinar. 2016. "*Plasmodium falciparum* Malaria in 1st–2nd Century CE Southern Italy." *Currrent Biology* 26 (23): R1220–r1222. https://doi.org/10.1016/j.cub.2016.10.016.

Marcone, Arnaldo. 1997. *Storia dell'agricoltura romana: Dal mondo arcaico all'età imperiale*. Rome: Nuova Italia Scientifica.

Maresch, Klaus. 1996. *Bronze und Silber: Papyrologische Beiträge zur Geschichte der Währung im Ptolemäischen Und Römischen Ägypten Bis Zum 2. Jahrhundert n. Chr.* Cologne: Westdeutscher Verlag.

Marfany, Julie. 2018. "Adapting to New Markets: The Income and Expenditure of a Catalan Peasant Family, 1686 to 1812." *Agricultural History Review* 66 (1): 18–42.

Martens, Marleen. 2004. "The Mithraeum in Tienen (Belgium): Small Finds and What They Can Tell Us." In *Roman Mithraism: The Evidence of the Small Finds*, edited by Marleen Martens and Guy De Boe, 25–48. Brussels: Instituut voor het Archeologisch Patrimonium.

Martens, Marleen, Anton Ervynck, and Richard Gordon. 2020. "The Reconstruction of a Banquet and Ritual Practices at the Mithraeum of Tienen (Belgium): New Data and Interpretations." In *The Archaeology of Mithraism: New Finds and Approaches to Mithras-Worship*, edited by Matthew McCarty and Mariana Egri, 11–22. Leuven: Peeters.

Martin, Dale. 1996. "The Construction of the Ancient Family: Methodological Considerations." *Journal of Roman Studies* 86: 40–60.

Martin, Stéphane. 2017. "Storage in a Non-Villa Landscape: The Batavian Countryside." In *Rural Granaries in Northern Gaul (6th Century BCE–4th Century CE)*, edited by Stéphane Martin, 106–27. Leiden: Brill.

Martiniano, Rui, Anwen Caffell, Malin Holst, Kurt Hunter-Mann, Janet Montgomery, Gundula Müldner, Russell L. McLaughlin, et al. 2016. "Genomic Signals of Migration and Continuity in Britain before the Anglo-Saxons." *Nature Communications* 7 (1): 10326. https://doi.org/10.1038/ncomms10326.

Martyn, Rachelle, Peter Garnsey, Luciano Fattore, Pierpaolo Petrone, Alessandra Sperduti, Luca Bondioli, and Oliver Craig. 2018. "Capturing Roman Dietary Variability in the Catastrophic Death Assemblage at Herculaneum." *Journal of Archaeological Science: Reports* 19: 1023–29.

Marzano, Analisa. 2007. *Roman Villas in Central Italy: A Social and Economic History*. Leiden: Brill.

———. 2013. "Agricultural Production in the Hinterland of Rome: Wine and Olive Oil." In *The Roman Agricultural Economy: Organization, Investment and Production*, edited by Alan Bowman and Andrew Wilson, 85–106. Oxford: Oxford University Press.

———. 2015. "Villas as Instigators and Indicators of Economic Growth." In *Structure and Performance in the Roman Economy: Models, Methods and Case Studies*, edited by Koenraad Verboven and Paul Erdkamp, 197–215. Brussels: Editions Latomus.

———, ed. 2020. *Villas, Peasant Agriculture, and the Roman Rural Economy: Archaeology and Economy in the Ancient World—Proceedings of the 19th International Congress of Classical Archaeology, Cologne/Bonn 2018*. Heidelberg: Heidelberg University Library.

Maschek, Dominik. 2023. "'Two of My Shops Have Collapsed . . .': Real Estate and Predatory Urban Practices in Late Republican Central Italy." In *The Real Estate Market in the Roman World*, edited by Marta Garcìa Morcillo, Cristina Rosillo-López, and Dominik Maschek, 191–228. London: Routledge.

Masotti, Sabrina, Nicoletta Onisto, Marta Marzi, and Emanuela Gualdi-Russo. 2013. "Dento-Alveolar Features and Diet in an Etruscan Population (6th–3rd c. B.C.) from Northeast Italy." *Archives of Oral Biology* 58 (4): 416–26.

Matthews, John. 2008. *The Journey of Theophanes: Travel, Business, and Daily Life in the Roman East*. New Haven, CT: Yale University Press.

Mattingly, David. 1988. "Oil for Export? A Comparison of Libyan, Spanish and Tunisian Oil Production in the Roman Empire." *Journal of Roman Archaeology* 1: 33–56.

———. 2006. *An Imperial Possession: Britain in the Roman Empire*. London: Penguin.

———. 2013. *Imperialism, Power, and Identity: Experiencing the Roman Empire*. Princeton, NJ: Princeton University Press.

Mau, August. 1882. "Scavi di Pompeii." *Bullettino dell'Instituto di Corrispondenza Archeologica* 6 (June); 7–8 (July/August): 137–48; 176–84.

Mayer, Emanuel. 2012. *The Ancient Middle Classes: Urban Life and Aesthetics in the Roman Empire, 100 BCE–250 CE*. Cambridge, MA: Harvard University Press.

———. Forthcoming. *Coinage, Political Economy, and Commerce from Tiberius to Nero*.

Mays, Simon, Tracy Prowse, Michele George, and Megan Brickley. 2018. "Latitude, Urbanization, Age, and Sex as Risk Factors for Vitamin D Deficiency Disease in the Roman Empire." *American Journal of Physical Anthropology* 167 (3): 484–96.

McCloskey, Donald. 1985. *The Rhetoric of Economics*. Madison: University of Wisconsin Press.

McIlvaine, Britney Kyle. 2015. "Implications of Reappraising the Iron-Deficiency Anemia Hypothesis." *International Journal of Osteoarchaeology* 25 (6): 997–1000.

McKendrick, Neil, John Brewer, and J. H. Plumb. 1992. *The Birth of a Consumer Society: Commercialization in the Eighteenth Century*. Bloomington: Indiana University Press.

Meinzer, Nicholas, Richard Steckel, and Joerg Baten. 2019. "Agricultural Specialization, Urbanization, Workload and Stature." In *The Backbone of Europe: Health, Diet, Work and Violence over Two Millennia*, edited by Richard Steckel, Clark Spencer Larsen, Charlotte Roberts, and Joerg Baten, 231–52. Cambridge: Cambridge University Press.

Menchelli, Simonetta, and Giulia Picchi. 2016. "Late Republican–Early Imperial Flat-Bottomed Amphorae: Some Remarks about Their Origins and Widespread Success." *Rei Cretariae Romanae Fautorum Acta* 44: 229–38.

Menten-Plesters, Ruben. 2017. "Weaving Tunics and Beyond: Rural-Urban Interactions in Roman Egypt." *Revue Belge de Philologie et d'Histoire* 95 (1): 109–30.

Mickwitz, Gunnar. 1937. "Economic Rationalism in Greco-Roman Agriculture." *English Historical Review* 52: 577–89.

Milanovic, Branko. 2005. *Worlds Apart: Measuring International and Global Inequality*. Princeton, NJ: Princeton University Press.

———. 2007. "Why We All Care about Inequality (but Are Loath to Admit It)." *Challenge* 1 (6): 109–20.

Milanovic, Branko, Peter Lindert, and Jeffery Williamson. 2007. "Measuring Ancient Inequality." *NBER Working Paper, 13550*. https://doi.org/10.3386/w13550.

Miller, Daniel. 2009. *Stuff*. Cambridge: Polity Press.

Millett, Martin. 1995. "Treasure: Interpreting Roman Hoards." *Theoretical Roman Archaeology Conference* 94: 95–106.

Millett, Martin, and Rebecca Gowland. 2015. "Infant and Child Burial Rites in Roman Britain: A Study from East Yorkshire." *Britannia* 46: 171–89.

Millett, Paul. 1991. *Lending and Borrowing in Ancient Athens*. Cambridge: Cambridge University Press.

Mills, Jessica. 2007. "Surveying the Claylands: Combining Aerial Survey and Fieldwalking Methods in Identifying Archaeological Sites on 'Difficult' Soils." In *Populating Clay Landscapes*, edited by Rog Palmer and Jessica Mills, 132–46. Stroud, UK: Tempus.

Milne, J. Grafton. 1900. "The Coins." In *Fayum Towns and Their Papyri*, edited by Bernhard Grenfell, Arthur Hunt, and David Hogarth, 64–73. London: Offices of the Egypt Exploration Fund.

———. 1908. "The Leaden Token-Coinage of Egypt under the Romans." *The Numismatic Chronicle and Journal of the Royal Numismatic Society* 8: 287–310.

———. 1938. "Report on Coins Found at Tebtunis in 1900." *Journal of Egyptian Archaeology* 21 (2): 210–16.

Minaud, Gérard. 2005. *La comptabilité a Rome: Essai d'histoire économique sur la pensée comptable commerciale et privée dans le monde antique*. Lausanne: Presses polytechniques et universitaires romandes.

———. 2006. "Des doigts pour le dire: Le comput digital et ses symboles dans l'iconographie romaine." *Histoire & Mesure* 21 (1): 3–34.

Minnen, Peter van. 1986. "The Volume of the Oxyrhynchite Textile Trade." *Münstersche Beiträge zur antiken Handelsgeschichte* 5 (2): 88–95.

———. 1994. "House-to-House Enquiries: An Interdisciplinary Approach to Roman Karanis." *Zeitschrift für Papyrologie und Epigraphik* 100 (1994): 227–51.

———. 1998. "Did Ancient Women Learn a Trade outside the Home? A Note on *SB* XVIII 13305." *Zeitschrift für Papyrologie und Epigraphik* 123: 201–3.

———. 2000. "Agriculture and the 'Taxes-and-Trade' Model in Roman Egypt." *Zeitschrift für Papyrologie und Epigraphik* 133: 205–20.

Minozzi, Simona, Paola Catalano, Carla Caldarini, and Gino Fornaciari. 2012. "Palaeopathology of Human Remains from the Roman Imperial Age." *Pathobiology* 79: 268–83.

Mirković, Miroslava. 2005. "Child Labour and Taxes in the Agriculture of Roman Egypt: ΠΑΪΣ and ΑΦΗΛΙΞ." *Scripta Classica Israelica* 24: 139–49.

Molina Vidal, Jaime, and Daniel Mateo Corredor. 2018. "Roman Amphorae Average Capacity (AC)." *Oxford Journal of Archaeology* 37 (3): 299–311.

Molinder, Jakob, and Christopher Pihl. 2023. "Women's Work and Wages in the Sixteenth Century and Sweden's Position in the 'Little Divergence.'" *Economic History Review* 76 (1): 145–68.

Momigliano, Arnaldo. 1982. "From Mommsen to Max Weber." *History and Theory* 21 (4): 16–32.

Monson, Andrew. 2012. *From the Ptolemies to the Romans: Political and Economic Change in Egypt*. Cambridge: Cambridge University Press.

Montana, Giuseppe, Bruno Fabri, Sara Santoro, Sabrina Gualtieri, Iannis Iliopoulos, Gabriella Giuducci, and Stefano Mini. 2007. "Pantellerian Ware: A Comprehensive Archaeometric Review." *Archaeometry* 49 (3): 455–81.

Monteix, Nicholas. 2016. "Contextualizing the Operational Sequence: Pompeian Bakeries as a Case Study." In *Urban Craftsmen and Traders in the Ancient World*, edited by Andrew Wilson and Miko Flohr, 153–82. Oxford: Oxford University Press.

Monteix, Nicolas, and Nicolas Tran, eds. 2011. *Les savoirs professionnels des gens de métier: Études sur le monde du travail dans les sociétés urbaines de l'Empire romain.* Naples: Centre Jean Bérard.

Montevecchi, Orsolina. 1936. "Ricerche di sociologia nei documenti dell'Egitto greco-romano." *Aegyptus* 16: 3–83.

———. 1950. *I contratti di lavoro e di servizio nell'Egitto greco, romano, e byzantino.* Milan: Vita e pensiero.

———. 1987. "La crisi economica sotto Claudio e Nerone: nuove testimonianze." In *Neronia III: Actes du IIIe Colloque international de Société internationale d'études néroniennes,* 139–48. Rome: L'Erma di Bretschneider.

Morduch, Jonathan, and Rachel Schneider. 2017. *The Financial Diaries: How American Families Cope in a World of Uncertainty.* Princeton, NJ: Princeton University Press.

Morel, Jean-Paul 2008. "Les céramiques hellénistiques et romaines et les problèmes de 'marchés.'" In *L'économie antique, une économie de marché?*, edited by Yves Roman and Julie Dalaison, 161–89. Lyon: Boccard.

Morelli, Cinzia, and Viviana Forte. 2014. "Il *Campus Salinarum Romanarum* e l'epigrafe Dei Conductores." *Melanges de l'École Française de Rome–Antiquité (Online)* 126 (1). https://doi.org/10.4000/mefra.2059.

Morley, Neville. 1996. *Metropolis and Hinterland: The City of Rome and the Italian Economy, 200 B.C.–A.D. 200.* Cambridge: Cambridge University Press.

———. 2000. "Markets, Marketing and the Roman Élite." In *Mercati permanenti e mercati periodici nel mondo romano,* edited by Elio Lo Cascio, 211–21. Bari, Italy: Edipuglia.

———. 2006. "The Poor in the City of Rome." In *Poverty in the Roman World,* edited by Robin Osborne and Margaret Atkins, 21–39. Cambridge: Cambridge University Press.

———. 2007. *Trade in Classical Antiquity.* Cambridge: Cambridge University Press.

———. 2011. "Demography and Development in Classical Antiquity." In *Demography and the Graeco-Roman World: New Insights and Approaches,* edited by Claire Holleran and April Pudsey, 14–36. Cambridge: Cambridge University Press.

Morris, Ian. 1999. "Foreword." In Moses I. Finley, *The Ancient Economy, Updated Edition,* ix–xxxvi. Berkeley: University of California Press.

———. 2010. *Why the West Rules—for Now.* New York: Picador.

———. 2011. *The Measure of Civilization: How Social Development Decides the Fate of Nations.* Princeton, NJ: Princeton University Press.

Motta, Laura. 1997. "I paesaggi di Volterra nel tardoantico." *Archeologia Medievale* 24: 245–67.

Motta, Laura, Lorenza Camin, and Nicola Terrenato. 1993. "Un sito rurale nel territorio di Volterra." *Bollettino di Archeologia* 23–24: 109–16.

Mouritsen, Henrik. 2011. *The Freedman in the Roman World.* Cambridge: Cambridge University Press.

Mouzelis, Nico. 2008. *Modern and Postmodern Social Theorizing: Bridging the Divide.* Cambridge: Cambridge University Press.

Muhs, Brian. 2016. *The Ancient Egyptian Economy, 3000–30 BCE.* Cambridge: Cambridge University Press.

Müldner, Gundula. 2013. "Stable Isotopes and Diet: Their Contribution to Romano-British Research." *Antiquity* 87 (335): 137–49.

Muldrew, Craig. 1998. *The Economy of Obligation: The Culture of Credit and Social Relations in Early Modern England.* London: Palgrave Macmillan.

———. 2011. *Food, Energy and the Creation of Industriousness: Work and Material Culture in Agrarian England, 1550–1780.* Cambridge: Cambridge University Press.

———. 2012. "'Th'ancient Distaff' and 'Whirling Spindle': Measuring the Contribution of Spinning to Household Earnings and the National Economy in England, 1550–1770." *Economic History Review* 65 (2): 498–526.

———. 2018. "What Is a Money Wage? Measuring the Earnings of Agricultural Labourers in Early Modern England." In *Seven Centuries of Unreal Wages: The Unreliable Data, Sources and Methods That Have Been Used for Measuring Standards of Living in the Past*, edited by John Hatcher and Judy Stephenson, 165–93. Cham, Switzerland: Palgrave Macmillan.

Muldrew, Craig, and Stephen King. 2003. "Cash, Wages and the Economy of Makeshifts in England, 1650–1800." In *Experiencing Wages: Social and Cultural Aspects of Wage Forms in Europe Since 1500*, edited by Peter Scholliers and Leonard Schwarz, 155–59. New York: Berghahn Books.

Mullen, Alex. 2014. "Sociolinguistics." In *Oxford Handbook of Roman Britain*, edited by Martin Millett, Louise Revell, and Alison Moore, 573–98. Oxford: Oxford University Press.

Murphy, Elizabeth. 2016. "Roman Workers and Their Workplace: Some Archaeological Thoughts on the Organization of Workshop Labor in Ceramic Production." In *Work, Labor and Professions in the Roman World*, edited by Koenraad Verboven and Christian Laes, 133–46. Leiden: Brill.

Musco, Stefano, Paola Catalano, Angela Caspio, Walter Pantano, and Kristina Killgrove. 2008. "Le complexe archéologique de Casal Bertone." *Dossiers d'Archéologie* 330: 32–39.

Nadeau, Carey, and Amy Glasmeier. 2016. "Minimum Wage: Can an Individual or a Family Live on It?" *Living Wage Calculator*. https://livingwage.mit.edu/articles/15-minimum-wage-can-an-individual-or-a-family-live-on-it.

Narotsky, Susana. 2016. "Where Have All the Peasants Gone?" *Annual Review of Anthropology* 45: 301–18.

Neesen, Lutz. 1980. *Untersuchungen zu den direkten Staatsabgaben der romischen Kaiserzeit: 27 v. Chr.–284 n. Chr.* Bonn: Habelt.

Nehlich, Olaf, Benjamin Fuller, Mandy Jay, Alice Mora, Rebecca Nicholson, Colin Smith, and Michael Richards. 2011. "Application of Sulphur Isotope Ratios to Examine Weaning Patterns and Freshwater Fish Consumption in Roman Oxfordshire, UK." *Geochimica et Cosmochimica Acta* 75 (17): 4963–77.

Netz, Reviel. 2002. "Counter Culture." *History of Science* 40: 321–52.

Neukom, Raphael, Nathan Steiger, Juan José Gómez-Navarro, Jianghao Wang, and Johannes P. Werner. 2019. "No Evidence for Globally Coherent Warm and Cold Periods over the Preindustrial Common Era." *Nature* 571 (7766): 550–54.

Neurwirth, Robert. 2012. *Stealth of Nations: The Global Rise of the Informal Economy*. New York: Anchor Books.

Noeske, Hans-Christian. 1977. "Studien zur Verwaltung und Bevölkerung der dakischen Goldbergwerke in römischer Zeit." *Bönner Jahrbucher* 177: 271–416.

North, Douglass. 1981. *Structure and Change in Economic History*. New York: Norton.

Northcott, Deryl, and Bill Doolin. 2000. "Home Accountants: Exploring Their Practices." *Accounting, Auditing & Accountability Journal* 13 (4): 475–501.

Nüsslein, Antonin, and Nicolas Bernigaud. 2018. "Les établissements ruraux du Haut-Empire." In *Gallia Rustica 2. Les campagnes du nord-est de la Gaule, de la fin de l'âge du Fer à l'Antiquité tardive*, edited by Michel Reddé, 133–234. Bordeaux: Ausonius Éditions.

Oerlemans, Annelieke, and Laurens Tacoma. 2014. "Three Great Killers in Ancient Rome." *Ancient Society* 44: 213–41.

Ogilvie, Sheilagh. 2001. "The Economic World of the Bohemian Serf: Economic Concepts, Preferences, and Constraints on the Estate of Friedland, 1583–1692." *Economic History Review* 54 (3): 430–53.

———. 2010. "Consumption, Social Capital, and the 'Industrious Revolution' in Early Modern Germany." *Journal of Economic History* 70 (2): 287–325.

Olcese, Gloria, ed. 2011. *Atlante dei siti di produzione ceramica (Toscana, Lazio, Campania e Sicilia)*. Rome: Quasar.

Omar, Sayed. 1979. *Das Archiv des Soterichos*. Opladen, Germany: Westdeutscher Verlag.

Osborne, Robin. 1987. *Classical Landscape with Figures: The Ancient Greek City and Its Countryside*. London: G. Philip.

Otter, Chris. 2007. *The Victorian Eye: A Political History of Light and Vision in Britain, 1800–1910*. Chicago: University of Chicago Press.

———. 2020. *Diet for a Large Planet: Industrial Britain, Food Systems, and World Ecology*. Cambridge: Cambridge University Press.

Ouzoulias, Pierre. 2006. "L'économie agraire de la Gaule: Aperçus historiographiques et perspectives archéologiques." Besançon: Université de Franche-Comté.

———. 2007. "Place et rôle de la petite exploitation dans la Gaule romaine: Un débat en cours." *Bulletin de la société française d'archéologie classique* 39 (August): 149–55.

———. 2014. "*Nos natura non sustinet*: À propos de l'intensification agricole dans quatre terroirs du nord des Gaules." *Gallia* 71 (2): 307–28.

Ouzoulias, Pierre, and Paul Van Ossel. 2009. "Petites et grandes exploitations agricoles: Le cas de la Plaine de France." In *Les formes de l'habitat rural gallo-romain: Colloque AGER VIII*, edited by Philippe Leveau, Claude Raynaud, Robert Sablayrolles, and Frédéric Trément, 111–21. Aquitania, supplément 17. Bordeaux: Fédération Aquitania.

Overmann, Karenleigh. 2022. "Early Writing: A Cognitive Archaeological Perspective on Literacy and Numeracy." *Visible Language* 56 (1): 9–44.

Overton, Mark, Jane Whittle, Darron Dean, and Andrew Hann. 2004. *Production and Consumption in English Households 1600–1750*. London: Routledge.

Packman, Zola. 1975. "Aurelia Tetoueis Revisited, or the Meaning of Price in Contracts of Sale on Delivery." *Chronique d'Égypte* 50: 285–96.

Padilla-Peralta, Dan-el. 2017. "Slave Religiosity in the Roman Middle Republic." *Classical Antiquity* 36 (2): 317–69.

———. 2020. *Divine Institutions: Religions and Community in the Middle Roman Republic*. Princeton, NJ: Princeton University Press.

Paine, Robert, Rita Vargiu, Carla Signoretti, and Alfredo Coppa. 2009. "A Health Assessment for Imperial Roman Burials Recovered from the Necropolis of San Donato and Bivio CH, Urbino, Italy." *Journal of Anthropological Sciences* 87: 193–210.

Papaconstantinou, Arietta. 2020. "Women in Need: Debt-Related Requests from Early Medieval Egypt." In *Living the End of Antiquity: Individual Histories from Byzantine to Islamic Egypt*, edited by Sabine R. Huebner, Eugenio Garosi, Isabelle Marthot-Santaniello, Matthias Müller, Stefanie Schmidt, and Matthias Stern, 195–205. Berlin: De Gruyter.

Papathanasiou, Anastasia, Nicholas Meinzer, Kimberly Williams, and Clark Spencer Larsen. 2019. "History of Anemia and Related Nutritional Deficiencies: Evidence from Cranial Porosities." In *The Backbone of Europe: Health, Diet, Work and Violence over Two Millennia*, edited by Richard Steckel, Clark Spencer Larsen, Charlotte Roberts, and Joerg Baten, 190–230. Cambridge: Cambridge University Press.

Pardini, Edoardo, and Piero Mannucci. 1981. "Gli Etruschi di Selvaccia." *Studi Etruschi* 49: 203–15.

Patterson, Helen, Robert Witcher, and Helga De Giuseppe, eds. 2020. *The Changing Landscapes of Rome's Northern Hinterland*. Oxford: Archaeopress.

Patterson, Orlando. 1982. *Slavery and Social Death: A Comparative Study*. Cambridge, MA: Harvard University Press.

Pecci, Alessandra, Emanuele Vaccaro, Miguel Ángel Cau Ontiveros, and Kim Bowes. 2015. "Wine Consumption in a Rural Settlement in Southern Tuscany during Roman and Late Roman Times." In *Le Forme Della Crisi: Cultura Materiale Nell'Italia Centrale Tra Romani e Longobardi*, edited by Enrico Cirelli, Francesca Diosono, and Helen Patterson, 229–35. Bologna: Ante Quem.

Peltonen, Matti. 2014. "What Is Micro in Microhistory?" In *Theoretical Discussions of Biography: Approaches from History, Microhistory, and Life Writing*, edited by Hans Renders and Binne de Haan, 105–18. Leiden: Brill.

Peña, J. Theodore. In press. "The Investigation of Portable Artifacts at Pompeii and the Pompeii Artifact Life History Project." In *Oxford Handbook of Pompeii and Environs*, edited by Joanne Berry and Rebecca Benefiel.

Peña, J. Theodore, and Miles McCallum. 2009. "The Production and Distribution of Pottery at Pompeii: A Review of the Evidence; Part 2, The Material Basis for Production and Distribution." *American Journal of Archaeology* 113 (2): 165–201.

Pennell, Sarah. 1999. "Consumption and Consumerism in Early Modern England." *The Historical Journal* 42 (2): 549–64.

Pennick Morgan, Faith. 2018. *Dress and Personal Appearance in Late Antiquity: The Clothing of the Middle and Lower Classes.* Leiden: Brill.

Perkins, Phil, and Ida Attolini. 1987. "An Etruscan Farm at Podere Tartuchino." *Papers of the British School at Rome* 60: 71–134.

Perring, Dominic, and Martin Pitts. 2013. *Alien Cities: Consumption and the Origins of Urbanism in Roman Britain*. Portslade, UK: SpoilHeap Publications.

Pestmann, Pieter. 1971. "Loans Bearing No Interest." *Journal of Juristic Papyri* 16–17: 7–29.

———. 1990. *The New Papyrological Primer*. Leiden: Brill.

Petersen, Lauren Hackworth. 2006. *The Freedman in Roman Art and Art History*. Cambridge: Cambridge University Press.

Petrone, Pier Paolo. 1994. "Indicatori bioculturali: Analisi dei dati di patologia dentaria e scheletrica in comunità di età sannitica (VI–IV sec. a.C., Molise)." *Bullettino di Paletnologia Italiana* 85: 493–507.

———. 2002. "Le vittime dell'eruzione." In *Vesuvio 79 A.D.: Vita e morte ad Ercolano*, edited by Pier Paolo Petrone and Francesco Fedele, 35–45. Naples: Fridericiana Editrice Universitaria.

Petrone, Pier Paolo, Alfredo Coppa, and Luciano Fattore. 2002. "La popolazione di Ercolano." In *Vesuvio 79 A.D.: Vita e morte ad Ercolano*, edited by Pier Paolo Petrone and Francesco Fedele, 67–73. Naples: Fridericiana Editrice Universitaria.

Petrone, Pier Paolo, Luciano Fattore, and Vincenzo Monetti. 2002. "Alimentazione e malattie ad Ercolano." In *Vesuvio 79 A.D.: Vita e morte ad Ercolano*, edited by Pier Paolo Petrone and Francesco Fedele, 75–83. Naples: Fridericiana Editrice Universitaria.

Pettegrew, David. 2001. "Chasing the Classical Farmstead: Assessing the Formation and Signature of Rural Settlement in Greek Landscape Archaeology." *Journal of Mediterranean Archaeology* 14 (2): 189–209.

Phang, Sara Elise. 2001. *The Marriage of Roman Soldiers: Law and Family in the Imperial Army*. Leiden: Brill.

Piccioli, Andrea, Valentina Gazzaniga, and Paola Catalano. 2015. *Bones: Orthopaedic Pathologies in Roman Imperial Age*. New York: Springer.

Piketty, Thomas. 2014. *Capital in the Twenty-First Century*. Translated by Arthur Goldhammer. Cambridge, MA: Harvard University Press.

Pirson, Felix. 1999. *Mietwohnungen in Pompeji und Herkulaneum: Untersuchungen zur Architektur, zum Wohnen und zur Sozial unde Wirtschaftsgeschichte der Vesuvstädte*. Munich: Verlag Dr. Freidrich Pfeil.

Pisante, Michele, Fabio Stagnari, Stefano Speca, Angelica Galieni, Giovanni Cafiero, and L. Ciciretti. 2013. "Legume-Wheat Rotation in Mediterranean Environments during Transition to Conservation Agriculture." *Green Carbon: Making Sustainable Agriculture Real*. Abstracts. Brussels: European Conservation Agricultural Association. https://ecaf.org/wp-content/uploads/2021/02/3-EDITORA-GCC-Book_of_abstracts-1.pdf.

Pitts, Martin. 2014. "Globalisation, Circulation and Mass Consumption in the Roman World." In *Globalisation and the Roman World: History, Connectivity and Material Culture*, edited by Martin Pitts and Miguel John Versluys, 69–98. Cambridge: Cambridge University Press.

———. 2018. *The Roman Object Revolution: Objectscapes and Intra-Cultural Connectivity in Northwest Europe*. Amsterdam: Amsterdam University Press.

Pitts, Martin, and Rebecca Griffin. 2012. "Exploring Health and Social Well-Being in Late Roman Britain: An Intercemetery Approach." *American Journal of Archaeology* 116 (2): 253–76.

Pohl, Benjamin. 2022. "Robert of Torigni's 'Pragmatic Literacy': Some Theoretical Considerations." *Tabularia: Sources écrites des mondes normands médiévaux*, 1–29. https://doi.org/10.4000/tabularia.5576.

Polanyi, Karl. 1944. *The Great Transformation*. New York: Rinehart.

———. 1992. "The Economy as Instituted Process." In *The Sociology of Economic Life*, edited by Mark Granovetter and Richard Swedburg, 29–51. Boulder, CO: Westview Press.

Porena, Pierfrancesco. 2016. "Il lavoro infantile." In *Storia del lavoro in Italia. L'età romana. Liberi, semiliberi e schiavi in una società premoderna*, edited by Arnaldo Marcone, 663–85. Rome: Castelvecchi.

Potter, Timothy. 1979. *The Changing Landscape of South Etruria*. London: P. Elek.

Powell, Kelly, Alex Smith, and Granville Laws. 2010. *Evolution of a Farming Community in the Upper Thames Valley Excavation of a Prehistoric, Roman and Post-Roman Landscape at Cotswold Community, Gloucestershire and Wiltshire. Volume 1: Site Narrative and Overview*. Oxford: Oxford Archaeology.

Prell, Marcus. 1996. *Sozialökonomische Untersuchungen zur Armut im antiken Rom: Von den Gracchen bis Kaiser Diokletian*. Stuttgart: Franz Steiner Verlag.

Prowse, Tracy L.. 2001. "Isotopic and Dental Evidence for Diet from the Necropolis of Isola Sacra (1st–3rd Centuries AD), Italy." PhD thesis, McMaster University.

———. 2011. "Diet and Dental Health through the Life Course in Roman Italy." In *Social Bioarchaeology*, edited by S. Agarwal and B. Glencross, 410–37. Oxford: Wiley-Blackwell.

Prowse, Tracy, J. L. Barta, T. von Hunnius, and A. M. Small. 2010. "Stable Isotope and Ancient DNA Evidence for Geographic Origins at the Site of Vagnari (2nd–4th Centuries AD), Italy." In *Roman Diasporas: Archaeological Approaches to Mobility and Diversity in the Roman Empire*, edited by Hella Eckhardt, 175–98. Portsmouth, RI: Journal of Roman Archaeology.

Prowse, Tracy, Chrystal Nause, and Marissa Ledger. 2014. "Growing up and Growing Old on an Imperial Estate: Preliminary Paleopathological Analysis of Skeletal Remains from Vagnari." In *Beyond Vagnari: New Themes in the Study of Roman South Italy*, edited by Alastair M. Small, 111–22. Bari, Italy: Edipuglia.

Prowse, Tracy, Shelley Saunders, Henry Schwarcz, Peter Garnsey, Roberto Macchiarelli, and Luca Bondioli. 2008. "Isotopic and Dental Evidence for Infant and Young Child Feeding Practices in an Imperial Roman Skeletal Sample." *American Journal of Physical Anthropology* 137 (3): 294–308.

Prowse, Tracy L., Henry P. Schwarcz, Shelley Saunders, Roberto Macchiarelli, and Luca Bondioli. 2004. "Isotopic Paleodiet Studies of Skeletons from the Imperial Roman-Age Cemetery of Isola Sacra, Rome, Italy." *Journal of Archaeological Science* 31 (3): 259–72.

———. 2005. "Isotopic Evidence for Age-Related Variation in Diet from Isola Sacra, Italy." *American Journal of Physical Anthropology* 128: 2–13.

Pucci, Giuseppe, ed. 1992. *La fornace di Umbricio Cordo: L'officina di un ceramista romano e il territorio di Torrita di Siena nell'antichità*. Florence: All'insegna del Giglio.

Pugliesi Caratelli, Giovanni, and Ida Baldassarre. 1990. *Pompei pitture e mosaici Volume II Regio I parte seconda*. Rome: Istituto della Enciclopedia italiana.

Quade, Leslie, and Rebecca Gowland. 2021. "Height and Health in Roman and Post-Roman Gaul: A Life Course Approach." *International Journal of Paleopathology* 35: 49–60.

Quigley, Jennifer. 2021. *Divine Accounting: Theo-Economics in Early Christianity*. New Haven, CT: Yale University Press.

Radicke, Jan. 2023. *Roman Women's Dress*. Berlin: De Gruyter.

Radman-Livaja, Ivan. 2013. "Craftspeople, Merchants or Clients? The Evidence of Personal Names on the Commercial Lead Tags from Siscia." In *Making Textiles in Pre-Roman and Roman Times: People, Places, Identities*, edited by Margarita Gleba and Judit Pástókai-Szeőke, 87–108. Oxford: Oxbow.

Ramli, Ainon, Rosmaizura Mohd Zain, Muhammad Ashlyzan Razik, and Abu Sofian Yaacob. 2017. "Micro Businesses: Do They Need Accounting?" *International Journal of Academic Research in Business and Social Sciences* 7 (9): 185–206.

Ramlugun, Vidisha Gunesh, Dineshwar Ramdhony, and Bissoon Poornima. 2016. "An Evaluation of Household Accounting in Mauritius." *International Journal of Accounting and Financial Reporting* 6 (2). https://doi.org/10.5296/ijafr.v6i2.9840.

Rani, Uma, and Nora Gobel. 2023. "Job Instability, Precarity, Informality, and Inequality." In *Routledge Handbook to the Gig Economy*, 15–32. Abingdon, UK: Routledge.

Rathbone, Dominic. 1990. "Villages, Land and Population in Graeco-Roman Egypt." *Proceedings of the Cambridge Philological Society* n.s. 36/216: 103–42.

———. 1991. *Economic Rationalism and Rural Society in Third-Century AD Egypt: The Heroninos Archive and the Appianus Estate*. Cambridge: Cambridge University Press.

———. 1996. "Monetisation, Not Price-Inflation, in Third-Century A.D. Egypt?" In *Coin Finds and Coin Use in the Roman World*, edited by Cathy E. King and David Wigg, 321–39. Berlin: Gebr. Mann.

———. 1997. "Price and Price Formation in Roman Egypt." In *Économie antique: Prix et formations des prix dans les économies antiques*, edited by Jean Andreau, Pierre Briant, and Raymond Descat, 183–244. Saint-Bertrand-de-Comminges: Musée archéologique départemental.

———. 2008. "Warfare and the State." In *The Cambridge History of Greek and Roman Warfare*, edited by Philip Sabin, Hans van Wees, and Michael Whitby, 158–97. Cambridge: Cambridge University Press.

———. 2009. "Earnings and Costs: Living Standards and the Roman Economy (First through Third Centuries AD)." In *Quantifying the Roman Economy: Methods and Problems*, edited by Alan Bowman and Andrew Wilson, 299–326. Oxford: Oxford University Press.

———. 2011. "*PPrag*. 3.240. Pay Records of Employees (Gr I 118+GR I 103+GR. I 143 g Verso)." In *Papyri Graecae Wessely Pragenses (PPrag. III)*, edited by Rosario Pintaudi and Dominic Rathbone, 110–20. Florence: Edizioni Gonelli.

———. 2013. "Village Markets in Roman Egypt: The Case of First-Century AD Tebtunis." In *Kauf, Konsum und Märkte: Wirtschaftswelten im Fokus—Von der römischen Antike bis zur Gegenwart*, edited by Monika Frass, 123–43. Weisbaden: Harrasowitz Verlag.

Rathbone, Dominic, and Peter Temin. 2008. "Financial Intermediation in Rome and England." In Pistoi Dai Tèn Technèn: *Bankers, Loans and Archives in the Ancient World*, edited by Koenraad Verboven, Katelijn Vandorpe, and Véronique Chankowski, 371–419. Leuven: Peeters.

Rathbun, Ted. 1987. "Health and Disease at a South Carolina Plantation." *American Journal of Physical Anthropology* 74: 239–53.

Rathbun, Ted, and Richard Steckel. 2002. "The Health of Slaves and Free Blacks in the East." In *The Backbone of History: Health and Nutrition in the Western Hemisphere*, edited by Richard Steckel and Jerome Rose, 208–25. Cambridge: Cambridge University Press.

Raux, Stéphanie, and Laurent Vidal. 2017. "Les sites de 'Torricella' et 'Saule' à Lucciana (Haute-Corse): Des unités d'exploitation 'saisonnière' du terroir de la colonie antique de Mariana?" In *Produire, transformer et stocker dans les campagnes des Gaules romaines*, edited by Frédéric Trément, 493–514. Bordeaux: Fédération Aquitania.

Ravallion, Martin. 2016. *The Economics of Poverty: History, Measurement and Policy*. Oxford: Oxford University Press.

Ravenelle, Alexandrea. 2019. *Hustle and Gig: Struggling and Surviving in the Sharing Economy*. Berkeley: University of California Press.

Ray, Nick. 2017. "Consumer Behavior in Pompeii: Theory and Evidence." In *Economy of Pompeii*, edited by Miko Flohr and Andrew Wilson, 87–109. Oxford: Oxford University Press.

Rebillard, Eric. 2009. "Les offrandes et dépots funéraires: nature, modalités et fonctions." In *Musarna 3: La nécropole impériale*, edited by Eric Rebillard, 101–10. Rome: École française de Rome.

Reddé, Michel. 2016. "Some Critical Thinking about Large and Small Rural Settlements in North-Eastern Roman Gaul." In *Méthodes d'analyse des différents paysages ruraux dans le nord-est de la Gaule romaine*, edited by Michel Reddé, 7–40. Paris: HAL.

———, ed. 2017a. *Gallia Rustica*. 2 vols. Bordeaux: Ausonius Éditions.

———. 2017b. "Native Farms and Roman Villae in 'Long-Haired' Gaul: A Confrontation between Classical Sources and Archaeological Data." *Annales: Histoire, Sciences Sociales* 72 (1): 43–68.

———. 2018a. "De La Tène finale à l'Empire. La dynamique d'occupation du sol." In *Gallia Rustica 2. Les campagnes du nord-est de la Gaule, de la fin de l'âge du Fer à l'Antiquité tardive*, edited by Michel Reddé, 485–500. Bordeaux: Ausonius Éditions.

———. 2018b. "The Impact of the German Frontier on the Economic Development of the Countryside of Roman Gaul." *Journal of Roman Archaeology* 31: 131–60.

Reddé, Michel, Nicolas Bernigaud, Sébastien Lepetz, and Véronique Zech-Matterne. 2018. "Les conditions du développement économique II: Les marchés." In *Gallia Rustica 2. Les campagnes du nord-est de la Gaule, de la fin de l'âge du Fer à l'Antiquité tardive*, edited by Michel Reddé, 519–84. Bordeaux: Ausonius Éditions.

Reden, Sitta von. 2010. *Money in Classical Antiquity*. Cambridge: Cambridge University Press.

Reden, Sitta von, and Dominic Rathbone. 2014. "Mediterranean Grain Prices in Antiquity." In *A History of Market Performance*, edited by R. J. Van der Spek, Jan Luiten van Zanden, and Bas van Leeuwen, 149–235. London: Routledge.

Redfern, Rebecca. 2017. *Injury and Trauma in Bioarchaeology: Interpreting Violence in Past Lives*. Cambridge: Cambridge University Press.

———. 2018. "Blind to Chains? The Potential of Bioarchaeology for Identifying the Enslaved of Roman Britain." *Britannia* 49: 251–82.

Redfern, Rebecca, Sharon DeWitte, John Pearce, Christine Hamlin, and Kirsten Egging Dinwiddy. 2015. "Urban–Rural Differences in Roman Dorset, England: A Bioarchaeological Perspective on Roman Settlements." *American Journal of Physical Anthropology* 157: 107–20.

Redfern, Rebecca, Rebecca Gowland, Andrew Millard, Lindsay Powell, and Darren Gröcke. 2018. "'From the Mouths of Babes': A Subadult Dietary Stable Isotope Perspective on Roman London (*Londinium*)." *Journal of Archaeological Science: Reports* 19: 1030–40.

Redfern, Rebecca, Andrew Millard, and Christine Hamlin. 2012. "A Regional Investigation of Subadult Dietary Patterns and Health in Late Iron Age and Roman Dorset, England." *Journal of Archaeological Science* 39 (5): 1249–59.

Redon, Bérangère. 2019. "Introduction: La petite société des fortins des routes du désert de Bérénice. Les réseaux personnels de Philoklès, Apollôs et Ischyras." In *Ostraca de Krokodilo II: La correspondance privée et les réseaux personnels de Philoklès, Apollôs et Ischyras: O.Krok. 152–334*, edited by Adam Bülow-Jacobsen, Jean-Luc Fournet, and Bérangère Redon, 2–31. Cairo: Institut français d'archéologie orientale.

Reece, Richard. 1988. "Interpreting Roman Hoards." *World Archaeology* 20 (2): 261–69.

———. 1991. *Roman Coins from 140 Sites in Britain*. Cirenchester, UK: Cotswold Studies.

———. 1996. "The Interpretation of Site Finds: A Review." In *Coin Finds and Coin Use in the Roman World*, edited by Cathy E. King and David Wigg, 341–55. Berlin: Gebr. Mann.

———. 2004. *The Coinage of Roman Britain*. Stroud, UK: History Press.

———. 2016. "Roman Coin Finds: Britain, France, Germany and Italy." https://www.academia.edu/22741727/Roman_coins_finds_Britain_France_Germany_and_Italy.

Reed, Adolph Jr. 2000. *Class Notes: Posing as Politics and Other Thoughts on the American Scene.* New York: New Press.

———. 2018. "Antiracism: A Neoliberal Alternative to a Left." *Dialectical Anthropology* 42 (2): 105–15.

Revel, Jacques. 1995. "Microanalysis and the Construction of the Social." In *Histories: French Constructions of the Past,* edited by Jacques Revel and Lynn Hunt, 493–502. New York: New Press.

Reynolds, Peter. 1992. "Crop Yields of the Prehistoric Cereal Types Emmer and Spelt: The Worst Option." In *Prehistoire de l'agriculture: Nouvelles approches expérimentales et ethnographiques,* edited by Patricia C. Anderson. Paris: Éditions du CNRS.

Rice, Candace. 2023. "Comparative Advantage, Specialized Viticulture, and the Economic Development of Gallia Narbonensis." *Journal of Roman Archaeology* 36 (2): 261–99.

Richards, M. P., R.E.M. Hedges, T. I. Molleson, and J. C. Vogel. 1998. "Stable Isotope Analysis Reveals Variations in Human Diet at the Poundbury Camp Cemetery Site." *Journal of Archaeological Science* 25 (12): 1247–52.

Richardson, John. 2015. "Roman Law in the Provinces." In *The Cambridge Companion to Roman Law,* edited by David Johnston, 45–58. Cambridge: Cambridge University Press.

Rieche, Anita. 1986. "Computatio romana: Fingerzählen auf provinzialrömischen Reliefs." *Bönner Jahrbucher* 186: 165–92.

Riggsby, Andrew. 2019. *Mosaics of Knowledge: Representing Information in the Roman World.* Oxford: Oxford University Press.

Rinehart, Nicholas. 2019. "Reparative Semantics: On Slavery and the Language of History." *Commonplace: Journal of Early American Life.* http://commonplace.online/article/reparative-semantics/.

Rippon, Stephen, Chris Smart, and Ben Pears. 2015. *Fields of Britannia: Continuity and Change in the Late Roman and Early Medieval Landscapes.* Oxford: Oxford University Press.

Rizzeto, Mauro, Umberto Albarella, and Pam Crabtree. 2017. "Livestock Changes at the Beginning and End of the Roman Period in Britain: Issues of Acculturation, Adaptation, and 'Improvement.'" *European Journal of Archaeology* 20 (3): 535–56.

Robb, John. 2019. "Beyond Individual Lives: Using Comparative Osteobiography to Trace Social Patterns in Classical Italy." *Bioarchaeology International* 3 (1): 58–77.

Roberts, C. H., and E. G. Turner. 1952. *Catalogue of the Greek and Latin Papyri in the John Rylands Library at the University of Manchester.* Vol. 4. Manchester, UK: University Press.

Roberts, Charlotte, and Margaret Cox. 2003. *Health and Disease in Britain.* Stroud, UK: Sutton.

Roche, Daniel. 2000. *A History of Everyday Things: The Birth of Consumption in France, 1600–1800.* Cambridge: Cambridge University Press.

Rodewald, Cosmo. 1976. *Money in the Age of Tiberius.* Manchester, UK: Manchester University Press.

Rohnbogner, Anna. 2018. "The Rural Population." In *New Visions of the Countryside of Roman Britain: Volume 3. Life and Death in the Countryside of Roman Britain,* edited by Alexander Smith, Martyn Allen, Tom Brindle, Michael Fulford, Lisa Lodwick, and Anna Rohnbogner, 281–345. London: Society for the Promotion of Roman Studies.

———. 2022. *Dying Young: A Bioarchaeological Analysis of Child Health in Roman Britain.* London: British Archaeological Reports.

Ronin, Marguerite. 2018. "Sharing Water in the Roman Countryside: Environmental Issues, Economic Interests, and Legal Solutions." In *Water Management in Ancient Civilizations,* edited by Jonas Berking, 107–15. Berlin: Edition Topoi.

Roselaar, Saskia. 2009. "*Assidui* or *Proletarii*? Property in Roman Citizen Colonies and the *Vacatio Militiae.*" *Mnemosyne* 62 (4): 609–23.

———. 2010. *Public Land in the Roman Republic: A Social and Economic History of* Ager Publicus *in Italy, 396–89 BC*. Oxford: Oxford University Press.

———. 2019. *Italy's Economic Revolution*. Oxford: Oxford University Press.

Rosenstein, Nathan. 2004. *Rome at War: Farms, Families, and Death in the Middle Republic*. Chapel Hill: University of North Carolina Press.

Rosenthal, Caitlin. 2018. *Accounting for Slavery: Masters and Management*. Cambridge, MA: Harvard University Press.

Rosillo-López, Cristina. 2021. "Destitute, Homeless and (Almost) Invisible: Urban Poverty and the Rental Market in the Roman World." In *Ancient History from Below*, edited by Cyril Courrier and Julio Cesar Magalhães de Oliveira, 104–21. London: Routledge.

Rostovtzeff, Michael. 1926. *The Social and Economic History of the Roman Empire*. 1st ed. Oxford: Oxford University Press.

Roth, Jonathan. 1999. *The Logistics of the Roman Army at War (264 B.C.–A.D. 235)*. Leiden: Brill.

Roth, Ulrike. 2005. "Food, Status, and the Peculium of Agricultural Slaves." *Journal of Roman Archaeology* 18: 278–92.

———. 2007. *Thinking Tools: Agricultural Slavery Between Evidence and Models*. Bulletin of the Institute of Classical Studies Supplement 92. London: University of London.

———, ed. 2010. *By the Sweat of Your Brow: Roman Slavery in Its Socio-Economic Setting*. London: Institute of Classical Studies.

Rothe, Ursula. 2009. *Dress and Cultural Identity in the Rhine-Moselle Region of the Roman Empire*. British Archaeological Reports, 2038. Oxford: Archaeopress.

Rouppert, Vanessa. 2017. "Identifier le logement des animaux de ferme à l'époque romaine: L'apport d'un référentiel architectural et agronomique." In *Produire, transformer et stocker dans les campagnes des Gaules romaines*, edited by Frédéric Trément, 525–48. Aquitaine: Fédération Aquitania.

Rowan, Erica. 2016. "Bioarchaeological Preservation and Non-Elite Diet in the Bay of Naples: An Analysis of the Food Remains from the Cardo V Sewer at the Roman Site of Herculaneum." *Environmental Archaeology* 22 (3): 318–36.

———. 2017. "Sewers, Archaeobotany and Diet at Pompeii and Herculaneum." In *The Economy of Pompeii*, edited by Miko Flohr and Andrew Wilson, 111–33. Oxford: Oxford University Press.

Rowlandson, Jane. 1996. *Landowners and Tenants in Roman Egypt*. Oxford: Oxford University Press.

———. 1998. *Women and Society in Greek and Roman Egypt: A Sourcebook*. Cambridge: Cambridge University Press.

———. 1999. "Agricultural Tenancy and Village Society in Roman Egypt." *Proceedings of the British Academy* 96: 139–58.

———. 2001. "Money Use among the Peasantry in Ptolemaic and Roman Egypt." In *Money and Its Uses in the Ancient Greek World*, edited by Andrew Meadows and Christy Shipton, 145–55. Oxford: Oxford University Press.

———. 2005. "The Organization of Public Land in Roman Egypt." *Cahiers de Recherches de l'Institut de Papyrologie et d'Égyptologie de Lille* 25: 173–95.

———. 2013. "Dissing the Egyptians: Legal, Ethnic and Cultural Identities in Roman Egypt." *Bulletin of the Institute of Classical Studies. Supplement* 120, 213–47.

Roymans, Nico, and Ton Derks. 2015. "A Roman Villa in a Peripheral Region." In *Méthodes d'analyse des différents paysages ruraux dans le nord-est de la Gaule romaine*, edited by Michel Reddé, 159–82. Paris: HAL.

Roymans, Nico, Ton Derks, and Henk Heddink, eds. 2015. *The Roman Villa of Hoogeloon and the Archaeology of the Periphery*. Amsterdam: Amsterdam University Press.

Rubini, Mauro, Elizabetta Bonafede, Silvia Mogliazza, Laura Moreschini, and Fulvio Bartoli. 1999. "Contributo alla conoscenza degli Etruschi: La necropoli del Ferrone, Tolfa." *Archivio per l'Antropologia e l'Etnologia* 1129: 123–43.

Rubini, Mauro, and Alfredo Coppa. 1991. "Studio antropologico sugli inumati della necropoli arcaica di Riofreddo (Lazio, VI sec. a.C.)." *Rivista di Antropologia* 69: 153–66.

Ruffing, Kai. 2008. *Die berufliche Spezialisierung in Handel und Handwerk: Untersuchungen zu ihrer Entwicklung und zu ihren Bedingungen in der römischen Kaiserzeit im östlichen Mittelmeerraum auf der Grundlage griechischer Inschriften und Papyri*. Rahden: Verlag Marie Leidorf.

———. 2016. "Driving Forces for Specialization: Market, Location Factors, Productivity Improvements." In *Urban Craftsmen and Traders in the Roman World*, edited by Andrew Wilson and Miko Flohr, 115–31. Oxford: Oxford University Press.

———. 2018. "Schriftlichkeit und Wirtschaft im Römischen Reich." In *Literacy in Ancient Everyday Life*, edited by Anne Kolb. Berlin: De Gruyter.

Ruffini, Giovanni. 2013. "B. Kelly, *Petitions, Litigation, and Social Control in Roman Egypt* (2011)." *Topoi. Orient-Occident* 18 (2): 603–11.

Rutherford, Stuart, and Sukhwinder Arora. 2009. *The Poor and Their Money*. Rugby, UK: Practical Action.

Sakellaridou-Soutiroudi, Alexandra. 1979. "*P. Lond.* 193 verso." *Hellenika* 31: 358–67.

Sallares, Robert. 2002. *Malaria and Rome: A History of Malaria in Ancient Italy*. Oxford: Oxford University Press.

Sallares, Robert, Abigail S. Bouwman, and C. Anderung. 2004. "The Spread of Malaria to Southern Europe in Antiquity: New Approaches to Old Problems." *Medical History* 48 (3): 311–28.

Saller, Richard. 1984. "'Familia', 'Domus,' and the Roman Conception of the Family." *Phoenix* 38 (4): 336–55.

———. 2002. "Framing the Debate over Growth in the Ancient Economy." In *The Ancient Economy*, edited by Walter Scheidel and Sitta von Reden, 251–69. London: Routledge.

———. 2013. "The Young Moses Finley and the Discipline of Economics." In *Moses Finley and Politics*, edited by William V. Harris, 49–60. Leiden: Brill.

———. 2022. *Pliny's Roman Economy: Natural History, Innovation, and Growth*. Princeton, NJ: Princeton University Press.

Salvadei, Loretana, Francesca Ricci, and Giorgio Manzi. 2001. "Porotic Hyperostosis as a Marker of Health and Nutritional Conditions during Childhood: Studies at the Transition between Imperial Rome and the Early Middle Ages." *American Journal of Human Biology* 13: 709–17.

Sancinito, Jane. 2023. *The Reputation of the Roman Merchant*. Ann Arbor, MI: University of Michigan Press.

Santomato, Emanuele. 2014. "Per una interpretazione dei graffiti privati e della economia quotidiana a Pompei (con particolare riguardo alle liste di prezzi)." *Ancient Society* 44: 307–41.

Santoro, Sara. 2017. "Crafts and Trade in Minor Settlements in North and Central Italy: Reflections on an Ongoing Research Project." In *The Economic Integration of Roman Italy: Rural Communities in a Globalizing World*, edited by Tymon de Haas and Gjis Tol, 263–95. Leiden: Brill.

Sarreste, Florian. 2017. "Une pale de roue à eau à deux jantes d'époque romaine découverte à Sorigny (Indre-et-Loire)." *Revue archéologique du Centre de la France* 56. http://journals.openedition.org/racf/2526.

Sayce, A. H. 1923. *Reminiscences*. London: Macmillan.

Sayer, Andrew. 2005. *The Moral Significance of Class*. Cambridge: Cambridge University Press.

Schärlig, Alain. 2001. *Compter avec des cailloux: Le calcul élémentaire sur l'abaque chez les anciens grecs*. Lausanne: Polytechniques et Universitaires Romandes.

———. 2004. "Un bas-relief à Tréves: Ces romains calculent, ils ne jouent pas!" *Antike Kunst* 47: 65–71.

Scheib, Christina L., Ruoyun Hui, Alice K. Rose, Anu Solnik, Eugenia D'Atanasio, Sarah A. Inskip, Craig Cessford, et al. 2023. "Local Population Structure in Cambridgeshire during the Roman Occupation." *bioRxiv*, 2023.07.31.551265. https://doi.org/10.1101/2023.07.31.551265.

Scheidel, Walter. 1996a. *Measuring Sex, Age and Death in the Roman Empire: Explorations in Ancient Demography*. Ann Arbor: University of Michigan Press.

———. 1996b. "What's in an Age? A Comparative View of Bias in the Census Returns of Roman Egypt." *Bulletin of the American Society of Papyrologists* 33 (1/4): 25–59.

———. 1998. "The Meaning of Dates on Mummy Labels: Seasonal Mortality and Mortuary Practice in Roman Egypt." *Journal of Roman Archaeology* 11: 285–92.

———. 2001. "Progress and Problems in Roman Demography." In *Debating Roman Demography*, edited by Walter Scheidel, 1–82. Leiden: Brill.

———. 2002. "A Model of Demographic and Economic Change in Roman Egypt after the Antonine Plague." *Journal of Roman Archaeology* 15: 97–114.

———. 2003. "Germs for Rome." In *Rome the Cosmopolis*, edited by Catherine Edwards and Greg Woolf, 158–76. Cambridge: Cambridge University Press.

———. 2005. "Mobility in Roman Italy II: The Slave Population." *Journal of Roman Studies* 95: 64–79.

———. 2007a. "Demography." In *The Cambridge Economic History of the Greco-Roman World*, edited by Walter Scheidel, Ian Morris, and Richard Saller, 38–86. Cambridge: Cambridge University Press.

———. 2007b. "Roman Funerary Commemoration and the Age at First Marriage." *Classical Philology* 102 (4): 389–402.

———. 2008. "Roman Population Size: The Logic of the Debate." In *People, Land and Politics: Demographic Developments and the Transformation of Roman Italy 300 BC–AD 14*, edited by Luuk de Ligt and Simon Northwood, 17–70. Leiden: Brill.

———. 2009. "In Search of Roman Economic Growth." *Journal of Roman Archaeology* 22: 46–70.

———. 2010. "Real Wages in Early Economies: Evidence for Living Standards from 1800 BCE to 1300 CE." *Journal of the Economic and Social History of the Orient* 53: 425–62.

———. 2012. "Roman Wellbeing and the Economic Consequences of the 'Antonine Plague.'" In *L'impatto della "peste antonina,"* edited by Elio Lo Cascio, 265–95. Bari, Italy: Edipuglia.

———. 2014. "'Germs for Rome' 10 Years After." In *Les Affaires de Monsieur Andreau: Économie et Société du Monde Romain*, edited by Catherine Apicella, Marie-Laurence Haack, and François Lerouxel, 310–15. Bordeaux: Diffusion de Boccard.

———. 2015. "The Early Roman Monarchy." In *Fiscal Regimes and Political Economy of Premodern States*, edited by Walter Scheidel and Andrew Monson, 229–57. Cambridge: Cambridge University Press.

———. 2017. *The Great Leveler: Violence and the History of Inequality from the Stone Age to the 21st Century*. Princeton, NJ: Princeton University Press.

———. 2020. "Roman Wealth and Wealth Inequality in Comparative Perspective." *Journal of Roman Archaeology* 33: 341–53.

Scheidel, Walter, and Steven Friesen. 2009. "The Size of the Economy and the Distribution of Income in the Roman Empire." *Journal of Roman Studies* 99: 61–91.

Scheidel, Walter, Ian Morris, and Richard Saller. 2007. "Introduction." In *The Cambridge Economic History of the Greco-Roman World*, edited by Walter Scheidel, Ian Morris, and Richard Saller, 1–12. Cambridge: Cambridge University Press.

Schmidts, Thomas. 2011. *Akteure und Organisation Der Handelsschifffahrt in den Nordwestlichen Provinzen des Römischen Reiches*. Monographien RGZM 97. Mainz: Römisch Germanisches Zentralmuseum.

Schmitz, Sascha David. 2013. "Nordgallische Produkte für Niedergermanien: Das Beispiel der Scheidt-Valley Amphoren." *Marburger Beitrage zur antiken Handels-, Wirschafts-, und Sozialgeschichte* 31: 121–51.

Schörner, Hadwiga. 2020. "The Rural Site of 'Il Cotone.'" In *The Vienna Orme and Pesa Valley Project*, edited by Günther Schörner, 171–85. Vienna: Phaidra.

Schrüfer-Kolb, Irene. 2004. *Roman Iron Production in Britain: Technological and Socio-Economic Landscape Development along the Jurassic Ridge*. Oxford: British Archaeological Reports.

Schubert, Paul. 2018. "Who Needed Writing in Graeco-Roman Egypt and for What Purpose? Document Layout as a Tool of Literacy." In *Literacy in Ancient Everyday Life*, edited by Anne Kolb, 335–50. Berlin: De Gruyter.

Schwartz, Jacques. 1964. "Une famille de chepteliers au IIIe s. p.C." *Recherches de papyrologie* 3: 49–96.

Scitovsky, Tibor. 1976. *The Joyless Economy: The Psychology of Human Satisfaction*. Oxford: Oxford University Press.

Scobie, Alex. 1986. "Slums, Sanitation and Mortality in the Roman World." *Klio* 68: 399–433.

Scott, James C. 1977. *The Moral Economy of the Peasant*. New Haven, CT: Yale University Press.

———. 2017. *Against the Grain: A Deep History of the Earliest States*. New Haven, CT: Yale University Press.

Sebesta, Judith Lynn, and Larissa Bonfante, eds. 1994. *The World of Roman Costume*. Madison: University of Wisconsin Press.

Semchuck, Lisa. 2016. "A Stable Isotope Investigation of Diet at Vagnari." MA thesis, McMaster University.

Sen, Amartya. 1983. *Poverty and Famines: An Essay on Entitlement and Deprivation*. Oxford: Oxford University Press.

———. 1985. *Commodities and Capabilities*. Amsterdam: North-Holland.

Shamir, Orit. 2017. "Textiles, Threads and Cordage from the Cave of Letters, 2000–2001 Excavations." In *New Discoveries in the Cave of Letters*, edited by Carl Savage, Philip Reeder, Richard Freund, and Harry Jol, 189–220. New York: Peter Lang.

Shamir, Orit, and Naama Sukenik. 2011. "Qumran Textiles and the Garments of Qumran's Inhabitants." *Dead Sea Discoveries* 18 (2): 206–25.

Shanin, Theodor. 1980. "Defining Peasants: Conceptualizations and Deconceptualizations." *Journal of Peasant Studies* 14 (4): 53–73.

———. 1988. "Expoliary Economies: A Political Economy of Margins." *Journal of Historical Sociology* 1 (1): 107–15.

———. 1990. "A Generalization: Peasantry as a Social Entity." In *Defining Peasants: Essays Concerning Rural Societies, Expoliary Economies and Learning from Them in the Contemporary World*, 21–36. Oxford: Oxford University Press.

Sharp, Michael. 1999. "The Village of Theadelphia in the Fayum: Land and Population in the Second Century." *Proceedings of the British Academy* 96: 159–92.

Shaw, Brent. 1982. "Lamasba: An Ancient Irrigation Community." *Antiquités Africaines* 18: 61–103.

———. 1984. "Latin Funerary Epigraphy and Family Life in the Later Roman Empire." *Historia: Zeitschrift für Alte Geschichte* 33: 457–97.

———. 1987. "The Age of Roman Girls at Marriage: Some Considerations." *Journal of Roman Studies* 77: 30–46.

———. 1996. "Seasons of Death: Aspects of Mortality in Imperial Rome." *Journal of Roman Studies* 86: 100–38.

———. 2006. "Seasonal Mortality in Imperial Rome and the Mediterranean: Three Problem Cases." In *Urbanism in the Preindustrial World: Cross-Cultural Approaches*, edited by Glenn Storey, 86–109. Tuscaloosa: University of Alabama Press.

———. 2013. *Bringing in the Sheaves: Economy and Metaphor in the Roman World*. Toronto: University of Toronto Press.

———. 2019. "Grape Expectations." In *Uomini, istituzioni, mercati: Studi di storia per Elio Lo Cascio*, edited by Marco Maiuro, 533–51. Bari, Italy: Edipuglia.

———. 2020. "Social Status and Economic Behavior: A Hidden History of the *Equites*?" *Ancient Society* 20: 153–202.

Shelton, John. 1971. *Papyri from the Michigan Collection*. Toronto: A. M. Hakkert.

Shuler, Kristrina. 2011. "Life and Death on a Barbadian Sugar Plantation: Historic and Bioarchaeological Views of Infection and Mortality at Newton Plantation." *International Journal of Osteoarchaeology* 21 (1): 66–81.

Sijpesteijn, Pieter. 1971. "Eine weitere Torzollquittung aus der Amsterdamer Papyrussammlung." *Zeitschrift für Papyrologie und Epigraphik* 7: 45–46.

———. 1987. *Customs Duties in Graeco-Roman Egypt*. Zutphen, Netherlands: Terra.

Silver, Morris. 2012. "The Nexum Contract as a 'Strange Artifice.'" *Revue internationale des droits de l'antiquité* 59: 217–38.

———. 2014. "The Market for Uncertainty Bearing in Roman Egypt." *Bulletin of the Institute of Classical Studies* 57 (1): 39–48.

———. 2016. "At the Base of Rome's Peculium Economy." *Fundamina* 22 (1): 67–93.

Silverman, Sydel. 1975. *Three Bells of Civilization: The Life of an Italian Hill Town*. New York: Columbia University Press.

Simelius, Samuli. 2022. "Unequal Housing in Pompeii: Using House Size to Measure Inequality." *World Archaeology* 54 (4): 602–24.

Smail, Daniel Lord. 2016. *Legal Plunder: Households and Debt Collection in Late Medieval Europe*. Cambridge MA: Harvard University Press.

Smith, Alex, Kelly Powell, and Paul Booth. 2010. *Evolution of a Farming Community in the Upper Thames Valley: Excavation of a Prehistoric, Roman and Post-Roman Landscape at Cotswold Community, Gloucestershire and Wiltshire. Volume 2: The Finds and Environmental Reports*. Oxford: Oxford Archaeology.

Smith, Alexander. 2016a. "Buildings in the Countryside." In *New Visions of the Countryside of Roman Britain. Volume 1. The Rural Settlement of Roman Britain*, edited by Alexander Smith, Martyn Allen, Tom Brindle, and Michael Fulford, 44–74. Britannia Monograph Series, 29. London: Society for the Promotion of Roman Studies.

———. 2016b. "The Central Belt." In *New Visions of the Countryside of Roman Britain. Volume 1. The Rural Settlement of Roman Britain*, edited by Alexander Smith, Martyn Allen, Tom Brindle, and Michael Fulford, 141–207. London: Society for the Promotion of Roman Studies.

———. 2017. "Rural Crafts and Industry." In *New Visions of the Countryside of Roman Britain. Volume 2. The Economy of Roman Britain*, edited by Martyn Allen, Lisa Lodwick, Tom Brindle, Michael Fulford, and Alexander Smith, 178–236. London: Society for the Promotion of Roman Studies.

———. 2018. "Lifestyle and the Social Environment." In *New Visions of the Countryside of Roman Britain. Volume 3. Life and Death in the Countryside of Roman Britain*, edited by Alexander Smith, Martyn Allen, Tom Brindle, Michael Fulford, Lisa Lodwick, and Anna Rohnbogner, 48–77. London: Society for the Promotion of Roman Studies.

Smith, Alexander, Martyn Allen, Tom Brindle, and Michael Fulford, eds. 2016. *New Visions of the Countryside of Roman Britain. Volume 1. The Rural Settlement of Roman Britain*. Britannia Monograph Series, 29. London: Society for the Promotion of Roman Studies.

Smith, Alexander, Martyn Allen, Tom Brindle, Michael Fulford, Lisa Lodwick, and Anna Rohnbogner, eds. 2018. *New Visions of the Countryside of Roman Britain. Volume 3. Life and Death in the Countryside of Roman Britain*. London: Society for the Promotion of Roman Studies.

Smith, Alexander, and Michael Fulford. 2016. "Conclusions: The Rural Settlement of Roman Britain." In *New Visions of the Countryside of Roman Britain. Volume 1. The Rural Settlement of Roman Britain*, edited by Alexander Smith, Martyn Allen, Tom Brindle, and Michael Fulford, 384–420. London: Society for the Promotion of Roman Studies.

Smith-Guzmán, Nicole. 2015. "Cribra Orbitalia in the Ancient Nile Valley and Its Connection to Malaria." *International Journal of Paleopathology* 10: 1–12.

Smolders, Ruben. 2011. "Kronion Son of Cheos." *Trismegistos: Leuven Homepage of Papyrus Collections*. https://www.trismegistos.org/archive/125.

———. 2013. "Patron's Descendants." *Trismegistos: Leuven Homepage of Papyrus Collections*. https://www.trismegistos.org/archive/66.

Sognini, Lucrezia, Luca Gnan, and Timu Maalmi. 2013. "The Role and Impact of Accounting in Family Business." *Journal of Family Business Strategy* 4: 71–83.

Solin, Heikki, and Paola Caruso. 2016. "*Memorandum sumptuarium pompeianum*: Per una nuova lettura del graffito *CIV* IV 5380." *Vesuviana* 8: 105–27.

Sombart, Werner. 1902. *Der moderne Kapitalismus*. Vol. 1. 2 vols. Leipzig: Duncker & Humblot.

Soncin, Silvia, Helen Talbot, Ricardo Fernandes, Alison Harris, Matthew von Tersch, Harry Robson, Jan Bakker, et al. 2021. "High-Resolution Dietary Reconstruction of Victims of the 79 CE Vesuvius Eruption at Herculaneum by Compound-Specific Isotope Analysis." *Science Advances* 7 (35): eabg5791. https://doi.org/10.1126/sciadv.abg5791.

Sonego, Fiorenza, and Caterina Scarsini. 1994. "Indicatori scheletrici e dentari cello stato di salute e delle condizioni di vita a Pontecagnano (Salerno) nel VII–V sec. a.C." *Bullettino di Paletnologia Italiana* 85: 1–25.

Speidel, Michael P. 1971. "The Pay of the Auxilia." *Journal of Roman Studies* 63: 141–47.

Speidel, Michael Alexander. 1992. "Roman Army Pay Scales." *Journal of Roman Studies* 82: 87–106.

———. 2014. "Roman Army Pay Scales Revisited: Responses and Answers." In *De l'or pour les braves! Soldes, armées et circulation monétaire dans le monde romain*, edited by Michel Reddé, 53–62. Bordeaux: Ausonius Éditions.

Sperduti, Alessandra, Luca Bondioli, Oliver Craig, Tracy Prowse, and Peter Garnsey. 2018. "Bones, Teeth, and History." In *The Science of Roman History: Biology, Climate, and the Future of the Past*, edited by Walter Scheidel, 123–73. Princeton, NJ: Princeton University Press.

Spurr, M.S. 1986. *Arable Cultivation in Roman Italy, 200 B.C.–A.D. 100*. Journal of Roman Studies Monographs, 3. London: Society for the Promotion of Roman Studies.

Stagnari, Fabio, Albino Maggio, Angelica Galieni, and Michele Pisante. 2017. "Multiple Benefits of Legumes for Agriculture Sustainability: An Overview." *Chemical and Biological Technologies in Agriculture* 4 (2). https://doi.org/10.1186/s40538-016-0085-1.

Stallybrass, Peter. 1998. "Marx's Coat." In *Border Fetishisms: Material Objects in Unstable Spaces*, edited by Patricia Spyer, 183–207. New York: Routledge.

Stannard, Clive. 2018. "The Crisis of Small Change in Central Italy of the 2nd and 1st centuries BC, and the Function of Overstriking." *Belgisch tijdschrift voor numismatiek en zegelkunde/Revue belge de numismatique et de sigillographie* 159: 97–170.

———. 2021. "Small Change in Campania, from the Fourth to the First Century BC, and the Roman Mint of Minturnae in the Second Punic War." In *Merchants, Measures and Money: Understanding Technologies of Early Trade in a Comparative Perspective*, edited by Lorenz Rahmstorf, Gojko Barjamovic, and Nicola Ialongo, 261–88.

Steckel, Richard. 1979. "Slave Height from Coastwise Manifests." *Explorations in Economic History* 16: 363–80.

———. 1986. "A Peculiar Population: The Nutrition, Health, and Mortality of American Slaves from Childhood to Maturity." *Journal of Economic History* 46 (3): 721–41.

Steckel, Richard, and Roderick Floud. 1997. *Health and Welfare During Industrialization*. Chicago: Chicago University Press.

Steckel, Richard, Clark Spencer Larsen, Charlotte Roberts, and Joerg Baten, eds. 2019. *The Backbone of Europe: Health, Diet, Work and Violence over Two Millennia*. Cambridge: Cambridge University Press.

Steckel, Richard, and Jerome Rose, eds. 2002. *The Backbone of History: Health and Nutrition in the Western Hemisphere*. Cambridge: Cambridge University Press.

Steckel, Richard, Paul Sciulli, and Jerome Rose. 2002. "A Health Index from Skeletal Remains." In *The Backbone of History: Health and Nutrition in the Western Hemisphere*, edited by Richard Steckel and Jerome Rose, 61–93. Cambridge: Cambridge University Press.

Sterling, Paul. 1965. *Turkish Village*. London: Charles Birchall and Sons.

Stern, Marianne. 1999. "Roman Glassblowing in a Cultural Context." *American Journal of Archaeology* 103 (3): 441–84.

Stevens, Chris. 2009. "The Charred Plant Remains." In *Cambourne New Settlement: Iron Age and Romano-British Settlement on the Clay Uplands of West Cambridgeshire Volume 2: Specialist Appendices*, edited by James Wright, Matt Leivers, Rachael Seager Smith, and Chris J. Stevens, 156–80. Salisbury, UK: Wessex Archaeology.

Stewart, Edmund, Edward Harris, and David Lewis, eds. 2020. *Skilled Labour and Professionalism in Ancient Greece and Rome*. Cambridge: Cambridge University Press.

Stiglitz, Joseph, Amartya Sen, and Jean-Paul Fitoussi. 2009. "Report by the Commission on the Measurement of Economic Performance and Social Progress." Organisation for Economic Cooperation and Development. https://www.stiglitz-sen-fitoussi.fr.

Stirn, Matthew, Rebecca Sgouros, and Maureen Carroll. 2022. "The Botanical Remains." In *The Making of an Imperial Estate: Archaeology in the* Vicus *at Vagnari, Puglia*, 188–205. Oxford: Oxbow Books.

Stodder, Ann, and Ann Palkovich, eds. 2012. *The Bioarchaeology of Individuals*. Gainesville: University Press of Florida.

Strid, Lena. 2009. "Animal Bone." In *Between Villa and Town: Excavations of a Roman Roadside Settlement and Shrine at Higham Ferrers, Northamptonshire*, edited by Steve Lawrence and Alex Smith, 287–300. Oxford: Oxford Archaeology.

Subramanian, Shankar, and Angus Deaton. 1996. "The Demand for Food and Calories." *Journal of Political Economy* 104 (1): 133–62.

Świderek, Anna. 1960. *La propriété foncière privée dans l'Égypte de Vespasien et sa technique agricole d'après* P. Lond. *131 recto*. Warsaw: Zakład Narodowy im. Ossolińskich.

Swift, Ellen, Jo Stoner, and April Pudsey. 2021. *A Social Archaeology of Roman and Late Antique Egypt: Artefacts of Everyday Life*. Oxford: Oxford University Press.

Taeuber, Hans. 2002. "Graffiti als Hilfsmittel zur Datierung der Wandmalereien in Hanghaus 2." In *Das Hanghaus 2 von Ephesos: Studien zu Baugeschichte und Chronologie*, edited by Friedrich Krinzinger, 93–99. Vienna: Verland der Österreichische Akademie der Wissenschaften.

———. 2005. "Graffiti." In *Hanghaus 2 in Ephesos. Die Wohneinheit 4. Baubefunde, Ausstattung, Funde*, edited by Hilke Thür, 132–43. Vienna: Verlag der Österreichischen Akademie der Wissenschaften.

———. 2010. "Graffiti." In *Hanghaus 2 in Ephesos. Die Wohneinheit 1 und 2. Baubefund, Ausstattung, Funde. Vol. 2*, edited by Friedrich Krinzinger, 472–78. Vienna: Verlag der Österreichischen Akademie der Wissenschaften.

———. 2016. "Graffiti und Inschriften." In *Hanghaus 2 in Ephesos Die Wohneinheit 7: Baubefund, Ausstattung, Funde*, edited by Johanna Auinger, Susanne Lorenz, and Elisabeth Rathmayr, 233–58. Vienna: Verlag der Österreichischen Akademie der Wissenschaften.

Tafuri, Mary Anne, Gwenaëlle Goudeb, and Giorgio Manzia. 2018. "Isotopic Evidence of Diet Variation at the Transition between Classical and Post-Classical Times in Central Italy." *Journal of Archaeological Science: Reports* 21: 496–503.

Takahashi, Ryosuke. 2021. *The Ties That Bind: The Economic Relationships of Twelve Tebtunis Families in Roman Egypt*. London: University of London Press.

Taliercio Mensitieri, Marina. 2007. "Rinvenimenti monetali a Pompei: Il caso delle Regiones VII, VIII, e IX." In *Presenza e circolazione della moneta in area vesuviana*, 27–70. Rome: Istituto Italiano di Numismatica.

———. 2012. "Ritrovamenti monetali, contesti archeologici, processi storici e socio-economici nel comprensorio vesuviano: Il caso di Oplontis." In *I ritrovamenti monetali e i processi storico-economici nel mondo antico*, edited by Michele Asolati and Giovanni Gorini, 191–216. Padua: Esedra editrice.

Tedesco, Paolo. 2018. "'The Missing Factor': Economy and Labor in Late Roman North Africa (400–600 CE)." *Journal of Late Antiquity* 11 (2): 396–431.

Temin, Peter. 2001. "A Market Economy in the Early Roman Empire." *Journal of Roman Studies* 91: 169–81.

———. 2004. "The Labor Market of the Early Roman Empire." *Journal of Interdisciplinary History* 24: 114–39.

———. 2006. "Estimating GDP in the Early Roman Empire." In *Innovazione tecnica e progresso economico nel mondo romano*, edited by Elio Lo Cascio, 31–54. Bari, Italy: Edipuglia.

———. 2012. *The Roman Market Economy*. Princeton, NJ: Princeton University Press.

———. 2020. "Statistics in Ancient History: Prices and Trade in the *Pax Romana*." In *Roman Law and Economics: Institutions and Organizations Volume I*, edited by Giuseppe Dari-Mattiacci and Dennis P. Kehoe, 137–62. Oxford: Oxford University Press.

Temple, Daniel, and Alan Goodman. 2014. "Bioarcheology Has a 'Health' Problem: Conceptualizing 'Stress' and 'Health' in Bioarcheological Research." *American Journal of Physical Anthropology* 155: 186–91.

Temple, Daniel, and Christopher Stojanowski, eds. 2019. *Hunter-Gatherer Adaptation and Resilience: A Bioarchaeological Perspective*. Cambridge: Cambridge University Press.

Tenger, Berhard. 1993. *Die Verschuldung im römischen Ägypten*. St. Katharinen: Scripta Mercaturae.

Tennant, Peter. 2000. "Poets and Poverty: The Case of Martial." *Acta Classica* 43: 139–56.

Terpstra, Taco. 2013. *Trading Communities in the Roman World: A Micro-Economic and Institutional Perspective*. Leiden: Brill.

———. 2014. "The Materiality of Writing in Karanis: Excavating Everyday Writing in a Town in Roman Egypt." *Aegyptus* 94: 89–119.

———. 2019. *Trade in the Ancient Mediterranean: Private Order and Public Institutions*. Princeton, NJ: Princeton University Press.

Terrenato, Nicola. 2005. "'Start the Revolution without Me': Recent Debates in Italian Classical Archaeology." In *Papers in Italian Archaeology VI: Communities and Settlements from the Neolithic to the Early Medieval Period*, edited by Peter Attema, Albert Nijboer, and Andrea Zifferero, 39–43. BAR International Series, 1452.1. Oxford: Archaeopress.

Terzani, Cristiana, and Maurizio Matteini Chiari, eds. 1997. *Isernia: La necropoli romana in località Quadrella*. Rome: Gangemi.

Thanheiser, Ursula, and Christiane König. 2008. "Plant Remains from Habitation Areas at Kellis: Some Considerations Concerning Their Accumulation." In *The Oasis Papers 2: Proceedings of the Second International Conference of the Dakhleh Oasis Project*, edited by Marcia Wiseman, 141–50. Oxford: Oxbow.

Thanheiser, Ursula, Johannes Walter, and Colin Hope. 2002. "Roman Agriculture and Gardening in Egypt as Seen from Kellis." In *Dakhleh Oasis Project: Preliminary Reports on the 1994–1995 to 1998–1999 Seasons*, edited by Colin Hope and Gillian Bowen, 299–310. Oxford: Oxbow.

Thibodeau, Philip. 2018. "Ancient Agronomy as a Literature of Best Practices." In *Oxford Handbook of Science and Medicine in the Classical World*, edited by Paul T. Keyser and John Scarborough. https://doi.org/10.1093/oxfordhb/9780199734146.013.28.

Thieme, Tatiana Adeline. 2018. "The Hustle Economy: Informality, Uncertainty and the Geographies of Getting By." *Progress in Human Geography* 42 (4): 529–48.

Thirsk, Joan. 1961. "Industries in the Countryside." In *Essays in the Economics and Social History of Tudor and Stuart England: In Honour of R. H. Tawney*, edited by F. J. Fisher, 70–88. Cambridge: Cambridge University Press.

———. 1978. *Economic Policy and Projects: Development of a Consumer Society in Early Modern England.* Oxford: Clarendon Press.

Thomas, David. 1975. "The Introduction of Dekaprotoi and Comarchs into Egypt in the Third Century A.D." *Zeitschrift für Papyrologie und Epigraphik* 19: 111–19.

Thomas, Rosalind. 2011. "Writing, Reading, Public and Private 'Literacies': Functional Literacy and Democratic Literacy in Greece." In *Ancient Literacies: The Culture of Reading in Greece and Rome*, edited by William Johnson and Holt Parker, 13–45. Oxford: Oxford University Press.

Thomas, Yan. 2004. "Travail incorporé dans une matière première, travail d'usage et travail comme marchandise: Le droit comme matrice des catégories économiques à Rome." In *Mentalités et choix économiques des Romains*, edited by Jean Andreau, Jérôme France, and Sylvie Pittia, 201–26. Bordeaux: Ausonius Éditions.

Thompson, E. P. 1963. *The Making of the English Working Class.* London: V. Gollancz.

Thonemann, Peter. 2020. *An Ancient Dream Manual: Artemidorus' "The Interpretation of Dreams."* Oxford: Oxford University Press.

———. 2023. *The Lives of Ancient Villages: Rural Society in Roman Anatolia.* Cambridge: Cambridge University Press.

Tietz, Werner. 2020. "Temporary Workforce in the Roman Villa." In *Villas, Peasant Agriculture, and the Roman Rural Economy: Archaeology and Economy in the Ancient World—Proceedings of the 19th International Congress of Classical Archaeology, Cologne/Bonn 2018*, edited by Annalisa Marzano, 7–13. Heidelberg, Germany: Heidelberg University Library.

Tilley, Lorna. 2015. *Theory and Practice in the Bioarchaeology of Care.* Cham, Switzerland: Springer Cham.

Todeschini, Giacomo. 2006. "La comptabilité à partie double et la 'rationalité' économique occidentale: Max Weber et Jack Goody." In *Écrire, compter, mesurer: Vers une histoire des rationalités pratiques*, edited by Natacha Coquery, François Menant, and Florence Weber, 67–76. Paris: Éditions rue d'Ulm.

Todisco, Elisabetta. 2011. *I vici rurali nel paesaggio dell'Italia romana.* Bari, Italy: Edipuglia.

Toepel, Lori. 1973. "Studies in the Administrative and Economic History of Tebtunis in the First Century A.D." PhD thesis, Duke University.

Tol, Gijs, Tymon de Haas, and Carmela Anastasia. 2016. "The Role of Minor Centres in Regional Economies: New Insights from Recent Archaeological Fieldwork in the Lower Pontine Plain." *Melbourne Historical Journal* 44 (2): 33–61.

Tol, Gijs, Tymon de Haas, Kayt Armstrong, and Peter Attema. 2014. "Minor Centres in the Pontine Plain: The Cases of Forum Appii and Ad Medias." *Papers of the British School in Rome* 82: 109–34.

Tomlin, Roger. 1988. "The Curse Tablets." In *The Temple of Minerva Sulis at Bath. Volume 2: The Finds from the Sacred Spring*, edited by Barry Cunliffe, 59–269. Oxford: Oxford University Committee for Archaeology.

———. 2016. *Roman London's First Voices: Writing Tablets from the Bloomberg Excavations, 2010–14.* London: MOLA.

———. 2018. "Literacy in Roman Britain." In *Literacy in Ancient Everyday Life*, edited by Anne Kolb, 201–19. Berlin: De Gruyter.

Torino, Marielva, and Gino Fornaciari. 2000. "Gli scheletri di Ercolano: richerche paleopatologiche." In *Gli Antichi Ercolanesi: Antropologia, società economia*, edited by Mario Pagano, 60–63. Naples: Electa.

Toulemonde, Françoise, Véronique Zech-Materne, and Alessio Bandelli. 2017. "Diversité des productions végétales et animales dans les campagnes champenoises et leur capitale de cité: Études archéobotaniques et archéozoologiques récentes à et atour de Reims/Durocortorum." In *Productions agro-pastorales, pratiques culturales et élevage dans le nord de la Gaule du deuxième avant J.-C. à la fin de la période romaine*, edited by Sébastien Lepetz and Véronique Zech-Materne, 91–102. Quint-Fonsegrives: Éditions Merogoil.

Tran, Nicolas. 2006. *Les membres des associations romaines: Le rang social des collegiati en Italie et en Gaule, sous le haut-empire*. Rome: École française de Rome.

———. 2013. *Dominus tabernae: Le statut de travail des artisans et des commerçants de l'Occident romain (Ier siècle av. J.-C.–IIIe siècle ap. J.-C.)*. Rome: École française de Rome.

Trentacoste, Angela, Ariadna Nieto-Espinet, Silvia Guimarães, Barbara Wilkens, Gabriella Petrucci, and Silvia Valenzuela-Lamas. 2021. "New Trajectories or Accelerating Change? Zooarchaeological Evidence for Roman Transformation of Animal Husbandry in Northern Italy." *Archaeological and Anthropological Sciences* 13 (1). https://doi.org/10.1007/s12520-020-01251-7.

Turner, Michael, John Beckett, and Bethanie Afton. 2001. *Farm Production in England 1700–1914*. Oxford: Oxford University Press.

Turner, Sasha. 2017. *Contested Bodies: Pregnancy, Childrearing, and Slavery in Jamaica*. Philadelphia: University of Pennsylvania Press.

Turner, Terence. 1980. "The Social Skin." In *Not Work Alone: A Cross-Cultural View of Activities Superfluous to Survival*, edited by Jeremy Cherfas and Roger Lewin, 112–40. Beverly Hills: Sage.

Turner-Bowker, Diane. 2001. "How Can You Pull Yourself up by Your Bootstraps, If You Don't Have Boots? Work-Appropriate Clothing for Poor Women." *Journal of Social Issues* 57 (2): 311–22.

Ulrich, Robert. 2007. *Roman Woodworking*. New Haven, CT: Yale University Press.

Vaccaro, Emanuele, Claudio Capelli, and Mariaelena Ghisleni. 2017. "Italic Sigillata Production and Trade in the Countryside of Central Italy: New Data from the 'Excavating the Roman Peasant Project.'" In *The Economic Integration of Rural Italy: Rural Communities in a Globalizing World*, edited by Tymon de Haas and Gjis Tol, 231–62. Leiden: Brill.

Vaccaro, Emanuele, Mariaelena Ghisleni, Antonia Arnoldus-Huyzendveld, Cam Grey, Kim Bowes, Michael MacKinnon, Anna Maria Mercuri, et al. 2013. "Excavating the Roman Peasant II: Excavations at Case Nuove, Cinigiano (GR)." *Papers of the British School at Rome* 81: 129–79.

Van der Veen, Marijke. 1998. "A Life of Luxury in the Desert? The Food and Fodder Supply to Mons Claudianus." *Journal of Roman Archaeology* 11: 101–16.

———. 2003. "When Is Food a Luxury?" *World Archaeology* 34 (3): 405–27.

———. 2008. "Food as Embodied Material Culture: Diversity and Change in Plant Food Consumption in Britain." *Journal of Roman Archaeology* 21: 83–109.

Van der Veen, Marijke, Charlène Bouchard, René Cappers, and Claire Newton. 2018. "Roman Life in the Eastern Desert of Egypt: Food, Imperial Power and Geopolitics." In *The Eastern Desert of Egypt during the Greco-Roman Period: Archaeological Reports*, edited by Jean-Pierre Brun, Thomas Faucher, Bérangère Redon, and Steven Sidebotham. Paris: Collège de France. https://books.openedition.org/cdf/5245.

Van der Veen, Marijke, and Terry O'Connell. 1998. "The Expansion of Agricultural Production in Late Iron Age and Roman Britain." In *Science in Archaeology: An Agenda for the Future*, edited by Justine Bayley, 127–43. London: English Heritage.

Van der Veen, Marijke, and Carol Palmer. 1997. "Environmental Factors and the Yield Potential of Ancient Wheat Crops." *Journal of Archaeological Science* 24: 163–82.

Van Horn, Mark. 2025. "The Economic Fabric(s) of a Roman Countryside: Rural Consumer Networks in First Centuries BCE/CE Southern Tuscany." PhD thesis, University of Pennsylvania.

Van Limbergen, Dimitri. 2018. "What Romans Ate and How Much They Ate of It: Old and New Research on Eating Habits and Dietary Proportions in Classical Antiquity." *Revue Belge de Philologie et d'Histoire* 96 (3): 1049–92.

Van Ossel, Paul, and Guillaume Huitorel. 2017. "Séchoirs et fumoirs: Réflexion autour de structures de transformation polyvalentes." In *Produire, transformer et stocker dans les campagnes des Gaules romaines*, edited by Frédéric Trément, 139–56. Bordeaux: Fédération Aquitania.

Van Oyen, Astrid. 2016. *How Things Make History: The Roman Empire and Its Terra Sigillata Pottery*. Amsterdam: Amsterdam University Press.

———. 2019. *The Socio-Economics of Roman Storage: Agriculture, Trade, and Family*. New York: Cambridge University Press.

———. 2020. "Innovation and Investment in the Roman Rural Economy through the Lens of Marzuolo (Tuscany, Italy)." *Past and Present* 248 (1): 3–40.

———. 2023. "Roman Failure: Privilege and Precarity at Early Imperial Podere Marzuolo, Tuscany." *Journal of Roman Studies* 113: 1–21.

Van Rossem, Ronan, and Isabelle Pannecoucke. 2019. "Poverty and a Child's Height Development during Early Childhood: A Double Disadvantage? A Study of the 2006–2009 Birth Cohorts in Flanders." *PLoS One* 14 (1): e0209170. https://doi.org/10.1371/journal.pone.0209170.

Vandorpe, Katelijn. 2011. "Archives and Dossiers." In *The Oxford Handbook of Papyrology*, edited by Roger S. Bagnall, 216–55. Oxford: Oxford University Press.

Varano, Sara, Flavio De Angelis, Andrea Battistini, Luca Brancazi, Walter Pantano, Paola Ricci, Marco Romboni, et al. 2020. "The Edge of the Empire: Diet Characterization of Medieval Rome through Stable Isotope Analysis." *Archaeological and Anthropological Sciences* 12 (196). https://doi.org/10.1007/s12520-020-01158-3.

Verboven, Koenraad. 2002. *The Economy of Friends: Economic Aspects of Amicitia and Patronage in the Late Republic*. Brussels: Latomus.

———. 2007a. "Demise and Fall of the Augustan Monetary System." In *Crises and the Roman Empire*, edited by Oliver Hekster, Gerda de Kleijn, and Daniëlle Slootjes, 245–57. Leiden: Brill.

———. 2007b. "Good for Business: The Roman Army and the Emergence of a 'Business Class' in the Northwest Provinces of the Roman Empire (1st c. BCE–3rd c. CE)." In *The Impact of the Roman Army (200 B.C.–A.D. 476): Economic, Social, Political, Religious and Cultural Aspects*, edited by Lukas de Blois and Elio Lo Cascio, 295–313. Leiden: Brill.

———. 2008. "*Faeneratores, Negotiatores* and Financial Intermediation in the Roman World." In Pistoi Dai Tèn Technèn: *Bankers, Loans and Archives in the Ancient World*, edited by Koenraad Verboven, Katelijn Vandorpe, and Véronique Chankowski, 211–29. Leuven: Peeters.

———. 2009. "Currency, Bullion and Accounts: Monetary Modes in the Roman World." *Belgisch tijdschrift voor numismatiek en zegelkunde/Revue belge de numismatique et de sigillographie* 155: 91–121.

———. 2014. "Attitudes to Work and Workers in Classical Greece and Rome." *Tijdschrift voor Sociale en Economische Geschiedenis* 11 (1): 67–87.

———. 2015. "The Knights Who Say NIE: Can Neo-Institutional Economics Live Up to Its Expectation in Ancient History Research?" In *Structure and Performance in the Roman Economy: Models, Methods and Case Studies*, edited by Koenraad Verboven and Paul Erdkamp, 33–57. Brussels: Editions Latomus.

———. 2016. "Guilds and the Organization of Urban Populations during the Principate." In *Work, Labour and Professions in the Roman World*, edited by Koenraad Verboven and Christian Laes, 173–202. Leiden: Brill.

———. 2017. "Currency and Credit in the Bay of Naples in the First Century AD." In *The Economy of Pompeii*, edited by Miko Flohr and Andrew Wilson, 363–86. Oxford: Oxford University Press.

Verboven, Koenraad, and Christian Laes, eds. 2016. *Work, Labour and Professions in the Roman World*. Leiden: Brill.

Verhagen, Philip, Maurice de Kleijn, and Jamie Joyce. 2021. "Different Models, Different Outcomes? A Comparison of Approaches to Land Use Modeling in the Dutch Limes." *Heritage* 4 (3): 2081–2104.

Vernant, Jean-Pierre. 1955. "Travail et nature en Grèce ancienne." *Journal de psychologie* 1: 1–29.

———. 1966. *Mythe et pensée chez les Grecs*. Paris: Maspero.

Vernhet, Alain. 1981. "Un four de la Graufesenque (Aveyron): La cuisson des vases sigillés." *Gallia* 39 (1): 25–43.

Veyne, Paul. 1961. "Vie de Trimalcion." *Annales* 16: 213–47.

———. 1976. *Le pain et le cirque*. Paris: Seuil.

———. 1979. "Mythe et réalité de l'autarcie à Rome." *Revue des Études Anciennes* 81 (3–4): 261–80.

———, ed. 1985. *Histoire de la vie privée, Vol. I. De l'Empire romain à l'an mil*. Paris: Seuil.

———. 2000. "La "plèbe Moyenne" Sous le Haut-empire romain." *Annales: Histoire, Sciences Sociales* 55 (6): 1169–99.

Visscher, Rudiger. 1965. *Das einfache Leben: Wort- und motivgeschichtliche Untersuchungen zu einem Wertbegriff der antiken Literatur*. Göttingen: Vandenhoeck & Ruprecht.

Vlassopoulos, Kostas. 2021. *Historicising Ancient Slavery*. Edinburgh: Edinburgh University Press.

Vuolanto, V. 2015. "Children and Work: Family Strategies and Socialisation in the Roman and Late Antique Egypt." In *Agents and Objects: Children in Pre-Modern Europe*, edited by Katariina Mustakallio and Jussi Hanska, 97–111. Rome: Institutum Romanum Finlandiae.

Waldron, Tony. 2009. *Palaeopathology*. New York: Cambridge University Press.

———. 2012. "Joint Disease." In *A Companion to Paleopathology*, edited by Anne Grauer, 513–30. Oxford: Blackwell.

Waldron, Tony, and Juliet Rogers. 1991. "Inter-Observer Variation in Coding Osteoarthritis in Human Skeletal Remains." *International Journal of Osteoarchaeology* 1 (1): 49–56.

Walker, Phillip, Rhonda Bathurst, Rebecca Richman, Thor Gjerdrum, and Valerie Andrushko. 2009. "The Causes of Porotic Hyperostosis and Cribra Orbitalia: A Reappraisal of the Iron-Deficiency-Anemia Hypothesis." *American Journal of Physical Anthropology* 139: 109–25.

Wallace, Sherman LeRoy. 1938. *Taxation in Egypt from Augustus to Diocletian*. Princeton, NJ: Princeton University Press.

Wallace-Hadrill, Andrew. 2008. *Rome's Cultural Revolution*. Cambridge: Cambridge University Press.

———. 2011. "Scratching the Surface: A Case Study of Domestic Graffiti at Pompeii." In *L'Écriture dans la maison romaine*, edited by Mireille Corbier and Jean-Pierre Guilhembet, 401–14. Paris: De Boccard.

Walther, Lauren. 2017. "All out of Proportion? Stature and Body Proportions in Roman and Early Medieval England." PhD thesis, University of Durham.

Walton, Philippa. 2012. *Rethinking Roman Britain: Coinage and Archaeology*. Wetteren, Belgium: Moneta.

Watson, G. A. 1958. "The Pay of the Roman Army: The Republic." *Historia: Zeitschrift für Alte Geschichte* 7 (1): 113–20.

Watts, Rebecca 2013. "Childhood Development and Adult Longevity in an Archaeological Population from Barton-upon-Humber, Lincolnshire, England." *International Journal of Paleopathology* 3: 95–104.

Weatherill, Lorna. 1988. *Consumer Behaviour and Material Culture in Britain, 1660–1760*. Cambridge: Cambridge University Press.

Weber, Max. 1891. *Die römische Agrargeschichte in ihrer Bedeutung für das Staats- und Privatrecht*. Stuttgart: F. Enke.

———. 1922. *Wirtschaft und Gesellschaft: Grundriss der verstehenden Soziologie*. Tübingen: Mohr.

———. 1976. *Agrarian Sociology of Ancient Civilizations*. London: NLB.

Weiss, Elisabeth, and Robert Jurmain. 2007. "Osteoarthritis Revisited: A Contemporary Review of Aetiology." *International Journal of Osteoarchaeology* 17 (5): 437–50.

Weisweiler, John. 2021. "Capital Accumulation, Supply Networks and the Composition of the Roman Senate, 14–235 CE." *Past & Present* 253 (1): 3–44. https://doi.org/10.1093/pastj/gtaa046.

———. 2022. "The Currency-Slavery-Warfare Complex: David Graeber and the History of Value in Antiquity." In *Debt in the Ancient Mediterranean and Near East: Credit, Money, and Social Obligation*, 1–35. Oxford: Oxford University Press.

Welch, Kimberly. 2018. *Black Litigants in the Antebellum American South*. Chapel Hill: University of North Carolina Press.

Welles, C. V. 1933. "Graffiti." In *The Excavations at Dura Europos: Preliminary Report of the Fourth Season of Work October 1930–March 1931*, edited by P.V.C. Bauer, Michael Rostovtzeff, and Alfred Bellinger, 79–181. New Haven, CT: Yale University Press.

Wendt, Peter Karl, and Andreas Zimmerman. 2008. "Bevölkerungsdichte und Landnutzung in den germanischen Provinzen des Römischen Reiches im 2: Jahrhundert A.D.: Ein Beitrag zur Landschaftsarchäologie." *Germania* 86: 1–36.

White, K. D. 1970. *Roman Farming*. Ithaca, NY: Cornell University Press.

Whittaker, Charles R. 1990. "The Consumer City Revisited: The Vicus and the City." *Journal of Roman Archaeology* 3: 110–18.

———. 1993. "The Poor in the City of Rome." In *Land, City and Trade in the Roman Empire*, VII. 1–25. Aldershot, UK: Variorum.

———. 2002. "Supplying the Army: Evidence from Vindolanda." In *The Roman Army and the Economy*, edited by Paul Erdkamp, 204–34. Amsterdam: Gieben.

Wild, John Peter. 2002. "The Textile Industries of Roman Britain." *Britannia* 32: 1–42.

———. 2009. *Textile Manufacture in the Northern Roman Provinces*. Cambridge: Cambridge University Press.

Wilfong, Terry. 1990. "The Archive of a Family of Moneylenders from Jême." *Bulletin of the American Society of Papyrologists* 27: 169–81.

———. 2002. *Women of Jême: Lives in a Coptic Town in Late Antique Egypt*. Ann Arbor: University of Michigan Press.

Williams, Kimberly, Nicholas Meinzer, and Clark Spencer Larsen. 2019. "History of Degenerative Joint Disease in People across Europe." In *The Backbone of Europe: Health, Diet, Work and Violence over Two Millennia*, edited by Richard Steckel, Clark Spencer Larsen, Charlotte Roberts, and Joerg Baten, 253–99. Cambridge: Cambridge University Press.

Wilson, Andrew. 1990. "Timgad and Textile Production." In *Economies Beyond Agriculture in the Roman World*, edited by David Mattingly and John Salmon, 271–96. London: Routledge.

———. 2002. "Machines, Power and the Ancient Economy." *Journal of Roman Studies* 92: 1–32.

———. 2006. "The Economic Impact of Technological Advances in the Roman Construction Industry." In *Innovazione tecnica e progresso economico nel mondo romano*, edited by Elio Lo Cascio, 225–36. Bari, Italy: Edipuglia.

———. 2009. "Large-Scale Manufacturing, Standardization, and Trade." In *The Oxford Handbook of Engineering and Technology in the Classical World*, edited by John Peter Oeleson, 393–417. Oxford: Oxford University Press.

Wilson, Andrew, and Miko Flohr, eds. 2016. *Urban Craftsmen and Traders in the Roman World*. Oxford: Oxford University Press.

Wilson, Jordan, David G. Pickel, Timothy Newfield, and Sierra Malis. 2022. "Nested Environments: A Biocultural Examination of Malaria, Disease Stress, and Mother-Infant Health in a Rural Community in Late Antique Umbria." *Environmental Archaeology*, 1–16. https://doi.org/10.1080/14614103.2023.2166652.

Witcher, Robert. 2006a. "Agrarian Spaces in Roman Italy: Society, Economy and Mediterranean Agriculture." *Arqueología Espacial (Paisajes Agrarios)* 26: 341–59.

———. 2006b. "Settlement and Society in Early Imperial Etruria." *Journal of Roman Studies* 96: 88–123.

———. 2012. "'That from a Long Way off Look like Farms': The Classification of Roman Rural Sites." In *Comparative Issues in the Archaeology of the Roman Rural Landscape: Site Classification between Survey, Excavation and Historical Categories*, edited by Peter Attema and Gunther Schörner, 11–30. Journal of Roman Archaeology, Supplementary Series, 80. Portsmouth, RI: Journal of Roman Archaeology.

———. 2020. "The Early and Mid-Imperial Landscapes of the Middle Tiber Valley (c. 50 BC–AD 250)." In *The Changing Landscapes of Rome's Northern Hinterland*, edited by Helen Patterson, Robert Witcher, and Helga Di Giuseppe, 117–207. Oxford: Archaeopress.

Wolf, Eric. 1966. *Peasants*. Englewood Cliffs, NJ: Prentice-Hall.

———. 1982. *Europe and the People without History*. Berkeley: University of California Press.

Wolff, Hans Julius. 1978. *Recht der griechischen Papyri Ägyptens in der Zeit der Ptolemäer und des Prinzipats, II: Organisation und Kontrolle des privaten Rechtsverkehrs*. 2 vols. Munich: Beck.

Wood, James, George Milner, Henry Harpending, Kenneth Weiss, Mark Cohen, Leslie E. Eisenberg, Dale L. Hutchinson, et al. 1992. "The Osteological Paradox: Problems of Inferring Prehistoric Health from Skeletal Samples." *Current Anthropology* 33 (4): 343–70.

Woolf, Greg. 1994. "Power and the Spread of Literacy in the West." In *Literacy and Power in the Ancient World*, edited by Alan Bowman and Greg Woolf, 84–98. Cambridge: Cambridge University Press.

———. 1998. *Becoming Roman: The Origins of Provincial Civilization in Gaul*. Cambridge: Cambridge University Press.

———. 2006. "Writing Poverty in Rome." In *Poverty in the Roman World*, edited by Robin Osborne and Margaret Atkins, 83–99. Cambridge: Cambridge University Press.

Wright, Gavin. 1988. "American Agriculture and the Labor Market: What Happened to Proletarianization?" *Agricultural History* 62 (3): 182–209.

Wright, James, Matt Leivers, Rachael Seager Smith, and Chris Stevens. 2009. *Cambourne New Settlement: Iron Age and Romano-British Settlement on the Clay Uplands of West Cambridgeshire*. Salisbury, UK: Wessex Archaeology.

Yamey, Basil. 1947. "Notes on the Origin of Double-Entry Bookkeeping." *Accounting Review* 22 (3): 263–72.

———. 1949. "Scientific Bookkeeping and the Rise of Capitalism." *Economic History Review* 1 (2/3): 99–113.

Yiftach-Firanko, Uri. 2003. *Marriage and Marital Arrangements: A History of the Greek Marriage Document in Egypt, 4th Century BCE–4th Century CE*. Munich: Verlag C.H. Beck.

———. 2016. "Quantifying Literacy in the Early Roman Arsinoitês: The Case of the Grapheion Document." In *When West Met East*, edited by David Schaps, Uri Yiftach, and Daniela Dueck, 269–81. Trieste: Edizioni Università di Trieste.

Youtie, Herbert. 1971. "*Bradeos Graphon*: Between Literacy and Illiteracy." *Greek, Roman and Byzantine Studies* 12 (2): 239–61.

Zamboni, Lorenzo. 2022. "L'insediamento rustico di Rivanazzano Terme: Cascina Boarezza." In *Edifici rustici romani tra Pianura e Appenino: Stato della ricerca*, edited by Stefano Maggi, Manuela Battaglia, and Lorenzo Zamboni, 113–25. Florence: All'Insegna del giglio.

Zanden, Jan Luiten van, Sarah Carmichael, and Tine De Moor. 2018. *Capital Women: The European Marriage Pattern, Female Empowerment and Economic Development in Western Europe 1300–1800*. Oxford: Oxford University Press.

Zuiderhoek, Arjan. 2013. "Workers of the Ancient World: Analyzing Labor in Classical Antiquity." *International Journal on Strikes and Social Conflicts* 1 (3): 32–48.

———. 2016. "Sorting out Labour in the Roman Provinces: Some Reflections on Labour and Institutions in Asia Minor." In *Work, Labour and Professions in the Roman World,* edited by Koenraad Verboven and Christian Laes, 20–35. Leiden: Brill.

INDEX

A NOTE ON THE TYPE

THIS BOOK has been composed in Arno, an Old-style serif typeface in the classic Venetian tradition, designed by Robert Slimbach at Adobe.